SETTING NATIONAL PRIORITIES
The Next Ten Years

SETTING NATIONAL PRIORITIES
The Next Ten Years

HENRY OWEN
CHARLES L. SCHULTZE
Editors

THE BROOKINGS INSTITUTION
Washington, D.C.

*In 1969 Kermit Gordon, President of the Brookings Institution, con-
ceived the idea of an annual publication devoted to an objective, timely,
and lucid analysis of the federal budget. As a former U.S. budget
director, he was keenly aware that the budget—the most important
single instrument for making national choices—was a highly complicated document understood by few. It was his imagination and persistence that gave birth to the* Setting National Priorities *series, and
his encouragement and intellectual drive that kept it going. This seventh
volume in that annual series represents both a continuation and an
innovation in whose conception and planning he was again the central
figure.*

*Kermit Gordon died on June 21, 1976. This book is dedicated to
his memory in affection and gratitude, both for the very direct role he
played in originating, planning, and continuing the series in which this
volume is the latest, and for his wise and effective leadership of the
Brookings Institution over the past decade.*

THE BROOKINGS INSTITUTION is an independent organization devoted to nonpartisan research, education, and publication in economics, government, foreign policy, and the social sciences generally. Its principal purposes are to aid in the development of sound public policies and to promote public understanding of issues of national importance.

The Institution was founded on December 8, 1927, to merge the activities of the Institute for Government Research, founded in 1916, the Institute of Economics, founded in 1922, and the Robert Brookings Graduate School of Economics and Government, founded in 1924.

The Board of Trustees is responsible for the general administration of the Institution, while the immediate direction of the policies, program, and staff is vested in the President, assisted by an advisory committee of the officers and staff. The bylaws of the Institution state: "It is the function of the Trustees to make possible the conduct of scientific research, and publication, under the most favorable conditions, and to safeguard the independence of the research staff in the pursuit of their studies and in the publication of the results of such studies. It is not a part of their function to determine, control, or influence the conduct of particular investigations or the conclusions reached."

The President bears final responsibility for the decision to publish a manuscript as a Brookings book. In reaching his judgment on the competence, accuracy, and objectivity of each study, the President is advised by the director of the appropriate research program and weighs the views of a panel of expert outside readers who report to him in confidence on the quality of the work. Publication of a work signifies that it is deemed a competent treatment worthy of public consideration but does not imply endorsement of conclusions or recommendations.

The Institution maintains its position of neutrality on issues of public policy in order to safeguard the intellectual freedom of the staff. Hence interpretations or conclusions in Brookings publications should be understood to be solely those of the authors and should not be attributed to the Institution, to its trustees, officers, or other staff members, or to the organizations that support its research.

Foreword

THIS is the seventh volume in a series published annually since 1970 by the Brookings Institution. Each of its predecessors was centered around analyses of the proposals set forth in the President's annual budget submission to the Congress. This year's volume differs from its predecessors in three respects. It is not focused on this year's federal budget, but rather examines a set of major national issues, only some of which entail significant budgetary decisions. Earlier volumes discussed the future budgetary implications of current decisions, but this one deals more explicitly with longer-run issues, as its subtitle implies. And the current volume, unlike earlier ones, consists of signed chapters, some by members of the Brookings staff and others by scholars not so affiliated.

Each chapter deals independently with a particular issue in foreign or domestic policy, yet, as the editors say in the introductory chapter, a common concern runs through most of them—a concern with the appropriate role of the nation abroad and the government at home. Ten years ago there was a widely held view that the nation could exert effective force virtually anywhere abroad and that the government at home could solve problems of almost any kind. In ten years the opposite view has gained many adherents—that the United States can and should do little to affect events abroad and that government intervention in domestic affairs often creates more problems than it solves. This book, however, gives little support to either view. As a group the authors plead for discriminating judgment. In foreign affairs they call for carefully distinguishing the areas and situations in which the nation should exert its influence from those in which it cannot or should not, and in domestic affairs for a similar case-by-case appraisal of what government can and cannot realistically expect to accomplish.

Five essays on foreign and defense policy follow the introductory chapter. They deal with the major threats to peace and to U.S. interests abroad, national defense policy and military budgets, nuclear proliferation, foreign economic policy, and organizational changes intended to improve the formulation and execution of foreign policy.

The next six chapters deal with domestic problems: economic stabilization policy, the size of the federal budget and of state and local budgets, energy and the environment, governmental regulation of health and safety for workers and consumers, and income security policy. The last chapter discusses executive-congressional relations as they affect the government's ability to frame and carry out economic and social policy.

Research underlying the chapter on national defense policy and military budgets was carried out as part of a continuing program of studies in defense policy supported by a grant from the Ford Foundation. The entire project was supported by grants from Carnegie Corporation of New York and the Richard King Mellon Foundation. The risk of factual error was minimized by the work of Penelope Harpold on the foreign policy and defense chapters and of Evelyn P. Fisher, assisted by Thang Long Ton That, on the domestic chapters. Elizabeth H. Cross and Ellen Alston edited the manuscript and prepared the book for publication.

The views expressed here are those of the authors and should not be ascribed to any of the persons whose assistance is acknowledged above; to the trustees, officers, or other staff members of the Brookings Institution; or to Carnegie Corporation or the Ford Foundation.

GILBERT Y. STEINER
Acting President

June 1976
Washington, D.C.

Contents

Tables

Figures

CHAPTER ONE

Introduction

HENRY OWEN *and* CHARLES L. SCHULTZE

AFTER conquering the depression, winning World War II, achieving postwar full employment, and containing Soviet expansion in the cold war, the American people had by 1965 concluded that the federal government was an effective instrument for accomplishing important and useful ends. That belief has been sharply eroded in the past ten years—partly because of failures (Vietnam and Watergate) and partly because of semi-successes (the Great Society and détente) that failed to fulfill exaggerated expectations. Skepticism about government's ability has been accompanied by suspicion about government's intentions. The public distrusts the government; the President and Congress distrust each other. Not unexpectedly, the loss of confidence and the growth of distrust, once begun, have become far greater than justified by the original causes. To remedy this condition, which could hinder us in coping with serious problems at home and abroad, we need to do two things.

First, distinguish more clearly between tasks the government can and those it cannot accomplish. Some of the current disillusion results from attempts by the government to resolve problems that it is ill suited to tackle. But an overreaction to past disappointments could prevent the government from addressing the problems it can handle.

Second, make the government and its policies more efficient in responding to problems that properly fall within its domain. It is a myth that government is incapable of operating effectively. But it is a reality that in many areas government is not living up to its capabilities.

1

The authors of this book discuss how these two needs can be met in selected areas of foreign and domestic policy. The main issues covered are described briefly below.

Foreign Policy

A quarter-century of playing a large role abroad has, on occasion, led us to venture beyond the limits of feasibility and good sense, as in Vietnam. It is time to review the prospect ahead, to see which problems can be dealt with effectively by U.S. action and which cannot.

In East-West relations, the limits of U.S. influence are evident. The USSR will remain a totalitarian, heavily armed state, determined to continue to dominate Eastern Europe and to extend its influence in the world, whatever we may do. We can seek business-like agreements with the Soviet Union, notably those that will limit the costs and risks of continuing U.S.–Soviet arms competition, but the possibilities of conflict will remain as long as the United States is committed to the defense of vital interests in Europe, Northeast Asia, and the Middle East. These possibilities are discussed in chapter 2—not because they are the ones most likely to materialize, but because they are the ones we want most to avert.

Conflict in Europe could be generated by the interaction of trends: one toward weakness and disunity in Western Europe, the other toward upheaval in Eastern Europe. Tempted by Western weakness and frightened by Eastern unrest, Soviet leaders might choose to follow policies—in response to a conflict in post-Tito Yugoslavia, for instance—that could trigger widening hostilities. Although we cannot prevent the Communist party from coming to power in France and Italy or Britain from continuing its descent into egalitarian stagflation, if that is what the voters in these countries want, we can try to bolster Western European strength by participating in the coordination of economic policies and by improving NATO's military posture. Although we can do little to mitigate the clash between Eastern European desire for greater autonomy and Soviet insistence on dominating the area, we can convey to the USSR our view of the risks that would attend its military intervention in a crisis in Yugoslavia—the "gray" area between East and West.

Chances of war in Northeast Asia hinge on the confrontation between two hostile and powerfully armed Korean states. The United States cannot resolve the confrontation but, over the short term at least, its military presence on the peninsula can probably deter war. In the longer run, even this is uncertain; our goal should be to disengage U.S. ground forces from Korea, where our interests and capability are both limited. Whether this can be done safely will depend on the constancy of our policies toward Japan. Continued Japanese confidence in the U.S. connection is needed if the gradual withdrawal of U.S. ground forces from Korea is not to lead to panicky and possibly dangerous military and political reactions in Japan.

Conflict in the Middle East is the most imminent and troublesome risk of all. We can encourage the parties to negotiate a general settlement committing the Arab countries to a genuine peace in return for Israeli territorial concessions, but our influence is limited and success is uncertain. Without a settlement, we can still provide enough military aid to Israel to maintain a local balance of military power and can manifest our naval and air presence in the area to deter Soviet armed intervention in any future conflict. If a settlement continues to elude us, however, these measures will not avert local conflict indefinitely: the danger of superpower military involvement will remain if a new Arab-Israeli war places any of the local parties in jeopardy.

Our stakes and our power in the rest of the third world are limited. We cannot use force effectively except in defense of vital interests that are widely recognized as such by the American public. Outside Europe, Japan, and the Middle East, few such interests can be perceived. Violation of this rule will waste our substance and divide our people.

As Blechman suggests in chapter 3, maintaining a clear balance of East-West military power in Europe, Japan, and the eastern Mediterranean means improving some elements of our military posture (forces for Europe), reducing others (forces for Asia), and making still others (personnel) more efficient and less costly. This probably means that the defense budget will continue to grow slightly in real terms from year to year, though probably more slowly than GNP or than the present administration seems to envisage. The decline of recent years in real defense spending cannot be continued. On the other hand, we cannot achieve clear-cut military superiority over the USSR by increasing spending. The prospect is for a continuing and expensive competition in arms which will maintain an uneasy peace at best—and then only if we approach defense policy in a more selective and innovative fashion than hitherto.

Peace will also be threatened by the increasing capability of some countries to produce nuclear weapons. We can retard proliferation by limiting exports of nuclear fuel and processing facilities; however, in chapter 4 Farley suggests that we cannot hope to contain it indefinitely by these measures. Our best hope is to help create a political and economic environment in which countries will not feel it necessary to proceed down the nuclear road. This means adopting U.S. defense and foreign policies that alleviate some countries' concern about security and cooperating with other countries to find non-nuclear ways of meeting their prestige and economic needs. But here again the limits of our influence are evident. We cannot convince countries that we will defend them when this is not the case, and we cannot readily confer on governments the prestige that goes with nuclear status. The greatest danger may lie in countries, such as Israel and Korea, that face serious external threats and believe they must rely on their own resources to meet these threats. We can reinforce obstacles to proliferation, which exist in most countries, but we cannot invent them in the few cases where they do not exist.

Despite talk of a declining U.S. role, Fried and Trezise point out in chapter 5 that our economic weight and potential leadership remain very great in the noncommunist world. We can use this influence to advance both our interests and those of other countries.

For one thing, we can press on with the General Agreement on Tariffs and Trade negotiations, which could provide both developed and developing countries with increased opportunities for world trade. Any realistic projection of export earnings suggests that the benefits developing countries can secure through commodity arrangements of the sort that currently preoccupy them are much less than those they could achieve by expanding exports of manufactured products to the developed world. The poor countries will also need large infusions of capital; the United States and other developed countries can provide these transfers—through private markets, the World Bank family, regional development banks, bilateral aid, and specialized international funds—to help the poor countries produce more food, energy, and needed raw materials. None of these actions are beyond our ability; wider trade would benefit the United States as well as others, and enlarged capital transfers would mean only a slight sacrifice. The danger to avoid is doing too little because of exaggerated fears about the costs and adjustments involved.

The United States has great potential for helping to bring about effective international economic action. It would be comforting to conclude that this prospect for economic progress outweighs the risk of military conflict; this is becoming, to some degree, the conventional wisdom. But if a combination of Eastern European upheaval and Western European weakness were to generate spreading European conflict, if a Korean war confronted us with a choice between intervention and inaction that might result in Japan's losing confidence in the United States, or if Arab-Israeli conflict prompted Soviet intervention that only U.S. action could offset, any economic progress we had achieved would be of little moment. The worst threat to our well-being remains what it has been ever since World War II—a clash between U.S. and Soviet armed forces. U.S. policy must address the threats to peace as well as the more likely economic opportunities.

We need instruments for carrying out foreign policy that will be more effective and responsive to public and congressional concern. This means, as Allison and Szanton suggest in chapter 6, new forms of partnership between the executive and legislative branches of government and new decisionmaking processes in the executive branch. Central to both is a perception that foreign policy should no longer be considered apart from domestic policy, with which it interacts increasingly. We need:

—to bring domestic and foreign policy agencies together in addressing economic issues of common concern and to involve in foreign policy people of experience and achievement in domestic affairs;

—to arrange for fuller congressional participation in the formulation and review of foreign policy and for more frank and frequent accounting to the American public about that policy.

Chapter 6 proposes the creation of an executive committee of the cabinet, on which would sit the principal officers of government handling domestic and foreign affairs. This committee would concern itself with all economic and security issues affecting both domestic and foreign policy. Its work would be intended to ensure that the domestic and foreign implications of these questions were considered and that the insight of officials concerned with both types of effects was brought to bear before the issues were decided.

These reforms could do something to restore public confidence. But the heart of the matter is policy itself. The security policies that the next administration will have to follow contain inherent contradictions: more defense in some areas and less in others; resistance to Soviet intervention as well as abstention, depending on where the intervention occurs; a larger role abroad in some fields and a declining role in others. In the economic field, we will face needs—concerting domestic economic policies among industrial countries and opening up these countries' markets to exports from the developing world —that will require patient effort, not grandiose initiatives. None of these policies will lend themselves to the kind of single-minded enthusiasm that marked the Marshall Plan, to the unambiguous aims that shaped the cold war, or even to the overblown hopes that accompanied détente. Even so, a large U.S. role abroad will be essential to the fulfillment of these tasks.

There is inevitably the question whether the public will support demanding foreign policies that cannot promise to solve quickly and safely the international troubles that surely lie ahead. Support depends partly on whether the long-term goal can be made clear. Lord Acton spoke of the "remote and ideal object" that captivates the imagination by its splendor and the reason by its simplicity, and thus evokes an energy that cannot be commanded by lesser and more proximate goals. Our remote and ideal object is to achieve a community of developed nations in which Western Europe, Japan, and the United States will arrange their defenses to deter war in the main areas of potential confrontation, will harmonize their political policies to lessen the prospect of conflict and proliferation, and will coordinate their economic policies to promote steady noninflationary growth in the industrial world and improve economic opportunities for developing countries. It should be our purpose to see the Soviet Union, the Eastern European countries, and many developing nations eventually drawn into this community's constructive business.

The means of attaining this long-term goal cannot be defined with precision. At best, it will provide a general direction in which to steer. Accomplishment will be a long process, and details will change as the process unfolds. But having some idea of what the process could eventually achieve may make it easier to accept the complex policies and subdued expectations that must shape our foreign and defense posture in the period ahead.

Domestic Policy

In domestic as in foreign policy, the place to start is with a sober analysis of what government can and cannot do well. Ten years ago a review of major economic and social problems would have concentrated on asking how government might best deal with them. In today's climate of public opinion the same kind of review must begin by asking whether government is capable of dealing with them. Ten years ago government was widely viewed as an instrument to solve problems; today government itself is widely viewed as the problem.

Belief in the government's ability to manage the economy so as to yield high employment, stable prices, and steady growth, generally heralded in the early and mid 1960s, has been shattered by the simultaneous appearance of the worst recession and the worst inflation of the past thirty years. A substantially increased portion of the public now sees government as too large, its budget as growing too fast, and its deficits as a major cause of persistent inflation. The social programs of the Great Society, launched only a decade ago to remove poverty, upgrade education, and restore urban quality, are now looked on largely as a failure or, at best, as delivering far less than originally promised. Instead of a safeguard against hazardous products, dangerous work places, and monopolistic practices, government regulations are increasingly perceived as generators of red tape, obstacles to efficiency, and intrusions on freedom.

As always, however, there are a number of contradictory themes running through public debate and public perceptions. During the long-drawn-out controversy on the energy crisis there was wide public support for tougher controls and regulations on energy prices and on oil companies. A Republican administration proposed a $100 billion program of government loans, guarantees, and investments for the energy industry. And the major program for economic growth and stability, endorsed by virtually every Democratic candidate in the primaries, is the Humphrey-Hawkins bill, which envisages a substantial expansion of federal economic planning and direct federal hiring of the unemployed. When questioned in polls, a large majority of the public believes that the federal government has a responsibility for ensuring a decent income for the poor, seeing to it that jobs are available for those wanting work, and controlling inflation. While the spread of government regulation is decried, more and more decisions about land use, mineral exploitation, and plant location are being subjected to governmental scrutiny and influence with apparent popular support.

In short, skepticism about the current size of government and about its ability to intervene successfully in the economic and social life of the nation coexists with a host of specific demands upon the government for further intervention. This book is not an attempt to analyze public perceptions of government. But the authors of the seven chapters dealing with domestic policy in a number of important areas do attempt to lay bare the realities underlying these perceptions.

First, despite some major failures and many disappointments, governmental policy can be credited with some impressive accomplishments. Perry reminds us in chapter 7 that the average level of unemployment has been kept lower and the depth of recessions far less in the years since the Second World War than in preceding periods. Palmer and Minarik, in chapter 12, evaluate how well we have done in meeting the four goals of income security policy: replacement of earnings lost from the death, disability, retirement, or unemployment of workers; provision of at least minimum levels of food, medical care, and certain other essential goods and services to everyone; alleviation of poverty; and reduction of income inequality. They conclude that considerable progress has been made toward the first three goals, largely as a result of such federal and state programs as social security, unemployment insurance, food stamps, and public assistance.

Second, chapters 8 and 9, which deal with the federal budget and with state and local budgets respectively, give comfort neither to those who believe that government spending is inexorably claiming an ever larger share of the national income nor to those who still look forward to a large fiscal dividend from economic growth. Chapter 8 concludes that, after adjustment for the effect of the current recession, total federal spending has grown faster than the rest of the economy in the past ten years, but only slightly, rising from about 18 percent to about 20 percent of the gross national product. The relative stability of the federal government's share of GNP, however, masks two opposing trends—a steady decline in the share of GNP taken by defense spending, and a slightly larger rise in the share accounted for by domestic spending. Since a continuation of the downtrend in the defense share at the rate of the past ten years is highly unlikely, domestic spending cannot continue to grow as it has in the past without a noticeable rise in the share of all federal spending in GNP. Although there is nothing built into the current structure of federal programs that will require a disproportionate rise in federal spending, neither is there much room to inaugurate substantial new programs without raising the size of the budget relative to GNP. In chapter 9 Sunley points out that state and local spending has risen much more rapidly than federal spending and has grown substantially relative to GNP. But many of the factors underlying that rise, especially the sharp postwar increase in the school-age population, have disappeared. Fiscal pressures on older central cities may continue unabated as needs mount more rapidly than revenues, but the growth of expenditures and the search for new revenue sources in most states and localities may moderate over the next ten years.

Finally, each of the chapters examines ways to improve the effectiveness of governmental policy. For instance, in the case of economic stabilization, Perry argues for more rather than less federal intervention. Past recessions have often been made worse because restrictive economic policies, adopted to fight inflation, were kept in force even after the economy had turned toward recession; more flexible response would require a standby authority for easier and quicker changes in taxes. He also argues that the present inflation in the United States is largely a matter of inertia, with prices and wages chasing each other up a spiral that originated several years ago. Rather than relying on high unemployment and excess capacity to slow the spiral, he urges direct government intervention in prices and wages—reducing employers' payroll taxes and other kinds of taxes that directly raise the price level, seeking wage moderation from labor in return for a labor-oriented tax reduction, and so forth. Over the longer term a variety of economic tools must be used by the government to reduce the inflation associated with low unemployment—buffer stocks of industrial and agricultural raw materials, changes in regulatory policies, manpower training programs, and other supply-oriented measures.

Three chapters—10, 11, and 12—deal with specific social issues:

energy and the environment, health and safety regulations, and income distribution policy. And in the final section of chapter 8, the many federal grants to state and local governments for social programs are examined.

The difficult social problems analyzed in these chapters no longer lend themselves to the drawing of battle lines chiefly on philosophical or ideological grounds or to the identification of heroes and villains. The secret of a sensible environmental policy is not finding out who are the good guys and the bad guys, but designing a system whereby society can rationally weigh the costs and benefits of alternative environmental standards and then intervene in the millions of individual decisions that affect the environment without smothering the economy in red tape and regulatory orders. In some cases the use of economic incentives—such as taxes on pollutants—rather than detailed regulations could prove a more effective way of dealing with environmental problems.

An industrial society that increasingly uses chemicals, electronics, and nuclear power and produces highly complex consumer products will have to find ways of dealing with the health and safety problems that result. A reasonable approach to this problem, in a nation of 3 million diverse business firms and 70 million families of consumers, requires great discrimination in sorting out the hazards that it is important to regulate from the kinds of lesser hazards that can best be dealt with by the normal prudence of consumers, workers, and business firms. The public interest may be better served by reallocating some of the resources of the health and safety agencies away from the pursuit of relatively minor violations toward the identification and analysis of important health hazards. Neither blanket condemnation nor uncritical urging on of governmental regulatory intervention comes to grips with the real problems.

In recent years, income security programs have constituted the fastest growing share of government expenditures. Unlike the situation ten years ago, the benefits provided by these programs are almost at the level necessary to cushion workers against income disruptions and furnish access to essential goods and services; with moderate additional expenditures, the welfare programs could provide benefits sufficient to meet the objective of alleviating poverty. The major policy problem is now not so much the aggregate level of benefits as their inequitable, uneven, and inconsistent structure. In particular, social security programs must be adapted to changing economic and demographic reality, and the welfare system needs restructuring to reduce unfairness, stimulate incentives, and eliminate the remaining poverty. There are also a number of changes in the tax structure that could help achieve these ends as well as contribute more generally to a fairer distribution of income. Some of these needed changes would increase federal expenditures or reduce revenues; others would have the opposite effects.

The highly complicated grant-in-aid relations between the federal government and state and local governments urgently need simplification and improvement. In some cases, such as reform of the welfare system, improvement should move in the direction of more federal responsibility and more uniform national standards; in others, improvement would mean relinquishing some of the detailed federal controls over the use of grant funds. But the problem cannot be dealt with by presenting the simple alternatives—more decentralization versus more central control.

In the final chapter of the book, Sundquist asks how our political system, with power divided between the executive branch and Congress and with its emphasis on the adversary process of political debate, can be expected to pursue the kinds of analysis and the fine distinctions that are required. In essence he concludes that, acting alone, neither institution can meet the needs of the country. The executive branch can look to the interests of the nation as a whole, frame sophisticated methods for dealing with complicated social problems, and balance conflicting objectives in selecting among alternative approaches. But independent congressional oversight, evaluation, and modification of presidential proposals are essential. Even when it does not lead to abuse, unchecked power gradually isolates the one who wields it from reality and converts objectivity into stubbornness.

Congress, on its own, can design and enact the kinds of programs simple enough to fall within the structure of individual committees, such as a major reform of the social security program or a new highway grant program. And Congress has recently made remarkable progress in organizing itself to cope with the overall federal budget. But a body of 535 separately elected representatives finds it extraordinarily difficult to originate such complicated and interrelated national policies as those needed for energy and the environment or the achievement of full employment and price stability, nor is it designed to deal promptly and independently with rapidly shifting economic trends.

If the American political system is to deal effectively with the social issues of the time, Congress and the executive branch must play separate roles, partly competitive but principally complementary. It is Sundquist's view that recent changes in the composition of the two political parties in the legislative branch have made it possible for a President and a Congress whose majority is of the same party to work together more fruitfully than at any time in recent history. But he also suggests that when the two branches are controlled by different parties the necessary complementary relations cannot be forged. Partisan politics in the narrowest sense prevails; deadlock and stalemate are frequent, and important new departures in policy are difficult to bring about. While Sundquist does not mention it in his chapter, it is the view of the authors of this chapter that under divided government public controversy about policy measures is more likely to be couched in simplistic, irrelevant ideological terms than to be a debate about realistic and useful alternatives.

Conclusions

This book does not provide a comprehensive review of all major foreign and domestic issues. In the compass of one volume this would have been impossible. The omission of a number of problems, such as arms control, crime, health insurance, and race relations, does not imply a belief on the part of the editors that these subjects are in any sense less important or less deserving of public attention than those treated here.

Taken together, the chapters in this book have a central message: there is no single truth about the performance, the capacity, and the limitations of government. Neither the view held in the 1950s that the United States should provide leadership in dealing with every world problem nor the currently fashionable view that the U.S. role should be retracted almost everywhere beyond its borders is much help in dealing with complex security and economic problems abroad. Neither the older hope that almost any problem could be solved by a piece of federal legislation and some money nor the new skepticism that government intervention inevitably makes things worse is accurate or useful. Neither the earlier belief that economic growth will generate a handsome fiscal dividend to support large new governmental initiatives painlessly nor the current view that government outlays are growing sharply out of proportion with the rest of the economy has much basis in reality. What emerges from all this is an implicit plea for discrimination, for a careful sorting out of the things the government can do reasonably well from those it cannot, and for a fundamental improvement in some of the ways the government traditionally goes about formulating domestic and foreign policy.

Questions about basic values will always be a feature of the debate about what the government should do and what limits should be placed on the instruments it uses. But in an affluent society and an interdependent world, both of which are growing more complex, the important issues are less ideological. Designing successful policies increasingly requires skills beyond the traditional political ones of negotiation and compromise among conflicting values and interests. In part, the need is for more analytical skills and technical competence. But even more important, we must abandon the traditional categories and alternatives that have characterized the political debate about issues. Should there be more or less defense spending, more or less government regulation of health and safety? Should the federal government keep its current control over federal grant funds or turn control over to the states? Should environmental regulations be made tighter or relaxed? Should U.S. forces withdraw from Asia or remain there? Is the federal government's role, at home and abroad, too big or too small? Such ways of stating issues are less and less relevant. The answers to all these questions must be "in some respects, yes; in some respects, no." Both the foreign and the domestic chapters of this book attempt to illustrate, for a selective range of issues, the kinds of analyses and types of distinctions that are necessary to frame realistic alternatives.

The similarity, as well as the interaction, of the changing demands of domestic and foreign policy underlie the proposals in this book to bring the two more closely together. The need to identify what can and cannot be accomplished by government action, to involve the public and Congress in choosing among difficult and imperfect courses of action, and to pursue these courses with more persistence than drama is evident in both fields. What is done in either domestic or foreign policy is bound to affect and be affected by what is done in the other. The conclusions that follow thus relate to *national* policy.

The American political system, with all its faults, has been a marvelously effective tool for providing both freedom and governance. Its institutions have been well suited to reaching the kinds of accommodations and compromises about national policy that are essential in a large and heterogeneous society. But that system has heretofore shown far more capability for making large value decisions than for achieving fine tuning in applying them to specific issues. The political debate—vigorous, impassioned, and sometimes raucous—was usually about general values: establishing a compulsory social security system, mobilizing for the Second World War, and later moving from isolationism to interventionism in the cold war. The political battle lines were arranged according to attitudes toward the role of the nation in international affairs and the scope of the government at home.

If the theme that runs through much of this book is correct, the older and simpler divisions no longer suffice as the basis for political debate and public decision. Lack of imagination, ingenuity, or technical competence will not be what prevents the nation from dealing with the growing complexity of society at home and interdependence abroad—the most fundamental challenge will be the ability of the political system to adapt. Can issues be drawn and alternatives debated along lines that are less ideological, more pragmatic, and necessarily more complicated at times than those to which we have become accustomed? It is not surprising that the growth of population, technology, communications, and interdependence requires increasingly discriminating choices of public policy. Correspondingly, it should be no surprise if this places ever greater demands upon the maturity of the electorate in a democratic political system. But maturity will not come unless government leaders also display more candor in defining the hard and complex choices that lie ahead—eschewing either easy retreats or the exaggerated promises that incur growing public mistrust.

The need for defining the ends and means of government is a continuing one, to be carried forward by each generation in light of changing circumstances. The coincidence of the Bicentennial and a presidential election furnish an occasion to make more than ordinary progress in meeting the need. The year 1976 should be one in which we debate again what purposes the government can best serve and how it can best be shaped to serve them. If we emerge from the debate with a clearer consensus on these points and with an administration determined to make this consensus effective, we will have given the best possible evidence that, after two hundred years, our political system is still vital and growing.

CHAPTER TWO

Peace or War

HENRY OWEN

TO SAY THAT NUCLEAR WAR is the central preoccupation of U.S. foreign policy is not to suggest that it is likely; merely that if it occurred its consequences would overshadow everything else. Hence its prevention must be our central objective. Only as long as this objective is achieved can we focus on the constructive goals described later in this book. Thus, the purpose of this chapter is to identify the prospects for large-scale conflicts that might involve the United States in the next ten years, and to consider how U.S. policy might seek to avert, contain, or resolve these conflicts.[1]

It has become fashionable in recent years to suggest that the risk of large-scale war involving the United States and the Soviet Union has been superseded by economic and social issues, and that it is a sign of hopelessly outdated thinking to take this risk seriously.[2] In the 1970s and 1980s foreign economic problems will no doubt become increasingly important; individual and group violence abroad may come to the fore; and nongovernmental actors will play a growing role on the international scene. But the most serious, though not most likely, threat to our well-being will continue to be what it has been in decades past: the possibility that U.S. armed forces might be drawn

1. This chapter does not purport to address all, or even the most important, issues in U.S. foreign policy. Its focus is on those areas of conflict that might lead to war.
2. Much the same was said about the prospect for war between the great powers in the early 1900s and in the 1920s; catastrophe followed.

15

into large-scale war with those of the USSR. If U.S. foreign policy accomplishes nothing but averting this threat during the coming decade, it will have served the nation well.

There is, of course, an obvious way to avoid all conflicts: to withdraw our forces to the United States (it being unlikely that the USSR would try to conquer North America) and abandon our commitments to the defense of overseas areas. This course of action would be predicated on the assumption that the United States does not have vital security interests outside its borders. The analysis in this chapter is based on the premise that we do have such interests in at least two main areas: Western Europe and Japan. Both these regions have sufficient economic and potential military power to make their policies and alignments of direct concern to the United States. If they were to come under the control of groups hostile to the United States, the international environment would be transformed in ways that, though unpredictable specifically, would increase the risk of nuclear war and make the values we prize more difficult to maintain. Americans, both in and out of government, have generally been willing to see the country bear the costs and confront the dangers of preventing such a development.

In addition to these two major areas, Israel makes a claim on the United States—a claim that is no less powerful for being based largely on intangible factors. It is hard to conceive of a U.S. administration remaining inactive while Israel was being overrun. We also have special interests in the Caribbean, partly because of its propinquity to the United States. Our security interests in the rest of the third world are of a different order. These countries lack the military power to threaten our security, and, as chapter 5 suggests, our vulnerability to the economic pressures these countries can exert (leaving aside the oil question) has been greatly exaggerated. Nonetheless, we have a general interest in promoting social and economic progress throughout the developing world, and we also have specific concerns, such as maintaining a free flow of oil from the Middle East and promoting majority rule and avoiding a racial bloodbath in Africa. These concerns would not generally warrant the involvement of U.S. forces in a conflict; they are best pursued by other means.

The main focus in examining prospects for involvement of the United States in large-scale war should thus be on the areas where industrial and potential military power weighs heavily in the global balance of power—Europe and Northeast Asia—and on the Middle East, where the threat of conflict is most urgent. The importance of our interests in these three areas is rarely questioned; debate focuses rather on how these interests can best be protected and what importance should be attached to our concerns elsewhere. It is to these questions that this chapter is addressed. After examining the areas of potential conflict, it turns to the big-power relations that affect them—relations between the United States and the Soviet Union, and between the United States and China.

In all of this, the object is not to predict the most likely contingencies but to identify those we want most to avoid. Inevitably, therefore, the focus is on the worst cases. These projections are also shadowed by the natural tendency to reason from the present and the recent past, which tends to obscure those sharp surprises that so often shape great events. It was easy to foresee that a major depression in Germany and continued allied refusal to accord the Weimar Republic equality with France and Britain would eventually bring an extreme nationalist regime to power in Germany. But it was almost impossible to foresee that this regime would take the form it did; in 1932 a prediction of what was to take place in the next twelve years (including the Holocaust) would have been received as science fiction.

So the future may well be dominated by events not even hinted at in the pages that follow. All we can hope to do is to sketch what now seem likely to be the main trends, illustrate their possible effects, and propose policies designed to respond to these trends in ways that will best sustain our interests.

The Middle East

The most dangerous international dispute now is that between Israel and its Arab neighbors. Although the Arab attitude toward Israel is not monolithic, this dispute evokes deep and widespread emotional responses among many classes of people in the Arab world. In neither of the two major Arab countries involved, Syria and Egypt, could governments long remain in power that were seen as being indifferent to demands to retract Israel's frontiers at least to the pre-1967 lines and to permit creation of a Palestinian state on some of the territory thus restored to Arab rule. Beneath these specific issues lies deep-seated resentment in the Arab countries at the creation of a Jewish state in their midst, and equally deep-seated Israeli suspicion and hostility toward neighboring countries that have so violently and implacably rejected this state.

Prospects for Conflict

Arab-Israeli tensions, reflecting also the hatred created by thirty years of war, will create a continuing risk of conflict. This risk will intensify in the coming decade if Syrian influence grows in Jordan, Lebanon comes under greater Moslem sway, and the Arab population of the West Bank becomes increasingly restive. There is little chance that useful opportunities for further interim Arab-Israeli agreements will arise. Israel will not make territorial concessions without a substantial Arab commitment to peace, and the Arab countries are unlikely to make that commitment without Israel's retreat to something approximating the 1967 lines. The obstacles to negotiations for a general settlement are also powerful. Even if these negotiations began, deep-seated suspicions on both sides would make rapid progress unlikely; if the negotiations stalemated, pressures for a new Arab-Israeli war would mount. That war could occur as a result of deliberate Arab attack, as in 1973, after Arab forces had been further strengthened; or it might arise out of a series of incidents that neither side could control, as in 1967, in which case it could erupt at any time. In short, the threat of violence will remain so long as there seems no prospect of change in the status quo by peaceful means. Opinion in the Arab countries and on the West Bank is predominantly for changing that status quo, by force if there seems no other way.

Soviet attitudes toward this situation are ambivalent: on the one hand, the USSR wishes to expand its influence in the Middle East, which means helping Arab countries in their conflict with Israel; on the other hand, it wishes to avoid a confrontation with the United States, which means promoting a settlement to resolve the Arab-Israeli conflict. So far, the first of these interests has been dominant; but if negotiations toward a general settlement began, Soviet leaders might be moved by fear of the hard choices that another war could pose for them—active support of the Arab countries or passive acceptance of an Israeli victory—to offer mild encouragement to Arab governments disposed to compromise. One should be careful not to exaggerate the extent of Soviet influence, however. Soviet leaders cannot allow their Arab allies to be destroyed, any more than we could accept the destruction of Israel, and this fact sets limits to their influence over Syria, as it does to our influence over Israel.

So far, each of the Arab-Israeli wars has been won by Israel without superpower combat involvement, both because Israel had a significant qualitative advantage and because it stopped the war before its victories threatened the Arab countries enough to induce Soviet military intervention. The Arab armies are improving, however, and the USSR has provided increasingly explicit wartime support of Arab countries—notably in 1970, when the Soviet Union reacted to Israeli bombing of targets deep in Egypt by deploying its own air defense forces in the area, and in 1973, when the USSR made serious military preparations to intervene if Israeli military pressure on the surrounded Egyptian Third Army continued. If Soviet forces should intervene in some future conflict, only counterintervention by U.S. forces could offset their effect.

Israel has at least a nuclear potential, if not a capability. It will be willing to hint at as much for deterrent purposes; but it is unlikely to be prepared to accept the opprobrium and other disadvantages of officially acknowledging the extent of its nuclear progress unless its leaders believe that it is facing the threat of imminent extinction. Israel has probably taken whatever protective measures are needed to make preemptive attack on its nuclear facilities an unattractive option for the Arab countries. The latter are unlikely to develop nuclear capabilities on their own in the next ten years, and decisive Soviet or Chinese help is improbable, unless Israel threatens to use its nuclear capability. Only if the balance of local conventional military power shifts decisively against Israel, therefore, is the nuclear issue likely to be posed in an agonizing way in the Arab-Israeli dispute in the next decade.

Prospects for Settlement

The main lines of a possible settlement of the Arab-Israeli dispute, suggested in U.N. Resolution 242[3] have been elaborated in a recent Brookings report,[4] signed by sixteen Americans of diverse views:

3. SC Res. 242 (1967), Nov. 22, 1967.
4. Morroe Berger and others, *Toward Peace in the Middle East: Report of a Study Group* (Brookings Institution, 1975).

—Arab commitment to full-fledged peace with Israel: open frontiers (insofar as any Middle Eastern frontiers are open), diplomatic recognition, a peace treaty, and an end to the boycott and official hostile propaganda against Israel. This commitment will, of course, be difficult for Arab governments. Their willingness publicly to face up to the fact that Israel is here to stay and that the Arab-Israeli issue has been settled once and for all will determine whether a settlement is feasible. If these governmental actions are taken, changes in Arab public opinion are likely to follow, albeit very slowly.

—Israel's withdrawal from territories occupied in the 1967 war, with such adjustments as may be mutually agreed upon. For Jerusalem, the report outlines three alternatives, all involving free movement of persons into and within Jerusalem: Israeli jurisdiction, divided jurisdiction between Israel and an Arab state, or international authority in an agreed area under either of these arrangements. The authors of the report wisely did not express a preference, feeling that only the parties directly involved in negotiations could choose in the circumstances then existing.

—Palestinian self-rule on the West Bank, either as an independent entity or in association with Jordan. It is difficult to see how an enduring Middle Eastern settlement can be achieved that does not concede, in some fashion, the right of self-determination to most of the people now living on the West Bank, given the strong and wide-spread support for this right in the Arab world. Many Israelis are understandably concerned over the threat that a separate Palestinian entity might pose to Israel; there is solid basis for this concern in the evident indisposition of important Palestinian leaders to accept any settlement that does not eliminate a Jewish state. There is some evidence that the major Arab states would urge postsettlement Palestinian leaders to accept the new status quo, and would refuse to provide aid for irredentist adventures. Moreover, the settlement would provide safeguards and guarantees against such adventures, including demilitarization of the West Bank. In any event, Israeli military superiority over any strength that Palestinian leadership could muster would be overwhelming. The present threat to Israel is posed not by Palestinian guerrillas but by the connection between the Palestinian movement and the regular armies of Syria and Egypt, supported by the oil-exporting states. The object of the proposed settlement would be to break that connection by creating a situation sufficiently acceptable to the major Arab states to cause them to disavow support for further Palestinian violence. This environment might also be conducive to the ascendance of elements in the Palestinian leadership that would accept the settlement and try to make it work. There would still be considerable risks, but fewer than in a continuing cycle of Arab-Israeli wars.

If a settlement along these lines is reached, it will have to be implemented in stages, each stage being dependent on the satisfactory fulfillment of the preceding one. This will be a long-drawn-out process, stretching over years. Misunderstandings and resulting conflicts will be possible along the way, the more so since it will be difficult to balance the different types of concessions required of the two sides: one—giving up territory—is tangible; the other—taking steps toward peace—is not. Defining the contents and duration of each stage, and ensuring that they are as nearly irreversible as possible, may be the hardest part of the negotiations.

Although primary responsibility for negotiating and implementing any settlement must rest with the parties concerned, the United States can play a useful role, both by helping the parties to overcome obstacles that arise and by providing postsettlement aid and guarantees, as needed and desired. The significance of U.S. guarantees should not, however, be exaggerated. Israel has good reason to believe, from its 1967 experience, that it cannot rely on outside intervention to assure its existence. The only real assurance will be its own strength and the changes in Arab policy that are prerequisite to a settlement: a public commitment to peace with Israel, and permanent acceptance of Israel's new frontiers. The Arab governments could not defend these provisions of a settlement to their own peoples without striking a posture that would entail large domestic political costs and that could be reversed only with great difficulty. This fact is both a major barrier to a settlement and the best assurance that, if achieved, it will last.

The U.S. role in helping the parties start negotiations and carry them forward will be one of great delicacy. Unless the settlement rests on solid commitments by the parties, it will not endure; and yet without some outside help, it may not be achieved. Walking the narrow line between an overly intrusive role and passivity will be a demanding task for the United States—the more so since the issue will also figure heavily in American domestic debate and politics. But there is no alternative if we are to remove what is now the most serious threat of conflict that could involve the United States and the USSR. Encouraging and supporting Arab-Israeli negotiations for a general settlement will thus be the most urgent foreign policy task facing the next administration.

There is, of course, a good chance that this task cannot be carried out—either because negotiations will not begin or because they will stalemate. A realistic U.S. policy must deal, therefore, with the possibility that the status quo will not be altered by negotiation. We must continue to arm the Israeli defense forces as necessary to deter or defeat Arab attack; and we must maintain powerful U.S. naval and air forces in the Eastern Mediterranean, which can be reinforced as necessary to deter Soviet involvement in any future conflict.

Here, as in Europe and Northeast Asia, we cannot rely on U.S. strategic nuclear power alone to protect our interests. In an era of nuclear parity, Soviet rulers will assume that this power is unlikely to be brought quickly into play for the defense of local interests. As indicated in chapter 3, we must avoid local conventional weakness that could present us with a choice between surrender and the early use of tactical or strategic nuclear weapons.

Providing weapons to Israel and maintaining U.S. forces in the Eastern Mediterranean to deter Soviet intervention will involve continuing strain on our relations with the Arab countries. We should be under no illusion that this can be avoided by economic aid to some of these countries, desirable though this may be on other grounds. Our policy of seeking an overall settlement will also involve intermittent strain on our relations with Israel, and this, too, must be faced.

The Arab countries will seek U.S. military aid and arms sales. Arms transfers to these countries could indeed strengthen moderate elements in their leadership and weaken their reliance on the USSR. But in the event of Arab-Israeli war we could hardly continue supplying spare parts and replacements to the Arab countries and thus enhance the threat to Israel; we would have to cut off that supply and rupture U.S. relations with the Arabs. To foresee that problem is to conclude that it is unwise for the United States to become a major supplier of arms to Israel's immediate neighbors and most likely adversaries: the so-called confrontation states, Egypt and Syria. It would be more prudent to encourage them to have recourse to Western European arms suppliers.

Other Areas of Conflict

Iran's ambition to dominate the Persian Gulf will continue to be resisted by bordering Arab states and by India. Iran will probably move slowly toward a nuclear capability in the next ten years, and its conventional superiority in the Persian Gulf is such that none of the bordering Arab states could plausibly contemplate a preemptive attack. As Iran comes increasingly into rivalry with India, however, the opportunities for introducing nuclear threats into local disputes will grow.

Disputes between conservative and radical groups in the Arab world are also likely to lead to intra- and interstate conflicts. Over the longer term, surviving feudal elites will probably decline, and regimes rooted in the nationalist middle class and its allies in the officer corps will become dominant. But these regimes are likely to become involved in conflict with each other as each seeks a role of regional leadership; and there will continue to be serious religious, ethnic, and political conflicts, even among the so-called radical Arab regimes. In short, a long period of turbulence is ahead.

The best U.S. policy toward these Middle East disputes will be nonintervention. Our interests would certainly be adversely affected if Iran and the Arab states fought over who should control the Persian Gulf, or if radical and conservative groups in the Arab world contested for influence; but we would only make the situation worse if U.S. armed forces and prestige were committed to one side or the other. We should do what we can to conciliate these disputes, and recognize that U.S. military commitment would only undermine this influence.

Middle Eastern conflicts that do not inflict widespread damage on oil production facilities or pipelines need not prevent oil exports from continuing, except in the event of an Arab-Israeli war, when some form of oil embargo would be likely. Failing this, higher prices are more likely to be sought by the Arab countries as a means of financial enrichment than of political leverage. As indicated in chapter 5, much will depend on how successful the developed countries are in cooperating to reduce consumption and develop alternative energy sources. Progress in these respects is likely to have more effect in limiting price increases than threats of U.S. military action. The only circumstance, and that an unlikely one, in which military action might receive allied support is if a total Arab oil embargo were imposed and continued for a long time.

We should not, however, go out of our way to allay any fears of the oil-exporting countries about U.S. military action. The threat of that action cannot be ruled out by them, if only because of our deployments in the Middle East and neighboring areas. Low-key though it is, this implicit threat may combine with economic considerations to reinforce those in the Arab world who argue against any attempt to use oil as a political weapon.

Another continuing dispute in the Eastern Mediterranean affecting the United States will be that between Greece and Turkey. This conflict is unlikely to be resolved, but it may abate as both sides come gradually to accept a partition of Cyprus; we should do what we can to help them move in this direction. The possibility of war cannot be excluded, but it is unlikely, given superior Turkish military power; again, pressures from the United States will help. This continuing dispute may compound the internal instability of both countries, as Greece and Turkey undergo the changes in political power and social outlook that accompany economic growth. Both countries will retain a lively interest in maintaining their independence from Soviet control; their relations with the United States will be shadowed by our inability to provide unqualified support for either side.

Europe

The potential for conflict in Europe results from the interaction of two possible trends: toward weakness in Western Europe and toward upheaval in Eastern Europe.

Western Europe

In contemplating Europe's future, we should be wary of projecting too much from our present fears. The last quarter century in Western Europe has been, after all, a period of stable democratic governments; powerful communist parties existed in France and Italy throughout this period, and it is not clear that the tendency of voters to favor the center (though not necessarily our idea of the center or the same center in all countries) has come to an end. Economic growth seems likely to continue, even if at a lower rate; and most people will wish to continue having new elections, as well as new automobiles. The European Community and NATO are likely to survive, even if in altered form. Still, serious problems lie ahead; they are most evident in southern Europe.

Although Portugal and Spain will move along different paths, reflecting their contrasting circumstances, both now lack the main prerequisite for peaceful political evolution: institutions that permit power to shift readily from one group to another, while surrounding the exercise of that power with subtle restraints. Over the longer term, economic growth will probably create the middle class needed to bring these countries' politics more into line with those of the rest of Western Europe, but this transition is unlikely to be completed in the next ten years. A considerable measure of political instability must be expected in the meantime.

The Italian economy is likely to continue to grow, but its social infrastructure will lag behind the needs of a modern state and its working class will remain outside the mainstream of Italy's society and body politic. High rates of inflation and a large Communist party are among the results. On the other hand, memories of fascism have created what appears to be a widespread desire to retain a democratic form of government. The communists may come to share in power, but to hold onto it they will probably have to respect the desire for democracy. Their growing alienation from Moscow may enable them to accept a continuation of something like Italy's present foreign policy. Nonetheless, the risks involved in communist participation in the national government could be great: a flight of capital could hasten deterioration of the economic situation; the competition for power between communists and noncommunists could cause violence; and all this could lead to a weakening of democratic institutions.

In France, as in Italy, inflation and a tradition of class conflict sustain a powerful Communist party; but its leadership has so far been less pragmatic and flexible than in Italy. If it came to power it would probably be in a coalition with the numerically stronger Socialist party; in this event, it would seek to dominate its ally, and might succeed. If so, an attempted military countercoup and even civil war could ensue. If a leftist coalition government remained in power the communists would probably eventually press for a break with France's present pro-Western foreign policy, an end to informal French cooperation with NATO, and withdrawal of the French Army divisions from Germany. Even if a centrist coalition remains in power, as seems somewhat more likely, these French divisions will remain below strength and weakly armed.

On present evidence, the unfavorable trend in Britain's economy seems likely to continue, with high inflation and low growth. Although this will not threaten the democratic system of government, Britain's contribution to the defense of the central front will probably continue to decline.

In Germany, prospects are better than in any other major European country for restraining inflation, keeping political power in moderate hands, and maintaining an effective contribution to NATO defense. Communist sharing of power in Italy and France could, however, lead to a change in German attitudes—either toward neutralism and loss of confidence or toward a more assertive and self-reliant national role. In either event, a strong and healthy Western Europe could be endangered.

The effects of these unfavorable trends will be limited, in some degree, by the workings of the European Community and the rudimentary economic discipline it imposes on its members. The Community is unlikely to become a superstate, but neither is it likely to disintegrate. It will continue to provide a framework within which moderate government and open economic policies are more likely to survive than otherwise.

By contrast, the outlook for a European defense entity, with which the United States could cooperate in reshaping and strengthening Europe's defense, is not bright. In its absence, the defense of the central front will increasingly devolve on the United States and Germany. These two countries are capable, with modest assistance from others, of maintaining an effective conventional defense of Central Europe; but growing recognition that NATO is essentially a U.S.–German alliance could generate increasing tension in both Eastern and Western Europe. Over the longer term, it might even weaken support for the alliance in Germany and the United States. If more effective cooperation on defense among Germany ,France, Britain, and the Low Countries becomes feasible ,we should make clear our strong support and be willing to accept the changes in NATO (including diminution of U.S. influence) that would be required to allow a larger European military role to emerge.

It is hard to see an explosion or major conflict in Western Europe, except by contagion from Eastern Europe. There will be considerable potential for upheaval in Eastern Europe in the coming decade, and it is not difficult to conceive of ways in which it could spread. How the Soviet Union would act in such a widening crisis would be influenced by the military balance in Europe. If something like the present balance had been maintained, Soviet leaders might perceive some advantage in restraint; but if it had changed greatly in their favor, they might be more tempted to act boldly. This shift could occur if on-going improvement of Soviet forces in Europe had created a widening gap between Warsaw Pact and NATO forces. This would be the more likely if, as for reasons indicated earlier, France had pulled its two divisions out of Germany, Britain had withdrawn most of the Army of the Rhine, and resulting European concerns over Germany's enlarged military role had created major rifts in NATO and the European Community.

Even in the absence of Eastern European upheavals, such a crumbling of NATO strength might tempt the USSR to apply greater pressure on Western Europe, and this could lead to miscalculation and some risk of conflict. But the chances of this occurring might be greater if Soviet leaders were already facing a violent challenge in Eastern Europe. In this event, they might conclude that a Soviet dominion in an Eastern Europe constantly exposed to the contagion of Western pluralism and influence would be difficult to preserve, that they must act to neutralize Western Europe or accept the prospect of continuing troubles in the East. The cost of these Eastern troubles would be obviously high; the costs of facing down a weakened Western Europe by precipitating a sharp crisis, say over Berlin, in order decisively to demoralize and disrupt NATO, might seem marginally more tolerable. None of these events is a strong possibility, no more than an outside chance at most.

The economic policies that would help maintain a healthy Western Europe and a sound U.S.–European connection are treated in chapter 5. If the cooperative U.S., European, and Japanese economic policies discussed there should reduce even moderately the rate of inflation in Europe, this might do more to limit communist strength in

Italy and France and to increase Britain's contribution to NATO than any other action we could take.

The defense policies that might help to maintain an evident balance of military power in Central Europe are discussed in chapter 3. The proposed U.S. commitment to maintain large U.S. forces in Europe runs counter to past congressional pressure for reducing our forces. These pressures, which have now abated, reflected two beliefs that have been discredited by events: that the European countries will do more if we do less, and that the Russians are so benign that it does not matter what we or the Europeans do. If Congress is persuaded to support the measures described in chapter 3, the USSR may become sufficiently convinced of the permanence of the U.S. military presence to pay something for its stabilization and eventual reduction in concessions at the talks on mutual balanced force reductions at Vienna.

Over the longer term, the economic and defense policies toward Europe suggested in chapters 3 and 5 should help to create an environment of confidence and security in which Western European integration can go forward. We should do what we can to encourage this trend. The larger European role that would result would pose some problems and risks for the United States, but it appears one of the more promising means of averting growing European weakness.

We should beware of the notion that a U.S. initiative could produce rapid progress in European affairs. We do not have the leverage to shape trends there, except over the very long term; and our withdrawal would surely make matters worse. Steadiness in seeking U.S.–European–Japanese economic concert and U.S.–European defense cooperation will be the most useful course, but it will not produce early and radical improvements. In fact, the most important factors in the European situation lie outside our control. Domestic trends in Britain, France, Italy, and other countries will be crucial, and we should resist the temptation to advise these countries how to arrange their affairs. Moderate leaders in France and Italy will be better judges than we of how to respond to growing communist strength in their countries. We should stick to what we *can* do, which is to help create an economic and security environment in which leaders of other countries will have freedom to make what they consider the right choices.

There will be some temptation in the United States to give up on the weaker European countries and focus our policies on Germany. This would stimulate fears that could weaken other Western European countries' attachment to the European Community and to NATO, thus making more likely the trend toward weakness that we should be trying to reverse. It would also stimulate Soviet and Eastern European fears that could impede any prospects for constructive East-West rapprochement. We cannot have a strong Western Europe that does not include Britain and France; support for European and Atlantic groupings that include them will be more promising than trying to build a bilateral alliance with Germany.

Eastern Europe

Nationalist pressures in Eastern Europe have overthrown two empires, Turkey and Austria-Hungary, in this century; and the death throes of each of these empires triggered major wars. Nationalist pressures will continue to threaten the Soviet empire in Eastern Europe; and this process, too, could be marked by substantial violence.

The Soviet Union has been unable to reconcile most Eastern European peoples to its hegemony: Yugoslavia has broken away; Rumania emphasizes its independence; nationalism is strong in Poland; the Hungarians are seeking to develop their own economic course; Czechoslovakia and East Germany are still garrisoned by Soviet divisions. The Eastern European peoples have learned the lessons of 1956 and 1968; they do not want violence. But nowhere, except perhaps in traditionally Slavophile Bulgaria, is there ready acceptance of continuing Soviet dominance.

Yet the Soviet Union is determined to maintain that dominance— to preserve docile allies and ready deployment areas for Soviet forces in the strategically important northern tier (Poland, East Germany, and Czechoslovakia); to ensure against a Yugoslav-type breakaway in Rumania or Hungary; and to make certain that Yugoslavia does not become the first country to abandon communism. In part, this determination reflects strategic concerns: Central and Eastern Europe is where many invasions of Russia have been launched. In part, it reflects the instinctive desire of heirs to an imperial tradition to hold what they have, if only because "losing" Eastern Europe could be seen by critics at home as a mark of incompetence. And, in part, it reflects the perceived need of a regime whose existence is rooted in ideology not to see that creed overthrown or weakened by pluralism close by, whence the challenge could spread to Russia itself. Soviet leaders may also be concerned lest the example of successful and assertive nationalism in Eastern Europe have an unhealthy impact on non-Russian nationalities in the USSR.

The clash between Soviet dominance and Eastern European nationalism has engendered substantial use of armed force three times since 1945—in Berlin in 1953, Budapest in 1956, and Prague in 1968. Fighting seemed imminent at other times—Warsaw in 1956 and Rumania in 1968. It would be unrealistic to assume that such clashes will never recur. If they do, rapid and massive Soviet action, Eastern European passivity, and the Western desire to avoid war will probably cause the violence to be contained, as in the past. But if Soviet repression did not succeed quickly, the success of détente in eroding barriers to communication and travel between Eastern and Western Europe over the last decade might make acceptance of that repression less ready, in both these parts of Europe and in the United States.

The most obvious danger is Yugoslavia. The chances are that this country will hang together after Tito, if only because the consequences of division are so unattractive to most Yugoslavs. But the possibility of conflict exists—notably between liberal and nationalist dissidents in the two northern republics and orthodox communists in Belgrade, whose ideological differences are compounded by older ethnic rivalries. Although both sides would prefer to resolve such a conflict without jeopardizing Yugoslav independence, the Soviet Union might be able to maneuver a plea for help from Belgrade if the orthodox cause seemed to be foundering. Bulgaria might join (or anticipate) Soviet intervention in order to assert its long-standing claim to Macedonia. The existence of strong local Yugoslav defense forces, as a result of their recent decentralization, might prevent Soviet intervention from succeeding quickly, however. If so, the reaction in Europe and the United States to appeals for help from anti-Soviet forces would probably be tepid, though one cannot be sure. The stage might be set for a widening conflict, the more so since the Adriatic might be patrolled by Soviet, Yugoslav, and NATO naval forces, and the air over Yugoslavia might be crowded with planes bringing supplies to the opposing forces.

Poland is another danger area. If internal disturbances—brought on, say, by economic troubles—threatened to end communist rule, Soviet forces might intervene. The Poles would not give in easily; the resulting clash could divert some Soviet forces from East Germany, whence Soviet forces were deployed to the Polish border in 1956. That diversion and, more importantly, the contagion of events in Poland could create opportunities for upheaval in East Germany.

Though events almost never turn out as predicted, the basic point is clear: the situation in Eastern Europe will remain potentially unstable until Soviet leaders reconcile themselves to a greater degree of Eastern European autonomy and a more pluralistic political life within these countries. This will not happen until basic changes occur in the Soviet Union, which is difficult to envisage happening in the coming decade.

U.S. influence will be limited in Eastern Europe. The Eastern European countries will want greater freedom, and the Soviet Union will try to prevent them from acquiring it, except within narrow limits, no matter what we do. Whether this results in upheavals will hinge on factors that are largely beyond our control.

Trade and economic cooperation between Western and Eastern Europe and between the United States and Eastern Europe will make sense—in contributing to useful exchanges of goods and ideas, in easing somewhat the plight of Eastern European peoples, and in helping to resolve certain common internal European problems. But this will not allow Eastern Europe to slip unnoticed out of Soviet control. The prerequisite to that change would be evolution in the USSR, not merely in Eastern Europe.

NATO–Warsaw Pact cooperation in the security field (for instance, advance warnings of maneuvers and exchanges of observers) would also make sense, in reducing fear of surprise attack. But the notion that Europe's security problems could be solved by an East-West security system anticipates changes in both sides' outlook that are unlikely to take place in the twentieth century.

President John F. Kennedy said in 1963 that there are some international problems for which an American answer cannot be found;[5] the clash between Eastern European nationalism and Soviet imperialism is one. This does not mean, however, that our actions

5. John F. Kennedy, "Commencement Address at American University, June 10, 1963," *Public Papers of the Presidents, 1963* (Government Printing Office, 1964), pp. 459–64.

cannot have some effect. We should make clear to the USSR the large price in interrupted détente it would have to pay if it used force against Eastern European countries. There is no reason to believe that the USSR would be more deterred in the future than it has been in the past by such warnings; its leaders probably believe, on the basis of past evidence, that any interruption would be brief. Still, the Soviet decision on Czechoslovakia was apparently taken only after a long period of doubt and debate, and we should do what we can to ensure that such decisions are not any easier in the future.

Warnings of possible U.S. military action were implicitly conveyed to the USSR by deployments of U.S. armed forces and by presidential speeches in 1968, when it seemed to be contemplating moves against Rumania and Yugoslavia. Only in the case of Yugoslavia, with its "gray" status between East and West, might future U.S. warnings be credible enough to be persuasive. We should make clear to the USSR that Soviet military intervention in a Yugoslav conflict could create the risk of a wider conflict that might prove difficult to contain.[6] We should, however, avoid overdramatizing the risk of a conflict in Yugoslavia and should do nothing that would limit our freedom to choose between action and inaction if conflict occurs.

Northeast Asia

After the Middle East, the most likely arena of conflict that could involve the United States is Korea, where two heavily armed and hostile states adjoin each other. Conflict in Korea might involve the United States both because we are committed to the defense of South Korea and because of the impact of events there on Japan, China, and the USSR. In the short term, our purpose must be to avert a Korean conflict. Over the longer term, we should try to distance ourselves from events in Korea, through measures discussed below, and to render the U.S.–Japanese connection less vulnerable to events on the peninsula.

Japan

The present U.S.–Japanese association serves our purposes well. It provides a framework both for close U.S.–Japanese cooperation in

6. The U.S. military policies in Europe and the Mediterranean that would help to make this warning persuasive are discussed in chapter 3.

meeting important economic problems, as discussed in chapter 5, and also for a continuation of Japan's low military posture. Although it is without precedent for a great power, the coexistence of that posture and great economic strength is likely to be maintained in Japan; some Japanese, indeed, see it as the wave of the future in a world in which nuclear war is plainly suicidal and economic issues are at the heart of foreign policy. Internal trends in Japan are not likely to change this combination. Economic growth may slow, but it seems likely to continue at a higher rate than in most developed countries. The leftist parties are solidly antinationalist, and the leadership of the conservative party is responsive to the desires of the Japanese business community, which has even less taste for foreign military adventures now than before the war. If domestic trends lead to any change in Japan's present foreign policy, it is likely to be in the direction of weakening the already modest defense program and making foreign policy more neutralist.

Japan's lightly armed nonnuclear status will, however, be vulnerable to external shocks. Japan adjoins two strongly armed and potentially hostile powers, China and Russia. Even the two Koreas, which are perceived by many Japanese as potentially hostile, have more powerful armed forces than Japan. The Japanese maintain their present low military posture primarily because they consider war in Northeast Asia unlikely, and because the Japanese leadership has confidence in Japan's continuing close defense association with the United States. Both these circumstances could change: war in Korea could persuade most Japanese that they live in a dangerous world; and U.S. inaction in such a war, a more nationalist U.S. economic policy, or near-total withdrawal of U.S. forces from Northeast Asia could persuade many Japanese that they could no longer rely on the United States as a main ally.

In any of these circumstances, pressures for large-scale Japanese rearmament might grow, at least among the elite. There might also be pressures to acquire nuclear arms, which would seem to some more effective and economical than a conventional arms buildup. A nuclear Japan would probably be increasingly nationalist and anti-American; indeed, only by such rhetoric could a Japanese government justify nuclear arms. China and other Asian countries would be alarmed, and the stage would be set for growing tension between them and Japan. Alternatively, a Japan that discounted its connection with the United States might move toward China or toward a neutralist foreign policy. In short, the results of a loss of Japanese confidence in the United States, while unpredictable, would almost certainly be highly adverse for the United States.

This course of events is unlikely, barring a Korean war or a major change in U.S. policy toward Japan. The change in U.S. policy we can preclude by our own decision; the war in Korea we cannot. In the long run, it is not in our interest to have our peace and the health of our relations with Japan dependent on events in Korea, where our influence and stake are both limited. If the U.S. defense and economic policies toward Japan discussed in chapters 3 and 5 are followed over a considerable period of time, Japanese leaders may be persuaded that they can count on the United States to support their interests, even if the gradual withdrawal of most U.S. ground forces from Korea discussed below is carried out.

Though the most evident U.S.–Japanese connection lies in the economic area, the heaviest penalty for not following a wise economic policy would be felt in the politico-military area. A Japan that had lost confidence in the U.S.–Japanese economic connection to assure its prosperity would be only a step removed from a Japan that had lost confidence in this connection to assure its security. Chapter 3 discusses the forces that need to be maintained in Northeast Asia to preserve Japan's continued confidence in the U.S. military connection. As in Europe, measures to sustain a powerful U.S. presence in Northeast Asia run counter to recent congressional pressure for the retraction of U.S. overseas military power. In the wake of Vietnam, however, Congress has shown increased sensitivity to the importance of Japan. If the maintenance of powerful U.S. naval and air forces in Northeast Asia can be balanced by the reduction in other U.S. forces in and for Asia, as recommended in chapter 3, the prospects for congressional support of the steps needed to maintain a healthy U.S. defense connection with Japan will be enhanced.

From time to time U.S. administrations will be tempted to encourage Japan to build up its own nonnuclear forces as a means of reducing the burden on the United States in Northeast Asia. Within limits, improvements in Japanese conventional military capabilities, particularly naval and air defense forces, would be useful, but they would not greatly reduce the need for U.S. forces in Northeast Asia to reassure the Japanese. A large-scale Japanese buildup could unhinge prospects for peace and stability in Asia.

Japan is one of the three great aggregations of economic and potential military power in the noncommunist world. It is a vital U.S. interest that this power not be directed against us, or used in other adverse and unpredictable ways. A close and confident U.S.–Japanese association will be the best way to protect this interest. This means an American willingness to give high priority to the needs of U.S.–Japanese interdependence in pursuing economic policies that are in our interest anyway; to continue deploying large U.S. forces to Northeast Asia, even if military reasons for deploying them are not readily evident; and above all, to avoid the independent U.S. actions on matters of great moment to Japan that have come to be known in Tokyo as "Nixon shocks."

Korea

If war broke out between the two Koreas, the Japanese reaction would be deeply ambivalent. On the one hand, many Japanese would be deeply concerned over U.S. military involvement in a war on their doorstep, and there might be moves to limit our use of bases in Japan to avoid Japan's being drawn into the war. On the other hand (and more importantly), if the United States remained inactive in the face of a successful North Korean attack, Japanese leaders might well conclude that this was decisive evidence of America's unreliability and that they had best pursue a more self-reliant military posture to assure their security. This would be the more likely if the war produced a unified and strongly armed Korea, which many Japanese would perceive as a threat to Japan. Either way a Korean war would adversely affect our vital interests in Northeast Asia.

Averting a Korean war should thus be a high priority for the United States in the coming decade. The roughly even balance of strength between the two Korean states and the constraints implicitly imposed by the major powers will probably continue to deter deliberate attack. Internal upheaval in either North or South Korea might, however, persuade its adversary to try to use force to unify the peninsula. If so, the external ties of China, the USSR, and the United States to the two Koreas and the tensions among these three great powers would make the conflict hard to limit; none of the great powers would wish to see its Korean ally destroyed.

It is sometimes suggested that Korean unification can be peacefully achieved by promoting dialogue between the two Koreas. We should not delude ourselves on this score; neither Korean regime will bend to foreign suasion on a matter of such moment, and neither will contemplate unification, except on its own terms.

The best way to deter war will continue to be to help maintain a situation in which neither government sees any chance of quick victory. We should provide South Korea with weapons on the scale needed for successful defense, while avoiding such large arms transfers as would threaten the balance of power on the peninsula. And we should use such influence as we have to try to persuade the South Korean regime to avoid repressive domestic policies that could create tempting opportunities for external intervention, and to restrain its enthusiasm if such opportunities occur in the North. But in matters of domestic policy, our influence will be limited, in Korea as elsewhere. The South Korean government will do what it considers necessary to remain in power, whatever we may do or say.

Prospects for violence in the Korean peninsula would be enhanced if South Korea moved overtly toward a nuclear weapons capability. This might generate pressures in North Korea for comparable nuclear weapons programs, or for preventive attack. And if South Korea achieved a nuclear capability, it might conclude that the best way to avoid North Korean preemption was to mount a first strike.

We should therefore try to dissuade South Korea from taking any steps that would seem to foreshadow a nuclear weapons program, and we should ask the USSR and China to urge similar restraint on North Korea. Over the longer term, this suasion will have only limited effect on Seoul. We should also try to cooperate with other potential suppliers, as suggested in chapter 4, to limit South Korea's capability for developing nuclear weapons. The South Korean interest in nuclear weapons rests, in part, on the fear that the U.S. security commitment will be attenuated. Continued stationing of U.S. forces in Korea is persuasive reassurance; their presence will slow, but it will not halt, Korean pressures for nuclear weapons. Our military presence in Korea is also welcome in Japan, and it helps to deter North Korean attack.

These considerations should not preclude immediate withdrawal of U.S. tactical nuclear weapons from Korea. Their use would be as dangerous in widening hostilities as it would be unnecessary in halting a North Korean attack. Such weapons are, moreover, available on aircraft carriers of the Seventh Fleet, which cruise in nearby waters. But withdrawal of the U.S. Army 2nd Division and the Air

Force Fighter Wing now in Korea would be a major step, affecting profoundly Japan as well as both Koreas. A distinction must be drawn between the two units, however: the Army division is not needed militarily, and its continued presence close to the border commits the United States to instant and automatic involvement in any Korean war; while the air force wing is needed to compensate for the relative weakness of South Korean airpower and is deployed somewhat further to the rear.

This issue should be resolved in close consultation with Japan. Our goal should be to withdraw the Army division over a period of some years, and to maintain the air force wing indefinitely, or at least until there is a basic change in the Korean situation or in Japanese attitudes toward Korea.[7] In this way, we would somewhat reduce both the risk of automatic involvement and the need to build up the South Korean air force to a level that might give Seoul an effective first strike capability, while giving some assurance to Japan and South Korea and some warning to North Korea. This goal should be subject to change if consultation with Japan or developments in Korea so indicate. In this area, a go-slow policy, testing the water and the wind as we go, will be wise; the consequences of a mistake would be great.

The Third World

Generalization about the third world is difficult because of its diversity, but one thing that can safely be said is that the prospects for conflict are substantial. Third-world countries have generally left behind the stagnation of their colonial and semifeudal past but often have not yet achieved the political, social, and economic development that would provide a new basis of stability. To do justice in a single chapter to resulting tensions among developing countries and between groups of them would be impossible; what follows is a brief description of those tensions and conflicts that might directly affect the United States.

Asia

The record suggests that there are likely to be periodic upheavals within Southeast Asian countries and occasional clashes between

7. For more details, see Ralph N. Clough, *Deterrence and Defense in Korea: The Role of U.S. Forces* (Brookings Institution, 1976).

them. Nationalist authoritarian governments will probably continue to hold sway in many of these countries. Economic growth is likely to continue, and there may be intermittent progress toward regional cooperation. No dominant regional power is likely to emerge; Indonesia and Vietnam, the most likely contenders, will probably be preoccupied with internal problems. On present evidence, communist parties are unlikely to be able to align themselves closely enough with nationalism in any of the countries where they have not yet come to power to be a decisive element. Direct military involvement by communist powers in this area is also likely to remain limited. Neither the USSR nor China now considers its vital interests to be so directly involved as to warrant commitment of substantial armed forces to this region, although this could change, in reaction, for instance, to a larger U.S. military role in the area.

India seems likely to make slow progress in its war on pervasive poverty and will probably remain under authoritarian rule. Its relations with Pakistan and Iran will probably remain tense; its nuclear capabilities are likely to increase slowly. None of the South Asian countries would benefit from fighting each other; the most pressing territorial issues have been settled and competition for prestige is being conducted largely by nonmilitary means. Nonetheless, local clashes between India and its neighbors are possible. These are unlikely, however, to involve the armed forces of great powers. China and the USSR will try to influence events in this area, but their success will be limited; and there is no evidence that either of them is prepared to increase decisively the commitment of its resources to this region.

The Soviet Union may increase its naval deployments in the Indian Ocean, but these are unlikely to have a dominant influence on events. India and Pakistan will continue to make their foreign policy decisions on other grounds; Iran and other countries will continue to expect vital oil supplies to move across this vast expanse, protected less by local forces than by the belief that large-scale war would result if they were molested.

Africa

Africa's future will be shadowed by racial struggles south of the Sahara. The Soviet Union and other communist countries are likely to provide weapons to black guerrilla groups and governments that wage war on the white government of Rhodesia. Eventually black

majority rule will be achieved in Rhodesia; but the communist countries will probably be disappointed by the speed with which their erst-
while allies turn to a policy of nationalist self-reliance, treating the
USSR and the United States with even-handed disdain, modified only
slightly by a desire for economic and military aid.

The communist countries will also offer help to militant groups
and governments willing to challenge white rule in South Africa; this
help is, as they see it, the main instrument they have to gain influence
in the region. But the white minority is large, well organized, and
well armed; it will continue to hold power in the Republic of South
Africa for at least the next decade.

The racial conflict in Africa will have a powerful and somber
effect on U.S. domestic opinion. There will be partisans and
pressures on both sides. Some will be alarmed by the prospect of
growing Soviet influence and will feel empathy for beleagured
whites; others will resent white domination and be anxious to promote majority rule. Casualties and atrocities in African fighting will
heighten American feelings. Any U.S. policy will be attended by
violent internal debate and dissension; it is highly doubtful a consensus could be secured for a policy that involved either use of U.S.
armed forces or provision of military assistance to any of the warring
parties.

Latin America

Large-scale wars have not occurred in Latin America for many
years. They are unlikely to recur, although major tensions will persist—notably between Argentina and Brazil in the east and between
Peru and its neighbors in the west. Internal conflict will probably
occur from time to time, since few Latin American countries have
reliable procedures for transferring power peacefully from one group
to another. The general trend now seems to be running toward
nationalist, authoritarian governments of conservative stripe.

Brazil's growth will continue to widen the gap between its economic and military power and that of other Latin American countries. The present military regime has so far proved agile in adapting
to changing conditions. Its substantial nuclear power program will
increasingly provide a base for a nuclear weapons program. If Brazil
moves toward nuclear weapons development, Argentina, technically
competent even though less wealthy and continually troubled by its
inability either to accommodate or repress its powerful labor move-

ment, will be tempted to follow suit. The resulting nuclear rivalry would be expensive, though unlikely to lead to war.

Mexico faces difficult internal problems, compounded by rapid population growth, whose effects are cushioned by economic progress and rising illegal emigration to the United States. The ruling party has shown some capacity to widen its base to encompass new groups, and will probably continue to do so. If not, we may find endemic disorder and extremism on our southern border.

In the Caribbean the trend seems to favor the left. Cuba is seen as the wave of the future, and there will probably be further would-be Castros in coming decades. If so, Cuba will probably give them help, and its influence may grow. The most likely trouble spot is the Panama Canal Zone. Panama's demands regarding the zone have widespread Latin American support. If they are not accommodated, guerrilla operations against U.S. forces and bases are likely to ensue.

Policy Guidelines

U.S. policy toward these possible sources of conflict—in Asia, Africa, and Latin America—cannot be dealt with in any depth here, but a few guidelines can be suggested. We should distinguish sharply between three types of conflict situations: where only the local parties are involved, where material assistance is being provided by outside communist countries, and where armed forces of outside communist countries are involved.

In a conflict of the first category, it would clearly be unwise to commit U.S. forces. Our vital security interests are not involved, and our capabilities are limited. If the South Asian or Southeast Asian states want to fight each other, if blacks and whites contest violently for control of parts of Africa, or if Castro seeks to spread his influence in Latin America, sending in U.S. forces will generally not be the answer. We should use what political influence we have to help these countries resolve their disputes; if this effort fails, the resulting wars will not be made less bloody or useless by our intervention. It does not follow, however, that we should be indifferent to the outcome. In Africa, we should come down firmly on the side of those seeking majority rule and avoid criticizing them for using force to that end, since it is unlikely to be achieved by peaceful means. In Latin America, we should be prepared to join any action by the Organization of American States (OAS) that may be agreed on in response to uses of force that extend across national frontiers, leaving it largely up to the Latin American countries to decide what that response should be; and we should be prepared to provide military assistance to threatened governments.

The problem becomes more complicated if we confront not merely a local conflict but also material assistance by outside communist countries to one of the parties. We should reject the notion that our relationship with the USSR requires us to offset its interventions, wherever they occur, even in regions of no intrinsic strategic importance to us. If the Soviet Union is encouraged by any successes it may achieve in such areas to challenge us in more vital regions, such as Europe, we will be better able to respond if we have not wasted our resources and political capital and divided our people by interventions elsewhere. Our refusal to respond in peripheral areas will be perceived as weakness by the Soviet Union only if we portray it as such in internal debate, failing to make clear the calculations on which it rests.

There may, however, occasionally be some advantage to the United States in making the Soviet Union and its allies pay for their involvement—to deny them cheap victories, if this can be done without excessive commitment of U.S. resources and prestige. This may mean asking Congress to provide a specified amount of military assistance, without any implicit or explicit commitment to raise the stakes if that assistance proves insufficient to achieve the desired end. This requires a considerable degree of national maturity and restraint. The present tendency is to believe that we should either go all the way or do nothing. But inaction may be costly, and the evidence to date does not support the proposition that military assistance need lead inevitably to involvement of U.S. forces.

The success of this policy hinges on the conflict being one in which the Soviet Union is playing a large role, in which we and our allies would like to see that role frustrated, and in which there seems a good chance that military assistance will have this effect. Perhaps such a case will not arise, but if it does we should not preclude a limited investment by our allies and ourselves, to stop Soviet intervention or at least to make it sufficiently expensive for the USSR so that it will think twice before repeating the experience. A good deal will depend on the nature of the conflict. The mere fact that communist countries are backing one side should not lead us to support its opponents. If, for instance, the USSR supports forces seeking black majority rule in Africa, we would only compound the damage by allying ourselves with white minority rule.

The third type of conflict is one where the forces of the Soviet Union or other communist countries are involved. Our decision regarding material assistance should be made according to the criteria described above. U.S. forces should be committed in only the most unusual circumstances. The risk that the United States and the USSR will be drawn into conflicts among local allies they cannot control is considerable in the Middle East, where we have a large security stake; we should avoid replicating this dangerous situation in areas where such important U.S. interests are lacking. Some possible exceptions may be noted. A full-scale Chinese invasion of Southeast Asia might warrant an American response, since it would portend such a large change in the Asian balance of power as to raise a question about Japan's future alignment. If Soviet forces should intervene in Latin America, this would be viewed as a challenge of sufficient proportions to U.S. hemispheric commitments that we could not ignore it without calling into question the validity of our other alliances, notably in Europe and Northeast Asia. Both these contingencies, however, are highly unlikely.

Since U.S. forces are not apt to fight in these areas of the third world, they should not be deployed there, or maintained especially for this contingency, on a substantial scale. This means that further reductions are possible, as indicated in chapter 3, in our Asian forces. Large-scale Pacific deployments outside Northeast Asia imply a threat that we would not wish to fulfill except, as noted above, in circumstances that are unlikely to come about. The U.S. resources involved could be put to better use in other areas.

Nor should there be large permanent U.S. naval deployments in the Indian Ocean. We have no good reason to intervene with force in future conflicts in South Asia; our main interest there is the oil traffic, which is protected by the fear that U.S. forces would intervene, rather than by local forces. In case of need, moreover, powerful U.S. naval forces could be moved to this area quickly. Otherwise, limited and largely symbolic U.S. deployments are all that is needed.

U.S. military assistance and arms sales policies should be geared to the policies outlined above. We should not seek to maintain a worldwide program of military aid as a matter of course; we should provide that aid only when special circumstances make it desirable, and with full public and congressional understanding of what is involved. Recent congressional reforms in the military aid program point in this direction. These reforms also affect military sales, which are the means by which most weapons now move from developed to developing countries. Our policy should shift from encouraging to regulating these sales. National security, rather than commercial, considerations should be dominant; where the national interest would not be served, no sale should be made. A resulting slow-down in arms transfers to poor countries will not make conflict less likely, but will diminish the scope of conflict if it occurs.

Outside of the Middle East and Northeast Asia, we should maintain a low military profile in the third world. We have important interests in these countries, but they are best advanced by nonmilitary means: development assistance, private investment, liberal trade policies, and other economic measures. Failure to recognize that these are not regions in which we have a sufficient direct stake or capability to involve U.S. armed forces will lead, first, to dangerous overextension and then to domestic discord and a general retrenchment that might endanger U.S. commitments in more important areas.

In the third world we will also face novel threats that do not arise solely, or even largely, out of interstate relations. Terrorism is likely to grow. Even if it does not involve nuclear theft, it could powerfully influence events—if, for example, it led to the assassination of major political figures or to increasingly large-scale terrorist raids and Israeli retaliation against Arab countries that aid terrorists. There may also be growing violence by nationals of developing countries against the peoples and goods of rich countries, whenever these can be attacked. Although the number of incidents will probably be limited, the effect on how the developed countries perceive the international environment may be great. In a world characterized by a large and increasing gap between rich and poor countries, the opportunities for ideologically motivated violence will be substantial.

The USSR

Having surveyed possible U.S. policies toward sources of conflict in specific regions, we now turn to our relations with the one power that could transform any one of these conflicts into another world war: the USSR. To say that the Soviet Union will remain a super-power in the coming decade is to acknowledge that it will remain the only country besides the United States capable of maintaining strategic nuclear forces that could obliterate civilized life in a large part of the world and the only country whose general purpose forces could dominate most of the developed world outside the Western Hemisphere, if unopposed by the United States.

There is every reason to expect Soviet leaders to maintain just such strategic and general purpose forces. As successors to the tsars, they are heirs to a long tradition of the use of military might to defend and expand the homeland. As Marxists they may anticipate clashes between Russia and what they believe to be the weakening but still basically hostile noncommunist societies that surround it, as well as with their Chinese rivals in the socialist commonwealth. Like most leaders of great powers, they probably perceive the maintenance of military strength as the best way to avoid war, and one way to extend their country's influence beyond its borders.

Soviet leaders will continue to assign the resources needed to maintain a steady rate of improvement in their general purpose and strategic forces, even though the Russian economy will continue to suffer the inefficiencies inherent in tightly centralized control. Although experts dispute the exact amounts involved, the USSR has in the last decade assigned a much larger proportion of its GNP to defense than has the United States.[8]

To reduce the risks and costs of arms competition, Soviet leaders will probably continue to seek strategic arms limitation agreements with the United States and to negotiate about mutual force reductions in Europe. The scope of any resulting agreements will probably be limited by their belief that large strategic forces are important both for fighting nuclear wars, if these occur, and for political purposes, and by a felt need to maintain sufficient conventional forces to balance those of China, Western Europe, and the United States and to control potentially unruly peoples in Eastern Europe.

There have been continuing improvements in Soviet strategic and general purpose forces over the past ten to fifteen years, and further improvement in the capabilities of these forces seems likely. How will Soviet leaders use this growing military power?

8. See chapter 3.

A good deal depends, of course, on the course of events within the USSR. The Communist party will almost certainly continue to hold a monopoly of power, and its desire to maintain that monopoly will probably produce a conservative leadership that is fearful of internal relaxation and anxious to maintain the dogma that legitimizes its power. All this may change over the longer run; and even in the short term the possibility of sharp reversals brought about by a struggle for power within the leadership or a clash between nationalities within the USSR cannot be precluded. The greater likelihood, however, is that we will not see such large upheavals in the coming decade.

The tasks facing the Soviet leadership involve inherent contradictions: trying to improve economic efficiency without conceding centralized political control, responding to pressures from the non-Russian nationalities that make up over half the population of the USSR without moving toward a federalism that would weaken Moscow's power, and containing internal dissidence without reverting to the harshest Stalinist methods. These domestic preoccupations, far from causing Soviet leaders to turn away from external affairs, will strengthen their desire to control Eastern Europe and make them even more reluctant to accept external defeats, which would further weaken their position vis-à-vis potential rivals. Conservative domestic policies will make them even less likely to change their predecessors' policies abroad; and emphasis on maintaining a strong ideological base in the USSR (and in the socialist commonwealth, in the face of Chinese competition) may sometimes make it difficult for them to refuse to support groups that claim they are trying to advance that ideology abroad.

Yet Soviet leaders can be expected to proceed with caution, constrained by the fear that large-scale war would destroy everything they have built up since the revolution. Soviet leaders know that at present, and for the foreseeable future, only one power poses this danger, so they will be anxious to avoid direct confrontations with the United States. The present leadership in the Kremlin evidently wants to maintain the appearance of détente, probably less because of its economic advantages, which can largely be obtained by trading with other Western economies, than because of its presumed impact on U.S. policy. The experience of recent years has probably made Soviet leaders confident that they can have their cake and eat it too: pursue détente, while proceeding with external policies that seek to expand their influence abroad. Whether a new leadership, which will surely come to power in the coming decade, will take the same view is uncertain. Much will depend on U.S. actions. It is too early to tell whether the recent shift in U.S. public opinion in favor of more defense and less détente has registered in the Kremlin and, if so, with what effect.

In any event, the USSR's relations with the United States will continue to be a mixture of cooperation and competition, which will vary within bounds set by its desires both to avoid war and to continue to play the role of a great power. Soviet leaders will not abandon that role for the sake of détente; nor will they knowingly allow it to propel them into a direct clash with the United States.

Over time, their perceptions of how far they can go in that role without provoking war may change if the military balance continues to move in their favor. Even if their military programs are not deliberately geared to this end, the effect might be the same. In future crises in the Middle East or Yugoslavia, for example, they might believe they could act more vigorously if they perceived a clear Soviet superiority in local conventional forces against a background of evident strategic parity or better.

It is probably U.S. determination that is most in question in the Soviet leaders' minds. The debate in the United States about our alleged defense weakness must be of interest to them. If they believe that Americans doubt U.S. military strength, they may expect that perception to moderate U.S. responses in future crises. On the other hand, if American statements and actions reflect self-confidence, aggressive Soviet action may seem less attractive to them. Their object is to face down, not fight, the United States.

Soviet leaders will be very sensitive to the specific state of U.S. forces; they will expect this to affect both U.S. attitudes and the military situation that they must confront if push comes to shove. For example, they might interpret the programs to improve U.S. forces in certain areas described in chapter 3 as portending an eventual change in the military balance, which they should either prevent by stepping up their own efforts or anticipate—by drawing back or by precipitating a crisis now, instead of later. More likely, they would continue their current policies until U.S. programs had proceeded far enough to change the actual military balance they would have to confront in specific areas of potential crisis, and then adjust pragmatically to these realities. There is little to suggest that their reaction would be to signal that they were prepared for some mutual restraint, in recognition that their own ambitious military programs had brought about U.S. countermeasures; but this response is not impossible.

The main risk in U.S.–Soviet relations is that of miscalculation and unintended war, and the main purpose of U.S. policy toward the USSR is to minimize this risk, by trying to avoid creating situations that will tempt the USSR to play an adventurous role and by making clear to Soviet leaders the advantages of businesslike cooperation and the disadvantages of aggressive pressures. Although this purpose has been more or less constant in U.S. policy during recent decades, the emphasis given its various elements has varied widely. Since World War II, relations with the Soviet Union have passed through several phases, each marked by some oversimplification in the attitudes of the American public. At the height of the cold war, the USSR was seen as the source of all our problems abroad; in this atmosphere, it was easy in 1960 to perceive a missile gap where none existed. Later President Richard M. Nixon presided over a period of détente, in which we were told that the United States and Soviet Union would join in building a generation of peace; in this environment, the notion of subsidizing the sale of grain to the USSR gained ready acceptance. As of this writing, the word détente is being excised from the official vocabulary; and exaggerated estimates of relative Soviet strength and aggressive intentions are again the coin of political debate.

The remarkable thing is that through all of this Soviet policy has shown considerable continuity. Soviet leaders have always exploited weakness where they found it, drawn back from direct confrontation with the United States, increased defense expenditures at about the same rate as their GNP, and negotiated advantageous agreements where they could. There has been some increased willingness to negotiate arms control agreements and some movement away from economic autarchy, but on the whole it has been our perception of Soviet policies and objectives, rather than reality, that has changed.

The first requirement in U.S. policy toward the USSR is, therefore, to avoid sharp changes of course without good reason. Year in and year out we must maintain evident and persuasive military strength without being provocative, at the same time as a receptivity to useful negotiations, without being soft-headed. If this is less exciting than periodic reversions to either cold war or euphoric détente, it is also a more promising guide to policy. We should be sensitive in adapting to changes in Soviet policy when they occur, without perceiving them when none are present.

The second requirement is not to succumb to an undue fascination with East-West relations. Soviet policy adjusts to what Soviet leaders like to call "objective realities." It is by creating these realities in the main areas of potential conflict—Europe, Northeast Asia, and the Middle East—that we are most likely to influence Soviet policy. We can only do this, however, if we have our priorities straight. During the Nixon administration, our preoccupation with the USSR tended to crowd out constructive action in other areas of the world; and local crises were sometimes viewed largely in East-West terms, slighting their local causes.

The third requirement is to focus our dealings with the USSR on specific issues, and to treat these issues on their merits. The notion that there is a seamless web of U.S.–Soviet relations, in which progress or setbacks anywhere make progress or setbacks elsewhere unavoidable, is a fanciful one. Nothing in the Russians' conduct suggests that by offering generous concessions in one area we can secure Soviet concessions elsewhere. Conversely, there is no evidence that the USSR sets such store by agreements in one area as to be willing to follow courses it considers highly disadvantageous in another to secure them.

With these three principles in mind, let us examine specific areas of U.S.–Soviet negotiation in the coming decade.

Arms Control

Competition between the superpowers in strategic arms will continue. To judge from experience, the costs will remain a lesser part of both countries' defense budgets (strategic arms now account only for about 20 percent of U.S. defense spending), and the competition should not engender a massive increase in tensions. The more important risk is that it will trigger the deployment or introduction of weapons that threaten stable deterrence, such as weapons whose vulnerability might invite attack in a first strike, whose accuracy might make a first strike appear feasible, or whose defensive power might persuade leaders in one country that it could launch such a strike and survive the other's retaliation. The main object in arms control should thus be to avoid destabilizing deployments that might increase the fear of a preemptive first strike in some future crisis.

The 1972 treaty barring antiballistic missiles (ABMs) was a notable step in this direction.[9] It should be maintained, whether or not a permanent agreement limiting offensive arms can be negotiated. There is no advantage in returning to a situation in which one side or the other might believe that it could build up sufficient defensive capabilities to make a first strike rewarding. It is paradoxical but true that an agreement that confirms the vulnerability of both sides to missile attack strengthens deterrence.

In any new agreement limiting offensive arms, attention should also be focused on eliminating weapons that detract from a stable strategic posture, such as fixed, land-based intercontinental ballistic missiles (ICBMs), whose vulnerability makes them attractive targets for a first strike. This can most readily be done in the context of an agreement that moves both the Soviet Union and the United States toward lower force levels.

Arms control negotiations will be prolonged, difficult, and complex. There will be a continuing temptation to abandon the process, to insist on one-sided agreements, or to succumb to Soviet pressures for unfavorable agreements. A great deal is at stake. We should stay the course; businesslike patience will be the key to success.

In seeking U.S.–Soviet arms control agreements, we should not form an exaggerated view of U.S. leverage. We will be doing well if we can secure agreements that reduce instability while leaving the present strategic balance between the United States and the USSR unchanged. Even this will require that we make clear our willingness to proceed with effective defense policies (although not to implement programs of dubious merit under the so-called bargaining chip theory), if negotiations fail.

The USSR may share our interest in preventing further nuclear proliferation. We should, as suggested in chapter 4, continue to seek its cooperation in limiting the export of sensitive materials and processing facilities to would-be nuclear powers, and in pressing nonnuclear countries not to join the nuclear club. Prospects for

9. For text, see *The Department of State Bulletin*, vol. 66 (June 26, 1972), pp. 918–20.

Soviet cooperation in offering joint U.S.–Soviet security guarantees to nonnuclear powers on acceptable terms are too remote at this time to make this approach a serious possibility.

Prospects for extending arms control to conventional forces do not appear bright. Two possibilities may be briefly noted:

—The effort to achieve mutual balanced force reductions at Vienna should be continued. Although enthusiasm on the Soviet side and among our allies appears slight, we should seek agreements that would reduce force levels by equal proportions, and thus preserve and regulate the existing balance of power in Central Europe.

—An agreement limiting naval deployments or permanent bases in the Indian Ocean, along the lines discussed in a recent Brookings study,[10] should be explored to see if there is sufficient Soviet interest and flexibility to make a mutually rewarding agreement feasible.

Regional Political Agreements

It would be well to involve the USSR, if it is prepared to participate constructively, in the search for a general Middle Eastern settlement; this might have some effect on Arab attitudes and help to make any resulting agreement more secure. The United States has appeared so far to exclude the USSR, lest its influence in the region be enhanced. While the Soviet Union's obstruction may make its inclusion in negotiations self-limiting, we should at least explore Soviet willingness to play a constructive role.

The Eastern European countries consider follow-up negotiations about the Helsinki agreement useful in enhancing their freedom of action. We should support such talks, without overdramatizing their importance. New regional political agreements in Europe would not cause the USSR to relax its grip on Eastern Europe or on the lives of its inhabitants; nor are further negotiations needed to make clear the NATO countries' willingness to accept present European borders.

There is something to be said for negotiations between the United States, the Soviet Union, and China to see if these great powers can agree that none of them will become involved in a future Korean conflict. In this way a climate might be created in which the United States could more readily disengage its forces from Korea without

10. Barry M. Blechman, *The Control of Naval Armaments: Prospects and Possibilities* (Brookings Institution, 1975).

the adverse consequences discussed earlier. Such an agreement probably could be reached only in the context of limited Sino-Soviet détente and continuing Sino-American détente.

It would be useful to conclude agreements with the Soviet Union banning external intervention in other areas, especially Africa. It is doubtful, however, that the United States has sufficient leverage to make such negotiation rewarding, given our own evident unwillingness to intervene in these areas; and we should not pretend to reverse that unwillingness to increase this leverage. It would be difficult to make an unwise and unpopular U.S. policy toward Africa sufficiently plausible to permit the United States to bargain for its renunciation with a leadership as shrewd as that of the USSR.

Economic Agreements

Economic relations with the USSR are discussed in chapter 5. Basically, the potential for trade and investment is limited. The Soviet economy is largely self-contained; U.S. demand for Soviet exports is not great; and there is no reason to expect a great upsurge in economic relations in the future. Over the longer term, there is some chance that slowly expanding trade will have a constructive effect, in the Soviet Union as in Eastern Europe, in exposing elites to wider outside contacts and in giving some elements of the regime a greater stake in peaceful ties with the outside world.

We should pursue economic ties for this reason, as well as because of their potential intrinsic value. The attempt to exploit them for short-term political purposes is unlikely to succeed. The Russians can get most of the technology they need from other industrial countries, if we set a political price on ours. In selling U.S. grain, the main object should be to get the Soviet Union to meet sensible economic terms—that is, to participate in an international arrangement to build up national reserves sufficiently to reduce the adverse impact of periodic national shortages on the global food situation. Whether the Soviet leaders would agree is in doubt; their rejection of political conditions is not.

Outside of international arrangements for food reserves, opportunities for drawing the Soviet Union into constructive cooperation in meeting global problems appear limited. It is difficult to identify areas in which the Soviet leaders are likely to perceive a sufficient coincidence between their interests and ours to provide an effective basis for that cooperation. This situation could change, however. If such areas emerge, they should be explored vigorously—both because this could contribute to solution of global problems and because, over the longer term, it could have some of the same constructive effects on Soviet evolution as wider trade. But we should not expect any trade agreements to have a large and immediate influence on internal developments in the USSR. This is not a reason for failing to make clear, on moral grounds, our distaste for Soviet policy; but we should not expect our distaste to weigh heavily in Soviet decisions. The refusal of the USSR to allow greater Jewish emigration in order to secure trade concessions illustrates the point.

China

It is not possible to consider the U.S.–Soviet relationship without taking account of Sino-Soviet and Sino-American relations. Any Chinese government will probably continue to fear and dislike the USSR as a powerful neighbor and a doctrinal rival. Even though limited Sino-Soviet détente may appear attractive for pragmatic reasons to post-Mao leaders, the long Sino-Soviet border is likely to continue to be manned by powerful deployments on both sides. Occasional clashes are possible but are unlikely to lead to war. Even if limited détente does not occur, neither government could readily perceive an outcome to hostilities that would be to its advantage. If large-scale civil conflict occurred within one of these two countries, however, the other might be tempted to intervene.

The most interesting peacetime effect of the Sino-Soviet conflict will be on the two countries' policies toward other areas. Both China and the USSR will seek to avoid confrontation with the United States, and both will be anxious to avoid war with other third parties, lest its communist rival try to exploit these situations. On the other hand, the two countries' competition for influence in North Korea may make them less able to restrain any tendency by that government to act aggressively toward South Korea—which is why limited Sino-Soviet détente may be a prerequisite to effective great-power dialogue concerning Korea. And global competition between the Russians and the Chinese may move them to try to outdo each other in supporting black nationalist pressure on Rhodesia and the Republic of South Africa.

So Sino-Soviet rivalry will both mitigate and exacerbate prospects for international conflict, depending on the region and the circumstances. The only certainty is that neither country will be likely to make any major foreign policy move without taking into account its effect on the other. In some situations, this may make for a greater willingness to compromise, in others for more dangerous rigidity. The importance of this factor may decline somewhat, however, if the present degree of hostility is eventually succeeded by limited Sino-Soviet détente.

Chinese foreign policy will, of course, have other goals. Any Chinese government will wish to regain Taiwan, to exert dominant influence in Korea, and to play a large role in Southeast Asia. It is unlikely that Peking will use force to attain these ends, except possibly with respect to Taiwan, unless it perceives a hostile coalition building upon its borders. Otherwise, it will probably limit itself to various forms of political pressure and to providing military and some economic aid to friendly groups and governments. Beyond this, China does not seem likely to play a major military or economic role on the world scene. Its offensive military power is now limited and will remain so through the 1980s; so will its external trade. Its oil deposits, while significant, are not likely soon to be a major factor in the world energy situation.

A revival of Sino-Japanese hostility, as the two nations seek to enhance their influence in Asia, cannot be precluded but now seems unlikely. In Japan, a pro-Chinese posture is popular; in China, there is no desire to add Japan to that country's list of potential enemies. The unlikelihood of past hostility repeating itself is enhanced by the asymmetry of the two countries' power: China is unable to compete economically with Japan, and Japan will be unable to compete militarily with China unless there is an abrupt shift in Japanese defense policy for other reasons.

This asymmetry might suggest that a Sino-Japanese bloc will be formed. But Japan's main economic ties are with the United States and Western Europe; and it relies for its security against external threats on U.S. naval and air power and on the U.S. nuclear deterrent. It is unlikely, so long as it retains confidence in the United States, to place these ties in jeopardy to secure the doubtful advantages of a tight alliance with China. Nor will Japan wish to align itself with China against the USSR. And a Sino-Japanese alliance that was perceived as hostile by the United States would be counter-productive for Chinese leaders anxious to maintain their country's freedom of action and good relations with the United States, as a counterbalance to the USSR.

Chinese military confrontation with the United States is even less likely than with the USSR or Japan. So long as Chinese leaders see the Soviet Union as their principal enemy, they will wish to maintain an accommodation with the other two great powers in the region —the United States even more than Japan. China is not likely, however, to move toward a security alliance with the United States. Chinese leaders may well solicit military assistance and wish to expand economic and technological ties, but they probably still perceive the United States more as a long-term rival than an ally in Asia; they would, moreover, consider an alliance with a capitalist country as a major liability in their ideological confrontation with the USSR. The outcomes sketched above now seem the most likely ones. They could be precluded, however, by sudden shocks, such as radical and unforeseen leadership shifts in the USSR or China.

Our policy toward China should be shaped with a view to two important U.S. concerns: our relations with the USSR and with Japan. The tension between China and the Soviet Union that results from pursuit of independent and competitive goals serves U.S. interests. Growing hostility leading to war would not: quite aside from the tragic human costs, the effects of such a war on wider prospects for peace are impossible to predict. A limited Sino-Soviet détente might serve our interest in some respects, in reducing any risk of war and permitting the two countries to enter into constructive discussions with each other and with the United States about threats to Asian peace, notably in Korea. A more wide-ranging Sino-Soviet détente could damage our interests, by reducing the diversion of Soviet forces to the Chinese border and mitigating the restraints that Sino-Soviet rivalry imposes on both countries' confrontations with the United States.

Our defense posture will probably have some effect on Chinese intentions toward the USSR. If the Chinese have confidence that we will maintain a military balance with the Soviet Union, they may be somewhat less likely to contemplate basic rapprochement with the USSR. From this standpoint what impresses them most (to judge from Chinese statements to date) is U.S. power in the main arena of potential U.S.–Soviet confrontation, Europe. Chinese leaders have repeatedly evidenced an interest in a strengthened NATO that is unequaled in most Western European countries. Just as we welcome China's tying up Soviet forces in Asia, the Chinese look for signs of continuing large NATO deployments, which will divert Soviet forces that might otherwise be assigned to their border.

Progress toward further normalization of U.S.–Chinese relations is unlikely unless the United States changes its policy toward Taiwan. The Chinese consider a break in U.S.–Taiwan diplomatic relations, denunciation of the U.S. mutual security treaty with the Republic of China, and withdrawal of remaining U.S. forces from Taiwan prerequisites to the establishment of full U.S.–Chinese diplomatic relations. Peking would presumably have no objection to the United States maintaining its economic ties with Taiwan by more informal means. It is unclear how far Peking would be prepared to see our commitment to Taiwan's security manifested unilaterally as part of an arrangement that would include full U.S.–Chinese diplomatic relations.

In the long run, things will probably move in this direction, but questions of timing and tactics are important. Some analysts of the Chinese scene have suggested that U.S. failure in the next few years to break relations with Taiwan would not only prevent our having full diplomatic relations with China but might strengthen groups in China that question friendship with the United States and hostility toward the USSR. The evidence on this point is limited. A good deal will depend on whether the Chinese are willing to accept more informal arrangements as a means of maintaining the U.S. security connection with Taiwan, and whether there are profound Japanese objections to the U.S. policy outlined above. The temper of American public opinion will also be important: would our disengagement from Taiwan generate a deeply divisive debate within the United States?

The major consideration, however, will be whether China would be likely to use force against Taiwan after a U.S. disengagement. At present, most analysts believe the Chinese are unlikely to attack the island, at least unless some unforeseen event on Taiwan changes the situation (for instance, Taiwanese movement toward a military nuclear capability that might make preemption an attractive option, or civil disturbances on the island that created an opportunity for external intervention). If U.S. protection of Taiwan were weakened, however, would Chinese calculations change? Might the Chinese then see a naval blockade of Taiwan as a useful way to keep the Taiwan issue alive and to slow Taiwan's march toward an independent status without ties to China?

In light of these considerations, it is premature here to do more than raise the question of whether an early shift in U.S. policy toward Taiwan is warranted. A decision should be postponed until further conversations with the Chinese and Japanese have shed more light on crucial variables.

Conclusions

Although U.S. involvement in a large-scale war is unlikely, it is still a sufficient possibility to make its avoidance the central purpose of our foreign policy. The popular notion that American foreign policy can now ignore security threats in focusing on international economic issues finds little basis in this survey of the next decade.

The greatest risk of war lies in the Middle East. The most urgent task facing the next administration is to help the Arab countries and Israel negotiate a general Middle Eastern settlement. The chances of failure are great enough that we must also rely on less promising means of averting war: helping Israel preserve a local balance of military power, and maintaining a sufficient U.S. military presence in the area to deter Soviet military involvement.

Risks in Europe are harder to assess, but the words of Pierre Hassner still ring true: "Almost any evolution in Eastern Europe is possible except a harmonious one."[11] While there is little we can do directly, at least in the short run, to temper the clash between Soviet dominance and local nationalism in Eastern Europe, we can make clear to the USSR the risks that would attend Soviet intervention in the one Eastern European country that lies outside the socialist commonwealth, Yugoslavia. And we can adopt defense and economic policies toward Western Europe that will help to maintain an environment in which Western weakness will not incite the Soviet leaders to a more adventurous European policy.

11. Pierre Hassner, "Europe East of the Elbe," in Robert S. Jordan, ed., *Europe and the Superpowers: Perceptions of European International Politics* (Allyn and Bacon, 1971), pp. 74–100.

In Korea, we best minimize the risk of conflict by a military presence that reinforces the deterrent created by our commitment to South Korea's defense. Over the longer term some reduction of this presence would make sense, if it could be accomplished without exciting Japanese fears. The measures that we take to maintain Japan's confidence in the U.S. connection should help to make this possible, and to reduce the risk of Japan's abandoning its nonnuclear posture.

In other areas of the third world, U.S. military restraint should be the rule. Only in the most extraordinary circumstances would a commitment of U.S. forces to combat be warranted. Our main concern should be with long-term economic and social progress rather than short-term security developments that do not involve our vital interests and cannot readily be shaped by U.S. intervention.

American policies aimed at prevention of conflict in Europe, Northeast Asia, and the Middle East should be reinforced by a businesslike posture toward the USSR: seeking agreements of mutual advantage, making clear our security commitments to allies, and maintaining a military posture that would reinforce both these courses. U.S. policy toward China should seek to sustain China's determination to maintain its independence from the USSR, without trying to play China and Russia off against each other in ways that might enhance the likelihood of conflict between them.

This set of policies will contain seeming contradictions; these tasks do not lend themselves to simplistic enthusiasms. There is some question, therefore, as to whether they will receive the necessary steady and sustained public support. This is the more uncertain in view of contradictory trends in U.S. opinion.

First, there is continuing tension between the executive and legislative branches of government over foreign policy, mitigated by a continuing public demand that the two branches act together in the face of major crises. Second, there is a strong desire both to avoid foreign military involvement and to avert what might be perceived as external defeats for the United States. Third, there is a widespread wish both to pursue U.S.–Soviet negotiations and to be assured that we get the best of any bargains struck with the USSR. And fourth, there is both growing recognition of global interdependence and, on present evidence, somewhat greater skepticism about all foreigners, friend and foe alike. This skepticism would probably be strengthened if communist parties came to power in France or Italy.

These trends ensure that whatever U.S. foreign and security policies are followed in the coming decade will face vigorous domestic
criticism. Still, certain areas of consensus can be discerned. The effort to reach mutually useful U.S.–Soviet agreements, notably on
arms control, seems likely to receive widespread support, as does
Sino-American détente. U.S. commitments to the defense of Western Europe and Japan rest on widespread public perception of our
self-interest; and our more informal commitment to Israel continues
to draw strength from a widely felt sense of shared values between the
two countries. There is a general willingness to provide defense funds
adequate to support these commitments, while avoiding U.S. military
involvement in other regions and limiting military spending where
this can be done without jeopardizing needed strength. To the extent
that this consensus can be discerned and exploited by an executive
branch that is willing to operate within the limits it imposes, and that
is also willing to accept Congress as an active partner in carrying it
out, U.S. foreign policy need not be inhibited by lack of public support.

The limits to our leverage abroad are evident. We cannot ensure
that a Middle Eastern settlement will be reached, resolve Soviet–
Eastern European tension, or be sure of averting a Korean war. Even
less can we prevent racial struggles in Africa or a variety of local
clashes elsewhere in the third world. The tempering of U.S.–Soviet
competition in strategic arms and other areas will be a slow business,
at best. Still, a large U.S. role abroad will be crucial. Without it, the
prospects for war and widening disorder will mount. The need is to
maintain such a role while adapting it to changing conditions and
basing it on more realistic expectations of what can be accomplished.

The United States will be living in a dangerous world during the
next ten years, whatever policies it follows. While these dangers can
be somewhat reduced by taking the steps to avert or resolve conflicts
discussed in this chapter, even more important may be the effect of
longer-term policies regarding defense, nuclear proliferation, and the
international economic scene designed to create an environment in
which such conflicts are less likely to arise. To these longer-term
policies the next three chapters are devoted.

CHAPTER THREE

Toward a New Consensus in U.S. Defense Policy

BARRY M. BLECHMAN
with ROBERT P. BERMAN, MARTIN BINKIN, *and*
ROBERT G. WEINLAND

IN RECENT YEARS, discussion of U.S. defense policy has tended to focus more on the political role of the armed forces than on their military functions. The military establishment helps to set the image of the United States as a great power. The mere existence of large military forces is evidence of the nation's ability to play an important part in international affairs. That the United States has chosen to allocate a significant portion of its resources to the military demonstrates its ability and its *willingness* to underwrite its announced role in the world. Thus by their existence alone, the armed forces serve important purposes.

By their location, military forces can be directed to specific ends as well. The deployment of armed contingents abroad makes U.S. commitments to the defense of various nations both more credible and more pointed. Placing these forces in areas of potential conflict makes it difficult for the United States to ignore threatening developments there and easier to respond to those developments. Consequently, overseas deployments make it more likely that the United States will live up to its announced policies. Moreover, during crises or at critical times in negotiations, changes can be made in the location, activity, or readiness of military units to buttress specific de-

The authors are grateful for the advice and comments of Shirley Bach, Philip J. Farley, Edward R. Fried, Stuart Johnson, Stephen Kaplan, Lawrence B. Krause, Jan Lodal, Edward O'Connor, and Frederick Young, and for the assistance provided by Georgina Hernandez and Ann M. Ziegler.

mands, to reinforce protests, and to make threats or promises more plausible.

Obviously, accomplishment of these purposes is not automatic—the credibility of the announced aims of military deployments sometimes must be tested by confrontation, if not violence. The point is that the main purposes of the military are political or psychological. A large military establishment is maintained not so much to provide for the direct defense of the United States as to affect the perception of leaders in foreign nations, prompting them to see things in such a way that they will make decisions that will help avoid the necessity for direct defense.

Because the effectiveness of the armed forces—on a first approximation, at least—must be measured by their influence on such subjective phenomena as perceptions, it is extraordinarily difficult to gain wide agreement on the military strategy and the numbers and types of forces that can best assure the nation's security. Considerable debate and alternative interpretations will always occur, even among well-informed people who begin with similar assumptions.

In recent years nothing has stirred up as much debate as the continuing growth of Soviet military power. The Soviet Union clearly is perceived as the nation's chief potential adversary. Its military establishment is large and technologically sophisticated—it is the only other nation whose military capability rivals that of the United States. Moreover, Soviet aims are viewed as generally hostile to U.S. interests and, more to the point, as susceptible to moderation mainly through policies founded on armed strength. Soviet leaders are believed to be deterred from hostile initiatives (or induced to behave cooperatively) only if they perceive their opponent to be strong, resolute, and militarily competent.

Calculations of relative U.S. and Soviet military power heavily influence U.S. decisions about its military posture in Europe and the Middle East. Comparisons of U.S. and Soviet nuclear capabilities are the dominant factors in decisions on U.S. strategic forces. Even the overall size of the defense budget, which is believed by some to be a politically important figure, may be in part governed by comparisons with Soviet military expenditures.

The buildup in Soviet military capabilities has been impressive. In the space of twelve years, Soviet long-range nuclear armed missiles have been transformed from a primitive force grossly inferior to that of the United States into a sophisticated and potentially devastating force. In conventional armaments, Soviet forces are also much improved. They can be, and have been, used far more flexibly and farther away from the USSR than they could be in the past. And they are being equipped with weapons, aircraft, vehicles, and other items of equipment which, if not the qualitative equal of equipment in the military establishments of the West, at least are not nearly so far behind as was once the case.

The continuing Soviet military buildup is proof of the importance the Soviet leadership attaches to military power. The Soviet Union devotes perhaps 15 percent of its national output to the military. This is a burden that no other country—except those, like Israel, living under the threat of imminent conflict—is willing to bear. The corresponding figure for the United States is less than 6 percent.[1] This unmistakable signal of Soviet priorities emphasizes the need for a careful evaluation of the implications of the growth in Soviet military capabilities.

Basing decisions about the U.S. defense posture on aggregate comparisons of military spending would not make much sense, however. If nothing else, any assessment of relative spending is most uncertain, as it depends on intelligence estimates derived from limited observations and on controversial assumptions and methodologies. Moreover, such an approach rewards inefficiency. If both superpowers had precisely the same military capabilities, the less efficient armed forces would have the larger budget and thus might appear— on the basis of aggregate comparisons—to be the more capable. Finally, each side has different needs for military power. There are glaring asymmetries between the United States and the Soviet Union —in history, in geography, in alliances, in technology, in strategy— that lead to different priorities in the way defense moneys are spent. These differences make comparing the two military establishments a difficult task.

It may well be that the U.S. defense budget should be increased as a means of ending, or even reversing, the trend in relative U.S.

1. Stockholm International Peace Research Institute, *World Armaments and Disarmament: SIPRI Yearbook 1974* (M.I.T. Press, 1974), pp. 208, 210, 214. See also U.S. Central Intelligence Agency, "A Dollar Comparison of Soviet and U.S. Defense Activities, 1965–1975," SR 76-10053 (February 1976; processed), and CIA, "Estimated Soviet Defense Spending in Rubles, 1970–1975," SR 76-10121U (May 1976; processed).

and Soviet military capabilities and thereby avoiding adverse political developments. But such a conclusion should rest not on gross budgetary comparisons but rather on individual comparisons of the trend in military capabilities in specific regions and in specific situations. It is necessary to understand how the two military forces might interact, what the result of such interaction might be, and how forecasts of such results might adversely affect U.S. interests. Only then can needed increases in U.S. military capabilities be identified and sufficient resources allocated for these purposes. And it is also only through such a review that areas of defense in which too many resources are being expended can be identified and moneys freed for more important uses.

Budgetary requirements are only one of many factors that determine decisions on defense policy. But consideration of the budget has one advantage: it makes brutally evident the need to make tough decisions. Resources are limited, after all; money spent in one area cannot be used in another. The review of U.S. defense policy that follows will make clear the need for several such trade-offs. Among the most important are those between:

—funds used to meet personnel costs and funds used to acquire military hardware;

—forces equipped and deployed to be primarily useful in wars in Asia and those more suitable for wars in Europe and the Middle East;

—force structures and weaponry oriented primarily to fight a protracted war along the lines of World War II and those geared to fight a short war of high intensity;

—weapons that, because they incorporate high performance features, are very expensive and thus can only be purchased in relatively small numbers and weapons that are individually less capable but that can be bought in larger numbers;

—resources allocated to the primary offensive arms of the U.S. military—tactical air power and armored formations—and resources allocated to antitank forces and air defense; and

—resources allocated to nuclear armaments and resources allocated to general purpose (or conventional) weaponry.

Throughout the chapter, the aim is to identify necessary redirections of the U.S. military posture so that this nation's armed forces can most appropriately be configured to meet its needs in a world of rapidly changing technology and political relations.

A Regional Survey

Latin America and Africa are omitted from this discussion. It is difficult to imagine that, except over a very long period of time, events will occur in Latin America or the Caribbean to threaten this nation's security to a degree or in a way that would require a significant military response. Consequently, except for the defense of the Panama Canal, some contingency planning regarding Cuba, and operations by naval vessels that are justified by other needs, Latin America plays only a small role in U.S. defense planning. Similarly, forces are not maintained specially for contingencies in Africa. The U.S. military posture is primarily determined by U.S.–Soviet relations and the nation's interests in Europe, East Asia, and the Middle East.

Military Requirements for Europe

The maintenance of close ties between Europe and the United States is a vital interest of this nation, perhaps its most vital interest abroad. The preservation of the North Atlantic Treaty Organization as an effective military and political alliance is viewed generally as a necessary (if not sufficient) condition for maintaining these ties.

Unquestionably, the United States and Western Europe have ample resources to balance Soviet power in Europe for as long as the competition is considered necessary. Comparisons of gross national products, manpower, technologies, or most other relevant measures all favor the West. Nor should these favorable comparisons be expected to change, at least for the next ten years.

Questions do arise, however, in two areas. First, does the West have the will to continue to allocate adequate resources to its common defense? Second, does NATO's strategy and force structure make sense in view of Soviet military doctrine and the organization and composition of Soviet military forces?

The prospects for future resource allocations to NATO defense are not easily assessed. Recent experience has been favorable. For example, arguments commonly heard in the early and mid-sixties for the reduction of U.S. forces in Europe no longer seem so compelling. In 1975 and 1976 there was virtually no pressure from Congress to reduce the U.S. presence on the Continent. And so far at least, the Western European nations have increased their defense expenditures

**Table 3-1. NATO Defense Expenditures and Military Manpower,
Excluding the United States, 1965 and 1974**

Country	Defense expenditures (millions of 1973 dollars)		Defense expenditures as percent of GNP		Total military manpower (thousands)	
	1965	1974	1965	1974	1965	1974
Belgium	984	1,320	3.1	2.8	115	100
Canada	2,370	2,530	3.0	2.1	120	80
Denmark	554	660	2.8	2.4	50	35
France	8,490	9,610	5.2	3.6	585	580
Greece	303	621	3.5	4.0	190	180
Italy	3,070	4,190	3.3	2.9	460	500
Luxembourg	20	17	1.4	0.9	2	1
Netherlands	1,590	2,100	4.0	3.5	125	105
Norway	504	609	3.8	3.1	35	35
Portugal	411	820	6.0	7.2	160	260
Turkey	630	871	5.0	3.7	490	535
United Kingdom	8,230	9,140	5.9	5.2	425	350
West Germany	10,700	12,500	4.3	3.6	440	490
Total NATO (excluding U.S.)	37,856	44,988	4.4	3.6	3,197	3,251

Sources: U.S. Arms Control and Disarmament Agency, "World Military Expenditures and Arms Transfers, 1965–1974" (1976; processed), pp. 15, 19–50; International Institute for Strategic Studies, *The Military Balance, 1974–1975* (London: IISS, 1974), p. 22.

sufficiently not only to offset inflationary price rises but also to finance the real increases in defense costs required by more advanced technologies (see table 3-1). Aggregate non-U.S. NATO defense spending rose nearly 20 percent, in real terms, between 1965 and 1974, while total Western European military manpower remained more or less constant and most military pay rates in Western Europe rose slowly—indications that most of the increase in real spending was used for qualitative improvements in equipment.

The long-term outlook is not so sanguine. Pressure is growing for significant increases in military pay rates in France, West Germany, and Italy—three countries that provide about half of NATO's manpower. Success in these efforts would probably mean sharp cutbacks in manpower levels, as already has happened in the United States and Great Britain. France makes only a small contribution to the crucial central front, and Italy makes none at all, but a decline in German military power could affect NATO's defenses. Even more important are the political and economic factors discussed in chapter

2. That a growing share of the NATO manpower burden is borne by West Germany has troubling implications. And while economic growth has so far made real increases in Western European defense spending possible even as the share of Europe's resources devoted to defense has declined, the modest rate of economic growth experienced in recent years, combined with domestic political pressures in the NATO nations, leads to more pessimistic forecasts of future Western European defense efforts.

This concern about Western Europe's defense outlook contrasts sharply with the apparent trend in the Soviet military posture in Eastern Europe. Over the past ten years, both the quality and quantity of Soviet forces deployed in Europe have improved markedly. The Soviet Union added five divisions to its Eastern European deployment when it invaded Czechoslovakia in 1968, and it has kept them there. Also, each Soviet division now contains more men and more tanks than it did before 1968. In 1975 there were 615,000 Soviet military personnel in Eastern Europe as against 418,000 in 1966.[2]

In the main, though, improvements in the Soviet military have been qualitative. New kinds of weapons, such as self-propelled artillery and mobile air defenses, have been introduced. In general, the equipment now entering the Soviet inventory is far more capable than that being replaced (see table 3-2).

Because superior air power has been a major Western advantage in the past, modernization of Soviet tactical aircraft is particularly significant. The new Soviet fighter and attack aircraft far surpass their predecessors in various measures of performance. Equally if not more important was the introduction, beginning in 1964, of a family of mobile air defense systems for the protection of Soviet ground forces. The nearly one dozen types of gun and missile systems now deployed in Eastern Europe provide a potent network of gunfire and antiaircraft missiles covering all attack altitudes. The improvement in Soviet air defenses is a significant new factor in the military balance in Europe.

Against these impressive gains on the Soviet side one must weigh

2. *Fiscal Year 1976 and July–September 1976 Transition Period Authorization for Military Procurement, Research and Development, and Active Duty, Selected Reserve, and Civilian Personnel Strengths,* Hearings before the Senate Committee on the Armed Services, 94:1 (GPO, 1975), pt. 5, p. 2241.

Table 3-2. Comparison of Selected Items of Soviet Equipment in the 1960s and 1970s

Item and characteristics	Mid-1960s	Mid-1970s
Armored personnel carriers		
Type	BTR-60	BMP-1
Range (miles)	312	312
Primary armament	14.5 mm heavy machine gun	73 mm cannon plus antitank missile
Number of troops carried	10	8
Weight (tons)	10	12
Mobility (horsepower–weight ratio)	18	23
Fighter aircraft		
Type	MIG-21PF (Fishbed)	MIG-23S (Flogger)
Maximum ordnance carried (tons)	1.0	2.2
Ordnance stations[a]	3	5
Maximum combat radius (miles)	350	600
Acceleration and climb (thrust–weight ratio)	0.53	0.80
Maximum speed (Mach number)	2.1	2.3
Cruisers		
Class	*Kresta I*	*Kara*
Displacement (tons)	6,500	10,000
Length (feet)	510	570
Maneuverability (shaft horsepower–displacement ratio)	15	10
Surface-to-surface missile launchers	4	8
Surface-to-air missile launchers	4	8
Antisubmarine mortars	4	4
Guns	4	8
Torpedo tubes	10	10

Sources: R. T. Pretty, ed., *Jane's Weapon Systems, 1976*, 7th ed. (New York: Franklin Watts, 1975; London: Jane's Yearbooks, 1975), pp. 372, 374; R. Meller, "Europe's New Generation of Combat Aircraft, Part I: The Increasing Threat," *International Defense Review*, vol. 8 (April 1975), pp. 180, 181; William Green and others, *The World Guide to Combat Planes*, vol. 1 (Doubleday, 1967), p. 142; John E. Moore, ed., *Jane's Fighting Ships, 1975–76* (Franklin Watts, 1975; Jane's Yearbooks, 1975), pp. 566–69.

a. A measure of versatility; the number of individual hardpoints to which bombs, missiles, spare fuel tanks, or electronics pods can be attached.

the continued modernization of NATO equipment made possible by the real increase in NATO defense spending, NATO's maintenance, so far, of roughly constant manpower levels, and the recent improvement in antitank weapons, a factor that, for the mid-term at least, seems to favor the West because of Soviet emphasis on armored formations and an offensive stance.

The net result is not at all clear. Nonetheless, although there certainly has not been any sudden or dramatic shift in the military balance in Europe, it is commonly believed that in the long run, under present trends, NATO's conventional force posture may become less credible.

To avert such a deterioration, it will be necessary to expand certain U.S. military capabilities relevant to the type of fighting likely to characterize any new war in Europe: (1) a step-up in the planned production rate of armored fighting vehicles so that armor could be added to units already in Europe and one or two of the three recently created U.S. divisions could be equipped to make them effective as reinforcements for Europe; (2) accelerated development and production of new types of antitank weapons; (3) greater investment in new forms of mobile and relatively inexpensive air defense systems; (4) additional purchases of artillery and free-fire rockets; and (5) increased U.S. airlift and sea lift capabilities so that forces in the United States could be deployed to Europe quickly in a crisis.

In addition, realistic projections of the budgetary resources likely to be made available to Western European military establishments make even more compelling long-standing arguments that NATO's force structure, organization, military doctrine, and tactics are in need of revision.

Soviet forces in Europe (and those of its Warsaw Pact allies) are organized primarily to fight a very short, intense conflict, one that might involve the use of tactical nuclear weapons from the onset. This is evident from the high concentration of armored units in the Soviet force structure in Europe; the high ratio of combat to support units in the Soviet army; design features of some Soviet weapon systems, particularly Soviet warships, that emphasize on-line firepower at the expense of an ability to conduct sustained combat; Soviet military doctrine, which stresses rapid advance into enemy territory; and Soviet military exercises, which usually feature nuclear strikes in conjunction with rapidly advancing armored offensives.[3]

All of this argues convincingly for increasing NATO's readiness and on-line firepower. What good is it, one may ask, for NATO to be able to muster forces capable of balancing those of the USSR in the 60th, 90th, or 120th day of a prospective conflict if the alliance is unlikely to survive the first ten days of a Soviet attack? The disposition and structure of NATO ground forces on the central front should

3. Thomas W. Wolfe, *Soviet Power in Europe, 1945–1970* (Johns Hopkins Press, 1970), pp. 198–99.

be altered so as to maximize NATO's combat capabilities in the early days of an attack; related changes in NATO air forces and navies also would be desirable. These reforms have been spelled out in some detail elsewhere, and within the past several years steps have been taken toward this end.[4] The question is whether these steps have gone far enough.

1. A further shift of U.S. army personnel in Europe from support to combat units may be possible. Considerable progress has been made during the past five years, most recently spurred by Senator Sam Nunn and former Secretary of Defense James R. Schlesinger.[5] Army spokesmen argue that the shift has already gone too far, resulting in too thin logistics. Whether this has happened is unclear. It is evident that if additional changes are to be made they will require fundamental changes in NATO policy, the most important of which is abandoning the notion that logistical support must be a national responsibility. Under a revised concept, U.S. forces would become partially dependent on European nations, especially West Germany, for the provision of various support functions such as transportation, medical care, rear-area construction activities, and equipment maintenance. Such a change is not without its risks, of course. But besides allowing a further increase in U.S. combat strength in Europe within constant overall manpower levels, it might promote military integration in the alliance.

2. Along similar lines, commonality in NATO weapon acquisition programs and interchangeability among NATO equipment should be emphasized. There has been much talk about this but few results. Perhaps this is because discussion of so-called standardization has usually focused on major items of equipment, such as tanks or aircraft, on which it is hard to reach agreement. Far more modest steps are possible, however, and would be useful. At present, for example,

4. See Richard D. Lawrence and Jeffrey Record, *U.S. Force Structure in NATO* (Brookings Institution, 1974); Jeffrey Record, *Sizing Up the Soviet Army* (Brookings Institution, 1975); Jeffrey Record with the assistance of Thomas I. Anderson, *U.S. Nuclear Weapons in Europe* (Brookings Institution, 1974); James R. Schlesinger, "Annual Defense Department Report, FY 1976 and FY 197T" (statement to U.S. Congress, February 5, 1975; processed), p. III-41.

5. "Annual Defense Department Report, FY 1977" (statement to U.S. Congress, January 27, 1976; processed), p. 296.

The Army's Project Fender (1971–74) reduced support personnel by 8,100 and increased combat strength by 9,000. Further shifts occurred in fiscal 1975 and 1976. All told, combat strength has been raised by 19,000 since 1971, at the expense of the support establishment.

German and American teletype machines cannot be linked together. Nor can many American aircraft be serviced at any but U.S. air bases. Standardization in support equipment and in subsystems of major combat items is a practical goal and could lead to considerable improvement in NATO's military punch.

3. The North German Plain has always been one of the weakest sectors in NATO's defense. Reductions in British, Dutch, and Belgian forces portend an even greater erosion of military capabilities in this area. One way to rectify this situation would be to shift some U.S. forces now in southern Germany to the north, shortening U.S. supply lines and making them less vulnerable. An alternative solution would be to have U.S. forces assume responsibility for a larger sector in southern Germany, freeing additional German army elements for the defense of the likely northern invasion route. Either move would be difficult, as land would have to be acquired—especially for training areas—and support facilities would have to be built, but the added expenditures and political costs in Germany will have to be incurred if this potential vulnerability is to be reduced.

4. The high cost of manpower provides great incentive to place more reliance on the reserve components.[6] Paid reservists, who train about sixty days a year, cost only 15 to 20 percent as much as their active Army counterparts. The primary disadvantage of reserve units is the relatively long time required for preparation and training before deployment. During the Korean War, for example, it took an average of about fifteen months for a National Guard division to get ready and deploy. The time needed to train the headquarters staff is the critical factor; it varies according to the size of the unit: about one week for a company, four weeks for a battalion, and eight to fourteen weeks for a division. The Army's reserve affiliation program, which links more than ninety reserve battalions and four reserve brigades with active Army divisions for training and concurrent deployment, is an important step toward making better use of reserves in planning for a war of short duration. But the eight full National Guard divisions still in the force structure would be of questionable value if they could not be deployed within fourteen weeks after mobilization. It would be desirable, therefore, to provide an active-duty cadre for each National Guard division, thus ensuring that these divisions

6. This discussion is based on Martin Binkin, *U.S. Reserve Forces: The Problem of the Weekend Warrior* (Brookings Institution, 1974).

would be ready to deploy as soon as the necessary air- and sealift became available. Manpower for these cadres could be obtained, without increasing the number of people on active duty, by relying even more on reserve units or designated individual reservists to fill out active divisions in time of war.

5. A shift in U.S. aircraft procurement away from large, long-range, multipurpose, and hence very expensive aircraft, designed mainly to achieve air superiority deep behind enemy lines and strike industrial and transportation targets, toward less expensive aircraft, specialized for the direct support of the ground battle, would increase NATO's on-line firepower. The destruction of targets far behind enemy lines can only be important in a protracted conflict. A shift from tactical air power to greater firepower in the ground units may also be desirable.

6. Finally, a shift in Navy planning away from the defense of peacetime civilian shipping levels in the Atlantic and the Pacific is warranted. Although defense of military convoys would be important, even in a short war, the Navy still bases much of its planning on a perceived need to defend a steady stream of shipping carrying both military and civilian supplies to Europe. This requires forces capable of controlling large areas for indefinite periods of time. Instead, the Navy's main mission should be to gain control of restricted seas, notably the Mediterranean and the Norwegian Sea, to enable it to project U.S. power on the flanks of NATO and to deny the Soviet Union access to these now vulnerable regions, while defending only those convoys of military goods that would be needed in Europe for a relatively short war.

In brief, much can be done to squeeze greater and more appropriate military capabilities from NATO's forces at whatever level they are funded. If such steps were taken, a favorable military balance could be maintained for some time, even if NATO's real defense spending did not grow more rapidly than, or even as rapidly as, it has in the recent past.

Military Requirements in the Pacific

There has been a remarkable change in the past decade in U.S. attitudes toward China and the threats posed by China to American interests. China's military capabilities are now believed to be limited. Its military hardware is largely obsolete and increasingly surpassed by U.S. and Soviet technological innovations. Chinese military expenditures seem to be on the decline and, as a result, the long overdue modernization of China's armed forces has proceeded only in fits and starts over the past few years.[7] Now, as in the past, China is unable to project its conventional military power beyond its own borders or the immediately contiguous regions. Even the development of its nuclear weapons has advanced far more slowly than was predicted for many years. Chinese nuclear deployments that have been identified seem to be directed at the Soviet Union.

Moreover, after belatedly recognizing in the mid-1960s that the Sino-Soviet split was genuine, the United States gradually came to the conclusion that improved U.S.–Chinese relations could help balance Soviet power. The dispute with China has been a major factor in the Soviet military buildup. So long as tensions between the two persist, planning for Chinese contingencies will continue to tie up a large share, perhaps one-fourth, of the Soviet force structure. Should the conflict be resolved, however, or even markedly de-emphasized, some of the forces now on the Chinese border might become available to bolster Soviet deployments in Europe and more directly threaten U.S. interests.

During the past few years the United States also has begun to define its interests in Asia more narrowly than in the past. It has placed tight constraints on the use of its armed forces in Southeast Asia and has increasingly recognized Japan as constituting the central U.S. interest in East Asia.

As a result of these shifts in American attitudes, U.S. forces in the Pacific—and those maintained in the United States as backup—now serve more narrowly defined purposes than before the Vietnam War. These purposes, which are discussed in greater detail by Owen in chapter 2, are threefold. First, the Asia-oriented forces help maintain the credibility of U.S. commitments to the defense of Japan, thereby ensuring that the U.S.–Japanese connection remains intact. Second, they support the U.S. commitment to the defense of South Korea, whose importance derives from Japan's interests. Third, U.S. forces in the Pacific help to buttress, in some vague sense, China's determination to resist Soviet demands, thereby somewhat reducing the like-

7. *Allocation of Resources in the Soviet Union and China—1975,* Hearings before the Subcommittee on Priorities and Economy in Government of the Joint Economic Committee, 94:1 (GPO, 1975), pt. 1, pp. 36–50.

lihood of the USSR's redeploying some of its military forces from the Chinese border to western Russia, where they would threaten NATO.

In calculating the most appropriate U.S. force posture for the Pacific, the main difficulty is that Asian contingencies have lost much of their plausibility. Although both China and the Soviet Union maintain large military establishments in the region, they seem to be directed far more at each other than at anyone else. Does a Soviet or Chinese invasion of Japan seem likely in the foreseeable future? Does Soviet or Chinese participation in a North Korean attack on South Korea seem a realistic prospect? Thus, even more than elsewhere, the function of U.S. forces in Asia is largely political: to convince Japanese, Chinese, Korean, and Soviet decisionmakers that the United States means what it says, that it would become involved militarily should one of its allies be attacked, and that it continues to have interests in Northeast Asia that must be accommodated when these decisionmakers formulate their own policies.

Forces maintained in Asia and the Pacific, or based in the United States but equipped to make them primarily useful for Asian contingencies, take up a large share of the U.S. force structure. The question is whether these forces can be reduced without creating doubt among Japanese about the credibility and the endurance of the U.S. commitment and among Chinese about the long-term role the United States will play in regional affairs. It seems evident that forces maintained in the United States as backup for those deployed in or near Japan have little political impact on either Japan or China. This suggests that one or two of the four Army and Marine infantry divisions on the U.S. West Coast and Hawaii, which are too lightly equipped to be effective in European or Middle Eastern contingencies, and portions of the Third Fleet, which operates from Hawaii and southern California, might either be eliminated from the force structure or reequipped (and in the Navy's case, redeployed) for European or Middle Eastern contingencies without causing strain in U.S.–Asian relations.

Making cuts in the forces deployed in the western Pacific is clearly more risky. Some reductions might safely be made if they were carried out gradually and in full consultation with the allies that might be affected and if the changes in the U.S. force posture were compensated for by appropriate diplomacy, economic policies, and military assistance. For example, the 2nd Infantry Division in Korea could probably be withdrawn gradually without causing grave difficulties in either U.S.–Japanese or U.S.–Korean relations.[8] Park Chung-hee, South Korea's president, has said that withdrawal of U.S. ground forces will be possible in a few years. So long as the United States maintains the 8th Air Force Tactical Fighter Wing and possibly the 38th Army Air Defense Artillery Brigade in Korea, the essential political function of the U.S. forces there would probably be fulfilled.[9]

Similarly, it may be safe to reduce the Seventh Fleet, which operates in the western Pacific and now consists of two aircraft carrier task groups. In a situation in which there is no specific military threat, one aircraft carrier task group in the western Pacific should meet U.S. political needs for Japan. The second carrier task group now in the western Pacific would be of greater use in the protection of U.S. interests if it were redeployed elsewhere.

Finally, the 3rd Air Force Tactical Fighter Wing, now deployed at Clark Air Force Base in the Philippines—a holdover from a time when the United States was heavily involved in Southeast Asia— might be eliminated. Dropping this wing from the force structure, together with a cut in the Seventh Fleet, would be tantamount to removal of the U.S. military presence in the Philippines. Whether such a step would be militarily desirable would also depend on decisions concerning the need for U.S. military deployments in the Indian Ocean.

Combining the possible cuts, or diversion to more important regions, of backup forces with potential reductions in forward-deployed forces would yield perhaps a one-fourth reduction in the U.S. Pacific force posture—say, three aircraft carrier task groups, one Air Force tactical air wing, and two Army or Marine infantry divisions. A cut or redeployment of this size should be implemented gradually, with careful attention to political effects and with pointed

8. See the discussion in chapter 2.
9. The U.S. Air Force presence could be streamlined. In addition to the 8th Tactical Fighter Wing, which consists of two F-4D squadrons, the 51st Tactical Composite Wing is stationed in Korea. The latter organization consists of one F-4E squadron and ten to twelve OV-10 observation aircraft. The reason for the separate existence of the 51st (which is not included in the twenty-six tactical wings that ostensibly make up the Air Force), and therefore the existence of an extra headquarters staff, is obscure.

demonstrations that the forces retained for Pacific contingencies would be adequate to support U.S. political commitments in Northeast Asia.

No doubt, although the essential components of a powerful force posture in Northeast Asia would have been retained, some risks would be associated with these reductions. These risks are slight, however, and should be accepted in order to protect more important and more threatened U.S. interests in Europe and the Middle East effectively. The forces cut in Asia would make it easier for the United States to counter the buildup of Soviet power in Europe and the eastern Mediterranean—either directly, if the Asian forces were redeployed or reequipped, or indirectly, if the Asian forces were removed from the force structure—thus freeing budgetary resources for more important defense needs.

The Middle East in U.S. Defense Planning*

The United States maintains a significant proportion—roughly one-third—of its general purpose forces abroad in defense of its vital interests in Western Europe and Northeast Asia. In defense of its interests in the area between Europe and Asia, the Middle East, it maintains only a token naval presence: the three-ship Middle East force. Of course, one major component of the forces deployed in defense of Europe, the Sixth Fleet, does operate in the Mediterranean Sea in direct proximity to the Middle East. And elements of the Seventh Fleet, which normally operates in the western Pacific, periodically deploy into the Indian Ocean. In each of these cases, however, defense of U.S. interests in the Middle East is a distinctly secondary consideration in naval planning.

In effect, to support its policies in the Middle East the United States relies mainly on its ability to redeploy quickly elements of its land, sea, and air forces stationed in or near Europe, Asia, and at home. Thus in addition to their primary missions these forces support the U.S. guarantee of the survival of Israel, help enhance U.S. influence in the region, and may also help ensure U.S. (and U.S. allies') access to energy supplies.

The credibility of the U.S. commitment to defend Israel depends on U.S. ability to defeat, if necessary, any Soviet military intervention in a new Arab-Israeli war. If Soviet leaders believe the United States

---

* This section was prepared by Robert G. Weinland.

has such a capability and that it will be used if needed, they are likely to be deterred from assuming any overt role in the fighting. Moreover, if the local actors share that belief and doubt Soviet threats (or promises) to intervene, U.S. influence in the region in peacetime is likely to be enhanced and U.S. attempts to bring the Arab-Israeli conflict to a peaceful settlement reinforced.

These goals place three requirements on U.S. armed forces. The first is to be able to gain and maintain control of the sea and the airspace in the eastern Mediterranean. The second is to be able to establish and keep functioning air and sea lanes to the area, primarily for the military resupply of Israel. The third is to be able to marshall adequate numbers of properly equipped air and ground forces for rapid deployment to the region if U.S. intervention became necessary.

The first task, which is a necessary though insufficient condition for the next two, is also the most difficult. It means that U.S. forces must be able to create a secure environment in the eastern Mediterranean, in which the United States could undertake whatever military operations it deemed necessary but the Soviet Union could carry out only those operations that the United States did not try to prevent. Given the present structure and disposition of U.S. forces, the task would fall largely upon the Sixth Fleet, but the fleet is likely to need help to carry it out successfully.

Even without assistance, the Sixth Fleet is certainly capable of prohibiting Soviet military use of the Mediterranean. If the United States chooses to oppose it, effective Soviet intervention in an Arab-Israeli conflict is not likely to be militarily feasible. No matter how or when Soviet ground forces were introduced into the conflict, they would have to be sustained by sealift. Since Soviet surface forces could not withstand a U.S. challenge, their sealift could be interdicted. Pre-positioning supplies for the Soviet intervening force and airlifting Soviet troops into the region would enable the sealift to begin later, but it would not obviate the necessity for it. And the airlift itself would be vulnerable to interdiction.

Establishing the ability of the United States to use the Mediterranean for its own military purposes is more difficult. It would be impossible if nuclear weapons were used. If only conventional armaments were used, the Sixth Fleet would probably sustain sizable losses. Nevertheless, if the fleet were reinforced before the outbreak of conflict to roughly double its normal complement and additional assistance were provided by land-based tactical aircraft, the Sixth Fleet could probably establish and maintain positive control of the eastern Mediterranean, despite Soviet counteraction.

Reinforcement of the carrier force would assure the presence of enough carriers to continue operations even if one carrier were put out of action. Moreover, if limited to its normal complement of two carrier task groups, the Sixth Fleet would have to allocate so much of its combat capability to self-defense that its remaining forces might be incapable of conducting offensive operations. Augmenting the carrier force would have a multiplicative effect on its overall effectiveness. Joint operations by two or more carriers would permit each to allocate a smaller proportion of its aircraft to defensive tasks, making a larger proportion of a larger force available for offensive tasks. Furthermore, joint operations by three or more carriers would permit air operations to be mounted around the clock for extended periods of time.

Land-based tactical air forces could also make a significant contribution not only to the control of the eastern Mediterranean, but also to the protection of the carriers. If they were based in range of the carriers, they could augment the air umbrella over the task force. Even if the carriers were out of range, land-based aircraft could establish barriers to intercept incoming Soviet strike aircraft before the attackers could fire their missiles at the carriers. Naturally, any use of land-based aircraft depends on the availability of airfields in the vicinity.

In the Indian Ocean, U.S. armed forces might help deter or, if necessary, help end any new interruption in the oil flow. Opinions differ on the feasibility and desirability of U.S. military action to restore a flow of oil if it were interrupted for political reasons. But one thing is clear: it is useful to sustain a healthy uncertainty in the Arab oil-exporting countries about whether military action might be taken. This requires maintaining a U.S. military capability for effective action.

All the types of military action that might be involved—seizure of the oil fields, blockades and other acts of coercive diplomacy, and protection of the sea lines of communication—would mean the deployment of additional forces into the Indian Ocean. The potential for Soviet counterintervention is the dominant consideration in estimating what U.S. forces, and how many, would be needed. In addition to those necessary to carry out the immediate task, the threat of Soviet involvement would necessitate the presence of major sea and air control forces capable of sustained operations in a relatively high-threat environment. Without that threat, only modest forces would be needed.

In any event, unless the Soviet Union drastically altered the size and character of its military activities in the Indian Ocean, neither its presence in the region nor the possibility of renewed interruptions in the oil flow require the United States to increase the size of its permanent deployments there. The main deterrents to a new embargo are U.S. and allied political will, cooperation, and overall military and economic strength, not the maintenance of a standing force in the region. Should there be another embargo, there would be adequate time to deploy sufficient forces to the region for whatever tasks the United States and its allies were able to agree on.

When one compares the tasks U.S. forces are likely to be called upon to perform in the Middle East with the resources that are currently available, a number of material and procedural shortfalls are readily apparent. Correcting them would be difficult, since most reflect long-standing principles of U.S. military practice, but it would not be inordinately expensive.

First, to successfully establish and maintain area control in the high-threat environment of the eastern Mediterranean—especially to be able to use the area for its own purposes as opposed to keeping the Soviet Union from so using the area—the United States would have to devote a larger proportion of its total carrier- and land-based tactical aviation to the region, and those forces would have to conduct more joint operations in the area during peacetime so that they could operate effectively within a very short time after the onset of a crisis. In essence, this requires the abandonment of two long-standing characteristics of U.S. peacetime operations: rigid forward aircraft carrier deployments at the highest sustainable level and single service operations. At present, the United States deploys as many of its aircraft carriers as far forward as it can, at the expense of the flexibility necessary for the rapid deployment and concentration of even larger forces. And U.S. land- and sea-based tactical air forces deployed abroad have each long been operated as though the other did not exist. Neither of these practices can be justified in view of the likely needs of combat. Weak and isolated forces in forward areas cannot be expected to survive the initial phase of combat, nor would they contribute as much separately as they could jointly.

Relaxing aircraft carrier operating schedules by reducing peacetime forward deployments would permit larger concentrations of sea-based tactical aviation in an emergency. As a benchmark, peacetime carrier operating schedules in the Sixth and Second Fleets (deployed in the Mediterranean and the Atlantic respectively) might be relaxed sufficiently to permit the United States to deploy four carrier task groups to the Mediterranean within fourteen days. The relaxation of carrier operating schedules in the Pacific is even more important, since the number of carriers located there is likely to be reduced.

Steps to increase the availability and effectiveness of land-based tactical aircraft in coordinated operations with naval forces are also necessary. For one thing, provisions could be made for Marine air wings to operate independently in situations where the ground forces they normally support are not likely to be employed. Marine aviation could support the Sixth Fleet from bases in southern Europe even if a Marine landing in the Middle East was not contemplated. For another, the frequency, size, and scope of joint operations conducted by Navy and Air Force tactical aviation deployed around the Mediterranean could be increased markedly.

Second, to have the capability to control and use the eastern Mediterranean or the Indian Ocean *when it is necessary to have that capability,* the United States must be able to anticipate events—to judge when and where crises are most likely to occur. This is particularly important since the United States has little control over events leading to confrontations and it takes time to move the requisite forces into the region. Having made such a judgment, the United States would have to deploy its forces before they were required and sustain those deployments until they were no longer needed. And it would have to do this in a potentially inhospitable environment, in which for one reason or another it might receive less support from its NATO allies than would be desirable. Naval forces are uniquely capable of operating for sustained periods in such an environment, but only with a large supporting fleet train. The latter has been neglected in the shipbuilding program in recent years by both the Defense Department and Congress, and is one area where increased expenditures may be required in the near future.

Third, and related to the last point, is the question of bases. In the Mediterranean, the key question is the availability of bases both for land-based tactical air operations and to support airlifts of men and equipment. The United States currently maintains one Air Force tactical fighter wing in the Mediterranean region—the 401st, located at Torrejón, Spain—with advance elements in Aviano, Italy, and Incirlik, Turkey.

Access to bases in Turkey or, possibly, Greece would be necessary if land-based fighter aircraft were to be used to help defend the carriers by intercepting Soviet strike aircraft operating from bases near the Black Sea. Turkish bases are also vital for intelligence collection. Recently negotiated agreements should permit the United States to retain access to these bases. But even then, additional arrangements would have to be made if they were to be available for use in non-NATO contingencies. The difficulty of negotiating such arrangements, however, should not be minimized.

Other bases in Europe are important too. Airfields in Spain and Portugal are important for any airlift to the Middle East. Airfields in Italy could be used to intercept Soviet aircraft originating in Central Europe. Important U.S. naval bases are located in Spain, Italy, and Greece. Past experience indicates that host nations are reluctant to permit the use of these facilities in non-NATO Middle Eastern contingencies. A major reason has been their fear of antagonizing the Arab oil-exporting countries. The recent agreement between the European countries and the United States for sharing oil in future crises, however, and the fact that the United States is only marginally dependent on Middle Eastern oil mean that, no matter how carefully the allies divorce their policies in the Middle East from those of the United States, they would be the primary target of any new embargo. The United States could only be pressured through an embargo directed at its allies. Allied awareness of these facts may reduce their concern about oil, but it is still uncertain whether they would provide access to military facilities, given their desire to avoid involvement in any U.S.–Soviet confrontation and their past substantive differences with the United States over Middle Eastern policy. The United States should discuss these considerations with its allies *before the next crisis* and attempt to reach clear understandings with nations providing facilities for U.S. forces about what operations would be permitted from their territories.

In the Indian Ocean, the principal question concerns facilities to support both sustained low-level and intermittent high-intensity operations. Without the recently approved construction of naval and air support facilities at Diego Garcia, it would be difficult and expensive to support any major force that might be sent to the Indian Ocean in a crisis. If nothing else, additional support ships would be necessary.

Without intermediate bases between the United States and Diego Garcia, it would also be difficult to supply the island itself, as well as the forces dependent on it for support. Studies are needed to determine if present U.S. bases on Guam fill this need, whether bases in the Philippines would have to be retained for this purpose, or if new, substitute facilities should be sought—perhaps in Australia. In any decisions about bases in the Philippines and Australia (as about the future of Diego Garcia), other factors—including political factors —will of course have to be considered.

Fourth, if the United States is to maximize its influence on the course of events in the Middle East and minimize the likelihood of a costly direct intervention in those events, it must have a better idea of what is going on in the area—that is, better intelligence concerning not only impending events but also the strength, location, and readiness of the Soviet forces the United States may have to confront. This applies particularly to the serious threat to U.S. carriers in the Mediterranean posed by Soviet submarines; to a lesser degree, it also applies to the threat Soviet submarines could present to the sea lines of communication in the Indian Ocean. In both cases, since accurate intelligence permits forces to be used more effectively, additional dollars spent on raising the level of U.S. military capabilities in those regions should go first to improving fixed and mobile ocean surveillance systems and other nonintrusive means of determining who is where, doing what, and to whom.

The Structure of U.S. Forces

Even if there were no dispute about the foreign policy best suited to secure U.S. interests around the world and the proper role of military power in supporting that policy, reasonable people would still disagree about a wide range of decisions concerning the necessary size, composition, and equipment of the armed forces. The reason is simple. A number of intervening factors play an important part in these decisions: projections of future capabilities of potential adversaries; technical evaluations of the relative cost and effectiveness of alternative weapon systems; forecasts of domestic economic (and eventually political) consequences; the private interests of individuals, groups, and the various parts of the defense bureaucracy; and, perhaps most of all, the momentum of past decisions. The choices that lie ahead are discussed under three main headings: strategic nuclear forces, general purpose forces, and manpower issues.

Strategic Nuclear Forces

The United States defines its strategic forces in a highly stylized fashion. They now consist of 1,054 land-based intercontinental-range nuclear-armed ballistic missiles; forty-one submarines, each carrying sixteen nuclear-armed intermediate-range ballistic missiles; twenty-one squadrons of B-52 long-range heavy bombers armed with air-to-surface missiles and gravity bombs; four squadrons of intermediate-range FB-111 bombers similarly armed; six interceptor aircraft squadrons on active duty and eleven squadrons with the Air Force National Guard used for continental air defense; various early warning, command, control, and communication systems; and a modest civil defense program. The United States has many other nuclear-armed weapon systems in its inventory, generally of lesser range. Many of these could strike the USSR because they are deployed within range of its territory. Other aircraft and some surface-to-air missiles located in the United States provide additional air defense capability. But for one reason or another, these last forces are not counted in the strategic category.

All told, expenditures on strategic nuclear forces were $17.3 billion in fiscal 1976, less than 18 percent of the total defense budget. According to administration projections, by fiscal 1981 the strategic forces' share of the defense budget will rise to about 20 percent. Even so, this share would be relatively low compared with earlier periods. These trends are shown in table 3-3. On the other hand, the strategic forces' share in the debate on U.S. defense policy is remarkably high and has been that way virtually as long as nuclear weapons have existed, a disproportion not too surprising considering the stakes associated with nuclear war.

Table 3-3. Costs of Strategic Nuclear Forces, Selected Fiscal Years, 1962–77[a]

Total obligational authority in billions of current and fiscal 1977 dollars

	Cost		Strategic forces as percent of total defense budget
Fiscal year	Current dollars	1977 dollars	
1962	17.1	40.7	34.1
1964	16.1	36.7	31.8
1965	14.3	31.8	28.2
1968	14.9	29.6	19.7
1972	16.3	24.5	21.0
1974	15.4	19.4	18.1
1975	16.7	19.1	19.0
1976[b]	17.3	18.5	17.6
1977[c]	20.6	20.6	18.3

Sources: Authors' estimates based on data appearing in *The Budget of the United States Government—Appendix*, appropriate years; Office of the Assistant Secretary of Defense (Comptroller), "National Defense Budget" (1976; processed); Office of the Assistant Secretary of Defense (Manpower and Reserve Affairs), "Manpower Requirements Report for FY 1977" (February 1976; processed); and unpublished computer printouts from the Department of Defense.

a. The costs of strategic nuclear forces are the sum of the strategic forces program (Program I of the Five-Year Defense Program), one-half of the intelligence and communications program (Program III), one-tenth of the National Guard and reserve program (V), four-tenths of the research and development program (VI), and a percentage of the three support programs—central supply and maintenance (VII), training, medical, and other general personnel activities, excluding retired pay (VIII), and administration (IX)—which varied each year in direct proportion to the operating cost ratio of strategic to all other forces.

b. Estimated.

c. Requested

Strategic planning is founded on three criteria.[10]

Secure retaliatory capability. The fundamental assumption is that the actual physical defense of the nation from nuclear attack—through the deployment of missile and air defenses combined with a massive program to protect the population from the effects of nuclear explosions—is impossible, or at least that it would be too risky, too costly, and too likely to encourage unstable relations between the United States and its adversaries. Instead, it is proposed that the United States deter nuclear attacks on this country or on nations to whose defense it is committed by making it known to potential attackers that, should they launch an attack, they themselves would suffer unacceptable and devastating levels of destruction. In brief, U.S. strategic forces are planned to be capable, under any conceivable circumstance, of absorbing an attack and inflicting massive damage on the attackers' industry, military forces, and population in retaliation. To ensure confidence in U.S. retaliatory capabilities, planning

10. See *U.S.–U.S.S.R. Strategic Policies*, Hearing before the Subcommittee on Arms Control, International Law, and Organization of the Senate Committee on Foreign Relations, 93:2 (GPO, 1974).

for strategic forces is based on the most pessimistic assessment of Soviet capabilities and of the circumstances surrounding the outbreak of hostilities. In addition, an independent retaliatory capability is maintained in each of three separate offensive systems—land-based missiles, submarine-launched missiles, and manned bombers. Because of the different modes of basing or penetration for each of the systems, the survivability of each component is considered to be relatively independent of the others.

Military flexibility. This factor, always important, has received new emphasis in recent years. Once the Soviet Union gained a believable secure retaliatory capability of its own, U.S. retaliatory threats—in certain situations—lost much of their credibility. For example, suppose that in a crisis the USSR launched a few missiles at isolated military targets in the United States. Should the United States respond with a massive attack on Soviet cities? Probably not, for the USSR would undoubtedly respond in kind to such retaliation, and both countries would be destroyed. Or suppose the USSR attacked a U.S. ally with nuclear weapons. Should this nation respond with an attack on Russian cities? Again, probably not; a more selective and more discriminating response, say, against military targets outside the Soviet Union, would be wiser. In short, the President should not have to choose between a nonnuclear response and an all-out nuclear attack on Soviet cities. U.S. strategic forces are therefore designed to provide a wide range of possible options—as regards targets and size and timing of attack—which could be tailored to the initial provocation. The availability of these options enhances deterrence by making potential adversaries realize that the United States could match whatever level of conflict they initiated.

Attainment of military flexibility requires the development of sophisticated command and control systems to permit the rapid retargeting of missiles, the launching of variable numbers of missiles, and similar steps. There has been virtually no opposition to this.

During the past several years, however, the administration also has pursued programs to increase the accuracy of U.S. missiles sufficiently to make them effective in destroying hardened point targets —primarily enemy missiles in concrete silos. This would give the United States options for limited nuclear war—notably, counterforce strikes at enemy ICBMs—heretofore not available. Criticism of these latter steps has been vigorous and widespread, based on a belief that the development of very accurate missiles decreases rather than enhances nuclear deterrence by giving an adversary an incentive to strike first in a crisis. If the opponent believes that its missiles are vulnerable and that a U.S. strike is imminent, it may be tempted to launch its missiles before they are destroyed. Thus very high accuracy may cause the superpowers' strategic postures to become relatively less stable in crises.

Defenders of the accuracy improvements, primarily former Secretary of Defense Schlesinger and other Pentagon officials, do not deny this possibility. They base their case on the fact that the Soviet Union —because its missiles are larger and can therefore carry more and higher-yield warheads—will almost inevitably develop the ability to destroy U.S. ICBMs, whether they also attain very high accuracies or not. The defenders argue that it behooves the United States to match this Soviet capability, which must be done by improving accuracy because of the relatively small size of U.S. missiles.

Political equivalence. In recent years, the most important factor in determining the U.S. strategic posture has been the perceived need to maintain forces that are judged at least equivalent to those of the Soviet Union. The reasons for this are political: to prevent the coercion or intimidation of the United States or its allies. The administration has argued that if a substantial imbalance should develop in total capabilities, or even in a specific type of strategic capability, a psychological atmosphere could be created in which the Soviet Union would be able to wrest various concessions from the United States even though the latter retained the capability—in extremis— to destroy Soviet society.

More specifically, it is argued that should an imbalance develop:
—in crises, Soviet leaders would be more bold and U.S. leaders more hesitant to risk confrontation;
—third nations—both allies and neutral states—would view any strategic imbalance as a sign of Soviet ascendancy and tailor their foreign policies accordingly; and
—the Soviet Union would have less incentive to negotiate new arms control or other cooperative arrangements with the United States.

The quest for political equivalence is used to justify the maintenance of numbers of strategic weapon systems comparable to those of the Soviet Union, even though some of the weapons may contribute only marginally to U.S. retaliatory or war-fighting capabilities.

And weapon modernization programs more rapid than those required by technical or military factors are justified in part by the political benefits imputed to increasing strategic capabilities.

Critics of political equivalence agree that a gross imbalance between the two sides could lead to adverse political developments, but they contend that virtually any static comparison of the two strategic forces is misleading. More important, in their view, are relative capabilities measured by qualitative as well as quantitative factors. In addition, they see only a loose relation between strategic capabilities and political consequences. They argue that, in view of the uncertainties inherent in strategic calculations, imbalances in the two forces could become fairly large before having any political effect. And finally, they point out that much of what the world thinks about the strategic balance depends on what American leaders say about it. Soviet leaders almost never discuss relative strategic capabilities publicly.

The administration's view—that political equivalence is an important factor in strategic force planning—is the ascendant one at present. Probably this is because of the major shift in the strategic balance in recent years, which is shown for various measures of strategic capability in table 3-4. As may be readily discerned, the Soviet Union has achieved parity with the United States during the past ten years in most static quantitative measures of strategic potential, and it seems likely to gain some advantage in various measures over the next ten years. When only missile characteristics are considered, the Soviet lead is already large and will probably increase. This troubles some observers, who feel that, because manned bombers are potentially vulnerable to air defenses (in which the USSR has invested vast resources), it is important to compare missiles and bombers separately. This is a questionable hypothesis. Presumably the United States acquires and operates bombers because it believes that they will be effective militarily; consequently, they should count politically as well. Besides, the United States retains various qualitative advantages not shown in the table, such as accuracy and missile reliability, some of which are much more important than the quantitative indexes listed in the table. Moreover, the United States seems likely to retain its advantage in the number of independently targetable warheads, even though this lead will narrow in the next ten years. Finally, relative counterforce capabilities,

Table 3-4. U.S. and Soviet Strategic Forces at End of Year, 1965, 1975, and 1985

| Index | 1965 | | 1975 | | 1985 projections[a] | | | |
| | | | | | Favorable for the United States | | Unfavorable for the United States | |
	United States	Soviet Union	United States	Soviet Union	United States	Soviet Union	United States	Soviet Union
Force levels								
Intercontinental ballistic missiles	854	224	1,054	1,603	1,054	1,409	1,054	1,409
Submarine-launched ballistic missiles	464	24	656	727	736	950	736	950
Strategic bombers[b]	807	155	497	135	509	0	509	0
Total launchers	2,125	403	2,207	2,465	2,299	2,359	2,299	2,359
Independently targetable warheads								
Total warheads	6,230	450	8,747	3,005	15,570	8,214	14,285	11,192
Missile warheads only	1,670	248	6,940	2,613	10,214	8,214	8,929	11,192
Payload capacity (millions of pounds)[c]								
Total payload	10.0	2.6	7.5	9.3	11.9	12.9	11.8	12.9
Missile payload only	2.2	1.1	3.9	8.2	5.1	12.9	5.0	12.9
Equivalent megatonnage[d]								
Total EMT	8,600	1,100	4,200	5,300	6,900	5,800	6,400	6,800
Missile EMT only	1,400	600	2,200	4,200	3,300	5,800	2,800	6,800
Hard target counterforce potential[e]								
Percentage of notional hard target set destroyed under ideal conditions by ICBM force	0	0	0	4	72	45	42	89

Sources: Authors' estimates derived from Stockholm International Peace Research Institute, *World Armaments and Disarmament: SIPRI Yearbook 1974* (M.I.T. Press, 1974), pp. 106–09; IISS, *The Military Balance, 1975–1976*, pp. 71–73; General George S. Brown, "United States Military Posture for FY 1977" (statement by Chairman of the Joint Chiefs of Staff, January 20, 1976; processed), pp. 31–48; Strategic Air Command, "The Development of the Strategic Air Command, 1946–1973" (September 19, 1974; processed), pp. 118–25; *Full Committee Consideration of Overall National Security Programs and Related Budget Requirements, Hearings before the House Committee on the Armed Services, 94:1* (GPO, 1975), pp. 228, 247; *U.S.–U.S.S.R. Strategic Policies, Hearing before the Subcommittee on Arms Control, International Law, and Organization of the Senate Committee on Foreign Relations, 93:2* (GPO, 1974), pp. 16, 45, 47, and 48; and General Electric, Heavy Military Electric Systems, "Missile Effectiveness Calculator" (Terrygraf Corp., 1965).

a. In all 1985 projections, it was assumed that both superpowers abided by the limits on strategic forces suggested by the Vladivostok guidelines. In the projection favorable for the United States, it was assumed that the United States carried out currently contemplated improvements in Minuteman III accuracy and yield, deployed a follow-on system for Minuteman (M-X) with an initial operational capability in 1983, and pursued present plans to modernize bombers and strategic submarines. For the Soviet Union, in the projection favorable for the United States it was assumed that (1) the deployment of three new kinds of ICBMs at the rates observed for existing Soviet missiles and commensurate improvements in their accuracy would continue; (2) a mobile ICBM would be introduced; (3) some "light" ICBMs with multiple reentry vehicles (MRVs) would be retained; (4) missiles on *Yankee*-class strategic submarines would not receive multiple independently targetable reentry vehicles (MIRVs); (5) production of *Delta*-type SSBNs, some with MIRVs, would continue.

In the projection unfavorable for the United States, the same assumptions as those listed above were made except: (1) the United States did not deploy the follow-on ICBM before 1985; (2) the Soviet Union deployed a version of the SS-18 with MIRVs instead of the single-warhead version; and (3) a more extensive MIRV program on the *Delta*-type strategic submarine was possible.

b. Following the International Institute for Strategic Studies definition, the Soviet Backfire bomber is not counted here as a strategic weapon system. This is a contentious point, one of the two or three issues that have delayed transforming the Vladivostok agreement into an explicit treaty.

c. The weight-carrying capacity of missiles and bombers is not directly comparable. This index includes the payload of each system that could be used to carry nuclear weapons, its protective structure, and associated guidance system.

d. Equivalent megatonnage is a measure of the area destruction capacity of a nuclear arsenal in light of the number and explosive yields of its various component weapons. It reflects the fact that the extent of the ground area that would be destroyed by a nuclear explosion does not increase one-to-one with increases in the yield of the nuclear warhead

e. The notional target set used in this calculation for both United States and Soviet ICBMs is 2,500 targets, each hardened to withstand blast over pressure up to 1,000 pounds per square inch. Two to three reentry vehicles are fired at each target; the target is assumed to be destroyed if they can produce a kill probability in excess of 85 percent. The "ideal conditions" refer to the assumptions of no degradation in accuracy caused by winds and similar environmental factors, and equal overall reliability for both United States and Soviet ICBMs.

now almost nonexistent, are extremely difficult to predict since they depend critically on the assumptions made about the characteristics (such as accuracy and hardness) of each side's missiles.

In the end, of course, the doctrinal controversies just described are translated into disputes over specific weapon programs. At present, there is little debate about force levels—the number of missiles and bombers the United States should maintain in its inventory. Essentially, the 1972 Interim Agreement on Offensive Weapons, which froze missile force levels as they then stood, and the promise, contained in the 1974 Vladivostok Accord, of a new agreement (which would extend the ceiling to include long-range bombers) have stilled such controversies at least for the time being. Current debate focuses instead on the pace and character of modernization programs: how quickly should the United States replace existing strategic weapons with more modern versions, and what are the most desirable features of the follow-on systems?

In the early part of this decade, the replacement for the existing Polaris/Poseidon strategic submarine and missile system was the most controversial modernization program. But that dispute clearly has been resolved in favor of the official nominee: the *Ohio*-class submarine carrying the Trident missile. Four of these submarines already have been authorized by Congress, and it seems likely that eventually the entire Polaris/Poseidon fleet will be replaced by this weapon system, at least up to whatever number is permitted under future arms control agreements.[11]

Currently, the main modernization issue concerns the strategic bomber force. For more than six years, the United States has been developing a new long-range bomber called the B-1; indeed, components of the B-1 can be traced to the advanced manned strategic aircraft program dating back to 1962. But the first significant production funds were requested in the 1977 budget proposal.

The B-1 is an impressive aircraft. Carrying eight short-range attack missiles and gravity bombs as its normal weapon load and using

11. Two missiles are planned for the new submarine, however. The first, Trident I, is endorsed by all observers—both for the *Ohio*-class submarine and for use in existing Poseidon submarines. The planned follow-on, Trident II, is more controversial. Some argue that there is no clear need for the greater range or throw-weight it would provide.

For a discussion of strategic submarine missile systems, see "Annual Defense Department Report, FY 1977," pp. 82–83.

a terrain-following radar, the B-1 would be able to penetrate even relatively thick and qualitatively advanced air defenses at altitudes as low as 100 feet and at speeds up to 400 knots. At higher altitudes, it would be supersonic.

Although some observers argue against the need for any replacement for the B-52s, opposition to the B-1 stems primarily from its cost. With a unit price of nearly $90 million, the cost of the planned B-1 program of 244 aircraft would exceed $21 billion. This estimate excludes the expense of acquiring a force of new tanker aircraft, which will be necessary if the B-1s are to operate effectively.

The most frequently cited alternative to the B-1 is a force of aircraft designed to stand off from enemy air defenses and launch a combination of long-range cruise missiles and shorter-range attack missiles at targets inside the Soviet Union. Eliminating the requirement that the aircraft itself be able to penetrate the enemy air defense system would greatly reduce the performance demanded of it, and thus its price tag, and make it unnecessary to buy tankers for the force. An earlier Brookings study concluded that a decision to buy a force of stand-off cruise-missile-carrying aircraft just as effective as the planned B-1 force would save between $10 billion and $15 billion in the ten-year period following such a decision.[12] Another alternative frequently cited, at least as an interim step, would be to equip existing B-52s with cruise missiles in addition to their current armament of short-range attack missiles.

In the future, the most important modernization decision is likely to concern land-based missiles. Follow-on programs to the present ICBM—Minuteman—are in relatively early development stages. But the administration has proposed increased spending for various research initiatives to develop land- and air-mobile ICBMs and fixed land-based missiles with much greater throw-weight than the existing systems, which would be placed in silos superhardened to withstand nuclear blasts.

Evaluations of the need for these programs, which would cost at least $30 billion over a ten-year period, hinge on assessments of the political consequences of potential outcomes. Such assessments begin with the common judgment that the present Minuteman force

12. Alton H. Quanbeck and Archie L. Wood, with the assistance of Louisa Thoron, *Modernizing the Strategic Bomber Force: Why and How* (Brookings Institution, 1976), pp. 27–29.

is likely to become vulnerable to a Soviet first strike sometime in the next decade, but that the relatively small size of the Minuteman ICBM would preclude the United States from gaining a comparable capability against the Soviet land-based missile force.[13] In essence, there are three choices. First, correct this imbalance by reducing U.S. vulnerability with superhardened silos while increasing Soviet vulnerability by upgrading the accuracy, yield, and number of U.S. ICBM warheads. (The last two features require the acquisition of missiles with much greater throw-weight than Minuteman.) Second, eliminate U.S. vulnerability either by replacing Minuteman with a land- or air-mobile missile or by building additional strategic submarines and submarine-launched missiles. Third, do not replace Minuteman as it becomes vulnerable but rely solely on the planned force of bombers and submarine-launched missiles for secure retaliatory capability.

Selecting the first option would suggest an emphasis in U.S. strategic planning on military flexibility. Both accuracy and responsive command and control systems, two features prerequisite for limited or very discriminating and time-urgent strikes against an enemy, are most reliably incorporated in fixed-site systems. The questions concerning this option are two. Is there any conceivable hardening program that would prevent fixed-site ICBMs from becoming vulnerable? If not, which situation is better: one in which both U.S. and Soviet ICBMs are vulnerable and the United States has the option of carrying out limited strikes or one in which neither is vulnerable and the United States does not have the option of carrying out limited strikes?

Choice of the second option (replacing Minuteman with a mobile system) would reflect continued emphasis on the need for political equivalence. It would mean that the nation recognized the dangerous instabilities implicit in vulnerable forces and was attempting to minimize the alleged political effects of abandoning fixed-site systems by replacing the warheads, throw-weight, and equivalent megatonnage now incorporated in the Minuteman force with alternative systems.

Choosing the third option (not replacing Minuteman) would im-

13. There are several reservations to this assessment, the primary one being the so-called fratricide effect. It has been suggested that the number of warheads that can be effectively targeted against a particular sector of a missile field or a single missile silo within a specific time period may be limited. It is theorized that, if not properly timed, the performance of warheads arriving after the first detonation is likely to be degraded by the effects of the earlier nuclear explosion.

ply a perception that the other two legs of the strategic triad were sufficient for secure retaliatory capabilities. In such a case, Minuteman could be retained for limited nuclear war-fighting, regardless of its theoretical vulnerability. Choosing this option would also imply, however, a discounting of the need for political equivalence.

It is difficult to evaluate these alternatives because of the uncertainty in the ongoing negotiations to limit strategic arms. If the SALT negotiations break down or if it is not possible to achieve a new treaty before the present interim agreement expires in October 1977, the size and composition of U.S. strategic forces might change markedly. Administration spokesmen have warned that in either of these eventualities they would request a sharp acceleration of missile and bomber modernization programs. No doubt the conservative wings of both political parties would urge increases in offensive weapon force levels as well. But more important, should the SALT process not produce a new agreement, the debate on U.S. strategic doctrine is likely to erupt with a vengeance. There could be strong pressure (1) to renounce the treaty barring more than token anti-ballistic missile systems; (2) to shift U.S. policy (and weapon deployments) toward rapid preparations for nuclear war-fighting, including the construction of massive missile, air, and civil defenses and an acceleration of programs to deploy large numbers of very accurate missiles; and (3) in general, to let nuclear weapons play a more central role in U.S. foreign policy.

There is already some evidence of a slow shift in U.S. policy on the last point. During most of the 1960s, the major thrust of U.S. defense policy was to curtail the role of nuclear weapons. The utility of these weapons was disparaged in official statements. Their function usually was described as being solely to deter nuclear attacks on this nation and its allies. Efforts were made to increase U.S. conventional military capabilities, and thus reduce the need for resort to nuclear weapons, and to regulate the nuclear competition.

Most of these policies have been continued, but with one difference. Since 1968 there have been persistent attempts, both in declaratory policy and through the acquisition of military hardware, to turn the nation's nuclear strength into political clout.

Although the roots of this new policy can be seen in the writings of Professor Henry A. Kissinger in the 1950s and although changes in U.S. nuclear doctrine were expounded in several documents in the early years of the Nixon administration, events did not gain momentum until 1972. That year Defense Secretary Melvin R. Laird conveyed the SALT agreements to Congress along with a request for an increase in funds to develop very accurate missiles—weapons that had previously been ruled out as too threatening to stable deterrence.

Strong indications of the new thinking were evident during the 1973 October War in the Middle East. Faced with Soviet threats to intervene in the conflict, the administration placed U.S. military units, *including strategic nuclear forces,* on alert. The nuclear threat was made apparent when the secretary of state, on nationwide television, spoke ominously of the "ashes of civilization."

Then, in January 1974, Secretary of Defense Schlesinger brought the changes in U.S. strategic doctrine pointedly to the attention of the public. He announced that the United States would retarget its strategic weapons to give the President additional nuclear options. He suggested that new war plans (and the hardware to back them up) would soon make it possible for the President to respond in crises with a tailored set of selected nuclear strikes on various target systems. He further emphasized the utility of nuclear weapons later in 1974 by making several statements to the effect that, under certain circumstances, the United States would consider first use of nuclear weapons. Moreover, he added, such first use conceivably could involve strategic weapons directed at targets in the Soviet Union.[14]

Essentially, Schlesinger only reaffirmed, but made more explicit, what had been a continuing theme in U.S. defense policy. This nation never had foreclosed the possibility of using its nuclear arsenal first if pressed to the wall in a conventional conflict, although it did tend to downplay it. The new emphasis on the possible use of nuclear weapons was evidently an attempt to halt a perceived erosion of U.S. influence in world affairs, resulting partly from the buildup of Soviet military capabilities and partly from communist victories in Southeast Asia.

If one fears that the American people are unwilling to pay the price necessary to match Soviet conventional military capabilities, it may be possible to secure deterrence cheaply by making it clear that any superpower confrontation could result in nuclear war. If one fears that small states, like North Korea, no longer find U.S. threats credi-

14. For discussion of retargeting and first strike policies, see *U.S.–U.S.S.R. Strategic Polices,* Hearing, pp. 7–17.

ble, perhaps raising the stakes will make them unwilling to challenge the United States. If one is apprehensive about the consequences of nuclear proliferation, emphasizing the vast superiority of the U.S. nuclear arsenal may minimize the status gained by new nuclear powers. And if one fears that allies are beginning to doubt the commitment of the United States, perhaps demonstrating its ability to look squarely at the possibility of nuclear war will reassure them.

The risks of such a policy are apparent. Suppose that in 1985, after the United States had clearly embraced a defense policy stressing the use of nuclear weapons, a naval confrontation developed between the United States and the Soviet Union in the Mediterranean. In such circumstances, might not the Soviet Union be the first to resort to nuclear weapons on the assumption that escalation to that level of conflict was inevitable? Or suppose the United States, after losing a warship to conventional Soviet weapons, made good on its new doctrine and launched a limited first strike at military targets in the Soviet Union. Given the widely proclaimed accuracy of U.S. missiles, how would the USSR react when its early warning systems picked up the launch of U.S. ICBMs? Would it wait to see what their targets were, thereby risking the destruction of a significant portion of its own strategic power, or would it launch its own ICBMs before they were destroyed? If the Russians did wait, what would be their response—a carefully tailored one or a massive attack on civilian targets? And even if they tried to avoid civilian targets, would the hardware work well enough to avoid tens of millions of deaths? Are these risks worth taking?

As anyone who has witnessed the manner in which governments reach and carry out decisions during crises can attest, the uncertainty among high-level decisionmakers, the pressure for action, the persistent failures in command and control systems, the frequent disruptions in communications all make it unlikely that the United States and the Soviet Union could coolly exchange nuclear-armed missiles without escalating to catastrophe.

In a nutshell, the danger of adopting a high-risk defense policy that relies on nuclear options is not that such a strategy would not work, but that it might work too well—that it would, by raising the stakes of virtually any conflict involving the United States, introduce new uncertainty into the calculations of decisionmakers around the world. Uncertainty might, in some cases, cause foreign leaders to behave more prudently, but would also raise the cost of failure to terrifying heights.

There are other disadvantages to emphasizing nuclear weapons, such as the encouragement it might give other states to develop their own nuclear capabilities, but these are less important.

The existing nuclear arsenals of the United States and the Soviet Union are sufficient to destroy civilization as we know it today. This is the inescapable reality of our time. When one speaks of nuclear gambles, it should not have the same connotation as a bluff in a penny-ante poker game. There are ways of emphasizing U.S. military power, restoring U.S. credibility in world affairs, and balancing Soviet power short of risking nuclear war—notably, by improving conventional capabilities. They should be actively pursued before nuclear weapons are given a central role in U.S. policy.

General Purpose Forces

In recent years, the technological revolution in military hardware has expanded and gained new momentum. Traditional concepts of proper military strategy and tactics in virtually all areas of conventional, or general purpose, armaments have been challenged on the premise that developments, mainly in missile guidance and propulsion systems but also in other aspects of military technology, will soon make available increases in conventional military capabilities of a magnitude that has not been seen since the introduction of firearms. Of these developments, the most important are (1) the advent of so-called hitting weapons—precision-guided munitions that can be used for various purposes and are characterized by accuracy so great that a single shot is almost certain to destroy most targets—and (2) sizable increases in the mobility, defensive capabilities, and offensive firepower of ground forces.

These developments, which have been brewing for some time, suddenly and dramatically surfaced during the October War in the Middle East. Rarely has a single short conflict witnessed so many affronts to traditional concepts of military strategy. Most of these innovations were demonstrated not by the U.S.-equipped Israeli army, but by the armies of Egypt and Syria, which were trained and equipped by the USSR and presumably, therefore, reflected Soviet military thought. In effect, the Arab armies were encased in a bubble of firepower, within which they could advance, even if slowly, despite the greater maneuverability and tactical innovations of Israeli armor and despite the inability of their own air forces to challenge the much superior Israeli air arm successfully.

Three aspects of the 1973 war are particularly noteworthy.

Augmented antitank capabilities. In the early days of the conflict, Arab armies equipped with large numbers of man-portable and vehicle-mounted antitank missiles took a high toll of Israeli armor. Tank attrition rates were cut down later in the war as the Israelis learned to defend against these weapons. But the Egyptian and Syrian (i.e., Soviet) antitank missiles were only first-generation and rather primitive versions of weapons that have since been introduced, or will be soon, into the armies of the world, and this promises even more serious future problems for armored formations. The net effect of this increased ground-based missile threat to armor, and of the reduced air threat to tanks discussed below, is difficult to judge. Probably there will be some reduction in the effectiveness of armor, but tanks will remain the dominant ground weapon in the next decade.

A marked reduction in the advantages of air superiority. Arab ground formations also were equipped with large numbers of relatively inexpensive man-portable short-range antiaircraft missiles, and were accompanied both by more capable longer-range mobile air defense missile systems and by large numbers of radar-directed rapid-fire mobile antiaircraft guns. These weapons contributed synergistically to an impressive air defense system which took a fearful toll of Israeli aircraft in the early days of the war. Again, the Israelis developed tactics and acquired equipment that reduced their losses as the war progressed. To some extent, however, these tactics decreased the effectiveness of close air support; for example, the Israeli Air Force appears to have destroyed fewer than ten tanks. Because the Soviet air defenses that NATO would face in Central Europe would be even more intense than those in the Middle East (the two newest Soviet surface-to-air missiles, SA-8 and SA-9, were not used in the Middle East), traditional methods of exploiting air superiority to blunt armored threats are unlikely to work. Instead, the antitank capabilities of ground units will have to be expanded, which is now possible. Also, air-to-ground ordnance that permits aircraft to remain farther away from their targets than do existing weapons, like "Maverick," would be useful. It seems likely that in future conflicts conventional methods for the exploitation of air superiority will no longer hold and that the large-scale use of aircraft for the close support of ground forces will be costly.

The first extensive combat between fast missile-armed patrol boats. These systems—particularly the Israeli *Saar*-class boat armed with the Gabriel missile—demonstrated their ability, if equipped with good electronic countermeasures and operated with tactical proficiency, to cripple opposing naval forces even when they are similarly armed.

Of course, no future war will be precisely the same as an earlier one. Terrain, weather, the skill of commanders, and many other factors will vary. Nonetheless, military planners have drawn a number of lessons from this Middle Eastern experience, which are now beginning to influence decisions about U.S. weapon modernization programs and the general purpose force structure. The new technology seems to favor the defense over the offense, ground forces over air forces, and larger numbers of cheaper weapons over fewer expensive ones. Analyses of the October War imply that the cost of any war between the United States and the Soviet Union would be extraordinarily high, thus making even more persuasive the argument that the United States should plan primarily for intense conflicts of relatively short duration, with only such hedges as steps to ensure that resources could be mobilized, if necessary, for more protracted wars. Even in a short war, however, the 1973 experience suggests that stocks of munitions should be much larger than they were previously.

The new technologies seem to improve the chances that NATO could defend itself against a Soviet attack if changes are made in traditional NATO weapon design criteria and in the priority NATO usually gives air power over ground power. The increase in antitank capability is particularly important, because armor plays an essential role in Soviet military doctrine. The new technologies also indicate that NATO should emulate the Soviet practice of buying larger numbers of relatively inexpensive weapons. These considerations and the broader political judgments discussed in chapter 2 are applied to each component of the general purpose forces in the following pages. There are four such components: ground combat forces, which account for about 30 percent of the baseline defense budget; tactical air forces, which account for about 25 percent; naval general purpose forces, more than 20 percent; and mobility forces, less than 5 percent.

GROUND COMBAT FORCES. The basic ground force building block is the maneuver battalion. Battalions are combined into brigades, which in turn are combined into divisions. The United States now has sixteen Army and three Marine divisions in active service, eight National Guard and one Marine division in reserve, plus three active and four reserve special mission brigades.[15] The data in table 3-5 show the various types of maneuver battalions, as well as their location and status.

The main problem concerning U.S. ground forces is that much of the force structure would be more useful in wars in Asia than in those in Europe or the Middle East. More than 40 percent of both the active maneuver battalions and the reserve force structure is made up of relatively lightly armed and immobile infantry, Marine, Ranger, airborne, or airmobile battalions. These units would not be as useful as armored or mechanized battalions in a conflict in either Europe or the Middle East, where they would have to face heavily armored and fully mechanized Soviet or Arab armies.

The disproportionate share of lightly armed ground forces is chiefly the result of two things. Over the past three years, the U.S. Army has grown from thirteen to sixteen divisions through the conversion of about 50,000 manpower spaces from support to combat categories. Two of the new divisions have been identified as infantry formations because current armor production rates will make it impossible to provide the vehicles necessary for an "armored" or "mechanized" classification for about four years; the third is a "mechanized" division.[16] On the other hand, the three Marine divisions are lightly armed by choice. The Marine Corps is organized, equipped, trained,

15. Office of the Assistant Secretary of Defense (Manpower and Reserve Affairs), "Manpower Requirements Report for FY 1977" (February 1976; processed), p. II-15.

16. As shown below, even infantry divisions have some tanks and armored personnel carriers (APCs) assigned to them; the amount of armor varies sharply, however:

	Typical number	
Type of division	Battle tanks	APCs
Armored	324	800
Mechanized	216	900
Infantry	54	150

Martin Binkin and Jeffrey Record, *Where Does the Marine Corps Go from Here?* (Brookings Institution, 1976), p. 18; *FY 1977 Authorization for Military Procurement, Research and Development, and Active Duty, Selected Reserve, and Civilian Personnel Strengths,* Hearings before the Senate Armed Services Committee, 94:2 (GPO, 1976), pt. 2, p. 674.

Table 3-5. U.S. Maneuver Battalions, by Type, Location, and Status, Fiscal Year 1977

Location, type, and status	Armored	Mechanized	Infantry	Airborne[a]	Airmobile	Ranger	Cavalry squadrons Armored	Cavalry squadrons Air[b]	Total
Europe, active[c]	25	28	3	1	...	...	10	...	67
Asia, active[d]	2	2	14	...	...	1	...	1	19
Total forward deployed	**27**	**30**	**17**	**1**	...	...	**10**	**1**	**86**
United States									
Active[e]	25	22	44	9	9	2	8	7	126
Reserve roundout[f]	7	6	9	...	...	...	...	...	22
Reserves[g]	37	38	65	2	...	...	18	...	160
Total reinforcement	**69**	**66**	**118**	**11**	**9**	**2**	**26**	**7**	**308**
Special mission[h]									
Active	...	1	5	...	...	...	...	...	6
Reserve	...	...	12	...	...	...	...	...	12
Total active	**52**	**53**	**66**	**10**	**9**	**2**	**18**	**8**	**218**
Total reserve	**44**	**44**	**86**	**2**	...	...	**18**	...	**194**
Total, all forces	**96**	**97**	**152**	**12**	**9**	**2**	**36**	**8**	**412**

Sources: Barry M. Blechman, Edward M. Gramlich, and Robert W. Hartman, *Setting National Priorities: The 1976 Budget* (Brookings Institution, 1975), p. 97; Office of the Assistant Secretary of Defense, "Manpower Requirements Report for FY 1977," p. V-4; and unpublished data from the Department of Defense.

a. Airborne battalions are easily transportable by fixed wing aircraft and can carry out parachute assaults.

b. Air Cavalry squadrons depend on helicopters for their mobility.

c. First Armored Division, 3rd Armored Division, 3rd Mechanized Division, 8th Mechanized Division, and the Berlin Brigade, all located in West Germany.

d. Second Infantry Division (South Korea) and 3rd Marine Division (Okinawa).

e. Second Armored Division (Fort Hood, Texas), 1st Mechanized Division (Fort Riley, Kansas), and 4th Mechanized Division (Fort Carson, Colorado); all have units deployed in West Germany. Fifth Mechanized Division (Fort Polk, Louisiana), 7th Infantry Division (Fort Ord, California), 9th Infantry Division (Fort Lewis, Washington), 24th Infantry Division (Fort Stuart, Georgia), 25th Infantry Division (Hawaii), 1st Marine Division (Camp Pendleton, California), 2nd Marine Division (Camp Lejeune, North Carolina), 1st Cavalry Division (Fort Hood, Texas), 82nd Airborne Division (Fort Bragg, North Carolina), 101st Airborne Division (Air Assault) (Fort Campbell, Kentucky), 75th Rangers (Georgia and Washington).

f. "Reserve roundout" means that reserve component battalions have been used to round out active divisions to standard configuration.

g. Eight National Guard Divisions and 4th Marine Reserve Division.

h. Includes 172nd Brigade (Alaska), 193rd Brigade (Panama), and four reserve component brigades.

and deployed mainly to conduct attacks from the sea. This emphasis on the amphibious mission, which stems from a variety of military, political, and institutional factors, has shaped the Corps into a distinctively tailored light infantry force—a force that, to be readily deployable and adaptive to helicopter and amphibious ship operations, conspicuously lacks armored fighting vehicles and heavy weapons.[17]

Since there is a reduced need for U.S. forces primarily suited for Asian contingencies, two changes are desirable. First, increased production rates for U.S. armored fighting vehicles would permit more rapid conversion of some infantry battalions to mechanized or armored battalions, thereby making U.S. military capabilities more applicable to Europe. And there are other reasons to increase the production of armored fighting vehicles: stocks of equipment pre-positioned in Europe for the use of U.S. troops that would be flown there in the event of a crisis have been drawn down to supply U.S. allies; deliveries of additional vehicles ordered by U.S. allies have been delayed in recent years; and the high attrition rates expected in any new conflict mean that reserve stocks of major items of equipment should be built up. It may seem paradoxical to be buying more armor at a time when antitank capabilities are improving, but the tank is likely to remain an essential ground weapon for some time, even if its effectiveness is reduced. Second, the infantry battalions no longer justified by U.S. interests or strategy in Asia could be phased out of the force structure, thus saving money. The precise number of battalions that should be equipped with armor and the number that should be phased out, and how many in each category should come from the Army or the Marine Corps, must be left to more precise analyses.

Modernizing equipment for ground forces does not attract the attention paid to air and naval forces, probably because of the relatively low price tags. Even the more expensive items of ground force equipment—for example, the tank at less than $1 million apiece—seem inexpensive compared to $5 million ballistic missiles, $20 million aircraft, and $1 billion to $2 billion ships. Like the other types of forces, however, acquisition programs for U.S. ground forces should begin to emphasize more of the relatively less expensive weapons. Of

17. Binkin and Record, *Where Does the Marine Corps Go from Here?* p. 2.

particular importance would be additional air defense systems for the forward combat area, increased densities of antitank guided missiles mounted on armored vehicles, and significant increases in fire-support weapons, such as free-fire multiple rocket launchers armed with improved munitions (for instance, scatterable antitank mines) to provide massive conventional firepower against concentrated attacking formations and tube artillery with sizable stocks of guided projectiles to provide accurate fire against high-value targets.

Over the longer term, there may be good cause to make fundamental changes in ground force doctrine, equipment, and tactics.

The United States has long relied on air power to provide fire support for its fighting men on the ground. This practice was carried to extremes in the "permissive" air environment of the Vietnam conflict. U.S. forces in Europe would also rely on air power for the destruction of opposing armor formations. But this support may be difficult to supply in the future even if the U.S. gains local air superiority over part of the battlefield. In part, heavy losses in close support aircraft may be made up for by new high-precision artillery and very accurate and longer-range air-to-ground munitions, but such losses will also have to be compensated for by greater defensive capabilities of the ground formations themselves.

A first step in this direction might be to increase the mass fire capability of the ground forces through the development and deployment of large numbers of inexpensive rocket systems. Rockets can be equipped with improved high explosive munitions that could destroy infantry formations, command and control facilities, and support activities. Rockets can also emplace antitank and antipersonnel mines quickly and effectively. Area rocket systems could be supplemented with tube artillery that would fire precision-guided projectiles to destroy point targets.

Second, despite the suggestion that increased armor production would be a good mid-term solution, considerable thought and solid research need to be devoted to the long-term future of the tank. Will developments in antitank missiles ultimately doom the tank as an effective offensive weapon? Could new tank designs or new weapons counteract the prospective increase in antitank capabilities? Would a greater number of cheaper tanks, with smaller crews, alleviate the problem? The answers to these questions, which are not yet evident, could have a profound effect on the structure of U.S. ground forces.

Third, the Soviet approach to air defense, which concentrates on acquiring enormous numbers of medium-technology and therefore less costly weapon systems, seems to have been successful. On the other hand, existing U.S. development programs—SAM-D (an area defense missile), STINGER (a man-portable system), and GLAADS (a low-altitude gun system)—are resulting in high-technology, high-cost weapons, of which fewer can be bought. Moreover, these systems are so sophisticated that they are likely to be unreliable, difficult to maintain, and possibly vulnerable to electronic countermeasures or even ambient electronic "noise."

Fourth, ground forces must move away from the concept of holding specific pieces of ground toward a more fluid battlefield. This means that a relatively fixed or semimobile defense may not be the most effective means of stopping an enemy attack. In a war in which the use of tactical nuclear weapons is implicitly threatened, combat forces will probably have to fight in dispersed formations from the start. The depth of the battlefield is likely to expand and several independent battles may be fought simultaneously. Such a concept would call for maneuver formations with their own integral combat support and logistic elements. Thus it seems sensible for the United States to move toward more independent ground formations—units with capable organic air defense, sizable antiarmor capabilities, their own fire support, and somewhat diminished logistic ties to rear echelons. These changes would be difficult to implement but are worth exploring.

TACTICAL AIR FORCES. More than to any other type of combat force, the United States has applied its ingenuity, technological prowess, and productive capacity to the development of aircraft, their electronic subsystems, and their ordnance. Consequently, U.S. aircraft today are unrivaled in performance and reliability. At the same time, this technical superiority is not without its price. As is shown in figure 3-1, the cost of U.S. tactical aircraft has been on a steady, steep upward curve since the Second World War, resulting, despite increasing budgetary allocations for the purchase of tactical aircraft, in a persistent decline in the number of tactical aircraft produced each year and thus in reductions in the number of aircraft in the inventories of the military services (table 3-6).

The dilemma for U.S. defense planners is by now a familiar one. Even though the newer and more expensive aircraft are far more

Figure 3-1. Average Flyaway Costs of U.S. Tactical Aircraft, Fiscal Years 1940–76

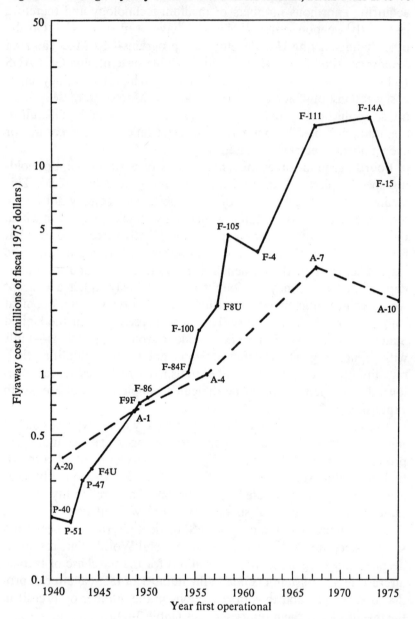

Source: William D. White, *U.S. Tactical Air Power: Missions, Forces, and Costs* (Brookings Institution, 1974), pp. 47, 56.

Table 3-6. Aircraft in Production and in Air Force and Navy Inventories,
Selected Fiscal Years, 1950–77

Fiscal year	In production	Inventory[a]
1950	2,268	31,400
1960	1,391	27,600
1965	1,448	24,400
1970	934	15,100
1975	407	12,300
1977[b]	460	11,500

Sources: *Aviation Week*, vol. 52 (May 1, 1950), p. 15; vol. 54 (February 26, 1951), pp. 14–16; vol. 56 (February 25, 1952), pp. 25, 27; vol. 70 (January 26, 1959), p. 30; vol. 74 (March 13, 1961), pp. 73, 80; and vol. 82 (February 1, 1965), p. 22; IISS, *The Military Balance, 1965–1966, 1970–1971,* and *1975–1976; Department of Defense Appropriations for Fiscal Year 1960,* Hearings before the House Appropriations Committee, 86:1 (GPO, 1959), pt. 5; Department of Defense, "Program Acquisition Costs by Weapon System: Department of Defense Budget for Fiscal Year 1977" (n.d.; processed).
a. Includes all strategic, tactical, and support aircraft and helicopters, whether assigned to operational squadrons or not.
b. Requested.

capable than their predecessors, no airplane can be in two places at the same time. At some point, trading quantity for quality may be disadvantageous.

Tactical aircraft are more flexible than ground forces; it is virtually impossible to identify a specific regional orientation for them unless they are deployed and explicitly committed there. These days, even land-based aircraft squadrons, along with their direct support facilities, can be relocated relatively quickly, and ordnance more suitable for one theater than another, even to the slight degree that one can identify such differences, can be easily replaced with more appropriate ordnance. Moreover, nearly three-fourths of the U.S. tactical air squadrons are based in the continental United States. These squadrons are primarily designated for European contingencies, but they could be used quite easily in the Middle East, in Korea, or anywhere else.

Two criticisms are often leveled at U.S. tactical air power: that there are redundancies in the force structure, and that certain design features of the aircraft unnecessarily increase their cost.

The United States now has four tactical air forces. The Air Force operates 91 active squadrons and 48 squadrons in reserve, the Navy has 99 active squadrons and 16 squadrons in reserve, the Marine Corps has 33 active and 9 reserve squadrons, and the Army operates 48 active and 16 reserve attack helicopter companies. The force structure is summarized, by service and by primary mission, in table 3-7.

Table 3-7. Structure of U.S. Tactical Air Forces, Fiscal Year 1977
Number of squadrons or helicopter companies

Service	Primary function				
	Air superiority[a]	Deep interdiction[b]	Multi-purpose[c]	Close air support[d]	Other[e]
Air Force[f]					
Active	6	12	41	7	25
Reserve	0	0	20	17	11
Navy[g]					
Active	12	12	14	27	34
Reserve	0	0	4	6	6
Marine Corps[g]					
Active	0	5	12	1	5
Reserve	0	0	2	6	1
Army[h]					
Active	0	0	0	48	2
Reserve	0	0	0	16	3
Total	18	29	93	138	87

Sources: Authors' estimates derived from *Fiscal Year 1977 Authorization for Military Procurement, Research and Development, and Active Duty, Selected Reserve, and Civilian Personnel Strengths: Tactical Air Power*, Hearings before the Senate Armed Services Committee, 94:2 (GPO, 1976), pt. 9, pp. 4859–71, and pt. 10, pp. 5330–35; Office of the Assistant Secretary of Defense, "Manpower Requirements Report for FY 1977," p. V-10; Martin Binkin and Jeffrey Record, *Where Does the Marine Corps Go from Here?* (Brookings Institution, 1976), p. 21; "Annual Defense Department Report, FY 1977" (statement to U.S. Congress, January 27, 1976; processed), p. 192. Aircraft types and capabilities from John W. R. Taylor and Gordon Swanborough, *Military Aircraft of the World* (Scribners, 1971).
a. Aircraft designed purely for aerial combat, in this case the F-14 and F-15.
b. Capable of long-range missions deep over enemy territory, such as the A-6 and F-111.
c. Capable of both aerial combat and long-range ground attack missions, like the F-4.
d. Intended to support ground troops in battle or to attack naval targets; includes fixed-wing high-performance aircraft like the A-4, A-7, and A-10; aircraft capable of vertical and short takeoff and landing (AV-8); and armed helicopters, like the AH-1.
e. Includes reconnaissance, electronic countermeasure, and early warning aircraft.
f. There are eighteen to twenty-four aircraft in each Air Force squadron; three to four squadrons of the same type of aircraft make up a wing.
g. Navy and Marine squadrons vary in size from four to twenty-one aircraft. A Navy wing consists of eighty to ninety aircraft, of different types, deployed on an aircraft carrier.
h. Army attack helicopters are found in attack helicopter companies and air cavalry troops. Attack helicopter companies have twenty-one helicopters. Air cavalry troops have nine attack helicopters assigned along with eighteen other transport and observation helicopters.

The military services do emphasize different missions. Army attack helicopters, for example, are useful only for close air support. The Marine Corps tends to emphasize this mission too, although it has 12 squadrons of F-4s and 5 squadrons of A-6s, which are not optimally configured and rather more capable (and expensive) than is necessary for close air support.[18] The Air Force, which presumably

18. Binkin and Record, *Where Does the Marine Corps Go from Here?* pp. 42–56, discuss Marine air capabilities.

would provide most of the Army's close air support, prefers to stress the air superiority and deep interdiction missions; this contributes to the Army's reluctance to give up its armed helicopters. To a lesser extent, this is the Navy's preference as well because of the need to intercept enemy aircraft far from the aircraft carriers and destroy them before they can launch their missiles. Thus considerable duplication exists among the four services, particularly in the support facilities necessary to maintain these aircraft. The overall costs of basic pilot training, aircraft maintenance and overhauls, and even research and development and procurement would be lower if each tactical air force were more distinctively tailored, and if the four shared more services.

The design criticism is essentially founded on the suspicion that too many U.S. tactical aircraft have been engineered to perform deep interdiction missions against very capable (Soviet) opponents. Deep interdiction refers to attacks on industrial and transportation system targets far behind the battle line that will interrupt the opponents' ability to support their military forces. To accomplish these missions, aircraft must be capable of carrying a large payload over a great range and of gaining air superiority at that distance. This requires an aircraft that performs well, is large enough to carry twin engines, advanced avionics, redundant pilot support systems, considerable fuel, and air-to-air ordnance, and has other features necessary to engage a sophisticated opponent far from the aircraft's own base. The incorporation of these features in first-line U.S. fighters is a major cause of the extremely high price tags of these aircraft.

Alternatively, aircraft could be designed for less demanding missions, such as providing fire support directly to troops on the battlefield, or they could be aimed at gaining air superiority against a sophisticated opponent, but only behind their own lines (as in air defense) or directly over the battlefield (as when providing air support). The United States has designed aircraft of both types—the A-10, now being acquired, is specifically designed for close air support, and both the F-18, a Navy aircraft, and the F-16, an Air Force plane, are designed to achieve air superiority but only at lesser ranges. The data in table 3-8 compare the costs and characteristics of these aircraft. The point is that if the United States purchased more of these specialized and less expensive aircraft and fewer of the more expensive ones, it would be able, for the same amount of expenditure, to

Table 3-8. Characteristics of "Competing" Tactical Aircraft

Characteristic	Primary function and type of aircraft					
	Air superiority		Close air support		Fleet air defense	
	F-15	F-16	A-7	A-10	F-14	F-18
Crew	1	1	1	1	2	1
Maximum speed (Mach number)	2.5	1.95	0.9	0.7	2.4	1.8
Empty weight (tons)	13.0	6.9	9.75	11.8	17.5	10.3
Maximum weight (tons)	27.0	16.5	21.0	22.7	34.5	22.0
Maximum combat radius (miles)[a]	500	650	700	750	500	650
Maximum bomb load (tons)[b]	6.0	5.0	7.5	8.0	7.0	5.0
Number of weapon stations[c]	5	5	8	11	6	5
Air-to-air missiles (typical load)						
Radar	4	0	0	0	4	2
Infrared	4	2	2	0	4	2
Thrust-to-weight ratio in combat[d]	1.48	1.35	0.34	0.40	0.76	1.15
Wing loading (combat weight in lb./sq. ft.)[e]	57.9	66.6	112.0	93.2	78.8	66.9
Program unit cost (millions of dollars)[f]	9.6	6.7	3.6	2.9	16.0	9.9

Sources: Authors' estimates derived from Taylor and Swanborough, *Military Aircraft of the World;* R. Meller, "Europe's New Generation of Combat Aircraft, Part 3: Variety Still the Rule," *International Defense Review,* vol. 8 (August 1975), p. 544; *Aviation Week and Space Technology,* vol. 102 (March 17, 1975), p. 81; Department of Defense, "Program Acquisition Costs by Weapon System . . . 1977"; "Selected Acquisition Reports, SAR Program Acquisition Cost Summary as of December 31, 1975," Department of Defense press release (February 17, 1976).

a. Actual combat radius will vary with the mission to be flown. A high speed–high altitude interception mission may yield a combat radius of only 150 miles, while if just flying from one base to another, the same aircraft's range may increase ten times. Similarly, trade-offs may be made between the amount of ordnance or fuel carried and range.

b. Maximum bomb load also is a function of how far the aircraft is to fly; range decreases markedly as bomb load increases.

c. The number of weapon stations (or "hard points") determine the aircraft's versatility.

d. Thrust-to-weight ratio is one indication of the aircraft's ability to climb and to accelerate, among other things. The higher the number, the better the aircraft.

e. Wing loading is a way of indicating the aircraft's maneuverability. It is derived from the weight of the plane and the area of its wings. The lower the number, the more maneuverable the aircraft will be. Wing loading can be improved at less expense than can thrust-to-weight ratio.

f. Program unit cost is the average cost, in dollars of equal purchasing power, of procuring the aircraft and its initial spares, plus a prorated share of the cost of research and development.

maintain a larger aircraft inventory and to increase the combat effectiveness of its air forces over the battlefield.

There is also some question whether the new "less-than-very-capable aircraft"—the F-16 and the F-18—incorporate more impressive design features than necessary. Recent significant gains in the capabilities of air-to-air and air-to-ground ordnance may make certain features—for instance, avionics necessary to penetrate air defenses—unnecessary. As the performance of these missiles improves, it should become possible to lower the performance requirements of the aircraft that launch them, reducing the price of these aircraft and permitting either budgetary savings or increases in the number of aircraft purchased.

The United States will have to come to grips with the marked improvement in the capabilities of air defense systems. Mobile systems incorporating gunfire, as well as several kinds of missiles, could make the close air support of ground units extremely costly. For a while, the gains in air defense capabilities may be offset by improvements in air-to-ground ordnance and electronic warfare systems. But some significant alteration in the overall trade-off between air power and ground defenses seems inevitable, which would call for a number of dramatic changes in traditional U.S. practices.

For one thing, the relative attention and amount of money accorded to air and ground forces by the United States might need revision, with increased emphasis on the latter.

Second, a concerted developmental effort might be aimed at replacing more aircraft with unmanned systems. Artillery might be substituted for some close air support, or cruise missiles used for deep interdiction missions. Remotely piloted vehicles might play a larger part—in reconnaissance, in electronic warfare, and particularly in the delivery of munitions to ground targets. The substitution of unmanned systems for aircraft would save money; life support systems and redundancies in various subsystems designed to reduce attrition rates contribute significantly to making modern aircraft so expensive. And personnel costs are the most important factor in the overall cost of tactical air forces. Above all, greater use of unmanned systems would reduce the toll of American lives in combat.

NAVAL FORCES. The Navy, which has gained for itself the largest share of the defense budget in recent years, is now at the center of the debate on defense policy.[19] This shift in the distribution of U.S.

19. The Navy will account for almost $38 billion of the $113 billion requested by the President for defense in fiscal 1977. "Annual Defense Department Report, FY 1977," p. B-1. It is the one service whose budget has increased in real terms since 1964. When their baseline budgets are compared in constant dollars, the Army shows a decline of more than 12 percent, the Air Force a decline of more than 31 percent, and the Navy an increase of about 3 percent between 1964 and 1976. U.S. Navy, Chief of Naval Operations, "Historical Budget Data" (March 1975; processed).

defense resources reflects a number of factors. Much of the change in each service's share of the budget is the result of shifts in strategic nuclear policies. Both the Army, which no longer mans surface-to-air missiles for continental air defense, and the Air Force, which has far fewer long-range bombers and interceptor aircraft than in the mid-1960s, have suffered significant budgetary reductions because of those changes. The Navy has also demonstrated considerable bureaucratic and political skill in promoting its interests in Washington during the past five years or so. Most important, however, the increasing attention paid to the Navy arises from important changes in the international environment in which U.S. defense policy must function.

One of these is that the U.S. Navy's primary opponent—the Soviet Navy—has made substantial changes in the quality of its equipment, in its deployment policies, and in its missions in the past fifteen to twenty years.

Beginning around 1958, the USSR started a sustained program to modernize its fleets.[20] New ships and submarines, which began to appear in the early 1960s, were markedly improved over earlier Soviet naval vessels, which more often than not were imitations of Western designs. These new ships also incorporated certain striking innovations, such as the use of cruise missiles for operations against opposing surface fleets. Beginning in the late 1960s, what may be called a second generation of indigenously designed Soviet naval ships and submarines began to appear, and these were very good indeed. Thus, even though the Soviet Navy is smaller than it was twenty years ago, it is a much more powerful potential adversary.

Moreover, beginning in the mid-1960s, the Soviet Navy for the first time left the close-in waters to which it previously had been confined and began to deploy its warships far from Soviet shores. A standing Soviet naval presence was established in the Mediterranean in 1964 and in the Indian Ocean in 1968. Intermittent Soviet deployments to the Caribbean were initiated a year later, and Soviet warships began to range further afield and to appear in greater numbers in the Atlantic and the Pacific. As shown in figure 3-2, this buildup has leveled off within the past few years. But the sudden appearance of the Soviet Navy on the oceans of the world has left an indelible

20. For a detailed discussion, see Barry M. Blechman, *The Changing Soviet Navy* (Brookings Institution, 1973).

Figure 3-2. Growth of the Soviet Naval Presence, by Region, 1964–75

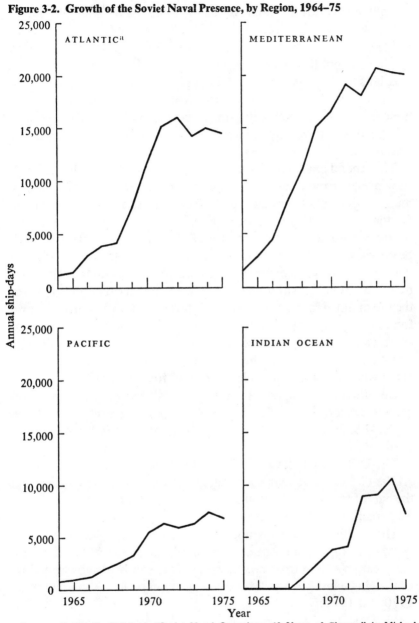

Sources: Robert G. Weinland, "Soviet Naval Operations: 10 Years of Change," in Michael MccGwire, Ken Booth, and John McDonnell, eds., *Soviet Naval Policy: Objectives and Constraints* (Praeger, 1975), p. 377; U.S. Department of the Navy, Office of the Chief of Naval Operations, *Understanding Soviet Naval Developments* (Philadelphia: Naval Publications and Forms Center, 1975), p. 12, and preceding issue, p. 12; Department of Defense, "FY 77 U.S. Defense Budget Perspectives" (March 8, 1976; processed).
a. Including the Caribbean.

imprint on worldwide impressions of Soviet naval strength and on U.S. planning.

Perhaps most troubling, the USSR then began to use its navy for various political purposes, in a traditional Western practice the Russians had long derided—gunboat diplomacy. They did this tentatively at first, in situations not involving the United States. When these early efforts met with some success, Soviet leaders became bolder; this was vividly demonstrated during the 1973 war in the Middle East.

The second important change is the marked decline in the U.S. military presence overseas. At the end of 1964, there were 719,000 U.S. military personnel abroad. Aside from the short-lived buildup in Southeast Asia, there has been a steady and steep decline in this overseas presence. At the end of fiscal 1977, for example, there will be only 462,000 U.S. military personnel abroad. Although there is a question whether naval forces can perform the functions of the land-based forces being withdrawn, a tendency in this situation is to favor the use of naval forces to support U.S. foreign policy initiatives. Naval forces can be deployed more flexibly, and because ships remain offshore (and out of sight if need be) they are less disruptive politically or psychologically. Thus the President is more likely to turn to the Navy when he wishes to make a show of force in a crisis.

Despite these changes in the international environment and the increased resources available to the Navy, both the present condition of the U.S. fleet and the state of naval planning leave much to be desired.

The U.S. Navy today is much smaller than it was twelve years ago. At the end of fiscal year 1964, there were 917 ships in the force; at the end of fiscal year 1976 there were only 476 ships, a reduction of 52 percent.[21]

The number of ships is not indicative because it includes everything from tugs to aircraft carriers and because the newer ships are more capable than their predecessors. This can be demonstrated by comparing a few gross indexes of the fleet's capabilities in fiscal years 1970 and 1977:[22]

21. Chief of Naval Operations, "Historical Budget Data"; *FY 1977 Authorization for Military Procurement,* Hearings, pt. 5, p. 2550.
22. Estimates based on unpublished data supplied by the Department of the Navy, April 1976.

	1970	1977	Percent change
Number of ships	769	489	−36
Standard displacement (millions of tons)	6.67	5.44	−18
Shaft horsepower (millions)	23.87	18.68	−22
Electrical generating capacity (megawatts)	1,949	2,029	+4
Average age (years)	16.7	14.0	...

From 1970 to 1977, for example, the total size of the fleet, as indexed by displacement, will have declined by roughly half as much as the reduction in number of hulls. Larger ships can have more endurance, bigger weapon magazines, more comfortable crew quarters, more powerful sonar, and so forth, all of which increase the capability of the individual vessel. In fact, electrical generating capacity, which may be the best single index of a modern navy's capabilities, actually rose during this period despite the more than one-third cut in numbers.

Nonetheless, like aircraft, no ship can be in two places at once. And even if qualitative improvements have been sufficient to compensate for the steep decline in the size of the fleet, so too has the Soviet Navy improved its capabilities. Indeed, it has probably improved proportionally more, leading many observers to fear that the U.S. Navy has become too small.

Yet so far official Navy force level objectives have been reduced consistently. In 1969 the objective for the mid-1980s was 850 ships. In the early 1970s this was lowered to 770 ships; and in 1975 it was dropped further, to about 600 ships. In 1976 it has become increasingly evident that even the 1975 objective is unlikely to be achieved. As a result, there have been calls for a sharp boost in the administration's proposed shipbuilding program (and appropriation), to attain a 600-ship force *by the end of the 1980s.*[23]

In addition, in 1976 there were evidently serious problems in the matériel readiness of the fleet. As shown in table 3-9, the Navy is experiencing a relatively large number of equipment breakdowns. It blames these problems on reductions in maintenance appropriations, which have led to a considerable portion of the fleet's being overdue for scheduled overhauls. This is probably not the sole answer, how-

23. *Force Structure and Long-Range Projections,* Hearings before the Task Force on National Security Programs of the House Committee on the Budget, 94:1 (GPO, 1975), pt. 1, p. 101.

Table 3-9. Indicators of Fleet Readiness, Fiscal Years 1972 and 1976

Description	1972	1976
Average number of items of equipment not functioning per ship		
All equipment	9.0	11.6
Critical equipment	2.8	2.9
Percentage of naval aircraft nonoperational because of lack of parts	15	21[a]
Production lead time for Navy and Air Force small parts (days)	190	270[a]
Percentage of ships overdue for overhaul	4	14
Officially acceptable maximum (percent)	5	5

Sources: *Full Committee Consideration of Overall National Security Programs and Related Budget Requirements,* Hearings, pp. 198, 200–02; *Force Structure and Long-Range Projections,* Hearings before the Task Force on National Security Programs of the House Committee on the Budget, 94:1 (GPO, 1975), pt. 1, pp. 32, 34, 46; "Annual Defense Department Report, FY 1977," pp. 259–61.
a. 1975.

ever. Indeed, the Navy may already be overhauling some of its ships too often. Other possible causes of the readiness problem probably include faulty equipment design, shortages of spare parts, and poorly trained personnel.

The shipbuilding appropriation began to decline in fiscal 1968.[24] It remained depressed for four years as first the cost of the U.S. involvement in Vietnam and then the soaring cost of manpower generated pressure for reductions in other sectors of the defense budget. After that, the shipbuilding appropriation grew slowly until fiscal 1976.

At the same time, the prices of new ships soared. Part of the rise is due to inflation; no other sector of the defense budget seems to have been struck quite so hard. Part was caused by the performance demanded of new ships—ships with missile systems instead of guns, ships with detection, communication, and other electronic systems at the leading edge of technology, ships with much larger than traditional spaces for weapon magazines, fuel storage, and crew quarters, and ships with nuclear rather than conventional propulsion systems are all far more expensive. Finally, part of the price rise is due to the structure of the American shipbuilding industry and the managerial skill (or lack thereof) demonstrated by both the Navy and private shipyards. Naval shipbuilding is one of the few sectors of the Ameri-

24. Chief of Naval Operations, "Historical Budget Data."

can economy that has experienced a decline in productivity in recent years.

As a consequence of these contrary trends, even the now increased appropriations for shipbuilding are barely sufficient to buy the 16 or so vessels that must be replaced each year, thus keeping the fleet level near 500, much less to add to the size of the fleet. In fiscal 1955 a shipbuilding appropriation of $1.2 billion paid for the construction of 30 new ships and the conversion of 17 others.[25] In 1977 the President's request for $6.3 billion would be enough to purchase only 16 new ships; no conversions were included in the request. Moreover, pressure to make more funds available for shipbuilding have caused the Navy and Congress to skimp on funds for operations and maintenance, which more than anything else has led to reductions in the operating tempo of the fleets and the problems of matériel readiness.

The solution is not nearly as obvious as the cause. Clearly, the shipbuilding program should be managed as efficiently as possible; efforts should be made to uncover the reasons for, and to correct, the decline in productivity and the steep inflation that have characterized the American shipbuilding industry for some time. Some have suggested that the solution in part may be to induce greater competition among private American, U.S. government, and foreign shipyards. This might mean reopening now closed, or expanding now open, government shipyards and allowing foreign shipyards to bid on some U.S. Navy ships. The last suggestion is not as radical as it sounds. Even the Soviet Union has some of its naval vessels built in East Germany, Finland, and Poland.[26]

This is not the place to examine the structure and the processes of the American shipbuilding industry in detail. In the light of recent performance, though, a hard look seems imperative.

But even if these efforts were successful, the price of new ships would continue to be driven higher by the improvements in performance demanded of new ships. The Navy tried to ease this problem earlier in the decade by adopting the so-called high-low mix acquisition strategy. Under this plan some very capable (and therefore very

25. *Department of the Navy Appropriations for 1955*, Hearings before the House Appropriations Committee, 83:2 (GPO, 1954), p. 515.

26. Alva M. Bowen, "Comparison of U.S. and U.S.S.R. Naval Shipbuilding" (Congressional Research Service, 1976; processed), p. 19.

expensive) vessels for the most demanding contingencies—those involving the Soviet Navy in regions close to Soviet shores—and larger numbers of less capable (and therefore less expensive) ships for less demanding contingencies would have been built. Obviously, one does not have to send a *Nimitz*-class nuclear-powered aircraft carrier every time one wants to impress a medium-rank or lesser power with a show of force or to outgun a single Soviet destroyer in some remote region. Unfortunately, the high-low mix seems to have fallen victim to politics—both electoral and bureaucratic. In 1974 Congress passed an amendment to the Defense Authorization Act requiring that all new major combatants for U.S. naval strike forces be nuclear-powered. This change would drive shipbuilding costs up tremendously. And in 1976 the House of Representatives added $1.7 billion to the $6.3 billion presidential request for shipbuilding to pay for some additional ships—all very capable and very expensive—and to replace some less expensive vessels with more expensive ones. The trouble with this approach is that it will lead inevitably to requirements that shipbuilding be funded indefinitely far above the level that Congress previously has supported: an $8 billion to $10 billion annual appropriation (aside from increases traceable to inflation) would be needed instead of the $3.8 billion appropriated in fiscal 1976. Perhaps Congress will make such funds available. But if the appropriation is lowered again, U.S. naval force levels will drop with it.

If the shipbuilding program is to be shaped so that the Navy will be sufficiently large and capable, and appropriately configured to carry out its missions at the least cost, a way will have to be found to deal with the potential vulnerability of surface ships.

It is becoming more and more evident that in some regions and in some situations the deployment of surface vessels at the very outset of a conflict is likely to be a dangerous and costly enterprise. As the fruits of the new revolution in military hardware ripen and are disseminated to a wider group of nations, the number of contingencies in which surface ships would be vulnerable is likely to grow larger.

The vulnerability problem centers on aircraft carriers, which dominate the structure of the Navy. Most of the Navy's escort and support vessels are designed primarily to protect and support the carriers. When the Navy decides how many escorts of a particular class to build, it usually bases that decision on a projection of the number of carrier task groups it will have in the future. When the President orders the Navy to deploy a force to a certain region, it usually sends a carrier task group.

Yet many of the aircraft based on the carriers are devoted to the ships's own defense. A typical load of about a hundred aircraft on a modern carrier is distributed something like this:[27]

Type of aircraft	Current model	Number of squadrons	Total number of aircraft
Fighter	F-4/F-14	2	24
Light attack	A-7	2–3	24–36
Heavy attack	A-6	1	9–12
Antisubmarine warfare, fixed-wing	S-3	0–1	0–10
Antisubmarine warfare, helicopter	SH-3	1	8
Early warning	E-2C	1	4
Electronic warfare	EA-6B	1	3
Tanker	KA-6A	1	4
Reconnaissance	RA-5C/RF-8	1	3
Carrier-on-board delivery	C-1/C-2	n.a.	1–2

The payload of the carrier is provided by the thirty-three to forty-eight attack aircraft, which can be used to strike surface vessels or land targets. The fighters and the other aircraft are mainly designed to protect and support the attack aircraft during their missions and to help defend the carrier. The fighters too could carry out strikes, and the fixed-wing antisubmarine warfare aircraft could help defend other ships from enemy submarines. But that is not why they are deployed on the carrier, and naval officers would be reluctant to divert them from their normal defensive mission.

Despite this large defensive allocation, the carriers' ability to survive for long in a high-threat environment is uncertain. The combination of missiles launched from a variety of platforms and submarine torpedoes would pose a threat that would be difficult to counter. This is particularly true in regions, like the eastern Mediterranean, where the full brunt of Soviet power could be brought to bear.

Carriers can, however, do some things that no other form of U.S.

27. "Annual Defense Department Report, FY 1976 and 197T," pp. III-81, III-99; and "Annual Defense Department Report, FY 1977," pp. 192–93.

military power can accomplish. They can protect U.S. maritime forces or attack enemy maritime forces in regions remote from land bases, such as the southern Atlantic or Indian Ocean. And they can bring U.S. air power to bear quickly and flexibly anywhere in the world. Still, if they are to carry out these tasks effectively in the future, a number of changes may be in order.

The United States could improve the effectiveness of existing carrier resources by changing the prevailing pattern of U.S. military operations. The point would be to make more carriers available for the most demanding contingencies—those in the Mediterranean—and to make greater use of land-based aircraft in joint operations with naval aircraft. Ways to do this have been discussed, including shifting naval units from the Pacific to the Atlantic and moving from rigid to flexible carrier deployment patterns. B-52s armed with air-to-surface missiles could help attack the Soviet surface fleet. For that matter, when the carriers are in immediate danger, it may be prudent to redeploy naval aircraft to land bases—say, in Israel.

Another useful step would be to rely on different types of naval task forces, instead of carrier groups, in regions such as the Indian Ocean, where enemy capabilities are not as great. For example, the United States has seven relatively small air-capable ships, known as LPHs, which it now uses for amphibious warfare. Five larger air-capable ships, known as LHAs, are now entering service or under construction. If some of these vessels were equipped with vertical or short takeoff and landing (V/STOL) aircraft and accompanied by a number of destroyers for air and submarine defense, they could form a potent naval force in many regions of the globe. This would free large attack carriers for the more demanding regions.

For the long term, the shipbuilding program must be designed so that the Navy can carry out its essential missions in support of the nation's foreign policy without exceeding realistic projections of the funds likely to be appropriated. Some very capable and therefore expensive vessels are necessary for the most demanding contingencies, but larger numbers of individually less capable and therefore less expensive ships are also needed for the many less demanding contingencies the Navy also will face. To this end:

—Whether or not a particular ship should be nuclear-powered should be decided on the basis of hard-headed technical analyses. There are many advantages in nuclear power, but it is also very expensive. Clearly, most submarines should be nuclear-powered, as should the largest aircraft carriers, but for smaller surface vessels the advantages of nuclear power are not so evident, particularly once it is realized that two, three, and sometimes four conventionally powered vessels can be acquired for the same cost as one similarly designed nuclear-powered ship.

—The key questions are the number and design of future aircraft carriers. It will be necessary to build a fourth, and possibly a fifth, *Nimitz*-class carrier, because sufficient funds have not been invested to develop alternatives. But it is far from obvious that all eight *Forrestal*-class carriers, built between 1955 and 1968, should or could be replaced with these very expensive vessels. If a medium-sized alternative to the *Nimitz* design is to become available in the 1980s, it will be necessary first to accelerate the development of V/STOL aircraft and lightweight nuclear reactors during this decade. Under present plans the U.S. attack carrier force, made up of some combination of older carriers, *Nimitz*-class, and perhaps the medium-sized alternative, would level off at twelve sometime in the 1980s.

—High priority should also be accorded the development and construction of small aircraft carriers as supplements to the attack carrier force. This third kind of air-capable ship, displacing around 20,000 tons rather than the 90,000 of the *Nimitz* and the perhaps 50,000 of the medium-sized carrier that might replace some of the *Forrestal* class, would carry helicopters and V/STOL aircraft. They would constitute an important addition to the U.S. ability to defend the sea lanes and to carry out other activities in remote regions.

—If the Navy is to accomplish its sea-control and peacetime missions within likely budgetary constraints, it will be particularly important to build a large number of conventionally powered destroyers and frigates over the next ten years. Many of these ships should be equipped with surface-to-surface missiles.

—More attention should be paid to support ships, which have been neglected too long. The Navy will be effective only if it can operate for protracted periods of time in hostile environments far from the United States; support ships are essential for such operations.

—Finally, the development of advanced technologies—such as hydrofoils and other surface effects ships—should be emphasized. Ultimately, radical technologies may offer the best prospects for coping with the growing threat to surface ships, thus permitting the Navy to carry out its vital missions in the high-threat areas likely to characterize the international scene in the next century.

MOBILITY FORCES. The smallest component of the general purpose force budget is consumed by mobility forces: aircraft and ships used to move military personnel and equipment between and within different theaters. Although in any major conflict most military equipment and supplies would necessarily be moved by sea, the emphasis in active U.S. forces is on the aircraft that would transport the lead elements. The United States relies on subsidized commercial shipping and the reserve fleet to furnish sealift over a more protracted period.

Requirements for U.S. mobility forces are determined by examining needs to move U.S. ground forces to Europe in a major crisis. Concern about the projected unfavorable balance between NATO and the Warsaw Pact countries in the early days of any mobilization has led the Department of Defense in the past several years to initiate a number of measures to improve U.S. airlift capabilities and to request authorization from Congress for several other steps. These include actions to increase the potential utilization rate and maximum range of C-141 and C-5A transport aircraft; modifications to the C-141s enabling them to carry larger loads and be less dependent on foreign bases; and modifications to civilian wide-bodied jets, such as the Boeing 747, and contractual arrangements with U.S. commercial air carriers, so that in a crisis, perhaps one hundred of these aircraft could be used to lift military cargoes.[28] Implementation of these proposals would be an important reassurance to European allies of the U.S. ability to reinforce peacetime forces in Europe to match increases in Warsaw Pact capabilities. The improvements, more specifically, would make it possible to counter a Soviet mobilization in the crucial early days more quickly, and thus seem appropriate in view of the emphasis on requirements to fight a short, intense war.

Airlift forces also serve important functions elsewhere. They have frequently been used to support U.S. allies through the prompt dispatch of needed items of military equipment. They can be, and have been, used to move U.S. ground troops to deal with minor contingencies. And they are a useful means of demonstrating American military capabilities for one political reason or another.

For the long term, the main question concerning mobility forces is how to modernize the existing air fleet most efficiently. In a few years, this will come up for the current force of tactical (shorter-

28. "Annual Defense Department Report, FY 1977," pp. 201–04.

range) airlift planes, mainly C-130s. Two prototypes are competing as replacements; both, however, incorporate features—particularly the ability to take off and land using relatively short runways—that some argue would be needlessly costly.

In the more distant future, a follow-on to the longer-range aircraft now in the force will have to be acquired. But these questions are technical and have few implications for broad policy.

Manpower Issues*

Whatever decisions are made about the size and character of U.S. armed forces, future defense spending will be influenced to no small degree by the success with which the cost of manpower is brought under control. Maintaining an adequate military capability without incurring substantial real increases in defense spending will hinge largely on a more efficient use of the defense work force. Some recent progress is visible; additional measures are possible.

The early 1970s were characterized by a marked structural shift in the defense budget. In contrast to the pre-Vietnam period, in which defense spending was dominated by the cost of acquiring and maintaining weapons, the 1965 U.S. involvement in Southeast Asia ushered in a period in which a rapid rise in manpower-related costs had a pronounced effect on the size of the defense budget. Since fiscal 1968 annual payroll costs have risen from $32 billion to close to $52 billion even though the defense work force has been reduced from nearly 5 million people to about 3.1 million.[29] In relative terms, the effect also has been dramatic. Payroll costs, which had consumed an average of about 44 percent of all defense appropriations during the early 1960s, constituted over half of the defense budget from 1968 to 1973.[30]

Three developments contributed to this result.

First, the price of defense manpower increased sharply. A series of pay raises—initially granted in the interest of equity and subsequently to underwrite the transition to an all-volunteer service—resulted in a twofold increase in average per capita military pay be-

---

* This section was prepared by Martin Binkin.

29. Payroll costs, as defined here, consist of military pay and allowances, the civilian payroll, and payments to retired military personnel.

30. Unless otherwise specified, figures in this section are derived from unpublished data supplied by the Office of the Assistant Secretary of Defense (Comptroller), 1976.

tween fiscal years 1968 and 1973. Average per capita defense civilian pay increased by roughly 50 percent over the same period.

Second, although defense manpower declined by one-third, or 1.6 million people, between 1968 and 1973, this cut did not keep pace with the decline in combat force levels. Advances in technology, the increasing complexity of military equipment, and the relatively large manpower component that does not vary closely with force levels—such as the people necessary to run the Pentagon—all helped bring this about. The relatively long time it took to dismantle the support establishment built for the Vietnam War was no doubt a factor too. Whatever the reasons, the result was that at the same time the cost of manpower was rising sharply, people were being used less rather than more efficiently.

Third, the rising cost of military retirements began to exact a noticeable toll on the budget. Amounting to just over $1 billion in fiscal 1964, the cost of retired pay began an inexorable and rapid climb, approximately doubling every four years, to $8 billion in fiscal 1977. Accounting for about 2.4 percent of the defense budget in 1964, retired pay consumed about 5.5 percent in 1973, and 7.4 percent in 1976.

Despite reductions in manpower levels, this rapid rise in the cost of manpower was sufficient to intensify fiscal pressures on the defense budget. Consequently, total investment in military weapon systems remained fairly stable. And because the price tags of the weapons on the Pentagon's shopping list also rose spectacularly, the result was delays in procurement programs, reductions in the total number of weapons purchased, and cuts in operating funds.

This trend, all the more disturbing to many observers in light of advances in Soviet military capabilities, did not go unnoticed for long. In 1974 the administration initiated major changes in U.S. defense policy. The new defense program called for greater emphasis on weapon development and increases in general purpose force levels, both to be financed in part by a slowdown in the growth of manpower costs. Plans to improve manpower efficiency were emphasized; three additional Army divisions were to be formed and four Air Force fighter wings filled out within current manpower levels by reducing the number of support personnel. Moreover, the administration, apparently of the view that federal pay rates already exceeded those for comparable jobs in the private sector, proposed a slowdown in the size of annual pay increases for both military and federal civilian personnel as well as changes in the method of calculating military pay raises. Also coming under closer scrutiny was the large number of supplemental benefits available to military personnel; changes in policies concerning subsidization of military commissaries and health care systems were proposed, as was a program to modernize the military retirement system. The success of recruiting under the all-volunteer system no doubt was partly responsible for the suspicion that military compensation might now be too high.

The consequences of this attention already are evident. With retired pay excluded, the proportion of the total defense budget consumed by the payroll began to decline. In the proposed 1977 budget, the share consumed by the payroll is below pre-Vietnam levels. In absolute terms, the rate of increase in the price of military manpower has been markedly curtailed. The average annual rate of growth in military pay since fiscal 1973 has been 6.5 percent as against 11.2 percent in the preceding five years.

But the rapidly rising cost of military retired pay has frustrated attempts to alter the proportion of the total budget allocated to manpower. When payments to retired military personnel are included, the total payroll continues to absorb about one-half of all defense appropriations.

Two proposals were made by the administration to Congress to slow the growth in retired pay costs; one would result in immediate savings, the other would initially raise costs but would eventually bring about large and growing savings. The first proposal would eliminate the "1 percent kicker" from retired pay increases—the 1 percent added to cost-of-living increases which is intended to compensate for the delay between the rise in prices and the retiree's receipt of a larger annuity. This change would apply to all federal retirees, military and civilian. The second proposal would bring military retirement a little more in line with the less liberal policies governing federal civilian retirement.

Measures taken to convert manpower spaces from support positions to combat jobs are also showing results. Improvements have been greatest in the Army; the number of total Army personnel employed for each maneuver battalion in the force structure is 10 percent lower than in 1964. Moreover, since contemporary battalions have far greater capability in firepower and mobility than those of the earlier era, the efficiency with which the Army now uses manpower has probably improved even more markedly.

The results of Navy and Air Force programs to improve efficiency are more difficult to measure. In total manpower per force unit (ships and aircraft), both services have moved toward a more intensive (less efficient) use of manpower. The Navy employs close to 50 percent more people for each of its ships than it did in fiscal 1964, and there are about 30 percent more Air Force personnel per aircraft than there were twelve years ago. When adjustments are made to account for increases in technology, complexity, and capability, however, a different picture is obtained. For example, if the size of ships or their engines' power is considered and men are counted per displacement ton or shaft horsepower, the Navy's loss of manpower efficiency is less marked; if electrical generating capacity—a proxy for electronic sophistication—is used as an output measure, Navy manpower is being used *less* intensively (more efficiently). By the same token, when a better measure of output, such as aggregate lift capacity of fighter and attack squadrons, is used for the Air Force, a more efficient use of Air Force manpower also becomes evident.

All of this suggests that improvements have been made in the past several years, with the savings used either to form additional combat units or to meet the demands for investment dollars imposed by advances in military technology. In some respects, manpower savings may be approaching their limits, given the present course. How many more times can pay rates be raised by less than the increase in the cost of living or fringe benefits be reduced before the morale, and hence the effectiveness, of the armed forces is seriously diminished and enlistments turn downward? How much more can the support establishment be squeezed without adversely affecting the readiness of military forces? There are no pat answers; the criteria for judging the price and use of manpower lack precision.

This is not to say that further savings are not possible. The average rank of military and civilian personnel could be reduced to earlier levels; the length of training courses could be shortened; more people could be trained on the job instead of in classrooms; tours of duty could be lengthened; ships and aircraft could be overhauled less frequently; marginal reserve units could be eliminated. All told, such measures, over a five-year period, could still eventually lead to savings of as much as $2 billion annually. Beyond this range, however, savings would depend on fundamental changes in the military compensation system and in the way manpower is managed. Far more than marginal changes in the present system would be required.

Controlling the price of manpower will depend largely on controlling military retired pay costs. If the major provisions of the military retirement system were aligned with the federal civilian retirement system, savings would be substantial. But this reform should be made as part of a broader and much needed effort to recast the entire military pay system. The current compensation system, perhaps appropriate for the paternalistic military establishment of an earlier era, is out of date. Members of the armed services, prospective volunteers, and legislators are often unaware of the full value of military compensation simply because some of its elements are not easily perceived or understood. Moreover, because its underlying rationale calls for paying people on the basis of their "needs" rather than exclusively for their contribution to national security, the compensation system in some instances attracts people who are costly in relation to their skill. As a result, the United States is paying more than is necessary for its present military forces.

Many of these problems could be resolved by paying the military in the same way as federal civilian employees are paid. The present hodgepodge of military pay, allowances, and benefits could be replaced by the payment of a single "salary." Earnings would become more apparent, more understandable, and hence easier for everyone to evaluate. These steps would reduce the need for the number and amount of differential payments (bonuses, proficiency payments, and so forth) now in existence and make it more likely that future increases in pay would be no larger than necessary to meet comparability standards.[31]

Over the long term greater efficiency in the use of defense manpower can be realized in three main areas: the personnel pipeline, maintenance policies, and the military base structure.

About one out of every six military personnel is now in the "pipeline"—either undergoing formal individual training or traveling between assignments.[32] Both training and travel requirements are chiefly

31. For a more detailed discussion of this proposal and its financial consequences, see Martin Binkin, *The Military Pay Muddle* (Brookings Institution, 1975).

32. Based on data in Office of the Assistant Secretary of Defense, "Manpower Requirements Report for FY 1977," pp. II-1, IX-2.

due to the turnover rate of enlisted military personnel—now about 22 percent. Each of the approximately 400,000 new recruits entering the armed forces every year is given basic recruit training, and most get initial training in a skill—usually at a separate location—before being moved to their first duty assignment. The rate of turnover, which stems from the desired distribution of military manpower—traditionally pyramid-shaped in grade, age, and experience—varies by service.

The Navy and the Air Force, the most technically oriented of the services, now have the lowest annual turnover. Turnover in the Army and the Marine Corps, which are interested in maintaining a youthful noncareer element, is higher. To the extent that the services could increase the average initial term of service and decrease the training received during the first enlistment period, they could reduce the number of new recruits they need and hence substantially reduce the cost of the personnel pipeline. For example, increasing by one year the average duration of the initial term of service, now running about 3.5 years, would cut the annual requirement for new recruits by 25 percent. How far initial enlistments could be lengthened without necessitating additional incentives in the form of higher pay or bonuses would have to be established through experimentation.

At least one-third of all defense employees are used to maintain military systems, and there may be room for economies. A major share of the defense resources are devoted to overhauling or repairing ships and aircraft. Yet little is known about the relation between the frequency of major overhauls, their duration, and the effectiveness of the overall force. In the past, frequency and duration of overhauls, which are based on engineering criteria, have varied widely because of fiscal or operational pressures. During World War II, for example, no aircraft carriers were overhauled, even though some sailed nearly 200,000 miles, an unheard-of distance without overhaul by today's standards. It is important that a reasonable balance be established between maintenance cost and readiness, and just as important that the design of future weapon systems take into account the need to reduce manpower requirements. If weapons are properly designed, the intensity of manpower use, particularly for their maintenance, can be reduced. The Minuteman missile program provides a good example: the selection of a solid rocket motor, gas-bearing gyros, and automatic remote testing all helped reduce maintenance manpower requirements.

Probably no area suffers more from piecemeal planning than military basing requirements. The links between a given combat force, its basing requirements, and the cost of acquiring and operating those bases have not been well established. There is little agreement on how to define a military base and even less on what "closure" means; infrequently are bases shut down and the land sold. But since neither Congress nor the administration is interested in pushing the basing issue, for obvious reasons, little attention has been paid to analyses of basing requirements. If these political and bureaucratic obstacles could be overcome, substantial manpower savings could be achieved by consolidating defense installations. To support a given military force, fewer large bases would be more efficient than a large number of small bases.

Only rough estimates can be made of the financial implications of actions to reform the military compensation system, reduce the personnel "pipeline," alter maintenance policies, and rationalize the military base structure. Together, however, they might eventually reduce the annual cost of defense manpower by at least $4 billion and perhaps by as much as $6 billion, depending on how far the reforms were pushed. At least half of these savings would result from reform of the compensation system. On top of the $2 billion possible as a result of the efficiency changes already mentioned, such savings could eventually reduce the annual cost of the defense work force by about 15 percent.

Toward a New Consensus

Except for the years immediately before the entry of the United States into the two world wars and the cold war years—say, from 1948 through 1963—activist peacetime defense policies have rarely gained wide support in this country. Instead, the strongest popular movements have formed around calls for the reduction of U.S. forces and the withdrawal of American power abroad, such as that during the Vietnam War in the late 1960s. The results are now evident: there are no U.S. forces on the mainland of Southeast Asia, the armed forces are smaller, and so is the defense budget. Some Americans still call for further reductions in defense spending, but many others feel that the retrenchment of American military power has gone too far. Prominent figures have warned of dire consequences for U.S. foreign policy and for the long-term protection of the nation's security if the trend in U.S. military strength is not reversed.

Perhaps it is time, then, for a new U.S. defense posture—one around which a new consensus could form. In both the preceding chapter and this one, proposals have been made for significant changes in defense policy, changes under which the nation's important interests would be protected, within realistic projections of the resources likely to be available for defense. Carrying out this new policy would require five basic decisions.

First, the nation's military posture should be tailored to changes in the international political system. In practical terms, this means two things.

—The U.S. force posture in East Asia and the Pacific—built at a time when it was believed both that the USSR and China constituted an aggressive monolith and that the United States had a need and a responsibility to protect the then-new states of Southeast Asia from aggression—should be scaled down further, providing either forces or budget dollars for more compelling military needs. The United States has important interests in East Asia, principally the maintenance of close relations with Japan, but protecting these interests does not require a force structure as large as that still in the region.

—The frequently expressed suggestion that Soviet forays in the third world necessitate added U.S. defense expenditures should be resisted. Strict criteria should be applied in determining when a Soviet action threatens important U.S. interests. Even for the few hypothetical cases in which a U.S. military response might be desirable, the necessary forces would be relatively small and characterized by just those features that the United States—unlike the Soviet Union—has already emphasized in its military planning: flexibility, sustainability, and the ability to operate in hostile environments far from the homeland.

Second, changes in the military balance that affect important U.S. interests should be offset by vigorous action.

Erosion of the military balance in Europe could eventually threaten peace and vital U.S. interests in Europe. Thus efforts to reverse the predicted adverse trend in the relative military capabilities of the NATO and Warsaw Pact countries should receive high priority.

Similarly, the trend in the naval balance on the periphery of Europe—in the Mediterranean and the Norwegian Sea—deserves new attention. A continuing erosion of U.S. naval capabilities in the Mediterranean could lead to precipitate behavior by the USSR in a new Arab-Israeli conflict and lessen U.S. influence in the region during peacetime. The changes in the operational patterns of U.S. tactical air and naval forces proposed in this chapter could go a long way toward defusing these risks in the short term. The proposed realignment of the shipbuilding program could help over the longer term.

Third, to finance the necessary improvements in the U.S. military posture without unnecessarily cutting into the resources available for domestic needs, the defense establishment should be made as efficient as possible. Once, perhaps, the United States could afford needlessly expensive weapons, excessive bases, a paternalistic compensation system, or reserve units whose usefulness was doubtful. It cannot any longer. The sources of inefficiency in military investment and, more important, in the price and use of manpower are evident. What must be overcome are political obstacles. This cannot be done by the administration, the military services, or the Congress alone. They must act together, with a clear, common vision of the national interest.

Fourth, current decisions on weapon acquisition programs and force levels must be based on an understanding of the implications of new technologies. This is the most rapidly changing influence on defense decisions. Technological advances in military hardware are making many traditional concepts of proper military doctrine, strategy, and tactics questionable—especially changes in the relative effectiveness of tactical air power and air defenses, of armor and antitank defenses. Because military hardware is with the armed forces for a long time, current investment decisions must foreshadow technological changes.

Finally, it must be recognized that the process of reducing the share of U.S. resources devoted to defense has more or less run its course. Additional savings are possible in some areas, but other sectors of the defense budget should receive more emphasis. In general, this means that defense spending will have to increase in real terms for at least the next five years, but probably more slowly than the expected growth in national output.

This outlook may be disheartening to some Americans, but the alternative is worse. Military power continues to play an important part in world affairs. The nation can only protect itself and its interests abroad if it is willing to spend what is necessary to maintain a credible military posture. If it does so, perhaps its adversaries will come to understand that the wisest course is to *mutually* reduce armaments and develop the necessary framework for more cooperative relations. Then, but only then, could the cost of defense safely renew its previous decline.

CHAPTER FOUR

Nuclear Proliferation

PHILIP J. FARLEY

THE LATENT DANGER of the further proliferation of nuclear weapons has gained unprecedented attention in the mid-1970s. The link between peaceful nuclear power programs and potential nuclear weapons capabilities has been exposed as it if were a novelty; the flaws in the policies and programs of the United States and other countries to forestall nuclear weapons proliferation have been dissected. There have been diverse reactions to the fact of our inability to guarantee that no more states will develop nuclear weapons. For some, the moral is that the United States should abandon its commitment to nonproliferation as futile and as interfering with beneficial relations and profitable sales abroad. Others urge that nonproliferation efforts be vigorously pursued or even dramatically strengthened by embargoes on the sale of sensitive equipment and by economic and political pressures on suppliers of nuclear materials and equipment, on nonsignatories of the nonproliferation treaty (NPT), and on countries with inflated nuclear programs.

There are several reasons behind this heightened sensitivity to the prospects and dangers of proliferation.

1. India's explosion of a "peaceful nuclear device" on May 18, 1974, made concrete reality out of what had been abstractly recognized for years. Many countries have, or shortly can have, the capability to conduct nuclear explosions and build nuclear weapons *if they choose*. The ten-year period of nonproliferation after the first Chinese nuclear test in 1964, during which no new members joined

the nuclear club, had obscured this fact, and the Indian explosion brought it into the light.

2. The Indian explosion came on the heels of the Arab oil embargo triggered by the Arab-Israeli hostilities of October 1973. The embargo gave new impetus to nuclear power. The uneven distribution of fossil fuels, particularly oil and gas, in the world, their eventual exhaustibility, and the ability of producers to cut off supplies and arbitrarily manipulate prices spurred interest in exploiting alternate sources of energy. Nuclear energy was becoming increasingly competitive in many regions before the embargo and the oil price hikes; its economic attractiveness was thereafter greatly enhanced. While uranium also is unevenly distributed, its compactness as an energy source lends itself to stockpiling. More important, as a heritage of the Atoms for Peace program, the establishment of the International Atomic Energy Agency in the 1950s, and the conclusion of the non-proliferation treaty in the 1960s, there is international cooperation and assistance in the peaceful uses of atomic energy that differs sharply from the cartelization and economic exploitation characterizing the world oil economy of the mid-1970s.

But if nuclear power is a promising alternative energy source, it can also be one base for nuclear weapons capability. As more and more nuclear power plants come into operation in the next few years (see the appendix to this chapter for a list of those now operating, under construction, or on order), there will be more and more countries (and their number is already considerable) that have the physical capacity to produce nuclear weapons but may be politically committed not to.[1]

1. A bit of technical background is in order here. The basic requirements for making any nuclear explosive device are fissionable material—highly enriched uranium or plutonium—and competence in physics, chemistry, and engineering. (Note that a "peaceful nuclear explosive" does not differ in kind from a nuclear weapon, but rather in what might be called the packaging.) The technical competence required is within the scope of any country with a balanced scientific and industrial establishment; see the appendix for a list of nations that have this capability now or will have in the next decade or two. Enrichment of natural uranium to the high concentrations of the isotope U-235 required for bomb design currently involves expensive, large-scale gaseous diffusion facilities, of high technology and large electric power input. Only the five nuclear-weapons states now have them. Other processes, of smaller scale and cost, greater potential simplicity, or more modest electric power requirements, are in various stages of development.

The most common nuclear power reactor fuel is slightly enriched uranium, which is not usable for explosives. A by-product of nuclear power reactor operation, however, is plutonium. For the plutonium to be usable for explosive devices (or for

3. To these familiar aspects of the proliferation problem, with which the international community has sought to cope through regulation of international nuclear trade, the NPT and other political agreements, and security guarantees to nonnuclear states, has been added a new threat. Large-scale generation of nuclear power is accompanied by large-scale accumulation of radioactive fission products, and by large-scale generation of plutonium as a by-product. Plutonium if separated is both highly poisonous and one of the two principal fissionable materials for nuclear weapons. Thus, to a world in which hijackings, terrorists acts, and coups or attempted coups by revolutionary or military groups have become dismayingly familiar, there is introduced the possibility of the capture of plutonium for bomb fabrication and blackmail or other use by such groups, or of nuclear power plants or fission products becoming the targets of terrorist acts. This kind of "subnational proliferation" may be as likely and as dangerous as the more familiar specter of proliferation of nuclear weapons states, and techniques for controlling the latter are of only limited avail in dealing with the new problem.

4. A further complication has been the sharp and active domestic debate (particularly but not uniquely in the United States) on nuclear power. The energy crisis and the determination to reduce dependence on foreign energy supplies have heightened government's and industry's interest in nuclear power as, along with coal, the major alternative to imported oil and to limited and increasingly costly domestic oil and gas. Simultaneously, however, concerns about the safety and environmental impact of nuclear reactors have been intensified. They have contributed to the rising costs of nuclear power plants, through design and siting requirements and lengthening construction periods. More radical critics challenged, at both the national and state levels, the public commitment to nuclear power. In addition to safety and environmental objections, there was the more fundamental ob-

---

fabrication into fuel elements) it must be separated out of the discharged fuel elements and their mixture of unburnt uranium and other fission products, many of them highly radioactive. While this is a difficult process, it is a chemical separation rather than an isotopic separation process and is not comparable in scale or difficulty to enrichment of uranium.

Excellent accounts of the basic considerations relating to nuclear weapons and explosives requirements, nuclear power technology, and safeguards to monitor nuclear power programs can be found in the widely available books by Mason Willrich and those published by the Stockholm International Peace Research Institute (SIPRI) on nuclear proliferation.

jection to what the National Council of Churches of Christ called "the plutonium economy"[2]—the commitment to an energy process producing and perhaps fueled by a poisonous man-made element directly usable in nuclear weapons. Some opponents of nuclear power pointed to the risk of theft or diversion by terrorists or blackmailers, as well as the prospect of international proliferation of nuclear weapon powers. They argued that in addition to a moratorium on nuclear power reactors in the United States there should be a moratorium on sales of nuclear fuel and reactors abroad, in the hope that U.S. action might be a catalyst and example for a worldwide abandonment of nuclear power that would undercut the trend toward nuclear weapons proliferation.

Containing Proliferation, 1945–75

There are thus weighty reasons why nuclear proliferation, along with the future of nuclear power, has become a topic of intense public interest in the United States as the world enters the fourth decade of the nuclear age. Yet the problems for world stability presented by nuclear proliferation have been well understood since 1945. Clearly apparent has been the military potential of even the purest civilian nuclear power program. Nuclear power reactors generate enough plutonium for some twenty to twenty-five nuclear bombs for each year of operation of a 1,000-megawatt nuclear electric plant. This civilian/military duality prompted many of the features of the first decade of the nuclear age. It was part of the logic of the radical Baruch plan of 1946 for an international authority to own and manage world nuclear activities; of the government monopoly of U.S. atomic activities under the McMahon Act from 1946 to 1954; of the extreme secrecy to protect the presumed U.S. monopoly of nuclear know-how; of the absence of international cooperation and trade in even peaceful uses of atomic energy.

The sharp change from monopoly and secrecy ushered in by the Eisenhower Atoms for Peace proposal of December 1953 and the revised Atomic Energy Act of 1954 was a recognition of changed circumstances, not an abandonment of America's concern with proliferation or of efforts to forestall it. U.S. secrecy and autarchy, it was

2. "The Plutonium Economy" (policy statement by the National Council of the Churches of Christ in the U.S.A., New York, October 1975; processed).

recognized, could no longer preserve a U.S. monopoly. The USSR and Great Britain had conducted nuclear weapons tests; civilian programs were launched in other countries. If the United States wished to shape the direction in which such programs moved, cooperation rather than isolation would have to be the choice.

The Atomic Energy Act of 1954 authorized international cooperation in nuclear power and other peaceful applications of atomic energy, both bilaterally and through the new International Atomic Energy Agency (IAEA). Any substantial cooperation, however, was rigorously constrained. Nuclear fuels and equipment could be exported only in conformity with a formal agreement for cooperation between the United States and the recipient country submitted in advance to Congress. The recipient would have to pledge not to use the assistance for weapons or for any other military purpose, and to accept verification of this pledge by inspectors from the United States, the IAEA, or (for members of the European Community) Euratom.

Appreciation of the benefits and risks of nuclear cooperation turned out to transcend ideological frontiers. The USSR was involved from the first in planning for international atomic energy cooperation, and the problem of nuclear proliferation was explicitly addressed in U.S.–Soviet exchanges. As summarized in an official U.S. aide-mémoire, one initial doubt expressed by the Soviet Union was "that any form of peaceful utilization of atomic energy must necessarily increase stocks of materials available for military purposes." The United States took the view that "ways can be devised to safeguard against diversion of materials from power producing reactors."[3] The first working paper submitted by the United States to the USSR to outline U.S. thinking on the proposed IAEA included the following provision: ". . . in order to assure that allocated fissionable material is being used for the purposes for which it was allocated, the Agency would have the continuing authority to prescribe certain design and operating conditions . . . require accountability and operating records, specify disposition of by-product fissionable materials and wastes, retain the right of monitoring and require progress reports. The Agency would also have authority to verify status of allocated material inventories and to verify compliance with the terms of

3. U.S. Department of State, *American Foreign Policy, 1950–55*, vol. 2 (Government Printing Office, 1957), p. 2819.

issuance."[4] The Soviet Union accepted this control and verification concept (usually referred to as "safeguards") for the charter of the new IAEA, which did not apply to the Soviet Union's territory though it would eventually apply within the boundaries of some of its East European allies.

In addition, long before the current nuclear suppliers' club, the United States took the lead during and after the establishment of the IAEA in the late 1950s in private consultations among countries possessing or controlling uranium ore supplies, both to encourage availability under controlled conditions and to discourage unrestricted sales that might feed new military programs.

Since 1960, nuclear cooperation and nuclear power facilities have grown enormously. The nonproliferation treaty, representing a major philosophical advance from leverage and constraint to accord and consensus, was negotiated in the 1960s, with provisions for voluntary renunciation of nuclear weapons and IAEA verification on the one hand, and for peaceful nuclear trade, cooperation, and assistance on the other. There are now ninety-five nonnuclear parties to the NPT, plus an additional thirteen signatories. The NPT five-year review conference in 1975 produced a good deal of lively and at times acrimonious debate over the effectiveness of safeguards and the extent to which the nuclear powers had carried out their NPT pledges of peaceful nuclear assistance and of movement toward nuclear disarmament. But on the whole, it reinforced rather than weakened international nonproliferation sentiment.

Of crucial importance are the countries who were not party to the NPT. As the appendix shows, a number of sensitive or potentially powerful states are not signatories (India, Pakistan, Brazil, Argentina, Chile, Israel, South Africa, and Spain, in addition to France and China) or have not ratified (Egypt, Indonesia, Turkey, Switzerland). Yet most of the nonparties give at least lip service to the principle of "peaceful uses of atomic energy only" (as do Brazil and India); and some give more than lip service to nonproliferation, despite political reservations about the treaty (as do France, Switzerland, and even South Africa, in different ways).

The global picture is a complex one. The ideal of nonproliferation has deep roots and a surprising vigor, both in practice and in international law—and in fact, nearly all the nuclear facilities in non-

4. Ibid., pp. 2807–08.

NPT countries are currently under bilateral or IAEA safeguards to verify their peaceful character. Yet the holdouts are a sobering reminder of the limits of consensus and mutual commitment; and even if there were universal adherence there would still be the iron reality of the military potential inherent in the fission process.

Current U.S. Policy

The U.S. government considers pursuit of a vigorous nonproliferation strategy to be a fundamental element of its overall foreign policy.[5] The purposes are to reduce the danger of nuclear war, particularly through escalation of regional conflicts; to avoid heightened political tensions and increased regional instabilities flowing from fears of use of nuclear weapons; and to eliminate enhanced security risks as a brake on expanded growth of peaceful nuclear power to meet energy needs.

Major practical steps in this direction include:

—Proposals for the major suppliers to strengthen and standardize nuclear safeguards.

—Efforts to gain the widest possible support for the international safeguards system and the nonproliferation treaty.

—Physical security measures to protect nuclear material against theft or diversion.

—Steps to restrain the spread of sensitive nuclear facilities, such as national reprocessing plants, uranium enrichment facilities, and heavy water production plants. Multinational regional facilities are viewed as a safer and economical way to meet needs for these services.

The basic strategy has been to seek these constraints and controls in conjunction with worldwide cooperation in the peaceful uses of nuclear energy. In such a context, the United States has offered to non-nuclear nations long-term assurances of enriched uranium supply and efficient U.S. reactor technology, thus seeking simultaneously to minimize the pressures for proliferation and to erect effective controls against it.

Such technical and legal measures are only part of the U.S. approach. In the long run, a secure international climate—including

5. Statement by Secretary of State Henry Kissinger before the Senate Committee on Government Operations (March 9, 1976; processed).

reduction of regional and global tensions, peaceful settlement of disputes, and satisfaction of legitimate security requirements—would be the key to removing the need felt by other states to develop nuclear weapons. There can be no assurance that this goal can be reached, but U.S. policy assumes that most nations, as well as the United States, are determined to pursue efforts to this end.

For some, however, the continued pursuit of nonproliferation is quixotic and costly. Over the long run, it is argued,[6] U.S. antiproliferation policy is doomed to failure: like all disarmament schemes, it will go aground on the predisposition of nations to look above all to their own defense. While a world of twenty or more nuclear nations may be unstable and prone to violence and destruction of unprecedented dimensions, it may also be a world where stable deterrence operates regionally as well as between the superpowers. In any case, so the argument goes, sooner or later we will have to live with proliferation; and trying to prevent this by embargoes or other restraints on nuclear exports and on nuclear industrial self-sufficiency will be ineffectual. Already, it is asserted, such a policy is depriving us of reactor sales abroad, among them $4 billion plus in sales to Brazil, a $7 billion sale to Iran, as well as other sales to Libya, Taiwan, and South Korea. And we lose influence also. By reestablishing our position as a reliable nuclear supplier, we could do much to calm the wasteful and dangerous movement toward self-sufficiency that we have helped to foster.

These sharply divergent views point up two important issues:
—How serious a threat to world and U.S. security and stability is further nuclear weapons proliferation? Is it worth pursuing efforts to forestall or drastically contain it?
—Is proliferation inevitable or likely? Do nonproliferation efforts offer prospect of success? Or should U.S. policy concentrate on coping with the consequences of proliferation?

Nuclear Proliferation: How Much Does It Matter?

Quite different assessments can be made of the likely consequences of the spread of national nuclear weapons programs. One prediction

6. See Tom Alexander, "Our Costly Losing Battle against Nuclear Proliferation," *Fortune* (December 1975), pp. 143–50, for a clear statement of a view that has many sympathizers but few public spokesmen.

is that the stable deterrence effect would spread, as new offsetting nuclear weapon capabilities created conditions for regional balances analogous to the stable deterrence of the U.S.–Soviet strategic balance. Nuclear proliferation might even enable middle-rank powers to provide minimal nuclear deterrence against the superpowers analogous to what some claim is the effect of the relatively small British and French nuclear forces on the Soviet Union. An opposite view predicts that, to the contrary, the result would be intensification of world and regional tensions, instabilities, and risks, perhaps to catastrophic proportions.

It is difficult to weigh these divergent views. Anticipating the future is hazardous at best, and analogies and precedents are but slender supports here. In particular, projecting the concept of stable deterrence into new regions may be unwarranted. Even after twenty-seven years of U.S.–Soviet interaction since the first Soviet nuclear test in 1949, stable deterrence remains theoretical, at best a goal not yet violated by actual nuclear conflict; as a description of the actual relationship, the concept summed up in the phrase "a delicate balance of terror"[7] is still more accurate. Whatever the exact nature of the U.S.–Soviet relationship, it is vastly different from that between other pairs of potential nuclear powers—Israel and its Arab neighbors, India and Pakistan, or North and South Korea (to say nothing of the Federal Republic of Germany or Japan vis-à-vis the Soviet Union). The United States and the Soviet Union, despite sharp ideological and more diffuse geopolitical differences, have no experience of direct hostilities (indeed were allies in World War II), have stable and prudent governments, have no common frontier, and enjoy some areas of cooperation or mutual toleration. The contrast with the regional situations enumerated above needs no comment; introduction of nuclear weapons into any of them can at best be described as having uncertain consequences. In any case, full analysis of what nuclear proliferation might mean in specific cases is not within the scope of this chapter; but as the particular cases just cited illustrate, *uncertainty* as to consequences is inevitable. This might mean some or all of the following:

1. In regional conflict situations—those where motivation for obtaining nuclear weapons might be considered strongest—instabilities

7. Albert Wohlstetter, "The Delicate Balance of Terror," *Foreign Affairs,* vol. 37 (January 1959), pp. 211–34.

would be heightened. In particular, a nuclear weapons program undertaken by one state would exacerbate regional tensions because neighbors would fear its motive to be aggression or dominance rather than deterrence; competitive nuclear weapons programs would result. Small or poorly dispersed and protected nuclear forces might then be tempting targets for preemptive attack, adding a dimension of "crisis instability" to the more general instabilities. And even if neighboring nations initially took a conciliatory posture, coups or internal conflicts might occur that would escalate tension, and conceivably could be attended by internal nuclear threats or acts with international repercussions.

2. Where rivals in a region are aligned with different major nuclear powers, the acquisition of nuclear capability by one would increase the risk that major-power involvement in any conflict would generate a nuclear confrontation.

3. Accident or miscalculation might occur in newly or poorly organized nuclear forces, with risks of misinterpretation both locally and globally.

4. Each new act of proliferation is likely to be in turn a focus of nuclear expansion. Additional neighbors and rivals might find it no longer possible to rely on the immunity afforded by nonnuclear status or on third-party guarantees and protection. In competitive situations, possession of a single nuclear weapon to qualify for the nuclear club will not suffice; growth, diversification, and sophistication of nuclear arsenals within local capabilities would be likely to follow, on the classic pattern of arms races.

5. Perhaps most troublesome of all—for it is conceivable that careful U.S.–Soviet and other international actions could at least contain the other consequences—would be the broader impact of proliferation. In a world of many nuclear states, it would become increasingly difficult for major states (Germany, Italy, Japan, eventually Iran or Brazil, and others) to continue to forgo nuclear weapons. Even if they were constrained to do so by external political pressure, serious and bitter internal debate and controversy, with resulting strains on alliances, are predictable.

6. As a related complication, the proliferation of nuclear weapons would increase and disperse the number of people with the practical knowledge needed to construct nuclear explosives and to handle them or the requisite plutonium. The pool of people from which terrorists,

blackmailers, or insurrectionists could be drawn would thus be significantly enlarged, at the same time that political and moral barriers to the use of nuclear weapons—now high—might be lowered.

7. The ultimate concern is the avoidance of the use of nuclear weapons. Even in the absence of formal nonuse agreements, there are powerful political inhibitions to the use of nuclear weapons against nonnuclear states. Proliferation might undercut these inhibitions and so increase the chances of recourse to nuclear weapons by major powers or local nuclear-capable states in future third world conflicts. An irreplaceable firebreak that has stood since 1945 would thus have been crossed and an important precedent for military restraint lost.

The foregoing predictions about the risks attendant on nuclear proliferation are only speculation. The alternate view of proliferation as expanding stable deterrence is no less speculative and uncertain, however. Unless nuclear proliferation is inevitable, then, the prudent course is to continue the present effort to slow down or avoid the spread of nuclear weapons.

Nuclear Potential: Spread and Constraints

Thus far we have been talking about attempts to stop the spread of an *exercised* capability to design and produce nuclear weapons. To attempt to halt the spread of a *potential* capability would be a different, and losing, battle. The inseparability of nuclear power and nuclear weapons capability, already emphasized, makes this fact inescapable.

Nuclear Weapons Potential

Nuclear power programs and capabilities are emphasized here because they are the focus of most nations' nuclear energy programs, and many of the policy issues involved have to do with cooperation and trade in power materials and technology. It must be borne in mind, however, that nuclear power reactors were not the means by which the present nuclear powers obtained fissionable materials for bombs. The other ways are:

1. Enrichment of uranium to high concentrations of U-235 (in contrast with the low-enrichment uranium used to fuel power reactors). Until recently, this called for massive, multistage gaseous diffusion plants—themselves heavy consumers of electricity—found only

in the United States, the USSR, the U.K., France, and China. Now enrichment techniques of smaller and potentially more manageable scale are being widely studied and are in various stages of development and installation: these include gas centrifuge separation (the U.K., Germany, and the Netherlands jointly); nozzle techniques (South Africa, Germany, and Brazil); and laser techniques, not yet fully demonstrated but potentially the simplest, most efficient, and most readily adaptable to high levels of enrichment.

2. Special plutonium production reactors fueled with natural uranium, maximized for output of weapons-grade plutonium, with heat a waste by-product.

3. Large research reactors incidentally yielding enough plutonium annually for one or a few weapons (such as the Israeli Dimona reactor and the Indian Trombay research reactor). Plutonium produced in these two ways is more efficient for bomb use than is most power-reactor plutonium.

One or more of these routes is available to any industrialized country with domestic uranium resources or access to uncontrolled supplies.[8] If there is an external constraint on self-sufficient nuclear programs in industrial nations, it lies not in technology but in materials. Uranium, like oil or coal, is not always available; it is widely dispersed in the earth's crust, but is less common in concentrated ores. Outside the communist nations, there are major known or indicated deposits in only a few countries: Canada, the United States, South Africa, Sweden, and Australia. Smaller but commercially significant deposits have been worked in Spain, Portugal, and France, and in the African states of Gabon, Niger, and the Central African Republic. Exploration has been limited to date in many countries but is likely to be given a powerful impetus by expanding nuclear power programs. New deposits are likely to be identified both in the territories of present major producers and elsewhere, but the size and location are unpredictable.

It will be noted that of the major countries producing or possessing uranium, several are NPT parties (Canada, the United States, Australia, Sweden, Gabon, and the Central African Republic). France and Niger are not parties, but France's stated and actual policy is to

8. Britain obtained its uranium mainly from members of the Commonwealth, and much of the French supplies came from associated African states, in ties predating the NPT.

act as if it were. South Africa is not a party. India, Brazil, Argentina, Israel, and some other nonparties have identified at least small quantities of uranium sufficient for a few nuclear weapons but have yet to find deposits to support a substantial power or weapons program.

Few states, of course, will follow the inefficient and duplicatory course of designing and building their own reactors or relying on domestic natural uranium. Proven reactors and enriched reactor fuel are available commercially under safeguards. Virtually all the present and prospective nuclear facilities in non-NPT countries as well as in the territories of parties to the treaty are subject to safeguards. Exceptions are the Indian, Argentine, and Spanish reprocessing facilities, the Indian and Israeli large research reactors, the fifth and sixth Indian power reactors under construction at Kalpakkam, Tamil Nadu, and the South African uranium enrichment plant under development—but all are in countries that also have other materials or facilities under IAEA or bilateral safeguards.

Even safeguarded facilities or NPT adherence do not mean absence of nuclear weapons potential in extreme circumstances. As the appendix shows, in the early 1980s more than twenty-five nonnuclear weapons states will have power reactors in operation,[9] each generating by-product plutonium annually sufficient for dozens of nuclear weapons. Six of these states are nonparties to the NPT (eight if Israeli and Egyptian power reactor programs firm up); others, as noted in the appendix, while NPT parties, are isolated, insecure, or ambitious states (South Korea, Taiwan, and Iran). If reprocessing facilities and stockpiles of separated plutonium were available, the step to nuclear weapons fabrication would be short. And the NPT

9. To illustrate the prospective spread of nuclear power, plants under construction, on order, or planned are tabulated. Even these data have substantial uncertainty—there may be slippage in completion, some planned plants may be deferred or canceled, and so forth. Such data are better, however, than more general forecasts of energy demands and nuclear power capacity, which are unreliable, particularly for developing countries. At the present time, the world energy economy is in a state of uncertainty as to both supply and cost. Oil availability and prices may improve over the short term, while nuclear power construction costs are rising. Thus large increases in total nuclear power capacity may not be forthcoming. But for the most part the plants listed appear likely to be built and operated; they thus constitute a base of nuclear experience and competence that allows us to establish a rough limit to the number of countries with a nuclear weapons potential. Other developing countries are unlikely to undertake nuclear programs in the next decade or so because of the size and capital cost of nuclear reactors, the lack of an integrated grid to exploit such large generating units, and uncertainties as to reliability and capacity utilization factors.

does not bar studies or laboratory experiments (such as "critical assemblies," which test the initiation and efficiency of the chain reaction process, relevant to either reactor or bomb design) that do not constitute the "manufacture or acquisition" of nuclear explosive devices. Under compelling external or internal threats or circumstances, withdrawal under the NPT escape clause and abrogation of bilateral safeguards agreements would make available a substantial initial stockpile of bomb material; indigenous natural uranium reactors or enrichment facilities could be brought into operation later. The political costs (and economic costs, where large power reactors contribute heavily to the energy base) would be heavy, but the physical possibility would be there.

The answer to whether the most stringent approach to nonproliferation is possible, then, is clear: additional countries cannot be prevented from achieving the material and technical wherewithal to make nuclear weapons. The technology for reactors, research or power, that generate plutonium in the course of operation is contained in the available scientific literature and is being mastered by scientists and engineers from dozens of countries. Only states with no indigenous nuclear materials or significant scientific and industrial capacity can be prevented by embargo from obtaining the base for a nuclear weapons option. Some states can decide to build natural uranium fueled reactors and associated facilities, or perhaps new simpler enrichment facilities if the technology tests out. And those which, from necessity or choice, import their nuclear reactors or fuel have the option—admittedly, at high political cost—of abrogating bilateral or NPT/IAEA commitments and safeguards and proceeding on weapons manufacture with a substantial plutonium stockpile.

The risks inherent in key facilities such as enrichment and reprocessing plants, and the case for limiting their spread, are clear, and are discussed below. It should be recognized, however, that there are motives other than the ambition to possess nuclear weapons, or the more temporizing desire to keep weapons options open, that lead countries to an interest in such technology and in nuclear self-sufficiency. Coal and oil deposits are absent or small, dwindling, and expensive in many countries, even populous and highly developed ones like Japan or Brazil or several in Western Europe. Alternate energy sources are needed. Energy independence in the form of complete self-sufficiency will generally be unattainable, but diversification will be sought to limit dependence on exhaustible or politically uncertain sources. Uranium will be especially attractive, not only because of its compactness and adaptability to stockpiling, but also because recycling and breeding plutonium offer prospects over the coming decades of multiplying manyfold the amount of energy obtainable from a given amount of natural uranium. For countries with their eye on this dimension of nuclear power, the ability to handle and even reprocess plutonium will be an element of a nuclear program. Beyond assured supplies of uranium (if not domestic, then through diversified sources of imports, stockpiles, and long-term contractual commitments), countries with heightened interest in nuclear power as a consequence of the 1973 oil embargo may also want to develop a balanced and independent chain of nuclear fuel-cycle facilities to the greatest extent possible.

The United States, with its trumpeted Project Independence in the energy field and its sensitivity to management of oil prices and supply by the Organization of Petroleum Exporting Countries (OPEC), should be able to understand the economic and political motivations at work in states that are even more vulnerable. Nuclear self-sufficiency prompted by such considerations is not inconsistent with non-proliferation in accordance with NPT commitments, but it does imply the extension of the physical base for a nuclear weapons option.

Still another complication from future technology may emerge from fusion research—sometimes touted as the risk-free inexhaustible energy process of the twenty-first century. No controlled fusion process has as yet been demonstrated; one of the more plausible approaches would be not to by-pass fissionable material but to use fusion reactors as sources of abundant cheap neutrons to convert U-238 into plutonium, or thorium into U-233. Familiar risks of proliferation and needs for safeguards would remain or increase.

Peaceful Nuclear Explosives

Under the NPT, nonnuclear-weapons states agree not to acquire or manufacture either nuclear weapons or other nuclear explosive devices. Prohibition of peaceful nuclear explosive devices (PNEs) for states other than the recognized five nuclear powers, though criticized as unwarranted discrimination by a few (India and Brazil), is logical: a PNE is not a different kind of explosion from that of a nuclear weapon. If PNEs were permitted, there is no verification means by which it could be ascertained that PNE tests or applications were not being used to test or advance weapons technology. Nonnuclear neighbors or rivals of states developing PNEs would have grounds for security concern that would be difficult to remove.

Skepticism about the motives of states insisting on developing PNEs, or using the desire to keep that option open as reason for withholding signature of the NPT, is supported by the dubious practical and economic value of PNEs. Though glamorous projects have been described by proponents of PNEs, technical, environmental, safety, and economic complications are numerous. In the United States, the PNE program (Project Plowshare) has almost dwindled away, and the current lively objections to nuclear power on safety and other grounds do not create an atmosphere propitious for revival. The USSR is thus the principal proponent of PNEs, for large-scale excavation, creation of underground storage cavities, and snuffing out oil field fires. If practical applications of PNEs do prove out, they will almost certainly be spinoffs of major weapons programs, charged off against the prior massive investment in research and production of weapons; to mount a PNE development program for its intrinsic benefits alone would be profoundly uneconomical. For any practical application, using PNE services made available by the nuclear weapons states would be surer and cheaper; and article V of the NPT commits nuclear powers to make such services available, under international observation, to nonnuclear-weapons states on a nondiscriminatory basis, at low cost and without reimbursement for research and development.

Incentives for Forgoing Nuclear Weapons

So the nuclear potential is inescapably there. And there exist today international conditions that will create continuing motivation for states to exercise the nuclear option. The grouping of nonnuclear-weapons states in the appendix identifies some of these motivations— regional rivalry, political isolation, and ambition for power or status.

The record of the past twelve years suggests that the pressures and incentives do not all operate in the direction of proliferation, however. After the first French weapons test in 1960 and the first Chinese test in 1964, no other state has unambiguously launched a nuclear weapons program. It is a sign of the force of nonproliferation sentiment that India publicly professes that its first nuclear explosion in 1974, and the program of which it is a part, are directed at peaceful nuclear explosives.

The principal disincentive to the development of a nuclear weapons program for key states has been not NPT/IAEA safeguards or supplier restraints but the dubious benefits of seeking nuclear weapons. For key states, the national decision is in the first instance a security one, with political overtones. Yet other constraints also weigh heavily. (1) Against a major nuclear power, nonnuclear status paradoxically can offer better protection against nuclear attack than does a small nuclear arsenal, which risks being more dangerous as an invitation to preemptive attack than effective as a deterrent. (2) Against a neighboring nonnuclear enemy nuclear weapons offer no great incremental advantage if a state is militarily and industrially superior, and they present a dangerous new area of rivalry against a more capable foe. (3) Association with a nuclear protector and ally has been the surest way of neutralizing any actual or potential nuclear threat. (4) And a heavy immediate cost of the nuclear commitment may be the risk of alienating a crucial ally and nuclear guarantor; South Korea, Israel, Taiwan, and even Japan and the FRG must weigh this risk, as South Korea may indeed have done in 1976 in deciding to defer acquisition of a plutonium separation plant in the face of U.S. opposition. Such considerations can be set aside or misjudged, of course, by unwise regimes or emotional tides of public opinion in times of perceived national peril or wounded pride. So far they have prevailed.

There are also broader political considerations that on balance weigh against the nuclear weapon option. First, there is a widespread sentiment against nuclear weapons, of varying strength in different places, which is a political fact even for authoritarian regimes. It is thus easier to keep the nuclear option open (or maintain a figleaf such as the PNE cover) than to launch an overt nuclear weapons program. Second, the agreement between the United States and the Soviet Union and their often concerted action on nonproliferation, while at times resented as superpower dictation, has undercut ideological rationales for going nuclear on anti-American or anticommunist grounds. Third, while north-south antagonisms may in time weaken the force of this unusual U.S.–Soviet convergence, the consensus in the third world has been more antinuclear weapons than antisuperpowers in this matter. Fourth, in this atmosphere the status gains of possessing nuclear weapons have been ambiguous. The critical but evanescent reaction to the Indian explosion, which did nothing for India's international standing, has if anything been deflating.

Not only have no new states joined the nuclear weapons club since 1964,[10] but there is striking evidence that an international consensus on nonproliferation has been growing. In contrast with the bitterness of much of the NPT negotiations, the five-year NPT review conference in 1975, while acrimonious on particular issues, did not shake or even question NPT foundations; criticisms were not of the NPT but of failures to implement or strengthen it (the nuclear powers asking for more effective safeguards and security measures, nonnuclear nations seeking more nuclear power aid and disarmament progress). Major NPT holdouts like Brazil and India feel compelled to stress their lack of interest in weapons and to excuse themselves for not signing on the grounds of political or PNE discrimination. Other holdouts have special regional problems (such as Argentina and Pakistan vis-à-vis Brazil and India, or Israel vis-à-vis Egypt) or internal problems (like South Africa and Spain). France, while not an NPT signatory, has professed and acted on the principle of "acting as if a signatory"; it has been cooperative in both the IAEA and the suppliers' group. China has been, if not cooperative, at least not disruptive; and the United States and the USSR have been able to agree on most principles and actions. Most basic of all, the isolated and insecure states (Israel, South Korea, and Taiwan) with growing nuclear potential, as well as the advanced industrial states with demonstrated potential (the FRG, Italy, Japan, and some of the East European states) have had the nuclear umbrella and security guarantee of a superpower ally or protector as a more powerful and less risky defense than a nascent nuclear force.

Is Nonproliferation a Losing Battle?

The situation foreseen more or less clearly in the postwar period is now at hand. In the next few years most of the advanced or indus-

10. There have been recurring allegations that Israel has fabricated either complete bombs or unassembled components. Israel's response has been to assert that it will not be the first to introduce nuclear weapons into the Middle East.

trializing nations will have one or more power reactors and will thus be generating fissionable material that can be used to make nuclear weapons; they will have the technical capability to take the final step. The 1974 Indian nuclear explosion shows not some special Indian aptitude, but what other countries are increasingly able to do if they choose.

Most countries do not so choose, for national considerations such as those reviewed above. Of the over 105,000 MWe (megawatts of electrical power) nuclear power capacity projected to be in operation in nonnuclear-weapons states by about 1982, five-sixths (nearly 88,000 MWe) will belong to NPT parties and one-sixth to non-NPT parties (17,000 MWe).[11] Of the reactors under construction or planned in non-NPT states, the great majority will be subject to IAEA safeguards—the exceptions being a joint Spanish-French reactor near the border of the two countries and the new generation of made-in-India power reactors.

Thus what is novel and surprising is not the growth of nuclear capabilities usable for nuclear weapons, but the preponderant degree to which this has taken place within a nonproliferation regime of NPT commitments supplemented by specific nonweapons pledges and IAEA safeguards covering facilities in non-NPT countries. The regime is clearly imperfect. A number of key states have refrained from ratifying or even signing the NPT. IAEA safeguards have weaknesses in their operation, plus the basic limitation that they cannot *prevent* diversion of nuclear materials, but only offer a high probability that diversion will be detected and reported, and thus *deter* it. To the extent that plutonium is actually separated and stockpiled in national facilities, or that new enrichment facilities lead to wider availability of highly enriched material, nuclear weapons ingredients will actually be in hand, thus decreasing the time needed for the manufacture of nuclear weapons once the decision to do so is made. These imperfections are conditions of life in the nuclear age; most of them cannot be removed, though they can be usefully lessened. They should not obscure the political fact that nonnuclear states have preponderantly come to *choose* that status (whatever the element of pressure and compulsion during the early years of limited sources of material and technology and compulsory safeguards), and that other

11. See the appendix to this chapter.

states adhere to a de facto even if not de jure nonnuclear status. Neither status is irreversible, but each can be confirmed and strengthened.

Nuclear weapons proliferation is thus possible but not inevitable; nonproliferation cannot at this time be considered a losing battle. The *potential* for building nuclear weapons will increase markedly with the growth of nuclear power. *Actual* nuclear weapon proliferation, if it does occur, will not do so easily or lightly, but for compelling national purposes in the face of political costs and even security risks. Drastic shifts in current alliances and international political alignments, the sharpening of regional or local tensions or conflicts, and other major international changes or developments may weight some national decisions toward nuclear weapons. In the absence of such adverse trends, however, continued and improved international cooperation in the exploitation of nuclear power, the institution of safeguards, and effective collective security or conflict control and resolution in international areas of tension can reinforce the non-proliferation consensus and thus prolong, perhaps indefinitely, the present de facto nonnuclear status of non-NPT parties.

One new element is the problem of subnational proliferation; it is perhaps more imminent than the more familiar threat of national proliferation. On the other hand, the ways of dealing with it are less politically sensitive and more manageable. Nuclear facilities and materials in transit might tempt terrorists, but both are sufficiently valuable so that the cost of guards and other protective measures is a tolerable incremental cost. The facilities can be isolated or screened and protected in a way that other targets of terrorists (airports, Olympic stadia, public figures, and international meetings) inherently cannot. Similar protective measures can be envisaged at substantial but not prohibitive cost to guard against diversion or seizure of bomb material. Even given the possibility of collusion by individual officials, the prevention of diversion is a different and more manageable one than when a government or plant management is assumed to be planning and executing the diversion. The necessity of providing physical security is beginning to get the attention it deserves from government and industry officials. If this is vigorously pursued in the United States, and accompanied by similar efforts in other countries and in international forums for cooperation on standards, exchange of technology and information, police coordination, and so forth, the problem should be manageable. It will *be* manageable, however, only if timely and concerted action is taken, nationally and internationally, not only to adopt principles and standards (perhaps in an international convention) but to put them into effect—and if this is done promptly rather than waiting until a dramatic terrorist incident galvanizes governments and public opinion.

How Effective Are U.S. Nonproliferation Policies?

How well do the main elements of current U.S. nonproliferation policy, as summarized above, fit the situation just described? These elements are, again: requirement of nonproliferation commitments (no weapons or other military or nuclear explosive use) for all nuclear exports, accompanied by safeguard procedures and inspections; encouragement of broad NPT adherence; supplier consultation to ensure uniform noncompetitive export and safeguard policies, particularly for non-NPT countries; national and international action to strengthen physical security; and security assurances and arms control efforts.

First, it should be noted that these measures are mutually reinforcing. The United States requires commitments and safeguards on its exports not only because of its obligations under article III of the NPT, but also because of the requirements of the domestic Atomic Energy Act. The NPT binds both supplier and recipient parties to the same principles and reciprocal obligations; these common groundrules mean that the United States has not taken itself out of competition in the international market by its own strict nonproliferation policy. Because of the NPT, coordination of suppliers within the limits of the treaty provisions is not resented as a cartel against developing countries but accepted as a technique for fairness and order in implementing the treaty (as is evidenced by the endorsement in the Final Declaration of the NPT five-year review conference in 1975).[12]

Supplier coordination within the bounds of the treaty not only prevents competition to cheapen or undermine the safeguards regime; it also clarifies and strengthens explicit provisions on a number of points, such as the application of safeguards to subsequent retransfer

12. "Final Declaration of the Review Conference of the Parties to the Treaty on the Nonproliferation of Nuclear Weapons," NPT/Conf./35/I, Annex I, pp. 3–4.

of exports and to the use of by-product materials or technology in local facilities. The NPT commitments and consultations of suppliers have special value with regard to exports to non-NPT parties. The FRG-Brazilian agreement is a case in point: it bars any use of FRG exports for PNEs (a sensitive point for Brazil), requires safeguards on and FRG consent for any reexport, and has tight provisions for application of these commitments and safeguards to any use of imported technology or by-product materials in other Brazilian facilities. The FRG negotiating leverage that obtained such far-reaching provisions, which apply to the greater part of Brazil's future nuclear program, was unassailable in view of Germany's NPT commitment on some of these points, and the common supplier position on others.

There is general recognition that IAEA safeguards are not perfect; and although they can be improved, with more men and money and instruments, they can never be made faultless. They can, in fact, be considered a deterrent and warning system, not a preventive one. But though imperfect, they have great value: any reactor system under safeguards is safer than one which is not. No less important, IAEA safeguards can become a device for mutual reassurance and confidence that a nuclear renunciation, once taken, remains a safe national decision. Most proliferation tensions are regional rather than global; one principal argument against NPT adherence is that a neighbor may overtly or clandestinely become a nuclear threat. If neighboring countries want to dispense with nuclear weapons, the way to cope with such fears and allegations is to exchange NPT commitments and open their nuclear energy programs to IAEA inspection. In such situations countries will have an interest in *cooperating* with inspections in order to demonstrate (and to encourage reciprocal actions by their neighbors) that the situation continues in fact to be unmenacing and stable.

Security Assurances

For many states, security assurances from nuclear powers are a prerequisite to their willingness to adhere to the NPT, and to justify this course to the domestic political opposition or to proponents of nuclear status: witness the protracted internal debate over the NPT in Germany and Italy, for example.

In the case of insecure and isolated states such as South Korea, Taiwan, and Israel, U.S. security assurances, by treaty or as a matter of firm policy, are particularly crucial. These are all states where attention has been given to the nuclear option. In the first two, the motives may well have been mixed—not only to signal a potential ultimate security recourse, but to remind the United States (with its known preoccupation with nuclear proliferation) of the possible consequences of a slackening of its support. The reminder should not be ignored in a period when political developments in Asia have put strains on the ties between the United States and South Korea and Taiwan; attrition of U.S. security commitments and of local confidence in them could indeed make interest in nuclear weapons more than a gesture. The nonnuclear status of Taiwan and South Korea, both currently parties to the NPT, is therefore one of the matters at stake in future U.S. decisions regarding security commitments and the visible measures to back them up in East Asia. And where we bear this degree of responsibility for defense of a beleaguered country, we have a corresponding right to ask for deference to our policies on so crucial a matter as steps toward nuclear independence (as, for instance, in the purchase of a reprocessing facility).

In other cases of isolated or imperiled states, direct U.S. security assurances are difficult or even infeasible; this is the case for Pakistan or South Africa, for example. Instead, broader international measures for settlement of harsh racial, religious, and national differences must be looked to if the threatened security situation is to be eased. The United States can support efforts to this end, but only in concert with other states in the regions or other interested powers.

Other nonparties to the NPT are concerned less with security (though there may be some such concerns, and nonadherence to the treaty may be rationalized domestically on such grounds) than with prestige or regional and international status. Brazil, India, and Spain can be put in this category; Iran, though now an NPT party, may at a later date incline in this direction, particularly if India undertakes an explicit weapons program. Security assurances cannot deal with this contingency: the essence of the prestige motivation is a desire to demonstrate a role as an independent actor on the international scene. But international approaches to security problems, combined with political and economic deference and cooperation, can in a more diffuse way offer alternatives to the nuclear option as a mark of status. The recent U.S.–Spanish treaty of friendship and cooperation may be a test case. Associated with it is a U.S. commitment for

$450 million in Export-Import Bank credits, principally for equipment for nuclear power plants—and this to a country that has not signed the NPT and has its own plutonium separation facility. The treaty can also be viewed as part of Spain's process of political liberalization and of its return to a place in Western European economic and mutual security institutions. Such a process, rather than continued isolation of Spain, may offer the best hope for circumstances in which the nuclear weapons option will be unnecessary and unattractive.

Arms Control

Article VI of the NPT commits the parties to pursue negotiation on cessation of the nuclear arms race and nuclear disarmament. This commitment is part of the NPT bargain; it is one of the promises of the superpowers in return for the nonproliferation commitments of the nonnuclear states. More radically, it is concerned with the discriminatory aspect of the NPT structure—the division of the world into nuclear weapon haves and have-nots. It holds out hope for long-term equalization in a peaceful international order moving toward more radical disarmament. Critics and nonsigners of the NPT have pointed to the limited and halting progress of the nuclear powers in the Strategic Arms Limitation Talks (SALT), on a comprehensive test ban, and on other nuclear measures as evidence that the treaty has not worked fairly. And indeed, uncontrolled continuation of U.S. and Soviet nuclear weapons programs or a cessation of SALT negotiations would underline the discriminatory aspect of the NPT, thus increasing political pressures on some NPT holdouts to keep their weapons option open. Progress in nuclear arms control, on the other hand, would undercut this objection to NPT adherence, by giving force to the argument that the discriminatory gap is diminishing.

SALT and other nuclear arms control negotiations should, of course, be pursued on their own merits, both for U.S. security and for a more stable world order. The NPT is unlikely to be successful over the long term if progress in such efforts is not substantial. But in the short term, so long as efforts are pursued in good faith and the major powers are responsible in their management of their nuclear arsenals, the fate of nonproliferation will be decided on other grounds. No nuclear arms control agreements foreseeable in the near future are likely to be decisive in moving significant holdout states toward NPT adherence. Major SALT agreements or a comprehensive test ban, however, might make it more difficult for a holdout actually to start nuclear testing.

Stiffening U.S. Policy

Proposals for a more aggressive nonproliferation policy are numerous. A clear and well-reasoned one was advanced by Senator John Glenn on the eve of Secretary of State Henry Kissinger's statement before the Government Operations Committee.[13] In his view, the NPT as currently implemented is not the answer to our proliferation problems. Joint U.S.–Soviet pressure might be brought to bear on all current nuclear suppliers to conclude agreements for at least the following: (1) a ban on the export of nuclear fuel production facilities and on stockpiles of fissionable material, except possibly under safeguarded multinational arrangements; (2) exports limited to NPT parties or states putting all nuclear activities under safeguards and forswearing nuclear explosions; (3) an international antiterrorist physical security convention; (4) commitments and procedures for IAEA member nations to recover diverted or stolen nuclear materials; and (5) strengthening IAEA inspection capabilities and eliminating the secrecy surrounding IAEA verification and reporting.[14]

It should be noted that Glenn's items 3, 4, and 5 are at most intensifications or variations of current policy; the novel element is the emphasis (applicable also to his measures 1 and 2) on U.S.–Soviet cooperation and joint pressure. This is an optimistic premise. U.S.–

13. John Glenn, "Biting the Nuclear Bullet," *Washington Post*, March 8, 1976.
14. More far-reaching suggestions have been proposed, but they do not appear practical in the near future. Some urge that the United States and the rest of the world abandon nuclear power and the "plutonium economy" with their attendant proliferation risks. ("The Plutonium Economy" [policy statement by the National Council of the Churches of Christ in the U.S.A.].) Senator Glenn has further suggested that ultimately the nations of the world may have to outlaw and punish countries that divert nuclear fuel to nuclear explosions. To relieve the security anxieties that might impel some states to proliferation, it has been suggested that the United States and the Soviet Union promulgate the following policy: "In the event of a nuclear attack on the territory of a nonnuclear state, the United States and the Soviet Union would undertake to make available to the victim a comparable number and scale of nuclear weapons with which to retaliate" (Alton Frye, *New York Times Magazine*, Jan. 11, 1976). To escape from the potential of diverting national nuclear power fuel and facilities to national nuclear weapons programs, the radical Baruch plan concept might be revived, and the nuclear fuel cycle or its sensitive stages put under international ownership, management, and control (Lincoln Bloomfield, *Foreign Affairs*, vol. 53 [July 1975], p. 749).

Soviet cooperation on the institutional aspects of peaceful nuclear energy has been quite good over the past two decades, but it has never involved the close concerted action envisaged here. Even if it were practical to work so intimately and concertedly with the Russians, the political costs of doing so against our industrial allies and the developing nations would be too high.

The United States and other suppliers have not followed the course Glenn proposes—withholding exports of nuclear equipment or materials to states that do not adhere to the NPT or accept IAEA safeguards on *all* their nuclear activities. Instead, exports are permitted if the recipient agrees not to use them or their by-products for nuclear weapons or other explosives and accepts IAEA safeguards on the related materials and facilities. The judgment behind this policy is a political one—that cooperation and consent are the most stable basis for long-term limitation of proliferation, even when non-NPT parties are the prospective buyers. Refusal to sell key technology may, most especially in the cases of the major NPT holdout states with strong national pride and emerging major nuclear programs, lead to totally or largely unsafeguarded programs. Sales in which reactors, fuel, and other facilities are committed to be used for nonmilitary and non-explosive purposes, under safeguards, with strict limits on retransfer and secondary use of imports, have the effect of involving many of the programs and nuclear and official establishments of these countries in a safeguarded regime. By working with these countries in such a manner it is hoped that a constructive mutual dependence will be created. It is impossible to predict which approach—cooperation on a safeguarded basis or pressure and perhaps isolation—maximizes chances that the recipient will move increasingly into the nonproliferation orbit, but the case for safeguarded cooperation is intellectually and pragmatically respectable. This course offers the opportunity for the United States to offer low-key encouragement to adhere to the NPT, and a likelihood of de facto exposure of the whole local program to safeguards.

The most sensitive and difficult issue is that raised by Glenn's proposal to ban exports of key facilities yielding fissionable material, as well as stockpiles of separated plutonium, except on a multinational basis. This is a critical area that has been officially recognized by Secretary Kissinger and others, who have made clear that in supplier consultations the United States has sought principles—particularly relating to withholding exports of technology for the sensitive

stages of reprocessing, enrichment, and heavy water production—
that the suppliers' group did not accept as binding. The U.S. argument is a simple one. These technologies either are the steps that
actually yield fissionable material in bomb-usable form (reprocessing and enrichment) or enable local natural uranium to be used to
fuel reactors and produce plutonium without dependence on imported (and safeguarded) slightly enriched uranium fuel (heavy
water plants). These are critical points; nonproliferation commitments would be more definitive if nonnuclear-weapon states did not
have independent national capabilities of this kind but had instead
to rely on external (perhaps multinational) facilities. While renunciation of such facilities might be politically difficult, they do require
heavy investment and are less economical than imports of fuel or
heavy water or reprocessing services. Their development should at
least be deferred, and the time so gained would be valuable for establishing a firm nonproliferation regime, both generally and in certain
insecure states that have expressed interest in nuclear weapons.

It must be understood that the reprocessing of fuel elements, the
separation of plutonium, is not a mystery:

Contrary to rather widespread belief, separation of plutonium from ir-
radiated nuclear fuel—that is, fuel that has been taken out of nuclear
powerplants—and its subsequent incorporation into nuclear weapons
suitable for military purposes, is not potentially beyond the capability of
most countries. A commercially competitive nuclear fuel reprocessing
plant that produces separated plutonium and uranium that meets the
stringent quality control specifications required by the nuclear industry is
a highly complex, sophisticated facility, costing at least several hundred
million dollars. But a reprocessing facility designed only to extract plutonium for nuclear weapons could be much smaller, simpler, and less expensive.

One could describe such a facility in a form that would require only a
few months for construction and an operating crew of less than a dozen appropriately skilled people, using information that is widely published and
materials and equipment that are commercially available worldwide. . . .
They could cost on a scale of tens of thousands of dollars.[15]

This may be an overstatement, but the essential point is important.
Small reprocessing facilities have been operated in a number of coun-

15. Statement of Theodore Taylor, Chairman of the Board, International Research and Technology Corp., in *Nuclear Proliferation: Future U.S. Foreign Policy
Implications*, Hearings before the Subcommittee on International Security and Scientific Affairs of the House Committee on International Relations, 94:1 (GPO,
1975), pp. 81, 88.

tries, including some not parties to the NPT—India, Argentina, and Spain. Others are being planned. Safeguards over such facilities are especially crucial and pose sensitive problems; the possibilities for reliance on multinational or regional rather than purely national facilities are receiving well-deserved attention. But now or in a few years many industrialized countries will be in a position to build a reprocessing capability.

But reprocessing capacity is not particularly urgent for nascent nuclear power programs. Plutonium recycling and breeder reactors, in which separated plutonium would be used, are still in the demonstration stage in the most advanced countries; the United States still has no operating commercial reprocessing facilities. There are adherents even in industry of the view that for at least a number of years storage rather than reprocessing of spent fuel elements will be the more economical course. (The IAEA is studying this alternative as one option in its regional fuel center study.) There is thus good basis for the argument that national reprocessing facilities, particularly for small power programs of one or two reactors, will not be needed for some time. It is more difficult, however, to justify the argument that states which can afford to plan major nuclear power programs should agree now to forgo national reprocessing facilities or give the United States a veto on subsequent selection of reprocessing locations. And states looking to ultimate major power programs will wish to have a completely national fuel cycle, if possible, and to understand major materials and processes by at least first-hand experimental experience (for instance, with plutonium).

The alternative suggested by the United States to a proliferation of sensitive national facilities is the establishment of multinational centers for reprocessing and perhaps other fuel cycle operations. The IAEA has already launched a study of the regional fuel center concept. The idea is attractive: in principle it can offer economies of scale and ease of safeguarding and physical protection, in addition to obviating the problem of national control of sensitive operations. There are problems, however: greater shipping distances exacerbate safety and security risks; modern multinational facilities and processes might defer the building of national facilities for a time, but meanwhile serve as channels for training and technological diffusion; efficient plants would quickly make separated plutonium available to participating states—just what we wish to avoid; arrangements for financing, organization, management, and siting would probably be difficult to negotiate and carry out. And could rival and suspicious states really agree on location and arrangements for facilities of such complexity and sensitivity, especially when they are in a tension-filled area?

There is an even more acute problem, with a similar possible solution, in the disposition of plutonium. Separated plutonium represents the penultimate stage before weapons manufacture, and the question of the disposition and protection of plutonium is a crucial one. In one sense, this is an extension of the general physical security problem; in another sense, it is the most sensitive test of the effectiveness of nonproliferation safeguards. Substantial national stockpiles of plutonium can be periodically inventoried, but they represent a ready resource for transformation into weapons. International custody of plutonium stocks not in process of separation, fuel fabrication, or reactor operation could alleviate fears of military use since plutonium would be distributed only in the form of fabricated fuel elements. A function of this kind is clearly consistent with the IAEA's authority, for example under articles III(A) (1), (5), and (7) of its charter.

Supporting action by the United States is possible. We have been the principal supplier of nuclear fuel, partly because we have the enrichment and fabrication capacity and have benefited from the exports, but also as part of a deliberate strategy of meeting the fuel needs of other countries, on a guaranteed long-term basis, in order to reduce economic and political incentives for constructing enrichment facilities. They key factor in the Brazilian decision to turn to the FRG as its major nuclear supplier was that the United States was unable, because of lack of production capacity, to enter into long-term supply contracts for the requisite reactor fuel. This incident underlines the importance for U.S. nonproliferation strategy of cutting through current domestic indecision regarding construction of additional enrichment capacity, so that we will be able again to enter into firm supply contracts that can be an economically attractive alternative to the expensive and difficult venture of new national enrichment facilities. Similarly, we and other suppliers should be in a position to offer reprocessing services where this is an acceptable alternative to premature construction of new national facilities.

The case for restraint in nuclear exports is so compelling that it is tempting to ascribe to commercial greed the reluctance of other suppliers to adopt obligatory guidelines restricting exports of key fuel cycle facilities. Such motives are not absent in any major trading nation, of course, but there is also a more rational basis for reservations on this score, one directly related to the issue of basic nonproliferation strategy.

The NPT can be conceived of as a bargain under which non-nuclear-weapons states agree to forgo nuclear weapons and accept safeguards, and are in turn promised full cooperation and assistance on nuclear power, PNE services, and arms control progress by the nuclear powers. How, then, can NPT parties justify refusal to sell relevant elements of a nuclear power program (which the sensitive stages outlined above undoubtedly are) if end-use commitments and safeguards are accepted and applied? The United States may have the economic and political weight to make unilateral interpretations of what its treaty obligations are regarding "full exchange" of peaceful nuclear programs and get away with it; this would not be so easy for lesser states. And the practical consequence can be that non-nuclear states, concluding that obligations to them are not honored, will claim to be released from their own obligations. And insisting on restrictions that go beyond the NPT requirements may be particularly risky vis-à-vis France, which, though not an NPT party, has adopted the public policy of acting as if it were, and has so acted in the suppliers' group; to ask France to go *beyond* the NPT is to remove the rationale for its cooperation.

Looked at in less of a horse-trading light, the basic question is how to broaden adherence and deepen commitment to the NPT. Pressures and embargoes may be appropriate on occasion—as when South Korea or Pakistan bruited about their interest in nuclear weapons—but as a primary incentive can be counterproductive. They may produce forced acceptance of restrictions, but only so long as necessary; when an unconstrained—and probably unsafeguarded—alternative turns up, it will be seized with redoubled determination to escape dictation. Even if we pressure key nonnuclear-weapons states to forgo peaceful nuclear options of importance to them, many of them can turn to more costly and time-consuming but still viable means of developing either weapons or nuclear power; and if our conditions seem unreasonable and impolitic, some suppliers will not be willing to fall in line.

The argument here is not for passivity. Thorough exploration of possibilities for regional and multinational fuel centers, the availability of reprocessing services when necessary from established nuclear programs, the extension and regularizing of coordination among suppliers, economic and technical arguments for delaying fuel-cycle decisions and investments and restraint in marketing such equipment in this stage of development—these are all prudent elements of U.S. policy. In individual cases, where desire for a national reprocessing facility seems too closely linked to political instability or recourse to the nuclear weapons option, stronger diplomatic action may be justified toward the aspirant and the potential supplier. Difficult judgments will be called for as to what is practical and how to achieve the goal, but a general embargo of sensitive fuel-cycle technology would be unlikely to gain supplier support and would risk imperiling the NPT bargain and regime among nonnuclear-weapons states.

Conclusions

The effort to halt further nuclear proliferation is no longer—if it ever was—a struggle by the nuclear haves against the nuclear have-nots, a kind of political cartel. It is an international venture, cutting across blocs and across the divisions between developed and developing countries, the basic logic of which is expressed in the final declaration of the 1975 NPT review conference, which records the parties as: "*Recognizing* that the danger of nuclear warfare remains a grave threat to the survival of mankind; *Convinced* that the prevention of any further proliferation of nuclear weapons or other nuclear explosive devices remains a vital element in efforts to avert nuclear warfare. . . ."[16]

The principal barrier to further proliferation is not NPT commitments and IAEA safeguards, or restraint and coordination on the part of the United States and other suppliers, important as these are. It is rather the perception by an increasing number of states that acquiring nuclear weapons will not enhance their security, that only a general practice of refraining from nuclear weapons acquisition can make them more secure. The principal thrust of nonproliferation policy in the United States and elsewhere must be to take action to ensure that a nation's decision to forgo nuclear weapons will be demonstrably in its security and welfare interests.

In a turbulent world in which nuclear weapons are a symbol not only of danger and catastrophe but also of international power and status, countries approach the decision to seek nuclear power from

16. "Final Declaration," Annex I, p. 1.

a variety of perspectives. To deal intelligently with the global situation we must have an understanding of the complex motivations behind nonnuclear countries' attitudes to proliferation. For many nonindustrial or small countries, of course, any significant military nuclear program is infeasible; for others, the burden would be heavy, and the opportunity to forgo it by mutual renunciation with the reassurance of IAEA inspections under a treaty is a welcome escape. Other states are less fortunate, either because they are exposed and isolated or because they are located in historic areas of conflict (Japan, India, Pakistan, Iran, and Central Europe). For them, security assurances—the nuclear umbrella of a major ally—may be a current prerequisite to forgoing nuclear weapons development.

It should not be forgotten that forgoing nuclear weapons, through NPT adherence or de facto, is not irrevocable. Indeed, it is only realistic to recognize that actions such as NPT signature, deferring purchase of a plutonium separation plant, and planning for participation in a multinational fuel cycle facility can be time-purchasing moves while technical capabilities and physical facilities enabling quick weapons development are built up. But if peaceful nuclear programs carry this inherent risk, they also constitute a hedge against failure of nonproliferation efforts, an assurance that countries which try the nonproliferation option will not be permanently disadvantaged if it fails. Meanwhile time will be bought for the constructive purposes of broadening adherence to the NPT, easing international tensions, and settling regional disputes, so that the nuclear weapons option will be less tempting in the future.

For some countries, suspicion of the nuclear powers will be a problem. It is true that the NPT is basically discriminatory, even if it is so with good reason. Not only are there nuclear and nonnuclear states; there are supplier states, and there are states with peaceful nuclear explosive devices. Excolonies suspicious that economic imperialism has been substituted for the political imperialism they recently escaped, and commercial competitors of the nuclear powers like Germany and Japan, will wonder, when asked to accept inspection or constraints on nuclear trade, whether the demand is motivated only by nonproliferation considerations or is also a device for preserving weapons monopoly or commercial advantage. Coordination among suppliers, when within the provisions of the NPT, can allay these doubts; but agreement among suppliers to withhold peaceful nuclear technology will feed doubts.

Some states will find the political discrimination of the NPT difficult to accept indefinitely. Some may be the traditional principal actors on the international stage—Germany, Italy, Japan—constrained by postwar political patterns to a more limited role; others will be rising states seeking an international role and status, globally or regionally, to match their size and wealth (Brazil, India, Iran, Spain, and before long perhaps Nigeria or Indonesia). Both the general state of the international system and the specific degree of recognition accorded their economic and political weight will affect their ability to accept a nonnuclear role. In the long run, pressure for nuclear status will be eased if substantial progress is made in nuclear arms control and arms reduction. But in addition to disarmament progress there must also be an easing of the superpowers' current preoccupation with the delicacy of the strategic balance and with the constant development and refinement of nuclear weapons systems, despite their lip service to the doctrine of nuclear deterrence and avoidance of nuclear war.

The viability of nuclear nonproliferation will also be imperiled if the thirty-year taboo is broken and even tactical nuclear weapons are ever used. Not only would a valuable firebreak against escalation of violence, maintained since 1945, be breached; but by making recourse to nuclear weapons in regional situations less unthinkable, it would become less feasible for nations to ensure their own defense and play a major regional role while forgoing nuclear weapons.

This review of some of the main perspectives of various groups of countries on nuclear proliferation identifies the major strains and problems. For none of the nuclear holdouts, however, is nuclear weapons acquisition a simple or attractive option. And for each there are alternative ways of easing the tensions, of reducing the motivation to turn to nuclear weapons, which U.S. foreign policy can help strengthen.

The primary thrust of our nonproliferation efforts should be, then, not to try to *force* nonproliferation on others, but to help them find ways to do without nuclear weapons. The risks of proliferation, which are at least indirectly grave for the United States, are vastly greater for other countries. For nations which out of sense of their own peril have hinted at recourse to nuclear weapons—South Korea, Pakistan, Taiwan, and Israel—the option is a matter of desperation, not bravado. In such cases, prudence will lead us to be cautious about making nuclear weapons material available while feelings run high, but our main effort should be to take such political and security steps as we can to ease the sense of insecurity that gives the nuclear option its desperate attraction.

At such international flashpoints of tension and conflict, early emergence of nuclear weapons material facilities would be risky, and strong diplomatic measures to forestall this are warranted. Elsewhere, a more cooperative and temporizing approach is indicated. Against the background of the oil embargo and uncertainty over the long-term durability of current alliances and international security arrangements, it is unrealistic to expect major or rising nations to accept the principle of incomplete nuclear power fuel cycles. Reluctance to renounce chemical processing or isotopic enrichment does not mean that a country is actively seeking nuclear weapons, though it may reflect a wish to hedge against political as well as economic uncertainty and dependence. Cooperative multinational approaches to both chemical reprocessing and isotopic enrichment deserve to be explored; countries in the market for such facilities might be encouraged to delay commitment to national facilities, a delay that would be warranted by technical uncertainties as to preferred enrichment technology and the economic and technical aspects of plutonium as a fuel. An orderly approach to such issues can be facilitated if the United States moves quickly to build the separation capacity that will enable it to resume supplying, and guaranteeing the long-term supply of, slightly enriched uranium fuel. Steps of this kind will be welcomed by nonnuclear NPT parties and meet with support and cooperation from suppliers and recipient states alike; export embargoes, or supplier cartels going beyond the NPT provisions, will not.

Implied throughout this chapter has been the importance of de facto nonproliferation. Increasing adherence to the NPT is certainly an important objective, but the basic objective is avoidance of any new nuclear weapons programs. A state may have reason to be reluctant to adhere to the treaty at present, but as long as it forgoes a nuclear explosives program it is contributing to the delicate balance of nonproliferation. Refusing such a country peaceful nuclear cooperation under the commitments and safeguards required by the NPT would serve no useful purpose and would risk pushing it into earlier and more active nuclear independence and self-sufficiency. Political judgments in particular cases, however, will have to be made and reviewed as regional and global security patterns change.

What then can we do? We *cannot* adopt an export policy of withholding any export of nuclear materials, equipment, or technology that would contribute to a nuclear weapons capability unless we are prepared to end cooperation with the peaceful nuclear power programs of other countries. We *can:*

—Require commitments from purchasing nations not to use imports for nuclear weapons or any nuclear explosive device and to accept IAEA safeguards over use of the imports. In so doing, we will not only be carrying out our own policy but also fulfilling our obligations under article II of the NPT.

—Encourage adherence to the NPT.

—Support the IAEA and its safeguards activities financially, technically, and diplomatically.

—Coordinate with other suppliers (including the USSR and nonparties such as France) to avoid undercutting safeguards and the NPT in international nuclear trade.

—Give impetus to the development and international application of procedures and measures to protect nuclear facilities and nuclear materials, in storage or in transit, from terrorist or other subnational seizure or diversion.

—Support and encourage deliberate and cooperative approaches to key stages of the fuel cycle.

—Relate our collective security, regional diplomacy, and other international security activities to the security concerns of other states in such a way as to encourage treaty or de facto commitments to nonproliferation.

Collective cooperative approaches can be of great significance to the nuclear fuel cycle and the handling of its risks. The practical difficulties are great but not insuperable; and U.S. policymakers should reflect on the fact that fuel cycle cooperative ventures—such as Eurochemic (the reprocessing facility at Mol, Belgium), the U.K.–French–German venture United Reprocessors, Eurodif (the French-led uranium enrichment venture involving also Italy, Spain, Belgium, Japan, and Iran), and Urenco (the U.K.–FRG–Dutch centrifuge enrichment project)—hitherto have involved other countries but not the United States. American imagination and leadership ought to be able to exploit our technical and financial capabilities in cooperative ways that are responsive to foreign needs and yet minimize proliferation risks.

None of the above approaches, even the most thorough-going, would solve the problem of nuclear proliferation. When nuclear chain reactions were shown to work, first in a reactor and then in a bomb, the risk of nuclear proliferation became a part of unfolding world history. Concern for the risks of nuclear proliferation (and for the underlying risk of nuclear war) is the beginning of wisdom. But these concerns should not obscure the unprecedented degree to which common interests have been perceived and pursued across the divisions of our disorderly world: between the United States and the Soviet Union, in the form of mutual deterrence and measures to reduce the risk of nuclear war and limit strategic arms; among most of the nations of the world, in the form of the IAEA and the NPT and other measures of cooperation and control of the peaceful uses of atomic energy. Although these are imperfect and fragile instruments, they should be valued and used and improved as they deserve—strengthened rather than abandoned, with emphasis on cooperation and accord rather than compulsion and pressure.

Appendix: World Nuclear Power Capacities

| Country (1) | NPT status* (2) | Status of nuclear power reactors | | | Forecast of energy capacity in 1982 (megawatts) (6) |
		Operational (3)	Under construction (4)	Planned (5)	
Nuclear weapons states					
United States	P	X			215,866
Soviet Union	P	X			14,400
United Kingdom	P	X	X	X	13,000
China	N	n.a.	n.a.	n.a.	n.a.
France	N	X	X	X	22,000
Insecure states					
Israel	N			X	0
South Korea	P		X		1,800
Taiwan	P		X	X	4,000
South Africa	N			X	
Status-seeking or hegemonic states					
Brazil	N		X	X	600
India	N	X	X	X	1,700
Iran	P		X	X	4,200
Spain	N	X	X	X	8,200

Appendix: World Nuclear Power Capacities (continued)

| Country (1) | NPT status[a] (2) | Status of nuclear power reactors | | | Forecast of energy capacity in 1982 (megawatts) (6) |
		Operational (3)	Under construction (4)	Planned (5)	
Rivals to the preceding					
Argentina	N	X	X		900
Pakistan	N	X			125
Egypt	N[b]			X	0
North Korea	N			n.a.	
Politically constrained major states					
Federal Republic of Germany	P	X	X	X	20,000
Italy	P	X	X	X	5,300
Japan	P	X	X	X	17,000
Czechoslovakia	P	X		X	1,870
Poland	P			n.a.	
East Germany	P	X	X		1,830
Other developed countries					
Australia	P			n.a.	
Austria	P		X		700
Belgium	P	X	X	X	5,500
Bulgaria	P	X	X		1,760
Canada	P	X	X	X	8,650
Finland	P		X		2,160
Hungary	P		X		880
Luxembourg	P			X	0
Netherlands	P	X			500
Romania	P			X	440
Sweden	P	X	X	X	7,500
Switzerland	N[b]	X	X	X	5,800
Other developing countries					
Chile	N				
Greece	P				
Indonesia	N[b]				
Mexico	P		X	X	1,320
Philippines	P			X	1,320
Thailand	P			X	500
Turkey	N[b]				
Yugoslavia	P		X		615

Source: Calculated from "World List of Nuclear Power Plants, June 30, 1975," *Nuclear News*, vol. 18 (August 1975), with adjustments for recent events. Classification of countries is the author's.

   n.a. Not available.

   a. P = party; N = nonparty.

   b. Signatory.

CHAPTER FIVE

The United States in the World Economy

EDWARD R. FRIED *and* PHILIP H. TREZISE

FOREIGN ECONOMIC POLICY has an uncertain place in an assessment of the nation's priorities. It does not involve government expenditures large enough to call for major budgetary choices. While having an important bearing on domestic economic prospects, it is clearly subordinate to internal macroeconomic decisionmaking. Yet concern about U.S. links with the world economy has been growing, stimulated by the economic turbulence of the past few years and by uneasiness about the future adequacy of food and raw materials. Even the assumption that the trend toward increasing international economic interdependence is a positive development, though still widely acceptable, is no longer taken for granted.

The purpose of this chapter is to explore some of the major issues that are likely to arise over the next decade, to assess their economic and political importance for the United States, and to outline directions for American foreign economic policy. Its major theme is that timidity is the main danger. Problems will not become notably more difficult to solve, but an exaggerated concern about adjustment to economic change and stubborn adherence to ideological preconceptions could cause the United States to make the wrong choices on some of the economic issues that lie ahead. Continued emphasis on averting short-term risks could entail excessive long-term costs.

The first section is devoted to a brief examination of the framework

The authors thank William Cline, Lawrence B. Krause, Walter S. Salant and Fred H. Sanderson for helpful comments on earlier versions of this chapter.

167

of the international economic order to determine whether the objectives and rules governing international economic relations are likely to evolve as part of an orderly continuum of the post–World War II past or whether power among nations has shifted, interests diverged, or new pressures arisen so that a radically different approach will be necessary. The second section takes up the major functional issues—trade, agriculture, energy, raw materials, East-West economic relations, investment and capital flows, and international monetary reform. In light of this discussion, the final section suggests how the United States should shape and organize its economic policies toward other countries.

The Changing International Economic Order

After two decades of impressive growth and marked stability, the world economy in the 1970s suffered a succession of severe shocks and extraordinary fluctuations. Merely to list them dramatizes their magnitude: the collapse of the Bretton Woods monetary system; a worldwide boom followed by the worst recession since the 1930s; a commodity price cycle more violent than anything recorded in a century; a quadrupling of oil prices, which transferred 2 percent of income from oil-importing to oil-exporting nations, depressed world demand and employment, and disrupted international payment positions; the virtual disappearance of world food reserves, leaving markets and the world's poor vulnerable to crop failures; and the persistence of worldwide inflation.

In the brief span of four years, general optimism about the outlook has been replaced by uncertainty, and assumptions about the adequacy of the international system are being questioned. Even with recovery well under way, concern about the potential vulnerabilities of the world economy is surely warranted. This is not to agree, however, with the view that there has been a distinct break with the past. The main economic forces and trends of the past quarter-century are still discernible and the habit and practice of international cooperation appear to be more firmly in place for having weathered so severe a test.

The Diffusion of Economic Power

It has become customary to attribute failings in the international economic system to the declining influence of the United States. During most of the postwar period, the argument goes, a preponderance of economic and military power enabled the United States to lead, if not to propel, the noncommunist world into an era of economic liberalism. It could afford to offer economic inducements when necessary, and its allies could not afford to forget that their security depended on U.S. military power. Supposedly, all this has changed. The United States is neither so able nor so willing to lead, Western Europe and Japan are strong economic rivals and less fearful for their security, exporters of oil and raw materials are newly powerful and bent on advancing their interests at the expense of importers, and the developing countries in general are self-assertive in pressing their demands. Hence, it is said, the orchestra is without a conductor and the musicians are playing from different scores.

Even though each element in this thesis has some basis in fact, the picture that emerges is misleading, in both its portrayal of the past and its implications for the future. In the first few years, when the machinery for the postwar system was being installed, the U.S. position was indeed almost hegemonial. But the notion that the United States could have imposed its will on subsequent economic negotiations even as early as the 1950s would surprise those American officials who carried on the negotiations. Hard bargaining and compromise were required then as now, and agreements depended on the demonstration of a mutuality of benefits. While leadership of the system centered on the United States, responsibility for its effective functioning over the past quarter-century has increasingly been distributed among all the major countries as the volume of world production grew threefold and of world trade sixfold. Growing capabilities and links strengthened the conviction among nations that cooperation was in their interest, and this enabled the international economic system to cope with the unusual disruptive events that began with President Nixon's emergency economic measures of August 1971 and continued through the deep world recession of 1974–75.

Nor is it evident that the United States is now little more than first among equals in national economic power and influence. A simplified but useful indication of what has happened and what the present situation is can be gained from examining the distribution of the world product since 1950. As shown in table 5-1, the U.S. share declined slowly from about one-third in 1950 to one-fourth in 1974. Western Europe's share stayed remarkably steady, but there were sizable increases in the shares of Japan and the developing countries

Table 5-1. Distribution of World GNP, Selected Years, 1950–74

Percent

Country or group	1950	1955	1960	1965	1970	1974
Industrial countries						
United States	34.2	33.3	29.7	29.4	26.5	25.1
Western Europe	24.4	24.9	25.2	25.0	25.3	24.8
West Germany	5.2	6.5	7.1	7.1	6.9	6.5
France	4.8	4.7	4.7	4.9	5.0	5.1
United Kingdom	5.5	5.0	4.6	4.2	3.6	3.3
Other	8.9	8.7	8.8	8.8	9.8	9.9
Japan	2.8	3.5	4.3	5.5	7.3	7.7
Other OECD countries	3.8	3.8	3.7	3.8	3.8	3.8
USSR	11.4	12.1	13.0	13.1	13.1	12.8
Eastern Europe	4.7	4.8	5.1	4.8	4.6	4.9
Developing countries						
Noncommunist	12.3	12.5	12.5	13.0	13.1	14.6
OPEC	n.a.	n.a.	n.a.	n.a.	n.a.	2.8
India	2.7	2.6	2.5	2.3	2.2	2.1
Brazil	1.0	1.1	1.2	1.2	1.3	1.7
Other	n.a.	n.a.	n.a.	n.a.	n.a.	8.0
China	3.1	3.6	3.9	3.7	3.7	3.7
Residual	3.3	1.5	2.6	1.7	2.6	2.6

Source: Adapted from U.S. Department of State, *The Planetary Product in 1974*, Publication 8838 (November 1975), p. 14.
n.a. Not available.

(mostly OPEC) and a small increase in that of the USSR. Living standards in Western Europe and Japan are now much closer to those in the United States than they were a generation ago, and their shares in world trade have grown. Nonetheless, it is striking that after a quarter-century of reconstruction and expansion and economic miracles, the U.S. economy is about equal in size to that of all Western European countries together and dwarfs those of Japan or West Germany or even the USSR.

Current prospects suggest that growth rates over the next ten years in the United States, Western Europe, Japan, and the USSR will be more nearly equal than they were during the 1950s and 1960s, which means that changes in relative economic positions of the major countries, if they occur at all, will be very small. If American influence among the advanced industrial states is destined to diminish, it will be by choice rather than because of a fundamental change in relative economic strength.

The noncommunist developing countries contain almost half the total world population but have a modest place in the world economy, accounting for barely 15 percent of world output. For a decade their economies have been growing by nearly 6 percent a year, well above the rate in the industrial countries. Their per capita incomes now average $500 a year, or about one-tenth the average in the industrial countries. These aggregates, however, as well as the rhetoric about chronic conflict between them and the industrial countries that has become customary in recent international discussions, should not be allowed to obscure the growing diversity among the developing countries and in their international economic requirements and priorities.

There are first the OPEC countries, which vaulted into prominence with the October 1973 oil crisis and the subsequent quadrupling of oil prices. Most of them can expect that oil revenues will underwrite their future economic expansion. Earlier fears that their large financial surpluses would disrupt the international economic system have proved groundless. The principal problems that remain stem from the unique characteristics of the oil trade: because of its large size and the concentration of export capacity in a few countries, sudden changes in the price and availability of oil could occur and subject the world economy to substantial shocks and political strain. This vulnerability poses special requirements for international economic policy.

Commodity power for the developing countries pretty much begins and ends with oil, however. While a large number of developing countries are heavily dependent on export earnings from primary commodities—notably tropical agricultural products, oil seeds, and minerals—in only a comparatively few instances are exports of these commodities unique to the developing countries. Even then, there are obstacles to the systematic exercise of market power, among them the weak financial position of most of the exporting countries, sharp competition from substitutes, and potentially large increases in supply from new sources. Unlike the countries exporting oil, developing country exporters of other primary products are hardly in a position to disrupt the economies of the industrial countries by withholding supplies, and certainly could not exact political ransom this way. They are concerned rather with improving world demand for their products, which traditionally has been sluggish and is dependent principally on the rate of economic activity in the industrial countries.

Their interests lie in working with the importing countries to bring about changes in the international economic system that might smooth fluctuations in investment in, prices of, and foreign exchange earnings from these products, and otherwise improve the benefits they receive from producing them.

A growing number of developing countries have achieved remarkable rates of economic expansion, stimulated by exports of manufactured goods and access to international private capital markets. Brazil, Korea, Taiwan, and Mexico are striking examples, but many other countries are moving in this direction. Their interests are now bound to liberalization of the rules governing industrial trade, and in part they must view commodity issues as importers rather than exporters.

Among those whose growth is well below average are such inwardly oriented countries as India and Pakistan. They already have the productive and technical capacity to become important members of the world trading community but, partly because of deliberate policy choices, have not realized this potential. On the other hand, the least developed countries—some twenty to thirty in number—have still to develop the basic social and economic structure for sustained economic expansion or close international economic involvement.

These differences illustrate the danger of lumping the interests of developing countries together in defining their international economic priorities. They differ significantly in levels of per capita income, in dependence on exports of raw materials, in capacity to export manufactured goods, and in needs for concessional capital. Their most important common feature is the growth of their populations and the pressure this imposes on their economies and societies.

Among the quantitative projections of the future, those for the world's demographic structure appear to have the greatest validity and should occasion the greatest concern. There is no plausible change in rates of population increase that will yield a world total of fewer than 6 billion by the year 2000. Projections by the United Nations of when and at what number world population might stabilize are more speculative: under optimistic assumptions this might happen within a century at about 10 billion, under pessimistic assumptions at about 16 billion. The *difference* between the two projections is roughly 50 percent greater than the present world population.

Which projection turns out to be more nearly correct will depend primarily on events in the developing countries, since that is where 90 percent of the increase in population will take place. Experience indicates that if per capita incomes rise sufficiently population growth rates will decline, though after a lag. In any event, the late years of the twentieth century will test this hypothesis, and the results could be the most fundamental measure of how well the international economic system performs. For unless forces are set in motion during the next two decades that will alter population trends in the most populous countries, the pattern—in numbers and age-sex distribution—will have been established for further growth to totals that would be unsupportable by standards now considered acceptable.

Finally, there are questions about the role of communist countries. The growth in their economies and in their foreign trade has about matched the average for the rest of the world. Over the past two decades, however, an increasing proportion of their foreign trade has been with the countries of the Organisation for Economic Co-operation and Development and a declining proportion within their own orbit. Although East-West trade is comparatively small—about 4 percent of world trade and 5 percent of the trade of the OECD countries—it is now substantial in absolute terms and requires heavy borrowing by the USSR and Eastern Europe from the West. (In 1975 net borrowing financed as much as one-fourth of the imports of the European communist countries from the West.) Specific aspects of this trade, moreover, are significant: Soviet and Chinese purchases of cereals are a key factor determining world prices, and the two countries export sizable quantities of energy fuels and other materials. Also, China's exports of labor-intensive manufactured products could become a source of international dispute.

Nonetheless, the communist countries are essentially passive members of the international economic system, participating little if at all in the General Agreement on Tariffs and Trade (GATT), the International Monetary Fund (IMF), the World Bank, or other organizations that set rules. This is likely to change, though slowly. As a practical matter, the USSR will have to accept major responsibility in any global arrangement for cereals, and both the USSR and Eastern Europe, to their dismay, are likely to become identified increasingly with the industrial countries in international negotiations with the low-income countries. More generally, the continued expansion of

East-West trade will raise questions about whether new guidelines are needed to regulate it.

Resource Constraints

Some of the worry occasioned by the 1972–74 disturbances in oil and in commodity markets centered on whether the functioning of the world economy will be threatened by scarcities and steadily rising costs of raw materials.

It is well to disclaim at the outset any pretense of knowing whether the neo-doomsday school, the technology optimists, the recycling enthusiasts, or those who emphasize other approaches to the analysis of resource adequacy will prove to have been right. The eventual outcome will depend on knowledge and experience that have not yet been accumulated and on forces that have not yet emerged.

What can be said now is that recent events have not radically altered the resource situation from what it was at the beginning of the decade. Natural resources are not in imminent danger of running out. Even finite materials, including mineral fuels, are nowhere near depletion. On the extreme assumption that technology will not be improved, there still would be no basis for predicting a resource constraint on production during the next quarter-century, and probably for a decade or two beyond.

In fact, the capacity to produce nonrenewable as well as renewable commodities continues to expand and the techniques of raw material exploration, development, and production undoubtedly will continue to improve. Historically, this combination has led to a decline in the real costs of producing raw materials and foods.

The future could be different. For some commodities, increased inputs of labor and capital may be required for the same amount of production, as it becomes necessary to exploit progressively less well endowed sources. In a few cases, such as oil, the producers may be able to manipulate markets so as to obtain permanently larger payments from consumers, and this in turn would be likely to raise the real costs of global production of energy and raw materials. And concern about the environment may increase the cost of obtaining natural resources.

None of these cost increases, however, should significantly threaten economic growth, as conventionally measured, or living standards. Primary commodities, including raw materials, primary energy fuels, and grains, are a small part of world output. Increases in their cost, which in most cases would come about gradually and thus could be adjusted to more readily, should have only a marginal effect on the potential for economic expansion.

It is of course true that some resources are exhaustible. In the long run, substitutes for them will have to be found if standards of life are not to be jeopardized. The most critical case is that of fossil fuels. Unless a genuinely alternative source of energy can be developed, the apparently predictable depletion of fossil fuel deposits could affect the prospects for supporting human life on the planet.[1] Here market forces do not assure a satisfactory outcome: rather, the market's discount rate is likely to be too high to encourage an optimal effort to develop a substitute energy source. Governmental—or, more accurately, intergovernmental—actions to press forward energy research and development clearly seem necessary.

Whether other exhaustible raw materials should be viewed similarly is unclear. The standard assumption is that, as costs rise, technology will produce suitable substitutes in time to allow a smooth transition from the use of one material to another. But if the market works imperfectly, there may be costly interruptions of supplies, leading to serious political and social tension. At the moment, no adequate basis exists for judging which, if any, of the exhaustible materials, other than fossil fuels, should be given special concern and attention—much more analysis is needed than has been directed to it thus far. The issue deserves international consideration, for its implications are truly global.

The Imperative of Growth

In most major respects, then, the international order that lies ahead will closely resemble that of the past. There will be shortages, in the self-evident sense that for an indefinitely long time to come human wants will far outrun the capacity to produce goods and services to satisfy them. On the other hand, the world economy has the productive base to support a steady expansion in output, incomes, and living standards. The bulk of this capacity will continue to be in the OECD countries, which necessarily must share the principal responsibilities for making the international economic system work.

1. See H. E. Goeller and Alvin M. Weinberg, "The Age of Substitutability," *Science,* vol. 191 (February 20, 1976), pp. 683–89.

For leadership, these countries perforce will continue to look to the United States, which remains by far the world's dominant economy. Nothing that has happened since 1971 has much changed these fundamentals.

One disquieting feature of the outlook is whether the industrial countries can keep their economies on a reasonably steady growth path. Attitudes developed over more than two decades of confidence-building experience have been shaken by the events of 1972–75. If the prospect in the OECD countries is for periodic bursts of inflation followed by strong measures to suppress demand, the growth potential of the world economy will not be realized and the international economic system will be severely strained.

A second has to do with the economic prospects of the poorest countries. If they cannot make much greater progress in the next decade, it is difficult to see how tension in the world can fail to increase.

All this is to say that raising output remains an imperative for any improvement in the world economic order. The primary task of economic policy, as in the past, is to achieve full and efficient use of resources. There is no conflict here with the requirements and priorities of the low-income countries. Efficiency must include measures to expand the international economic opportunities open to these countries and to improve their capacity to take advantage of these opportunities. Nor is there an inherent conflict with environmental concerns. Efficiency obviously must be defined to include the preservation of a livable habitat, or the point of the whole effort will have been lost. It is therefore still appropriate to emphasize the output objective as an essential element of any satisfactory long-term international future.

New perceptions of international economic relations may also have a significant effect on the future. The inflation and recession, the wild swings in food and raw material prices, and the oil crisis—all global in their incidence and consequences—have sharpened public awareness of the increasing economic links among nations and created concern about their implications. Mainly, they have cast some doubt on the postulates underlying economic interdependence. Some prescriptions call for greater national self-sufficiency or policy autonomy. Others, emphasizing the supposedly conflicting interests of the industrial North and the developing South, would create a vaguely defined "new" international economic order.

None of these departures from established policy are likely to make much sense for the United States. That interdependence creates problems is plain enough. It also has substantial rewards in improved prospects for economic growth and for sane political relations. In a world where deprivation, not affluence, is the common human situation, the search must still be for solutions that will promote the effective use of resources and the growth of global output. This means that neither a retreat from interdependence nor calls for confrontation offer any useful bases for a rational foreign economic policy.

Policy Issues

In this section seven specific areas of foreign economic policy—trade, food, oil, raw materials, East-West economic relations, investment and foreign assistance, and international money—are discussed. In each, the emerging problems call for international cooperation—sometimes in novel ways.

Should Trade Liberalization Continue?

No feature of the postwar economic scene has been more remarkable than the expansion of world trade. From 1953 to 1973 the volume of trade grew by an average of 8 percent a year, double the rate of the four decades preceding the First World War and in sharp contrast to the two interwar decades of relative stagnation.

In due course this phenomenon swept virtually all countries, even the communist autarchies. The largest export increases, however, were achieved by Japan, Western Europe, and North America, and these consisted mostly of manufactured goods. In a break with earlier patterns of trade, in which manufactured goods and primary products grew at about the same rate, postwar exports of the former rose more than half again as much as exports of the latter.

Despite the growth of trade, and the large share of it represented by industrial products, problems of domestic adjustment apparently have been minor. For example, exports of the members of the European Community (EC) to one another quadrupled during the first ten years of the customs union without triggering the Community's escape clause. In fact, the EC's customs duties on industrial goods were eliminated ahead of schedule. The removal of industrial tariffs within the European Free Trade Association followed much the same course. On a global scale, the industrial nations were able with little apparent difficulty to cope with the adjustments necessitated by successive reductions in world tariffs negotiated under the GATT, the Kennedy Round in the 1960s being the most comprehensive and far-reaching of the series. Evidently, the elected leaders of the OECD countries considered further liberalization politically acceptable, for they agreed to a new negotiation immediately after the Smithsonian monetary discussions in 1971. The most impressive evidence is in the recent record. Neither the extraordinary swings in trade and payments balances of the past few years nor the high levels of unemployment in 1974–75 have led to any general backsliding into restrictionism.

The chief sources of trade growth have been rising output and income, improvements in communications and transport, and the reduction of preexisting official obstacles to trade. But trade itself has been a causal force—raising per capita productivity, permitting economies of scale, stimulating innovation, and invigorating competition. The interaction of trade with other elements in the process of economic growth helped greatly to drive and shape postwar prosperity.

Nonetheless, it should be asked if potential gains from the further growth of international trade warrant the pursuit of policies designed for this purpose. Specifically, should the current Tokyo Round be pushed, and should American foreign economic policy continue to hold trade liberalization as an important objective?

A negative reply might rest on the supposition that specialization based on international markets has already proceeded so far that additional shifts of resources will bring notably smaller real returns. If this is so, the possible benefits may not significantly exceed the economic and social costs of reallocating capital and labor as imports and exports increase.

One argument might be that the customs tariff, the most ubiquitous barrier to trade, is now so low that further cuts will contribute to specialization and efficiency in only minor ways, and that other trade barriers are intractable, or that their trade-inhibiting effects are for the most part marginal, or at least speculative.

Another might be that the burdens and hazards associated with a growing volume of imports and exports suggest the need for caution. At issue is not only the extraordinary example of oil. In times of bad harvests, U.S. commitments to supply other nations with cereal grains could make life difficult for American consumers and ultimately for the government in power. Industries relying on foreign sources for raw or processed materials or components face the risk that political decisions will be made abroad to restrict or interrupt supplies. So do industries that rely heavily on export markets. Worries about possible disruptions from outside may be widely enough shared among the principal trading nations to make a consensus on new efforts to liberalize trade doubtful.

These arguments, if accepted, would amount to at least a go-slow signal for foreign trade policy. There are also frequent proposals to restore old trade restrictions and install new ones. Adoption of enough of these could alter the whole course of an American policy that has been followed with some consistency for four decades. It seems safe to assume that the costs of such a return to a basically protectionist position, including the repercussions from the retaliatory actions it would provoke throughout the world, would deter almost any conceivable administration from choosing it. Nonetheless, the positive arguments for continued trade liberalization need elaboration.

In a static system, trade, like all other economic activity, assuredly would be liable to diminishing returns. But the world economy is not static. The unexpectedly vigorous postwar growth of trade in manufactured goods has been marked by specialization within as well as between industries, so that the range of traded products has widened greatly. When this process might end or what new developments will come from technological advances or from enlarged markets cannot be predicted. But recent experience indicates that trade is inherently an unsettling economic phenomenon. Its growth is based on and provokes innovation and change. To discount the prospects for further gains from trade liberalization is to conclude, without evidence, that the dynamic elements have been almost wrung out of the advanced industrial economies.

This conclusion is particularly difficult to accept when one considers how much of the world economy has been touched only in passing by the growth and liberalization of trade. The example of temperate agricultural products will be discussed in a later section, but it can be noted here that few of the prospective gains in efficiency from freer trade in these products have been realized after more than two decades of trying.

Nor have tariff barriers to trade been reduced enough to make fur-

Table 5-2. Average Tariffs on Major Import Categories of the Industrial Countries, 1971[a]
Percent

Import category	Average tariff for all imports[b]	Average tariff for imports subject to duty[b]
Raw materials	1.5	5.7
Semifinished manufactured products	6.6	10.5
Finished manufactured products	9.4	11.3

Source: Adapted from General Agreement on Tariffs and Trade, *Summary by Industrial Product Categories: Basic Documentation for the Tariff Study* (Geneva: GATT, 1974).
a. Countries included are: Australia, Austria, Canada, the countries of the European Community, Finland, Japan, New Zealand, Norway, Sweden, Switzerland, and the United States.
b. The GATT secretariat uses four procedures for calculating average tariffs. The table uses the one in which rates are weighted by imports from countries subject to most-favored-nation duty. This produces the lowest average.

ther cuts irrelevant. Tariffs that remain on manufactured and semi-manufactured products are on the average about twice as high as the cuts achieved in the Kennedy Round. The averages, moreover, conceal the full extent of existing protection. The secretariat of the GATT has compiled and organized data on present tariffs on industrial goods in the OECD countries. This extensive documentation shows a progression, summarized in table 5-2, from low tariffs on industrial raw materials through much higher tariffs on semimanufactured goods to highest tariffs on finished manufactured products.

Tariffs not only rise with the degree of processing, but their application also becomes much wider. In 1971 duties were imposed on 22 percent of imported raw materials, on 65 percent of semimanufactured goods, and on 84 percent of finished goods.

Broadly, then, tariffs are levied on most manufactured products and at average rates that cannot fail to have a deterrent effect on trade. But throughout the tariff schedules of the advanced industrial countries are found much higher duties on such products as textiles, footwear, toys, plastic articles, and plywood; for these, duties average between 15 and 20 percent. Their protective impact, moreover, is commonly greater than the nominal rates imply. This is because the materials or components that make up a manufactured product typically are not themselves subject to tariffs, which means that the tariff on the finished product is actually effective for the value added in manufacture rather than for the total cost of production.

The most disturbing aspect of these tariff distortions is that they impede the integration of the developing countries into the international industrial system, hindering their economic progress and im-

Table 5-3. Composition of Exports from Developing Countries, Selected Years, 1955–73

Year	Exports in billions of 1973 dollars[a]				Manufactured goods as percent of nonoil exports
	Total	Oil[b]	Nonoil	Manufactured goods[c]	
1955	41.1	10.2	30.9	5.3	17.2
1959	40.2	11.4	28.8	5.1	17.7
1964	50.7	15.6	35.1	8.3	23.6
1969	59.5	19.3	40.2	13.7	34.1
1973	108.8	43.0	65.8	27.0	41.0

Source: United Nations, *Monthly Bulletin of Statistics*, relevant issues. Figures are rounded.
a. Current dollars converted to 1973 dollars with GNP deflator.
b. Includes all fuels, most of which were oil.
c. Included in nonoil exports. Consists of standard industrial trade classification categories 5–9.

posing losses in efficiency. Tariffs in the United States and other industrial nations are skewed to give the greatest protection to those industrial and raw material processing sectors where the lower income countries are, or can be expected to be, competitive. Lowering such barriers would give these countries an opportunity to expand their export earnings and improve their terms of trade.

Future progress on this score could well be the most crucial test of the adequacy of the world economic system. Exports of manufactured goods have been a major factor in the achievement of high rates of economic growth in a limited number of developing countries. This process will have to be extended widely if the developing world is to have any hope of a satisfactory economic future.

From 1959 to 1973 the developing countries increased the volume of their exports of manufactured goods by almost 13 percent a year (see table 5-3). Manufactured goods, as a proportion of total nonoil exports, grew from 18 percent in 1959 to 41 percent in 1973. Even so, these exports in the boom year of 1973 were less than 8 percent of total world exports of manufactured goods. Most of the possible economic gains from the exchange of labor-intensive industrial products from the developing countries for capital- and technology-intensive products from the industrial countries are still to be exploited.

The relation of manufactured goods exports to development goals is a key point. In the 1974 Lima Declaration, spokesmen for the developing world set as an objective for the year 2000 a threefold or greater increase in the developing country share of world industrial output, or from the present 7–8 percent to at least 25 percent. Attainment of this objective would bring about a significant restructuring of the world economy and would assure substantial economic growth for the largest part of the developing world.

The most important prerequisites of course relate to the domestic policies of the developing countries. As for OECD policies, the requirements consist primarily of there being strong markets in the industrial countries and adequate access to those markets for imports. The secretariat of the United Nations Conference on Trade and Development has calculated that the industrialization objective would have to be supported by a 12 percent annual rate of increase in exports of manufactured goods and that this implies a level of exports in the year 2000 equal to twenty times the 1973 level. While such an objective may be ambitious, it is not farfetched, since the projected rate of growth is no greater than that achieved over the past fifteen years. It will require steady economic expansion in the industrial countries, further reductions in tariffs, and a sustained attack on nontariff barriers to the import of labor-intensive products.

Legal and administrative obstacles to trade other than tariffs are found in all countries. The members of the GATT have identified more than 800 national laws, rules, and practices that adversely affect trade. Not all of these are equally burdensome, to be sure, but the total weight of subsidies, quotas, discriminatory public procurement policies, cumbersome customs procedures, product standards applied protectively, and other trade-distorting practices must be heavy. The present round of trade negotiations is the first in which the nontariff barriers have been taken up comprehensively. The extent to which these barriers can be dealt with will be an important measure of the success of the Tokyo Round.

This point may apply with particular force to controls on exports. How widespread the resort to export restrictions was during the peak of the 1973–74 inflation is not well recognized. Although the OPEC oil embargo and U.S. controls on soybean exports captured most of the publicity, all major trading countries put restraints on some exports in the hope of diverting inflationary pressures to foreign customers. Rules to check this new version of bad-neighborliness will have to be devised. Otherwise, the issue is likely to remain a major threat to the orderly functioning of the world economy.

Thus there are substantial gains in efficiency to be achieved and costs to be avoided through continued reductions of tariffs and other barriers to trade. By spurring domestic competition and producing a more effective allocation of resources, trade liberalization could be a significant anti-inflationary tool. This would return a dividend of potentially large proportions, since a reduction in inflationary pressures by this means could diminish the need for employment-restricting measures to achieve greater price stability.

A further growth of trade and a widening of international specialization unquestionably will add to adjustment problems. To judge from the past, these should be readily manageable in circumstances of steady economic growth and of shared responsibilities among nations for absorbing the impact of economic change. Greater dependence on trade also adds to the risk that other nations peremptorily will either restrict their exports of specific commodities or block access to their domestic markets. But with common rules, mutual obligations, and effective sanctions, such a risk would be greatly diminished.

In general, the best answer to the problems of economic interdependence in trade is to continue to negotiate understandings that will progressively reduce the areas within which sovereign nations wish or can afford to take arbitrary actions. Such a course is clearly in the interest of the United States as the dominant industrial nation, and it could not succeed without active U.S. support. Even if the United States should consider the economic costs of a reversion to protectionism acceptable, the damage to other nations would make the U.S. political position in the world untenable and its security ties meaningless. The fact is that trade liberalization, while the most accustomed form of international cooperation, is also the most important means of strengthening the world economic system.

Redefining the Ever Normal Granary

International agricultural issues in the next decade will be dominated by the food problem: will food supplies be adequate to meet rising world requirements and will food prices be a recurring obstacle to containing inflation?

At the core of the question are the cereal grains—wheat, rice, and coarse grains—which directly or indirectly provide more than two-thirds of the calories consumed in the world. A series of poor grain harvests in the USSR, South Asia, and the United States set off the food price explosion of 1972–75 and gave rise to anxieties about the world's ability to feed its growing numbers. What had been seen as

Table 5-4. World Cereal Grain Production, Consumption, and Net Exports, Selected Periods, 1960–76[a]

Annual average, millions of metric tons

Description	1960–61 to 1962–63			1969–70 to 1971–72			1973–74 to 1975–76		
	Pro-duction	*Con-sumption*[b]	*Net trade*[b]	*Pro-duction*	*Con-sumption*[b]	*Net trade*[b]	*Pro-duction*	*Con-sumption*[b]	*Net trade*[b]
Developed countries	315	299	20	399	375	30	439	382	60
United States	168	140	33	209	169	40	228	159	72
Other exporters[c]	41	24	19	55	33	27	62	37	26
Western Europe	90	115	−27	122	144	−22	137	156	−20
Japan	16	21	−5	13	28	−14	12	30	−19
Centrally planned countries[d]	276	279	−3	375	391	−7	421	441	−20
USSR	123	116	7	165	170	4	184	193	−9
China	95	99	−4	137	140	−3	150	154	−4
Developing countries[e]	213	224	−12	289	302	−22	306	342	−35
South Asia	82	88	−6	108	114	−6	116	126	−9
Rest of world	5	6	−1	5	6	−0.4	6	7	−1
Total, world	808	808	f	1,069	1,074	f	1,173	1,172	f

Source: U.S. Department of Agriculture, Economic Research Service, *World Agricultural Situation* (USDA, 1975), p. 27. Figures are rounded.

a. Total of wheat, coarse grains, milled rice.

b. Includes changes in stocks.

c. Canada, South Africa, Australia–New Zealand.

d. USSR, other Eastern European countries, People's Republic of China.

e. Central and South America; Africa; Middle East; South, Southeast, and East Asia.

f. Net trade does not always balance out because of minor discrepancies in the data.

a problem of the distant future became for some observers the much more immediate prospect of chronic food scarcity.

Aside from the unlikely contingency of permanent adverse climatic changes, world food production will probably continue to keep ahead of population growth. But as in the past, many developing countries, particularly the densely populated countries of South Asia, will experience difficulties in meeting their food needs. And there is the ever-present possibility of a recurrence of serious crop failures in major grain-producing countries. In this situation, prudence argues for policies aimed at three principal objectives:

—increased cereal grain output in the developing world;

—efficient use of agricultural productive capacity in the industrial countries;

—building of reserve stocks to cushion temporary shortages.

Progress toward attaining these objectives will depend largely on international or multilateral actions. As background for a discussion of them, table 5-4 summarizes the major variables involved.

Several points stand out. First, both developing and communist country deficits have been on an upward trend. Since population and incomes will probably grow for some years at rates not much different from those of the past decade and a half, world demand for cereals can be expected to increase steadily in any case. In view of the institutional and structural obstacles to changes in agricultural practices and productivity, output in the developing countries is likely to lag behind requirements. Increasing demands on the supplies of a relatively few surplus grain producers are thus to be expected.

Second, only a few countries produce grain in excess of domestic consumption. In recent years the major and regular exporters have been the United States, Canada, Australia and New Zealand, South Africa, Argentina, and Thailand.

Third, the predominance of the United States as an exporter is apparent. This applies not only to wheat and coarse grains but even to rice, which is not a major American crop.

THE IMPORTANCE OF DEVELOPING COUNTRY DEFICITS. Although the developing nations account for less than 30 percent of world grain consumption (table 5-4), their deficits seem certain to be an important factor in determining the nature of future cereal markets. The United Nations Food and Agriculture Organization estimated in 1974 that the total cereal deficits of the developing countries would increase from 30 million tons in 1974 to 87 million tons in 1985.[2] Western Europe's deficit in 1985, if there is no change in farm support policies, might be on the order of 10 million to 15 million tons (the average for the past three years was about 20 million). Japan's import needs could easily rise from the current 19 million tons to 30 million tons. It is difficult to predict for Eastern Europe, the Soviet Union, and China, but a conservative estimate of their combined deficit for 1985 would be 10 million to 15 million tons, based on an average of 20 million tons for the past few years.[3] Summed up, the margin to be supplied by imports in 1985 might be 140 million to 150 million tons, up from about 100 million tons in 1975.

This is not a projection of an impending food catastrophe. With world import demand growing by 4 million to 5 million tons a year, the countries that normally produce surpluses could be expected to grow enough to easily cover all needs except in years of exceptionally bad harvests in some major producing region. In fact, it might be a reasonable allocation of economic effort if the developing countries were to expand their exports of manufactures to finance gradually increasing imports of food from the most efficient producers. This has been the trend in the world economy for the past fifteen years; if markets can be progressively opened to developing country industrial products, this trend can be expected to gain strength.

But complacency is not warranted. The estimates of deficits for the developing countries rest on the assumption that their cereal output will grow at more or less the annual average rate of 2.6 percent attained in the years 1961–73.[4] Any significant slowing of this rate of increase would raise their import requirements sharply. Capacity in the exporting countries would be strained. Rising prices would threaten to shut low-income countries out of the commercial market, and escalating costs would make it difficult to mobilize food aid.

Further, lumping the developing countries together obscures distinctions between those with higher incomes and the poorest. The

2. UN Doc. E/Conf. 65/3 (November 15–16, 1974), p. 89. The 87 million tons is an adjustment of the FAO's estimate of 100 million tons to take account of the FAO's use of paddy rice rather than milled rice.

3. Fred H. Sanderson, "Export Opportunities for Agricultural Products: Implications for U.S. Agricultural and Trade Policies," Columbia Journal of World Business, vol. 10 (Fall 1975), pp. 19–20.

4. UN Doc. E/Conf. 65/3, p. 87.

projected 1985 grain deficit divides about equally between the nations with very low incomes—principally in South Asia and Africa south of the Sahara—and the better-off developing countries, most of which have prospects of being able to finance their imports of food on commercial terms. In the best of circumstances, the low-income countries will have difficulty earning enough foreign exchange to pay for their growing needs. And it is of course these countries that have the lowest levels of nutrition; if per capita caloric intake could be raised to more acceptable standards, their prospective requirements for imports would also increase.

Finally, the problem of feeding the world's population should be viewed in its long-term aspects. Even if it may be a sensible division of labor for the developing world to depend essentially on North America for a substantial part of its food imports, there will be physical and financial limits to the volume of grains that can move in international trade. Neglect of the agricultural sector, especially in the most heavily populated regions, could end in an unmanageable food situation.

Food policy therefore should incorporate measures to raise productivity and output in the developing countries. The potential for expanding cereal production through increases both in cultivated areas and in yields appears to be large,[5] but its realization will depend on the provision of increased agricultural inputs, more adequate extension services, investments in irrigation and land development, and policies that give farmers incentives to raise production. The principal responsibility for accomplishing all this, and most particularly for adopting appropriate domestic farm policies, clearly will lie with the developing countries. In the most critical cases, however, external aid will be necessary. The OECD countries and the World Bank have shifted their development assistance priorities toward agriculture, but the volume of their assistance to agriculture is still too low. In view of the critical and long-term character of the food problem in the developing countries, these priorities will have to be maintained and the total effort expanded for an indefinite period.

EFFICIENT USE OF AGRICULTURAL CAPACITY. The present outlook for the grain-exporting countries is good. Growing export markets plus growing domestic demand plus stock rebuilding provide

5. UN Doc. E/Conf. 65/4 (November 1974), pp. 23–68.

a picture of strong markets. For the short run, therefore, it can be expected that returns to producers will be adequate to ensure that cultivable acreage will be fully used and that, barring natural disasters, output available for export will grow at satisfactory rates.

This is not to say that agricultural productive capacity is going to be used prudently, however. Agricultural protection and subsidies are common in all the industrial countries and are the cause of a great waste of agricultural and other resources. Furthermore, the grain economy of the industrial world is segmented into insulated markets, as in Western Europe and the USSR, and comparatively open markets, as in the United States and Japan. Market forces, in other words, do not have sufficient room to function, since world prices influence only a part of world production and consumption. Fluctuations in production in major producing countries or regions therefore tend to have a disproportionate effect on internationally traded supplies and prices and on agricultural policies in the open grain economies, notably that of the United States.

This situation could easily bring a recurrence of past difficulties. Should new crop disasters occur before stocks have been rebuilt, world market prices would again rise steeply and create pressure for export controls. The United States came perilously close to applying them to grain exports in 1972–73 to protect the economy from the inflationary impact of world grain prices. Other exporting countries did cut back grain sales abroad for this reason.

If, on the other hand, there were to be a succession of good harvests in the world, stocks would accumulate once again in the United States and Canada, and demands for acreage restrictions would again be heard. A return to limitations on North American output would greatly increase the world's vulnerability to bad harvests, for it is on the margin provided by American and Canadian surpluses that the rest of the world is essentially dependent in periods of short supply.

All of this argues for a more rational organization of agricultural production in the OECD countries. The emphasis should be on actions to use agricultural resources so as to meet rising demand most efficiently. Agricultural protectionism is so widespread that the benefits of specialization are largely forgone. If trade liberalization brought about even a modest redirection of agricultural effort— away from grains and toward livestock and poultry in Western

Europe and Japan, and away from dairy products in the United States—real income would rise and a more stable and more productive agricultural base would exist for meeting future food needs in the world.

Actions to free agricultural markets will have to be gradual since agricultural protectionism is deeply embedded in the political structure of all countries, including the United States. This attitude persists even though the ostensible income and employment effects that justify protection could be obtained more surely with liberalized agricultural trade. There will be pressure on governments to use the recent extreme fluctuations in world cereal markets as an argument against exposing domestic markets to more imports. They will have to have guaranteed supplies—that is, assurances that reserve stocks will be available—to justify even small steps toward more open markets. The rebuilding of grain stocks is thus critical to prospects for more efficient use of agricultural resources in the OECD countries, as it is to other aspects of a rational world food policy.

AN INTERNATIONAL GRAIN RESERVE. Between 1955 and 1972, the variations in world cereal prices were small, even in years of serious production shortfalls in Eastern Europe and South Asia. The reason, of course, was that supplies could be drawn from large reserve stocks, held mainly in the United States, but also in Canada. These stocks were accumulated reluctantly, incident to domestic price support policies. Eventually they were reduced, largely through cuts in acreage, when they were seen to be fiscally and politically burdensome. In 1972 American and Canadian stocks had already been partially drawn down, and when the Soviet Union entered the market as a buyer on a large scale, prices rose sharply.

Two important lessons should be drawn from this experience. On the one hand, sizable stocks made stable prices possible in a period of wide swings in world output and could do so again. On the other, national stocks are subject to national political decisions: there can be no assurance either that they will be maintained or that they will be released for export when supplies are short.

A central argument for an international grain reserve system, therefore, is simply that a sharing of responsibilities and costs is the surest guarantee that benefits will be there to be shared as well. The United States as the largest producer and exporter of grain would have to be a major contributor to a reserve scheme, but it should not

and need not take the responsibility unilaterally. Other putative beneficiaries, including the USSR, have a basic interest in achieving more
stable grain markets; a multilateral system that pools risks is a better
choice for them than the alternative of national stocks.

A multilateral reserve arrangement might involve a stock target
to be negotiated among the industrial nations that would share in the
financing of the reserve. Calculations based on the experience of the
past decade and a half suggest that a minimum initial target should
be 60 million tons of wheat and coarse grains (the costs and short
storage life of rice make it less suitable for stock purposes) to be
accumulated by the individual countries when world supplies are
ample and prices low and drawn on when supplies are tight and
prices high.[6] The floor price at or near which stocks would be bought
would have to be set to cover the costs of the efficient suppliers. The
floor-to-ceiling price range would then need to be wide enough—
say, a spread of 40 percent of the floor price—to give market forces
a major role in discouraging consumption and encouraging output
when supplies were low. Conversely, if world stocks grew beyond
levels considered adequate for stabilization and emergency purposes,
the floor and ceiling prices would be reduced.

With agreement on the target and the price spread, reserve shares
could be divided among participants in proportions that would take
account of consumption levels and export or import positions. The
actual reserves would be national, stored either in the country that
owned them or in the exporting countries. Each country would ear-
mark a part of its reserve for emergency allocation should famine in
a developing country or region threaten. Stocks allocated to famine
relief would be applicable primarily to South Asia, where a serious
crop failure could require huge shipments to prevent mass starvation.

A multilateral grain reserve would be a general departure in international economic arrangements. Its negotiation would present novel
issues and its management would require close, continuing cooperation, since any agreement in this unfamiliar field could hardly be self-

6. See Philip H. Trezise, *Rebuilding Grain Reserves: Toward an International
System* (Brookings Institution, 1976). If reserves are assumed to be equally divided between wheat and coarse grains and the floor price per ton in 1975 dollars to
be $110 for wheat and $100 for other grains, the total investment would be approximately $6 billion, with carrying charges of $600 million a year. If reserves proved
to be an effective stabilizing device—that is, if stocks were acquired at generally
low prices and sold at generally high prices—real costs would be zero.

executing. Among other things, it should provide for withholding benefits from nonparticipants; the USSR, specifically, could not stand aside from an agreement and expect to enjoy nondiscriminatory access to available supplies in times of bad domestic harvests. Agreement on a price range, on operating guidelines, and on the distribution of reserve stock shares would all be hard to negotiate.

But the main objection to a reserve system is not these predictable negotiating and management problems but rather the view held by some parts of the U.S. government that the provision of reserves can safely be left to the private market. If public authorities resolutely refuse to hold stocks, it is said, farmers and grain processors will do so. One form in which stocks will be held is livestock, whose feeding can be adjusted in times of shortage to free grain for other uses, just as happened after a poor American corn crop in 1974.

This objection has force only to the extent that world grain markets are likely to be free of governmental intervention. If there were free trade in grain, if export controls could be prohibited, if consumer prices everywhere were allowed to fully reflect bad harvests, and if all these conditions infallibly prevailed even in times of shortage, the need for reserves would be relatively small and the private sector might hold a substantial share of what was needed. But of course these conditions will not be approximated, even in this country. As noted, trying to achieve freer trade in grain is worthwhile. But gross market imperfections will not disappear soon. Reliance on private stock accumulations to cope with the next major crop shortfall is a prescription for:

—large price increases that will probably have a ratchet effect, through wages, on the general price level;

—unnecessary hardship for the poorest people in the developing world, as high costs force reductions in both commercial imports and food aid;

—strong pressures for export controls, which if indulged could more or less permanently damage the international trading system;

—the stimulation of even more agricultural protectionism than already exists.

It is understandable that there should be resistance in the United States to a return to officially held grain reserves. Past experience with unilateral stocks saw this country accepting most of the costs of holding the world price within a narrow range. There is every reason for insisting that other affluent nations should henceforth share the responsibilities as well as the benefits; one reason is that should the United States once more rebuild its own stocks no administration could guarantee that they would be freely available for export in another period of inadequate world supplies.

FOOD AND FOREIGN POLICY. It is clear that the United States, as the largest exporter of grain, will play a principal part in determining developments in the world food economy. This has given rise to heady notions of an American food diplomacy patterned on the model of Arab oil diplomacy. Little consideration is needed to see how ill conceived these notions are.

If the main target of food diplomacy were to be the Soviet Union, the requisite vulnerability is not there. The USSR is a big, relatively affluent nation; much of its grain consumption is in the form of meat and poultry. When its harvests are bad, it has the option of reducing livestock herds rather than importing grain. A realistic estimate of Soviet decisionmaking would be that its choice will always be to cut meat rations rather than concede to American demands.

The import needs of the OPEC countries are small and can easily be satisfied from other sources. The argument that the United States might derive political or economic leverage from its grain exports to them has no substance. Concessional sales of grain by the United States to some of the low-income countries obviously can be helpful to political leaders whom it wishes to favor; but almost any concessional aid from anyone can have the same effect. In the end, the object of food diplomacy would narrow down to Japan, which has deliberately allowed its diet patterns to develop on the basis of imports, especially of feed grain, and is the largest commercial market for the United States. But that the United States might attempt to pressure Japan through food supplies is too farfetched for discussion.

U.S. policy toward the world food problem will have to take a more useful course. This country can use its influence to promote increased cereal production in the developing countries; if it can once again pick up its fair share of development aid, that influence will be greater. It can commit itself to full domestic production, subject to international agreement on the conditions that will make the commitment practicable. And it will have to take the lead in negotiating an international system of reserve stocks.

Containing the Oil Problem*

Oil, more than any other international economic issue, dramatizes the close connection between foreign and domestic policies and the difficulties, if not the illusory character, of a go-it-alone approach. The experience of the past few years emphasizes the special characteristics of oil and the formidable questions it poses for international economic policy.

In size alone, oil is in a class by itself. In 1974 the direct and indirect effects of the sudden jump in oil prices added substantially to inflationary pressures in the industrial countries and caused their combined output to fall almost 3 percent from the level that might otherwise have been reached. Also, the oil price hike brought a virtual upheaval in world trade and payments positions. In one year, oil exports as a percentage of total world exports rose from 5 percent to 13 percent and the increase in payments for oil affected the current accounts of the major industrial countries dramatically. The oil import bill of the United States rose by $15 billion, and higher oil prices cost the nonoil developing countries $10 billion, enough in the aggregate to offset their 1974 receipts of concessional assistance from the OECD countries. There is no record of such a sudden and far-reaching change having ever before been imposed on the world economy in peacetime.

Other considerations contribute to disquiet about oil. For one thing, the oil-exporting countries are in an extremely strong position to manipulate the market for their product. This is based on a number of factors: notably, the slow response of energy demand and supply to higher prices; the concentration of two-thirds of export capacity and reserves among half a dozen countries; the strong financial position of these countries; and the comparative ease with which production can be cut back quickly. Then, there is the political dimension: the Arab oil-exporting countries, which achieved near unanimity in applying the oil embargo in October 1973, account for well over half of world exports and thus could use the oil weapon again.

There have been countervailing developments, to be sure. The

* This section draws on calculations appearing in Edward R. Fried and Charles L. Schultze, eds., *Higher Oil Prices and the World Economy: The Adjustment Problem* (Brookings Institution, 1975).

quadrupling of the price of oil is bringing in alternative sources of primary energy fuels and is reducing the growth of energy consumption. Demand for oil has been sharply, if temporarily, reduced by the recession. As a result mainly of the check on demand, a large export capacity surplus has emerged, amounting to about 9 million barrels a day in early 1976, or almost one-third of total exports. OPEC has held ranks extremely well under the pressure of surplus capacity, but its cohesiveness as a cartel is only at a first stage of testing. Shut-in productive capacity of the present magnitude, furthermore, diminishes the threat of a new political oil embargo, for even large cutbacks in exports by the Arab countries could be made up by increased shipments by non-Arab exporters.

The process of adjusting to higher oil prices is going forward in other ways as well. Increasing sales of goods and services to the oil-exporting countries and rising domestic investment in energy are stimulating the economies of the oil-importing countries, in contrast to the demand-depressing effects of the oil price jump in 1974. Because of the rapid rise in exports to OPEC, the special impact of oil on the balance of payments of the OECD countries as a group should end soon, although some countries will fare less well than others. The earlier fears that financial surpluses from oil would place an unbearable strain on the international trade and payments system or that members of OPEC would accumulate huge and constantly growing claims on the assets of the oil-importing countries prove to have been grossly overstated.

Can the world afford the real burden of higher oil prices? Eventually, higher energy prices must be fully paid in real resources—the transfer of a larger volume of goods and services to the oil-exporting countries and the application of larger amounts of capital and labor to the production of domestic energy fuels. How great a burden is this likely to be? Here again the answer depends on whether the industrial countries can resume their trend levels of economic growth. Higher oil prices, in themselves, will not prevent them from doing this. If they are successful in pursuing satisfactory growth policies, the costs of adjusting, say, to the present level of oil prices, though large in absolute terms, would not be so high as to threaten living standards. In the second half of this decade, for example, the growth of consumption in the OECD countries might be reduced an average of one-half percentage point from a trend growth of around 4 percent a year. High levels of economic growth in the industrial countries would also ease adjustment in the nonoil developing countries, although the burden of higher oil prices on these countries would be proportionately heavier and more difficult for them to offset.

In sum, oil presents a special problem for foreign economic policy, primarily because a few exporting countries have the potential power, through their control of supplies, to administer sudden large shocks to much of the world economy, including the United States. This condition will endure for some years, for no early end to the world's dependence on OPEC oil—rather, Persian Gulf oil—can be foreseen. But the vulnerability of importing countries can be reduced by policy actions that may be politically difficult but need not be unduly burdensome.

For the short run, the requirement is for measures that will deter or, if deterrence fails, cope with an embargo or a sharp cutback of OPEC exports. The oil stockpile and sharing understandings reached in the International Energy Agency are the central elements in a program of defense against embargo or near-embargo actions by OPEC. Stockpiling large quantities of oil is expensive, but, like defense forces, it is a cost-effective way of warding off potential damage. The emergency sharing principle is necessary to ensure against attempts to embargo importing countries selectively. The IEA agreements on stockpiles and sharing may need to be strengthened, but the basic policy course here is quite clear.

A longer term policy aim should be to diminish the ability of the principal OPEC countries to control the oil market. It can reasonably be assumed that in the next five to ten years neither technological breakthroughs nor discoveries of large new non-OPEC oil fields are likely. Policy must therefore focus on restraining energy consumption growth and increasing production of conventional energy fuels in the oil-importing countries. To the extent that these policy measures succeed, oil import requirements will be held stable or reduced and the oil cartel's power over prices will decline.

The scope for reducing oil imports in each of the major importing countries or group of countries can be seen in the breakdown of energy consumption and sources of energy production in 1975 shown in table 5-5. In the United States, Western Europe, and many of the developing countries, possibilities for conserving oil imports exist across the board. They could take the form of reductions in the

Tab'e 5-5. Estimated Consumption and Sources of Energy
of the Oil-Importing Countries, 1975

Millions of barrels of oil or oil equivalent a day

Country or group	Total energy consumption	Nonoil sources of energy	Domestic oil production	Oil imports
United States	34.9	18.9	10.2	5.8
Western Europe	23.4	9.7	0.9	12.8
Japan	7.0	2.2	a	4.8
Other industrial countries	2.4[b]	1.4[c]	0.4	0.6
Developing countries	8.5[b]	2.9[c]	1.7	3.9
Total	76.2	35.1	13.2	27.9

Source: Joseph A. Yager and Eleanor B. Steinberg, "Trends in the International Oil Market," in Edward R. Fried and Charles L. Schultze, eds., *Higher Oil Prices and the World Economy: The Adjustment Problem* (Brookings Institution, 1975).
  a. Negligible.
  b. Estimated on the basis of the 1970 ratio of oil consumption to total energy consumption, as calculated from data in United Nations, *World Energy Supplies, 1969–1972*, Series J, no. 17 (UN, 1974).
  c. Difference between oil consumption and total energy consumption.

growth of energy consumption or increases in domestic output of coal, nuclear power, natural gas, and oil. The point is that the effective market for OPEC exports can be kept stable or even be reduced by a variety of specific actions. The effect on the world oil market of an increase in India's coal production or a cut in the growth rate of Japan's energy consumption could be the same as an increase in the output of oil in the United States or the North Sea. Economies in the use of oil in any country potentially will benefit the importing countries as a group.

The possibilities for restraining oil imports can be stated more dramatically still. As shown in table 5-5, imported oil is responsible for a little more than one-third of world energy consumption. Since primary energy fuels are widely though not completely substitutable at present levels and patterns of consumption, a given percentage reduction in world energy consumption could bring close to a threefold reduction in oil import requirements.

If the efforts of the importing nations were reasonably successful— if total world oil imports continued at or below present levels— OPEC's ability to manage oil prices would in due course be severely strained. Saudi Arabia, Iran, and a few other large exporters, which at present support prices by acting as residual suppliers, would have to accept a steady decline in their exports as export capacity grew elsewhere. Or the stronger members of OPEC might aid the weaker

Table 5-6. World Net Imports of Oil, 1974, and International Energy Agency
Forecasts for 1980 and 1985

Millions of barrels a day

| | | 1980, under assumption I[a] | 1985[a] | | |
| | 1974, actual | | Under assumption 2 | Under assumption 3 | Under assumption 4 |
Country or group					
United States	5.9	7.8	4.3	8.6	10.9
European Community	11.3	9.0	8.5	9.5	10.4
Japan, Australia, New Zealand	5.5	7.5	9.0	9.8	11.7
Other industrial countries[b]	2.4	3.0	2.3	4.2	4.8
Developing countries[c]	3.8	4.6	4.2	4.2	5.7
Total imports	28.9	31.9	28.3	36.3	43.5
OPEC exports[d]	28.9	31.3	27.7	35.7	42.9

Source: *The Economist*, vol. 259 (April 10, 1976), p. 107.

a. *Assumption 1:* OECD annual GNP growth rate of 4.3 percent in 1974–80; no extra conservation. *Assumption 2:* OECD annual growth rate of 4 percent in 1980–85; conservation program and accelerated investment in alternative fuels. *Assumption 3:* OECD annual growth rate of 4 percent in 1980–85; no policy change. *Assumption 4:* OECD annual growth rate of 4.5 percent in 1980–85; no policy change.

b. Excluding communist countries.

c. Excludes OPEC countries, but includes other oil-exporting developing countries.

d. Difference between projected total imports and OPEC exports in 1980 and 1985 equals projected net exports from communist countries plus changes in stocks.

members to hold prices firm and help them wait for an eventual rise in OECD oil consumption and imports. If this did not happen, these countries sooner or later would cut prices. The cartel would probably be reconstituted thereafter, but it would operate at a lower price level.

It must be stressed that the position of OPEC would be easier, and its control over the oil market more firm, should world import requirements grow steadily, even at a moderate rate. In that circumstance, the larger, well-off exporters might continue as residual suppliers in the interest of sustaining high prices. They could hold their export volume steady, realize satisfactory total returns, and still permit the smaller or poorer oil exporters to take advantage of market growth.

What happens in the United States will be the key to future shifts in OPEC's market power. According to projections of the International Energy Agency (table 5-6), world imports in 1985 could range from a low of 28 million barrels a day, with conservation and an accelerated stream of alternative energy sources (assumption 2), to 43 million barrels a day under business-as-usual conditions (assumption 4). (Oil prices are assumed to stay at present levels in real terms.) U.S. oil imports would be 4 million barrels a day in the low case and 11 million in the high case, the difference being almost enough to determine whether the market will be tight or relatively soft. These projections should not be taken literally, but their message about the decisive role of the United States is clear. Without higher prices to restrain consumption and encourage domestic production and without additional tax incentives, tax penalties, and regulatory measures to supplement market forces, U.S. imports will gradually rise; by 1985 they are likely to be near the upper end of the range. Then prospects for coping with the market power of OPEC would be poor.

Even successful import restraint measures would present a dilemma for the OECD countries. A policy that produces lower world oil prices will eventually lead to an increase in oil imports. Energy conservation and production programs have long lead times. If they were put aside in favor of higher imports, vulnerability to OPEC actions would necessarily increase. This argues for steps to insulate domestic energy prices from a fall in the world price of oil sufficiently to keep the import restraint program on a steady course.

The concept of a minimum safeguard price for oil, which is now part of the International Energy Agency program,[7] is directed at achieving this objective. It represents a policy trade-off in the competition with OPEC for oil market power. To achieve economic and political security despite the cartel, the importing countries would agree not to take maximum advantage of any reduction of world oil prices that their policies of import conservation might achieve. They would elect, rather, to continue to restrict the growth of consumption and to protect domestic fuel production so as to avoid any undue resurgence of OPEC's capability to control the market.

For the longer term, substitutes will have to be developed not only for OPEC oil but for all the nonrenewable energy fuels now in use. Experts differ on how long reserves of conventional fuels will last, but there seems to be no doubt that as the readily exploitable supplies are depleted their real cost will rise quite steeply.

Against these relative certainties, there are substantial uncertainties about the technologies that may eventually make current sources

7. The members of the IEA have agreed on an initial minimum safeguard price of $7 a barrel. This price will be periodically adjusted in light of future developments.

of energy obsolete. This is at least one area in which prudence seems to argue for a research and development effort that may have to be sustained for some decades. By its nature, such a program is an issue for public policy rather than one that can be left to market forces.

As is true of policies aimed at shorter range objectives, the search for substitute energy sources is likely to be more successful if it is international. Although there is obviously room and necessity for competition in energy research, the coordination of national programs might well lead to cost savings and earlier results than a series of independent efforts. Also, international investment consortia may be the only feasible way of realizing some of the exotic or high-cost prospects for new sources of energy.

Until now, the response of the world community to the oil crisis has emphasized the importance of cooperation in dealing with a problem whose magnitude and pervasiveness make purely national solutions appear impractical. The United States could conceivably be the exception to this generalization. With its large remaining domestic reserves of oil, natural gas, and especially coal, as well as the vast shale deposits in the western states, energy self-sufficiency at relatively high rates of consumption is probably not automatically foreclosed. The Federal Energy Agency considered this possibility in its revised *National Energy Outlook* (published in early 1976). According to the FEA, the achievement of energy self-sufficiency by 1985 would require a U.S. domestic oil price of $16 a barrel (in 1975 dollars); an accelerated use of coal, causing additional environmental damage; radical policy changes to reduce the time from inception to operation of nuclear plants; and incremental capital investments for energy conservation. To hold imports in 1985 to 6 million barrels a day (somewhat below present levels) would require a domestic oil price of $13 a barrel (in constant 1975 dollars) and would be much less damaging to the environment. These estimates are highly tentative, principally because so little is known about future effects of high prices on energy demand and supply, but the incremental costs of self-sufficiency evidently would be significant.

It is well to recognize the implications of American energy independence for the rest of the world. If this country were able to withdraw from the world energy market gradually, that alone would tend to depress world oil prices. In due course energy costs in the United States would probably diverge quite widely from those in other industrial countries, becoming higher perhaps by a factor of 2. The United States, by its own efforts, might thus present the other oil-importing countries with a greatly improved energy cost position, in which it could not share.

Whether the policy choice of energy independence really exists is doubtful. The experience of the past two years has shown widespread resistance to higher energy prices, and this attitude would surely grow stronger if energy prices rose in the United States while they declined elsewhere and if the competitive position of American industry were being progressively weakened by the difference in energy prices.

In the real world, therefore, energy policy is most likely to be linked to cooperation with the other OECD countries. This is essentially the course outlined in the long-term program of the International Energy Agency, which the United States has strongly supported. It provides a framework for sharing the burdens of a concerted program to restrain imports of oil and to expand energy research and investment. This is not a simple matter, because standards of comparable performance will be hard to establish and even harder to enforce and the temptation for individual countries to seek a free ride will be strong. Nonetheless, for the United States—as for other industrial countries—the essential point is that action taken together to reduce the vulnerability to OPEC's power will be more effective and cost less than action taken alone.

Eventually it may be possible for oil importers and exporters to reach an international agreement on oil, which might provide for an assured quantity of imports, at an agreed price, for a stated period. Such an agreement would have to be revised periodically in light of changes in market conditions. If safeguards against abrogation could be made strong enough, a producer-consumer accord might permit importers to invest less heavily in high-cost sources of domestic energy fuels and give exporters a larger market and greater stability in export earnings. But this possibility lies well in the future. The present positions of the two sides are far apart and are unlikely to move closer together until the underlying market strength of the consumers improves.

In any circumstances, a rational energy policy for the United States must have three components. The first is a domestic program to reduce or at least check the growth of U.S. oil imports. The second is cooperation with other OECD countries. The third is patience.

Other Primary Commodities: A Mixed Approach

When oil and food are set aside, commodity questions take on an entirely different dimension. Trade in all other primary commodities taken together is comparatively small, fits no clearly defined pattern, and makes fears that raw material cartels will spread and become a growing source of economic disruption unrealistic. A rough breakdown of world exports in 1973, shown in table 5-7, provides the necessary perspective.

Fuels (mostly oil) and food clearly dominate world trade in primary commodities, with all other raw materials making up less than one-fourth of the total. No item in this other group is overwhelmingly large. In 1973 combined exports of the seven largest—copper, cotton, iron ore, wool, rubber, tin, and phosphate rock—accounted for about half the total for the group. The other half was spread over twenty-five to thirty additional commodities for most of which world exports were under $500 million a year. Possibilities for substituting among these raw materials are considerable and shifts occur between primary and secondary sources according to price.

Industrial countries (including the Soviet Union and Eastern Europe) account for the major share of exports of primary commodities other than oil. This is the case for each of the nonfuel categories—food (where the dominance of industrial country exporters is exceptionally large), ores and minerals, and other raw materials. In the

Table 5-7. Origin and Composition of World Exports, 1973
Billions of U.S. dollars

Category	Developing countries	Non-communist industrial countries	Communist countries	Total world exports
Primary commodities				
Agricultural raw materials	9.2	17.4	3.8	30.4
Ores and minerals[a]	5.1	7.1	1.7	13.9
Food	22.8	51.2	6.9	80.9
Fuels	43.0	13.7	5.8	62.5
Manufactured and processed products	27.9	296.0	36.6	360.5
Residue	1.5	6.9	3.1	11.5
Total	109.5	392.3	57.9	559.7

Source: General Agreement on Tariffs and Trade, *International Trade, 1974–75* (Geneva: GATT, 1976), table E.
a. Nonferrous metals—as distinct from ores—are included in manufactured and processed products.

aggregate, only 30 percent of the exports of nonfuel primary commodities originate in the developing countries.

The developing countries, moreover, have much larger export interests in agricultural commodities than in nonfuel minerals. More than four-fifths of their nonoil primary commodity exports in 1973 consisted of food (principally oil seeds, coffee, sugar, cocoa, and bananas) and agricultural raw materials (raw cotton, natural rubber, and hard fibers). Mineral ores (copper, bauxite, tin, and phosphate rock, for example), which are often cited as materials that lend themselves to cartelization and market manipulation, account for a comparatively small proportion of the commodity trade of these countries.

Programs designed to hold the prices of raw materials at artificially high levels are not the most effective way to transfer resources to the developing countries. These countries are not only exporters of raw materials; they are also importers of raw materials and to that extent their interests will be adversely affected (as with oil) by high prices. For a number of raw materials, moreover, a successful high price policy would benefit some rich countries more than poor countries. In general, the final consequence of artificially high prices is market shrinkage, as the growth of demand is checked and the search for alternatives and substitutes is stimulated. Capital resources are then locked in to products that have a poor economic future.

These considerations are enough to cast doubt on the proposition that producer cartels will govern primary commodity markets in the future. When it is further recalled that the developing countries concerned usually have small financial reserves and are not drawn together by shared political aims, the outlook for more OPECs can be seen in proper perspective. Cartel experiments among the primary commodity exporters will be few and most of those attempted will be short-lived.

Some aspects of the primary commodity markets require closer international attention, however.

Wide fluctuations in commodity prices such as in 1973–75 are not in the common interest. On the downswing, the fall in foreign exchange earnings can disrupt otherwise feasible economic development programs in the developing countries. For the industrial countries, the upswing of a commodity cycle is often built into the general price structure, adding to the problem of controlling inflation.

Hostility to foreign investment in natural resource industries, a phenomenon not wholly restricted to developing countries, is cause for concern. It will not necessarily halt development or expansion, for investment funds will still flow to areas that are or appear to be politically safe. But second-best investment choices mean higher real costs for commodities. And to the extent that resistance to foreign investors slows down the growth of commodity output, bottlenecks will appear earlier in the next boom.

Even though the possibilities for the effective cartelization of raw materials can be largely discounted, attempts to restrict export supplies of some commodities may be made for a variety of reasons. The potential costs of such supply interruptions could go well beyond the immediate difficulties of coping with bottlenecks or like problems. Industries and distributors in importing countries will be forced to look for other supply sources and for substitutes. Once these are found or developed, it will seem rational to protect them from lower-cost but unreliable suppliers. A proliferation of restrictions along these lines could damage world trade generally and the development prospects of particular countries directly.

A single policy approach to the varied problems of primary commodity markets is infeasible. If the primary commodity sector is to become less controversial and contribute more to growth and stability, policies will have to be fitted to specific situations.

Price stabilization arrangements between producers and consumers are possible for a limited number of commodities exported principally by the developing countries. The candidates here include coffee, cocoa, and tin, for which international agreements already have been negotiated, and copper, rubber, tea, sugar, and hard fibers, for which the prospects are at least worth serious exploration. In such agreements buffer stocks, financed principally by the industrial countries on an individual commodity basis, are likely to be more useful than export quotas as the principal stabilizing device. It must be recognized, however, that buffer stocks can work only if it is agreed that substantial changes in their size will be decisive signals for changing the price objectives.

Compensatory financing facilities can supplement individual commodity agreements as a means of bringing greater stability to the earnings of developing countries. The recent liberalization of the compensatory financing facility of the International Monetary Fund is an important step in this direction. Additional measures to strengthen the IMF's capability to carry out a countercyclical lending program for the developing countries could be the next step.

A reduction in tariffs and other barriers to trade would increase the benefits that producing countries receive from primary commodities and reduce the waste that occurs when the location of processing plants is determined by artificial factors. As pointed out earlier, existing tariff structures discriminate against processing in the primary producing countries.

Investment in primary commodity industries can be supported by more extensive use of intergovernmental financing facilities. The possibilities include increased World Bank lending for raw material development projects, a more ambitious program of participation investment by the World Bank's International Finance Corporation, and a new multilateral investment facility specifically designed to promote primary commodity development.

Finally, for some commodities—notably among the minerals—where buffer stock arrangements between producers and consumers prove neither negotiable nor appropriate and where sources of supply could be unreliable, industrial countries could work out economic stockpiling arrangements for stabilization as well as defensive purposes. They could agree to acquire stocks on a coordinated basis when markets are soft and to dispose of them when markets are tight. This would help avoid wide swings in prices and smooth the flow of investment in raw materials, and could provide security against price gouging and panic buying in times of shortage.

Measures to stabilize prices and earnings and to promote investment in lowest cost sources of supply would at least help to depoliticize primary commodity issues. The ideological fervor brought to commodity questions is real enough but is hardly warranted by the facts. If producers err in believing that prices can be raised permanently above market levels, consumers who argue that all price fluctuations, however wide, can be justified as necessary to restore equilibrium are also wrong. The truth is that commodity markets are both imperfect and the best allocative mechanisms available. Official intervention can make matters worse or better, depending on how it is conducted; the possibility of worse outcomes argues for case-by-case caution but not for hands off in any circumstance.

Because the resource position of the United States is relatively favorable, insulation of the domestic market from world commodity markets might be an attainable goal. It would require a system of commodity stockpiles, supported by a readiness to apply export controls without restraint in times of stringency. To state these conditions is to suggest how devastating to the international system the policy would be. The trading partners of the United States would be driven to defensive measures: the development of substitute supply sources, regional sharing arrangements, and restrictions on imports or exports, commodity by commodity. At the end of this process the world economy would be moving back to where it was in the 1930s.

East-West Economic Relations

Much of the discussion of East-West economic relations is based on shaky premises. One is that the Soviet Union, Eastern Europe as a whole, or Eastern Europe plus China promise to become very large export markets for the United States or for all the industrial market economies. A second is that the communist states gain excessively from trade with the West; this finds its ultimate expression in the declaration, "We should not *give* them anything." A third is that access to Western technology is the key to Soviet or communist economic progress and, by an easy extension, that it gives the United States and other Western states special bargaining power vis-à-vis the USSR or China.

Little time should be spent wondering about the size of the market in the communist countries. After fifteen years of steady growth, the imports of what the GATT calls "the Eastern trading area" make up only 5.3 percent of the total exports of North America, Western Europe, and Japan and 3.6 percent of the exports of the developing countries. It should be evident that any marked upsurge is not probable, or even possible.

China is a very large but very poor country whose low per capita output is a severe and lasting limitation on trade prospects. With the exception of the USSR, the Eastern European countries are small and per capita incomes are three-fourths the average for Western Europe. Even if the economies of these communist states became much more open, the resulting trade opportunities for the West could not be very great.

The USSR is a large country with per capita income probably slightly higher than that in Italy. If the economic system were to be redirected sharply away from central dictation and an emphasis on self-sufficiency, the USSR, at the extreme, might develop a dependence on trade similar to that of the United States now—with imports amounting to 7 or 8 percent of GNP rather than the present 4 percent or less. On this abstract assumption, Soviet imports today would be about $50 billion, or considerably less than those of Japan.

No such change in the Soviet system is in sight. Meanwhile, nearly half of the quite modest volume of imports into the USSR comes from its Eastern European neighbors in a trading pattern that is at least in part politically imposed and unlikely to change soon.

As for the belief that the USSR or any communist state inevitably will get the best of things in trade with the West, the logic is thin to the point of invisibility. Given time for things to work themselves out, comparative advantage applies to the trade of the nonmarket as well as of the market economies. All parties to commercial exchanges may be expected to gain—from realizing opportunities to use resources more efficiently—but nobody is "given" anything.

As for which parties to trade are in the best position to maximize gains, a planned economy is at a distinct disadvantage compared with a private enterprise system. This is because the gains from trade depend on shifts of capital and labor among industries and economic sectors. In a market economy, relatively small changes in returns to capital and labor will induce movements into export industries and out of import-competing industries. In a centrally managed economy, the decisions must be made from the top according to procedures that are bound to be slower and more prone to error than in a decentralized system.

There is also the notion that the communist states are able to make undue gains from trade simply by operating as single buyers in markets where sellers are in competition with one another. State agencies acting as monopsonists allegedly can play would-be suppliers from the West against each other until prices have been shaved to a profitless minimum, while communist exports sell at world prices, which include normal profits.

It is never explained why Western exporters should continue to try to sell to the planned economies in these circumstances. Since interest in the Soviet and Chinese markets remains high and the trade from all accounts is profitable, the explanation may be that it is not easy in a big, fragmented bureaucracy to operate a monopsony, that the suppliers are less competitive and more oligopolistic than is assumed, or both. But any factual foundation for fears about predatory communist monopsonists having their way with gullible capitalists is not apparent.

International trade in technologically advanced equipment, patent rights, blueprints, or various forms of expertise is commonly considered more helpful to the East and thus less desirable to the West than exports of, say, wheat or feed grain or blue denim trousers or shoes.

This generalization implies that the communist countries are backward in technological knowledge rather than in its application. But the least productive of communist industries—and this is certainly true of the Soviet Union—is agriculture, followed closely by consumer goods. Industries producing technically more advanced items, though lagging behind the best Western practice, seem to do better; and the production of military hardware requiring a high level of technology is believed by observers of the Soviet economy to be the most efficient of all. To maximize its gains from trade, Moscow should be importing grain and trousers, where the Soviet system works badly, and transferring capital and labor to the so-called advanced technology sectors, where it does better.

The Soviet leaders do seem to believe that Western equipment and technical knowledge can help them with their chronic domestic economic difficulties. But access to foreign machines and knowledge cannot solve the problems of running a command economy. The USSR is a big industrial country, demonstrably capable of making complex technical equipment as well as goods of all other kinds. That this equipment is less good than the best, or even than the average, in the West is a relevant but hardly decisive consideration. Imported machines, or the technology needed to construct them, may improve matters by allowing some reshuffling of resources, leading to increased production. But a comparatively small amount of imported technology—which must be paid for in exports of real goods or services—will not suddenly and radically expand the volume of domestic output in an economy that is already generating $700 billion of goods and services, that has its own scientists and skilled technicians, and that can build computers and missiles and spacecraft. Lags in Soviet productivity derive far more from inadequate motivation and an unwieldy organizational structure than from technical shortcomings.

China differs from the USSR in that China is technologically far less advanced. Its industries may thus have more bottlenecks that Western technique or equipment could relieve. On the other hand, China's poverty limits what it can afford to buy abroad, and its prevailing backwardness limits its ability to absorb and apply advanced technology.

Once the mystification surrounding East-West economic relations is lessened, the lines of sensible policy for the United States fall into place. Since there is no objective basis for believing that trade in non-military goods with the East either raises special security risks or affords special political leverage, an essentially hands-off official approach ought to be the objective.

Neutral policy does not imply equal treatment in all respects. There is a genuine problem of reciprocity in the application of GATT most-favored-nation treatment to the USSR and other non-market economies. When trade is entirely determined by governmental fiat, the GATT premise that equalizing trade opportunities is enough does not hold, and bilateral agreements to assure equality of treatment are justified. To be most effective, these should be negotiated within the terms of a standard OECD agreement that would establish uniform East-West trade practices.

Nor should trade be subsidized. Although its material significance is small, Western governments' practice of underwriting better than commercial terms for exports to the USSR and China is collective foolishness; an agreement among the OECD countries to end these minor but still indefensible subsidies is long overdue.

For the United States to follow an essentially neutral policy in economic relations with the East does not require a judgment that increased East-West trade (and eventually investment) will modify in desirable ways the character of communist regimes. Normal—or as normal as possible—economic relations will not affect the relative power positions of the West or the East enough to matter. If the trend of developments in the USSR is otherwise favorable to U.S. interests, the economic benefits from what will still be a comparatively small volume of commerce will be more welcome. In the event of unacceptable Soviet political behavior, the option of a break in economic relations will be available, not as a powerful lever in itself, but as an unmistakable political response and one that is not now open to the United States.

Foreign Investment and Development Assistance

Long-term capital outflows have preoccupied American foreign policy since immediately after the war. The premise has been that foreign investment, like trade, helps bring about a more efficient allocation of resources among all countries. As the world's richest nation, the United States would normally be expected to be a net contributor of capital to the rest of the international economy, a role that would advance its interests at home and abroad.

At an early point, it was decided that market forces alone would not induce an outflow of funds sufficient to achieve U.S. foreign policy objectives. The Marshall Plan, and later Point Four and development assistance, were created to help fill this perceived gap. Incentives were given to private investors for much the same purpose. These elements of policy remain in force still, though they are attenuated, applied selectively, and involve much soul-searching about their pertinence to the pursuit of U.S. interests in the developing countries.

The persisting balance-of-payments deficits of the 1960s turned official policy to restraints on private capital exports other than those to developing countries. At the same time, misgivings were growing abroad about the increasing volume of direct investment by American private firms, which became, by virtue of their having subsidiaries abroad, multinational corporations. The official restraints on capital exports have since been dropped, but controversy over the merits of foreign direct investment—in addition to allegations of specific sins of commission by multinational firms—has heightened. At home, opposition is based on the belief that direct investment abroad is harmful to domestic employment, skews income distribution against labor, or is a vehicle for evading taxes. In many countries that are hosts to U.S. foreign investment, antagonism toward the multinationals arises from a variety of sources, ranging from fear of excessive political influence to the conviction that this form of investment is inherently exploitative. Even in the United States, apprehension was aroused when the inflow of direct investment appeared in 1973–74 to be reaching an unusually high level.

Policies toward private investment flows, outgoing and incoming, thus bear on American foreign relations generally. If outflows are in fact at the expense of employment and income at home, should policy not be outright restrictive rather than neutral or encouraging? If, on the other hand, flows from capital-rich to capital-poor countries (or, for that matter, between capital-rich countries in response to market-determined opportunities) do make economic sense, can policies be devised to foster private investment where it promises to be most productive? It is as well to sort out these issues before considering the special case of capital exports in the form of development aid.

PRIVATE FOREIGN INVESTMENT. The United States is of course the world's largest exporter of private capital. Table 5-8 presents data on long-term private investment flows to the rest of the world, earnings therefrom, and for comparison, gross domestic private investment.

The comparatively small size of net direct investment outflows casts doubt on the proposition that they can have had any marked influence on domestic employment in the United States or on the distribution of income between capital and labor. Even on the extreme assumptions that all past outflows, direct and portfolio, preempted savings that otherwise would have been invested at home and that no repatriated earnings were invested, the numbers seem hardly to justify all the excitement.

A return to first principles may be a more useful approach, especially since the advent of flexible exchange rates has much diminished worry about the impact of investment abroad on the balance of payments. It is reasonable to suppose that the relatively marginal

Table 5-8. Relation of Net Outflow and Income from U.S. Private Long-Term Investment Abroad to Gross Domestic Investment, Five-Year Averages, 1960–74

Billions of dollars

Description	1960–64	1965–69	1970–74
Net long-term outflow[a]	−2.9	−1.8	−2.8
Net direct investment	−1.8	−2.9	−3.7
Other long-term investments	−1.1	1.1	0.9
Net income from investments abroad[b]	3.1	3.8	7.4
Direct investment	2.8	3.7	7.1
Other long-term investments	0.3	0.1	0.3
Gross domestic private fixed investment, nonresidential	51.9	84.6	121.2
Net long-term outflow as percent of gross domestic private fixed investment	5.6	2.1	2.3

Sources: Calculated from data in *Survey of Current Business*, vol. 55 (June 1975), pp. 30–31, and *Economic Report of the President, January 1976*, pp. 181, 184.

a. Minus sign indicates outflow.
b. Income does not include fees and royalties.

amounts of American savings invested outside the country are made in the expectation of higher than normal returns. It is also reasonable to suppose that the countries receiving foreign investments benefit in rising incomes, or else presumably they would act to prevent inward flows. The process allows exploitation of comparative advantages all around, bringing positive returns net of any adjustment costs. As with international trade, both parties gain from the transactions. To ignore these dynamics of foreign investment is to forget the central point.

Moreover, the term "multinational corporation" colors thinking in unfortunate ways. A subsidiary of a foreign corporation is an integral part of the domestic economy of the country in which it operates, using that country's labor and materials and, in many cases, its capital. As a vehicle for foreign investment the corporation can bring together management, technology, and capital in a single package; the postwar growth of direct foreign investment suggests that this advantage is important. But the multinational firm is not beyond the reach of governments. It is subject to—sometimes hostage to—the sovereign power of the nations in which it operates. Should individual companies act in antisocial ways, recent experience is ample proof that adequate sanctions are available to national governments.

The issues that do deserve attention relate to artificial factors or social inefficiencies in foreign investment. Not all investment flows take place in environments comparatively free of distorting forces. Tax or tariff or other policies may lead to an international allocation of savings different from what more neutral policies would bring. Governments can and do seek to manipulate foreign investment in ways they conceive to be domestically advantageous. And because multinational firms often are large and operate in oligopolistic industries, there are legitimate questions about the effect of some direct investments on competition.

The solutions to these kinds of problems seem to lie in specific remedies rather than in a blanket condemnation of foreign direct investment. If tax policy favors foreign over domestic investment— a point that ought to be susceptible of factual determination—tax laws should be changed in the direction of neutrality. Similarly, if competition is the issue, antitrust statutes should be made effective against multinational as well as against wholly domestic companies. The U.S. policy of providing official insurance against political risks as a stimulus to investment in the developing countries is questionable on allocative grounds, as well as because it can engage the government more than may be desirable in nationalization and expropriation issues.

To be fully effective, these remedies would require international collaboration, but the policies of other governments obviously are beyond U.S. control. Where governments find the local presence of foreign corporations politically embarrassing or otherwise undesired, there can be little point in insisting on an American right to invest, even when treaty commitments ostensibly guarantee that right. The United States cannot enforce an international leveling of corporate tax rates or outlaw other nations' investment incentives (the less so because in many of its own states and regions similar incentives are offered to investors, foreign as well as domestic). Nor can it prevent host countries from imposing onerous regulations on foreign investors, from expropriating them without compensation, or from tolerating or encouraging monopolistic practices. Some sources of distortion—tariffs, for one—can be alleviated by negotiation, however. Others, like tax rates, may be open to greater harmonization, although corporate tax differences are already quite small among the industrial countries. Still others may be to some extent self-correcting as their efficiency costs are further assessed by governments.

A code for foreign investment could be helpful. Just as the GATT has reduced the arbitrary elements in national trade policies, international agreements could reduce distortions in the flows of private investment. If a suitable text could be agreed upon, political leaders might be able to take a less polemical position toward foreign investment. A code would be particularly useful if it established, along with guidelines for corporate conduct, the goal of official investment neutrality and recognized the importance of internationally accepted procedures for settling investment disputes.

The OECD countries have taken a step in this direction. They have agreed on a code that includes guidelines both for government policies toward foreign investment and for the behavior of multinational corporations. Its provisions are not binding but they form a basis for consultation and should reduce distortion and friction.

Prospects that this or any other acceptable code could be extended to the developing countries are likely to be poor for a number of years ahead. Hostility to foreign investment has been spreading in these countries and in many cases investment issues have become politically sensitive. Where this is so the United States and other industrial countries have only limited possibilities for changing matters. They should attempt to deal with the problem as much as possible through multilateral approaches—international rather than national investment guarantee programs, greater reliance on joint ventures, including the active participation of international financial institutions, and renewed attempts to negotiate rules for the settlement of disputes. In the end, however, the principal antidote to hostility toward foreign investment will be evidence that it is making an economic and politically acceptable contribution in countries where development is succeeding.

A commonsense view also ought to apply to U.S. policy toward foreign investment in the United States. The anxiety so widely expressed in 1974 about the dangers of possible OPEC investments in American industry reflected a curiously inverted idea of the capacities of the U.S. government to enforce its own laws and administrative rules, as well as an unrealistic perception of the likely motives of OPEC investors. Measured against the enormous mass of domestic assets, incoming foreign investment, whether portfolio or direct, will have only a modest place in the American economy. But within its limits it ought to be accepted as benefiting American welfare.

OFFICIAL DEVELOPMENT AID. Measures to promote capital exports to the developing countries represent a major departure from the policy of letting the market determine capital flows. Outright grants, concessional loans, and subsidies to private lenders and investors can be seen as means either of supplementing market-oriented private lending and investment or of compensating for their absence. These measures are justified by the belief that their contribution to economic growth and welfare in the low-income countries will sustain and advance U.S. interests. The basic proposition may be stated as follows: to be able to avoid a situation in which poverty and population pressure create intolerable moral, political, and economic tension, global material well-being must improve; this requires larger flows of capital to poor countries than market forces alone will provide.

There are many more particular arguments in support of this belief that need not be repeated or reviewed here. Suffice it to say that all industrial countries[8] have long since accepted the premise that

8. Including the Soviet Union and the Eastern European countries and, for that matter, a conspicuously low-income nonindustrial country, China.

development aid policies advance a national purpose. Development aid can thus be expected to be a part of foreign economic policy in this country, and in Japan and the Western European nations as well, indefinitely.

The most pertinent issues come down to three main questions. To which countries should development aid be extended? How much aid is required, or desirable, or feasible? Through what mechanisms or institutions should aid be provided?

Which countries qualify as being dependent on concessional capital flows should surely be principally determined by levels of per capita income or GNP. The poorest countries—those, say, where the World Bank estimated per capita GNP in 1973 to be less than $300 —are precisely those least likely to be able to generate domestic savings and to attract enough foreign loans and investments to achieve rates of economic growth running much ahead of population increase. If development assistance is to promote its central objective, special emphasis must be placed on flows of funds to the lowest income countries.

Of the 2 billion people in the developing world (excluding China), some 1.2 billion are found in the poorest countries. Roughly three-fifths are concentrated in four countries of South Asia (India, Pakistan, Bangladesh, and Sri Lanka) and another one-fifth in Africa south of the Sahara. The common thread among these countries is that the margin of resources for development is narrow. This hard core of very poor nations will be in need of external capital on easier than market terms for an extended period.

The remaining claimants for development aid are the countries falling between the lowest income category and the high-income oil producers. This group includes the rapidly growing countries in Asia and Africa, most of the Latin American nations, and the poorer countries of southern Europe. Many of them already rely on private capital inflows for much of their external resources. They are also the principal borrowers of long-term funds at near-commercial rates from the World Bank and the regional banks, they draw on the temporary credit facilities of the IMF, and they receive bilateral loans from OECD and OPEC governments.

Thus the flow of capital to developing countries is of a mixed character. In 1974 the total from all sources (OECD, OPEC, and the communist countries) came to roughly $41 billion, net of amortization payments. Private capital (direct investment, Eurocurrency borrowing, and other private loans) amounted to $21 billion, almost all of which went to the higher income countries. Another $6 billion consisted of government export credits and loans from the international financial institutions. Most of these also went to the higher income countries. The remaining $14 billion was concessional, consisting of $3 billion in technical assistance grants, $2 billion in grant-like loans from multilateral institutions, and $9 billion in a variety of bilateral loans and grants, including food aid. The poorest countries—those with per capita income below $300 a year—received perhaps half the total concessional aid.

Some other aspects of the present situation should be kept in mind. Concessional aid, which provokes the most difficult problems for appropriations and burden sharing, amounted in 1974 to only one-third of 1 percent of the gross national product of all OECD countries, the proportion for the United States being below this average. In real terms, the volume is down almost 10 percent from the level of a decade ago. On the other hand, because private capital expanded so rapidly, the volume of total capital flows to developing countries is about one-third larger than it was in 1964. In part, this change is the result of recent extraordinary borrowing by the developing countries to maintain economic growth despite higher oil import costs. Nonetheless, the figures are evidence that many of these countries have been able to lessen their dependence on concessional capital and rely more heavily on external capital obtained at market or near-market terms.

A substantial increase in concessional loans and grants probably will be necessary to help solve the food and population problems in the poorest countries. The volume of this capital may be an important determinant of the long-term prospects of the international system. It is true that the economic future of even the poorest nations will be decided chiefly by their own efforts; no conceivable flow of external resources alone could be sufficient to deal with their problems. Nonetheless, external funds can be important, if not critical, as both a stimulant and supplement to the mobilization of domestic capital.

South Asia and Africa south of the Sahara represent most of the problem. In 1974 aid flows equaled about 15 percent of gross investment in South Asia and probably a considerably higher percentage in the poorest countries of Africa. These amounts suggest only that concessional aid must have figured significantly in economic development in the two regions. Without aid, investment and per capita income growth would have had to be smaller, the capacity to save and invest in the future lower. As matters stand, however, with a few exceptions among the African states, the countries of both regions have been lagging well behind the developing countries as a whole in per capita growth. There is a prima facie case that without much larger external resource flows the prospects of these poorest regions are quite bleak. For, based on the present outlook, it would be quixotic to expect private investors or lenders to risk substantial resources in these poor, low-growth countries. Increased development aid, however, could improve the prospect of mobilizing domestic savings, which is the key to more rapid economic growth.

In the more dynamic economies, the trend toward declining concessional aid and increased reliance on private capital should continue, but here again a larger volume of official capital may be decisive. Despite their impressive economic performance over the past decade, the financial position of these countries could become precarious, essentially for reasons beyond their control. Their credit position is vulnerable to cyclical downturns in industrial countries, which quickly depress their export earnings; to shifting judgments of foreign lenders and investors about their long-term prospects; and to the heavy foreign exchange cost imposed by higher oil import prices, a burden that will probably continue well into the future. To make an orderly transition to economic self-reliance at high rates of economic growth, these countries will need increased access to foreign official capital, not necessarily on concessional terms, to strengthen as well as supplement their access to foreign private capital.

One major means of boosting the volume of this type of official capital could take the form of a large expansion of the long-term hard lending of the World Bank and the regional financial institutions. This would require periodic increases in their authorized capital, which enables them to borrow on private markets for relending at market rates to creditworthy developing countries. Through this mechanism the donor member countries of these institutions are in effect guarantors for a flow of funds moving from private lenders to developing country borrowers. Because the loans are long term they improve the general financial position of the developing countries and hence their ability to borrow directly from private markets. Because they are made through the international institutions, the credit risks can be equitably apportioned among the industrial countries.

Another requirement would be an increase in the capacity of the developing countries to borrow official capital for countercyclical purposes and thus protect their economic programs against recession in the industrial countries. Here the IMF could play the primary role. This would be facilitated by periodic increases in Fund quotas, and by authorizing the Fund to use its compensatory financing facilities to lend against a cyclical deterioration in the terms of trade in addition to a shortfall in export earnings. Increased borrowing by developing countries in a recession and repayment during an economic upswing would have the additional benefit of reducing the severity of cyclical disturbances in the industrial countries.

Thus future requirements strongly indicate the need for a multilateral approach to the problem. Bilateral aid will continue to exist and to serve its diverse national purposes, but it cannot be relied upon to meet future development assistance needs and its political disabilities are likely to increase. It is becoming an anachronism.

This applies especially to aid for the poorest countries, where the very intractability of the economic problem argues for concessional and nonpolitical flows of external capital, continued over long periods. The multilateral institutions—the World Bank and the regional banks—are now the channels for a large share of official development lending and are in a position to deal with the recipient countries on a professional basis. It makes more sense than ever for the donor countries to pool their aid resources and let such institutions handle them. The World Bank's International Development Association and the soft loan facilities of the regional banks are particularly important here. If a sustained and determined effort to break the poverty-breeds-poverty cycle is to be assured, these multilateral agencies will have to be given a central responsibility for it.

A next step in aid policy should be to regularize, as much as possible, a lending program for the poorest countries through periodic world aid budgets. The World Bank could be requested to assemble experts from the regional banks and the United Nations to prepare three-to-five-year estimates of soft loan requirements as part of an assessment of total capital needs for the developing countries. This budget could be submitted for review to the Development Committee (a joint ministerial committee of the boards of governors of the World Bank and the IMF), which could then make recommendations to governments.

Progress in building a strong world development effort depends heavily on U.S. actions. The United States now accounts for 40 percent of the production of the OECD countries; it need not supply more than its share of foreign aid but should not supply less, as it does now. A lagging U.S. performance could ultimately cause other industrial countries also to do less, and would certainly preclude improvements. The same point applies to the conduct of foreign aid. At present, world policy is in a vacuum. While the United States will have occasion to supply bilateral, politically motivated aid, its emphasis should be on strengthening the international development system. A phasing out of U.S. bilateral development lending and a willingness to substantially increase U.S. contributions to the international financial institutions would invigorate the world development program and create a promising foundation for relations between industrial and developing countries.

The International Monetary System: Will Prosperity Be Divisible?

After the failure of attempts to replace the Bretton Woods monetary arrangements with a similarly structured system, the major financial powers appear to be set on a course of experiment and evolution in international monetary affairs. This is not a disturbing turn of events. The lack after 1971 of well-defined monetary rules did not lead to a disruption of international trade and investment or to a breakdown of international cooperation. There seems no reason to expect that private markets will be less resilient or governments more inclined to economic isolation in the future.

The limited monetary understandings that have been arrived at seem likely actually to promote rather than impede trends toward economic cooperation. The essentials that have been agreed upon are that exchange rates between the major currencies will continue to be flexible, that governments may choose to manage the extent of that flexibility, and that intergovernmental coordination will be required to ensure that policies for managing exchange rates are reasonably consistent.

The accord reached at the IMF meeting in Jamaica in January

1976 specifically recognizes, moreover, as the Bretton Woods articles did not, that "underlying conditions"—that is, domestic macro-economic policies—ultimately determine exchange market developments. The coordination process therefore seems bound to go beyond the tactics of central bank intervention to consideration of the demand management policies of the major countries and their interactions with one another. How far coordination of policy will go is still uncertain, to be sure, but the logic for making the effort is compelling.

Apart from the formal agreement on a flexible exchange rate regime, monetary reform has stalled, leaving to some indefinite later date action on the other principal issue: the control of international liquidity. As matters stand, the situation is certainly untidy. Monetary reserves are held in multiple forms: principally dollars, marks, sterling, gold, IMF quotas, and IMF special drawing rights (SDRs). Eurocurrency markets, swollen with deposits of oil producers, have been a channel for creating large reserves through official borrowing. Total reserves as customarily counted more than doubled in the five years between the end of 1970 and the end of 1975; if gold were generally valued nearer its market price, the increase would be much greater still. All this is a far cry from the expectation of a monetary system based on the carefully monitored issuance of an international reserve asset, the SDR, with other forms of reserves being greatly reduced or simply retired.

There are hazards in the prevailing disorganization. Reserves created by revaluing gold, by borrowing OPEC surpluses, or by financing a reserve-currency country's deficit could strengthen inflationary forces. Futhermore, central bank decisions to shift reserves from one asset to another could cause undesirable and possibly costly exchange rate movements.

These dangers are real enough, but it is much less certain that measures to cope with them are a matter of urgency. Although reserves have increased greatly since 1970, their size in relation to the value of international trade has declined; and reserve growth in 1974–75 was almost entirely confined to the OPEC countries. To revalue official gold effectively requires that buyers be found, but private markets could not and central banks probably would not be ready to buy unlimited amounts of official gold at anything close to present free market prices. Eurocurrency borrowing cannot be continued indefinitely. Shifts of reserve currency holdings do take place but largely in response to differences in interest rates and to expectations about inflation—factors that would cause instability in exchange rates in any circumstances.

In practical terms, technical, political, and economic complexities preclude another round of monetary reform in the near future. Eventually international liquidity issues will have to be faced. The most obvious approach to solving them would be the building of an SDR-centered system, much of which could be achieved by consolidating reserve currencies into SDRs and by creating a gold substitution account in the IMF in which national gold stocks could be deposited and ultimately disposed of in private markets. The IMF's Committee of Twenty offered some cautious thoughts along these lines when it made its interim recommendations for reform in 1974. These and other proposals ought to be fully developed and argued because the subject is too important to be shelved, even though it cannot be settled now. Meanwhile, more experience with a flexible exchange rate system will improve understanding of how much international liquidity is needed, how best to manage intervention in exchange markets, and the urgency of reserve consolidation.

One aspect of reform, the disposal of IMF gold stocks, could be improved upon under the new IMF Articles. The Jamaica accord stipulates that one-sixth of the IMF's gold be sold at the low official price to Fund members in proportion to their quotas and one-sixth be sold by the IMF in the private market over a four-year period, with the profits, or the difference between the realized price and the official price of $42 an ounce, going directly or indirectly to the developing countries. The agreement to return IMF gold to members was an unfortunate compromise, since it gives the OECD and OPEC countries gold to which they have no legal claim and on which potentially large profits could be realized—profits that should properly accrue to the international community and be used for internationally agreed upon purposes. The Fund should be authorized to sell the remaining two-thirds of its gold in an orderly way and use the proceeds entirely for the benefit of the developing countries, particularly the poorest countries among them. This would provide a useful supplementary source of highly concessional development assistance—the most urgently needed form of foreign aid.

Meanwhile the focus of policy must be on the performance of the exchange markets and on their links with demand management. This subject was considered by the heads of government of the largest OECD countries at the Rambouillet conference in November 1975 and the Puerto Rico conference in June 1976 and will continue to be a major question for international policy in the future.

For more than a decade the chief OECD countries have been persistently if gropingly seeking greater consistency of domestic economic decisionmaking. The OECD charter (circa 1961) commits its signatories to the pursuit of "policies designed to achieve economic growth and internal and *external* financial stability and *to avoid* developments which might endanger their economies *or those of other countries*" (emphasis added). The consultation process that was developed under this article has been conducted with a regularity that certainly suggests a general acceptance of the necessity for a systematic exchange of information on basic policies among the main industrial countries.

The 1972–75 sequence of synchronized global boom and recession has raised more acutely the question of international policy coordination. Worldwide inflation accompanying the boom was the worst in peacetime history; the subsequent world recession the sharpest since the 1930s. The distortions flowing from the inflation and the enormous losses in output incurred during the recession will continue to affect all economies for years to come. Surely the inflation was heightened and the recession deepened because demand-management policies in each of the major industrial countries were formulated without taking sufficient account of the policies of other countries.

To recognize that interdependence implies causal connections between national macroeconomic decisions is not to say that policy coordination is readily achievable. In the 1960s economists pointed out that to maintain fixed exchange rates required more nearly common monetary policies than were being followed, but the prescription or warning was for the most part cheerfully ignored. Even within the tightly knit trading community of Western Europe, all efforts so far to keep demand management policies aligned have had only partial success. The difficulty is not mere political perversity. Differing degrees of concern about inflation or unemployment can create different pressures on national governments. Or if the efficacy for short periods of either monetary or fiscal policies varies from country to country, the intended coordination of policies may be hampered by longer or shorter lags between policy actions and economic responses. Demand management is not a certain enough procedure to make policy coordination among the big economies a simple matter.

All the same, the pull is likely to be toward coordination, since the notion of wholly independent macroeconomic policies is in varying degrees a political and economic illusion. This pull will be felt at first through developments in exchange markets.

Exchange rate flexibility is an incomplete means of insulating an open economy from policy decisions taken abroad or from external constraints on domestic policy decisions. The hope that under a flexible regime small changes in rates normally will set off stabilizing speculation has not been realized. Instead, exchange rate swings have been wide and often erratic. This can be partly explained by international flows of short-term funds in response to yield differences or in reaction to expectations about variation in inflation rates, which in turn are strongly affected by the monetary policies of the major countries. In any event, large, irregular fluctuations in exchange rates complicate the problems of achieving price stability and create distortions in the competitive position of internationally traded goods industries. If private speculative movements do not offset these disturbances, it is sensible, or at least understandable, for governments to intervene themselves rather than permit what might be unnecessarily costly corrections in the trade accounts. Following the Jamaica accord, central banks (ultimately national political authorities) will continue to attempt to stabilize exchange markets; daily consultations are intended to assure consistency in the intervention activities of monetary authorities.

The same central banks and political authorities that decide on exchange market intervention, however, will be responsible for shaping the national macroeconomic policies affecting short-run exchange rate movements. Inevitably the consultation process will have to go beyond questions of exchange market intervention and cover domestic demand policies as well. The test will be whether countries modify their domestic policies in the interests of a closer international concert of policies.

The commanding position of the American economy and the status of the dollar as the leading reserve currency give this country a capability for independent action no other industrial market economy has. Since the impacts of decisions by others can be absorbed more readily here, the case for coordinating U.S. policies with those of others may be viewed as less compelling than for other countries. Nonetheless, the effect on the U.S. economy of changes in demand in other countries is not trivial, and the United States has a clear interest in how exchange rates are managed elsewhere, which suggests a significant concern about aggregate demand policies that are proposed or adopted in other countries. Since U.S. policies can have a pervasive influence on other countries, the process of consultation and coordination will have to be mutual.

Whether international coordination will require modifications in U.S. domestic policies or in the combination of U.S. policy instruments will depend in the first instance on the performance of the U.S. economy. Probably the most important contribution the United States could make to the world economy would be to run its domestic economy on a noninflationary course at or near its growth potential. At the same time, in formulating policies to achieve this objective the United States will have to take into account the policies and problems of its major trading and financial partners and the effect of its own policies on others. The economic summit meetings and the Jamaica accord recognized that the economies of the United States, the European Community, and Japan are intimately linked. A stable prosperity may be either a phenomenon common to the principal economic powers or an unsustainable goal for any of them.

A Strategy for U.S. Foreign Economic Policy

The administration that takes office in 1977 presumably will wish to reassess the country's foreign economic policies. Priorities are not frozen and the most durable policy lines require periodic reexamination. After the recent turbulence in world economic affairs, stocktaking may well seem even more necessary.

Such a review will have to encompass specific policies—trade, energy, foreign aid, and so on. Each of these presents its own issues, to be pursued in separate negotiations. But the country needs a broad strategic framework for its external economic policies, as it does for foreign policy in general.

The objective of foreign economic policy is to shape global economic events so as to advance the material well-being, the security, and the humanitarian objectives of the American people.

It has been argued in this chapter that economic growth is a global imperative. American policies that successfully promote a fuller, more efficient use of global resources will mean higher standards of living at home. That economic progress abroad enhances domestic prosperity has been amply demonstrated by the positive impact on the U.S. economy of recovery and growth in Western Europe and Japan.

Foreign economic policy must also play a role in containing and reducing political tension in the world. This is far from an assertion that the sources of conflict among nations are or will be mainly economic. But U.S. political and security aims abroad can be pursued effectively only if economic policies are outward looking and directed toward fostering conditions in which all economies can prosper.

Since U.S. foreign economic policy will have to be globally oriented, perennial suggestions for an inter-American economic bloc or other exclusionist economic arrangements are unrealistic. In the conduct of the country's policy, however, the association with Western Europe and Japan, where security and economic interests are intertwined, must be emphasized. The United States cannot be insensitive to economic developments that could impede its continuing close association with its main allies.

Security interests apart, U.S. constructive actions will hardly be possible unless they are taken in common with the other principal OECD nations. For example, a crucial test for foreign economic policy in the decade ahead will be the provision of improved market access for exports of manufactured goods from the developing countries. Yet no country will be able alone to liberalize imports of low-wage goods, for fear of having its domestic industries overwhelmed. Similarly, defenses against potentially predatory OPEC pricing policies will require that the main importers, the OECD nations, present a common front. So will the creation of food reserves or the rationalization and strengthening of the development assistance regime or any other significant advance in international economic cooperation.

If current policies are to have a positive influence on the world a quarter-century hence, their bearing on economic developments in the low-income regions must be a central consideration. One requirement is that per capita income in the developing countries must steadily and substantially improve. While the OECD countries cannot assure this, they can help to establish some of the preconditions—not by a single policy but by a range of actions pertinent to the divergent situations of the developing countries. In some cases commodity policies will be important; in others, private capital flows; in still others, concessional aid. And trade policy will be a factor everywhere. The general aim is to accelerate the integration of the developing countries into the world economy.

As in the past, a sharing of responsibilities by the OECD countries could result in hesitant, stilted policy decisions, aimed principally at averting short-term risks. If so, the international economic system will not break up or collapse; the structure of international cooperation will rock along. Rather, the danger is that slow and inadequate international responses to serious economic problems, because the industial countries will underestimate their combined capacities for managing economic change, will involve very high long-term costs. Problems will build up, particularly in the critical area of North-South relations, that will call for much larger efforts and expenditures at a later time.

At present, the wrong choices are either being made or seem likely to be made on the central economic questions of the times. These wrong choices include putting off reducing barriers to labor-intensive imports out of exaggerated worry about the difficulties of making domestic adjustments; permitting OECD oil consumption to rise unchecked and thereby giving OPEC unhampered control of the world oil market; forgoing the creation of a reserve of cereals because it is a difficult task and because of a wishful belief that private markets will do the job; and failing to make possible the capital flows needed to assist the developing countries to maintain otherwise feasible rates of economic growth on the ground that the burden of exporting capital, much of it on essentially commercial terms, is too great.

A strategy fitted to a longer vision would find unacceptable the costs of deferring these feasible and necessary actions.

The decision will hinge to a large degree on U.S. attitudes. Initiatives in world economic affairs will have to come mainly from this country. Not only is the American economy still overwhelmingly large, but other potential leaders are subject to much greater political limitations on foreign economic policy than is the case in this country. The European Community must accommodate the differing outlooks of nine sovereign states. Japan sees itself as being uniquely vulnerable to external pressure. Passivity on the part of the United

States will thus mean inaction all around. There is no substitute for American leadership if a system of shared responsibilities and joint management is to work.

Leadership in foreign economic affairs does not mean that the United States would have to undertake large new budgetary outlays. The reduction of tariffs and other trade barriers doubtless would require expenditures for adjustment assistance, but these would be small in any foreseeable circumstance. Capital needs for developing countries increasingly could be supplied on market terms; the grant or concessional element could hardly exceed 1 percent of future federal budgets. A multilateral cereal reserve should balance costs and returns over a grain price cycle; even worst-case losses should be relatively small. Much the same considerations would apply to American shares in the financing of buffer stocks for other primary commodities.

The material gains to the nation from a successful foreign economic policy would far exceed any of these direct expenditures. Returns in the form of higher GNP would come from a more efficient allocation of productive resources, increased competition, lessened inflationary pressures, and less need for costly stop-go economic policies.

More speculative are the savings in security costs that could be realized from reduced tensions in the world, but these might be very large. A demonstration that the industrial democracies could cooperate effectively for their mutual well-being and at the same time deal rationally with the problems of the developing world could not fail to alter the world's political environment favorably. Potential gains here could swamp all other considerations, bringing long-lasting and extraordinary benefits to Americans and all other peoples.

CHAPTER SIX

Organizing for the Decade Ahead

GRAHAM ALLISON *and* PETER SZANTON

IF YOU ASKED a friend who had just dined with others at a Chinese restaurant what he had for dinner and why, the answer would almost certainly be posed in terms of personal preference—for twice-cooked pork, for example—and it would seem both accurate and complete. But the overriding fact would have been missed: namely, that the meal had been eaten at a Chinese restaurant. The friend may or may not have chosen the restaurant, but once that choice was made, the question of having a hamburger or *coq au vin* simply did not arise. The effects of the organization of the federal government on the "menu" of problems brought to the President's attention, on the information presented about them, on the alternative responses proposed, and on the execution of the course of action selected are equally pervasive, and equally easy to overlook.

As it turns to the conduct of our foreign relations, the next administration will find itself atop a "restaurant" whose influence on the substantive issues discussed in the preceding chapters will be profound, and whose limitations are as important as any problems of policy. Wittingly or not, the next President will begin to resolve or compound these deficiencies immediately with his first appointments to major office. Shortly thereafter, Congress will also be involved—

The diagnoses and proposals of this chapter, together with a broader analysis of recent organizational performance and a variety of additional recommendations, are developed in the authors' *Remaking Foreign Policy: The Organizational Connection* (Basic Books, forthcoming).

confirming or rejecting appointees, creating or disapproving new agencies, mandating new procedures. Progress in managing the policy issues of the next decade, therefore, will require early attention to organizational problems as well, and to the interactions between the two.

Some aspects of the organizational problem seem obvious. The view is quite common—and it is largely right—that many agencies of the federal government do not work well. That is so even when they work alone. When several departments interact, the results are often worse: delayed, piecemeal, disjointed. Clichés capture other pieces of the problem: the urgent drives out the important; government never foresees but always reacts; the postwar consensus is gone; Vietnam and Watergate have hobbled presidential leadership. But what relation do these half-truths have to each other, which are most important, and what can be done about them?

Our approach begins with the proposition that there is a central organizational problem of which many of the other problems are part: how to conduct a foreign policy that serves the nation's collective interests when power is broadly diffused among organizations that represent more particular concerns. The problem is not new in kind, but it is quite new in degree, and it is compounded by a constraining organizational legacy. The present structure of the U.S. government for the conduct of foreign policy dates largely from the late 1940s, and especially from 1947, when the National Security Act at one stroke unified the Department of Defense, created the Central Intelligence Agency, and established the National Security Council as the principal forum for presidential deliberation in foreign affairs. That structure was appropriate to its time, a time when foreign relations were dominated by an apparent military threat, when the U.S. economy was relatively autonomous, when "politics stopped at the water's edge," and when in foreign policy matters Congress deferred to the White House.

Times have changed. "Foreign" policy has almost disappeared as a distinct and specialized realm. The tightening economic and physical interdependence of nations now means that actions of one country affect the daily lives and consequently the domestic politics of others. Responsibility for policies that concern foreign governments is now shared within the executive branch not only among the Departments of State, Treasury, and Defense, but also among Agriculture, Labor, Transportation, Interior, the Federal Energy Administration—in fact, virtually every major agency other than Housing and Urban Development. Furthermore, authority is now divided between the executive and Congress, not only in constitutional theory but in fact, partly as a consequence of reaction to Vietnam and Watergate, but more importantly because interdependence has thrust foreign policy into domestic politics. Power is also far more broadly dispersed within Congress, partly because foreign policy issues cut across committee jurisdictions, partly because recent congressional leadership has been weak. Moreover, important influences on the formulation of foreign policy are now divided between the government and the private sector, a result both of the multinationalized industries and of the growing importance of economic factors—food production, inflation, the growth of the nuclear power industry—in the foreign policy agenda. Finally, power is somewhat more widely spread among nations, held not solely by two superstates or a "Big Five," but by six or eight nations of great population or productive strength and a dozen others of middling size, ambition, technical accomplishment, or important natural resources. Yet the organizational framework—"the restaurant"—in which America's foreign policy options are presented and decisions made remains largely unchanged.

The recent history of the oil issue illustrates vividly the resulting difficulties. A decision by a dozen oil-producing countries in 1973 to reduce oil exports and quadruple oil prices caught the United States unaware. The direct results included long lines at American filling stations, higher prices for gasoline, and a strong push toward double-digit inflation in 1974. Oil price hikes posed an even greater threat to the prosperity and political stability of our allies in Europe and Japan and to economic development in the fourth world. The immediate effects of the embargo were managed with more success than anyone had a right to expect, less by governments than by the multinational oil companies that allocated available oil equitably among the consuming nations and by the international banks that arranged the financing. After too long a period of stalemate between Secretary of State Henry Kissinger and Secretary of the Treasury William Simon, the United States did devise international initiatives that yielded important results, including agreements on oil stockpiles, sharing of available supplies in the event of future embargoes, and creation of the International Energy Agency.

But coping with this issue abroad depended on meeting it effectively at home. Here, the record is bleak. President Richard M. Nixon's response, "Project Independence," offered a rhetorical palliative rather than a realistic program. Eleven congressional committees or subcommittees undertook hearings. The Departments of State, Treasury, Commerce, Transportation, Interior, Justice, Defense, and Agriculture, the Federal Power Commission, the Interstate Commerce Commission, the Civil Aeronautics Board, and the Environmental Protection Agency asserted jurisdiction over pieces of the problem. The administration was unable to assemble an energy bill until 1975; the bill finally submitted to Congress represented the least common denominator, simply avoiding most of the hard choices. And Congress weakened that bill even further before passing it. Neither substantial conservation of energy nor expansion of domestic production was achieved. In mid-1976, the United States finds itself even more heavily dependent on imported oil than it was just before the embargo of 1973.

Secretaries of state once complained about the intrusion of Defense and Treasury in foreign affairs; as a result of the more general dispersion of power, they now complain about the "domestic" departments and Congress. Future secretaries will have to broaden their complaints to include recalcitrant private interests. Secretary Kissinger is inclined to Spenglerian pessimism about the possibility of effective foreign policy in a participatory democracy. "Accommodating special or parochial interests through a series of compromises does not necessarily produce coherence," he has said. "Contention between the executive and Congress risks falling between two stools on too many grave issues."[1] The issue Kissinger identifies is central, but the solution he implies—reversion to the old deference to executive judgment—is not a likely one; at least not in the near future. It may be that by the 1990s the complexity and importance of international relations and our continued inability to manage them effectively will have forced fundamental shifts of authority: constitutional changes within the United States, or grants of what are now national powers to supranational bodies, or both. But such changes are not likely in the decade just ahead. The task of this next period will be to see whether less radical measures will suffice; whether the shared authority of existing constitutional arrangements can be so exercised as to

1. *Department of State Bulletin*, September 15, 1975, p. 396.

meet the minimum conditions of coherence, speed, and decisiveness that effective foreign policy requires.

This chapter addresses that task. It outlines the major problems in the present organization of the U.S. government for dealing with foreign affairs and suggests a number of reforms that we believe are feasible and likely to facilitate much more effective performance. Change, we think, will be required in three related realms: the relations between President and Congress; the presidency itself; and the performance of the departments of the executive branch. First, however, we had best specify what we mean by organization, why we believe organization matters, and how we approach the problem of organizational design.

Does Organization Matter?

We define government organization to include three factors: the *structure* of government—that is, the existence of agencies having particular missions, authorities, and competences, and the nonexistence of others; the *processes* by which issues are identified and assessed and decisions made and put into effect; and the *people* whose energy, skills, and values make the machinery work. This definition is broader than that traditionally used, but processes (as we will suggest) and people (as everyone knows) have fully as pronounced an effect on performance as does formal structure. Improving government requires attention to each.

The popular notion that neither structure nor process really matters but "it's all a matter of good people" has a certain merit. The competence, energy, and values both of key officials and of the members of large bureaucracies do matter more than any other single factor. Good people can find ways to make an illogical structure work; a brilliant structure cannot save incompetents. But people, processes, and structure interact. Especially at the top of the government, the roles assigned to key positions must match the skills and energies of their occupants. Who could confidently assign certain roles to the secretary of state and others to the President's assistant for national security affairs without knowing whether Henry Kissinger would be the first and William Rogers the second or vice versa?

To change organization is to alter the terms and conditions of peo-

ple's jobs: their routines, expectations, power. Those adversely affected resist such changes. That resistance, combined with the subtle
and partly unforeseeable effects of organizational change, means that
the net results of "reforms" are often meager or unintended. In 1947
advocates of the National Security Council believed it would con-
strain footloose presidential initiative in foreign affairs. The NSC
was to be "Forrestal's revenge" on Franklin Roosevelt's practices of
war management;[2] it would force the President to confront the counsel of his senior advisers and chief lieutenants before taking action.
But President Truman demonstrated that even Presidents inexperienced in foreign affairs need not be awed by such an institution.
President Kennedy largely ignored it; and President Nixon transformed the NSC into a mechanism for centralized presidential control.

Because of such bureaucratic and intellectual difficulties, discussions of organizational reform tend to be driven by either high ab-
stractions or quite specific tactical concerns. In the first case, discussion is dominated by such concepts as "coordination," "efficiency,"
"responsibility," and "centralization" (or "decentralization"). In the
second case, tactics for achieving particular policy objectives are
advanced; they may be nakedly substantive (cutting the defense
budget) or plausibly organizational (giving the Office of Management and Budget more influence over the defense budget). Here we
apply a more operational conception. It is built on the proposition
that government organization has three principal functions: to create
capabilities; to vest and weight certain interests and perspectives;
and to assure the legitimacy of decisions.

Most obviously, organization *creates capabilities* for doing jobs
beyond the capability of single individuals. An idealized list of foreign policy tasks to be thus addressed would include: developing a
coherent conception of U.S. interests; scanning for problems, collecting information, and identifying issues that may require decision or
action; developing alternative courses of action and analyzing their
relative benefits and costs; making decisions, without delay and at
the lowest level having the requisite perspective and authority; implementing action promptly and effectively; and assessing results and

2. Richard E. Neustadt, "Reorganizing the Presidency in 1961: A Preview of
the Issues" (paper prepared for delivery at the 1960 annual meeting of the American
Political Science Association; processed).

revising policy accordingly. Creating capabilities adequate to each of these tasks means establishing structures (the Federal Energy Administration, for example); rearranging processes (for inter-agency consultation on fuel requirements); and choosing and placing key people (creating an "energy czar").

Second, organization *vests and weights particular interests* and perspectives. Organizational arrangements—the existence or non-existence of specific departments or agencies, the distribution of powers among them, procedures for concurrence or consultation, the presence or absence of particularly forceful officials—raise or lower the probability that particular considerations will be included in policymaking. A key question in organizational design, therefore, is which substantive perspectives should be introduced, and with what weights, in the processes of decision and action.

An interest can be vested in a number of ways. The most obvious instance is the establishment of a new agency dedicated expressly to that interest. The Arms Control and Disarmament Agency, for example, was set up in 1961 exactly to provide an institutional voice for the arms control perspective. Interests can also be vested by establishing units within existing organizations, such as the Arms Control Directorate in the Office of the Secretary of Defense; or by establishing procedures that require existing agencies to take an underrepresented perspective into account, through an "arms control impact statement," for example. Giving weight to an interest or perspective is a different matter. Weight is power. It may arise from formal authority (to take actions or make decisions, or to impose limits on the actions or decisions of others); from control of resources, mainly money and personnel; from special competence at some important task; or from links to sources of power outside the government, principally money, votes, and publicity. But weight does not follow automatically from vesting; ACDA illustrates that point too.

Third, organization *legitimates*. It makes decisions broadly acceptable by ensuring that parties having stakes in the matter, or relevant competence, are heard, and that decisions are taken by duly constituted authorities. Contrast the nation's probable acceptance of a decision to use military force made by the President alone with the likely response to the same decision taken only after the cabinet, the Joint Chiefs of Staff, and Congress had all publicly concurred. As in all spheres where reasonable men can disagree about ends, legitimacy depends on observance of established procedures. Constitutional government consists of processes designed to give competing interests a fair hearing in the making of decisions that concern them. Congress represents the many particular interests of citizens in districts and states; the President stands as the sole official elected by all the people; the departments embody specialized knowledge and capacity for action. Effective interaction among them assures the representation of multiple interests and the application of relevant knowledge and makes more likely the acceptance and cooperation even of those who sought a different result.

This triple conception of the purpose and effect of organization underlies the discussion that follows. For each of the arenas of foreign policymaking, we ask: What *capabilities* should the government possess? Which *perspectives* should be introduced, and with what weight, in the major processes of decision and action? What interests must be represented to assure the *legitimacy* of decisions?

Organizational Objectives

There are a number of specific policy recommendations proposed in this book whose adoption and effective implementation can be facilitated by changes in organization. But an agenda for organizational reform in the decade ahead must locate these specific objectives in the context of larger goals. From a review of recent failures in American foreign policymaking (and in government generally), and from a judgment that the foreign policy issues of the future are likely to be complex, politically sensitive, and important to many interest groups and organizations, we have drawn six such larger objectives.

1. *Rebuilding trust in government and a measure of consensus about the main lines of foreign policy.* The ability of government to act and to gain acceptance for its actions depends only partly on the soundness of particular decisions. Its deeper source is a more general belief that the processes of decisionmaking are balanced and fair and that the key officers of government are honorable and competent. The perception that those conditions are present is a precious national resource, perhaps the most precious. During the last decade it was rapidly depleted—to the point of bankruptcy with Vietnam

and Watergate. The number of citizens expressing "a great deal of confidence" in either the executive branch or Congress dropped from over 40 percent in 1966 to 27 percent in 1973.[3] A January 1975 survey found 69 percent of the population agreeing with the proposition: "Over the past ten years this country's leaders have consistently lied to the American people." More recent polls show no important improvement.[4]

The broad consensus that supported postwar American foreign policy is a lesser resource, but still an important one, and its breakdown has been equally dramatic. The Chicago Council on Foreign Relations found in December 1974 that the public put "containing Communism" ninth in importance in a list of eighteen foreign policy goals, behind "securing adequate supplies of energy," "protecting the jobs of American workers," and "combating world hunger." Defense treaties continue to commit the United States to more than forty nations. But when asked whether they would favor sending U.S. troops to defend particular nations under external attack, a majority of Americans replied yes for only one country: Canada. Fewer than one in four Americans favored sending troops to defend West Berlin or Israel.[5] Public opinion changes rapidly with events; the reemergence of a clear and direct threat of Soviet expansion would undoubtedly change those priorities. But the impact of the past decade and its implications for the next should not be underestimated.

Public confidence in U.S. leadership and a measure of consensus about the nation's goals are indispensable to effective foreign policy. Viable international action requires steadiness of purpose and tolerance for the compromises unavoidable in bargaining among nations. To effect such compromises, negotiators need some discretionary authority, an authority based on trust. Rebuilding public confidence in government and a measure of consensus about the nation's foreign policy are therefore priority tasks. That reconstruction should figure centrally both in the substance of foreign policy choice, and in the process by which decisions are made.

3. See *Confidence and Concern: Citizens View American Government,* Hearings before the Subcommittee on Intergovernmental Relations of the Senate Government Operations Committee, 93:1 (GPO, 1974), p. 8.
4. Patrick H. Caddell and Albert C. Pierce, "Alienation in Politics: What Is the Electorate Telling Us?" (Cambridge Research Institute, 1975; processed), p. 9.
5. John E. Reilly, ed., "American Public Opinion and U.S. Foreign Policy, 1975" (Chicago Council on Foreign Relations, February 1975).

2. *Rethinking and restating U.S. objectives in the world.* Few Americans, in government or out, are confident that they understand even the broad lines of current policy; fewer still understand its basis. A main cause of that uncertainty is the gap between rhetoric and reality in recent foreign policy: a lost war merchandised as "peace with honor"; relaxation of tensions with the Soviet Union treated as an end to hostility; a presidential visit to China staged as "the event of the century"; a fragile international environment declared a "stable structure of peace." Another factor has been a decisionmaking process in which, for too many issues, only Secretary of State Kissinger, the President, and a few key assistants have been privy to the "real" definition of the problem or the "true" reasons for our actions. The need to rethink and restate U.S. purposes, like the necessity to reconstruct trust and consensus, suggests that the processes by which the main lines of our foreign policy are laid down should become far broader and more open, that policy, once established, be articulated not only by the President and secretary of state but by numbers of cabinet and subcabinet officials as well, and that informed debate in Congress and in the press be regarded as an opportunity, not an encumbrance.

3. *Advancing "national" interests—that is, collective and longer-run interests—as against their opposites.* Current American foreign policymakers look back to the late 1940s and 1950s with some nostalgia. Though the risks of the cold war were grave, the fear that communist expansion would mean disaster for all Americans did wonderfully concentrate the national mind, and it provided a clear hierarchy of objectives. Distinctions between "security," "economic," and "domestic" considerations seemed tolerably clear and, where a choice was necessary, security objectives dominated.

Fundamental changes in the nature of international politics have shattered the simple clarity of the postwar period. The perception of an immediate and overriding threat to our security has faded. Our apparent preponderance in military, economic, and political power among noncommunist countries has been reduced. The current foreign policy agenda contains many issues that divide rather than unite Americans. Wheat sales to the Soviet Union, arms sales to Egypt, the Panama dispute, a 200-mile fishing zone—each requires goring some domestic oxen and feeding others. Such issues confuse—quite literally—"domestic" and "foreign" affairs. Most major national issues now have both domestic and foreign implications.

The problem is compounded by the diffusion of governmental responsibility for such issues. Decentralization of authority inevitably pulls toward the disintegration of policy. The corresponding responsibility of government—there is none more important—is to ensure that special interests are accommodated within a coherent conception of the nation's larger needs. That task is now weakly undertaken even in the executive branch, the branch with a chief. In Congress, where power is more systematically diffused, the problem is inherently harder, doubly complicated, as chapter 13 suggests, by the weakness of congressional leadership and the long experience of opposing parties controlling the two branches.

4. *Adjusting to interdependence.* In the past Americans took pride in their "splendid isolation" from the rest of the world. During the last quarter-century, that kind of independence ended for all time. Soviet strategic nuclear forces make that fact clear: at any moment, a Soviet decision can cause immediate death to tens of millions of Americans. The further proliferation of nuclear weapons presents a medium-term risk of less catastrophic but still devastating attack, or of environmental damage resulting from a nuclear war among third parties.

Over the last quarter-century, the economic connections between America and the rest of the world have also become more direct, numerous, and powerful. In the spheres of money, investment, trade, production, and entrepreneurial labor, a world economy has emerged. Though degrees of interdependence vary—most nations being more dependent on the United States than the United States is on them—dependencies now run both ways, a fact made vivid for Americans by the oil embargo.

The principal significance of these developments can be summarized in a single assertion: during just that period in which the U.S. government, like all central governments, assumed responsibility for the nation's economic stability and growth, its power to meet that responsibility through autonomous action has been eroding. Economic events in Germany, Japan, or member states of the Organization of Petroleum Exporting Countries have important, direct, short-run impacts on jobs, wages, profits, and prices in the United States. Attempts to achieve U.S. domestic economic objectives through traditional instruments of monetary and fiscal policy can be hampered (or facilitated) by developments in other countries that affect the flow of U.S. short-term money to foreign markets or change worldwide demand, and thus the U.S. trade balance. Indeed, the degree of interdependence among member nations of the Organisation for Economic Co-operation and Development in 1976 is probably greater than that among the thirteen American colonies in 1776.

A major challenge for the last quarter of the twentieth century, therefore, will be to create and strengthen international processes and institutions capable of managing the conditions of interdependence, promoting cooperative problem solving among nations, and discouraging beggar-thy-neighbor practices. Satisfactory adjustment to interdependence will also require the creation of various nets and cushions—oil stockpiles, loan guarantees, import adjustment assistance, and the like—to protect against the dangers and share the costs of interdependence.

5. *Meeting new threats and opportunities.* Three years after a 1969 presidential task force had warned of the threat of an oil embargo, the embargo occurred; in the interim, the United States had taken no action to avert the embargo or to lessen our vulnerability to it. The split between the Soviet Union and China persisted for over a decade before the United States took advantage of it by establishing closer relations with China. While the capacity of man to foresee the future is limited, and the ability of bureaucracies to adjust their behavior to remote contingencies smaller still, the United States must find ways of responding more quickly and flexibly to increasing rates of change. Potential areas of danger, now familiar but little discussed five years ago—icecap melting, nuclear terrorism, ozone depletion—suggest how unfamiliar the problems of the future may be. In the next decades, therefore, the challenge to foresight will prove particularly demanding, and failures to meet that challenge may be particularly dangerous. Organizational change must increase government's ability to recognize new circumstances of importance, and to act on them. The ability of Congress to raise both public and governmental awareness of novel issues through investigations and hearings should be fully exploited.

6. *Making government work.* There is a deep and growing feeling within the United States, reflected in polls as well as in the anti-Washington campaign rhetoric of 1976, that the U.S. government is doing its job poorly. In part, this view results from inflated expectations, but in larger part, it reflects genuinely poor performance. The problem has several dimensions. First, there is the relation of the President to

Congress. As James Reston recently observed: "There have been so many puzzles here over the conduct of American foreign policy in the last couple of years that the notion is getting around that the President and Congress can't agree on anything, but this is not precisely true. On at least one thing they are in total agreement: that the present decision-making system, if that's the right word, is an incoherent mess, excessively irritating to both branches of the government and dangerous to the national interest."[6]

Relations between the "appointive government" and the "permanent government" are not much better. Over the past thirty years a permanent government has emerged in Washington. In the foreign affairs–oriented agencies, it consists of over three million people (some two million of them in the military), who do not change with Presidents and administrations. Organized by department and agency, each with its separate professional career lines, protected by Civil Service regulations and now largely unionized, the permanent government does most of the day-to-day business of government. Atop this structure sit fewer than a thousand members of an administration, appointed officials charged with managing the various departments and making and supporting national policy.[7] Because the permanent government often resists the initiatives of new administrations, political appointees are tempted to depend solely on small groups of trusted assistants, to circumvent or distract the bureaucracy, and largely to ignore the wide range of problems—especially those of implementation—on which such practices provide little leverage. Treated in this way, members of the permanent government resort to doing their business around and beneath appointed officials, pushing favorite projects when they can be given labels attractive to the present "boss," working through congressional or private allies, or delaying action they oppose until a secretary or assistant secretary moves on.[8]

Uncertain relations between government and the private sector complete the trilogy. Particularly as economic components of the foreign policy agenda have expanded, governmental objectives have

6. *New York Times,* Feb. 1, 1976.
7. Numbers of employees estimated from data in *The Budget of the United States Government, Fiscal Year 1976—Appendix;* and Civil Service Commission, data on administration appointments under Schedule C.
8. In the last two decades assistant secretaries have averaged roughly eighteen months on the job, secretaries less than two years.

come to require action by oil companies, nuclear construction firms, farmers, unions. As a market-oriented, capitalist economy, we have no central mechanism for directing such industries. Indeed, the U.S. government is often not even well informed about activities in the private sector.

The Organizational Agenda

This is a formidable set of problems. Any serious attempt to address them will require many changes in the way our foreign policy-making machinery is structured, staffed, and led. But it is well to recall that the organizational pattern that we seek now to change was established in the late 1940s as an even more fundamental revision of previous arrangements. The time is now ripe for similarly farsighted change in three related domains: relations between the President and Congress; interactions between the President and the departments; and activities within departments.

The President and Congress

The central tasks here are to reconstruct comity and trust between the branches, to establish mechanisms able to offer some resistance to the pressures for fragmented treatment of issues, and to differentiate more clearly the roles of the two branches.

Current discussions of the relative virtues of Congress and the executive branch in the conduct of foreign policy bring to mind the story about the judge in a singing competition who awarded the prize to the second of two contestants after having heard only the first. In the wake of Vietnam, many observers seemed inclined to follow the judge's example and give the prize to Congress. Students of Congress, however, will anticipate the end of the story. The judge was made to listen to the second contestant, whereupon he retracted his judgment and cut the trophy in half. That conclusion might have been inspired by the Founding Fathers, for the Constitution declines to choose between the executive and Congress. In foreign as in domestic affairs, it creates a government of "separated institutions sharing power."[9]

Yet historically the President has played the dominant role in directing foreign relations. The reasons for this are several and they

9. Richard E. Neustadt, *Presidential Power: The Politics of Leadership* (John Wiley and Sons, 1960), p. 33.

appeared early. The necessities of management in the first decades of national independence moved Jeffersonians and Hamiltonians alike to accept greater executive leadership in foreign affairs than the Constitution had envisioned. Congress could not stay abreast of the details of relations with foreign states; only rarely could it act as a unified body; it could not conduct negotiations nor keep a secret. By 1790, Secretary of State Thomas Jefferson had come to the view that "the transaction of business with foreign nations is Executive altogether."[10]

When the business involved meeting crises, the advantages of the executive became all the more important. They had been laid out clearly in *The Federalist:* unity, constancy, expertise, decision, secrecy, and dispatch.[11] Thus, though the dominance of executive authority over foreign affairs ebbed and flowed, recurring crises led gradually to widespread acceptance of what Arthur Schlesinger has called the "executive perspective," the view that in foreign affairs "the Executive branch, with superior information and direct responsibility was the source of judgment to which Congress should customarily defer."[12]

War was the ultimate test, and the Second World War placed in the President's hand virtually unlimited powers in foreign affairs. After a decade of congressional attempts to enforce neutrality and limit preparedness (the House had come within a single vote of repealing the draft just five months before Pearl Harbor), the war seemed clear evidence that Congress as a body could not be trusted to play a major role in foreign policy. The dominance of the President in the postwar period had other forces behind it as well. His prerogatives as commander-in-chief had special weight in a period of sharp external threat. The emergence of a huge federal bureaucracy put at the President's service hundreds of thousands of eyes, ears, and hands, enlarging the knowledge, expertise, and capacity for action of the executive. A classification system kept from Congress (and the public) enormous stores of information on which wise decision-making might depend. The growing involvement of the federal government in the domestic economy greatly increased the President's

10. Arthur M. Schlesinger, Jr., *The Imperial Presidency* (Houghton Mifflin, 1973), p. 14.
11. Alexander Hamilton, James Madison, and John Jay, *The Federalist,* ed. Max Beloff (Oxford: Basil Blackwell and Mott, 1948), no. 75, p. 384.
12. Schlesinger, *The Imperial Presidency,* p. 14.

bargaining power vis-à-vis Congress. The growth of the mass media and especially television gave him ready access to every voter, largely on his own terms. The decline of political parties made the President the central focus of political emotion.

The protracted failure of a presidential war in Vietnam eroded the presumption that in foreign affairs the President knew best; the revelations of Watergate washed it nearly away. Congress is now deeply immersed in foreign policymaking and, in our judgment, it will remain so. Indeed, we believe that the factor likely to most distinguish American foreign policymaking in the last quarter of this century from that of the preceding decades will be a shift in power from the executive to Congress. The balance of power at any moment will depend on many factors: whether the same party controls both branches; the degree to which dominant issues are controversial; patterns of presidential and congressional behavior expected by press and public; the strength of congressional leadership; and the unity of the political parties. But whatever the particulars, Congress will play a more substantial role than it has since World War II.

The reason for this shift is not that public suspicion of presidential adventurism will remain high; it may or it may not. The emergence of any severe threat to important U.S. interests will align the electorate where such threats always align it—behind the commander in chief. Instead, the fundamental reason for the changing relation of Congress to the executive in foreign policy is the changed content of that policy. Our relations with other countries are no longer dominated by the terms of alliances, the duration of base rights, or the breadth of security guarantees; they are also shaped by issues arising from the tightening economic and physical interdependence among nations. Those issues affect prices, jobs, and the conditions of daily life; they are the stuff of domestic politics. It is this fact that makes congressional activism inevitable.

A number of secondary factors reinforce congressional involvement. One is the explosive growth of congressional staff. Since 1954 Congress has more than tripled its personal and committee staffs, and they now comprise some 17,000 persons.[13] Though perhaps half this

13. Including the congressional service agencies (such as the General Accounting Office, the Congressional Research Service, and the Office of Technology Assessment), the number exceeds 25,000. Alan Schick, "The Supply and Demand for Analysis on Capitol Hill" (Congressional Research Service, June 1975; processed), p. 14.

number attend primarily to constituent services, the dramatic increase in the number of professional staffers dealing with policy matters gives congressmen the ability to dig more deeply into a wider range of issues and generates staff pressure for further pieces of the action. Second, the composition of Congress itself is changing; the number of representatives and senators with broad experience, advanced education, and considerable understanding of the world outside the United States has increased sharply and seems likely to continue to grow. Third, in the absence of direct threats to U.S. security producing an overriding need for a unified response, Congress will give voice to the special claims of particular ethnic and national as well as economic interests. Fourth, the lesson of Vietnam and Watergate has deeply affected the public conception of necessary and proper congressional behavior. A senator can no longer explain to himself or his constituents that he defers to superior executive expertise in foreign affairs. Moreover, recent relaxation of demands for deference to congressional barons, especially in the Senate, enables junior members to seize issues themselves and to build sufficient support to block or deflect an administration's proposals.

Increased involvement of Congress in foreign policymaking therefore seems certain. But involvement can be deep without being either effective or responsible. The authors of *The Federalist,* though determined that Congress should provide the ultimate check and balance to executive power, were skeptical about the capacity of so large and diverse a body to play a leading role in foreign policymaking. "The fluctuating and . . . multitudinous composition of that body forbids us to expect in it those qualities which are essential to the proper execution of such a trust. Accurate and comprehensive knowledge of foreign politics; a steady and systematic adherence to the same views; a nice and uniform sensibility to national character; decision, *secrecy,* and dispatch, are incompatible with the genius of a body so variable and so numerous."[14] Time has confirmed their skepticism. A larger congressional role in foreign policymaking may both fail of its constitutional purpose and further distort executive policymaking. Feasible change in the processes of interaction between the branches and in congressional organization itself can diminish those probabilities. What are the changes?

RESTORING COMITY. The first and probably most important

14. *The Federalist,* ed. Beloff, no. 75, p. 384.

group of proposals seeks to reestablish comity and minimum conditions of trust between the branches. For more than half a decade, executive-congressional relations have been poisonous—far worse than diverging party loyalties require—and the costs to the stability, coherence, and wisdom of U.S. foreign policy have been high. Congress now feels ill used by Presidents—manipulated, deceived, treated with indifference or contempt. Indeed, the recent insistence of Congress on quite particular changes in policy (often of dubious merit) —the high and explicit quota for Jewish emigration from the Soviet Union and the cutoff of arms to Turkey—appears to have been motivated almost as much by congressional pique at the administration as by the influence of Greek and Jewish constituencies. As Congressman Donald Fraser has observed: "The distrust of the executive branch runs so deep in this chamber that members are afraid that any discretion, any grant of authority to the executive branch will open the door to allow the executive branch to again try to make one more effort to do what ten years failed to do."[15] A major opportunity open to the next President is to end that situation.

Party affiliations, presidential attitudes, and the substance of policy proposals will importantly affect the results of efforts to resolve this problem, but setting up procedures can help. Steady and genuine informal coordination between the White House and the limited number of congressional leaders who strongly influence congressional action on any particular issue is the first requirement. The President, his assistants for congressional liaison, and his cabinet and subcabinet officials must all make such consultation priority business. It must come ungrudgingly and early, not after reports in the media of administration action inconsistent with prior assurances to Congress. And the staffs of those officials should develop working relationships with the relevant congressional staffers. On numerous foreign policy issues, especially those that do not arouse strong emotions in particular districts or states, the votes of many members of Congress are not politically constrained. Under these circumstances, congressmen, unless personally expert in the matter, tend to follow the lead of colleagues whose values and knowledge they trust. Engaging a sizable fraction of that informal leadership group in executive decisionmaking would produce benefits far greater than its likely costs in time or

15. Quoted in Robert A. Pastor, "Coping with Congress's Foreign Policy," *Foreign Service Journal,* vol. 52 (December 1975), p. 16.

compromise. Such consultation should extend to both the development of policy and the creation of institutions capable of carrying it out. A good model was provided by the Asian Development Bank, where, after several years of stalemate, the Treasury Department solicited and received genuine and substantive congressional participation, which produced not only initial appropriations but also a proprietary and protective attitude in Congress toward a valuable international institution.

Executive willingness to share credit with Congress will also be required. A President must not only involve congressmen, but also be seen to involve them. Truman's dealings with the congressional leadership provide a model both of manner and of result. Even as an apparent lame duck and with Congress controlled by the opposite party, he succeeded (with the assistance of a number of cabinet and subcabinet officials) in enlisting active congressional support for so sharp a departure in foreign policy as the Marshall Plan. The recipe included steady consultation, informal and formal; willingness to forgo partisan advantage; and a determination to share credit as widely as necessary.[16]

RESISTING FRAGMENTATION. A second major objective of organizational change should be to reinforce congressional incentives to view major foreign policy issues more comprehensively, thus at least partially offsetting the powerful pressures in Congress to deal with issues by carving them up to fit committee jurisdictions. To this end, many reformers recommend sweeping congressional change: random and rotating assignments to committees; a lengthening of representatives' terms to four years running concurrently with presidential terms; sharp reductions in the number of subcommittees, combined with a "sunset" rule limiting the life of new subcommittees; and broadening the jurisdictions and reducing the number of standing committees. But the implications of such reforms reach far beyond the realm of foreign relations. We focus here, therefore, on more modest and more feasible reforms that still might have quite substantial effects.

Probably the most important step would be presidential assistance in strengthening congressional leadership through political support and practices of consultation. Here, the President who takes office in 1977 may have a unique opportunity. For the first time in this cen-

16. Neustadt, *Presidential Power*, pp. 47–52.

tury, both houses will simultaneously acquire new leaders certain to be more forceful than their predecessors. Such leaders can find many ways to encourage a greater measure of policy consistency among committees. In addition, the President should take the initiative in making the case for hard foreign policy decisions, especially where they impose significant domestic costs. A President deeply and publicly committed to a major policy on grounds that it well serves the general interests of the nation provides an indispensable rallying point for congressional support.

A naturally reenforcing pair of more formal mechanisms also seems worth considering. One is that the President submit to Congress every second year a comprehensive statement of U.S. purposes and commitments in the world, a document that would articulate basic foreign policy goals and specify their relation to proposed and continuing policy. Such biennial statements might be amplified by occasional white papers dealing with specific issues in more detail. Second is the creation within each house of a new Committee on Interdependence to receive and debate the biennial statement and the various white papers, to prepare comprehensive congressional responses, to study issues arising from these documents that transcend the jurisdictions of existing committees, and to propose means of coordinating congressional action accordingly.

For the biennial statements there are, we recognize, a number of unpromising precedents: the Basic National Security Policy documents of the Eisenhower administration, the National Policy Papers of the Kennedy years, and Nixon's "State of the World" messages. Their preparation absorbed enormous effort in the departments and the White House; they tended to resolve disagreements by resorting to assertions so general as to be meaningless; and they provided little usable guidance for decisionmakers faced with particular choices. Nonetheless, we believe that, in conjunction with the proposed Interdependence Committees, such statements could be made to serve a number of important purposes. Relevant portions of the biennial statements could provide the policy basis for Defense budget requests; white papers on foreign policy and force posture, presented and defended jointly by the secretaries of state and defense, would serve the same purpose in alternate years. Other portions of the biennial statement could preface presidential requests for authorizations and appropriations of foreign economic aid, military assistance, contributions to international financial institutions, and the like. Specific white papers could provide the framework for congressional hearings and debate on issues of particular concern, such as U.S. policy toward southern Africa, current U.S. interests in Southeast Asia, and U.S. policy on the spread of nuclear reactors and related technology. In this way the statements and papers could encourage rethinking in the executive branch of the adequacy of current policies and the relations among them, publicly articulate policy in a form that invited argument, discussion, and increased public understanding, and offer a framework for more coherent congressional debate and action.

It is particularly to help achieve the last of those purposes that we propose establishing the Committees on Interdependence. Without encroaching deeply on the jurisdiction of any present committee, these new committees would make possible comprehensive and sustained congressional review of the larger concepts behind U.S. foreign relations, and of the consistency of those concepts with particular programs and actions. The committees would review the biennial statements and white papers, hold hearings on them when appropriate (sometimes jointly with other committees), prepare congressional responses, and attempt to influence the numerous related actions of other committees. Membership of these committees would be drawn from the leadership of each House, plus the Appropriations, Armed Services, Foreign Relations, and economic Committees (Ways and Means, Finance, Banking and Currency, and Commerce) and the Joint Committee on Atomic Energy. It should include a number of more junior members, and, to broaden the experience of the membership and avoid a hardening of the committees' perspectives, membership should rotate, appointments being limited to four or six years.

The proposal takes the Joint Economic Committee as its model. The JEC, established by the Employment Act of 1946, receives and reviews the President's annual economic report, studies means of coordinating programs to further the policy of the act, and, as a guide to the several committees of Congress dealing with economic legislation, reports its findings and recommendations to both houses. The committee has no legislative jurisdiction, but it has provided a focus of congressional response to presidential economic proposals, has kept disparate committees of Congress aware of the potential macroeconomic effects of issues before them, and has speeded the education

—both of members of Congress and of the country—in the complexities of national economic policy.

In theory, the new Budget Committees of the two Houses might provide a more forceful model. Those are the committees through which Congress now limits appropriations and spending to conform to prior decisions about the total budget and its allocations to major program areas: health, agriculture, defense, and the like. While not yet in full effect, the budget process has passed its early tests. If it operates as designed, it will represent effective coordination of the most sensitive and difficult kind and itself encourage a more coherent treatment of national priorities affected by spending. But two circumstances make the budget process unique. Its quantitative nature makes setting an overall policy relatively simple—a ceiling can be expressed in numbers—and the current political climate gives strong support to a reform designed to limit federal expenditure. Foreign policy objectives cannot be so precisely stated, and, more important, there is no comparable pressure for their consistency and integration.

Creation of Committees on Interdependence would, by itself, change nothing. Much would depend on the skill, energy, and seriousness of the chairmen, the capacity of staffs, and the chosen modes of operation. But while the existence of such committees would guarantee little, it could facilitate much. Hearings and reports might dramatize the growing interactions among societies (European concern about New York City's solvency, the impact abroad of U.S. inflation). The committees' staffs could serve as brokers among other congressional staffs, encouraging the consistent treatment of related issues. Foreigners might be asked to testify directly (as was done in Secretary of Transportation William Coleman's hearing on the *Concorde*), symbolizing the breadth of the population now affected by congressional action. The committees might over time become a natural focal point for executive-congressional coordination.

Related proposals have been made before. The Joint Committee on National Security advocated by Senator Humphrey and Representative Zablocki is similar in its purpose and design. The difference—and it seems to us important—is that the Humphrey-Zablocki bill proposes, in effect, a congressional counterpart to the National Security Council. It is designed to meet the coordination problem of the past—that of integrating military and diplomatic considerations—but not the broader difficulty of coordinating military, economic,

political, and technological policies. The changing nature of international relations requires far more inclusive forums for high-level
coordination and decision in both the executive branch and Congress. If new committees are to facilitate understanding of the growing links among nations they will need broader membership and
responsibility.

A related reform would be a longer foreign affairs authorization
cycle. Until the last decade, appropriations—the approval of particular budgets—were voted annually by Congress but authorizations
—the entitlements of departments and their major programs to continued existence—were renewed only at longer intervals. Partly as
a result of the deepening conflict between Congress and the executive
branch, partly because the legislative committees that control authorizations sought to regain power that had shifted toward the appropriations committees, more and more authorizations are now required annually. State, the oldest cabinet department, now depends
on annual authorization; so do foreign aid, atomic energy, and the
major defense programs.

The result has been largely pernicious. Fundamental rethinking
is not possible on an annual basis, and the costs of trying it are protracted and unnecessary executive testimony and annual delay and
uncertainty within the departments. A biennial authorization cycle
would link congressional debate of the biennial statement to decisions about authorizations and would help reestablish the distinct
purposes of authorization and appropriation. Such a cycle would
have in the biennial statement a comprehensive and coherent basis
for reviewing the agencies and programs being authorized, and it
would schedule authorizations neither so infrequently as to dilute
congressional influence nor so frequently as to limit serious debate in
Congress or make executive programming impossible.

Related reforms should provide Congress with better means and
greater incentive to deal substantively with the major questions of
policy choice. Congressman Les Aspin has rightly cautioned against
efforts to convert Congress "into a kind of Brookings Institution or
Systems Analysis office."[17] It is in the nature of Congress to deal with
issues through specialized committees, and therefore in specialized
aspects, rather than comprehensively; to respond to the politics and

17. "The Defense Budget and Foreign Policy: The Role of Congress," *Daedalus*
(Summer 1975), p. 163.

symbolism of a problem as much as to its basic facts; and to view issues in terms of the desires of constituents as much as the exigencies of national interest. Organizational reforms predicated on transforming congressional values and purpose will fail, and so they should. But changes with a more modest objective are both legitimate and feasible.

Defense is an obvious arena for change. Congressional treatment of defense issues has been generally superficial and unrealistic. Blechman and Fried have aptly characterized the problem: "Being unwilling either to permit defense budgets to rise beyond inflation or to challenge fundamental military policies, the Congress . . . has temporized. It seeks short-term economies by reducing the numbers of weapons purchased in a single year, without changing the total number in the program. Or it slows down development programs without killing the proposed new weapons altogether. Or it reduces operating budgets without cutting manpower significantly, thus causing longer queues of equipment waiting for over-haul, smaller stockpiles, and other reduction in readiness."[18]

The biennial statements should be helpful here by specifying the linkages between budgets, force levels, and foreign policy objectives. Such a specification, and the assessment of alternative budgets and forces in the light of other possible levels of policy aspiration, offers the best hope of rationalizing U.S. force structure and making it an effective instrument of policy. The growing availability to Congress of technically competent analytical staffs gives some promise that such assessments will be made and used.

ROLE DIFFERENTIATION. A final objective is to expand the role of Congress in some areas and to enlarge the discretion of the executive in others. Especially in the last few years, executive-congressional relations have been regarded as a single zero-sum game. This is an inadequate conception. The differing constitutional roles and the varying comparative capabilities of the two branches strongly suggest that both particular and national interests are well served by enlarging the discretion of the President in some areas, particularly economic affairs and expanding congressional involvement in others, particularly war making and national commitments.

The Constitution gives Congress alone the power to declare war. For the last quarter-century, however, the actual role of Congress

18. Barry M. Blechman and Edward R. Fried, "Controlling the Defense Budget," *Foreign Affairs*, vol. 54 (January 1976), p. 240.

in war making has been to approve executive action after the fact, or to provide a blank check beforehand. Both the Korean and Vietnam wars were undeclared. In the Cuban missile crisis, the only occasion when major nuclear war was seriously contemplated, Congress played no direct role. The War Powers Resolution of 1973 now requires that within forty-eight hours of the initiation of hostilities the President must report to Congress on the causes for such action; it requires termination of American involvement unless Congress approves it within sixty days. It is a pale reflection of the constitutional intention that a decision to go to war be made collaboratively by the whole body of citizens elected to national office. Finding a functional equivalent of the original intention under current conditions is difficult, and after passing the War Powers Resolution Congress has little enthusiasm for further change. But further steps are desirable. Perhaps most useful would be a personal and explicit presidential commitment to take seriously the mandate of the War Powers Resolution to consult with Congress *before* the fact of military action. Such a commitment might specify that, unless it were physically infeasible, the President would seek the approval of the leaders of each House and of the chairmen of both Armed Services and Foreign Relations Committees before either committing U.S. troops to hostilities or authorizing the first use of nuclear weapons. In an actual crisis, the President might still act alone, letting the electorate and history judge. But the commitment would strengthen the presumption of serious consultation, and effectively require it in less extreme cases.

According to Congress a larger role in undertaking and periodically reviewing U.S. obligations abroad is equally important. If, for example, the President regards the political complexion of Angola to be important to the United States, that proposition should be demonstrable to Congress. If Congress cannot be persuaded, there is a powerful presumption that U.S. security and economic interests are not so deeply engaged as to justify any substantial intervention, overt or covert. Nor will it do to drag Congress into the act in the middle of a crisis. An effectively organized administration will seek congressional approval or support for major commitments abroad— whether embodied in treaties or not—long before they are challenged by force of arms. Given the prospects for conflict outlined in chapter 2, this should be an important element of executive-congressional relations for the next administration.

But in the negotiation of detailed agreements toward objectives

set collaboratively by the President and Congress, especially where
the final terms will be subject to congressional ratification or rejection, executive officials should have wide discretion. Tariffs provide
a good example. The nation as a whole benefits from free trade, but
that fact cannot determine the views of those whose jobs or profits
are threatened by imports of shoes or textiles or steel. Nor can it
persuade their congressmen. The processes for decisionmaking within Congress, and between Congress and the executive, should therefore structure tariff decisions so as to limit the opportunities of small
groups of congressmen to exercise item vetoes. Instead, on the model
of reciprocal trade negotiations since 1934—a model from which the
1974 Trade Act took several steps backward—Congress should
restrict its role to collaboration with the executive in setting the general objectives of trade reform and the guidelines to govern negotiations. Other areas in which Congress should grant greater discretion to the executive branch include aid to developing countries,
support of international lending organizations, and the adjustment of
national tax rates within a narrow band as an instrument of macroeconomic management.

The Presidency

A President plays many roles. Perhaps most evident is that implied by the famous sign on Harry Truman's desk: "The buck stops
here." The President must make the hard choices forced upon him
by events, by officialdom, by Congress, by leaders abroad. He must
respond to the needs, agendas, and schedules of others. But the President must do more than just respond; he must establish his own priorities, understand which of them he can affect by decisions that will
come to him unbidden, identify those which only his initiatives can
advance, and then find ways of advancing them. In this second and
larger role, the President does not decide individual issues as they
come to him; instead, he organizes, leads, and manages an administration.

As discussed in chapter 13, Vietnam and Watergate made plain
the dangers of an imperial presidency and the need for effective
checks on presidential domination. But the problems analyzed by
chapters 2 through 5 demonstrate that for the effective conduct of
foreign affairs a strong and active president is necessary. The diffusion of power within the U.S. government in the face of the serious

challenges the next decade will present permit no alternative. Only as broadly based a body as Congress can legitimately confer legislative authority. Only as insulated a system as the courts can be trusted to pronounce the meaning of our basic law. But only the President can articulate the nation's immediate purposes, propose policies and actions appropriate to advance those purposes, and induce the machinery of government to formulate and to execute them. A system as diffuse, plural, and complex as ours requires an active President to make it work. "Energy in the executive is a leading character in the definition of good government. It is essential to the protection of the community against foreign attacks; it is not less essential to the steady administration of the laws . . . to the security of liberty against the enterprises and assaults of ambition, of faction, and of anarchy."[19] That conclusion of *The Federalist* retains its validity.

As leader and manager of an administration, a President faces two main organizational tasks that no one else has the perspective, the incentive, or the authority to undertake. First, he must look to the balance of organizational arrangements. He must ensure that in the forums of national decision the many relevant interests are represented in some rough relation to their real importance. If the performance of the U.S. economy powerfully affects Europe and Japan, then officials concerned with our foreign relations need some voice in economic decisionmaking. If physical threats to the United States include climatic changes and terrorist activity, then national security cannot be adequately safeguarded simply by a strong conventional defense establishment. Second, the President must seek the integration of policy. Only he can ensure that the decentralized actions of many departments and agencies bear some consistent relation to each other and cumulatively serve the nation's larger interests. If twenty departments and agencies own pieces of energy policy, they must be held to a conception of national purpose advanced from the center. This is the overriding problem of policymaking under conditions of diffused power.

The scale and complexity of the President's problem in seeking to balance and integrate policy is suggested by a glance at the several concentric circles of the executive branch. The innermost circle contains the White House itself, the President and his closest staff. Until Henry Kissinger moved from the National Security Council to the

19. *The Federalist*, ed. Beloff, no. 70, p. 358.

Department of State, assistants to the President for national security affairs had for more than a decade overshadowed the secretary of state. From two personal assistants in the time of President Hoover and eleven White House aides to FDR during World War II, the number of assistants to the President grew to fifty-two in 1972.[20] While President Gerald Ford achieved some reduction, pressures for expansion persist, generated by major issues that cut across departmental lines, major domestic departments that resist reorganization, and the increasing political attention focused on the President personally. The numbers make it clear that few such assistants can have responsibilities sufficiently broad or a relationship sufficiently close to the President to offer him advice that reflects much appreciation of his own central concerns.

Just beyond the White House lies the Executive Office of the President, the "institutional presidency." This circle too has swelled, from 1,175 persons in the early Eisenhower period and 1,664 in Kennedy's last year in office, to over 5,000 under Nixon.[21] The Executive Office is intended to serve only the President, but its growing size makes it both distant from him and hard to distinguish from the cabinet departments.

The third circle is the "appointive government," consisting of several hundred secretaries, under secretaries, assistant secretaries, and their deputies, expected to direct the departments and link the President with the operating levels of government. But the ascendancy of key White House advisers has reduced many members of the appointive government, especially in domestic affairs, to ministerial tasks. Recent Presidents have seen many appointees rarely or not at all—and then for purposes more ceremonial than substantive. Presidents know that many members of their administrations are hostage to special interests, and doubt the competence of others.

Finally, there is the "permanent government," which does not change with administrations but carries on the day-to-day work of all administrations. For so large a body, its levels of skill, expertise, and devotion to duty are high. Yet it appears to a new President as a behemoth: huge, slow, at least independent, perhaps hostile. Beyond the executive branch—which, for all its unwieldiness, at least is *his* (or so he thinks; Congress believes otherwise)—lies Congress,

20. *Congressional Record*, vol. 118, pt. 17, 92:2 (1972), p. 21512.
21. Ibid.

alien territory. And beyond that the private sector of an economy that has itself become a participant in the making and execution of foreign policy; and even beyond that the larger public whose support or acquiescence he must gain and hold.

The President's major organizational challenge is to energize and lead this conglomerate so that its interactions with the external world serve his best conception of the nation's broadest interests—checked, corrected, and constrained though that conception must be by Congress and the public. The task is easy to state and difficult in the extreme to perform. As Harry Truman commented in contemplating the prospect of Eisenhower as president: "He'll sit here, and he'll say, 'Do this! Do that!' *And nothing will happen.* Poor Ike—it won't be a bit like the Army."[22]

In the absence of effective presidential leadership, three key tasks can only be handled poorly.

—Development and articulation of a new policy framework, and of strategies and guidelines for carrying it out. Unless the President takes the lead in conceiving, articulating, and enforcing a new framework, and in presenting and explaining it to Congress and the public, the government's actions will follow old assumptions and procedures.

—Central decisionmaking, coordination, and management. The particular importance of economic issues in the current foreign policy agenda create a special need for central coordination and management. Such issues as energy, nuclear proliferation, or tariffs do not fall exclusively within the domain and control of a single department. Most day-to-day business is inevitably conducted on a decentralized basis by various departments, subject to routine clearance. But primary reliance on decentralized operations and cabinet officers' initiatives encourages inconsistency, inattention to important considerations about which the department taking action cares little, and inability to face hard trade-offs where choices are necessary. The most distinctive feature of foreign economic policy, for example, is that its principal issues constitute the hinge between foreign and domestic policy. Only the President can assess the weight of the varied considerations bearing on such issues, make the trade-offs, and impose decisions on his subordinates.

—Changing structure, procedures, and personnel to serve a coherent policy. Successful policy depends not simply on wisdom in high-level

22. Quoted in Neustadt, *Presidential Power.* p. 9.

decision, but on the energy, intelligence, and values applied to the processes of gathering information, devising alternatives, interpreting intentions, and taking actions at lower levels. Only persistent presidential interest can ensure that structures, processes, and people capable of making these choices and taking these actions effectively are put in place.

The President cannot perform these tasks alone. But neither should he rely as heavily as all recent Presidents have done on White House staff. At bottom, the organizational strategy of each of the last four Presidents has been so to strengthen the Executive Office of the President as to make it possible to do without the departments, and then to look for counsel not to cabinet officers but to White House assistants. The long-term costs of that strategy are unacceptably high. White House staff cannot represent the breadth of concerns now affected by major issues, nor can it deal with issues in substantive depth or manage implementation. Staff is responsive to the President—that is its principal virtue, but also its worst defect. Staff is too responsive. It has no purpose but to serve its single superior. It brings to that service no counter-pressure from statutory responsibilities, bureaucratic loyalties, professional identification, or congressional supervision. Staff members tend to become courtiers. This is true everywhere, but nowhere more so than in the White House. And the result is deepening presidential isolation and unrealism as the White House becomes, in Senator Charles Mathias's words, a presidential "house of mirrors in which all views and ideas tend to reflect and reinforce his own."[23] The mirror effect has been most evident in the Johnson and Nixon presidencies, but it is not a new or passing phenomenon; the pressures and powers of the modern White House tend to disorient all Presidents.

One reliable antidote to the mirror effect is steady contact between the President and his chief line subordinates, the major cabinet secretaries. Cabinet members face both ways, combining presidential loyalties and departmental responsibilities; they cannot merely echo a President. Effective cabinet officers watch for issues that affect their domains; they can deploy substantive expertise, and they can manage processes of implementation. The question is how to link them to each other and to the President—that is, how to organize the processes of central coordination and decision.

23. *Executive Privilege: The Withholding of Information by the Executive,* Hearings before the Subcommittee on Separation of Powers of the Senate Judiciary Committee, 92:1 (GPO, 1971), p. 17.

The mechanisms used for central decisionmaking and coordination in foreign policy have varied widely with presidential styles and preferences. But the record displays clear patterns, and it justifies several conclusions. One is that two perennially attractive mechanisms tend to prove unworkable: reliance on the Department of State, and dependence on formal interagency committees.

The central direction of foreign affairs, subject only to presidential guidance, turned out to be impossible for the Department of State when its two principal competitors in foreign affairs were Defense and Treasury—next to itself the agencies most nearly "presidential" in viewpoint. Today, the increasingly direct domestic effects of "foreign" policy (such as the relation of fuel availability to U.S. support of Israel) and the multiplying consequences abroad of "domestic" decisions (such as how fast to reflate the U.S. economy in 1975 or whether to grant landing rights to the *Concorde* in 1976) mean that the business of the State Department is shared not merely with Defense and Treasury but also with most of the major domestic agencies. It means too that State's business, far more than before, is political. Issues of large political import typically engage many departments and generate sharp disagreements. Within the executive branch such issues can be settled only by the President. Processes of consultation and machinery of coordination can affect the shape and timing of such issues but cannot resolve them. Resolution requires that some important interests that are the special responsibility of particular departments be sacrificed to others. Departments do not accept such losses if the decisions can be appealed. Final resolution of such issues, therefore, can be made only by the highest political authority. The President has such authority; State does not. State's disability is all the more limiting because many foreign policy issues of peripheral importance to State are of central concern to other cabinet departments, as a tariff on canned hams is for Agriculture, the Strategic Goods List is for Commerce, and exchange rate adjustments are for Treasury.

Formal interagency committees like the Council on International Economic Policy share the same handicap: the absence of a chairman capable of making decisions stick. They compound that problem with others. They tend to operate apart from mainline foreign policy decisionmaking, thus missing connections between their issues and others. They encourage departmental principals, surrounded by committed and watchful retainers, to argue only their own agencies' briefs. They typically expand in numbers and decline in level of representation over time. Their real work then shifts to other forums.

THE CABINET. Instead of reliance on either a lead department or formal interagencies committees, we propose the parallel use of two other mechanisms. The first is built on that perennial loser, the cabinet. Presidents have frequently taken office promising to use the cabinet fully; they have uniformly behaved otherwise. "With regard to the Cabinet as an institution, as differentiated from the individuals who compose it, as I have seen it operate under three Presidents, it is a joke. As a collegium, it doesn't exist. Its members, serving as a Cabinet, neither advise the President nor engage in any meaningful consideration of serious problems or issues."[24] So said Abe Fortas, and his is not a minority view. The persistent failure of the cabinet as a collegial body reflects two inherent defects. Many issues engage only a small number of cabinet departments. Secretaries of other departments thus become extraneous, and extraneous participants inhibit serious discussion. Moreover, many cabinet members are rapidly socialized into departmental roles, becoming spokesmen for the interest groups and congressional committees to which their departments are oriented. They appear to a President, therefore, not as counselors but as special pleaders. "The members of the Cabinet are a President's natural enemies," is Charles Dawes's famous comment.[25]

The first of these defects is serious: the full cabinet is simply too large. But the second, we believe, can readily be turned to advantage. If foreign and domestic issues are intertwined, and if foreign policy is more politically sensitive than before, then a decision process that exposes the President to less than the full spectrum of interests affected by major issues cannot serve him well. It will not reliably reveal the full implications of proposed decisions, nor warn of the nature and intensity of potential opposition. Such a restricted process will fail, in short, to weight appropriately the relevant perspectives; it will gain ease of decision at costs to balance and legitimacy.

Broader use of cabinet members would confer other benefits as well. Presidents need stronger and more responsive performance from key cabinet departments, and strength and responsiveness are not easy to combine. But making key cabinet officers the primary sub-

24. Quoted in Emmet John Hughes, *The Living Presidency* (Coward, McCann and Geoghegan, 1972), p. 335.
25. Quoted in Neustadt, *Presidential Power*, p. 39.

stantive counselors to the President and ensuring steady face-to-face relations between them and the President would tend to induce both. The recognized participation of secretaries in presidential decision-making strengthens their command of their own subordinates; it also sensitizes them to presidential perspectives and to interests other than those of their own departments.

A less obvious advantage may be equally important. Councils and cabinets are not only forums; they are also reasons for the creation of staffs. Indeed, no consequence of the NSC has proven more important than the development of its staff. The broad use of a cabinet-like forum for decisionmaking would facilitate creation of a single integrated cabinet staff. Combining the three principal White House staffs that are now autonomous—those of the NSC, the Domestic Council, and the Economic Policy Board—would be an important advance. Some specialization within a broader and integrated staff would obviously be necessary, but a single staff preparing issues for a central forum of broad jurisdiction could address the interacting issues of the future far more effectively than the three specialized staffs do now.

We propose, therefore, that the National Security Council be abolished and that an executive committee of the cabinet become the chief forum for high-level review and decision of all major policy issues that combine substantial "foreign," "domestic," and "economic," implications.[26] Most major decisions about the U.S. economy would fall in this category; so would virtually all key national security issues. Such a committee, which might be called ExCab, should surely include the secretaries of State, Defense, and Treasury. As the official normally best situated to represent the concerns of domestic social policy, the secretary of HEW should also be a member. ExCab should also include an additional representative of U.S. economic interests, ideally, the secretary of a new department resulting from a merger of Commerce and Labor. Opposition from interest groups and Congress has so far made such a merger impossible; that being so, the President might appoint whichever head of either department embodied the larger perspective and higher competence. John Dunlop, George Schultz, and Elliot Richardson are recent reminders that men capable of representing larger economic perspectives than those of either department have occupied those offices.

These officials might form ExCab's permanent membership, but

26. A similar body was proposed by Maxwell D. Taylor in "The Exposed Flank of National Security," *Orbis*, vol. 18 (Winter 1975), pp. 1011–22.

other cabinet officers and agency heads would be asked to join the discussion of issues that concerned them. (Congressional leaders might also occasionally be invited to ExCab meetings, though on a wholly informal basis.) Depending on the issues being discussed, several additional officials might attend: the President's chief substantive staff members and congressional liaison officers; his science adviser, chief intelligence officer, and the director of OMB. At least in the early months of an administration, and at subsequent times of major uncertainty when broad changes in policy are contemplated, issues should be prepared for ExCab deliberation through formal and intensive interagency studies.

A body such as ExCab would yield most of the advantages of the the collegial participation of major department heads, while avoiding the unwieldiness of the full cabinet. In doing so, it would also establish an implicit hierarchy of cabinet and "supercabinet" positions, a means of improving the integration of policy throughout the government that has attracted many Presidents but proven impossible to achieve through formal reorganization in the face of congressional opposition. ExCab would possess no formal authority of its own but might still prove a powerful innovation. It would widen the circle of advisers the President normally consults before making major decisions. It would put those advisers directly in touch not only with the President but also with each other, helping to generate a collegial comprehension among all the President's principal subordinates of the varied dimensions of the issues the President confronts. It would reinforce the standing of cabinet officers as the primary substantive counselors to the President and greatly improve the odds that major decisions were taken with an eye to both their domestic and foreign effects. The size, formality, and title of the forum used to accomplish these purposes are quite secondary. What is essential is that some such forum regularly bring together for substantive discussion and decision the senior line officials of the government, the officers who together can best assess the full implications of major issues and who individually and jointly must understand, support, and manage the processes by which decision becomes action.

ExCab would clearly have to be supplemented by various cabinet subcommittees and by ad hoc task forces—groups consisting, in Francis Bator's characterization, of "a small number of people who are senior enough to marshall the resources of their agency; not so senior as to make it impossible for them to keep up with detail or spend the time needed for comprehension and sustained exploration of each other's minds; and close enough to their Secretaries and to the President to serve as double-edged negotiators (each operating for his Secretary in the task group bargaining, and in turn representing the group's analysis of the issues and choices to his Secretary)."[27] Such task forces would utilize subcabinet officials, together with White House staff members, in some instances providing staff work for presidential decision, in others managing the continuing processes of implementation, review, and redecision. Presidential assistants might more appropriately chair groups engaged in the first function; departmental officers, selected for personal competence as well as departmental position, would normally chair those engaged in the second.

PRESIDENTIAL STAFF. What the President cannot rely on the machinery of coordination to produce is what he needs most from his staff: help in ensuring that issues requiring his attention are identified; that decisionmakers are faced with maps of such issues that reveal their full dimensions and facilitate knowledgeable choice; that choices made are faithfully implemented; and that the President's own judgments benefit from advice sensitive to his personal and political concerns.

Before issues are brought to a forum such as ExCab, the President's staff must see to it that studies have tested the purported facts, highlighted uncertainties, explored feasible alternatives, and identified linkages to other issues. For issues handled by more informal and lower-level arrangements, staff has several other tasks: to ensure timely formation of working groups and the balance of their memberships, and to communicate presidential perspectives where these should inform decisions but the President need not be directly involved. At all levels, staff must see that all affected parties are apprised of decisions taken, that their responsibilities resulting from those decisions are specified, and that their subsequent actions meet the intent of policy. The principal role of staff, in short, is to help the President ensure the balance, depth, and integrity of the processes of decision. It is a hard role, requiring self-restraint in a place—the

27. *U.S. Foreign Economic Policy: Implications for the Organization of the Executive Branch*, Hearings before the House Foreign Affairs Committee, 92:2 (GPO, 1972), p. 114.

White House—where that discipline is hardest to maintain. And it has not often been well performed in recent years. Instead, staff members have frequently become the President's chief substantive advisers and assumed major operating responsibilities—for continuing negotiations, for the authoritative statement of policy, and for relations with press, Congress, and foreign leaders. The result has been a confusion of staff and line functions, and poor performance of both.

The organization of White House staff must depend largely on the President's own preferences and disposition. The roles of staff and of line officers sketched above, however, suggest that the total number of White House staff be reduced, though a slightly larger number than has recently been common should have direct access to the President. It also suggests that if the President wishes to place a close substantive adviser in the White House, he should allow such a person no role in managing the flow of advice from other sources. If a forum such as ExCab were established, the President's substantive staff[28] might consist of four principal assistants to the President— one monitoring the flow of predominantly "foreign policy" issues, one for "domestic" affairs, and one for "economic" issues. (The director of the Office of Management and Budget might be regarded as an equivalent, fourth principal assistant.) The first three of these would be assisted by two or three deputies. The assistant for foreign affairs, for example, might have a deputy for foreign economics and a deputy for defense. The three presidential assistants and their deputies would be backed by an ExCab staff of several dozen members responsible to them jointly—a single, unified staff replacing the currently autonomous staffs of the NSC, the Domestic Council, and the Economic Policy Board.

In such a system, the sensitive task of assigning particular issues to one or more of the principal assistants, of ensuring that they worked effectively together, and of controlling jurisdictional disputes generated by the necessarily ambiguous boundaries between them should be assumed not by a chief of staff but by the President himself. Presidents of particularly reclusive temperaments might find that responsibility unwelcome. But most modern Presidents would have performed it willingly enough in view of the probable benefits. For the first time, the President would possess a substantive staff ori-

---

28. We ignore here other assistants such as press and appointments secretaries, speech writers, and the like.

ented toward a central task previously performed only in his own mind or not at all: assessing trade-offs among domestic, foreign, economic (and political) considerations, and integrating policy across those boundaries.

The Departments

However organized, neither mechanisms of central coordination nor presidential staffs conduct foreign policy. The day-to-day business of foreign affairs is carried on by the cabinet departments. Their performance has often been poor. The three principal sources of failure are mismatches between cabinet appointees and their jobs, presidential unwillingness to provide cabinet officials the mandates and support necessary to make them the managers of their departments, and the inability of the appointive government to work effectively with the permanent substructure on which it is placed.

The greatest single opportunity a President possesses to address these problems and to establish the character and competence of his administration arises in the choice of cabinet and subcabinet officials. The President must begin by selecting for his cabinet men and women of breadth and substance, capable of both managing their departments and advising the President. He should then permit them to select their own subordinates. If they are to manage their departments effectively, cabinet officers will need strong and compatible deputies, under secretaries, and assistant secretaries—all the more so if cabinet officers are to spend substantial time assisting the President in matters that transcend their own departmental responsibilities. Just as presidential performance is likely to be improved by broader and more collegial consultation with key cabinet members, so departmental performance would be strengthened by the collegial use of subcabinet officials. But such practices will succeed only if subcabinet officials understand that they work for their secretaries—an understanding the President can reinforce or undermine. Insofar as he can, the President should resist selecting subcabinet officials. Where campaign debts or prior loyalties make such self-restraint impossible, the appointed officials should know that though they may owe their jobs to the White House, they owe their loyalties to their secretary. Fortunately, a President who chooses cabinet officers of strength and scope and who deals with them directly is likely to find it easier to abstain from making subcabinet appointments. Having good two-way communication with his cabinet officers, he will feel less need than previous Presidents to protect himself with special agents and personal loyalists at lower levels of the departments.

A President whose cabinet officers meet those standards should also be inclined to keep them longer in office, a most desirable change in itself. Understanding the work of a major department, identifying its points of leverage, learning to deal with the political constraints within which it works, establishing effective relations with its permanent officials—these are all large tasks. It typically takes at least a year for senior officials to understand both what they are up to and what they are up against. Their second years are often their first productive ones. Yet the average tenure of cabinet officials since Truman's presidency has been under two years. The price of such rapid turnover includes uncertainty of policy, ragged implementation, and disincentives to long-range thinking, costs underappreciated in recent years.

Having appointed competent secretaries to head his ExCab departments and encouraged them to create departmental teams of strong and collegial subordinates, the President must make clear his major objectives for their departments. He and his staff must also periodically assess progress toward those objectives. A President will have particular priorities for specific departments, but several more general objectives apply throughout the government. One addresses the problem that time horizons in the top echelons of all departments are too short. The President must encourage organizational change to counteract the pressures on high officials to focus only on Tuesday's congressional testimony or next month's budget submission. Several proposals discussed above may be helpful: multiyear authorizations and appropriations; biennial statements and white papers that set current policy in a longer-run framework; and longer tenure for appointed officials. Several additional devices are worth considering. The President should require that proposals made to ExCab be presented with attention to their possible consequences five and ten years forward. Requests for major capital expenditures for defense and foreign aid should be justified in terms of the probable environment in the years when the products generated by those expenditures (Trident submarines, steel plants, dams) are operating—two or even three decades later. To retain their own sensitivity to the longer-run problems and purposes of their departments, secretaries may find it useful to establish small groups of knowledgeable private citizens whose judgments they value, and to meet with them informally for wide-ranging discussions several times each year.

To meet the demand for longer-run thinking that devices such as these should stimulate, many secretaries may wish to establish small staffs with special responsibilities for future projections. Their purpose will not be to monopolize such projections but to stimulate and improve their development throughout the departments. Experience shows that, if capable, such staffs are drawn into short-run business; if not, they lack influence. Coping with this dilemma requires that the director of such a staff seek a personal working relationship with his principal, that he find ways of linking longer-run analysis to current deadlines, and that the principal hold his staff to these purposes.

A second general objective is that cabinet officers come more rapidly to understand the processes they are charged with managing. Secretaries, like Presidents, find it natural to focus on decisionmaking. But decisions become action only through the work of subordinates, mostly members of career services. The values and incentives of such services are typically different from those of political appointees. Appointive officials cannot manage their departments without far deeper understanding of the motivations of their bureaucracies than has been common. In very large and complex agencies, particularly in the Department of Defense, this requirement might well be pressed to the point of establishing staffs specifically dedicated to what has been called "implementation analysis": predicting the bureaucratic response to policy proposals and designing whatever changes may be necessary in the form of those proposals, or in the implementing organizations themselves, to ensure that the policies chosen are feasible, and that they are then made to work.

The larger issue here, of course, is the systematically underattended problem of the relationship between the appointive and the permanent governments. The mutual suspicion and hostility that mark that relationship must be sharply reduced, but improvement will require long-sustained effort, an effort no postwar President has been willing to make. Viewed from the perspective of individual Presidents, such reluctance is understandable, but its cumulative effect is dismaying. Methods for dealing with the problem will vary by department. Among the measures worth considering in each are: creating some form of the long-proposed "federal executive service"; giving agency heads more flexibility in administering supergrade executives; broadening the perspectives of career officers through rotation among related agencies; abolishing the "merit system" embodied in the current civil service; and assuring the career services genuine participation in departmental decisionmaking. The underlying objective of all such reforms is the same. It is to establish conditions in which the skill, knowledge, and energy of the permanent government can be deployed on the issues of greatest importance to the administration, and thereby to create a relationship between the permanent and appointive governments of greater respect, trust, and productivity.

Finally, the department needing closest presidential attention is the Department of State. For two decades, State has most cherished and been repeatedly assigned a role it is not capable of performing, that of "preeminent director and coordinator of all U.S. foreign and national security policy." "Coordination" and "direction" are functions of power. As we argued above, coordination across departmental lines requires that the interests of some departments be sacrificed to others. Imposing such sacrifice requires authority that State does not, and cannot, possess. Even in the 1960s, when Defense and Treasury were its only main competitors, State could not coordinate or direct; on matters of importance to them the other departments would appeal to the President, and they frequently had greater weight in presidential councils than did State. In the decade ahead, when issues having import abroad will engage multiple agencies, interest groups, and congressional committees, the role that State found impossible even in the 1960s must clearly be abandoned. Assigning State a different and feasible role is essential to making the department effective.

There is a role that is appropriate for State, which with feasible reforms it can perform well, and whose effective performance would greatly improve the making of U.S. foreign policy. It is to advocate, forcefully and at every stage of the decision process, the interest of the United States in policies and actions that advance our security and well-being by meeting the legitimate requirements of other nations. Such advocacy must respond to longer-run American interests rather than to immediate foreign concerns; must focus on decisionmaking in Washington rather than on representation abroad; and must actively engage in the bureaucratic and political warfare from which policy emerges. State has sometimes performed exactly this function, though as one among many and rarely to the level its importance demands. What we think essential is that the department accept such advocacy as its central role and main responsibility, and that its structure, processes, and staffing be rethought in those terms.

Well played, such a role cannot be popular. It will frequently require opposition to proposals that serve powerful domestic interests, and whose costs to the United States may appear only after some remote and contingent foreign reaction. But its performance is essential. Policymakers must be kept steadily aware that America's security depends on a fragile network of international relations, and that actions serving short-run U.S. interests, or venting nationalistic emotions, can damage that network or provoke costly foreign reactions. Fortunately, State will not stand alone. The domestic interests directly affected by foreign reactions are becoming more conscious of their own stakes in responsible American policy—the support of free trade by the Department of Agriculture is an example. Moreover, most agencies of the government are now deeply engaged in foreign relations of their own, especially with their counterpart agencies abroad. And all have substantial international staffs attuned to the interests of other societies and aware of the ways foreign actions can affect U.S. interests. An important element in State's role as advocate, therefore, is to mobilize these potential supporters.

Making State an effective advocate for this perspective will take not only clarity about the primacy of the role, but attention to its organizational requirements. One is an appropriate secretary. At every stage of the policy process—in the articulation of national purposes, in the formulation of specific decisions, in the resolution of lower-level differences, in leading or monitoring implementation— the qualities State needs most are aggressiveness backed by relevant competence. Those requirements have implications everywhere in the department, but nowhere so clearly as at the top. The secretary of state must possess not only intellectual breadth, relevant experience, and political sense, but initiative and energy. Lacking these, he will not long remain the President's chief foreign policy adviser. Nor will his department intrude into policy debates over issues more central to other departments than to itself. The secretary will need the support of a team of top officials, each having his confidence and each assured his support. But most secretaries of state have presided over a department in which under secretaries, assistant secretaries, and ambassadors were appointed separately by the President, and many operated as independent entrepreneurs. Others—Kissinger among them—have so dominated their subordinates that little of substance could be undertaken without their explicit direction. Neither is an adequate model. An effective secretary requires allegiance and support from his subordinates; an effective department requires guidance and delegated authority from its secretary. Both requirements argue that all principal officers of the department should be appointed and employed as part of a single team.

Effective advocacy will also require far higher levels of functional competence than State now commands. State cannot and need not supplant Treasury in monetary expertise, or Defense in military judgment, or the Federal Energy Administration in estimating national fuel requirements, but it must become a respected participant in discussions of those subjects. It must be able to hold its own in interagency argument, developing its own proposals and analyzing those of others on the basis of solid technical skills. Achieving that capability will require a clearer focus and better staffing for the department's military and economic responsibilities. Curiously, there is no high-level point of focus within the department for politico-military affairs. A small staff is now headed by a director nominally equivalent to an assistant secretary, but not confirmed by the Senate. The department's third-ranking official, the under secretary for political affairs, has sometimes assumed responsibility for State's high-level involvement in national security issues, but sometimes has not. His job is not so defined and neither is anyone else's. Responsibility within State for defense-related issues should be clearly assigned as the main business of a single under secretary, probably the under secretary for political affairs. His position might be retitled accordingly. The Bureau of Politico-Military Affairs should be placed under his direction and its staff upgraded—principally by recruiting from outside the department—until its competence in strategic doctrine, military planning, logistics, and costing is solid.

Responsibility for economic affairs is already well focused in the department, although the under secretary for economic affairs has only rarely played a key role since the late 1950s. The problems here are that the under secretary lacks direct authority over what should be his principal staff—the department's semiautonomous Bureau of Economic and Business Affairs—and that this bureau is grossly undersupplied with trained economists.[29] The department's tactic of filling economic slots with foreign service officers having some interest or brief intensive training in the subject serves passably abroad and in the geographic bureaus of the department in Washington. But the absence of full professional competence in the staff designed to support the department's intervention in economic issues of high policy is a mistake.

Improving State's performance in defense and economic matters is thus partly a matter of clear assignments of responsibility and appropriate lines of authority, neither now present, but both relatively easy to establish. The harder problem will be to acquire and retain high competence, energy, and skill at the staff level. This is not a matter of numbers: if the functional staffs need expansion, it is by tens, not by hundreds. The difficulty will be creating a working environment in which specialized, Washington-based, functional talents are respected and rewarded in a department dominated by a generalist tradition, an overseas orientation, and a regional pattern of organization.

A final set of reforms in State looks to stronger foreign assessment. If State is to argue effectively against policies whose domestic and political implications are attractive, it will require some resource that other advocates do not possess. State's major resource can only be its ability to assert with authority the probable foreign responses to such policies and the resulting consequences for the United States. Such assertions must be based on an understanding of the governments and societies with which the United States is dealing that is firm enough to provide accurate predictions of foreign positions and to suggest those formulations of U.S. positions with the greatest chances of success. State's current political reporting does not commonly reach that level.

Ensuring that State's capacity for foreign assessment meets this need will require, first, that assessment be given express recognition as the central skill and great comparative advantage of the missions abroad and of State's country and regional desks in Washington. The secretary should make manifest his own belief that high performance here is essential. Responsibility for managing the institutional changes required to this end should probably be lodged in a single senior

29. Out of a professional staff of 126, only 3 have a Ph.D. in economics (based on unpublished information from the Department of State).

official. One concern of that official should be to improve the ability of U.S. overseas missions to anticipate the kinds of information and analysis most important to policy debate in Washington. The burden here is on the department to ask pointed questions and to insist on usable answers. Informal techniques are probably most useful, especially expanded use of the telephone, and more routine visits of desk officers to the field and of senior mission officers to Washington.

Equipping the missions to provide penetrating answers, once pointed questions are asked, may require innovations of several kinds. Entry into the department for persons with training, experience, or demonstrated capacity in area studies, political behavior, policy analysis, decision theory, and the like should be made easier and more attractive. Special training of foreign service officers might be tried, using courses yet to be devised. Assignment patterns should permit extended experience with particular nations and regions. Perhaps most important, the performance of foreign service officers should be evaluated in terms that give high priority to policy-relevant reporting, and promotion decisions should weigh those evaluations heavily.

This list of reforms is long and ambitious. But the work is genuinely important; and if ever the nation and the government were ripe for organizational reform, the time is now.

CHAPTER SEVEN

Stabilization Policy and Inflation

GEORGE L. PERRY

MODERN stabilization policy, born officially in the Employment Act of 1946, is now thirty years old and, to judge by the current volume of criticism, no longer to be trusted. Ten years ago, on the twentieth anniversary of the act, economists, the press, and the public all celebrated the then five-year-old expansion, already the longest in the modern record books. Early in the expansion, a 4 percent unemployment rate had been established as the proximate goal of policy, and by the end of 1965 it was achieved. But in 1976 the economy is just beginning to recover from its longest and deepest postwar recession and the administration, in its 1977 budget, projected a long-term path of economic growth that will not restore a 5 percent unemployment rate—a level last achieved in 1973—until 1981. The problem that emerged during these past ten years to complicate policymaking, and now to lower the goals for output and employment, is of course inflation.

Even taking account of the recent deep recession, the postwar record of economic performance is far superior to the record before modern stabilization policy came into being. Before World War II and the government's commitment to promote full employment, the U.S. economy experienced frequent sharp downturns in economic

I am grateful to Merriann Panarella for her research assistance in the preparation of this paper. George von Furstenburg of the American Enterprise Institute for Public Policy Research and Keith M. Carlson of the Federal Reserve Bank of St. Louis kindly provided data.

271

activity. The Great Depression of the thirties is the best remembered but hardly the only flaw in the record. A severe slump brought six straight years of double-digit unemployment rates in the 1890s. Before World War I unemployment jumped to recession levels with dismal regularity—in 1908, 1910–11, and 1914–15. Another severe slump raised the unemployment rate to 11.7 percent in 1921, following the boom years of the war. Although modern stabilization policy has unquestionably improved economic performance, it has still, in recent years, failed to live up to the expectations for high employment and price stability that had developed.

The current concern about inflation is not new. Although the Employment Act officially specified "maximum employment, production, and purchasing power" as its goals, politicians and economic policymakers have always accepted the avoidance of inflation as an implicit part of their mandate. Fiscal policy, comprising changes in federal taxes and expenditures, and monetary policy have been the principal tools used to meet the goals of the Employment Act. Both operate through their effect on the overall demand for goods and services in the economy. And throughout the past thirty years policy has been concerned with inflation arising from excess demand, strained capacity, and tight labor markets just as it has been concerned with recession and unemployment arising from insufficient demand.

However well demand management worked for much of the postwar period, it is painfully obvious that the conflict between high employment and price stability has steadily worsened in recent years. Inflation has existed alongside idle capacity, unemployed labor, and no excess of demand. In this situation there is no froth of inflationary excess demand to be skimmed off; restrictions of demand through monetary and fiscal policy cannot reduce inflation without interfering with the reduction of current high unemployment.

Past conflicts between price stability and high employment were resolved in different ways by different administrations. On three occasions, specific attempts were made to moderate wage and price increases as an adjunct to aggregate demand policy. Price controls were used to contain the sharp inflation engendered by the Korean War. Some twenty years later, a price freeze followed by a much looser set of controls were used in an attempt to end a far milder, though chronic, inflation. And from 1962 to 1966 guideposts for wage-price behavior were tried as a way of moderating wage and price increases. Each of these attempts to control, or at least influence, wage-price behavior had at least some success, but each also had drawbacks that eventually led to its abandonment.

In the following sections, the record of fiscal policy and monetary policy is reviewed with the aim of analyzing what they have done well and where they have failed. An analysis of recent and contemporary experience with inflation then illustrates why tools that influence only aggregate demand are inadequate to meet the current stabilization objectives of both high employment and a much lower rate of inflation than has been experienced. It is hard to escape the conclusion that the scope of stabilization policy must be expanded to deal with inflation directly, as well as indirectly through aggregate demand management, and a number of proposals for doing this are discussed.

The Record of Fiscal Policy

Fiscal policy refers to changes in taxes and expenditures as they affect the level of total demand in the economy. To examine historical experience with fiscal policy, a quantitative characterization of it is needed. It has long been recognized that changes in taxes and expenditures, and thus in the surplus or deficit,[1] come about from two causes: first, deliberate changes in tax rates and expenditure policies made by Congress and the President; and second, the "automatic" changes in taxes and expenditures brought about, under unchanged policies, by variations in the level of economic activity. During recession, personal income and corporate profits are depressed, lowering the tax base and reducing revenues from their normal levels. At the same time, unemployment compensation and other transfer payments are enlarged, raising the level of expenditures above normal.

These induced changes in the budget are called automatic stabilizers and help level off swings in economic activity. Because the federal budget shares in the ups and downs of private incomes, the swings in private demand for goods and services are moderated, thus automatically restraining the swings in economic activity. The importance of automatic stabilizers can be seen from their operation in the

1. From here on, the term surplus will be used with the understanding that it can be negative and hence a deficit.

recent recession. In the first quarter of 1975, before the antireces-
sionary tax rebates and tax cuts took effect, the budget deficit was $57
billion larger than it would have been with unemployment rates,
incomes, and profits at prerecession levels. If private incomes and
profits had instead been depressed by this $57 billion, private demand
would have been weaker and the recession much worse.

The High Employment Surplus

The induced changes are passive changes, responding to economic
conditions, rather than active changes that cause movements in the
economy. To get an indicator of fiscal policy that measures the active
influence of the budget on the economy, revenues, expenditures, and
the surplus in the budget calculated at some standardized level of
economic activity are estimated.[2] The most widely used indicator is
the high employment surplus in the budget—the surplus that would
prevail with the economy operating with a 4 percent unemployment
rate. The choice of 4 percent is historical convention. A surplus calculated at any other constant level would do just as well.

To directly compare policies in different periods, the ratio of the
high employment surplus to high employment gross national product
is used and will be referred to as the potential surplus ratio. At any
one time, this potential surplus ratio conveys the same information
as the high employment surplus itself, and it keeps comparisons
among different periods from being distorted by the growth of GNP.

Figure 7-1 depicts the potential surplus ratio and the ratio of the
actual surplus to potential GNP for fiscal years 1952–75.[3] The difference between the two in any year, which is shown in the bottom part
of the figure, measures the relative size of the surplus or deficit that
is induced by deviations in actual economic activity from the high-
employment path. As the figure shows, recessions generate large
deficits. In 1975, that part of the deficit induced by recession was
nearly 4 percent of potential GNP.

No level of the potential surplus ratio is "correct" for all time. The
whole object of stabilization policy is to offset variations in total demand that would move the economy from the desired level of activity.
As for fiscal policy alone, if total demand threatens to be too strong

2. E. Cary Brown first did this in "Fiscal Policy in the 'Thirties: A Reappraisal,"
American Economic Review, vol. 46 (December 1956), pp. 857–79.

3. The data on the high employment surplus and high employment GNP used in
constructing the figure and elsewhere in the paper were provided by George von
Furstenburg while he was with the Council of Economic Advisers.

Figure 7-1. Actual and High Employment Budget Surplus and Induced Deficit as Percentages of Potential GNP, Fiscal Years 1952–75

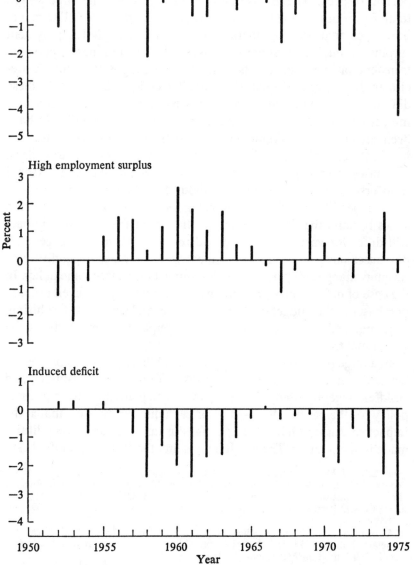

Sources: Actual surplus, COMETS data bank; other data, Council of Economic Advisers.

for whatever reason, stabilizing the economy calls for increasing the high employment surplus; if total demand prospects look too weak, stabilization calls for reducing the high employment surplus.

The case having been made for using the high employment surplus as an indicator of fiscal policy, its limitations should be noted as well. As a measure of economic impact, it is imprecise in at least two important respects. The first is that it implicitly assigns the same weight to all forms of revenue and all forms of expenditure. A dollar reduction in personal or corporate income taxes moves the full employment surplus as much as a dollar increase in defense purchases, personal transfers, or increased grants to state and local governments. A precise analysis would distinguish among the economic impacts in these different cases. Standardized surpluses assigning individual economic impact weights to different types of revenues and expenditures have been calculated by Oakland and Gramlich, among others.[4] These adjustments characteristically assign a full weight of 1.0 to federal purchases, with weights of about 0.9 for personal taxes and personal transfers. There is less agreement about the weighting appropriate to other expenditures and revenue categories. The second imprecision arises because the timing as well as the size of the economic impact will differ for various spending and revenue categories. In general, purchases have an immediate impact whereas other expenditure or revenue changes may have their full impact only after some delay. In the case of defense procurement, economic activity can even precede purchases in the budget, as contracts are let and suppliers start hiring, ordering, and producing before the receipt of payments from the government.

In a large formal econometric model, all these problems of weighting and timing are automatically taken into account. Blinder and Goldfeld recently used a large model to calculate the effects of fiscal policy for the period 1958–73.[5] For each quarter, they estimated the impact on future GNP of all changes in tax rates and expenditures made in the quarter. The catch here is that the Blinder-Goldfeld esti-

4. Edward M. Gramlich, "Measures of the Aggregate Demand Impact of the Federal Budget," in Wilfred Lewis, Jr., ed., *Budget Concepts for Economic Analysis* (Brookings Institution, 1968), pp. 110–27; William H. Oakland, "Budgetary Measures of Fiscal Performance," *Southern Economic Journal*, vol. 35 (April 1969), pp. 347–58.

5. Alan S. Blinder and Stephen M. Goldfeld, "New Measures of Fiscal and Monetary Policy, 1958–1973" (Princeton University, revised August 1975; processed). They used the MPS model for their simulations.

mates are specific to the particular model they use. And alternative large models differ in their estimates of how long it takes the different expenditure and revenue changes to exert their influence on GNP and how large the ultimate effects of different changes will be.[6] In short, economic model building is still far from providing any widely accepted characterization of fiscal impact as a substitute for the high employment surplus. In practice, for analysis over relatively short time periods, it turns out that the changes in the high employment surplus tell the basic story of the impact of fiscal policy on aggregate demand. Special care in interpreting periods when defense spending is rising or falling sharply probably will catch the only cases when a more elaborate calculation would be worthwhile.

Finally, during periods of rapid inflation, the interpretation of increases in the potential surplus ratio as deliberate fiscal policy actions differs slightly from that in noninflationary times. Inflation raises federal revenues more rapidly than expenditures. The consequent increase in the potential surplus ratio comes about not because of deliberate budget changes but because of rising prices and incomes. Interpreting this as a restrictive move in fiscal policy does make sense. Permitting the potential surplus ratio to rise from zero in the first quarter of 1973 to 2.1 percent in the third quarter of 1974 clearly reflected the administration's belief that fiscal restriction was desirable.

Fiscal Policy in Recession

Antirecession action has been a widely accepted priority in stabilization policy. This meant trying to avoid recessions, limiting their severity if they occurred, and promoting recovery from recession so as to restore high employment levels. This commitment to avoiding or minimizing the downward swings of the business cycle makes periods of recession and recovery a natural center for an analysis of fiscal policy.

In table 7-1, potential surplus ratios are shown for the quarters immediately preceding and following the last five recessions. The top half of the table is based on each quarter's ratio; it offers a view of policy on a current basis. The bottom half of the table is based on the

6. The whole issue is discussed in Alan S. Blinder and Robert M. Solow, "Analytical Foundations of Fiscal Policy," in Blinder and others, *The Economics of Public Finance* (Brookings Institution, 1974), pp. 3–115.

Table 7-1. Fiscal Policy as Measured by Full Employment Surplus Ratios, Five Recessions, 1953–75

		Quarters from peak (P) or trough (T)										Changes (percentage points, sign reversed)[a]		
Peak	Trough	P−4	P−3	P−2	P−1	P	T	T+1	T+2	T+3	T+4	P−4 to P	P to T	T to T+4
		Full employment surplus ratios (percent)												
1953:2	1954:2	−1.1	−2.2	−1.6	−2.1	−2.5	−0.7	−0.5	0.0	0.4	1.1	1.4	−1.8	−1.8
1957:3	1958:1	1.6	1.6	1.3	1.2	1.6	1.2	0.5	−0.1	−0.4	0.7	0.0	0.4	0.5
1960:1	1960:4	0.7	1.2	1.2	1.4	2.8	2.5	2.2	1.8	1.7	1.4	−2.1	0.3	1.1
1969:3	1970:4	0.0	0.4	1.1	1.4	1.1	0.6	0.3	−0.1	−0.1	−0.1	−1.1	0.5	0.7
1973:4	1975:1	−1.6	0.0	0.5	0.8	0.9	0.9	−2.0	−0.4	...	...	−2.5	0.0	1.3[b]
		Four-quarter average of full employment surplus ratios (percent)												
1953:2	1954:2	...	...	−1.3	−1.8	−2.1	−1.7	−1.3	−0.8	−0.2	0.3	0.8[c]	−0.4	−2.0
1957:3	1958:1	1.4	1.5	1.5	1.4	1.4	1.4	1.2	0.8	0.3	0.2	0.0	0.0	1.2
1960:1	1960:4	0.2	0.4	0.7	1.1	1.7	2.6	2.4	2.2	2.0	1.8	−1.5	−0.9	0.8
1969:3	1970:4	−0.8	−0.4	0.1	0.7	1.0	0.6	0.4	0.3	0.2	0.0	−1.8	0.4	0.6
1973:4	1975:1	−0.7	−0.6	−0.3	−0.1	0.5	1.6	0.7	0.1	...	...	−1.2	−1.1	1.5[b]

Source: Calculated from full employment GNP and full employment surplus series provided by the Council of Economic Advisers.
a. A positive change is stimulative, a negative change restrictive; thus a change to a higher potential surplus ratio is shown as a minus.
b. Change through quarter T + 2.
c. Change from quarter P − 2.

average of the ratio over the four quarters ending in the quarter shown; this averaging blurs the effect of current policy changes, but also reduces the possibility of erratic quarterly movements distorting the true ongoing thrust of policy. Because the four-quarter average builds in a lag and there is some lag in the response of the economy to fiscal changes, it should also come closer to measuring the economic impact of the budget in the quarter shown.

The last three columns in the table give changes in the surplus ratio for three intervals: in the four quarters leading up to the cyclical peak, between the peak and the trough of the recession, and in the first four quarters of recovery from the trough. As the signs on the changes have been reversed, a restrictive policy is shown as a negative change. In interpreting the magnitude of the changes shown, a reduction of 1 percent in the surplus ratio—which would be a positive change of 1.0 in the table—can be thought of as roughly equivalent to a $17 billion tax reduction in today's economy. To give an idea of which changes are "significant" compared to the normal variability in the potential surplus ratios, changes greater than one standard deviation are shown in bold type.[7] Over the 1953–75 period, one standard deviation was 1.2 percent of potential GNP for the changes in the top half of the table and 0.9 percent for the changes in the bottom half. A restrictive change this large or larger occurs in about one-sixth of all quarters.

The most striking finding from table 7-1 is that fiscal policy has contributed to the last three recessions. In each case, the surplus ratio grew substantially in the four quarters leading up to the downturn in business activity, using either the current or moving average measure of fiscal policy. Only in the quarters leading up to the 1953–54 recession was policy moving in a stimulative direction. And that was fortuitous, resulting entirely from the boom in Korean War spending. On that occasion, the decline from the spending crest coincided with the onset of recession. The drop in defense orders preceded it and helped bring on the economic downturn.

Policy was only a little more timely once the economy actually headed into recession. The current-quarter surplus ratios in the top

7. One standard deviation is a number that statistically measures the variability in a series. If their signs are ignored, approximately two-thirds of all quarterly changes in the 1953–75 period will be smaller than that number and one-third will be larger. The third that is larger will in turn be approximately divided into half restrictive and half stimulative changes.

Table 7-2. Econometric Model Estimates of the Effects of Fiscal Policy on the Economy as Percent of GNP, Four Recessions, 1957–75

Peak (P)	Trough (T)	Changes		
		P−4 to P	P to T	T to T+4
1957:3	1958:1	...	...	+0.8
1960:1	1960:4	−2.3	−0.4	+2.1
1969:3	1970:4	−2.3	0.7	+1.4
1973:4	1975:1	−1.5	...	...

Source: Derived from Alan S. Blinder and Stephen M. Goldfeld, "New Measures of Fiscal and Monetary Policy, 1958–1973" (Princeton University, revised August 1975; processed), table 2.

half of the table show fiscal policy growing quite restrictive between the peak and trough of the 1953–54 recession, doing nothing in 1973–75, and becoming slightly more expansionary in the other three cases. By the moving average measure in the bottom half of the table, only in the 1969–70 downturn had policy become even moderately more supportive between the peak and trough of business activity. In the recessions of both 1960–61 and 1973–75, this averaged measure of fiscal policy grew markedly more restrictive right through the worst of the economic downturn.

Policy usually got going the right way by the end of the recession. Only in 1954 did the surplus ratio grow in the four quarters following the trough in business activity. Here the conclusion is much the same with either the current-quarter or moving average measure of fiscal action.

The picture of fiscal policy around recessions that emerges from the potential surplus ratio is confirmed by the alternative measure of fiscal impact calculated by Blinder and Goldfeld using the large MPS econometric model.[8] Their estimates of how fiscal policy affects the economy each quarter have been divided by real GNP to remove scale effects over time and reduced by the trend growth of real GNP in order to make a neutral policy one that would just keep up with the trend growth rate in the economy. The resulting estimates of fiscal impact shown in table 7-2 for the limited period for which they are available confirm the verdict of the potential surplus calculations. Fiscal policy was pulling down real GNP relative to trend before each of the last three recessions. It turned expansionary only in the quarters after the recession had bottomed out.

Before the recessions in 1957, 1969, and 1973, inflation compli-

8. "New Measures."

cated fiscal policymaking. Indeed, in 1969 taxes had only recently been increased to cool off an economy overheated by the Vietnam War. And in both 1969 and 1953, the aim of policy was probably a modest increase in unemployment from the very low levels that had been reached in the two wars. Only in 1960 did policymakers muff the stabilization job completely, bringing on a downturn when no conflict of goals complicated the outlook. But the other recessions give warning that, so long as policy must rely on restricting aggregate demand to slow inflation, it seems likely to push the economy toward recession in the process.

Delays in Taking Action

Whatever importance one assigns to any conflict of objectives in assessing fiscal policy, the failure to turn more promptly from restrictive to expansionary policy is troublesome. Policy has also erred by moving too late to moderate excessive booms, notably at the outset of the Korean War and when spending for the Vietnam War escalated. The overall impression is that fiscal policy has responded too slowly to changing economic conditions to be a successful countercyclical tool. Some have argued that lags are inherent in the fiscal policy process and there is little chance for improving on the record. But this is not clear. To be timely, policy would have to react to forecasts and would have to use tax and expenditure changes that could be implemented quickly. The one bright note that came out of the last recession is the speed with which countercyclical action was taken once the need for it was accepted. Congress and the President became seriously concerned about halting the recession in early 1975; by May and June tax withholding rates were lowered and checks for tax rebates and transfer bonuses were mailed out. The delay in sounding the call to action on that occasion is of course another matter.

Tax reductions were made before the recession trough in 1954 and 1970. In both cases, temporary taxes that had been imposed during wars were reduced or eliminated. Beyond these cases—1954, 1970, and 1975—tax reductions have never been used during recessions, although the investment credit, which had been suspended in 1966, was reinstated in early 1967 in a deliberately countercyclical move when capital goods spending threatened to weaken seriously.

A standby authority to change taxes would be a useful addition to the countercyclical arsenal. Such an authority should explicitly provide the apparatus, and hence the responsibility, to raise taxes as well as to lower them. It should specify the particular combination of taxes that would be changed if the authority were invoked. In this way, matters of equity would have been settled beforehand and would not become an issue when prompt stabilization action was needed. The authority should be available both to the President and Congress, with either branch having veto power over a change initiated by the other.

Policy Activism

Behind the issue of timeliness in policy changes lies a broader issue of how actively policy should be conducted. Activism is a recurring theme in discussions of stabilization policy. Its advocates believe they can improve the performance of the economy by managing aggregate demand. Its critics believe attempts to do this are likely to destabilize the economy and so support fixed rules for the conduct of policy. The difference between the two positions comes down to whether information about changes in the economy should influence policy-setting. Activists would adjust policy in light of recent or prospective changes. Rules advocates would not.[9]

Strict rules for the conduct of policy, as opposed to discretionary activism, make an illogical distinction between economic surprises stemming from the public and private sectors. If the economy were near its desired operating rate and there were a sudden big rise in defense spending, both rules and an activist strategy would call for an offsetting tax increase or a slowdown in other government spending, in effect to stabilize the high employment budget. But under the same economic conditions, rules would not call for a response to a prospective sudden surge in capital goods spending because it would not affect the budget. Activist advisers would respond.

Fortunately, policy is seldom guided by such strict adherence to budget rules. Some feedback from economic developments eventually gets into fiscal policymaking. The desire to speed up the response time and anticipate the need for changes in policy are the main distinguishing features of activist economists. And whatever the stated stabilization philosophy of an administration has been, political decisions and the force of economic events have often overridden it.

---

9. The issue of activism is analyzed in detail in Arthur M. Okun, "Fiscal-Monetary Activism: Some Analytical Issues," *Brookings Papers on Economic Activity*, *1:1972*, pp. 123–63. Hereafter *BPEA*.

Table 7-3. Variability of Fiscal Policy, 1953–75

| | | | | Kennedy-Johnson | |
| | | | | Pre-Vietnam buildup (1961:3–1965:4) | Post-Vietnam buildup (1966:1–1969:2) |
Description	Eisenhower (1953:3–1961:2)	Kennedy-Johnson (1961:3–1969:2)	Nixon-Ford (1969:3–1975:3)		
Potential surplus ratio	1.27	1.00	0.92	0.66	0.85
Quarterly change in potential surplus ratio	0.49	0.49	0.79	0.48	0.46

Standard deviations (column group header)

Source: Calculated by author from source cited in table 7-1.

The activism issue has distinct political associations. As always happens, this stresses differences and blurs the real analytic issues. But the political split is clear. Following the three recessions of the preceding eight years, the economic advisers who took over in 1961 advocated activist policies.

The business cycle does not have the inevitability of the calendar. The Government can time its fiscal transactions to offset and to dampen fluctuations in the private economy. Our fiscal system and budget policy already contribute to economic stability, to a much greater degree than before the war. But the time is ripe, and the need apparent, to equip the Government to act more promptly, more flexibly, and more forcefully to stabilize the economy—to carry out more effectively its charge under the Employment Act.[10]

Following the inflation of the 1960s, the economic advisers who took over in 1969 advocated an end to activism:

we must achieve a steadier and more evenhanded management of our economic policies. Business and labor cannot plan, and consumers and homebuyers cannot effectively manage their affairs, when Government alternates between keeping first the accelerator and then the brake pedal to the floor.[11]

In view of these positions, it is remarkable that one cannot tell who is on which side of the argument from the statistical record of actual changes in fiscal policy as measured by the potential surplus ratio. Table 7-3 shows the variability of fiscal policy in two ways: by the standard deviations of the potential surplus ratio (which expresses variations in the absolute level of the ratio, capturing major swings)

10. *Economic Report of the President, January 1962*, pp. 17–18.
11. *Economic Report of the President, February 1970*, p. 10.

and by the standard deviations of quarterly changes in that ratio (which expresses variations from the major trend in the ratio). For changes in the ratio, the Nixon-Ford years are easily the most variable, with a standard deviation of 0.79 as against 0.49 in both the Eisenhower years and the Kennedy-Johnson years. For the level of the ratio, the Nixon-Ford years are the least variable, with a standard deviation of 0.92, just below the 1.00 for the Kennedy-Johnson years and well below the 1.27 for the Eisenhower years. The last two periods exhibited pronounced downward and upward trends, respectively, in the surplus ratio, which add to the variation by this measure. If the 1960s are broken at the end of 1965 to separate the period when fiscal policy was dominated by the war, both halves show less variation than either Republican period, with a standard deviation of only 0.66 during the supposedly activist "new economics" era of 1961 to 1965. Apparently all administrations are activist, but some are willing and some unwilling.

The 1960s

The hallmark of fiscal policy in the first half of the 1960s was the deliberate use of major tax reduction to reduce the potential budget surplus and restore full employment. It took time to sell the President and then the Congress on this plan, which flew in the face of fiscal orthodoxy because the actual budget was in deficit. But the eventual success of policy in that period was widely celebrated when the economy reached the 4 percent unemployment goal by the end of 1965.

Unfortunately, the buildup of defense spending for the Vietnam War was under way and, again, it took time to sell another needed fiscal initiative, this time to raise taxes. A number of things contributed to the delay. The Council of Economic Advisers was initially ignorant of the size of the defense spending buildup that was coming. The council was nonetheless urging a tax increase by December 1965, but the President resisted, in part for fear it would jeopardize his new Great Society programs with Congress. Another opportunity was missed the next year. A midyear tax increase was proposed in the Economic Report and Budget Message at the start of 1967, but the brief economic slowdown in the first half of the year made it difficult for the administration to sell a tax increase to Congress. Industrial production was well below the peak it had reached in the last quarter of 1966. The rise in wholesale prices had slowed or, in many lines, reversed itself. And the general tone of discussion in the press was against any restrictive policy measures. As a result, the proposed tax increase was not seriously debated until late in 1967 and did not pass and become effective until mid-1968. This was two and a half years after the President's activist economic advisers had urged higher taxes to offset rising defense outlays. The great failure of economic policymaking in the 1960s resulted from inaction in stabilization policy despite activist economic advice.

The 1970s

The major economic move of the Nixon years was the New Economic Policy launched in the summer of 1971. Impatient with lingering excess unemployment, balance-of-payment deficits, and stubborn inflation, the President went for a program that devalued the dollar, first froze and then controlled prices, and sharply reduced the potential surplus ratio in the budget from close to balance in the summer of 1971 to a deficit of 1.2 percent by the fourth quarter of 1972 (calculated after allocating half that quarter's retroactive revenue sharing grants to the third quarter). Except for devaluing the dollar, this was hardly a program favored by the Nixon economic advisers. Yet for all the faults of the price control system, 1972 was objectively the best year of economic performance in the 1970s, with real GNP growing 5.7 percent, unemployment declining 0.8 point to 5.1 percent, and the consumer price index rising only 3.4 percent during the year.

In 1973 and 1974 the whole process was reversed. The potential surplus ratio rose by nearly 3 percent between the second half of 1972 and the second half of 1974. This restraint, maintained as long as it was, helped aggravate the recession and send unemployment soaring. But inflation accelerated sharply as the dollar was again devalued, food and fuel prices soared, and controls were ended. In October 1974, with the recession nearly a year old, the administration proposed further restrictive fiscal measures.

Finally, 1975 saw another dramatic reversal in fiscal policy. As the recession deepened, Congress and the administration agreed on rebates and tax reductions to turn the tide. Six quarters after the economy peaked, a major swing toward fiscal stimulus was taken. Between the second half of 1974 and the second half of 1975, the surplus ratio dropped by more than 2 percent. In the second quarter of

1975, the drop was temporarily much greater as a result of the rebates and special transfers made in that quarter.

These huge reversals in fiscal policy during the 1970s—first sharply expansionary through 1972, then sharply restrictive through 1974, then sharply expansionary again in 1975—were hardly inadvertent. Nor were they necessarily out of step with the economic developments of their time given the joint objectives of high employment and price stability. But the experience shows the ineffectiveness of aggregate demand management in coping with these joint objectives in recent years, and it can also be read to show that the reluctance to make gradual and timely responses may lead to the need to make larger and late ones. Heller emphasized this possibility in his discussion of activism: "given the limited margin for error in a high-employment economy, it is better to rely on many smaller monetary-fiscal moves than a few large ones."[12]

The Record of Monetary Policy

Monetary policy is the second major instrument for influencing total demand in the economy. Fiscal and monetary policy affect GNP independently and can either complement or substitute for each other. If differences in timing, which point to somewhat prompter effects from most fiscal policy changes, are ignored, the same overall economic impact could be achieved with either a combination of tight fiscal policy and easy monetary policy or one of easy fiscal policy and tight monetary policy. The former would involve relatively large high employment surpluses and would require lower interest rates and, for a time, more rapid money supply growth on the part of monetary policy; the latter would involve relatively small high employment surpluses and would require higher interest rates and slower money supply growth. In other words, to achieve any given GNP target, a tight fiscal policy would require an easy monetary policy, which would include both lower interest rates at the target GNP level and faster money supply growth until the target was achieved.

Because it has a potent, independent influence on aggregate demand, monetary policy plays an important role in economic stabilization. The Federal Open Market Committee of the Federal Reserve

12. Walter W. Heller, "What's Right with Economics?" *American Economic Review*, vol. 65 (March 1975), p. 13.

System meets frequently to assess the condition of the economy and adjust monetary policy. Its instructions guide the daily conduct of open market operations through which the Fed can influence the quantity of money and the level of interest rates.

Important as it is, monetary policy is a surprisingly elusive subject. The trouble begins when a simple way is sought to characterize it. The layman, people in the financial community, and many economists would characterize it by the level of interest rates. Many other economists, a group including but by no means limited to those loosely thought of as monetarists, would characterize it by the growth rate in the money supply.[13] The trouble arises because money, interest rates, and GNP are interrelated. The less money is supplied for a given GNP, the higher interest rates will be. The higher GNP is for a given interest rate, the more money will be demanded. And the higher GNP is with a given money supply, the higher interest rates will be.

The level of interest rates affects total private demand and thus the level of GNP. Higher interest rates especially discourage demand that depends directly on borrowing, such as the demand for consumer durable goods, business investment, and housing. The effect on housing is particularly severe because high interest rates drain funds from the primary source of mortgage loans—the thrift institutions—which cannot raise the rates they pay depositors to competitive levels. High interest rates may also influence demand less directly by reducing the net value of private wealth.

Because the impact of monetary policy on economic activity works primarily through interest rates and their effect on total spending, it may seem natural to use interest rates to characterize policy. For all practical purposes, the Federal Reserve can directly affect some rates and through them influence others. It pegged rates at low levels through World War II and the immediate postwar years. Then in 1951 it reached an accord with the Treasury to stop doing so to allow freedom for countercyclical action. However, because interest rates are so sensitive to economic activity, it is not very useful to label all of

13. The money supply is defined as the sum of currency and demand deposits. When the discussion starts getting technical, interest-bearing time deposits are sometimes added to this to provide an alternative version of "money." Some would go further, adding savings and loan shares and so on, each addition to the total representing a close substitute for the one before it. Others would back up and analyze bank reserves since they are directly controllable by the Federal Reserve and come close to defining how large the money supply will be.

their rise and fall over the business cycle as discretionary monetary policy, even if the movements are, in principle, controllable by the Federal Reserve. By analogy with the high employment surplus, one might estimate a high employment interest rate to characterize monetary policy (that is, the interest rate that would be generated by the actual money supply and a high employment GNP). Actual movements in the interest rate above and below its high employment level could then be treated as an automatic stabilizer. But the monetary relationships among the money supply, GNP, and interest rates necessary for such a calculation are not very reliable, and it has not been pursued.

Many economists opt for characterizing monetary policy by the rate of growth of the money supply on the grounds that this ultimately will determine the growth rate of GNP. Since the demand for money is related to GNP, if GNP is "too high," money demand will run ahead of supply and interest rates will rise, bringing GNP down to where the demand for money equals the supply. But there is a good deal of professional controversy over the stability of this ultimate link of GNP to the money supply, and even more controversy over the strength of this link in the short run.[14]

A further difficulty in characterizing policy arises from inflation. As the demand for money grows with the price level, the rate of money growth must be discounted by the inflation rate to get the growth rate in the real money supply, the measure that is relevant to real economic activity. Four percent money growth might be expansionary with a stable price level. But if prices are rising at 6 percent a year and if that price increase is not very sensitive to short-run variations in the level of economic activity, a 4 percent money growth unavoidably leads to a decline in the real money supply of 2 percent a year. Simply

14. Though this is less obvious than in the case of interest rates, the money supply is not logically free of contamination from induced as opposed to discretionary movements either. Of course, under a policy of holding interest rates constant, variations in GNP will induce variations in the money supply. But even a policy of holding high employment interest rates constant, if they could be computed, would lead to induced variations in money growth to the extent that the demand for money itself shifted, as it frequently does. Pursuing this line of reasoning, one might choose between the money supply and interest rates for characterizing policy according to whether the relation between interest rates and economic activity is more or less reliable than the relation between economic activity and money demand. William Poole uses this distinction in "Optimal Choice of Monetary Policy Instruments in a Simple Stochastic Macro Model," *Quarterly Journal of Economics,* vol. 84 (May 1970), pp. 197–216.

characterizing policy by the real money supply, however, leads to the definition that policy is neutral when it is providing for normal real growth in the economy plus fully accommodating whatever ongoing rate of inflation exists. This is correct if real output is the only object of policy. But the definition is arguable if slowing inflation is a policy objective as well, especially if the inflation arises from excess demand. With no totally acceptable answer to all these questions, both real and nominal money growth rates as well as interest rates will be examined in viewing the performance of monetary policy.[15]

A final complication arises because of the lags between monetary policy and its effects on economic activity and because brief variations in money growth rates are of little importance. For the present purpose, policy in a given quarter will be characterized by money growth rates in the four quarters ending with the given quarter, which both allows for some lags and smooths erratic movements.

Monetary Policy in Recession

In table 7-4 monetary policy around the last five post-Korean recessions is characterized in various ways. The top two banks of the table show measures based on the nominal and the real money supply. Columns 1 through 10 give four-quarter growth rates, measured as deviations from trends,[16] for the period from four quarters before cyclical peaks to four quarters after cyclical troughs. The bottom third of the table shows the four-quarter change in interest rates on three-month Treasury bills during the same quarters. Columns 11, 12, and 13 give changes in the money growth measures (in the top two banks of the table) for different intervals around the recessions. These changes are most relevant if one believes that accelerations or decelerations in money are what matter, as opposed to departures from some fixed norm for money growth.

As with the earlier analysis of fiscal policy, it is useful to have some

15. Inflation also presents the problem of how to interpret interest rates since they will incorporate some premium to make up for rising prices. This is considered when changes in interest rates are discussed.

16. In measuring deviations from trends, zero should be neutral. The overall 1949–75 annual trends of 3.6 percent for the money supply and 0.3 percent for the real money supply were thus adjusted to allow for changes in the trend growth of potential GNP. After this adjustment, the annual trend for the money supply was 3.4 percent from 1949 through 1962, then 3.7 percent through 1968, and 3.9 percent thereafter. For the real money supply, the trends for the three periods were 0.1 percent, 0.4 percent, and 0.6 percent.

Table 7-4. Monetary Policy as Measured by Money Supply and Treasury Bill Rates, Five Recessions, 1953–75

Peak	Trough	Quarters from peak (P) or trough (T)										Changes (percentage points)		
		P−4 (1)	P−3 (2)	P−2 (3)	P−1 (4)	P (5)	T (6)	T+1 (7)	T+2 (8)	T+3 (9)	T+4 (10)	P−4 to P (11)	P to T (12)	T to T+4 (13)
		Money supply growth relative to trend (annual percent)												
1953:2	1954:2	1.8	1.6	0.7	−0.2	−0.3	−2.7	−1.9	−0.9	−0.1	0.3	−2.1	−2.4	3.0
1957:3	1958:1	−2.6	−2.3	−2.5	−2.7	−2.7	−4.0	−2.9	−1.9	−0.2	1.3	−0.1	−1.3	5.3
1960:1	1960:4	1.3	1.0	0.5	−1.3	−3.1	−3.0	−2.1	−1.1	−1.4	−0.6	−4.4	0.1	2.4
1969:3	1970:4	2.9	3.5	4.0	3.2	1.7	0.9	1.7	2.8	3.2	2.6	−1.2	−0.8	1.7
1973:4	1975:1	4.2	4.2	3.8	3.1	2.1	−0.3	0.1	0.8	0.4	0.9	−2.1	−2.4	1.2
		Real money supply growth relative to trend (annual percent)												
1953:2	1954:2	4.2	3.4	2.5	1.2	0.9	−0.9	0.7	0.6	1.7	1.9	−3.3	−1.8	2.8
1957:3	1958:1	−2.7	−2.7	−3.0	−2.9	−2.7	−2.7	−1.3	0.0	1.6	2.7	0.0	0.0	5.4
1960:1	1960:4	2.7	1.8	1.5	−0.3	−2.1	−1.2	0.5	1.2	1.0	1.6	−4.8	0.9	2.8
1969:3	1970:4	1.6	2.0	2.7	1.7	−0.3	−0.8	0.0	1.0	1.4	1.2	−1.9	−0.5	2.0
1973:4	1975:1	3.4	3.3	1.9	0.2	−1.7	−7.5	−5.8	−3.9	−2.8	−1.1	−5.1	−5.8	6.4
		Change in Treasury bill rate (percentage points over past four quarters)												
1953:2	1954:2	0.2	0.2	0.3	0.4	0.5	−1.4	−1.1	−0.5	0.2	0.7	...	...	...
1957:3	1958:1	0.7	0.7	0.8	0.6	0.8	−1.3	−2.2	−1.7	−0.6	1.0	...	...	...
1960:1	1960:4	1.0	2.0	1.9	1.5	1.1	−1.9	−1.5	−0.7	−0.1	0.2	...	...	...
1969:3	1970:4	0.9	0.8	1.0	0.7	1.8	−2.0	−3.4	−2.4	−1.3	−1.1	...	...	...
1973:4	1975:1	0.6	2.3	2.8	4.1	2.6	−1.9	−2.8	−1.9	−1.7	−0.8	...	...	...

Sources: Calculated from data on money supply and Treasury bill rates from *Federal Reserve Bulletin*, various issues, and the official gross domestic product deflator from COMETS data bank.

idea of variability in the monetary measures against which to judge their movements around recessions. From 1949 to 1975 the standard deviation of money growth over four-quarter intervals is 2.0 percent and of real money growth 2.3 percent. For the changes shown in columns 11–13 the standard deviations are 2.2 and 3.0 for money and real money, respectively. Changes larger than these standard deviations are shown in bold type in the table. Of these, changes larger than one standard deviation can be expected in about one-sixth of all the postwar quarters. They can be thought of as "significantly" large movements in monetary policy.

REAL MONEY GROWTH AND INTEREST RATES. The rate of growth in the real money supply bears a clear, if imperfect, relation to recessions. The real money supply grew significantly more slowly than trend (column 5) up to the peak in 1957 and had been doing so throughout the preceding year as well. It was also growing considerably more slowly than trend up to the peaks in 1960 and 1973, but not in any immediately preceding quarters. Clearly, in 1957 and possibly in 1960 and 1973, tight money contributed to the downturns by this criterion.

The slowdowns in growth rates of the real money supply (column 11) show an even stronger relation to recessions. The growth rate had slowed noticeably at all peaks except 1957, with only the 1969 slowdown smaller than one standard deviation in this measure.

Interest rates offer another way of judging when policy was tightening before recessions. Rates were higher than a year earlier at all cyclical peaks (column 5). Real GNP grew 5.6 percent, 2.1 percent faster than trend, in the four quarters before the 1953 peak. It grew only 0.6 percent faster than trend before the 1960 peak, and 0.9, 2.0, and 0.8 percent more slowly than trend before the 1957, 1969, 1973 peaks, respectively. Thus an induced rise in interest rates stemming from a particularly rapid advance in the economy can explain the 1953 behavior of rates. But the justification that the rise was induced does not fit 1960 well since growth was only a little above trend and unemployment was still high. And it does not fit the other cases at all.[17]

17. If one believes the current rate of inflation should be subtracted from short-term interest rates to get a measure of restrictiveness, the picture becomes quite unclear. The change in the annual rate of inflation in the GNP deflator between peaks and four quarters earlier exceeded the corresponding rise in the Treasury bill rate at the cyclical peaks in 1953, 1969, and 1973. These inflation rates, however, vary a

Monetary policy was not becoming less restrictive before any of the recessions. The uniform rise in interest rates before peaks is one sign of this, and it is confirmed by the changes in real money growth rates (column 11), which slowed down before all recessions except 1957 (when real money growth remained significantly slower than trend for an extended period).

Nor did policy usually move decisively against recession even after it started. Real money growth was slower than trend at every recession trough (column 6), and significantly so at the troughs in 1958 and 1975. In three recessions, real money growth slowed between the peak and trough (column 12). Interest rates fell in every recession, but this cannot be regarded as expansionary policy since declining real output will lower interest rates under all but extremely perverse monetary policies.

Around the 1957, 1969, and 1973 recessions, monetary policy was faced with the same conflict between goals for unemployment and price stability as faced fiscal policy. Monetary policy has no special power to control inflation other than by affecting aggregate demand. It thus runs the same risks of causing recession when it becomes restrictive and of worsening inflation should it become stimulative when demand is already too strong.

THE MONEY SUPPLY. A very simple view that holds deviations from trend growth in the money supply responsible for real economic developments gets little support from this analysis of recession periods. Only at the 1957 and 1960 peaks was money growth significantly restrictive by this measure. Allowing for a longer lag in the impact of money loses even the 1960 case, for money growth was faster than trend in the year ending two quarters before the 1960 peak and faster still four quarters before. Money growth was faster than trend at both the last two peaks, in 1969 and 1973, and was faster still in quarters preceding these peaks. Of course, postwar changes in the inflation rate influence these calculations since rising prices cause approximately

---

great deal from quarter to quarter. More important, the significance of adjusting by such an average price increase is not clear. A potential borrower is presumably interested in the prospective price of particular goods and services when trying to decide whether to borrow for them. This may bear little or no relation to any one price index. For instance, in 1973 the GNP deflator accelerated primarily because of soaring food prices; borrowing costs were low if one was borrowing to hold food and other raw commodities and high if one was borrowing for most other purposes. Also, to the extent that higher rates affect demand by diverting funds from thrift institutions and hence housing, the rate of inflation is immaterial since these institutions operate with nominal interest rate ceilings.

proportional increases in the demand for money. Thus the trend of the whole period reflects the faster growth in money demand that came with the inflation of the latest years. With this inflation, even substantially faster money growth rates than the trend for the whole period may be noticeably restrictive and contribute to economic downturns. Slowdowns in money growth (column 11) are related to recessions, though not as strongly as the corresponding slowdowns in real money growth already discussed.

Monetary Activism

Monetary policy has hardly been identical in all recessions. Yet by at least some criteria it has been in general pro-cyclical, not fighting and perhaps worsening some recessions, if not actually causing them. Monetarist economists have used observations such as this to argue against activist monetary policy, advocating in its place a constant rate of growth for the money supply.[18] Without entering deeply into this debate, a few observations can be made on the basis of the experience surrounding recessions.

First of all, the money supply was growing faster than trend before the last two recessions and as fast as trend before the first recession examined here. A fixed rule of trend growth would have worsened matters in two cases and helped in two. Compared to what was done, keeping the real money supply growth at trend would have eased policy in 1957, 1960, and 1973 and tightened it somewhat in 1953. But monetarist prescriptions are rarely written in terms of real money growth, for that misses the whole point of controlling inflation with monetary policy. It is much more difficult to assess what would have happened with trend growth in the money supply not only just before and during recessions, but in all earlier periods as well. An evaluation would depend on what trend growth rate was chosen and, beyond that, on what other factors were affecting economic performance and on how stable the demand for money was from period to period.

Rising interest rates were a more persistent precursor of recession than below par growth in money or real money. It would be even harder to prescribe fixed rules for interest rates than for monetary aggegates since they exhibit such pronounced cyclical movements. But attention to rates should improve on stabilization policy based on monetary aggregates alone. When the economy is past the early stages

18. Milton Friedman is the foremost proponent of this view, but it is shared by many other monetary theorists.

of recovery and output is not growing noticeably faster than trend, a significant rise in interest rates should alert the authorities that policy is becoming restrictive no matter what the monetary aggregates are doing. Conversely, even if the real money supply is declining, monetary policy should not be viewed as restrictive if real output is growing normally or better and interest rates are stable or falling. This was precisely the situation in the half-year after the summer of 1975.

In the 1960s a monetary policy not oriented to fixed money growth rules performed well both in accommodating a desired above par expansion and later in restricting excessive demand. It pursued an accommodative policy when the tax cut of 1964 was passed in an effort to restore high employment levels. And it tightened up in 1966 when the war started overheating the economy and successfully slowed the surge in demand without causing recession.

The hardest problems are not easily handled with either activist policy or rules. During 1973 a new burst of inflation resulting primarily from a shortage of world food supplies came on top of a modest but persistent inflation in the domestic nonfood sector. This was followed at the end of the year by a new round of inflation arising from world fuel prices. Monetary policy was particularly impotent against these price increases. Not only did they not stem from excessive aggregate demand in the United States, but they were clearly reducing effective real demand by transferring real income away from most consumers to oil producers and the farm sector. Money supply rules would have ignored these special developments, and the Federal Reserve pretty much ignored them too. Private short-term interest rates were driven to historic peaks in 1973 and again in the summer of 1974, well after the start of the downturn. Monetary policy thus played a part not only in starting the 1973–75 recession, but in deepening it as well. On the other hand, a policy that fully accommodated the new burst of inflation in 1973 might have led to a larger growth in wages and a higher and more persistent inflation in subsequent years.

Autonomy and Coordination in Monetary Policy

The relation between the Federal Reserve and the President is ambiguous. The Federal Reserve is an independent body but hardly immune to the wishes of the administration; historically the Fed's chairman has maintained an informal working relation with the President.

However, there is no statistical evidence of fiscal policy and monetary policy working systematically together. Of several postwar intervals analyzed, none showed a significant negative correlation between money growth and changes in the potential surplus ratio. And in the period from the first quarter of 1966 to the second quarter of 1969, there was a noticeable (0.7) positive correlation, indicating policies pulling largely in opposite directions: changes in the money supply were positively related to changes in the potential surplus.

Recently, the Fed's independence has been of some concern to Congress. As an outgrowth of this concern, the Federal Reserve chairman has been reporting each quarter to congressional committees with targets for growth rates of the money supply and for other monetary aggregates. In view of the imprecise relation between the money supply and real economic activity, this focusing of concern on money growth targets has little merit. On the other hand, Congress has a legitimate interest in airing the economic goals being pursued by the Fed, particularly when the economy is suffering both inflation and unemployment and policy must choose a balance between the two.

Inflation in the 1970s

Traditional stabilization policy, as pursued by both fiscal and monetary authorities, has always been concerned with avoiding inflation by avoiding excessive aggregate demand. Translated into unemployment targets, this has meant not trying to run the economy with "too low" an unemployment rate. By bearing this in mind, the special problems that inflation has posed for stabilization policy in the 1970s can be easily appreciated. The best-known and most widely followed price measure is the consumer price index. From the end of the Korean War through the 1960s, the CPI rose an average of 2.0 percent a year while unemployment averaged 4.8 percent. The best year for price stability was 1955, when prices declined 0.4 percent, and the worst was 1969, when they rose 5.4 percent. Up to the end of the 1960s the only other years consumer prices rose more than 3 percent were 1957 and 1968. By contrast, in the first six years of the 1970s, the CPI consistently rose more than 3.0 percent despite a price control program and two recessions. When controls came off, consumer prices rose 11.0 percent in 1974 and 9.1 percent in 1975, and these were years of severe recession.

The rise in the prices of food and fuel was exceptional after 1972, but for reasons largely unrelated to the state of aggregate demand in the U.S. economy. The special difficulties that food and fuel prices posed for stabilization policy in this period will be taken up below. But it is easier to start analyzing the general problem of inflation without considering them. The private nonfarm deflator is a useful aggregate price index for this purpose. It excludes the wages and salaries of government workers and the prices of agricultural production, as well as the prices of imports, and so provides a good measure of inflation in the main part of the American market economy. Here, the index will also be adjusted to remove the effects of the rise in energy prices after the fall of 1973.

A Basic View of the Inflation Process

Two questions lie at the heart of the inflation issue: what starts it or accelerates it, or the *initiation* problem, and what keeps it going, or the *inertia* problem. The ability of traditional monetary and fiscal instruments to achieve the joint objectives of high employment and price stability simultaneously hinges largely on the answers to these two questions. If inflation is set off during an economic recovery, well before the unemployment rate drops to a reasonably low level, the dilemma for policymakers is obvious, and the dilemma is compounded if inflation, no matter what its origin, persists for a long time in the face of rising unemployment and idle capacity.

The historical record in table 7-5 shows that price inflation is closely related to the inflation in current wage costs. Here wage costs are measured by average hourly compensation, which includes fringe benefits as well as wages, and within fringe benefits includes the employers' share of payroll taxes. In the twenty-two years since the end of Korean War controls, the annual increase in the private nonfarm deflator (excluding the extraordinary energy price increases of 1974–75) averaged 2.36 percent less than the annual increase in hourly compensation. This difference provides an estimate of the average growth trend in labor productivity in the private nonfarm sector. The increase in hourly compensation less this trend increase in productivity equals the increase in standard unit labor costs shown in the third column.

A simple rule of thumb is that each year's price increase will equal the increase in standard unit labor costs; in other words, each year average prices will rise 2.36 percent less than average hourly compen-

Table 7-5. Effects of Wage Costs on Prices, 1954–75
Percent

	Annual change			Actual less predicted price changes	
Year	Compensation per hour (1)	Private nonfarm deflator[a] (2)	Standard unit labor cost (3)	When prediction equals change in standard unit labor cost (4)	When prediction is from estimated equation[b] (5)
1954	4.2	1.6	1.9	−0.3	−0.4
1955	2.9	2.0	0.6	1.5	1.3
1956	5.8	3.1	3.4	−0.3	0.4
1957	5.4	3.5	3.1	0.4	0.4
1958	4.5	0.9	2.2	−1.2	−1.3
1959	4.4	2.2	2.1	0.1	0.2
1960	3.8	1.6	1.5	0.1	0.0
1961	4.0	0.8	1.6	−0.8	−0.8
1962	3.7	1.4	1.4	0.1	0.0
1963	3.6	1.3	1.3	0.0	0.0
1964	4.0	1.2	1.6	−0.4	−0.3
1965	3.5	1.7	1.1	0.6	0.5
1966	5.7	2.8	3.3	−0.5	−0.1
1967	5.7	3.0	3.3	−0.3	−0.4
1968	7.1	4.0	4.7	−0.7	−0.5
1969	6.4	4.7	4.1	0.6	0.4
1970	7.2	4.7	4.9	−0.1	−0.1
1971	6.8	4.6	4.5	0.1	−0.1
1972	5.8	3.0	3.5	−0.4	0.1
1973	7.1	4.0	4.7	−0.7	0.3
1974	9.6	8.1	7.3	0.9	0.3
1975	9.7	8.6	7.3	1.3	0.1

Sources: Column 1, official compensation per man-hour series provided by the U.S. Bureau of Labor Statistics, adjusted for overtime and interindustry shifts from *Business Conditions Digest* (December 1975), series 740, and *Economic Report of the President, January 1976*, table B-28, fifth column. Column 2, *Economic Report of the President, January 1976*, table B-30, last column. Column 3, column 1 less 2.36, which is the mean difference between columns 1 and 2. Columns 4 and 5, see description in text. Figures are rounded.
a. Energy is excluded in 1974 and 1975.
b. The equation is given in footnote 19.

sation. Up to the Nixon price control years, the largest deviations from this rule, shown in column 4 of the table, were an underprediction of 1.5 percent for prices in 1955 and an overprediction of 1.2 percent in 1958. As these extremes suggest, cyclical changes in aggregate demand may temporarily modify the relation between prices and standard wage costs, with prices falling slightly behind standard wage costs when demand suddenly weakens, and getting slightly ahead, or catching up, when aggregate demand surges. From 1962 to 1969, when the growth of demand was not interrupted by any sharp cyclical swings, the largest deviation from the simple rule relating price and wage inflation was an overprediction of 0.7 percent in 1968. In the four years from 1972 to 1975, the Nixon controls interfered with the normal relation. They held down prices relative to wages in 1972 and 1973; and when controls ended, prices rose to overcome this squeeze, contributing to an underprediction of 1.3 percent in 1975.

The simple rule for explaining prices can be improved by allowing for some lag in adjusting prices to wage costs and for some change over the years in the productivity trend. A statistically estimated relation that makes these allowances and also allows for the distortions of the Nixon controls explains the price performance since the Korean War quite well.[19] Ninety-two percent of the variation in price inflation during these twenty-two years is explained by the relation that makes this year's rate of price inflation equal to 80 percent of this year's rate of increase in hourly compensation plus 21 percent of last year's rate of compensation increase, discounted by an annual productivity trend that slowed gradually from 2.5 percent at the start of the period to 2.2 percent in 1975.[20] The largest errors from this statistical relationship are the 1.3 percent under- and overpredictions in 1955 and 1958, as shown in column 5 of table 7-5, but the average absolute error for the whole period is 0.4 percent. According to this statistical relation, the Nixon controls held down prices relative to standard wage costs by 0.9 percent in 1972–73; in 1974–75 prices made up for this shortfall.

If the analysis of price changes starts with wage costs, the analysis of wage behavior starts with the effect of aggregate demand on labor markets. When demand increases relative to the economy's potential, employment grows faster than the labor force and unemployment

19. The estimated relation is

$$\Delta \ln P = -2.6 + 0.804 \, \Delta \ln C + 0.210 \, \Delta \ln C_{-1} + 0.015 \, T + 0.90 \, DNIX,$$
$$ (5.7) (1.6) \phantom{\Delta \ln C_{-1} +} (0.5) (2.7)$$

$$R^2 = 0.92; \text{Durbin-Watson statistic} = 2.2$$

where P is the price deflator, C and C_{-1} are current and previous year's compensation per hour, T is a time trend that equals 1 in 1949 and 27 in 1975, and $DNIX$ is the dummy variable that equals -1 in 1972 and 1973 and $+1$ in 1974 and 1975. The period of fit is 1954–75. The numbers in parentheses are t-statistics.

20. Reasons to expect such a slowdown based on demographic changes are given in George L. Perry, "Labor Force Structure, Potential Output, and Productivity," *BPEA, 3:1971*, pp. 533–65.

declines. The lower unemployment rate is only one manifestation of the stronger demand for labor and tighter labor markets. Firms lay off fewer workers, and more workers quit their jobs to take better ones. There are fewer short work weeks and more overtime. Employers reach further down the scale of training and experience to fill job vacancies. Participation rates increase as job opportunities expand. Exactly how all these characteristics of tighter labor markets are related to more rapid rates of wage increase is still the subject of research. But that they are is a persistent empirical fact, and no postwar wage inflation has *started* without low unemployment.

The two basic propositions discussed thus far—first, that prices are closely related to wage costs, and second, that wages are closely related to unemployment—have characterized much of the thinking about aggregate demand management. How far can one get explaining inflation by combining the two? As figure 7-2 shows, about as far as the start of this decade. A close relation between unemployment and inflation is apparent in the first fifteen post-Korean years. Inflation was low in the recession years 1954, 1958, and 1961, and generally quickened when unemployment fell. Although there is a strong year-by-year link, on close inspection the expected lagged effects appear as well. Unemployment remained low in two periods, 1955–57 and 1965–69, and the rate of inflation increased each year in both periods.

The 1970s differ from previous experience both in the amount of inflation experienced and in the relation between the current inflation and the current unemployment rate. Although recession raised the unemployment rate in 1970 and 1971, the rate of inflation scarcely slackened. The price-wage control program slowed prices in 1972 and 1973 while unemployment was declining. But with the end of controls, the private nonfarm deflator rose more than 8 percent in both 1974 and 1975 in the midst of a recession that brought the unemployment rate to a postwar record high of 8.5 percent.

A More Complete View of Inflation

In trying to explain the price performance of the 1970s, the basic description of the inflation process presented thus far must be expanded in several ways. First, the aggregate unemployment rate has been understating both the degree of overall labor market tightness and the upward pressure on wages resulting from it. Second, prices

Figure 7-2. Inflation and Unemployment Rates, 1953–75

Sources: Official unemployment rate provided by U.S. Bureau of Labor Statistics, adjusted from 1953 to 1966 by the author to make series consistent with the 1967 BLS revision; deflator from *Economic Report of the President, January 1976*, table B-30, p. 206.
  a. Private nonfarm deflator (excluding 1974 and 1975 energy contribution).

are not wholly determined by wage costs, and the importance of other influences on U.S. prices, particularly the prices of foreign goods, has been evident in recent years. Third, prices do respond to wages, but the reverse is true as well. To some degree, wage changes are linked to changes in living costs, to changes in product prices (to the extent that these reflect changing margins), and to changes in other wages. Such links have contributed to a wage-price spiral in recent years that has given inflation a great deal of inertia. As a result, today's inflation is closely linked to past inflation as well as to current levels of demand and labor market tightness.

LABOR MARKET TIGHTNESS. The labor force experience of different demographic groups varies widely. On the average, men in their middle years have by far the highest participation rates, the longest work weeks, the highest wages, and the lowest unemployment rates of all groups. People in their teens are at the opposite end of the distribution in these characteristics. In any age group, blacks average more unemployment and lower wages than whites. And in most age groups, women average more unemployment and lower wages than men.

While such distinct characteristics have existed throughout the postwar years, the differences between the unemployment rates for most groups and that for adult males have widened steadily in the post-Korean period. Compared with earlier years, a given overall unemployment rate today represents an average of lower rates for adult males and higher rates for other groups, especially young workers. Because adult males have the largest impact on overall wage movements and experience the lowest unemployment rates of any group, the growing disparities among groups means that the same aggregate unemployment rate has been representing an increasingly tight, and hence more inflationary, labor market.[21]

A weighted unemployment rate constructed to allow for these changing demographics and unemployment patterns tells a somewhat different story about labor market tightness than the official rate.[22] Figure 7-3 shows how far above or below its 1955 level the weighted unemployment rate was in each postwar year; 1955 is an arbitrary but convenient reference point because it was considered an example of a noninflationary high employment situation when policy targets were being discussed in the early 1960s.

As measured by weighted unemployment, labor markets were tighter than in 1955 throughout the 1965–69 period. In 1968 and 1969 they were about as tight as during the Korean War, when wage-price controls were employed. From 1970 to 1974 markets were not as slack as in any year from 1958 to 1963.

21. This phenomenon and its implications for inflation are analyzed extensively in George L. Perry, "Changing Labor Markets and Inflation," *BPEA, 3:1970*, pp. 411–48.

22. The weighted unemployment rate maintains the relative demographic composition of the labor force as it was in the mid-1960s and weights the persons in each group according to estimates of how much they would add to output if they were employed.

Figure 7-3. Labor Market Tightness, 1948–75

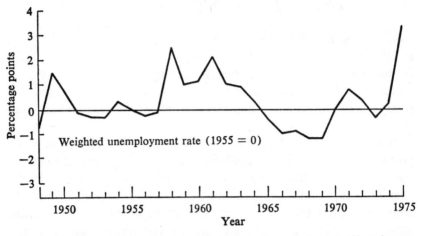

Source: Weighted unemployment series as developed by George L. Perry in "Unemployment Flows in the U.S. Labor Market," *BPEA, 2:1972*, pp. 245–78, taken from the Brookings data bank.

There is no precise aggregate unemployment rate that marks the boundary line between excessively tight and excessively slack labor markets. Rather, there is a high employment region with the characteristic that still lower unemployment rates risk noticeably more inflationary pressure from wage increases. This region, which in the 1950s was thought to be around 4 percent unemployment, drifted upward in the 1960s and 1970s when there were demographic changes and increasing dispersion of unemployment rates among demographic groups. Labor markets were tighter during this period than was commonly perceived on the basis of unemployment comparisons with earlier years.

Today, the high employment region is probably between 5 and 6 percent unemployment. Manpower policies that improved the productivity and employability of the groups in the work force that experience the highest unemployment rates and the greatest difficulty in finding stable jobs would lower the aggregate unemployment rate attainable without excessive inflationary pressure. Policies to directly moderate the wage and price increases that occurred in the high employment region could also allow the achievement of a lower unemployment rate.

Part of the explanation for the inflation of the past decade is thus the traditional one of a tight labor market leading to rapid wage increases. But this is hardly the whole explanation. Even measured by weighted unemployment, the labor market in 1975 had more slack than in any previous postwar year, and from 1970 to 1974 it was not as tight as in 1955–57 or 1964–66. Yet the increase in average hourly earnings averaged 6.7 percent in 1970–74 as against 4.3 percent in 1955–57 and 3.5 percent in 1964–66. Comparisons using the private nonfarm deflator or other price indexes tell a similar story. The wage-price guideposts may have contributed to the relatively good inflation record of the mid-1960s, but there is more than just current labor market tightness behind the inflation of the 1970s.

OTHER INFLUENCES ON PRICES. In recent years, the link between inflation and labor market conditions has been loosened by the unusual importance of other influences on prices. The increased prices of foreign goods with which U.S. output competes has raised the private nonfarm deflator, even with energy excluded. These increases have passed into the consumer price index, which has also been driven up by rising food and fuel prices and by the direct weight of import prices in U.S. consumption.

After being nearly stable in the late 1960s, world export prices of manufactured goods rose about 6 percent in 1970 and 1971, 8 percent in 1972, and then 16 percent, 19 percent, and 21 percent (based on data through the second quarter) the following three years. The average price of U.S. imports, including oil, rose 7 percent in 1972, 17 percent in 1973, 44 percent in 1974, and 12 percent in 1975. The dollar price of foreign goods rose as a result both of increased prices in producing countries and of the declining value of the dollar in some years in this period.

While the acceleration in prices of internationally traded goods is evident in these figures, their impact on U.S. prices is hard to quantify. Merchandise imports are about 8 percent of gross private product. Imported goods that are used in further production rather than consumed directly become costs that are passed on to consumers. Thus the direct effect of rising import prices on a final price index such as the CPI can be approximated very roughly as 8 percent of the annual import price increases just given. But the impact on U.S. prices goes beyond this direct effect. U.S. and foreign goods compete both in the U.S. market and around the world. Automobiles and steel, and of course oil to the extent its price is uncontrolled, are examples of products whose U.S. prices are influenced by import competition.

Chemicals and machinery are examples of products whose U.S. prices are influenced by competition in world export markets. Because neither the quantity of goods whose price is influenced in this way nor the exact effect on prices can be accurately measured, one can only say that, after 1972, foreign prices probably contributed noticeably to inflation in competing U.S. products. This is a distinct change from years before 1972 when world prices of manufactured goods changed very little and, if anything, may, through competition, have restrained U.S. prices.

During 1973 and 1974 soaring prices of food and fuel were major sources of acceleration in the overall price level. In neither of these areas were prices driven up by wages or other costs or by the level of U.S. aggregate demand. Food prices rose when world production fell short of demand and stockpiles were inadequate to close the gap. This also raised the price of nonfood agricultural products that compete for land use with food. An international oil cartel raised world oil prices, with the increase spreading to other fuels that are competitive with oil. The impact on domestic fuel prices, although considerable, was limited by government controls on part of natural gas and oil production.

Domestic fuel prices added 1.5 percent and 0.8 percent to the non-farm deflator in 1974 and 1975. In the three years 1973–75 farm prices added 1.5 percent, 1.2 percent, and 0.6 percent to the private product deflator. These measures of domestic production prices do not translate directly into consumer prices, as part of farm output is exported while a substantial amount of oil is imported. In the consumer price index, prices of food, fuel, and utilities rose 44 percent between the end of 1972 and the end of 1975, and added 2.8 percent and 2.7 percent to the annual increases in the CPI in 1973 and 1974. In 1975 they made little difference in the CPI, as the rate of increase in the rest of the index caught up with the increases in these categories.

Perpetuating Inflation via Wages

If bursts of inflation—whether from periodic episodes of excessive demand and an overtight labor market such as in the late 1960s or from direct effects on prices such as those just described—were confined to a specific sector or time, the problem would not be hard to manage. But inflation is not confined to a particular part of the

economy or a particular time for long. Rather, it spreads to other sectors and declines only gradually even after the initial inflationary impulse is gone.

The response of wages to price inflation and to changes in other
wages is an important part of this process. This response, which operates in addition to the effect of labor market conditions on wage
changes, became increasingly important in the 1970s. At the start of
the period, it perpetuated the inflation that had originated in the tight
labor market of the late 1960s long after that market had slackened.
In the past two years, it has spread the step-up in inflation resulting
from fuel, food, and foreign prices throughout the economy.

COST-OF-LIVING EFFECTS. Wages may be influenced by prices
in at least two distinct ways. The first is the influence of the cost of
living on wage increases. This channel is perhaps the most obvious to
the layman, who knows that union wage contracts often contain automatic cost-of-living escalator provisions. But only an estimated 5
million workers, or about 6 percent of all those employed, are covered
by wage contracts with cost-of-living protection. So the strength of
any direct causal link between the CPI and wages must depend on the
importance of living costs in wage setting when it is not part of formal
contract provisions. Here both the conceptual arguments and the
empirical evidence become inconclusive.

It is sometimes argued that the supply of labor depends on real
wages—that is, wages adjusted for purchasing power—so that CPI
increases will be passed completely through into higher wages. But
there is simply no evidence that the labor supply depends on real
wages in any systematic way.

As a variation on this theme, it is axiomatic that employees want
higher wages to make up for the inroads of higher prices on their purchasing power. But this tells less than it seems to, for it is also axiomatic that employees would like higher wages at all times. Thus what
the employer is willing and able to pay becomes an essential part of
wage determination during inflation just as it is in noninflationary
times.

The rather imprecise notion that an environment of rising prices
will increase the importance of the consumer price index in wage setting is probably nearest the truth. Employers have a stake in keeping
their employees satisfied; if rising living costs become a source of dissatisfaction, they are more likely to become a factor in wage setting.

In addition, employers' perceptions of how readily they can pass higher wage costs on in higher prices will be influenced by what is happening to the general price level.[23] As a result, the extent to which CPI increases push up wages probably changes with general perceptions about inflation, how long it has been going on, and how likely it is to continue. Empirical estimates covering a long period, such as the past twenty years, indicate that wages are pushed up by only 10 to 20 percent of past changes in consumer prices.[24] Once inflation has become a prominent issue, however, the impact of living costs on wages may become stronger. It was this risk that led some economists to urge the adoption of measures for keeping the food and fuel inflations of 1973 and 1974 from pushing up wages and thus spreading into a more generalized inflation throughout the economy.

PRICE MARGIN EFFECTS. In considering pure CPI effects on wages, one is dealing with the response to a rise in the general price level that does not change profitability. This happens when prices rise in response to higher costs, rise in response to higher excise or payroll taxes, or rise from outside the sector as in the case of the food price explosion. The situation is quite different when prices increase in a way that raises the margin between prices and standard wage costs. When this happens, the wage the employer is willing and able to pay rises, and more of the initial price inflation is likely to show up in higher wages. The CPI increase that came from soaring food costs in 1973 did not make it easier for automobile companies to pay higher wages. The automobile price increases that came in the wake of higher prices for competing foreign cars did.

While changes in competitive foreign prices are one potential source of margin-expanding price increases, margins can also expand for other reasons. Not all excess demand inflations are expressed initially with rising wages which then drive prices up. When the Korean War broke out, prices rose more rapidly than wages. After controls were imposed in early 1951, wages rose rapidly for two years, restoring more normal margins, while prices generally stabilized below their ceiling levels. And a recent analysis of price behavior in

23. Arthur M. Okun discusses how relations between employers and their employees and customers lead to price and wage inflexibility and add to inflationary inertia in his "Inflation: Its Mechanics and Welfare Costs," *BPEA*, 2:1975, pp. 351–90.

24. See Robert J. Gordon, "The Impact of Aggregate Demand on Prices," *BPEA*, 3:1975, pp. 613–62.

1974–75 concludes that price margins have widened by more than enough to make up for any price squeeze that developed during the Nixon control years.[25]

WAGE-WAGE EFFECTS. Finally, it is important to recognize that wages respond not only to prices but to other wages as well. Wage inflation in one sector of the economy can spread to other sectors, either through competitive effects, as other employers push up their wage scales to maintain their position in the job market, or through imitative effects in wage bargaining and in less formal wage-setting arrangements. Students of collective bargaining often emphasize pattern-setting and pattern-following to explain the outcome of negotiated wage settlements. Nonunion employers are probably under more pressure to keep up with wage increases elsewhere than to make up for rising consumer prices.

The wage-wage spiral that all these responses lead to reinforces the tendency for an inflation to be perpetuated through the price-wage spiral of living costs pushing up wages. It is hard to isolate the importance of one process relative to the other because wages are a business cost that moves prices and so prices and wages move together at most times. Statistical analysis has supported the importance of wage-wage effects in the past.[26] And the acceleration of wages in 1974–75 following the acceleration of prices suggests the price-wage effect may be significant as well.[27] But whatever the precise mechanism, the result is inflation with a lot of inertia. Either way, the price-wage or wage-wage spiral, which then leads to another round of generalized wage-price inflation, does not exist because of currently excessive aggregate demand or a labor market that is too tight. And this raises special problems when attempting to control it by reducing aggregate demand.

Inertia in Inflation

Because of price-wage-price interactions, today's inflation rate is much higher than suggested by the state of aggregate demand and the

25. See Charles L. Schultze, "Falling Profits, Rising Profit Margins, and the Full-Employment Profit Rate," *BPEA, 2:1975*, pp. 449–71.

26. See Robert E. Hall, "The Process of Inflation in the Labor Market," *BPEA, 2:1974*, pp. 343–93.

27. It may seem that this period would offer conclusive estimates of the relative importance of different mechanisms for perpetuating inflation, but there are complications. Margin-widening price increases took place alongside wage accelerations in 1974, so it is not easy to separate out pure CPI effects on wages in this period.

Table 7-6. Errors from Equations Predicting Inflation with and without Strong Inertia Effects, 1970–75

Actual minus predicted percentage price change

	Last year of estimation period	
Year of prediction	1969[a]	1975[b]
1970	2.2	−0.2
1971	2.8	0.1
1972	1.0	0.2
1973	1.7	2.1
1974	6.2	2.2
1975	7.2	0.1

a. The equation fitted to annual data from 1954 to 1969 is:

$$\Delta \ln P = -2.9 + 22.3\ U^{-1} + 0.21\ \Delta \ln P_{-1} - 0.7\ DGP,$$
$$\quad\quad\quad\quad (9.4)\quad\quad (1.8)\quad\quad\quad\quad (-2.6)$$

$$R^2 = 0.903;\ \text{Durbin-Watson statistic} = 2.2$$

where P represents the private nonfarm deflator excluding the effects of rising energy prices in 1974–75; U^{-1} is the inverse of the unemployment rate; and DGP is the wage-price guidepost dummy and equals +1 in 1964, 1965, and 1966 and zero in all other years. The numbers in parentheses are t-statistics.

b. The equation fitted to annual data from 1954 to 1975 is:

$$\Delta \ln P = -1.7 + 9.5\ U^{*-1} + 0.88\ \Delta \ln P_{-1} - 0.5\ DGP + 1.8\ DNIX.$$
$$\quad\quad\quad (2.7)\quad\quad (6.0)\quad\quad\quad (-0.6)\quad\quad\quad (3.2)$$

$$R^2 = 0.762;\ \text{Durbin-Watson statistic} = 1.6$$

The definitions for P and DGP are given above; U^{*-1} is the inverse of the weighted unemployment rate; and $DNIX$ is a dummy variable for the Nixon wage-price controls and equals −1 in 1972 and 1973, +1 in 1974 and 1975, and zero in all other years. The numbers in parentheses are t-statistics.

tightness of the labor market. Prices continue to move with wage costs in the private nonfarm sector, as shown in table 7-5. And unemployment continues to affect the rate of wage inflation. But the inertia in the inflation process caused by the price-wage spiral delays the full effect of weaker labor market conditions for many years.

To see the force of this inertia, one must turn to statistical explanations in which the significance of the spiral shows up in the weight given recent inflation in predicting the present inflation rate. Table 7-6 shows the prediction errors for 1970–75 from two inflation equations. The first equation was estimated for the years 1954–69 and explained inflation using the unemployment rate and the previous year's inflation rate as a way of capturing the inertia effects of price-wage-price interactions. It also estimated an effect for the wage-price guideposts. The estimated inertia effect was modest, with only 21 percent of one year's inflation rate perpetuated into the next. The second equation was estimated for the years 1954–75 and used the weighted unemployment rate as the appropriate measure of labor market tightness. It also allowed for the Nixon controls shifting some price increases from 1972–73 to 1974–75. The estimated inertia effect is considerable, with 88 percent of one year's inflation rate perpetuated into the next. The errors for predicting inflation in recent years are very large for the first equation, with the annual rise in the deflator underestimated by an average of 4.0 percentage points the last four years. The second equation tracks the period fairly well, although the inflation rate is still underestimated by over 2 points in 1973 and 1974.

This is not a definitive analysis, as it greatly simplifies the wage-price interactions that lead to inertia.[28] But it does characterize the dilemma of controlling inflation today through aggregate demand policy. Keeping unemployment high is still a means of slowing inflation, but it is a long-drawn-out, costly process. Raising the official unemployment rate two points, from 5.5 to 7.5 percent, and keeping it there will eventually stop inflation. But it will slow inflation less than 1 percentage point the initial year. In six years this policy will have had only half its ultimate effect. By then, it will have reduced the annual inflation rate by 3 to 4 percentage points.

Stabilization Policy for the Future

Today's continuing inflation poses serious problems for stabilization policy. The cost of reducing inflation by maintaining a slack economy is enormous. Just in readily measurable losses, some $45 billion in output and incomes is lost each year for every extra point of cyclical unemployment. The burden is more lasting for those near the back of the hiring line. The avenues out of poverty narrow as good jobs remain scarce for minorities. Permanent job handicaps and social problems are created when access to stable, career-oriented jobs for young workers without seniority or established skills is limited. And reducing investment and the modernization and productivity improvements that come with it steals from the future.

The problem can hardly be avoided by framing policy in terms of policy instruments rather than economic goals. The monetarist prescription for a fixed, low rate of growth in the money supply dramatizes rather than solves the problem. If the prescription for money

28. Recent papers that deal with the issue more fully and come to comparable conclusions include Gordon, "The Impact of Aggregate Demand," and Michael L. Wachter, "The Changing Cyclical Responsiveness of Wage Inflation," *BPEA, 1: 1976.*

growth without inflation were 3 percent a year and inflation was actually 5 percent, the real money supply would decline by 2 percent in a year. If nothing else special were happening to affect the economy, interest rates could be expected to rise sharply, real output to rise slowly or to fall, and unemployment to rise. This slack would have some effect on inflation—the rise in prices might have been nearer 6 percent than 5 percent if the economy had expanded normally. But the main effect of slow money growth will have been to raise interest rates and unemployment. Only by imposing that kind of cost for an extended period will slow money growth, tight fiscal policy, or any combination of the two that adds up to a brake on total demand eliminate the current inflation.

In view of these costs, it is often suggested that stabilization policy ignore inflation as the lesser evil and concentrate entirely on reducing excessive unemployment and slack capacity. But inflation is a real evil, even if a lesser one. It redistributes real incomes, often to the strong and well organized at the expense of the rest of society. It inhibits investment by making the future less certain as projects must count on inflation to pay for part of increased borrowing costs. And inflation always threatens to get worse. If it starts to, and they have no other way to combat it, policymakers can be expected to step hard on the aggregate demand brakes; if the past is any guide, this runs a considerable risk of again sending the economy into recession. In order to resolve this dilemma, ways must be found to cope directly with inflation rather than relying on the costly and delayed indirect effects that come from restraining aggregate demand.

The present inertia in inflation benefits no one. If, in place of the present standard forecast of 5 to 6 percent price increases and 7.5 to 8.5 percent wage increases for 1976, 2 percent slower rates of increase in both wages and prices could be achieved, the relative positions of labor and business would be unchanged and the general interest in price stability would be advanced. But individual workers or unions and individual firms and industries cannot, in their own best interests, lead the way to this de-escalation. This is the essence of the case for a government role in slowing the spiral.

The experience of 1972–73 demonstrated once again the inherent difficulties of a comprehensive program of price and wage controls. Although it is not hard to point out the mistakes of that particular program, any alternative version of comprehensive controls would suffer at least some of the same problems of limiting the needed flexibility of prices and restraining prices and wages unevenly. Technical points aside, that experience has discredited controls by general consensus and they would have little political support today.

Without resorting to controls, a number of initiatives are available to the government to help slow the present inflation and to help maintain wage-price moderation as employment expands. Any steps that moderate price increases will help moderate wage increases and vice versa. Thus the initiatives discussed below include a variety of measures that would complement each other in an overall anti-inflation strategy.

Incomes Policies

The informal and flexible approach of wage-price guideposts during the Kennedy-Johnson years avoided the rigidities and bureaucracy of controls. The program was abandoned when the Vietnam War brought tight markets and excess demand inflation. The present absence of those conditions recommends another look at this form of restraint. Even without government enforcement powers, a new guidepost program could be helpful. Its centerpiece could be a 6 percent standard for annual wage increases, a standard one or two points below what is currently expected. Employers that are currently raising wages faster than this because other wages are also rising faster would have an interest in enforcing the new rule. The historical links between wages and prices indicate employers could also be expected to raise prices correspondingly less. But a program for wage restraint alone would be unacceptable. Labor cannot be expected to accept a call for wage restraint without a companion call for price moderation that was comparably specific or some other assurance that it was not losing real income.

The old guideposts enunciated both a wage standard and a rule that price increases should be less than wage increases by the amount of the trend in labor productivity. As table 7-5 showed, this is approximately the result that market forces produce in the aggregate economy. For individual prices, this rule raised questions about how fast the productivity trend was and about unusual increases in other costs. In practice, price increases in major concentrated industries had to be justified on a case-by-case basis. A similar set of operating rules, backed with more formal authority, is generally contemplated as a necessary part of any new guidepost program. But to help gain labor's acceptance of a new program, two ways of linking tax relief and wage moderation have recently been suggested.

TAXES AS A BARGAIN. The latest upward thrust in the wage-price spiral came when wages started responding to the escalation in prices in 1974. At that time, if a tax cut aimed at working class incomes had been offered as part of a renewed effort at wage moderation, the spiral might have been kept under better control.[29] Labor incomes are still chasing prices as well as other labor incomes, and the possibility of using tax reduction to bargain for wage restraint may still be worth a try. To a worker earning $12,000 to $14,000 a year, a tax cut of $100 is worth about as much in after-tax income as an extra 1 percent wage hike. As slower wage increases translate into slower price inflation, the tax cut becomes a pure real gain, not just an offset to wages "lost" through moderation.

A reduction in payroll taxes would be a particularly useful form of tax reduction because it automatically focuses the benefits in the wage earners' income range. In addition, it would have desirable complementary effects in reducing prices. The social insurance trust funds, which depend on the payroll tax, would be reimbursed by earmarking funds from general revenues for the program. This would make overall fiscal policy more expansive, but a somewhat more expansive policy would be appropriate in view of the reduced inflation that would accompany any given rate of unemployment. If the resulting fiscal policy were still considered too expansionary, other parts of the budget could be adjusted to reach the desired high employment surpluses. At present, a budget initiative that slowed inflation while maintaining aggregate demand deserves some priority over other programs.

TAXES FOR INSURANCE. Tax reduction can also be offered in the form of real wage insurance as part of a wage restraint program.[30] A guidepost target for wage increases would be linked to a commensurate target for price increases. If at the end of the year consumer prices exceeded the price target, a special tax rebate would be pro-

29. Offering tax cuts in a social compact with labor was originally suggested by George L. Perry in "Statement before the Joint Economic Committee, Congress of the United States" (February 20, 1974; processed). The British government adopted just such a program in the spring of 1976.

30. Arthur M. Okun proposed such a scheme in his "Statement Before the Joint Economic Committee, Congress of the United States" (October 16, 1974; processed).

vided to make up the shortfall in real after-tax incomes in the lower and middle income groups.

An attractive feature of this program is that, if it worked and wages and prices moderated on schedule, the tax guarantee would never have to be paid. This would also ensure the government's interest in other initiatives to keep down the price level.

TAXES FOR EMPLOYER RESISTANCE. Finally, a proposal that is not tied to any call for wage moderation, but rather uses taxes to penalize employers for rapid wage increases and reward them for moderate increases, has been developed by Henry Wallich and Sidney Weintraub.[31] Their "tax-based incomes policy" would place a surcharge on corporations for any wage increase they allowed above a guidepost figure announced by the government. This proposal is the most complex of the three, requiring complicated calculations of average wage increases for a firm. But it has the virtue, which its authors regard as particularly important, of not requiring any direct government enforcement activity beyond its traditional one of enforcing the tax laws. Like any guidepost for wages alone, it is unlikely to be well received by labor.

All programs to slow inflation will have to slow wages and prices in tandem. Wages are not the cause of today's inflation, but their momentum is an important part of what keeps inflation from slowing now that it is here. Conversely, to make wage restraint, however achieved, acceptable, prices will have to rise more slowly. Anything the government can do to slow price inflation, even if it cannot repeat the act year after year, will help slow the whole spiral, whether as part of a total package that includes direct attempts at wage restraint or without such a package.

Taxes and Prices

Many taxes directly affect prices. Yet economic policy has ignored the potential this offers for coping with inflation. Analyses of taxes by economists have usually focused either on their impact on aggregate demand or on their effects on relative prices, real income distribution, and resource allocation. Less attention has been given to short-run nominal incidence of different taxes, which is to say their impact on the price level.

31. Henry C. Wallich and Sidney Weintraub, "A Tax-Based Incomes Policy," *Journal of Economic Issues*, vol. 5 (June 1971), pp. 1–19.

Empirical knowledge of price level effects is incomplete and imprecise, but some generalizations can be made. Excise taxes appear directly in price levels with little or no delay.[32] Payroll taxes on employers are treated like any other wage cost. And, as shown earlier, wage costs pass fully and quickly into prices.

The nominal incidence of personal income taxes and employees' payroll taxes has not been as easy to analyze. These taxes may have no direct impact on the price level; if they do have some, it is almost surely slight, which is to say only a small part of each dollar of tax is offset by a higher wage. There would be an impact if the supply of labor were affected by after-tax income; for most workers, this does not seem to be the case, with high-income professionals who work for themselves a possible exception. At the extreme, one might expect the effects of income taxes on wages to be similar to the effect of increases in the cost of living since both affect real after-tax incomes. It has been noted that the direct effect of living costs on wages has historically been modest, with perhaps 10 to 20 percent of CPI increases inducing offsetting wage increases. But income tax impacts are surely less. No union contracts contain "cost of income tax" escalators, and there is no evidence that an income tax surcharge, such as was imposed in 1968, generates compensating wage increases as a show of goodwill by employers.

The effect of the corporate income tax on the price level is even harder to pin down. The standard profit-maximizing model suggests there is none since, given a firm's cost schedule, the price that maximizes before-tax profits also maximizes after-tax profits. Markup models of pricing are usually founded on a loose concept of after-tax rate of return; but while empirical studies confirm a prompt pass-through of cost changes, they find no response to the profits tax rate.[33] In the long run, the after-tax return should help determine investment, the capital stock, labor productivity, and real wages. But even in the long run, it is the ratio of wages to prices that would be affected, and this can come about through lower wages as well as higher prices. In short, there is little evidence pointing to any short-run effect on prices from profit taxes and considerable reason to suspect any effect is small if not negligible.

32. See Oswald Brownlee and George L. Perry, "The Effects of the 1965 Federal Excise Tax Reductions on Prices," *National Tax Journal*, vol. 20 (September 1967), pp. 235–49.
33. One of the most recent is Gordon, "The Impact of Aggregate Demand," especially p. 644.

As these characteristics of different taxes indicate, the price deflator for gross business product, which now totals about $1,400 billion, would be directly reduced approximately 1 percent for each $14 billion reduction in excise taxes or employer payroll taxes. Such reductions would also be expansionary fiscal policy boosting aggregate demand, and their desirability from that standpoint would have to be judged in light of economic conditions and the position of the budget as a whole. If, to keep total revenues unchanged, income or corporate taxes were raised by the same amount, most and possibly all the price level reduction would still be achieved.

Sales taxes, which are the predominant excise tax levied in this country, exist in forty-five states. Arthur Okun has suggested that the federal government make grants to states in exchange for their reducing or doing away with their sales taxes.[34] In fiscal 1974 revenues from state sales taxes totaled $46 billion, so there is plenty of scope for price reductions from this source; the five states that still have no sales tax would have to receive comparable grants, but this would weaken the effect hardly at all since they are relatively small states economically. As sales taxes are paid predominantly on consumer purchases, the effect of reducing them would be concentrated on consumer prices. A 1 percent reduction in the consumer price index could be achieved through a reduction of about $10 billion in sales taxes. Import duties are a principal excise tax levied by the federal government. Reducing them would have comparable effects on the price level and would put downward pressure on the prices of competing domestic goods as well.

Revenues from employer payroll taxes are approaching $50 billion, most of it coming from the 5.85 percent social security tax on the first $15,300 of wage and salary income. To preserve the actuarial position of the social security trust fund and to maintain the present balance between employee and business contributions to the fund, any reduction in the employer tax rate could be made up by diverting the same amount of corporate profits tax revenues into the fund.[35] Each one-percentage-point reduction in the employer's payroll tax would reduce the private price deflator by 0.7 percent.

34. See Arthur M. Okun, "Income Inflation and the Policy Alternatives," in "The Economists' Conference on Inflation" (report of conferences held on September 5 and 23, 1974; processed), vol. 1, pp. 371–72.
35. Since matching reductions in employee contributions would not have the same price-reducing effect, they are not discussed here. Reducing the employee part of the tax was discussed above in connection with achieving wage moderation.

The beneficial effects of such tax changes on the inflation rate would be magnified by any further response of wages to living costs. This would reverse the recent experience when extraordinary increases in living costs stemming from the rise in food and fuel prices in 1973–74 contributed to speeding wage increases. Even though these direct effects of living costs on wages are probably not large, neither are they negligible, especially when wages that respond directly to the CPI affect other wages through imitative and competitive effects.

Stabilizing Volatile Prices

Prices of raw industrial and agricultural commodities fluctuate sharply in response to shifts in the world balance of supply and demand. And once major price moves start, speculation can become an additional force driving up the prices of raw materials. Worldwide industrial production peaked relative to trend in mid-1973, but the prices of industrial materials continued rising until April 1974, by which time an average index of these prices had climbed 127 percent above its level two years earlier.[36]

Although the costs of raw materials are only a small component of final product prices, their movements can be so large that their effect on final prices is significant despite their small size. And the price increases they initiate can spread. High prices of raw materials pass into the prices of final goods. And from there, they can affect wages through the cost of living. To the extent that this ultimate passthrough takes place, the original cyclical rise in raw material prices contributes to a generalized inflation. This, in turn, keeps the prices of raw materials themselves from returning to original levels as the inflation in other prices adds permanently to the cost of producing raw materials.

BUFFER STOCKS. By accumulating stocks of raw materials and selling them when prices threaten to rise sharply, the government can reduce the price fluctuations in these markets. Until recent years, the government maintained buffer stocks of agricultural commodities. The 1973–74 food price explosion came after these stocks had been run down as a deliberate policy of the Department of Agriculture. The government maintains a stockpile of strategic industrial materials and stocks in excess of strategic needs are available. Only limited

36. See the analysis in Richard N. Cooper and Robert Z. Lawrence, "The 1972–75 Commodity Boom," *BPEA, 3:1975*, especially p. 673.

sales were made from these stocks in 1973, however, because regulations governing sales were not geared to stabilizing prices.[37]

One fear that inflation will re-escalate in the years ahead stems from the danger of another commodity price explosion. This danger would be greatly reduced and the extent of any price rise could be minimized by the aggressive use of buffer stocks to stabilize prices. Such use would damp down variations in the supply-demand balance, and the mere threat of such use would reduce speculative movements in prices as well. For industrial raw materials, the carrying costs of buffer stocks are modest and should not inhibit a stabilization program. For agricultural commodities, storage and carrying costs are more significant, and some international sharing of the burden becomes more important. If direct sharing of the costs of buffer stocks cannot be negotiated with some countries, serious attention should be given to developing an agricultural export policy that would reflect the true cost of large fluctuations in purchases by other countries.

SHIELDING U.S. PRICES. If a suitable buffer stock program cannot be worked out to limit food price fluctuations on a worldwide basis, the economy of the United States can still be shielded from extreme movements in prices without compromising its interest in developing stable export markets for agricultural output. One possibility would be to separate the domestic market, together with any export customers that wished to commit themselves for a steady supply from the United States, from the incremental demand from elsewhere in the world. U.S. production beyond that needed to meet steady demand would be available for sale on world markets to meet incremental demand. By placing the risk of large price fluctuations on those customers that were unwilling to stabilize their demands on U.S. production, such a marketing arrangement would encourage other nations to join the "steady customer" part of the program. A marketing arrangement making the separation described here would not impose special hardships on other nations simply because their own supplies were unreliable from year to year. By becoming steady customers, they would end up bearing the cost of holding their own buffer stocks to meet the fluctuations in their own import requirements.

Finally, if there were no other arrangements to avoid large fluctuations in agricultural food prices, temporary subsidies could be used to smooth out these fluctuations at the consumer level. If direct price

37. Ibid., p. 713.

subsidies—negative excise taxes—had been used to shield consumer prices in 1973–74, the inflation that followed the food price explosion might have been noticeably modified. Such subsidies may seem perverse at a time when prices are rising because of excess demand for the particular commodity. But the demand for food is so inelastic that the additional consumption encouraged by a countercyclical subsidy would be small. In exchange, the benefits from stabilizing the consumer price index could be substantial.

Competition and Regulation

A broad range of individual prices are affected by specific laws and regulations. In some cases, such as many parts of the power and transportation industries, regulation directly controls prices. Regulation also affects prices less directly by controlling the degree of competition in various industries. And in other instances, such as trades and professions that require licensing and unions that restrict apprenticeships, competition is limited by the acquiescence of the government in these private arrangements.

Economists broadly agree on the benefits of competition. But the role of regulation and the less competitive parts of the economy in the inflation process is less clear. In many instances, prices are sluggish in the less competitive sectors, with oligopolistic prices and union wages lagging behind other prices and wages during periods of strong demand. These same sectors can perpetuate inflation long after excess demand has vanished, and their price unresponsiveness to weak demand is an important element contributing to the inertia of inflation that currently plagues the economy.

As far as anti-inflation policy goes, the less competitive areas have to be treated on a case-by-case basis. They cannot be identified as a cause of inflation over the whole cycle. But they are candidates for supervision under an incomes policy aimed at slowing an ongoing inflation in the absence of excess demand.

In recent years regulations arising from environmental and health and safety concerns have increased and will continue to do so in the years immediately ahead. These affect a wide range of industries and often add noticeably to business costs. In some instances, where individual industrial processes or techniques have to be substantially modified or replaced, the regulations can lead to temporary bottlenecks in capacity. It would be sensible to coordinate these new initiatives in regulation with stabilization and anti-inflation objectives. Compliance generally raises costs, and ultimately the general public absorbs these costs. Efforts should be made, however, to pay these "public costs" without inflating prices. This goal can be pursued by allowing the flexibility to choose least-cost methods of meeting regulatory goals, by employing subsidies where appropriate rather than forcing all cost increases to pass into the price level, and even by permitting some delay in compliance where a little more time would permit a less inflationary solution.

FOREIGN COMPETITION. Maintaining free foreign trade and the benefits of import competition can provide important protection against inflation. Foreign supplies can be vital when capacity bottlenecks appear in domestic industries. They may prove to be particularly valuable if isolated capacity shortages develop, as some industry sources maintain they will, as a result of U.S. environmental regulation of some industrial processes. More generally, foreign supplies add to the competitive price pressures on domestic industries. This can be particularly important where concentrated industries bargain with strong unions. Resistance to excessive wage demands depends on an industry's ability to pass the higher costs along in higher prices, and foreign suppliers are the only ones not subject to the common wage settlement. The political temptation to inhibit foreign competition always mounts when unemployment is high, as it is at present. Yet by maintaining downward competitive pressure on prices and offering protection against shortages from any isolated bottlenecks in domestic supplies that might occur, unencumbered imports make it easier to pursue expansionary demand policies that create jobs. Any policy to slow inflation, particularly when reducing unemployment is also a goal, should avoid tariffs, quotas, and marketing arrangements that would limit imports and competition from abroad.

Conclusions

Most postwar recessions have been associated with a restrictive fiscal policy, a tight or tightening monetary policy, or both. These restrictive moves usually reflected the desire of policymakers to slow inflation. Today, stabilization policy is more difficult because of the persistence of inflation accompanied by excess unemployment and underutilized capacity. The foregoing analysis of stabilization economics and of the current problem of inflation leads to several suggestions for improving the effectiveness of stabilization policy.

In mid-1976, the U.S. economy continues to operate with a historically high level of unemployment and a large amount of idle industrial capacity. The main barriers to achieving a higher level of output and prosperity are the still unacceptable rate of inflation and the fear that policies to stimulate total demand would accelerate it. Thus a policy for enhanced prosperity must deal directly with the problem of inflation.

The present inflation in the United States is largely a problem of inertia, with prices and wages chasing each other in an upward spiral that originated in earlier years. Rather than relying simply on high unemployment and excess capacity to slow this spiral, policy can slow wages and prices directly, permitting a prompter return to high employment. Price inflation can be slowed by reducing employers' payroll taxes, sales taxes (which are levied primarily by state and local governments), and import duties, all of which directly raise the price level. Although the direct effect would be a one-time price reduction, by slowing inflationary expectations and the part of wage increases that results from increased living costs, such price-reducing policies can be significant in slowing the wage-price spiral, thus providing anti-inflation benefits beyond the direct effect on the price level.

The tax system can be used to elicit wage moderation in a variety of ways. Tax reductions aimed at working-class incomes can be offered as an inducement for wage moderation in a social compact with labor. Such an exchange would provide an opportunity to raise after-tax real wages while moderating the rate of inflation. As part of a program to enlist labor's support in moderating wages, contingent tax reductions could also be offered as a guarantee against any erosion of real wage gains. Either of these proposals would fit into an overall incomes policy that monitored wage and price developments in sectors of the economy where competitive forces are weakest and discretion for the setting of wages and prices is considerable. It might also be feasible to give business an incentive to moderate wage increases by establishing standards for increases and taxing businesses at rates that varied according to their wage increases relative to the standard.

But beyond the need to slow the current unique wage-price spiral, policies should be developed to protect the economy from inflationary shocks and to reduce the tendency of inflation to emerge while unemployment is still excessive among many groups. Maintaining buffer stocks in industrial and agricultural raw materials and using them to reduce fluctuations in raw material prices would lessen the risk of these sources increasing inflation. Along with the buffer stock program, an export policy aimed at making steady rather than sporadic customers for U.S. grains would help maintain stability in food prices. Regulatory policies should be reviewed for their inflationary impact; new regulations in particular may contribute to inflation by raising costs and, in isolated areas, reducing industrial capacity. Without neglecting the goals of new regulatory policies covering health, safety, and the environment, the nation's overall economic well-being will best be served if alternative ways of reaching those goals are evaluated in light of their consequences for the price level.

The changing demographic composition of the labor force and the especially high unemployment rates of young workers—high relative both to other workers and to the experience of young workers in earlier postwar periods—have combined to increase the aggregate unemployment rate at which inflationary wage pressure becomes noticeable. Unless specific policies are successful in altering this situation, aggregate demand policies will hold the unemployment rate at an undesirably high level or court renewed inflationary pressure from rapid wage increases. The kind of incomes policy that would help moderate wage and price increases in today's economy should also prove useful in reducing the unemployment rate that could be achieved before inflation reemerged. Steps to improve the productivity and employability of members of the work force who experience the highest unemployment and the greatest difficulty in getting jobs would also permit the pursuit of a lower unemployment target.

Finally, the traditional tools of fiscal policy should be made more flexible. Past recessions have often resulted from attempts to slow an expansion by the use of policy. If discretionary policy were used more continuously to stabilize aggregate demand, the big policy swings that have been made in the past would be less necessary in the future. In addition, a standby authority to change taxes for countercyclical purposes would provide fiscal policy with a highly desirable quick-response capacity that it has not had. If aggregate demand overshot the target, in the direction of either too much demand threatening inflationary pressure or too little causing recession, the use of the authority to raise or lower taxes could have a prompt stabilizing effect.

CHAPTER EIGHT

Federal Spending: Past, Present, and Future

CHARLES L. SCHULTZE

CONTROLLING THE GROWTH of federal spending and reassessing
the federal government's role in society have become two of the
major themes of the 1976 election campaign. Federal spending, federal deficits, and government bureaucracies have never been popular.
Some part of the rhetoric of political campaigns has almost always
concerned itself with these subjects, but after bowing to the rhetoric,
the political debate usually moved on to other subjects.

Lately, however, things have changed. Many candidates have been
running against Washington. Even where this has not been the case,
the traditional catalog of proposals for new federal programs, in education, urban rehabilitation, child development, and similar areas,
has been noticeably truncated if not missing entirely from the precon-
vention speeches and position papers.

The perceived shift in attitudes toward the federal government
takes several forms and has several apparent causes. A large number
of people believe that the growth of federal spending and the budget
deficits of recent years were the principal source of the current inflation. Related to this is a belief that federal spending is, in some
sense, out of control and without draconian action will eventually
gobble up a frightening proportion of the national income. Moreover, the rapid pace of recent inflation combined with social security

The author thanks John L. Palmer, Emil M. Sunley, Jr., Henry J. Aaron, and
Lawrence B. Krause for their helpful comments, and Leonard Herk for extensive
research assistance.

323

tax increases has pushed many salaried and blue-collar workers into higher and higher tax brackets, even when their real incomes have risen little, if at all, and despite the reduction in income tax rates enacted in 1975. As a consequence, many people find themselves paying a larger fraction of their incomes in taxes and often associate the growing burden with programs that provide assistance to the poor and near-poor.

There is also rising public skepticism about the federal government's ability to perform effectively. During most of the 1960s, the prevalent belief was that some kind of federal budgetary program could be designed to deal with almost any social problem—deteriorating central cities, juvenile delinquency, low reading scores of poorer children, rat infestation, or inefficient local police departments. Scores of programs were enacted, usually in the form of federal grants-in-aid to state and local governments, to deal with those problems. This conventional wisdom of a few years ago seems now to have been replaced by its polar opposite: most federal programs do not work well and consist principally in "throwing money at problems." While most of the numerous social grant programs enacted in the 1960s remain on the books, recent appropriations for them have barely kept up with inflation and the pressure for large-scale expansion has sharply dwindled.

Finally, the combination of public opposition to Vietnam, exposés of questionable activities by intelligence and law enforcement agencies, the trauma of Watergate, and the revelation of past instances in which the government has dissembled about the nature of its activities and intentions to its own citizens has taken its toll. Washington, D.C., and the politicians who work there appear to occupy a very low place in the public's esteem. Attitudes toward the government's budget, programs, and taxes are influenced by this more general malaise.

If the polls and general observation are right, both the overall size and the specific programs of the federal government are now subject to greater questioning by citizens than has been true for a long time. This chapter takes a look at these two aspects of the budget. The first part examines the growth of federal spending over the past twenty years. How rapid has it been, both absolutely and relative to the national economy? How much of this growth has been due to rising prices and how much represents "real" increases in spending? What have been the principal sources of growth, and how has the composition of the federal budget changed over time? Is the budget out of control; do rising prices and growing numbers of beneficiaries of social security, Medicare, welfare, and other federal programs threaten an inexorable increase in the proportion of national income accounted for by federal spending? More generally, given current policies and programs, what is the likely course of federal spending over the next decade?

Other chapters in this book deal with two of the three major components of federal spending—national defense and income security programs. The concluding section of this chapter examines the third component—the complex array of federal programs that provide grants-in-aid to state and local governments.[1] It is through such programs that the federal government tries to deal with domestic social problems—education, manpower training, criminal justice, and the like. The degree of federal financial support and of federal control over the use of grant funds varies substantially from one program to the next. The desirable level of support and the appropriate degree of control are the central issues of this part of the budget. The final section develops two broad sets of criteria as aids in thinking about these questions. First, what characteristics of a particular social problem or social need warrant the federal government's playing a role rather than leaving the problem in the hands of state or local governments or the private sector? Second, aside from sheer financial support, what kinds of activities can the federal government reasonably expect to direct fairly and effectively and what kind can only be directed well at the state and local level?[2]

The Size and Composition of the Federal Budget

For the first one hundred and forty years of the Republic, until the 1930s, federal spending never exceeded 3 percent of the gross national product except during wars and their immediate aftermath. Of that amount most was devoted, even in peacetime, to paying for the

1. National defense, income security, and grant-in-aid programs, together with interest payments on the national debt, now make up nine-tenths of the total federal budget.

2. This chapter does not deal with the revenue side of the budget or with the problem of tax expenditures—that is, the various subsidies for businesses and individuals contained in the tax code. Recent short and readable summaries of these subjects are U.S. Congressional Budget Office, *Budget Options for Fiscal Year 1977: A Report to the Senate and House Committees on the Budget* (GPO, 1976), pt. 2, pp. 381–90, and *Five-Year Budget Projections, Fiscal Years 1977–81* (GPO, 1976), chap. 3.

Table 8-1. Federal Expenditures as Percent of Gross National Product, Selected Periods, 1869–1957[a]

Period	Total expenditures	Spending on defense or past wars[b]	Other spending
1869–73	4.5	3.3	1.2
1877–81	2.8	2.0	0.8
1889–93	2.5	1.6	0.9
1902–06	2.3	1.5	0.8
1912–16	1.8	1.1	0.7
1925–29	3.0	2.2	0.8
1935–39[c]	7.7	2.8	4.9
1947–49	15.7	10.2	5.5
1955–57	17.7	12.6	5.1

Source: Charles L. Schultze, Edward R. Fried, Alice M. Rivlin, and Nancy H. Teeters, *Setting National Priorities: The 1973 Budget* (Brookings Institution, 1972), p. 395.
a. Calendar years, 1869–1939; fiscal years thereafter.
b. Outlays for military purposes plus veterans' programs and net interest on the debt.
c. Potential rather than actual GNP is used to avoid the effect of depression or recession on the ratios. For the same reason, federal expenditures have been adjusted to exclude the added federal unemployment compensation resulting from unemployment rates in excess of 4 percent.

armed forces and for the costs of past wars (veterans' benefits and interest on the debt, principally accumulated during wartime). Until the 1930s spending for civilian purposes never significantly exceeded 1 percent of GNP (see table 8-1).

The New Deal programs of the 1930s expanded the scope of the federal government's domestic activities. Domestic spending rose to 5 percent of GNP and remained at that level for the next twenty years. In the decade after the Second World War, a combination of large veterans' readjustment payments, interest payments on war-accumulated debt, and the rise in military outlays associated with the cold war pushed up the level of spending related to defense or past wars to record peacetime levels. By the mid-1950s, total federal spending was running at a fairly steady 17 to 18 percent of GNP.

The total federal budget in fiscal 1955 was $68.5 billion. In the new budget for fiscal year 1977, expenditures are likely to amount to $414 billion,[3] a sixfold increase in the short space of twenty-two

3. Throughout this chapter the 1977 expenditures are an estimate, by the author, of what the level of spending is likely to be. The President submitted in January 1976 a budget calling for spending $394.2 billion. At this writing, Congress is in the process of debating a budget resolution calling for spending of somewhere between $413 billion and $415 billion. The author's estimates of 1977 expenditures used throughout this chapter are based on *The Budget of the United States Government, Fiscal Year 1977;* Congressional Budget Office, *Five-Year Budget Projections, Fiscal Years 1977–81,* and *Staff Working Paper for Five-Year Budget Projections, Fiscal Years 1977–81* (CBO, 1976).

years. During that period, of course, prices have risen and the economy has expanded. But after growing in line with the rest of the economy until 1965, federal spending rose relative to the growth of the economy:

	Percent of GNP
1955	18.4
1960	18.5
1965	18.0
1970	20.5
1975	22.5
1977 (estimated)	22.2

Continued expansion at this rate would raise federal spending to 27 percent of GNP by 1985 and require a similar expansion in the proportion of income paid in taxes to the federal government. It is this line of argument that has led to the recently expressed fears about the excessively rapid increase in federal spending.

Closer examination of the course of federal spending, however, casts serious doubt on this conclusion. In the first place, 1970 was a year in which some $17.4 billion, or 1.8 percent of GNP, was devoted to the still active war in Vietnam. Liquidation of the war removed that source of spending. And 1975 was a year of deep recession—the worst since the Great Depression. The unemployment rate by the end of fiscal 1975 was 9 percent, and the GNP was some 11.6 percent below the level that would have been reached had unemployment remained at 5 percent of the labor force. When unemployment rises, federal expenditures for a number of programs automatically increase—unemployment compensation, food stamps, welfare payments, and other similar programs. Recession therefore pushes the numerator of the federal-spending-to-GNP ratio up and the denominator down, and consequently raises the ratio well above its basic trend. Table 8-2 corrects for these aberrations by measuring the GNP in each year at a constant unemployment level (the GNP that would be produced at a 5 percent rate of unemployment, or nonrecession GNP); by similarly adjusting federal expenditures to the level that would accompany 5 percent unemployment; and by subtracting, for 1970, the incremental costs of the Vietnam War.[4] For

4. The use of a 5 percent unemployment rate to define the nonrecession GNP and the baseline budget is simply a convenience. It is the average rate of unemployment over the years 1955–75. In no sense does its use imply that 5 percent is an appropriate target for economic policy. A similar calculation at 4 percent or 6 per-

Table 8-2. Baseline Budget as Percent of Nonrecession GNP,
Selected Fiscal Years, 1955–77

Billions of dollars and percent

Description	1955	1960	1965	1970	1975	1977[a]
Total federal outlays	68.5	92.0	118.4	196.6	324.6	413.7
Less: Vietnam War costs	...	...	0.1	17.4	...	...
Less: recession-related outlays	...	...	...	−1.7[b]	7.8	14.5
Equals: baseline budget	68.5	92.0	118.3	180.9	316.8	399.2
Nonrecession GNP	377	507	652	954	1,588	1,990
Baseline budget as percent of nonrecession GNP	18.2	18.1	18.1	19.0	19.9	20.1
National defense and foreign affairs	11.2	9.5	8.1	6.9	5.7	5.4
Domestic programs	7.0	8.6	10.0	12.1	14.2	14.7

Sources: Vietnam war costs from U.S. Department of Defense (Comptroller), *The Economics of Defense Spending: A Look at the Realities* (Department of Defense, 1972), table 16-1, p. 149; other data, *The Budget of the United States Government*, relevant years, and author's estimates.

a. See footnote 3 to this chapter.

b. In fiscal 1970 unemployment averaged less than 5 percent; hence outlays on unemployment compensation and similar programs were lower than the baseline level.

convenience the resulting expenditure level is called the baseline budget.

Measured in a way that excludes the short-term fluctuations caused by recession, the overall level of federal spending has risen less sharply relative to the size of the national economy. Very roughly, federal spending in the first decade of the twenty-year comparison, from 1955 to 1965, remained at an almost constant 18 percent of GNP. Over the next ten years the ratio rose modestly, to about 20 percent at present.[5] What is also clear from the analysis, however, is that the relatively stable overall relationship between federal spending and GNP was achieved by large offsetting movements in two major components: defense spending as a fraction of GNP fell stead-

---

cent unemployment would reveal basically the same trends so long as every year was adjusted to the same common level. (A very slight difference in trends might show up because of long-term improvements in unemployment insurance, which would have a different impact depending on what constant level of unemployment was used to define the baseline budget.) An outline of the procedures used to estimate the volume of recession-related expenditures is available on request from the author.

5. Some two-fifths of the 20 percent of GNP devoted to federal programs in 1977 represents cash transfer payments and net interest payments. The recipients may spend the money as they wish. Hence, the fact that 20 percent of gross national income flows through the federal government does not imply that the federal government controls the allocation of 20 percent of the national output.

ily, while domestic spending rose sharply, outweighing the fall in defense. During the past twenty years the fall in the defense share has made it possible to start and then rapidly expand a large number of new domestic programs with only a small rise in the portion of national income taken in federal taxes. Whatever the course of defense spending may be in the next decade, it is virtually certain that its share of GNP cannot continue to shrink at the same pace. As a consequence, constraints on domestic programs will be more severe than they were in the previous two decades unless the overall share of federal spending in GNP rises significantly above 20 percent.

Federal Spending in Constant Dollars

As in all other sectors of the national economy, the prices of what the federal government buys or finances have risen, moderately until 1968, more sharply thereafter. Unfortunately, the prices of what the federal government buys have risen faster than the average price level.

Outside of defense procurement, a small volume of other purchases from the industrial sector of the economy, and cash payments to individuals, the federal government deals mainly in either buying services and construction or in financing similar purchases by state and local governments. It has long been recognized that the prices of services tend to rise faster than the prices of goods. The central reason for this is that technological improvements and capital investment can, and usually are, more fruitfully applied to improving productivity in goods production than in service production. New machinery can substantially reduce the labor costs of producing textiles or automobiles. But it takes a specified number of players to perform a Brandenburg Concerto or to play *Hamlet*. New kinds of furnaces raise the productivity of labor in turning out steel, but in education a drop in the number of teachers per class is normally associated with a deterioration in quality rather than an increase in productivity. While new equipment can perhaps improve the efficiency of police forces, it is generally much less likely to lead to productivity gains than is the case for the production of TV sets.

In general, therefore, the service industries experience much lower productivity gains than do the goods industries. But in the long run, wages tend to rise at about the same rate in both sets of industries (otherwise barbers, teachers, and policemen would suffer a steady erosion of their income relative to their neighbors). The effect of these wage increases on costs and prices in the goods industries is moderated significantly by productivity gains; in the service industries, much less so. As a consequence, prices tend to rise more rapidly in the service than in the goods industries.

To some extent this phenomenon is a statistical artifact. The output of TV sets, steel, and textiles can be counted and measured, but not the output of policemen, teachers, doctors, and government statisticians. In estimating prices and national output, it is customary to *assume* that no productivity gains are occurring in such occupations. If 5 percent more teachers or policemen are hired each year, it is assumed that the output of education or law enforcement increases by only 5 percent a year—not 7 or 8 percent as would be the case if productivity were rising. Correspondingly, it is assumed that a 6 percent wage increase for teachers or policemen is a 6 percent price increase for education or law enforcement (whereas one can actually observe the price increase that accompanies a 6 percent wage increase for workers in textile plants and it is usually less than 6 percent). Despite this statistical problem, it is undoubtedly true that the "prices" of services purchased or financed by government tend to rise more than the average price level for the economy as a whole.

The federal government also purchases, or finances the purchases of, a substantial amount of construction whose prices have tended to rise more than other prices. Between 1955 and 1975 the price of "structures," as estimated in the national income accounts, rose 114 percent while the average price of all goods production rose 82 percent.

Since the prices of what the federal government buys or finances tend to rise faster than the average price level, devoting a constant share of the nation's *real* output to the federal government sector requires an increase in the share of total income flowing to the federal government, taking the form of a higher share of income paid out in taxes. Conversely, a steady share of income taken in taxes by the federal government would buy a steadily smaller share of real national output. Table 8-3 shows how the divergence in price trends between the price of federal expenditures and the average price of GNP has affected the federal budget.

During each five-year subperiod of the past twenty years, the price

Table 8-3. Relation of Federal Baseline Expenditures to Nonrecession GNP, in Current and Constant Dollars, Fiscal Years 1955–77

Description	1955– 60	1960– 65	1965– 70	1970– 75	1975– 77
Annual percentage chang? in price indexes					
Federal baseline expenditures	3.8	2.3	5.3	7.7	8.0
Total GNP	2.5	1.5	3.9	6.5	7.1
Annual percentage change					
Real nonrecession GNP	3.5	3.6	3.8	4.0	4.5
Constant dollar baseline expenditures	2.2	2.8	3.4	3.8	4.0
	1955	*1960*	*1965*	*1970*	*1975*	*1977*
Federal baseline expenditures as percent of GNP						
Current dollars	18.2	18.1	18.1	19.0	19.9	20.1
Constant dollars[a]	18.2	17.0	16.4	16.1	15.9	15.8

Sources: Price index for GNP from U.S. Department of Commerce, *Survey of Current Business*, vol. 56 (January 1976), pt. 1; price index for federal baseline expenditures calculated by the author. A description of the methodology underlying the calculations is available on request.

a. Implicit deflators for both GNP and federal expenditures were calculated with calendar year 1972 = 100 and then shifted to a fiscal year 1955 = 100 base.

of what the government buys or finances has risen annually about 1.0 to 1.3 percent faster than the overall price index. From fiscal 1955 to fiscal 1977 the average price of federal expenditures will have risen some 27 percent more than prices in general. As a consequence, the rough stability of the federal expenditure share in total national income from 1955 to 1965 was translated into a falling federal share in real output, from 18 percent in 1955 to roughly 16 percent in 1965. Real federal outlays during the period rose at a significantly slower rate than real GNP. From 1965 to 1977, however, real federal outlays will have grown at approximately the same rate as real GNP. But this equality in real growth rates, when combined with the faster increase in prices for federal expenditures than for GNP as a whole, has caused the share of total national income flowing to the federal government to rise to about 20 percent.

So, because it tends to purchase and finance the purchase of services and other categories of output whose prices rise faster than average, channeling a constant share of the nation's output into federal programs requires that a growing share of the national income be devoted to governmental purposes. Conversely, holding the tax burden constant so that only a stable share of income is devoted to government necessarily leads to a fall in the share of national output being used for public purposes. Paradoxically, in an affluent nation where productivity in the manufacture of goods rises rapidly, the relative cost of providing public services tends to increase sharply. The wealthier the nation grows, the more likely are its people to complain about the "outrageous" cost of government.

The Sources of Growth in Domestic Expenditures

As noted, the relatively small increase in the overall share of federal expenditures in GNP masks two offsetting trends—a steady decline in the ratio of defense spending to GNP and a slightly larger and equally steady rise in the ratio of domestic spending to GNP. Even after allowing for the increase in the price of federal expenditures related to other prices, the real share of national income devoted to the domestic programs of the federal government rose steeply (see table 8-4).

What were the major sources of the large increase in the federal government's domestic programs?

There are approximately 1,200 separate appropriations in the federal budget, many of them providing funds for more than one program or activity. To gain some understanding of the changing character of the budget and the factors underlying the growth in domestic spending, it is obviously necessary to group these highly varied programs into a reasonable number of categories. There are

Table 8-4. Share in Nonrecession GNP of Federal Baseline Expenditures on Domestic Programs, and Price Ratios, Selected Fiscal Years, 1955–77[a]

	Share in GNP (percent)		Price ratio, domestic expenditures to GNP
Fiscal year	Current dollars	Constant dollars	
1955	7.0	7.0	1.00
1960	8.6	7.8	1.11
1965	10.1	8.7	1.15
1970	12.1	9.8	1.24
1975	14.2	11.1	1.28
1977[b]	14.7	11.3	1.30

Sources: Baseline domestic expenditures from table 8-6; nonrecession GNP from table 8-2; price indexes for domestic expenditures derived by the author
a. Domestic expenditures equal total budget expenditures less outlays on budgetary functions "national defense" and "international affairs."
b. Estimated.

Table 8-5. Federal Expenditures on Domestic Programs, by Major Category, Fiscal Years 1955 and 1977

Category	Billions of dollars		Percent of nonrecession GNP	
	1955	1977	1955	1977
Baseline domestic expenditures	26.4	292.2	7.0	14.7
Payments to individuals (in cash and in kind)ᵃ	12.1	167.4	3.2	8.4
Grants to state and local governmentsᵃ	1.7	43.5	0.5	2.2
Outlays for net interest	4.8	33.0	1.3	1.7
Other	7.8	48.3	2.1	2.4
Addendum: Recession-induced expenditures	...	14.5	...	0.7

Sources: Baseline domestic expenditures, payments to individuals, and net interest from table 8-6; nonrecession GNP from table 8-2; 1955 grants-in-aid from *Special Analyses, Budget of the United States Government, Fiscal Year 1977*, table O-5, p. 264; 1977 grants-in-aid from the same source, adjusted by the author to be consistent with a $414 billion estimate of total federal expenditures; see footnote 3 to this chapter.

a. Some individual payments, principally aid to families with dependent children (AFDC) and housing assistance payments, are made through grants to state or local governments. These are shown in the "payments to individuals" rather than the "grants to state and local governments" category. The amounts are $1.5 billion in 1955 and $25.0 billion in 1977.

several ways of doing this. One is to classify expenditures by the end purpose served, that is, by *function:* education, manpower training, environmental control, and so on. Another way is to classify expenditures according to the *method* used by the federal government in going about its tasks. It makes payments to individuals in two forms: cash payments for social security, unemployment compensation, or veterans' pensions; and goods or services provided directly to individuals—food stamps, medical benefits, and housing subsidies. It gives grants-in-aid to state and local governments for general financial support or to induce them to deliver specific services to their citizens. And it directly provides some goods and services—it builds dams, delivers mail, collects statistics, enforces federal laws, regulates pollution, and so forth. In what follows, different methods of classification will be used as the need arises.

In 1955 and still in fiscal 1977, three broad groupings of federal activities account for the bulk of domestic spending (see table 8-5). Individual payment programs and grants-in-aid accounted for virtually all of the growth in the ratio of domestic federal expenditures to GNP—6.9 out of 7.7 percentage points of increase. The rising fraction of GNP going to interest payments is not due to a growth in

Table 8-6. Federal Expenditures on Domestic Programs, by Category, Selected Fiscal Years, 1955–77

	Billions of dollars						As percent of nonrecession GNP			
Category	1955	1960	1965	1970	1975	1977	1955	1965	1970	1977
Baseline domestic expenditures	**26.4**	**43.8**	**65.7**	**115.4**	**225.8**	**292.2**	**7.0**	**10.1**	**12.1**	**14.7**
Payments to individuals	12.1	21.9	31.1	61.3	131.4	167.4	3.2	4.8	6.4	8.4
Retirement, disability, and unemployment	10.4	19.4	27.2	51.8	107.2	136.5	2.8	4.2	5.4	6.9
Low-income assistance	1.7	2.5	3.9	9.5	24.2	30.9	0.5	0.6	1.0	1.5
Physical investment and subsidies	6.1	10.7	20.7	23.8	32.5	41.4	1.6	3.2	2.5	2.1
Natural resources and environment	4.7	4.3	6.9	8.8	11.2	16.4	1.2	1.1	0.9	0.8
Transportation	1.0	4.2	5.8	7.0	10.4	15.5	0.3	0.9	0.7	0.8
Commerce, science, research and development, and other	0.4	2.2	8.0	8.0	10.9	9.5	0.1	1.2	0.8	0.5
Social investment and services	2.4	3.5	4.9	16.3	32.3	40.9	0.6	0.8	1.7	2.1
Education	1.0	1.0	1.3	6.0	12.2	14.2	0.3	0.2	0.6	0.7
Health	1.0	1.8	2.3	5.0	9.7	12.4	0.3	0.4	0.5	0.6
Manpower training	0.1	0.2	0.5	1.6	2.8	4.7	...	...	0.2	0.2
Social services and other	0.3	0.5	0.8	3.7	7.6	9.6	...	...	0.4	0.5
Revenue sharing	0.1	0.2	0.2	0.5	7.0	7.4	...	...	...	0.4
Outlays for net interest	4.8	6.9	8.6	14.4	23.3	33.0	1.3	1.3	1.5	1.7
Other	1.1	1.8	1.6	1.7	5.7	9.6	0.3	0.2	0.2	0.5
Less: intragovernmental transactions, etc.	−0.2	−1.2	−1.4	−2.6	−6.4	−7.5	...	...	...	...
Addendum: Recession-oriented expenditures (all classified as "payments to individuals")	0.0	0.0	0.0	−1.7	7.8	14.5	...	...	...	...

Sources: Total baseline domestic expenditures equal total expenditures less expenditures on "national defense" and "international affairs," and recession-oriented expenditures. Recession-oriented expenditures derived by the author; see footnote 4 to this chapter. All other expenditure data, except for fiscal 1977, taken from various issues of *The Budget of the United States Government*, and grouped in categories by the author; for 1977 expenditures, see footnote 3 to this chapter.

federal debt—debt declined sharply as a percentage of GNP—but to the large rise in interest rates over the past two decades.

Another, more detailed analysis of the sources of growth in federal spending is given in table 8-6. Outlays for individual payments are separated into two major components: (1) payments for retirement, disability, and unemployment—principally social security, medical care for the elderly (Medicare), veterans' pensions and compensation, and unemployment insurance—and (2) assistance to low-income recipients—principally cash welfare, food stamps, housing assistance, and medical care for the poor (Medicaid). The next major category of expenditures is composed of federal programs dealing with the physical or economic environment—agriculture, natural resources, transportation, pollution control, subsidies to business, and science and technology. About 40 percent of these expenditures are made in the form of grants to state and local governments for construction of highways, waste treatment plants, mass transit facilities, and the like. The third largest category, which became important only in the past ten years, is composed of programs providing assistance for social services and social investment—education, health (apart from Medicare and Medicaid), manpower training, urban development, and social services. About two-thirds of these outlays are made in the form of grants to state and local governments. Net interest, revenue sharing, and a miscellaneous category (principally the overhead costs of running the federal government) make up the rest of the budget.

Developments in three major types of program explain almost nine-tenths of the growth in the ratio of domestic federal expenditures to GNP between 1955 and 1977. (1) The rapid expansion of retirement, disability, and unemployment compensation was responsible for slightly more than half of the growth. (2) The introduction of new low-income assistance programs providing food, medical, and housing benefits to the poor, and the subsequent increase in both those benefits and the older cash welfare payments, accounted for 14 percent of the growth. (3) The introduction and the rapid expansion, especially between 1965 and 1970, of new social service and social investment programs contributed about 18 percent of the growth.

Below, the highlights and developments in these and other budget programs are briefly examined.

Table 8-7. Estimated Federal Baseline Expenditures on Individual Payment Programs, and Recession Increment, Fiscal Year 1977

Billions of dollars

Program	Baseline	Recession increment[a]	Total
Retirement, disability, and unemployment	**136.5**	**8.2**	**144.7**
Old age, survivors, and disability insurance[b]	87.2	...	87.2
Medicare	20.5	...	20.5
Federal civil service retirement	10.1	...	10.1
Veterans' compensation and pensions[c]	8.4	...	8.4
Unemployment compensation	9.1	8.2	17.3
Coal miners' "black lung" benefits and other	1.2	...	1.2
Low-income assistance	**30.9**	**6.3**	**37.2**
AFDC and SSI ("welfare")	10.5	1.8	12.3
Food stamps	5.2	0.8	6.0
Medicaid	8.2	1.2	9.4
Child nutrition	3.1	...	3.1
Public service employment	0.8	2.5	3.3
Housing assistance	3.1	...	3.1

Sources: Author's estimates, based on *The Budget of the United States Government, Fiscal Year 1977;* and U.S. Congressional Budget Office, *Five-Year Budget Projections, Fiscal Years 1977–81* (GPO, 1976).
a. See footnote 4 to this chapter.
b. Includes railroad retirement.
c. Includes veterans' insurance programs.

Individual Payment Programs

The programs making up this category, and the estimated expenditures for them in fiscal 1977, are shown in table 8-7. While some of the increase during the past twenty years simply reflects inflation and the growth of population, by far the most important cause has been new legislation broadening coverage and raising the real level of benefits.

Expenditures under the *social security* program—old age, survivors, and disability insurance (OASDI) plus Medicare—will amount to $107.7 billion in fiscal 1977. Expenditures have risen more than twentyfold since 1955, and they alone explain more than 50 percent of the rise in the ratio of domestic expenditures to GNP. Although the basic program of cash benefits for retired people and survivors was begun in 1935, the benefit levels were still very low and the number of older people who had qualified for benefits was still relatively small as late as the mid-1950s (see table 8-8). In

Table 8-8. Changes in Number of Beneficiaries and Benefit Levels under OASDI, Selected Years, 1954–75

Year	Number of beneficiaries* (millions)		Retirement benefits[b]	
	Old age and survivors insurance	Disability insurance	Monthly (1975 dollars)	Wage replacement rates[c]
1954–55[d]	7.4	...	263	0.48
1965	19.1	1.7	311	0.47
1975	27.5	4.3	420	0.61

Sources: Number of beneficiaries, 1954–65, from *Social Security Bulletin, Annual Statistical Supplement, 1973*, table 30, p. 60; 1975, from *Social Security Bulletin*, vol. 39 (February 1976), table M-9, p. 54. Replacement rates and median wages, furnished by the U.S. Department of Health, Education, and Welfare, Office of the Assistant Secretary (Planning and Evaluation). Average monthly benefits were calculated by multiplying the median wage for each year by the replacement rate for that year.

a. At end of December, 1954, 1955, and 1965; end of October 1975.

b. First year of benefits to a retired couple; husband retired on July 1 of the year shown, having earned median wages during his working life.

c. Ratio of first-year retirement benefits to wages in year immediately before retirement, both in constant dollars.

d. Because the replacement ratio in 1954 was temporarily very low and in 1955 was temporarily very high, 1954 and 1955 were averaged.

several legislative steps since then, Congress has steadily widened the scope and coverage of this program: real benefit levels were greatly increased; the disabled were added to the list of eligible persons; Medicare was enacted in 1965; and coverage was extended to many older people who had not worked long enough under the original program to qualify for benefits. Liberalizing legislation enacted between 1955 and 1965 was principally directed toward expanding the coverage of the program, including the introduction of disability insurance. The benefit formula was adjusted periodically just enough to keep retirement benefits for an average newly retired worker and spouse at slightly less than 50 percent of preretirement earnings. Starting in 1970, benefit liberalizations have raised this earnings replacement ratio to over 60 percent.

Until recently all benefit increases, including those designed simply to offset cost-of-living increases for workers already retired, were periodically enacted by Congress. By a law passed in 1972 (and amended in 1973), benefits are now automatically increased each year to keep pace with the cost of living.[6]

In 1977 Medicare will add some $20.5 billion to budget outlays.

6. The formula by which cost-of-living increases are incorporated in the benefit schedule, however, is seriously defective. See chapter 12.

Since medical costs have had a tendency to rise much faster than prices in general, Medicare outlays have almost tripled since 1970.

Even though the "baseline expenditures" exclude the extra *unemployment compensation* attributable to the recession, the level of compensation that goes with 5 percent unemployment has grown rapidly (from $3 billion in 1965 to $9 billion in 1977). As wages have risen, the average benefits paid to the unemployed have grown apace. This is a joint federal-state program; the federal government sets certain minimum standards, and individual states can and often do go beyond them. A combination of liberalizing federal legislation and state action has tended to extend coverage and improve benefits over the past two decades, in addition to the increases that accompany rising wages.

Retirement benefits for federal civilian workers have become an important component of the budget, rising from $0.4 billion in 1955 to $10 billion in 1977. The federal work force grew substantially in World War II and again during the Korean War. Although it has increased little since that time, the last decade has seen a large rise in retirements as those hired twenty to thirty years ago began to retire. In addition, growing federal salaries, substantial liberalization of benefits, and a particularly generous technique for giving cost-of-living adjustments have produced large gains in average benefits per retiree. *Veterans' pensions and compensation* (for service-connected disabilities) follows a course of its own, depending on the age structure of the veteran population, the number disabled in recent conflicts, and congressional liberalization of benefits.

All the above programs (except Medicare) are of long standing. All of them provide benefits to people based on age, health, employment status, or being a veteran. Except for the veterans' programs, all of them involve special taxes or contributions, collected from workers and employers and placed in special trust funds.[7] Most of them are thought of as insurance. That is, beneficiaries who have been taxed or assessed to pay for the programs see them as an earned right, even though the benefits paid out may have little relation to past contributions.[8] While many of the benefits go to people who are poor, or who

7. Under pending legislation, black lung benefits for coal miners, now paid for by general revenues, would be converted to a trust fund financed by a tax on coal.

8. And even veterans can be said to have paid for their benefits by their military service.

Table 8-9. Recipients of Aid to Families with Dependent Children and Average Real Benefits, Fiscal Years 1955, 1965, and 1975

Fiscal year	Number of recipients, average monthly case load[a] (thousands)	Average annual benefits per recipient[a,b] (1975 dollars)
1955	2,173	542.2
1965	4,238	621.6
1975	11,077	771.3

Source: Data from Department of Health, Education, and Welfare, Social and Rehabilitation Service.
a. Recipients include not only parents receiving the payments but their children as well.
b. Payments include both federal and state and local contributions.

would be poor were it not for their benefits, the programs were not designed for the poor, but for everyone meeting certain employability criteria (retired, disabled, or unemployed). These programs are not looked on as "welfare," nor do they engender widespread hostility on grounds that they are subject to abuse or that the taxpayer is being "ripped off." But it is precisely these benefits, going to the average citizen, that account for more than half the growth in domestic federal expenditures relative to GNP.

In the *low-income assistance* category there are six major programs that provide individual payments, in cash or in kind, to the poor and near-poor. Total expenditures under such programs were relatively small until as late as 1965 ($3.9 billion, 0.6 percent of GNP).

In the 1930s, at the same time social security was introduced, the federal government began making grants to state governments to provide a bare minimum of cash income to families whose earner was unable to earn a living and had no other source of income: the aged poor, the blind, the permanently and totally disabled, and families with children whose breadwinner had died, deserted, or otherwise left. Each state set its own criteria for eligibility and benefit levels, subject to certain federal standards. Over the years, benefits were gradually raised and eligibility widened.

Starting in the 1960s, the program of aid to families with dependent children (AFDC) began to expand rapidly (see table 8-9) as a result of three developments. The number of families with children headed by females mushroomed, standards were loosened, and a larger proportion of those eligible began claiming payments. According to one set of estimates, the proportion of eligible families

Table 8-10. Changes in Number of Recipients of Medicaid and Food Stamps, and in Average Benefits, Fiscal Years 1965–75

Money amounts in 1975 dollars

Fiscal year	Medicaid		Food stamps	
	Number of recipients (millions)	Average annual benefit per recipient[a]	Number of recipients (millions)	Average annual benefit per recipient
1965	...	...	0.4	129
1970	16.1	419	4.3	174
1975	22.9	566	17.1	258

Sources: Medicaid recipients, U.S. Department of Health, Education, and Welfare, Social and Rehabilitation Service; Medicaid benefits, 1970, HEW, *Trend Report, 1971*, DHEW(SRS)73-03101 (HEW, 1972), p. 9, and 1975, HEW, Division of Finance; food stamp recipients, U.S. Department of Agriculture, Food and Nutrition Service; food stamp benefits, *The Budget of the United States Government—Appendix*, relevant years.

a. Includes federal and state and local contributions.

receiving benefits monthly rose from 39 percent in 1967 to 61 percent in 1970 to 86 percent in 1975.[9]

In 1972 Congress converted the other cash welfare program— aid to the aged, blind, and disabled—into a wholly federal program with uniform benefits and standards (the supplemental security income program, or SSI). Some states supplement that federal payment with their own funds. In 1977 federal payments for AFDC and SSI are estimated to be $6.4 billion and $5.9 billion respectively, of which about $1.8 billion appears to be the result of the recession (table 8-7).

Three federal programs provide the poor with medical care, food, and housing assistance. All of them are relatively new and have grown rapidly in the past six or seven years. Table 8-10 shows, for example, how greatly the numbers of recipients in the Medicaid and food stamp programs have grown. Unlike virtually all other programs of assistance for the poor, which require the recipient to be aged, disabled, or from a broken family, *food stamp* benefits are based solely on income and asset levels. This means, among other things, that the large number of working poor whose families are intact can receive

9. The 1967 and 1970 percentages are from Barbara Boland, "Participation in the Aid to Families with Dependent Children Program (AFDC)," in *Studies in Public Welfare, Paper No. 12 (Part 1)*, Prepared for the Subcommittee on Fiscal Policy of the Joint Economic Committee, 93:1 (1973). The 1975 percentage is based on estimates furnished by the Urban Institute; the estimates may not be precisely comparable with the earlier ones.

food stamps. The program was introduced on a small scale in 1961 and remained relatively modest until about 1970. Thereafter, the income level at which a family is eligible to receive benefits was steadily increased, and the program was converted into a purely federal one, available in every county of the nation. The number of beneficiaries has grown rapidly, as has the average real value of the benefits. Despite the greater number of beneficiaries, it has been estimated that only about half the people eligible to receive food stamps are actually participating in the program.

Medicaid, which provides health care for the poor, is a joint federal-state program. The federal government sets certain minimum criteria for eligibility for the health services covered, and shares the costs (the federal share averages 55 percent) with the states. The program was introduced in 1966 as an outgrowth of several smaller programs of medical care for the poor. Since participation in AFDC usually makes a family eligible for Medicaid, the rapid growth in the former program has been accompanied by similar growth in the latter.[10] And as with Medicare, rising medical costs have swelled outlays still further. Federal expenditures under the program grew from $2.7 billion in 1970 to an estimated $9.4 billion in 1977.[11]

For many years the federal government provided support for low-rent public housing projects constructed by local housing authorities —about $200 million to $300 million a year in the mid-1960s. The Housing and Urban Development Act of 1965 inaugurated a new set of programs under which the federal government made annual *housing payments* to families with low and moderate income, usually tied to the construction of new housing for those families. The government entered into contracts providing these subsidies on new rental or homeowner units for up to forty years. A constant annual flow of new subsidized housing units results in continually increasing budget outlays, as each year's new subsidies are added to payments made under earlier long-term commitments. In 1973 the administration ceased making new commitments under this program but in 1974 reinstituted it in a new form (differing principally in that the "contract" is not tied to the construction of new housing but may be used to pay for existing housing as well). About 400,000 new contracts a year are being written. Even if this level continued for many years,

10. In many states, poor families not eligible for AFDC are eligible for Medicaid.
11. About $1.2 billion of the $9.4 billion was generated by recession.

the number of families receiving subsidies would be only a small proportion of those whose incomes make them eligible for assistance.

The *public service employment program* is counted here as part of the individual payments category since its principal purpose is to provide people with income. The administration has proposed phasing this program down in 1977; the majority of Congress apparently wants to maintain and expand it. To avoid having too many budget groupings, it is included in the "low-income assistance" subcategory, although the demographic and educational characteristics of those hired under the program suggest that, before they became unemployed, many of them were not poor. In any event, under the laws governing the current public service employment program, outlays would be much reduced if the unemployment rate fell to the 5 percent level used here as a measure of nonrecession conditions and would account for a very small portion of the individual payments category.

Taken together, the individual payments programs designed explicitly for the poor will have grown very sharply between 1965 and 1977, accounting for about 0.9 of the 4.6 percentage-point increase in the share of baseline domestic expenditures in GNP. Even so, their overall magnitude is still a relatively modest fraction of national income (1.5 percent of GNP in 1977). Though they are not a major burden on taxpayers, they are apparently perceived as such. The widespread dissatisfaction with these "welfare" programs probably arises from the fact that, taken all together, they provide a jumble of overlapping and inconsistent benefits and treat people in similar economic circumstances unequally because of a host of arbitrary factors, including sheer luck.

Physical Investment and Subsidies

Some $82 billion of federal expenditures in 1977 (4 percent of nonrecession GNP) will be about equally divided between two major groups of programs: physical investment in and subsidies for natural resources and for industrial and commercial development; and investment in and services for social purposes.

In the first broad category of spending, *physical investment and subsidies* outlays grew rapidly, much faster than GNP, between 1955 and 1965. Thereafter they rose much more slowly, and there was a marked realignment of priorities. In the early part of this period federal spending for agricultural subsidies, the interstate highway pro-

Table 8-11. Major Growth Programs in Physical Investment and Subsidies, Selected Fiscal Years, 1965–77

Billions of dollars

Year	Mass transit	Energy	Environ- mental control	Total	Total as percent of nonrecession GNP
1965	0.0	0.5	0.1	0.6	0.1
1970	0.1	0.6	0.4	1.1	0.1
1975	0.9	1.6	2.5	5.0	0.3
1977	1.8	3.4	4.4	9.6	0.5

Sources: *The Budget of the United States Government*, relevant years; GNP from table 8-2.

gram, water resource projects, and (starting somewhat later) space exploration bulked large in the federal budget. (Space is included in the "commerce, science, research and development, and other" sub-category in table 8-6.) Major growth in highway spending ceased after 1965; agricultural subsidies peaked in the late 1960s, declined slowly for a while, and then in recent years fell sharply as worldwide crop shortages and other events drove farm prices up; space outlays reached their highest level in 1966, declined until 1975, and are now rising slowly (somewhat less than prices).[12]

The large reduction in these outlays as a proportion of GNP has been partially offset by increasing expenditures on mass transit, environmental control, and energy investment (see table 8-11).

Social Investment and Services

In 1955 the federal government provided little support for health care, education, manpower training, social services, or community development. Only about 9 percent of the domestic budget went for these purposes, and more than half of that ($1.4 billion out of $2.3 billion) was for veterans' health and education programs. As late as 1965 the social investment programs were only $4.9 billion, less than 9 percent of the domestic budget. Starting in 1965 the introduction of a large number of Great Society programs and their subsequent expansion led to substantial growth in this broad area of the

12. In 1977 the administration plans to sell a large volume of mortgages from its portfolio of rural loans and to take other actions that will reduce outlays under the mortgage programs of the Department of Housing and Urban Development. The recorded outlays in the "physical investment and subsidies" category, which includes these activities, will be temporarily depressed below their long-term level in 1977.

budget. The simultaneous increase in the number of Vietnam veterans entitled to educational benefits and a decision to improve the government's medical care programs for veterans also added to the growth of spending. (Veterans' health and educational expenditures rose from $1.3 billion in 1965 to $9.6 billion in 1977.) Relative to GNP, the major growth in these programs occurred between 1965 and 1972; thereafter, they grew about in line with GNP:[13]

	As percent of nonrecession GNP			
	1965	1972	1975	1977
Veterans' health and education	0.2	0.4	0.5	0.5
Other social investment and services	0.6	1.7	1.5	1.6

The 1977 budget estimates used here assume that Congress rejects most of the cuts in these programs proposed by President Ford. Should the cuts be accepted, the $41 billion of expenditures (see table 8-6) would drop about $7 billion.

Of the $31 billion (excluding veterans' programs) going to social investment and services in 1977, about $21 billion will be grants-in-aid to state and local governments. Most of the federal assistance for elementary and secondary education, social services, manpower training, and community development is in the form of grants-in-aid, whereas federal support for higher education is principally accomplished through scholarships and loans to students. In the health field, federal grants of about $2 billion are made to state and local governments, but the bulk of the spending is for medical research, food and drug control, and assistance to medical and other professional health schools (see table 8-12).

As much as any other development in the past ten years, it is the $21 billion of social grants that have come in for criticism. The $21 billion is composed of a large number of categorical grant programs, each with its own set of regulations and controls, often imposing, or attempting to impose, relatively detailed federal control over the state and local recipients. In addition to criticism about the excessive number of such programs, questions have also been raised about their effectiveness in reaching the goals they were designed to attain —improved skills and employability for the hard-core unemployed, higher quality education for the disadvantaged, more effective deliv-

13. *The Budget of the United States Government,* relevant years.

Table 8-12. Grants and Other Forms of Federal Support for Social Investment and Services, Fiscal Year 1977[a]

Billions of dollars

Function	Total	Grants-in-aid	Other
Elementary and secondary education	5.4	4.9	0.5
Higher education[b]	3.8	0.9	2.9
Manpower training[c]	4.7	4.1	0.6
Health	7.7	2.2	5.5
Social services	4.0	3.9	0.1
Community development	4.7	4.0	0.7
Law enforcement assistance	0.9	0.8	0.1
Total	31.2	20.8	10.4

Sources: *The Budget of the United States Government, Fiscal Year 1977;* Congressional Budget Office, *Five-Year Budget Projections, Fiscal Years 1977–81,* and *Staff Working Paper for Five-Year Budget Projections* (CBO, 1976).

a. Totals exclude expenditures for veterans' education and medical service.

b. Includes subfunction "research and general educational aids."

c. Excludes public service employment programs, both temporary assistance and transitional assistance under Title II of the Comprehensive Employment and Training Act of 1973.

ery of health services in central cities and rural areas, rehabilitation of central cities, and more efficient law enforcement.

The $21 billion of social grants and the $30.9 billion of payments to low-income families and individuals (table 8-7) are the lightning rods for most of the criticism of domestic spending, especially, though not exclusively, from conservatives. While other domestic programs are criticized, these seem to draw most of the attacks. If expenditures for these two broad categories had remained at the same percentage of nonrecession GNP as they were in 1965, they would now account for $17.9 billion of federal spending instead of $51.9 billion. The difference represents some 8.5 percent of the 1977 baseline budget, or about 1.7 percent of GNP. In a sense, one might say that the great political debate about federal spending for social welfare revolves around the propriety and effectiveness of the way 1.7 percent of the national income is being spent. The modest size of these amounts emphasizes the point made earlier—it is probably the perceived lack of equity or efficiency in the structure of these programs, rather than their real burden on the taxpayer, that is the underlying cause of the dissatisfaction.

Net Interest, Revenue Sharing, and Other Expenditures

Net interest payments on the national debt will account for almost 14 percent of domestic baseline expenditures in 1977. Through 1965 they remained a more or less constant share of GNP, but in the past twelve years they have grown more rapidly. This did not occur because the national debt was rising more rapidly than GNP—indeed the debt–GNP ratio fell throughout most of the period. But interest rates have increased enough to raise total interest payments substantially:[14]

	Fiscal year			
	1955	1965	1975	1977
Federal debt held by the public as percent of nonrecession GNP	59.9	39.8	23.4	26.7
Net interest payments as percent of debt held by the public	2.1	3.3	6.3	6.2

The small expenditures under "revenue sharing" in the early years (shown in table 8-6) arise principally from several long-standing arrangements under which the federal government makes payments to the District of Columbia and shares certain revenues with Puerto Rico and the Virgin Islands. In 1971 the new federal program of general revenue sharing with state and local governments was introduced. The "other" category in table 8-6 consists of various overhead expenditures (the Internal Revenue Service, the construction and operation of federal buildings, and so forth) and the direct law enforcement activities of the federal government. For 1977 it also includes an allowance of $1.5 billion for unanticipated contingencies.

The Next Ten Years

The historical review just presented emphasized several points. First, the total federal budget, adjusted to remove the passing effects of recession, has grown only slightly faster than the national economy over the past twenty years. Second, the stability of the total budget in relation to GNP masks two divergent trends—a continuing fall in the relative size of defense spending and a steady rise in the relative size of domestic spending. Third, a major part of the growth in domestic spending has arisen from legislation creating new programs or expanding the scope and coverage of old ones; with no liberalizing new legislation, the growth of spending would have been much smaller.

14. *The Budget of the United States Government*, relevant years.

Table 8-13. Basic Economic Assumptions for Budget Projections, No Policy Change, Selected Calendar Years, 1975–86

Description	1975	1977	1981	1986	Average annual percentage change	
					1975 –81	1981 –86
Nonrecession GNP						
Billions of 1972 dollars	1,329	1,434	1,657	1,970	3.7	3.5
Billions of current dollars	1,680	2,036	2,834	4,097	9.1	7.6
GNP deflator (1972 = 100)	126.4	142.0	171.0	208.1	5.2	4.0

Source: Derived by the author.

These observations about the past immediately suggest several conclusions about the future. Even under the most "dovish" policies, it is highly unlikely that defense spending can continue to fall as a percentage of GNP. Thus future increases in domestic spending at the same rate as in the past would soon begin to raise the overall share of spending, and hence of taxes, in GNP by quite substantial amounts. But there is nothing built into the nature of existing federal programs that would automatically lead to a continuation of past growth rates. The growth of the domestic budget relative to GNP resulted from legislative actions, not from automatic expansion of outlays in response to outside forces.[15]

To amplify these general observations some specific numerical projections must be made.

To start, what would happen to federal spending if today's basic laws and policies were left in force, if current programs were neither cut back nor expanded in real terms, but allowed to rise only with prices and, in the case of individual payment programs, with the growth in the number of beneficiaries under existing benefit laws? The results obtained under these assumptions are compared with the projected growth of GNP under nonrecession conditions.

Table 8-13 lays out the basic economic assumptions used in the projections. The projected future price inflation may be considered

15. In view of both the large growth in the number of retired people relative to the working force that will occur after the turn of the century and the current formula for determining social security benefits, there could be a very substantial rise in social security expenditures relative to GNP even if further liberalizations were not enacted. But this will not happen during the next ten years.

by some as optimistic between now and 1980 and pessimistic for the long run, since a decline in the inflation rate to 4 percent by 1980, but no drop below that thereafter, is projected. A faster or slower rate of inflation, however, would not significantly change the ratio of spending to GNP (since both numerator and denominator would be changed by roughly the same amount).[16]

For purposes of making projections under a "no-policy-change" assumption, government programs can be divided into two basic groups.

First, there are a number of programs, chiefly those for making individual payments, in which the law stipulates eligibility requirements and provides a formula for calculating benefits. The actual volume of spending on these "entitlement" programs then depends on the number of people who claim the benefits and the way in which economic circumstances (for instance, inflation) affect the benefit formula. By now most entitlement programs have automatic cost-of-living or other price escalation features. For the few that do not (veterans' benefits and AFDC), it is assumed that benefits are legislatively adjusted to keep up with price changes.

Second, in most other programs the basic authorizing laws do not specify the level of benefits; this is determined annually by appropriation action of Congress. In the absence of a long-term budget plan, any definition of what constitutes a continuation of current policy on such programs is bound to be arbitrary, since Congress has not committed itself beyond the current budget year. It is assumed that, unless there are explicit reasons to make exceptions, the maintenance of current policy implies keeping the level of these programs unchanged in real terms; future appropriations are increased solely to cover inflation.

Several special cases had to be dealt with. The number of social security beneficiaries, recipients of unemployment compensation (at 5 percent unemployment), and veterans is predictable. But in programs for the poor and near-poor—principally AFDC, SSI, Medicaid, and food stamps—predictions are more difficult. They depend on changes in income at the bottom of the income distribution and, in the case of AFDC, on trends in the number of families with

16. Under existing tax laws, however, the rate of inflation does make a difference to the ratio of revenues to GNP, since price increases raise taxes faster than they raise nominal GNP.

children headed by females. In general, heavy reliance has been placed on two sets of projections developed by the Congressional Budget Office,[17] but some changes have been made where this seemed reasonable. In the case of food stamps, one additional problem was encountered. In 1976 about 40 to 50 percent of those eligible for the program were receiving benefits. A large growth in expenditures could occur simply because more of those eligible decided to claim benefits. The projections assume only a small further growth in the percentage of those eligible receiving benefits.[18]

In the defense program, it was assumed that the real value of defense procurement would remain at 1977 levels. But actual spending in 1977 reflects chiefly the volume of defense contracts let some years ago—there is a lag between ordering defense equipment and paying for it as it is produced and delivered. The 1977 volume of new contracts is significantly higher than several years ago. Hence, even though the real volume of defense contracts remains unchanged, the real volume of spending continues to rise for several years as it catches up with the current level of contract placement. In several other programs, where the current level of appropriations and new orders is running higher than spending, this same phenomenon will occur.

The national debt is assumed to continue growing for several years because of the federal deficits caused by recession, but thereafter to remain constant. Interest rates are assumed to remain unchanged, on the average, over the projection period.[19] General revenue sharing is assumed to be fixed in dollar terms at the current level through 1981 and to rise with inflation after that.

Table 8-14 shows the results of the projections in current and in constant (1972) dollars. Defense spending in constant dollars rises

17. *Staff Working Paper for Five-Year Budget Projections, Fiscal Years 1977–81;* and *Growth of Government Spending for Income Assistance: A Matter of Choice,* Prepared by the Congressional Budget Office for the Senate Committee on the Budget, 94:1 (GPO, 1975).

18. This projection was influenced by the likelihood of the passage, this year, of some kind of reform legislation that would at least modestly restrict the number of people eligible. While technically this would lower the total number of eligibles, not the percentage claiming benefits, it should moderate program growth.

19. The baseline federal budget excludes recession-caused expenditures in the individual payment programs, but includes the interest payments incurred by the recession-generated increase in the federal debt. Even with a return to high employment, that debt would remain. Moreover, in this projection it has not been assumed that there will be any future reduction in the debt held by the public.

Table 8-14. Federal Expenditures under a No-Policy-Change Assumption, Selected Fiscal Years, 1977–86

	Billions of current dollars			Billions of 1972 dollars		
Category	1977	1981	1986	1977	1981	1986
Baseline budget	**399.2**	**534.0**	**719.0**	**271.8**	**296.0**	**316.0**
National defense and foreign affairs	107.0	146.0	190.0	72.8	80.0	81.0
Payments to individuals	167.4	233.0	334.0	117.8	136.0	160.0
Physical investment and subsidies	41.4	52.0	65.0	28.6	29.0	28.0
Social investment and services	40.9	50.0	60.0	28.1	27.0	24.0
Revenue sharing	7.4	8.0	11.0	5.0	4.0	4.0
Net interest	33.0	40.0	50.0	18.1	17.0	16.0
Other	9.6	13.0	17.0	6.5	7.0	7.0
Intragovernmental transactions, etc.	−7.5	−8.0	−8.0	−5.0	−4.0	−4.0
Recession increment	**14.5**	...	...	**10.2**	...	...
Total federal budget	**413.7**	**534.0**	**719.0**	**282.0**	**296.0**	**316.0**

Source: Derived by the author.

between 1977 and 1981, as outlays adjust to the higher level of new contracts. The small rise thereafter is due solely to the growth of military retirement programs. Two factors account for the fall in real outlays in the social investment and services category: the number of Vietnam veterans eligible for educational benefits declines, and inflation reduces the real value of the federal grant program for social services, on which Congress has placed an absolute dollar ceiling. In the physical investment category, real highway expenditures decline as the interstate highway system is finished, and the current large backlog of federal construction grants for municipal waste treatment plants is reduced. Real expenditures on energy and on air navigation facilities increase. The total for the category remains about constant in real terms.

Current dollar outlays for all categories increase throughout the period, both because of the general inflation and because the prices of what the government buys or finances are expected to continue rising slightly faster than prices generally.

Table 8-15 expresses the projected no-policy-change budget as a percentage of nonrecession GNP. Several sets of factors will affect this share. For most programs other than defense and individual payments, it would take specific policy decisions to raise real expenditures—there is nothing inherent in the programs to increase

Table 8-15. Projected No-Policy-Change Budget as Percent of Nonrecession GNP, Selected Fiscal Years, 1977–86

Category	1977	1981	1986
Baseline budget	20.1	19.2	17.9
National defense and foreign affairs	5.4	5.2	4.7
Payments to individuals	8.4	8.4	8.3
Physical investment and subsidies	2.1	1.9	1.6
Social investment and services	2.1	1.8	1.5
Revenue sharing	0.4	0.3	0.3
Net interest	1.7	1.4	1.2
Other	0.5	0.5	0.4
Intragovernmental transactions, etc.	−0.4	−0.3	−0.2
Recession increment	0.7	...	...
Total federal budget	20.8	19.2	17.9

Source: Derived by the author. Figures are rounded.

outlays unless the President and Congress decide to do so. Since real GNP will rise, the ratio of expenditures to GNP in these programs will therefore decline under a no-policy-change assumption. For several years, real defense outlays will rise, but simply as expenditures catch up with current policy decisions as expressed by the volume of new contracts being let.[20] But this increase will be less than that of real GNP so the share of defense will fall, and after 1980 or 1981, when real outlays level off, it will fall somewhat faster. Under a no-policy-change budget, however, the fall in the defense share will be much less rapid than in the past, when the absolute value of real outlays declined.

In the case of individual payments programs, the growth in the number of beneficiaries, and in some cases in real benefit levels, is likely to be sufficient under current laws to increase real outlays almost as fast as real GNP. Hence the share of these programs in GNP would fall only slightly under a no-policy-change budget.

Finally, the somewhat faster rate of growth in prices paid by government than in prices generally will prevent the ratio of expenditures to GNP from falling as much as it might have with no policy changes. Had no increase in government prices relative to other prices been projected, baseline expenditures in 1986 would fall to 17.0 percent of GNP instead of 17.9 percent. (In current dollars, 1981

20. Real outlays for military retirement will continue to rise as the number of retirees increases and real benefit payments grow.

Table 8-16. Implications of Holding Federal Baseline Expenditures to 20 Percent of Nonrecession GNP in Fiscal Years 1981 and 1986

Billions of current dollars

Description	1977	1981	1986
Baseline expenditures			
(20 percent of GNP)	398	557	805
Projected no-policy-change budget	399	534	719
Difference	−1	23	86
Less: allowance for contingencies	...	10	20
Available leeway I	...	**13**	**66**
Defense increases proposed by the			
administration[a]	...	7	17
Available leeway II	...	**6**	**49**

Sources: GNP and baseline expenditure projections from tables 8-13 and 8-14.
a. See text.

expenditures would be $8 billion and 1986 expenditures $36 billion lower than shown in table 8-13.)

A budget projected on the assumption of no policy changes over the next five or ten years is useful neither as a prediction nor as a goal. But it does provide a benchmark against which potential changes can be judged. Once probable expenditures based on this assumption have been estimated, the consequences of pursuing a number of alternative policies can be examined.

Given the growth in federal expenditures that would occur even without policy changes, how much room is left to expand existing programs or inaugurate new ones without raising the share of expenditures in GNP above its current 20 percent level? Determining future leeway in the budget cannot be put off. Actions to expand existing programs or to launch such new initiatives as health insurance and welfare reform will not immediately increase expenditures, but only after several years. As a consequence, current budget planning must have, as one component, an estimate of the budgetary situation several years from now.

Table 8-16 shows future budgetary leeway under a criterion of not allowing baseline expenditures to exceed 20 percent of GNP. By 1981 total outlays could be raised about $23 billion above the no-policy-change projection. But in planning ahead for major new program initiatives, some allowance must be made for a modest and routine expansion in real outlays under existing programs or for unanticipated developments that could cause outlays to exceed the no-policy-change projection. Expanding facilities and personnel to handle growing work loads at national parks is an example of the first category of contingencies; a larger than expected rise in the number of eligible beneficiaries receiving food stamps is an example of the second. The further ahead one looks, the larger the prudent allowance for contingencies must be.

With a $10 billion contingency allowance in 1981, the leeway for additional outlays shrinks to $13 billion. In turn, should some moderate increase in real defense procurement be undertaken, as is implicit in current administration defense planning, the 1981 leeway shrinks to only $6 billion.[21]

There is of course no economic or social law that sets 20 percent of GNP as the limit for federal spending beyond which catastrophe occurs. An alternative benchmark from which to begin future budget planning would be to hold expenditures at a level consistent with the yield from current tax laws. The individual income tax, which contributes 44 percent of federal revenues, is progressive. As national output and income rise, individual taxpayers find themselves in higher tax brackets and pay a higher proportion of their income in taxes. The other major federal taxes, social security and corporate income, rise at roughly the same rate as GNP.[22] As a whole, federal revenues tend to rise faster than GNP, whether the rise in GNP is due to increases in real output or to inflation. Table 8-17 shows the leeway for future budgetary action in relation to the revenues generated under existing tax laws. In projecting future revenues, it has been assumed that the current temporary reductions in income and corporate profits taxes are made permanent. With the projected growth in GNP and in prices, federal revenues would increase from 20.1 percent of GNP in 1977 to 21.3 percent in 1981 and 22.7 percent in 1986.[23] By 1981 high-employment revenues would be $58 billion higher than a no-policy-change expenditure budget; by 1986 the difference would be $197 billion.

21. An estimate of 1981 outlays under the administration's current defense plans was derived from data in Congressional Budget Office, *Budget Options for Fiscal Year 1977*, pt. 2-1.

22. Since many federal excise taxes are based on physical quantities (for instance, gasoline and cigarettes), they do not respond to inflation. But also they constitute only a small percentage of total revenues.

23. Unlike its impact on the ratio of expenditures to GNP, a change in the assumptions about inflation would change the ratio of federal revenues to GNP.

Table 8-17. Leeway for Future Policy Action Based on Revenues under Current Tax Laws, Fiscal Years 1977, 1981, and 1986

Billions of dollars

Description	1977	1981	1986
Nonrecession revenues under current tax laws	400	592	916
As percent of nonrecession GNP	*20.1*	*21.3*	*22.7*
Projected no-policy-change budget	399	534	719
Difference	1	58	197
Less: allowance for contingencies	...	10	20
Less: nonrecession surplus[a]	...	14	20
Available leeway I	...	**34**	**157**
Defense increases proposed by the administration[a]	...	7	17
Available leeway II	...	**27**	**140**
Size of tax reduction permitting expenditures to remain at 20 percent of GNP and allowing nonrecession surplus of 0.5 percent of GNP	...	21	91
As percent of revenues	...	*3.5*	*9.9*

Source: Derived by the author.
a. See text.

Before gauging the possibilities for expenditure increases or tax cuts, however, it is necessary to ask whether provision should be made, in long-range planning, for a budget surplus when employment is high. No convincing answer can be given now since it depends on economic circumstances at the time. Several recent studies have suggested that to sustain long-run economic growth, to meet environmental cleanup objectives, and to move toward greater self-reliance in energy, some increase in the share of GNP devoted to business investment will be necessary.[24] Even with recovery from the recession levels of 1974 and 1975, housing investment is likely to be a lower fraction of GNP than between 1955 and 1975, but the decline in its share will be less than the projected increase in the share devoted to business investment.[25] The total share of GNP going to investment

24. See, for example, Barry Bosworth, James S. Duesenberry, and Andrew S. Carron, *Capital Needs in the Seventies* (Brookings Institution, 1975), p. 9 and chap. 2; and *Economic Report of the President, January 1976*, pp. 41–47.
25. In the nonrecession years between 1963 and 1973, total fixed investment was 14.5 percent of GNP. Bosworth and others, *Capital Needs*, project an increase to 14.8 percent in 1980, a 1.2-percentage-point rise in the business investment share

—business plus housing—may have to rise if generally accepted economic and social goals are to be met. This implies that, without an increase in private saving rates, some government "saving," that is, a government budget surplus, may be needed at nonrecession levels of GNP.

An examination of federal surpluses in postwar periods of prosperity, when combined with estimates of investment requirements in the future, suggests the desirability of planning for a small nonrecession surplus in the neighborhood of 0.3 to 0.5 percent of GNP. On the other hand, the estimates assume that the target level of GNP is one that produces a 5 percent level of unemployment. Should it prove possible to push (and sustain) unemployment below that level without reigniting inflation, a smaller surplus, or even a slight deficit, might be desirable.[26]

There is no need at present to commit the government to any particular choice about the appropriate balance in the budget as far ahead as 1981 (and obviously 1986). But in making a tentative judgment about the leeway for long-term expenditure commitments or permanent tax reductions, prudence suggests not going beyond a point that would make attainment of a small surplus impossible in 1980 and 1981. Should events over the next few years indicate that business investment and other private spending are weaker than current estimates suggest, additional tax reductions or expenditure increases could be set in motion. The opposite possibility—making commitments that imply a balance or deficit and then reducing outlays or raising taxes if private demand is stronger than anticipated—is a much more difficult course of action. For these reasons, table 8-17 includes an allowance for a nonrecession budget surplus equal to 0.5 percent of GNP in 1981.[27]

After allowing for contingencies and for the possibility of a surplus, there is still room—under existing tax laws—for moderate expenditure increases or tax cuts between 1977 and 1981 (see table

---

being only partially offset by a 0.9-percentage-point fall in the housing share. The Council of Economic Advisers estimates a rise of about 2.0 percentage points in business investment requirements.

26. In all cases the nonrecession budget is measured here in terms of the revenues and expenditures yielded at 5 percent unemployment. The *target* for unemployment can of course be different.

27. The inclusion of a similar surplus in 1986 is purely for the sake of symmetry of treatment; it does not imply a judgment about the strength of private demands in 1986.

8-17). The leeway that would build up between 1981 and 1986 is naturally much larger. The last line in table 8-17 shows the tax reductions that would be feasible by 1981 and 1986 if overall budget expenditures were kept at 20 percent of high-employment GNP; taxes could be cut by 3.5 percent by 1981 and 10 percent by 1986. The reason for this was emphasized earlier: the federal tax system tends to generate a growth in revenues faster than the growth in GNP.

There are two central messages contained in the projections. First, without a significant further reduction in the real level of defense spending or an increase in the share of GNP devoted to federal spending, little leeway is left in the next five years to expand domestic programs or to inaugurate large new ones. The leeway would be even less, indeed would virtually disappear, if it were decided to expand the real level of defense outlays modestly during the next several years.

Reducing expenditures in some areas below the no-policy-change projections would afford some room for altering priorities. Some programs could be terminated, others de-emphasized. For the most part, such reductions would have to come in four places: cutting real defense outlays; modifying the laws that provide benefits in the large, older individual payments programs (social security, unemployment compensation, and veterans' benefits); narrowing the eligibility criteria or reducing the real benefits in programs that make individual payments to the poor (principally food stamps, Medicaid, and cash welfare); or reducing the real level of federal financial support for state and local governments.[28] While there are other areas for possible action—merchant marine subsidies, federal research and development, postal subsidies, and so forth—the chances that reductions in these areas could be large enough to provide significant program expansion elsewhere are remote.

But since there is nothing magic about the figure of 20 percent of GNP, the second major import of the projections is that the simple maintenance of existing tax laws would yield a growth in high-employment federal revenues exceeding the growth in the economy (see table 8-17). Even after tentatively planning for a high-

28. How much to streamline and consolidate the large number of existing categorical grants-in-aid, however, is a question that should be addressed independently of the overall *level* of such financial support to state and and local governments. A reduction in the level of support might, in part at least, simply transfer taxes from the federal to state and local tax systems.

employment budget surplus and providing a modest reserve for un-foreseen contingencies, there would be room in 1981 for about $30 billion in program expansion or new federal activities. The increase in the average share of income paid in federal taxes that automatically accompanies economic growth can either be allowed to occur, and the proceeds used to finance additional federal expenditures, or it can be returned to private uses through tax cuts. What combination of these two courses of action should be taken depends on the relative weight given three considerations: the merits of existing programs that might be abolished to provide savings for other uses; the value of new programs like health insurance or expansion in existing programs like federal aid to states and cities; the value of additional private investment or consumption that would be made possible by tax cuts.

Extrapolating past trends is not a very good way of projecting the areas in which the federal government might increase its outlays be-yond a no-policy-change level. It is highly unlikely, for example, that future legislation will lead to an expansion of individual payments programs at anywhere near the rate of the last decade. Much of the past growth in these programs relative to GNP was due to three fac-tors: the inauguration of new forms of assistance such as Medicare, Medicaid, and food stamps; legislative improvements in coverage and benefit levels in social security and unemployment insurance; and a rise in the percentage of the eligible population actually claim-ing benefits, as in the AFDC program. With a few exceptions these developments are unlikely to be repeated. By now virtually everyone is covered by social security, and for the average retired couple benefits have already been raised to over 60 percent of earnings just before retirement.[29] Medicare is available to all of the elderly. In most states the combined value of food stamps and AFDC payments now provides a level of support to families with dependent children that needs only to be supplemented with a modest amount of part-time earnings to bring family income above the poverty line. Food stamps give some assistance to the working poor. In the AFDC program the proportion of those eligible who claim benefits has already risen to about 90 percent. The food stamp participation rate is still not high

29. According to estimates by several analysts, an elderly couple needs an in-come that amounts to about 60 to 65 percent of income during working years to keep living standards unimpaired. For the average worker, OASI already provides this. See chapter 12, footnote 8.

but most of its growth, if it occurs, will not be among the poorest families receiving large food subsidies (since their participation rate is already high), but among the near-poor where the food subsidy per family is much lower.

Adoption of a national health insurance plan, under which the federal government picked up a sizable proportion of the medical bills now paid by private individuals, would be a major exception to these conclusions. A more modest approach, incorporating a full federal takeover of the Medicaid program and federal support of insurance against catastrophic illness for all citizens, would indeed increase outlays under the individual payments category, but by an amount not nearly large enough to make those payments rise at the rate of the past ten years. A full-scale housing allowance program, added to the present welfare programs, could produce a significant jump in expenditures.[30] On the other hand, a comprehensive welfare reform proposal, in which the federal government took over the current federal-state AFDC program, consolidated it with food stamps and perhaps with SSI, and expanded the benefits available to the working poor, would require some increase in outlays for individual payments but need not raise them sharply as a percent of GNP.

A major expansion of the existing categorical grant programs for social purposes, which grew so rapidly between 1965 and 1972, is unlikely. Measured as a percent of GNP, these programs stopped growing in 1972, and with a few exceptions pressures for future growth have lessened. There are, however, two possible areas in which large growth in federal grants is possible. Continuing financial problems in older central cities might call forth some form of federal assistance, either through a special supplement to general revenue sharing or through some entirely new program.[31] And a new approach to the achievement of full employment, emphasizing a permanent program of public service employment, could add a major increment to budget outlays, principally in the form of grants to state and local governments for job creation.

Finally, one outcome of the current debate over the defense budget and over the significance of increased arms spending by the Soviet Union could be some step-up in the real level of U.S. defense expenditures.

30. See the analysis by Palmer and Minarik in chapter 12.
31. See the discussion by Sunley in chapter 9.

Current programs and policies therefore do not portend a continued growth of domestic federal spending relative to GNP. In fact, unless new initiatives are launched, spending as a share of GNP will decline slightly in the years ahead. To the extent that new initiatives are undertaken, they are unlikely to be a simple continuation of past trends but will probably occur principally in areas quite different from those that have been responsible for past growth.

Federal Grants to State and Local Governments

Other chapters in this book discuss the major long-term issues associated with the defense budget and with the individual payment programs. To conclude this chapter on the federal budget as a whole, federal grants to state and local governments are examined. The three components—defense, individual payments, and grants-in-aid—together with interest payments on the public debt account for nine-tenths of the total budget.

Federal grants-in-aid to state and local governments amounted to $60 billion in fiscal 1976 and are likely to total about $69 billion in 1977. Quite different purposes are served by these grants and very different problems must therefore be considered in judging their current and future role in the federal budget.

Table 8-18 divides the $60 billion of grants in 1976 into three major categories: individual payments programs; general revenue sharing and block grants for broad functional purposes; and categorical grants for very specific purposes. Within the $23 billion of grants in the last category, there are three very large grant programs—highways, urban mass transit, and municipal waste treatment plants. The remainder, some $13 billion, is spread among a huge number of specific grant programs, a system by which the federal government exerts or seeks to exert substantial control over the use of the funds.

Virtually all the federal *grants for payments to individuals* are associated with programs of direct assistance to the poor and near-poor. Except for food stamps, SSI, and some housing payments, all the federal income payments for the poor and near-poor are grant programs in which the federal government shares the cost of making payments to individuals under eligibility criteria and benefit levels set by the states, subject to certain federal standards. Palmer and

Table 8-18. Federal Grant-in-Aid Programs by Major Category, Fiscal Year 1976
Billions of dollars

Category	Amount
Payments to individuals	22.8
AFDC	5.9
Medicaid	8.2
Public service employment[a]	3.4
Other	5.3
Revenue sharing and block grants	14.0
General revenue sharing	6.3
Comprehensive manpower training[b]	2.3
Community development	2.6
Law enforcement assistance (part)	0.4
Social service grant programs	2.4
Categorical grants	23.0
Major capital grants	10.1
Highways	6.2
Urban mass transit	1.5
Municipal waste treatment plants	2.4
Other categorical grants	12.9
Education	4.0
Health	1.8
Social services	1.6
Manpower training	0.8
Other	4.7
Total	59.8

Source: *Special Analyses, Budget of the United States Government, Fiscal Year 1977,* Special Analysis O.
a. Includes $800 million from Title II of the Comprehensive Manpower Act.
b. Excludes $800 million of grants for public service employment.

Minarik, in chapter 12, discuss possible ways of reforming and improving these programs to reduce overlaps, inequities, and abuses. Consolidation and integration of such programs, transforming them into direct federal assistance to individuals with a minimum nationwide standard of benefits (allowing states to supplement them on their own if they choose), is the direction toward which most proposals for reform point.

The federal government cannot efficiently control the delivery of educational, health, and social services in thousands of localities throughout the nation. Hence, reform of grant programs that deal with the delivery of services will in many cases require moving toward less federal and more state and local control over the use of grant funds. But making payments to individuals and providing medical care for the poor through a health insurance program are things the federal government can do. More important, reaching a more equitable distribution of income is basically a national responsibility. Leaving basic decisions about these matters to state and local governments is unfair both to their taxpayers and their poor. A person might be perfectly willing to vote for income assistance or medical care for the poor but balk at doing so if only his or her state or locality were providing such assistance. States and localities with lower levels of assistance to the poor would have an advantage, via lower tax rates, in attracting industry and thereby lowering tax rates still further. Voting for higher levels of income assistance to the poor, confined to one state, would thus cost taxpayers in that state twice: first, the direct cost of the assistance, and second, an indirect cost associated with the worsened competitive position of the state. In the long run it would be almost impossible to have a system in which some parts of the country carried on major programs of assistance to the poor, and taxed accordingly, while other parts of the country ignored the problem of poverty. Quite apart from other aspects of welfare reform, there are therefore powerful reasons for federalizing such kinds of assistance and gradually moving away from the current grant-in-aid technique for dealing with direct assistance to the poor.

By now, a significant part of federal grants-in-aid is in the form of *general revenue sharing and block grants*—that is, financial support provided for broad general purposes with many fewer controls than in the past. Altogether $14 billion of grants were paid out in this form in 1976. General revenue sharing, inaugurated in 1972, amounted to $6.6 billion. Under general revenue sharing, funds are paid out according to a statutorily determined formula to state and local governments as general financial support with virtually no strings attached to their use.[32]

Besides introducing general revenue sharing, the Nixon administration made the blocking together and simplification of federal grant programs a centerpiece of its New Federalism policy. After much effort with Congress, the administration had some of its proposals accepted. A large number of individual grant programs for manpower

32. In any event, these funds are fungible in state and local budgets. Whatever strings are theoretically attached, they become, in fact, a general source of revenue, are merged with other funds, and can be used as state and local governments see fit.

training and for urban development were consolidated into two large block grants—comprehensive manpower training and community development grants. Most, though not all, federal direction over the allocation of funds within the broad grants was removed and state or local matching requirements were largely eliminated. About half the funds for the law enforcement assistance program are paid out as block grants.

In the early 1970s an older federal grant program, which underwrote 75 percent of the cost to state and local governments of providing social services designed to reduce welfare dependency, suddenly began to grow at an exceedingly rapid rate. State and local officials had discovered that many long-time social services, such as mental health clinics, juvenile delinquency programs, and compensatory education programs, could qualify for support on the theory that such efforts were, among other things, designed to prevent people from ending up on welfare. They began to call upon the federal government to finance a large part of their budgets under the provisions of this open-ended program.[33] At first the federal government sought to slow the growth by exerting control over the particular uses to which the funds could be put. But the ingenuity of the grant applicants outran the ability of the regulators to keep up. Finally Congress imposed an absolute ceiling of $2.5 billion a year on the program and parceled the money out to states in accordance with population. With this ceiling, controls eased up and states can now, within wide limits, treat the program as a broad block grant for social services with little detailed federal direction.[34]

The major issues in this part of the federal grant structure no longer have to do with simplification, consolidation, and the degree of federal controls. That issue has been settled in favor of de-federalization. Rather, current issues revolve around two basic questions. First, what should be the level of federal financial support for state and local governments, both for their general operations and for the four broad purposes—manpower training, community development, law enforcement, and social services? Second, are the present criteria

33. In 1972 the state of Mississippi proposed that the federal government support more than half of its budget costs under the provisions of this social service program. For a discussion of the program, see Martha Derthick, *Uncontrollable Spending for Social Services Grants* (Brookings Institution, 1975).

34. In 1976 the Ford administration proposed removing the 25 percent state matching requirement and taking the remaining few steps to convert the programs from a de facto to a de jure block grant.

for distributing these funds among state and local governments equitable, and do they channel the support to areas of the greatest legitimate need?

The third group of grant-in-aid programs, the *categorical grants*, can best be analyzed by first setting aside the three major capital investment grants—for highways, urban mass transit, and municipal waste treatment plants. Each of these has its own set of issues that arise not so much from its status as a grant program, but from special questions about national transportation and environmental control policy. The remaining $13 billion of federal grants, although constituting only about one-fifth of the total dollar amount, account for the majority of them: there are about one thousand, principally in the fields of education, health, social services, and local economic development. Their purposes are usually narrowly defined, and the services delivered or the activities carried out are closely supervised by the federal granting agency. While called "grants," many of these programs are really federal activities in which state and local governments (and often nonprofit private institutions) act as agents of the federal government.

In education, for example, there are eighty-five separate grant programs run by the Office of Education of the Department of Health, Education, and Welfare. Among them are grants for:
—bilingual vocational education;
—group projects abroad for non-Western language and area training;
—training of physical education and recreation personnel for handicapped children;
—media services and captioned film loan program centers;
—undergraduate instructional equipment;
—university community services programs;
—projects in environmental education;
—interlibrary cooperation projects;
—consumer and homemaking education.

For health services there are somewhat fewer grants, but the number is still large and for some grants, at least, the purposes are quite narrow: rat control and prevention of lead poisoning are examples. Moreover, some of the grants for broader purposes are subdivided and parceled out for particular activities. In the field of mental health, for example, there are separate grants for research, training, construction of mental health centers, staffing of centers, children's services, and operations.

On the other hand, there are a few large grants within this broad category in which federal control is specifically designed to ensure that the funds are channeled to the beneficiaries for whom the assistance was intended. Title I of the Elementary and Secondary Education Act, for example, provided in fiscal 1976 some $2 billion for compensatory education of disadvantaged (principally low-income) children. There are few school districts in which disadvantaged children make up the majority. Without control or supervision, there is a clear possibility that the federal funds, while formally allocated to schools with high proportions of disadvantaged children, will substitute for local moneys that otherwise would have been spent on those schools,[35] and the savings used for tax reduction or other purposes. The federal interest and control is (or ought to be) not so much directed toward precisely what forms the compensatory education takes as toward ensuring that the funds reach the group for which they are intended.

In his 1977 budget, President Ford proposes to continue the trend of the past four years by consolidating into large block grants many of the categorical programs in health and education. The health proposal would include, in the consolidated grant, not only the categorical grants for delivery of health services but also the Medicaid program.

To evaluate proposals for further consolidation and removal of federal control over the current categorical grant programs, and more generally to think through the long-term future of the federal government's complex system of grants, it is essential to have a set of general criteria about the appropriate roles of the federal and state and local governments in the provision of public services and in affecting the distribution of income.

If one examines the major reasons the federal government currently makes grants to state and local governments, a number of objectives emerge:

1. Providing general financial support for state and local governments through general revenue sharing.[36]

---

35. If it is public policy to provide additional educational resources to compensate for the disadvantaged background of low-income children, *more* must be spent on their education than on education elsewhere in the school system.

36. There are several rationales for such general support: among them, making possible a more even provision of public services in areas of widely different fiscal capacity and transferring part of the tax burden from state and local tax systems to federal tax systems (which is generally considered to be a more equitable and

2. Supporting state and local efforts to make individual payments, in kind and in cash, to the poor and near-poor.

3. Supporting state and local expenditures for broad general purposes, such as education, highways, and manpower training, whose benefits accrue to citizens beyond the boundaries of individual states or local governments. People from all over the nation travel on highways built in each state. In a society as mobile as ours, a large percentage of the children educated in one community end up living and working in other communities. Treating municipal wastes from a community along a river benefits not only the citizens of that community but all of those who live or vacation downstream.

4. Developing new or improved means of delivering public services. The use of community mental health clinics instead of large state mental hospitals to deal with the mentally ill was an innovation that might have become nationwide eventually but that was accelerated by federal grant funds. Neighborhood health centers in low-income sections of central cities were seen as a new way of furnishing health services for the poor in areas where few private physicians were located. Federal grant funds supported the establishment of such centers throughout the country and continue to supply much of their operating costs.

5. Supporting the provision of particular public services for the poor or for those otherwise disadvantaged. As spelled out earlier in the case of individual payments, it may be difficult for the average taxpayer in one locality to vote funds for public services that benefit principally the poor if other localities gain a competitive advantage by not taxing themselves to the same extent for these needs.

6. Using state and local governments (or private nonprofit institutions) as agents to provide, at the state and local level, particular kinds of public services deemed "desirable" by federal legislators and agencies. Usually programs that attempt to do this are almost fully financed by federal funds; the state or local matching requirement is nominal. Many specific education and health grants were started in response to the belief that some special problem or need was not being met in most communities.

Some of the problems associated with federal categorical grant programs—excessive federal control and ineffectual or high-cost delivery of services—stem from a failure on the part of legislators or

efficient one). It is not the aim here to support or attack these rationales but simply to sort out the various purposes for federal grant support.

agencies to distinguish among these different objectives. Grants for neighborhood health centers, for example, now seek to serve two purposes: first, to inaugurate new and effective institutions for delivering health care; and second, by providing free access to such health centers, to remove financial barriers to medical care for the poor. But in trying to use neighborhood health centers to achieve both objectives, the federal government has run into major difficulties. In the first place, since the services are free (or require minimal fees), only the poor or near-poor are allowed to use them. This tends to create a two-class medical system. Second, the health centers do not have to stand the test of consumer acceptance—obviously, if they charge nothing, they will be preferred to other sources of medical care delivery that do charge. The federal government thus not only supports the initial establishment of such centers, but is permanently committed to supplying the annual operating funds, and hence to exerting continuing oversight.

If on the other hand, the two objectives were recognized as being different, a more reasonable approach could be followed. Removing financial barriers to medical care for the poor can be accomplished by a system of medical insurance for the poor, either as a reform of the current Medicaid program or as part of a broader national health insurance system. In turn, after providing the seed money to help new institutions like neighborhood health centers get started, the federal government could gradually withdraw the operating funds and require the institutions to charge fees covering costs. This would be no hardship on the poor, since their medical bills would be covered by federally supported insurance. But the neighborhood health centers would then have to stand the test of the marketplace, since potential clients would be able to choose whether to use the centers or to buy their medical care elsewhere. Moreover, it would not be necessary to limit the centers' services to the poor, since everyone would be paying fees covering costs.

At least on an experimental basis, similar principles could be applied in other areas. If vouchers for manpower training programs were available to eligible recipients, government-sponsored and private training programs could compete for clientele. Government support for particular training institutions could be limited to developmental help for innovative approaches or for areas where private institutions do not exist. But all institutions would ultimately be required to stand the test of consumer acceptance. And the same principle suggests concentrating federal support for higher education on direct assistance to students rather than on subsidies to colleges and universities.

Many federal categorical grants for restricted purposes, such as the educational grants listed earlier, probably serve no major national purpose but simply reflect the substitution of the judgment of federal legislators and agency officials for that of state and local officials about what specific local services should be available. No one can say, a priori, who is the wiser. But there seems little reason not to leave this kind of judgment to state or local officials, who are much closer to the people being served, and much merit in consolidating these numerous grants into a few broad groups supporting the delivery of educational and social services at the state and local level, with discretion for the precise allocation of funds left to the recipient government.

In a number of cases the federal government seeks to support some national objective by making grants for the purchase of equipment or construction—that is, it supports the capital costs of particular activities. Federal capital grants for urban mass transit and construction grants for hospitals and municipal waste treatment facilities are cases in point. Unfortunately, these types of grants often lead to inefficient state and local choices and to misdirected resources. If capital costs are subsidized, it is quite natural for grant recipients to choose ways of doing things that emphasize capital costs, which the federal government pays, and to minimize operating costs, for which the local taxpayer foots the bill. Capital grants for urban mass transit encourage the building of capital-intensive subway systems instead of bus systems or other "lighter" modes of mass transit. And they encourage municipalities to skimp on the maintenance and repair of bus systems and to replace buses prematurely.[37] In the case of municipal waste treatment plants, the federal capital subsidy encourages municipalities to spend excessively on plant construction and to economize on subsequent operations.[38] If federal incentives for municipal services like mass transit and waste treatment are to be

37. One study found that such premature replacement of buses could add some 20 to 25 percent to the costs of mass transit. William B. Tye, "The Capital Grant as a Subsidy Device: The Case Study of Urban Mass Transportation," in *The Economics of Federal Subsidy Programs,* A Compendium of Papers Submitted to the Subcommittee on Priorities and Economy in Government of the Joint Economic Committee, 93:1 (GPO, 1973), pt. 6, pp. 796–826.

38. See Allen V. Kneese and Charles L. Schultze, *Pollution, Prices, and Public Policy* (Brookings Institution, 1975), pp. 36–38, 43.

provided, the incentive should apply to outputs, not to capital inputs. A federal transit subsidy per passenger or passenger-mile would be much more conducive to efficiency than a subsidy for capital costs. A federal subsidy per unit of pollution reduction or a federal tax on pollution effluents would generate more effective incentives for pollution reduction than construction grants for waste treatment plants.[39]

Several criteria can be suggested to guide long-term reform of the federal grant programs.

First, the provision of basic income and medical assistance to the poor is a national problem. It is poorly met by the use of grants-in-aid to support a wide variety of eligibility standards and benefit levels set by state and local governments. Reform should be a gradual attempt to supersede the grant programs with a uniform federal system of benefits, principally cash and medical care. States or localities should be allowed to supplement the federal standard, but at their own expense.

Second, once federal financial support is available for medical insurance for the poor, federally supported institutions for the delivery of medical care should be weaned from federal assistance and required to cover their costs by charging fees. Institutional support grants should be converted to temporary development assistance for promising innovations in the delivery of health care; the temporary nature of this initial assistance, combined with the availability of medical insurance for the poor, would guarantee that the new institutions would eventually have to meet the hard test of consumer acceptance. On an experimental basis, at least, such an approach might be tried in the manpower training area.

Third, narrow categorical grants through which the federal government determines the detailed allocation of funds to very specific kinds of services should be consolidated into broad grants for such major purposes as elementary and secondary education and social services. State or local officials should decide on the exact types of educational or social services to be offered.

Fourth, while there is little national purpose served in retaining federal control over the detailed specification of what kinds of services are delivered within broad categories, a case can be made in some instances for retaining federal supervision over who gets the

39. Ibid., chap. 7.

benefits. Under a consolidated educational grant, it would be desirable to continue efforts to channel part of the funds explicitly toward schools with large proportions of children from low-income families. It can be advantageous for local taxpayers to know that channeling special educational assistance to poor schools will not put their locality at a competitive disadvantage. Similar controls may be needed under the existing community development block grants.[40] Federal grant programs, in other words, would be significantly improved if federal control over the *kinds* of services delivered were sharply reduced but federal control over *who* got the benefits were maintained or even intensified in selected cases.

Finally, federal grants that seek, through capital subsidies, to increase the delivery of certain state and local services should be replaced by subsidies tied to service output.

These criteria do not provide guidance about the appropriate level of federal grant support for various activities or about the formulas by which the grants should be apportioned among the individual state and local governments. In particular, they do not suggest the appropriate federal role in assisting the older central cities with their financial problems. These are obviously critical matters and will always remain at the center of political debate, as they should. But substantial improvements in the effectiveness and equity of federal, state, and local fiscal relations can be made if the quite different objectives of federal grant programs are carefully sorted out and individual programs are more closely adjusted to the objectives. Readers who do this may arrive at particular suggestions for reform that differ significantly from those made above. But without some set of general guidelines, reasonable reform will be impossible.

It has become fashionable to believe that the federal government is generally fumbling and ineffectual in dealing with domestic social problems. This conventional wisdom is as wrong as the earlier view it replaced—that a federal program could be devised to solve any social need. What is needed is discrimination in separating the things the federal government can and should do from those it either should not do or cannot do effectively. There are some of both.

40. Since the funds are fungible, ensuring that low-income schools and low-income areas within larger governmental units receive additional money is very difficult. But within reasonable limits, continued federal efforts would be helpful, as much for the focus it could give local public interest groups as for the effectiveness of its formal accounting controls.

CHAPTER NINE

State and Local Governments

EMIL M. SUNLEY, JR.

THE FINANCIAL CRISIS of New York City has made the fiscal condition of all state and local governments newsworthy. It has focused attention on the spiraling growth of state and local taxes and expenditures. Politicians are now responding to indications of mounting public opposition to increased taxes. In January 1975 Governor Hugh Carey of New York called for expanding the sales tax base to balance his budget; a year later he pledged to put the state's fiscal affairs "in touch with reality again," called for cutbacks and retrenchment, and strongly opposed further increases in taxes. Governors Edmund Brown, Jr., of California and Michael Dukakis of Massachusetts gained national attention in 1975 by championing a smaller role for government. Perhaps 1975 was the turning point separating years of accelerating expansion of state and local taxes and expenditures from years of much slower growth.

The state and local sector has been one of the most rapidly growing sectors of the economy for the past twenty years. Unlike the federal government, whose expenditures have risen only slightly faster than

This chapter benefited significantly from the comments of Charles L. Schultze, Lawrence B. Krause, Joseph J. Minarik, Richard P. Nathan, and Kenneth Vogel of the Brookings Institution; Maurice Criz of the Bureau of the Census; Robert D. Reischauer of the Congressional Budget Office; Robert P. Strauss of the Joint Committee on Internal Revenue Taxation; Robert D. Ebel, Ronald C. Fisher, and Michael E. Bell of the Advisory Commission on Intergovernmental Relations; Steven D. Gold of Drake University; Nancy D. Sidhu of Northeastern Illinois University; and George E. Peterson of the Urban Institute. Wendy Holt provided valuable computational assistance. Any errors that remain are the author's alone.

the gross national product, state and local expenditures have grown nearly 50 percent faster than GNP. There are a number of reasons for this. The postwar surge in births placed heavy demands on state and local governments for building and staffing new schools. Higher education also grew rapidly both because of the increase in the school age population and because a higher percentage of that population enrolled in public colleges and universities. During the war the salaries of state and local employees fell sharply in relation to those of other workers. Since then they have been catching up, raising state and local expenditures very quickly. Moreover, much of state and local expenditure consists simply of wages and salaries, and there is little chance for productivity gains. Hence costs have increased faster than for the economy generally. Finally, federal grants-in-aid have necessitated large matching spending.

Economic growth has been too slow to bring in the revenue needed to cover expenditures, which have climbed rapidly. State and local taxes have continually been raised and new taxes have been introduced. Although there have been increases in all kinds of taxes, the income tax has been expanded the most.

Over the next decade many of the factors making for the expansion of the state and local sector may not grow as rapidly; the catch-up in state and local salaries may be over; and federal grants-in-aid are likely to rise more slowly, requiring smaller increases in matching expenditures. The decade may thus be one of relatively low growth in expenditures and taxes. The financial problems of the deteriorating central cities will continue, but the pressures on state and local governments in general may ease.

Growth of the State and Local Sector, 1955–74

The state and local sector is characterized by great diversity and this makes generalizations difficult. New York City is facing bankruptcy, but Houston is enjoying a budget surplus equal to its payment under federal revenue sharing. Many older central cities in the Northeast are experiencing declines in population, but many newer central cities in the South and West are growing. The northeastern and north central states have traditionally had a much greater "taste" for public expenditures than the southern and western states. A particular problem in comparing different cities and different states is that the responsibility for carrying out various government activities varies across states. For example, in many states local education is controlled by independent school districts; in others it is controlled by municipal or county governments; and in one, Hawaii, it is a state responsibility. Also, state governments support local education with state grants-in-aid, but the percentage of local education costs financed by state aid varies considerably from state to state and even within states.

Total Expenditures

Between 1929 and 1955 state and local expenditures showed only a small increase as a percentage of GNP. In the ensuing twenty years, however, expenditures increased from $34.9 billion, or 9.2 percent of GNP, in 1955 to $207.7 billion, or 15.3 percent of GNP, in 1974 (see table 9-1). In dollars, expenditures rose almost sixfold. While the increase in expenditures as a percentage of GNP is not quite as striking, it does indicate that the state and local sector is now much more important in the overall economy than it was twenty years ago.

Two adjustments to data on state and local expenditures will put

Table 9-1. Expenditures of State and Local Governments in Current and Constant Dollars and as Percent of GNP, Selected Fiscal Years, 1955-74
Money amounts in billions of dollars

Description	1955	1960	1965	1970	1972	1974
Total expenditures[a]						
Current dollars	34.9	53.6	77.8	135.9	173.0	207.7
Percent of GNP	9.2	10.8	11.8	14.2	15.6	15.3
Constant dollars[b]	34.9	45.5	57.9	76.8	85.9	89.5
Percent of GNP	9.2	10.3	10.7	11.8	12.6	12.1
Total less federal grants-in-aid						
Constant dollars[a]	31.7	39.5	49.6	64.3	70.3	71.5
Percent of GNP	8.3	9.0	9.2	9.9	10.3	9.7

Sources: State and local government data, U.S. Bureau of the Census, *Governmental Finances in 1973-74* (GPO, 1975), and preceding relevant issues; Bureau of the Census, *Summary of Governmental Finances in 1955* (GPO, 1956); information on contributions to state-administered and locally administered retirement systems obtained from Bureau of the Census, Governments Division. GNP in current dollars, U.S. Bureau of Economic Analysis, "Benchmark Revision of National Income and Product Accounts: Advance Tables" (BEA, 1976; processed), Set 1, table 1.1. GNP in constant dollars and implicit price deflators for personal consumption expenditures and state and local government expenditures, BEA, "Benchmark Revision," Set 2, tables 1.2, 7.1.

a. Total expenditures differ from the standard Bureau of the Census classification, as explained in footnotes 5 and 6 and in the notes to table 9-2.

b. Transfer payments are adjusted by the deflator for personal consumption expenditures. All other state and local expenditures are adjusted by the deflator for state and local governments. Deflators with 1972 = 100 were used for the individual functions; then the total was converted to 1955 = 100.

the growth in this sector in better perspective. First, if both GNP and state and local expenditures are expressed in terms of constant (1955) dollars, the apparent growth of the state and local sector is reduced. Constant dollar expenditures increased 33 percent, from 9 percent of GNP in 1955 to 12 percent in 1974. Thus about half of the apparent increase in the state and local sector is due to greater price increases in that sector than in the rest of the economy.[1]

A second adjustment is needed for federal grants-in-aid. Since 1955 an increasing proportion of state and local expenditures have been financed by federal revenue given to the states (see table 9-7). The effect of federal grant programs on the growth of state and local expenditures is not clear-cut. The relatively new program of general revenue sharing provides overall financial support whose proceeds can be used by state and local governments to undertake additional expenditures or to avoid tax increases, or some combination of the two.[2] Some other federal grants probably support expenditures that state and local governments would have undertaken in any event. But a large part is distributed through some 600 categorical programs[3] under which state and local governments have little discretion on how the money is spent. These governments are acting essentially as agents of the federal government even though they are not required to participate in the various categorical programs and often have to allocate some of their own funds to match federal grants. In many categorical programs, state and local expenditures of grants-in-aid should therefore be considered federal expenditures. Because of the complex effects of federal grants on state and local decisions, one

1. Since government services are valued in the national income accounts at labor cost, most increases in the price index for the state and local sector are simply the result of increases in average employee compensation. See table 9-5 below for the trend in average employee compensation.

It is very difficult to separate price increases from productivity gains. In the national income accounts, it is arbitrarily assumed that state and local workers have no productivity gains. This is further discussed by Schultze in chapter 8 of this volume.

2. Gramlich and Galper have estimated that for state and local governments taken together about two-fifths of the additional revenue is used to increase expenditures and about three-fifths to reduce taxes or avoid tax increases. See Edward M. Gramlich and Harvey Galper, "State and Local Fiscal Behavior and Federal Grant Policy," *Brookings Papers on Economic Activity, 1:1973*, pp. 42–46.

3. Just how many categorical programs there are is confusing. Some claim that there may be more than 1,200. For a discussion of the "numbers game," see the testimony of David B. Walker, assistant director of the Advisory Commission on Intergovernmental Relations, in *Fiscal Relations in the American Federal System*, Hearings before the Intergovernmental Relations and Human Relations Subcommittee of the House Committee on Government Operations, 94:1 (GPO, 1975).

cannot simply subtract such grants from state and local expenditures and assume that the remainder is an accurate estimate of how much those governments would have spent without the grants. Nevertheless, that measure does provide a useful fiscal indicator—state and local expenditures from own sources of revenue. In constant dollars such expenditures rose from $31.7 billion in 1955 to $71.5 billion in 1974, and from 8.3 to 9.7 percent of GNP.

The rate of increase in state and local expenditures from own sources (in constant dollars) appears to have slowed recently. For the years 1955–60 the increase in real expenditures was 4.5 percent a year. This growth accelerated to 4.7 percent a year during 1960–65 and to 5.3 percent a year during 1965–70. For 1970–72 the rate of increase slowed to 4.6 percent, and for 1972–74, to 0.8 percent.

The following table summarizes the three measures of the growth of state and local outlays relative to the national economy:

	Percent of GNP		Increase
Total expenditures	*1955*	*1974*	*(percentage points)*
Current dollars	9.2	15.3	6.1
Constant dollars	9.2	12.1	2.9
From own sources, constant dollars	8.3	9.7	1.4

Of the 6-percentage-point increase in the ratio of state and local spending to GNP since 1955, about half was related to the greater rise in the prices of what state and local governments bought than in prices generally. Another one-quarter was associated with (although not necessarily caused by) the growth of federal grants-in-aid.

Major Expenditure Categories

As shown in table 9-2, over the twenty-year period general expenditures decreased slightly, from 97 to 96 percent of total expenditures.[4] Subsidies to public utilities[5] and contributions to retirement

4. In this chapter, total expenditures include three categories—general expenditures, subsidies to public utilities, and contributions to retirement systems.

5. The standard Census Bureau classification of expenditures and revenues treats utility receipts as a revenue source and utility outlays as an expenditure. Outlays have consistently exceeded revenue. In table 9-2, the difference between utility outlays and utility receipts is considered an expenditure and this expenditure is called "subsidies to public utilities." This is consistent with the classification scheme of the national income accounts, which treats publicly operated utilities as part of the business sector with only the subsidy to public utilities considered an expenditure of state and local governments.

Table 9-2. Expenditures of State and Local Governments, by Type, as Percent of GNP and of Total Expenditures, Selected Fiscal Years, 1955–74

Type of expenditure	1955	1960	1965	1970	1972	1974
	As percent of GNP					
General expenditures	8.8	10.4	11.4	13.7	15.0	14.6
Capital outlays	2.8	3.0	2.8	2.8	2.8	2.5
Other than capital outlays	6.0	7.4	8.6	10.8	12.2	12.1
Subsidies to public utilities[a]	0.1	0.1	0.2	0.1	0.2	0.2
Contributions to retirement systems[b]	0.2	0.3	0.3	0.4	0.4	0.4
Total[c]	**9.2**	**10.8**	**11.8**	**14.2**	**15.6**	**15.3**
	As percent of total expenditures					
General expenditures	96.6	96.8	96.4	96.6	96.5	95.8
Capital outlays	30.7	28.2	23.9	20.0	18.1	16.6
Other than capital outlays	65.9	68.7	72.5	76.6	78.4	79.2
Subsidies to public utilities[a]	1.1	0.9	1.3	0.9	1.1	1.5
Contributions to retirement systems[b]	2.3	2.4	2.3	2.5	2.4	2.7
Total[c]	**100.0**	**100.0**	**100.0**	**100.0**	**100.0**	**100.0**

Sources: See table 9-1. Figures are rounded.

a. Utility expenditure minus utility revenue.

b. Includes only government contributions to self-administered retirement systems; contributions to other retirement systems are included in general expenditures.

c. The components of total expenditures differ from the standard Census Bureau classification in that (1) public utility revenue is netted against public utility expenditure to derive "subsidies to public utilities"; (2) liquor store and trust fund expenditures are omitted; and (3) contributions to retirement systems are considered an expenditure.

systems[6] increased from 3 to 4 percent of total expenditures. Of course, as a percentage of GNP, general expenditures, subsidies to public utilities, and contributions to retirement systems have all increased since 1955. Most of the growth in general expenditures has not been in capital outlays—that is, bricks and mortar—which de-

6. "Contributions to retirement systems" includes only government contributions to state-administered or locally administered retirement systems. Contributions to other retirement systems are included in the various functional categories under general expenditures. Also, unlike the accounting convention used both by the Census Bureau and in the national income accounts, employee retirement trust funds are not consolidated with state and local governments. Thus contributions to the trust funds is the appropriate expenditure item rather than benefits and withdrawals from the trust funds. When the primary concern is the fiscal condition of state and local governments, the trust funds should be kept separate; however, if the concern is the impact of the state and local sector on the economy, state and local governments and their trust funds should be consolidated.

Table 9-3. Expenditures of State and Local Governments for Higher Education, Public Welfare, and Interest on General Debt as Percent of GNP, Selected Fiscal Years, 1955–74

Function	1955	1960	1965	1970	1972	1974
Higher education	0.4	0.6	0.9	1.3	1.4	1.4
Public welfare	0.8	0.9	1.0	1.5	1.9	1.8
Interest on general debt	0.2	0.3	0.4	0.5	0.5	0.6

Sources: See table 9-1.

clined slightly as a percentage of GNP but from almost one-third to less than one-fifth of total expenditures.

Within the various general expenditure functional categories, three categories more than doubled as a percentage of GNP—higher education, public welfare, and interest on general debt (see table 9-3). Three other categories each increased by 45 to 100 percent—local schools, health and hospitals, and police and fire protection and correction. The reasons for the very rapid increases in expenditures for these functions are fairly clear. Those born during the "baby boom" of the early 1950s reached college age in the late 1960s and early 1970s; the proportion of high school graduates going on to college increased significantly; and low tuition in state and municipally supported colleges, junior colleges, and universities attracted a growing number of students to these schools. Whereas in 1955 only 17.8 percent of persons of college age (eighteen to twenty-four years) attended public colleges and universities, by 1973, 32.3 percent attended these institutions.

Welfare expenditures of state and local governments increased from 0.8 percent of GNP in 1955 to 1.8 percent in 1974. Federal grants to state and local governments cover almost one-half of these expenditures, and these grants require substantial matching funds. The sharp increase in state and local expenditures for welfare might better be viewed as a sharp increase in federal programs administered by the states.[7]

The increase in interest on general state and local debt as a per-

7. The trend in increased state and local expenditures for public welfare as a percentage of GNP appears to have halted between 1972 and 1974 as a result of the conversion of the public assistance program for the aged, blind, and disabled, which was a grant-in-aid program, to supplemental security income (SSI), which is a federally administered program. Some state and local governments, however, supplement the SSI program with funds of their own.

centage of GNP is mainly due to the increase in interest rates rather than to an increase in debt outstanding.[8] It is estimated that in 1955 the average interest rate on outstanding debt was 2.0 percent. By 1974 it had risen to 3.9 percent.

Expenditures for local schools have not grown as rapidly as expenditures for higher education. Between 1955 and 1974 the number of schoolchildren rose from 34 million to 50 million, but the percentage increase was much less than that for students at publicly supported colleges and universities.[9] The growth of expenditures for health and hospitals is largely explained by the sharp increases in health costs and the improved medical care for the aged under Medicare. The rise in crime and the greater number of automobiles are mainly responsible for higher police and correction expenditures.

Finally, expenditures for three functions—highways and parking, financial administration and general control, and sewerage and other sanitation—as a percentage of GNP remained about the same between 1955 and 1974. As a percentage of total state and local expenditures, these three functions decreased from 26.1 percent in 1955 to 16.2 percent in 1974.

One convenient way of analyzing the growth of state and local expenditures is to separate the three major factors generating growth. First, even if prices were steady and services per capita remained constant, increasing *work loads*—as the number of school age children rose or the volume of motor vehicle traffic grew—would require higher expenditures. Second, *prices* increased—higher salaries for employees, higher medical care costs, and the like. Third, all other expenditure increases can be allocated to improvements in the *scope and quality* of services; more teachers per hundred students, for example, or a greater portion of the poor receiving welfare payments or the provision of more free or inexpensive medical care. Table 9-4 shows a rough attempt to allocate the increase in expenditures between 1962 and 1972 to the three factors.[10] Price increases were the major factor explaining higher expenditures, accounting for 52 percent.

8. See table 9-8 for data on the trend in indebtedness of state and local governments.

9. There has been a shift in the distribution of the school age population with a greater proportion of students now enrolled in high school. The average expenditure for high school students is greater than that for elementary school students.

10. For similar estimates for 1955–69, see Charles L. Schultze and others, *Setting National Priorities: The 1972 Budget* (Brookings Institution, 1971), pp. 138–40.

Table 9-4. Increase in Expenditures of State and Local Governments, by Function, Fiscal Years 1962-72

Function	Expenditures			Percentage distribution of increase by generating factor		
	Amount (billions of dollars)		Percentage increase,	Work		Scope and
	1962	1972	1962-72	loads	Prices	quality
General expenditures						
Local schools	17.7	45.7	157	10	59	32
Higher and other education	4.5	19.2	329	26	38	36
Public welfare	5.1	21.1	314	−6	16	90
Highways and parking	10.4	19.2	84	37	81	−18
Health and hospitals	4.3	12.9	196	37	55	9
Police and fire protection, and correction	4.0	10.7	163	39	63	−1
Interest on general debt	2.0	6.0	196			
Financial administration and general control	2.3	5.9	152	10	65	25
Sewerage and other sanitation	2.0	4.7	142	11	71	18
Other and unallocable	7.8	21.6	178	10	52	37
Subsidies to public utilities[a]	0.4	1.9	356	...	...	...
Contributions to retirement systems[b]	1.4	4.2	189	...	...	...
Total	62.1	173.0	179	13	52	35

Sources: Expenditures, *Governmental Finances in 1963-64*, table 3; *Governmental Finances in 1971-72*, tables 3, 13; Bureau of the Census, *Census of Governments, 1962*, vol. 6, no. 1, *Employee-Retirement Systems of State and Local Governments* (GPO, 1963), table 3. Distribution of increase by work load, price, and scope and quality factors prepared by Robert D. Reischauer. Figures are rounded.

a. Utility expenditure minus utility revenue.

b. Includes only government contributions to self-administered retirement systems; contributions to other retirement systems are included in individual functional categories and in the category "other and unallocable."

This conclusion is consistent with the data presented in table 9-1, which indicated that the increase in state and local expenditures as a percentage of GNP measured in constant dollars is one-half the percentage measured in nominal dollars. The remainder of the increase is accounted for by population or work-load pressures (13 percent) and quality improvement (35 percent). Thus from 1962 to 1972 the scope and quality of government services improved significantly.

The importance of the three factors varies considerably between one functional category and another. For example, population is not important in explaining the growth in welfare expenditures for there was actually a decline in the low-income population between 1962

Table 9-5. Average Annual Earnings per Full-Time Employee, 1955 and 1973

Industry	Amount (dollars)		As percent of average earnings in all industries	
	1955	1973	1955	1973
All industries	3,851	9,106	100.0	100.0
Federal government[a]	4,589	12,984	119.2	142.6
State and local governments[b]	3,562	9,448	92.5	103.8

Sources: U.S. Department of Commerce, *The National Income and Product Accounts of the United States, 1929–1965: Statistical Tables* (GPO, 1966), table 6.5, p. 108, and *Survey of Current Business*, vol. 54 (July 1974), table 6.5, p. 37.
a. Excludes employees of government enterprises and members of the armed forces.
b. Excludes employees of government enterprises.

and 1972; the increase is due mainly to scope and quality improvements—a larger proportion of the eligible population being served and real benefits per recipient being improved.[11] Population and work-load pressures were important factors in explaining the increase in expenditures for higher education; police and fire protection, and correction; and health and hospitals.

The data in table 9-4 permit a rough estimate of what would have happened to state and local expenditures if there had been no improvement in the scope and quality of government services in 1962–72. Since 65 percent of the rise in expenditures was due to price and work-load increases, these factors alone would have pushed expenditures up to $134.2 billion in 1972. This would have represented an increase in expenditures from 11.4 percent of GNP in 1962 to 12.0 percent in 1972, and tax rates would have had to rise during the decade just to maintain the 1962 level of government services. But this rise would have been slight if only prices and work loads had increased. These increases would have occurred in any case; it is the growth in the scope and quality of services that drove up state and local expenditures.

The compensation of government workers represents almost half of all state and local expenditures, and higher average compensation constitutes the major price increase faced by state and local governments. As indicated in table 9-5, average annual earnings of state and

11. Barbara Boland has estimated that the AFDC participation rate for families headed by females increased from 63 percent to 91 percent between 1967 and 1970. "Participation in the Aid to Families with Dependent Children Program" in *Studies in Public Welfare*, Paper no. 12, part 1, Studies Prepared for the Subcommittee on Fiscal Policy of the Joint Economic Committee, 93:2 (GPO, 1974), p. 139.

Table 9-6. Full-Time Equivalent Employees, 1955 and 1973

Industry	Number (thousands)		As percent of employees in all industries	
	1955	1973	1955	1973
All industries	54,864	75,948	100.0	100.0
Federal government[a]	1,716	2,010	3.1	2.6
State and local governments[b]	4,138	9,083	7.5	12.0

Sources: Department of Commerce, *National Income and Product Accounts*, table 6.4, p. 104, and *Survey of Current Business*, vol. 54 (July 1974), table 6.4, p. 37.
a. Excludes employees of government enterprises and members of the armed forces.
b. Excludes employees of government enterprises.

local government workers almost tripled between 1955 and 1973, moving from 92.5 percent to 103.8 percent of the average earnings of workers in all industries. (The position of federal government workers improved even more dramatically between 1955 and 1973.) This catch-up has not quite restored the relative position of state and local government workers in 1929, when their average earnings were 106.7 percent of the average earnings of all workers, and it is still considerably below their position in 1939, when their average earnings were 116.4 percent of the average for all workers. But the relative position of state and local workers fell during World War II, and by 1945 their average earnings were only 88.5 percent of the average for all workers.

The major explanations for the increase in wages and salaries of state and local workers are that their average earnings had to rise rapidly to restore the relative position they had enjoyed before World War II and that state and local governments had to be able to attract workers away from the private sector as they expanded their share of the labor market. Between 1955 and 1973 employment by state and local governments rose from 7.5 percent to 12.0 percent of all workers (see table 9-6).[12] In contrast, federal civilian employment as a percentage of total employment declined between 1955 and 1973. To bid successfully for workers, state and local governments had to raise wages and salaries faster than the private sector. Unionization, which

12. The large increase in state and local workers as a percentage of the work force would appear to be inconsistent with the much smaller increase in deflated expenditures as a percentage of GNP. If, however, increases in productivity in the state and local sector are small relative to those in the private sector, the trend in the employment share is not an indicator of the trend in state and local expenditures as a percentage of GNP in constant dollars.

has grown rapidly, has also been important in improving the position of state and local workers.

Revenue

Expenditures are one side of the budget; revenue, the other. State and local governments must finance increased expenditures with increased taxes, federal grants-in-aid, or debt. It is therefore not surprising that the revenue of state and local governments has increased as rapidly as expenditures, rising from $31.3 billion in 1955 to $208.2 billion in 1974. Table 9-7 indicates that, whereas the growth of revenue has kept pace with the growth of expenditures, the importance of the various sources of revenue has shifted.

The most significant shift is the increase in grants-in-aid from 10 percent of total revenue in 1955 to 20 percent in 1974 and the decrease in taxes from 76 percent of total revenue in 1955 to 63 percent in 1974. Charges and miscellaneous general revenue, such as fees, tolls, and college tuition, have increased slightly, from 14 percent of total revenue in 1955 to 17 percent in 1974.

There have also been shifts in the importance of various taxes. Property taxes, selective sales taxes, and other taxes (motor vehicle

Table 9-7. Sources of Revenue of State and Local Governments,
Fiscal Years 1955 and 1974

Source of revenue[a]	Amount (billions of dollars)		As percent of GNP		As percent of total revenue	
	1955	1974	1955	1974	1955	1974
Federal grants-in-aid	3.1	41.8	0.8	3.1	10.0	20.1
Taxes	23.6	131.2	6.2	9.7	75.7	63.0
Property	10.7	47.8	2.8	3.5	34.3	22.9
General sales and gross receipts	3.1	26.3	0.8	1.9	9.9	12.6
Selective sales	4.8	20.2	1.3	1.5	15.2	9.7
Individual income	1.2	19.5	0.3	1.4	3.9	9.4
Corporation income	0.7	6.0	0.2	0.4	2.4	2.9
Other	3.1	11.4	0.8	0.8	10.0	5.5
Charges and miscellaneous general revenue	4.5	35.2	1.2	2.6	14.3	16.9
Total	31.3	208.2	8.2	15.3	100.0	100.0

Sources: See table 9-1. Figures are rounded.
a. The sources of revenue differ from the standard Census Bureau classification in (1) the omission of insurance trust revenue, (2) the netting of liquor store expenditure against liquor store revenue and including this net amount in selective sales taxes, and (3) the omission of utility revenue.

and operator licenses, severance, death, and gift) have declined in importance as a source of revenue.

The taxes that increased in importance are the broad-based ones —general sales and gross receipts, individual income, and corporation income. Of these, the individual income tax increased the most. The three taxes together rose from 16 percent of total revenue in 1955 to 25 percent in 1974, and from 22 percent of total taxes in 1955 to 40 percent in 1974. The shift toward broad-based taxes has increased the responsiveness of state and local tax collections to economic growth, but it has also increased their responsiveness to economic downturns. Countercyclical revenue sharing, which is discussed later in this chapter, is a means of reducing the vulnerability of state and local governments to economic downturns.

Federal Tax Subsidies

In addition to providing intergovernmental revenue, the federal government aids state and local governments indirectly by means of two important tax subsidies. These subsidies reduced federal revenue in fiscal 1974 by $15.8 billion, a sum equal to 37.8 percent of the amount of federal grants-in-aid received that year by state and local governments.[13]

First, interest on state and local government debt is exempt from federal taxation, lowering interest costs for these governments. The cost to the federal government of this exemption, $3.9 billion in 1974, is greater than the amount saved by state and local governments on interest costs.[14]

Second, individuals who itemize personal deductions on their federal income tax returns may deduct general sales taxes and state and local taxes on property, income, and gasoline. Deductibility of these taxes, which lowered federal revenue by $11.9 billion in 1974, reduces the burden of paying them. The higher the taxpayer's marginal tax rate, the more this subsidy is worth. For a taxpayer in the 50 percent bracket who itemizes deductions, a dollar of state or local

13. *Special Analyses, Budget of the United States Government, Fiscal Year 1977,* pp. 125–27, 259.

14. The inefficiency of the tax-exempt interest subsidy has been widely discussed. See, for example, David J. Ott and Allan H. Meltzer, *Federal Tax Treatment of State and Local Securities* (Brookings Institution, 1963), pp. 14–17. The optimal taxable municipal bond, an alternative that would increase the efficiency of the tax subsidy, is discussed later in this chapter.

taxes costs 50 cents. For a taxpayer in the 25 percent bracket, the cost is 75 cents. But the taxpayer who claims the standard deduction gets no federal tax saving from paying state and local taxes. Since most low-income families do not itemize, deductibility of these taxes mainly benefits high-income families and the states and municipalities in which they live. One might view the deductibility of state and local taxes as a kind of indirect revenue sharing for high-income suburbs and wealthy states or as an incentive for state and local governments to adopt progressive taxes so as to maximize the value of this indirect revenue sharing. It is very likely that this tax subsidy offsets the equalizing or redistributive effect of general revenue sharing.

Indebtedness

Expenditures not covered by revenue must be financed by increasing the amount of indebtedness or decreasing any cash surplus accumulated in earlier years. State and local governments have traditionally financed capital expenditures such as school construction with long-term borrowing. Benefits from these capital expenditures are realized over a number of years, and long-term debt financing permits their cost to be spread over the lifetime of the asset. State and local governments have also traditionally borrowed in the short-term market to smooth out seasonal fluctuations in revenue. In addition to borrowing to finance capital expenditures and to reduce fluctuations in revenue, New York City in recent years has borrowed extensively in the short-term market to cover current account deficits. It is estimated that in fiscal year 1976, New York City will have had to borrow $2.6 billion in the short-term market just to roll over the debt accumulated from financing operating deficits incurred in prior years.[15]

Although a few other cities have made a practice of covering operating deficits in the short-term market, New York City is not representative of the entire state and local sector. Between 1955 and 1974 the indebtedness of state and local governments increased from $44.3 billion to $206.6 billion and grew from 11.6 percent of GNP in 1955 to 15.2 percent in 1974 (see table 9-8). Most of this growth occurred

15. U.S. Congressional Budget Office, *New York City's Fiscal Problem: Its Origins, Potential Repercussions, and Some Alternative Policy Responses*, Background Paper 1 (GPO, 1975), p. 5.

Table 9-8. Indebtedness of State and Local Governments, Fiscal Years 1955 and 1974

Indebtedness	Amount (billions of dollars)		As percent of GNP		As percent of total revenue	
	1955	1974	1955	1974	1955	1974
Total debt outstanding at end of fiscal year	44.3	206.6	11.6	15.2	141.5	99.2
Long-term	42.3	190.0	11.1	14.0	135.1	91.3
Full faith and credit	30.5	111.0	8.0	8.2	97.4	53.3
Nonguaranteed	11.7	79.0	3.1	5.8	37.4	37.9
Short-term	2.0	16.7	0.5	1.2	6.4	8.0

Sources: *Governmental Finances in 1973–74*, p. 28, and *Summary of Governmental Finances in 1955*, p. 32; GNP, see table 9-1; revenue, from table 9-7. Figures are rounded.

between 1955 and 1960; in view of the rise in state and local expenditures, this increase is not worrisome. When the outstanding indebtedness is measured against state and local revenues, it declined from 141.5 percent in 1955 to 99.2 percent in 1974.

The composition of the indebtedness of state and local governments shifted after 1955. Short-term debt increased in importance relative to long-term debt, and there was also a shift toward nonguaranteed debt. But full faith and credit debt, for which the credit of the government is unconditionally pledged, increased very little.

Variation in Expenditures per Capita

There is great variation across states and municipalities. In 1974 state and local expenditures from own revenue sources averaged $742 per capita, but state averages ranged from $422 in Arkansas to $1,848 in Alaska (see table 9-9). Except for Maryland, the seven states that averaged over $850 per capita were located either in the western or in the eastern and north central regions of the country. Except for New Mexico and Missouri, the twelve states with the lowest state and local expenditures from own sources, less than $575 per capita, were in the South.

Interstate comparisons of state and local expenditures are fraught with difficulties. States such as Alaska with high expenditures per capita are generally states with high costs, and the apparent differences in expenditures per capita would be greatly reduced if the comparison could be made in terms of real expenditures per capita. Also, population may be inadequate for measuring the need for government expenditures. States with a high proportion of aged, poor,

Table 9-9. Direct State and Local General Expenditures from Own Revenue Sources per $1,000 of Personal Income and per Capita, by State, Fiscal Year 1974

Amounts in dollars

State	Per $1,000 of personal income		Per capita	
	Amount	Rank	Amount	Rank
U.S. average	148	...	742	...
Alaska	318	1	1,848	1
New York	209	2	1,202	2
Hawaii	194	3	1,049	3
Vermont	190	4	762	17
Wyoming	174	5	801	14
Nevada	171	6	942	4
Wisconsin	169	7	805	13
Washington	165	8	840	9
Minnesota	163	9	832	10
Arizona	162	10	725	21
California	162	11	880	5
Massachusetts	162	12	851	7
Maryland	160	13	870	6
Oregon	158	14	748	18
Louisiana	156	15	613	32
Utah	152	16	612	33
Colorado	151	17	741	19
Michigan	150	18	828	11
Maine	149	19	596	36
South Carolina	149	20	565	42
New Mexico	146	21	556	45
Mississippi	146	22	509	49
Delaware	145	23	844	8
Montana	143	24	656	29
Pennsylvania	140	25	701	22
Florida	139	26	651	30
New Jersey	139	27	815	12
Idaho	138	28	588	39
West Virginia	137	29	545	46
Virginia	137	30	657	28
Georgia	137	31	590	38
Tennessee	136	32	558	44
Rhode Island	135	33	680	24
Alabama	134	34	513	48
New Hampshire	134	35	614	31
Oklahoma	133	36	566	41
Connecticut	131	37	777	16
Iowa	130	38	699	23
South Dakota	128	39	605	35
Kansas	126	40	674	25

Table 9-9 (*continued*)

State	Per $1,000 of personal income		Per capita	
	Amount	*Rank*	*Amount*	*Rank*
Nebraska	126	41	664	26
Kentucky	126	42	506	50
Texas	126	43	562	43
Illinois	126	44	731	20
North Carolina	124	45	522	47
District of Columbia	121	46	790	15
Ohio	120	47	607	34
Indiana	119	48	594	37
Missouri	118	49	569	40
North Dakota	115	50	658	27
Arkansas	108	51	422	51

Source: *Governmental Finances in 1973–74*, tables 22, 24.

school age, or urban population may require higher per capita expenditures.

Variations in state and local expenditures per capita are in part due to variations in the fiscal capacity of states. Although the term "fiscal capacity" is somewhat vague, personal income is probably an adequate proxy for it. Expenditures from own revenue sources per capita and expenditures from own revenue sources per $1,000 of personal income are positively correlated, but ranking states by the two measures gives somewhat different pictures. States such as Alaska, Hawaii, and New York rank high in both expenditures per capita and expenditures per $1,000 of personal income. Other states such as Mississippi, South Carolina, and New Mexico rank low in per capita expenditures but quite high in expenditures per $1,000 of personal income. This may be because the low per capita expenditures in these states are a reflection of their low fiscal capacity to pay for expenditures. Farming states such as Nebraska, Kansas, and Iowa ranked low in 1974 in expenditures per $1,000 of personal income but higher in per capita expenditures, largely as a result of unusually high farm incomes that year. Still other states, such as Arkansas, Missouri, North Carolina, and Texas, rank low in both expenditures per capita and expenditures per $1,000 of personal income. The per capita expenditures of these states cannot be explained simply by their low fiscal capacity. Part of the explanation must be that they prefer goods and services provided by other means than government.

Not only is there considerable variation in expenditures per capita across states; there is similar variation among municipalities within a state. The variation is not just between central cities with high expenditures for welfare and police and suburbs with high expenditures for local schools; it is also between poor suburbs and wealthy ones. For example, in the Detroit metropolitan region, per capita general expenditures (other than capital outlay) ranged from $83 in Garden City, a low-income residential suburb, to $509 in Highland Park, an enciave in Detroit with considerable industrial property in the tax base. Of the forty-five municipalities with 10,000 or more population in the Detroit metropolitan region in 1970, the central city spent $258 per capita and ranked sixth in expenditures.

The fragmentation of metropolitan regions into separate municipalities, counties, and often school districts results in unequal fiscal burdens which citizens in the various jurisdictions must bear to provide equivalent government services. This led the Supreme Court of California in 1971 in *Serrano* v. *Priest* to condemn reliance on existing forms (essentially the local property tax) of financing local schools because it makes the quality of a child's education a function of the wealth of his or her parents and neighbors. It has been proposed that state aid to local school districts be distributed under a power-equalizing formula, in which the number of dollars produced in local and state funds per schoolchild per mill in the local tax rate would be the same for each school district. This would ensure that the funds available to support local education did not depend on the property values in the local school district. Spending equal dollars on education, however, does not ensure that the quality of education will be the same. It may be desirable to go beyond power-equalizing and provide additional state funds to school districts with greater numbers of disadvantaged children.

The problem of unequal fiscal burdens is complicated by the fact that families and individuals often live in one local government jurisdiction, work in another, and shop and seek recreation in still others. Also, a local jurisdiction may have opportunities to "export" tax burdens by taxing industrial property located within it. It is not clear, however, that jurisdictions gain fiscally from the presence of commercial and industrial property. Although increasing the tax base, it also increases the need for government services, and it is difficult to attract new industry without attracting new residents who require still more government services. Nevertheless, local governments actively compete to attract industry, particularly high technology industry, where the increased property values may be high, the additional workers few, and the income of these workers above average. At the same time local governments try to zone out "bad ratables" (such as housing projects requiring sewers, streets, and new schools).

Declining Cities

The financial crisis of New York City has turned the spotlight on the special problems of the older central cities characterized by an economy going nowhere and a population going elsewhere.[16] George Peterson divided the twenty-eight cities (excluding Washington, D.C.) with population of over 500,000 (in either 1960 or 1970) into three groups: "growing" cities that gained population between 1960 and 1973, cities that gained population between 1960 and 1970 but are now losing population, and "declining" cities that lost population continuously between 1960 and 1973; New York City with its special problems was treated separately. For the twenty-eight cities, spending on the common functions—highways, police protection, fire protection, sanitation, parks and recreation, financial administration, and general control—was compared. The fourteen declining cities spent $264 per capita in 1973, which is 74 percent more than the $152 per capita spent by the seven growing cities. The per capita expenditures of the six cities that grew in population between 1960 and 1970 and are now losing population was $195, which is in between the expenditure level of the growing cities and that of the declining cities. New York City spent $396 per capita, considerably more than the average expenditures in the declining cities. New York, however, is required to assume a much greater portion of welfare costs than most other cities. The high expenditures of New York and of the declining cities do not necessarily reflect a higher quality of services.[17] Rather they probably indicate greater need for services, particularly welfare, police protection, and housing and urban re-

16. This section borrows from George E. Peterson, "Finance," in William Gorham and Nathan Glazer, eds., *The Urban Predicament* (Urban Institute, 1976).

17. Expenditures for higher education, public hospitals, and public transportation are more generous in New York than in other large cities.

newal. But declining cities, most of which are in the northeastern and north central states, find it increasingly difficult to support needed expenditures with a shrinking tax base and a shifting population. They are surrounded by other incorporated municipalities, which makes annexation of the more affluent surrounding suburbs very difficult.[18] Some of the immediate fiscal problems of New York and other central cities may be due to loose fiscal management in the past, and part of the burden of adjustment may have to take the form of a scaling down of budgets that are excessively ambitious on the expenditure side. But an important part of these cities' malaise is the result of factors beyond their control. Hence their fiscal problems can be fully met only by increased state or federal aid.

Selected Problems

A survey chapter such as this must be highly selective. It is not possible to discuss adequately or even to mention all the important policy issues facing state and local governments. Three topics have been selected for more detailed discussion: (1) state and local retirement plans; (2) tax-exempt municipal bonds; and (3) counter-cyclical revenue sharing. Each of these topics has important long-term consequences for state and local governments, and each is currently before Congress. Two other important issues are taken up in other chapters in this volume: Palmer and Minarik discuss federal takeover of welfare in chapter 12, and Schultze, block grants in chapter 8.

State and Local Retirement Plans

The Employee Retirement Income Security Act of 1974 (ERISA) provides for a comprehensive overhaul of the pension rules that affect almost every pension plan. It establishes mandatory participation rules, which in general state that a new employee over the age of twenty-five is eligible to participate in the pension plan after a maximum waiting period of one year. Each plan must meet minimum standards for vesting and funding. Vesting means that an employee does not lose his right to benefits from contributions that have been made on his behalf even if he leaves his job. Funding is setting aside adequate reserves for future pension claims. A plan is fully funded if

18. Richard P. Nathan, "Complexifying the Problems of Cities" (Brookings Institution, n.d.; processed).

the assets held by the plan are sufficient to pay all promised benefits. Most plans are not fully funded. To increase the solvency of pension plans, the ERISA requires that employers make contributions to the plan to amortize unfunded liabilities over thirty years. Since a minimum funding standard will not ensure that a plan can pay all vested benfits when it terminates, the ERISA provides for mandatory termination insurance to protect participants with vested benefits from losses from plan terminations. The ERISA also tightens fiduciary standards and requires audited financial statements for plans.

State and local government plans are exempt from the requirements of the ERISA. This is not the result of an accident or of congressional oversight. State and local governments lobbied hard to be exempted. The ERISA does stipulate a congressional study of state and local retirement plans, to be completed by the end of 1976, which is to include an analysis of the adequacy of existing levels of participation, vesting, funding, and fiduciary standards.

Pension plans administered by states or by local governments have become an important element in the economic security of millions of state and local government workers and their families. Almost all such full-time workers are now covered by retirement plans, whereas only 44 percent of wage and salary workers in private industry are covered. State and local plans pay periodic benefits to about 1.6 million people. Assets of these plans increased from $9.9 billion in 1955 to $87.5 billion in 1974.

The New York City financial crisis raised two important questions about all state and local pension plans. First, how do benefits under these plans compare with those under private plans? Second, are state and local plans financially sound?

Benefits under state and local plans typically are more generous than benefits under private plans.[19] The normal retirement age is often fifty-five or sixty; in the case of police and firemen normal retirement may be at any age after twenty or twenty-five years of service. The vesting rules of state and local plans, however, often do not meet the requirements of the ERISA, and this ties state and local workers to their jobs. State and local employees who meet minimum age and service requirements generally retire at about 50 percent of preretirement earnings, which is a higher earnings-replacement rate than

19. See, for example, Philip M. Dearborn, Jr., *Pensions for Policemen and Firemen* (Washington, D.C.: Labor-Management Relations Service, 1974).

under most private plans.[20] State and local plans, unlike private plans, are beginning to make limited adjustments in benefits to offset the inflationary erosion of pension benefits during retirement years.

When state and local salaries were low, high retirement benefits and greater job security were the major financial inducements to government employment. Before the 1950s these workers were not covered by social security, so that state and local plans served as both private pension plans and social security. Once social security coverage was extended to most state and local workers, the public plans were not adjusted downward to reflect the additional economic security afforded by social security.[21]

Public employee unions usually bargain for both liberalized pension benefits and current wage and salary increases. Unless the pension benefits are currently funded, increased pension promises can be negotiated outside the normal budget constraint, whereas increased wages and salaries must be financed by increased revenue. It may be a matter of indifference to a union whether it receives for its membership increased wages and salaries worth $10 million a year or increased pension benefits that would require, say, $12 million a year to fully fund.[22] Government negotiators, however, may prefer the increased pension benefits because, if the plan is only partially funded, current government contributions to the pension plan might amount to less than $10 million a year. In short, government negotiators can mortgage the future by agreeing to an increase in unfunded pension benefits. It is unlikely that the benefits under state and local plans would be as generous as they are if the governments had to fund promised benefits currently.

When pension benefits are not currently funded, it means that governments are incurring future liabilities that will have to be paid for by future taxes and that when these taxes are collected they will not

20. Systematic data on benefit rules of public plans are not available. For a discussion of what might be considered a typical public plan, see Robert Tilove, *Public Employee Pension Funds* (Columbia University Press, 1976).

21. State and local governments may opt out of social security. New York City has given the required two-year notice that it intends to do this. It would be the first large state or local government unit to opt out.

22. This example assumes that the union would prefer a $10 million wage and salary package to a $10 million pension package, because the wage and salary package would give the workers greater financial flexibility. If they do not have to wait until retirement to receive the money, they can save it or consume it. There are, however, federal income tax advantages which conceivably could tip the scales toward increased pensions.

be paying for any current government services. It is not much different from incurring indebtedness today to cover current operating deficits. In fact, if governments increased the funding of pension plans by contributing more to them and did not raise taxes or cut other expenditures, the governments would have to incur additional indebtedness to cover the resulting operating deficits.

But how unfunded are the promised benefits? It is estimated that Washington, D.C., has unfunded pension liabilities exceeding $1 billion and that New York City would have to spend an additional $400 million to $700 million a year for full funding.[23] Washington, Indianapolis, and Pittsburgh maintain only negligible assets in their plans, relying on annual appropriations to cover benefits being paid currently. Most plans do maintain some assets. In 1974 the $6.6 billion in benefits and withdrawals paid out by state and local plans was equal to 7.5 percent of the end-of-year assets of the plans. Aronson has attempted to measure empirically the extent of underfunding.[24] He concludes that amortization of unfunded liabilities over a twenty-seven-year period would require state and local governments, at a minimum, to double the amount they contribute annually to the pension plans. The required increase may be as much as sixfold. With state and local government contributions amounting to $7.8 billion in 1974, this is a significant increase.

The issue of funding state and local pension plans is similar to that of funding social security. In a *growing* national economy, current workers are taxed to pay social security benefits to those who are retired. When the present workers retire, their social security benefits can be paid for by taxing the next generation of workers. If the proportion of the population working remains constant and real wages rise, social security benefits can increase, giving each generation of workers, in effect, a return similar to interest on the taxes it paid to support the social security benefits of the previous generation. Similarly, in a *growing* state or local economy, current taxpayers can be

23. Senator Thomas F. Eagleton, "The Crisis in Public Pension Systems," speech delivered to the New York Society of Security Analysts, January 13, 1976. For data on New York City plans, see Bernard Jump, "Financing Public Employee Retirement Programs in New York City: Trends Since 1965 and Projections to 1980," Occasional Paper 16 (Syracuse University, Maxwell School of Citizenship and Public Affairs, Metropolitan Studies Program, 1975; processed), pp. 13–24.

24. J. Richard Aronson, "Projections of State and Local Trust Fund Financing," in David Ott and others, *State-Local Finances in the Last Half of the 1970s* (American Enterprise Institute for Public Policy Research, 1975), pp. 63–89.

taxed to pay pensions to retired government workers, and the next generation of taxpayers can be taxed to pay pensions to the next generation of retired workers. Because of this analogy to social security, the congressional study of state and local pensions required by the ERISA is supposed to take into account "the taxing power of the government maintaining the plan" in evaluating whether state and local plans are adequately financed.[25]

While the assumptions—a growing economy, rising real wages, and a constant proportion of the population working—are valid enough for the U.S. economy as a whole to permit social security to be on a pay-as-you-go basis,[26] they clearly cannot be applied to some states and to many local governments. Declining cities with large unfunded pension benefits, in particular, will have fewer taxpayers in the future to finance pension benefits promised long ago. Some state and local pension plans are in danger of insolvency.

Rapid growth of state and local employment may hide the burden of paying future pension benefits. When employment is growing, present workers far outnumber retired workers. Once growth stops or slows down, however, the ratio of retired workers to present workers increases. Pension costs then rise much more rapidly than payrolls. It is estimated that after 1975, if salaries of New York City workers do not increase and employment declines at 2 percent a year, the city's total retirement and social security costs will increase from the $1.1 billion of 1975 to a peak of $1.5 billion in 1978 and will fall only to $1.4 billion in 1980. Even under these conservative assumptions concerning employment and wage and salary increases, the retirement contribution rate will have to increase from 19 percent of payrolls in 1975 to 23 percent in 1980.[27] This suggests that cities can do little in the near future to cut pension costs. It is even possible that a slowdown in the rate of pay increases will induce some workers to retire earlier and thus actually increase short-term pension costs. The increase may be offset if personnel costs can be reduced by paying lower salaries to junior grade replacements. Some government units may consider forcing earlier retirement to achieve downgrading.

25. Public Law 93-406 (September 2, 1974), sec. 3031(3).
26. For a discussion of the long-term problems of social security financing, see chapter 12 below.
27. These estimates assume that New York City does not move toward more current funding of its retirement systems. See Jump, "Financing Public Employee Retirement Programs," pp. 61–64.

The New York City financial crisis, however, may have focused too much attention on the adequacy of funding and the risk of insolvency. It should be remembered that funding is essentially a question of when pension promises are paid for. Except for a few plans that may become insolvent, funding is not a matter of never paying for the promised benefits.

The most serious problem with state and local pensions may be that the level of promised benefits is too high relative to current compensation. If state and local governments were required to amortize unfunded pension liabilities over thirty years—the ERISA rule for most private plans—increases in promised benefits would be subject to the budget constraint. This would make the true cost of liberalized benefits clear to taxpayers and would increase the resistance of state and local governments to benefit increases that currently may appear to cost very little.

Tax-Exempt Municipal Bonds

The New York City financial crisis was triggered in April 1975 when the municipal bond market closed for the city. New York was unable to roll over its short-term debt, which had been issued to cover operating deficits. Although a few other cities have made a practice of covering operating deficits in the short-term market, the New York crisis increased both awareness of some of the shortcomings of tax-exempt financing and interest in alternatives for subsidizing state and local governments.

Tax exemption permits state and local governments to float debt at a lower interest cost than would be possible if the interest on state and local obligations were taxed under the federal income tax. Traditionally there has been about a 30 percent difference in yield between taxable and tax-exempt bonds with the yield differential being about 40 percent for short-term bonds and about 20 percent for long-term bonds.[28]

The major criticisms of tax-exempt financing are that it is inefficient and inequitable.[29] If the yield differential for all tax-exempt bonds were 30 percent and if the holders of tax-exempt bonds were all in

28. The yield differential is greater for short-term tax-exempts because commercial banks invest most heavily in this side of the market.

29. See, for example, Ott and Meltzer, *Federal Tax Treatment of State and Local Securities;* and Richard Goode, *The Individual Income Tax,* rev. ed. (Brookings Institution, 1976), pp. 133–38.

the 30 percent tax bracket, the after-tax yield on taxable bonds would be the same as the yield on tax-exempt bonds and investors in tax-exempts would receive no tax advantage from buying them. The average marginal tax rate of holders of tax-exempt securities, however, is about 45 percent. As a result, the cost to the federal government in forgone revenue (about 45 percent of the interest that would be paid if state and local obligations were taxable) exceeds the benefit to state and local governments of the lower interest rates. It therefore costs the federal government about $1.50 to reduce the interest costs of state and local governments by $1.[30] In aggregate, state and local governments saved about $2.7 billion on interest in 1975 at a cost of $4.1 billion to the federal government. The difference of $1.4 billion is the cost of the inefficiency of the subsidy, and this wastage went to the holders of tax-exempt securities.

The 30 percent difference in yield between taxable and tax-exempt securities can be viewed as a kind of "tax" paid by the holders of tax-exempt securities. This is obviously a bargain for taxpayers subject to marginal tax rates of over 30 percent on other income. These taxpayers can better their after-tax income position by holding tax-exempt instead of taxable securities. The higher the marginal tax rate, the greater is the incentive to hold tax-exempts and in effect to pay taxes at the 30 percent bargain rate. Tax-exempt securities therefore erode the progressiveness of the individual income tax and reduce the vertical equity of that tax.

For investors subject to marginal tax rates below 30 percent, there is no incentive to hold tax-exempt securities. Thus state and local governments cannot market their obligations to pension funds or other tax-exempt organizations such as colleges and universities.[31]

The three major holders of tax-exempt securities are commercial banks, fire and casualty insurance companies, and individuals. During periods of tight money when the demand for bank loans is high, commercial banks desert the tax-exempt market. Only by offering higher interest rates are state and local governments able to attract new investors into the market and to induce existing holders to acquire more tax-exempt bonds. The yield differential then narrows,

30. See Goode, *Individual Income Tax*, p. 136.
31. New York City pension funds agreed to hold New York City obligations after the municipal bond market was closed for the city. Special federal legislation is needed to ensure that these purchases will not adversely affect the tax-exempt status of the pension funds.

reducing the effective subsidy to state and local governments and raising its cost to the federal government.

The taxable municipal bond proposal included in the House version of the Tax Reform Act of 1969 and endorsed by the administration in 1973 and again in 1976 would broaden the market for tax-exempt bonds, reduce the cyclical instability in that market, and reduce the inequity of tax-exempt financing. Under this proposal state and local governments would have the option of issuing taxable municipal bonds. The federal government would agree to pay, say, 40 percent of the interest on such issues.

Because the taxable municipal bond would be an option, state and local governments would only issue such bonds if their interest cost, net of the subsidy, were less than the interest cost of tax-exempt bonds. Since they would still be able to issue tax-exempt bonds, they could not be worse off under this proposal. State and local governments could be expected to issue taxable bonds until the yield differential on tax-exempt bonds approached the subsidy rate. As the supply of tax-exempt bonds decreased, the yield differential would rise. Only when the yield differential equaled the subsidy rate would the net borrowing costs be the same in both markets. Then it would not matter to state and local governments whether they issued taxable or tax-exempt bonds.

If the subsidy rate were 40 percent, taxpayers with marginal tax rates above 40 percent would continue to prefer tax-exempt bonds while taxpayers with marginal rates below 40 percent, including tax-exempt organizations, would prefer taxable bonds. The market for state and local bonds would be broadened and its instability reduced because the new taxable bonds would be attractive to investors who at present are effectively excluded from the tax-exempt market.

Proponents of the optional taxable bond differ on the appropriate subsidy rate. The administration has recommended 30 percent.[32] Stanley S. Surrey, former assistant secretary of the treasury for tax policy, has recommended 40 percent.[33] At the lower rate, few taxable bonds would be issued since the average yield differential is about 30

32. See "Statement of the Honorable Edwin H. Yeo III, Under Secretary of the Treasury for Monetary Affairs, before the House Ways and Means Committee on Proposals Relating to Tax-Exempt Financing," January 21, 1976, Department of the Treasury *News*, WS-585 (no date).

33. "Statement of Stanley S. Surrey," Hearings before the House Ways and Means Committee on Optional Taxable Bonds (January 1976; processed).

percent. A 40 percent rate would ensure that a significant quantity of taxable bonds would be issued; possibly as much as 40 percent of all state and local obligations with a maturity over one year would be issued as taxable bonds.[34] There is some fear, however, that if the subsidy rate were set too high it would eliminate the tax-exempt market. Above 70 percent would clearly be such a rate because the yield differential would then be greater than 70 percent, and all investors could improve their after-tax income position if they purchased taxable bonds and paid the tax on the interest income. At a rate above 48 percent the market for tax-exempt bonds might become very thin. Commercial banks, which are subject to a 48 percent marginal rate of tax, would switch from tax-exempt to taxable bonds. Thus a 30 percent rate is too low and a 48 percent rate is probably too high. This suggests that a rate in between, possibly 40 percent, would ensure that a significant number of taxable bonds would be issued and that the number of tax-exempt bonds would not fall too low.

A 40 percent subsidy rate for taxable municipal bonds would reduce, though it would not eliminate, the inequity of tax-exempt financing. It would raise the yield differential to 40 percent, thus increasing from 30 to 40 percent the implicit tax paid by the holders of tax-exempt securities. These investors would still be able to improve their after-tax income position by holding tax-exempt securities but the advantage would be less than at present. As the yield differential approaches the average marginal tax rate of holders of tax-exempt securities, the tax-exempt subsidy becomes more efficient. The difference between what tax exemption costs the federal government in forgone revenue and what tax exemption saves state and local governments in reduced borrowing costs becomes smaller.[35]

In addition to adopting the proposal for taxable municipal bonds, Congress should limit the amount of tax-exempt bonds state and local governments may issue to finance the purchase of pollution control equipment leased to business enterprises. Interest rates on all tax-exempt bonds must rise to make municipal bonds issued for traditional purposes as well as bonds issued for pollution control attractive to investors. To sell the increased volume of tax-exempt securities,

34. Ibid.
35. The taxable municipal bond option would raise the average marginal tax rate of the holders of tax-exempts, possibly to 50 percent. With a yield differential of 40 percent, it would then cost the federal government $1.25 to provide $1 of subsidy to state and local governments.

new buyers with lower marginal tax rates must be attracted into the tax-exempt market. But that requires an increase in the yield of tax-exempts. When taxable bond rates are 9 percent, a taxpayer in the 40 percent marginal tax bracket will be interested in buying tax-exempt securities with yields of about 5.5 percent. But to attract a taxpayer in the 30 percent bracket, yields would have to rise to 6.3 percent. Hence, extending the tax exemption privilege to pollution-control bonds would raise interest costs on state and local bonds generally, increase the windfall to upper income taxpayers, and raise the subsidy cost to the Treasury. One study estimates that tax-exempt rates will be 0.25 percent higher in 1976 to induce investors to hold the new issues of pollution control bonds.[36]

These bonds are issued under an exception to the general limitations Congress placed on industrial development bonds in 1968. At that time, no pollution control bonds were being issued. Increased federal and state requirements for pollution control since then have led to around $3.5 billion in public issues of pollution control bonds a year and possibly an equal amount in private placements.[37]

The fundamental question is, who should pay for cleaning up the environment? Even if it were decided that taxpayers in general should pay some of the costs of cleaning up industrial pollution, doing so by the issuance of tax-exempt bonds would cost the taxpayer more per dollar of subsidy than other alternatives. In any event, there are good economic reasons for requiring that industrial products carry, in their prices, the full costs of the pollution cleanup necessitated by their production. Public subsidies tend to hide the true costs of production and thereby encourage excessive production of goods causing heavy pollution. Tax incentives also are unattractive because they are unlikely to increase investment in pollution control, which is probably determined solely by the pollution control standards set by the federal government.

Making pollution control bonds subject to the same limitations as other industrial development bonds would improve the market for state and local securities by lowering borrowing costs and increasing

36. The projections of pollution control investment assumed in this study should probably be revised downward in view of the easing of some environmental standards since the energy crisis. See George E. Peterson and Harvey Galper, "Tax Exempt Financing of Private Industry's Pollution Control Investment," *Public Policy*, vol. 23 (Winter 1975), pp. 81–103.

37. See "Statement of Surrey," Hearings, pp. 13–14.

the yield differential between taxable and tax-exempt bonds. It would also ensure that the general taxpayer did not bear the cost of pollution control. Congress should consider too eliminating tax exemption for all industrial development bonds or eliminating all exceptions to the general limitations on industrial development bonds. At present, in addition to pollution control bonds, tax-exempt financing is allowed for (1) residential real property, (2) sports facilities, (3) convention facilities, (4) airports, docks, wharves, and mass commuting and parking facilities, and (5) water and waste disposal facilities. Although these other exceptions are not very important today, they may become so in the future, particularly if pollution control bonds are limited.

Countercyclical Revenue Sharing

Congress enacted revenue sharing in 1972 to reduce intergovernmental fiscal disparities, to give more decisionmaking power to state and local governments, to reduce state and local taxes, and to shift the overall tax burden toward the income tax, which is primarily a federal tax, and away from the property tax, which is primarily a local tax. Although these various reasons for adopting revenue sharing may be somewhat inconsistent,[38] short-run stabilization was not one of the reasons advanced during consideration of revenue sharing. The debate focused instead on the long-term advantages of transferring federal funds to state and local governments with few strings attached.

Revenue sharing was enacted in October 1972 at a time when many observers concluded that federal aid was not needed. The surplus of the state and local sector in the national income and product accounts reached an all-time high of $16.3 billion, at an annual rate, for the second quarter of 1972. If the surplus on the insurance funds is excluded, the state and local sector had swung from a deficit of $6.4 billion in the last quarter of 1970 to a surplus of $8.3 billion in the second quarter of 1972.

The combination of recession and inflation since 1973 has caused

38. See, for example, Henry Aaron, "The Honest Citizen's Guide to Revenue Sharing," in National Tax Association, *Proceedings of the Sixty-fourth Annual Conference on Taxation* (1972), pp. 18–25, and Richard P. Nathan, Allen D. Manvel, and Susannah E. Calkins, *Monitoring Revenue Sharing* (Brookings Institution, 1975), pp. 4–5, 344–72.

a serious deterioration in the fiscal condition of the state and local sector. The surplus or deficit (excluding the social insurance funds) shifted from a surplus of $13.4 billion in the fourth quarter of 1972, when the first revenue sharing checks were mailed out, to a deficit of $5.0 billion in the first quarter of 1975. The economic downturn induced revenue shortfalls, particularly for state and local governments that rely heavily on sales and income taxes. The greater reliance of states on progressive income taxes increased the exposure of state tax systems to recessions. In addition, recessions intensify the need for public expenditures for welfare, health, food stamps, and even education as students tend to stay in school longer when employment possibilities are bleak.

Inflation in the long run may tend to boost expenditures and revenues in proportion. In the short run, however, it may cause state and local expenditures to rise more rapidly than revenues.[39] This is true even though inflation pushes taxpayers into higher effective income tax rates. Property tax receipts generally do not keep up with inflation because assessments are apt to lag and increases in nominal property tax rates face political obstacles.

In addition to the short-run problem of expenditures rising faster than revenues in periods of inflation, state and local governments are usually restricted in their access to the credit market to cover operating deficits. Recession- and inflation-induced deficits must be offset by decreases in current services, postponements or cancellations of capital outlays, or increases in taxes. While employee layoffs in the state and local sector are much less pronounced than in the private sector, it is no longer true that government employment is recession-proof. It is estimated that cutbacks in expenditures and increases in taxes, measured at the full-employment levels of GNP, together amounted to $14 billion between the third quarter of 1974 and the third quarter of 1975.[40] This occurred at the same time that the federal government was shifting to a stimulative fiscal position by cutting the taxes of individuals and businesses.

Countercyclical revenue sharing, if properly designed, could make state and local budget-related action more consistent with federal

39. See Roy Bahl and others, "The Impact of Economic Base Erosion, Inflation, and Employee Compensation Costs on Local Governments," Occasional Paper 23 (Syracuse University, Maxwell School of Citizenship and Public Affairs, Metropolitan Studies Program, 1975; processed).

40. *Economic Report of the President, January 1976*, p. 57.

government efforts to stimulate the economy. In principle, it could completely fill the gap between expenditures and revenues caused by recessions. It may be undesirable to go quite this far because economic downturns can serve the socially useful purpose of requiring governments to examine priorities closely and to reduce or eliminate programs of low priority.

The Local Public Works Capital Development and Investment Act of 1975 (which President Ford vetoed—a veto Congress failed to override) contained a provision for emergency support grants to state and local governments for five calendar quarters beginning April 1, 1976. Although this provision was not enacted, a similar provision may be added to the bill extending general revenue sharing which Congress must act on in 1976. The public works bill would have authorized $500 million annually for countercyclical revenue sharing[41] when the seasonally adjusted national unemployment rate reached 6 percent and an additional $250 million for each half of a percentage point it rose above that. Because of lags in the collection of unemployment data, payments for a given quarter would have been based on average unemployment two quarters earlier. Since unemployment averaged just under 8.5 percent for the last quarter of 1975, the public works bill would have authorized annual emergency grants totaling $1.75 billion to be paid to state and local governments during the second quarter of 1976.

As in general revenue sharing, one-third of the funds would have gone to the states and two-thirds to local governments. The amount of funds allocated to each state would have depended on the amount of taxes collected in that state and its unemployment rate.[42] The same general formula—taxes collected and unemployment—would have allocated the local funds within each state.[43] No individual state or local government would have received any funds if its unemployment rate was under 6 percent. The program would have ended for all state and local governments when the national unemployment rate fell

41. The bill uses the term "emergency support grants" instead of "countercyclical revenue sharing."

42. The unemployment factor was excess unemployment, defined as the unemployment rate during the most recent quarter minus the state's unemployment rate during 1967–69, the last period the national unemployment rate was below 4.5 percent. Presumably this meant only positive deviations from the base period.

43. The unemployment factor was again excess unemployment. Because of the lack of historical data, excess unemployment was defined as the local government's unemployment rate minus 4.5 percent.

below 6 percent. Amounts allocated but not paid to jurisdictions with unemployment below 6 percent would have been reserved for a contingency fund from which the secretary of the treasury could have made additional grants to state and local governments in severe fiscal difficulty.

Countercyclical revenue sharing can only be evaluated by comparing it with the major alternatives for stimulating the economy and aiding state and local governments.[44] These alternatives include (1) public service jobs, (2) public works programs, (3) additional spending on transfer programs such as unemployment insurance, (4) tax cuts, and (5) an increase in general revenue sharing or community development block grants. The two main criteria for evaluating these alternatives are the fiscal effectiveness of the program and whether the program would introduce any socially undesirable side effects. Public service jobs may have a role to play in alleviating the problem of the so-called hard-core unemployed. A program of public service jobs, however, is unlikely to be a useful countercyclical tool because it would have the undesirable side effect of encouraging state and local governments to replace present employees with employees eligible for the subsidized jobs. This would lead to little reduction in the overall unemployment rate but some relaxation of the fiscal squeeze on state and local governments. Public works programs, in practice, have not proved to be an effective countercyclical tool mainly because the length of time it takes to get new projects under way means that the economic stimulus comes too late. They also lead to a bunching of capital investments, which may be socially undesirable. If the primary justification for countercyclical revenue sharing is the loss of jobs in the state and local sector, liberalized benefits, which make it possible to get money into the economy quickly, might be the answer. But liberalization, such as extending the maximum period for benefits beyond sixty-five weeks, is not necessarily the most effective means of dealing with the problems of the long-term unemployed—it may have perverse labor market effects. Tax cuts can also get money into the economy quickly, and clearly tax cuts are an important antirecession measure. They cannot, however, be targeted

44. See, for example, statements of Richard P. Nathan and Charles L. Schultze in *Intergovernmental Anti-Recession Assistance Act of 1975,* Hearings before the Senate Subcommittee on Intergovernmental Relations of the Committee on Government Operations, 94:1 (GPO, 1975), pp. 26–53, 16–26; and Ray D. Whitman, "The Future of Revenue Sharing," *Challenge,* vol. 18 (July–August 1975), pp. 14–21.

to areas of high unemployment nor do they make state and local budget actions more consistent with federal fiscal policy. An increase in general revenue sharing or community development block grants would not necessarily get the money to the state and local governments that have been hardest hit by recession. Also, when the economy recovered, it would be difficult to phase out the program. General revenue sharing and community development block grants are aimed at long-term problems in the state and local sector of the economy. They are not suited for meeting short-term problems caused by economic downturns. A countercyclical program of community development block grants, like a public works program, would involve loss of time in getting new projects under way. Compared to the alternatives, countercyclical revenue sharing could get money into the economy quickly, and it would obviate undesirable cutbacks in state and local spending or tax increases during recessions.

The formula contained in the public works bill for distributing the countercyclical revenue sharing, however, had a number of serious weaknesses. The unemployment rate that triggers the emergency support grants is usually a lagging indicator of recession. In the 1974–75 recession, for example, the unemployment rate did not rise above 6 percent until the last quarter of 1974. If the countercyclical program had been in effect, the first payments would not have been made until the second quarter of 1975. Real personal income, however, declined in the first quarter of 1974, and in some states it fell even earlier.[45] In addition, unemployment data are available for only about 1,500 local governments whereas general revenue sharing covers almost 39,000 governments. The countercyclical revenue sharing program contained in the public works bill also set up a contingency fund which would have given the federal government considerable discretion to direct federal money toward favored state and local governments. The distributional formula in the public works bill could surely be improved by making the trigger depend on a decline in real personal income (or a growth in personal income of less than 2 percent) and eliminating the contingency fund.

45. Because the first effect of recession is to increase the deficit (or reduce the surplus), this problem is somewhat mitigated. Cutbacks in state and local expenditures occur only after a lag. See Schultze, statement in *Intergovernmental Anti-Recession Assistance Act of 1975*, p. 17.

Projections for the State and Local Sector to 1981 and 1986*

The growth of state and local government spending over the next decade will be influenced by events, forces, and developments that can only be speculated about today. Principal among these is the overall strength of the nation's economy. For example, if long periods of sluggish growth or recession occur, unemployment will remain high and welfare costs could escalate far above the levels needed during an era of prolonged full employment growth. Such adverse economic conditions similarly could generate a greater demand for the services of public hospitals and educational institutions because fewer people would be able to afford the services offered by private institutions. The general level of inflation will also play an important part in determining how rapidly state and local government expenditures grow. If price increases continue at 6 to 10 percent instead of gradually moderating to the low rates experienced in the early 1960s, billions of dollars will be added to state and local budgets. Public demands for new and better services as well as altered priorities will also influence the pace at which state and local spending grows. New programs for dealing with pollution and environmental control or day care and early childhood education could push state and local spending up significantly, although federal initiatives in national health insurance and welfare reform could have the opposite effect. Finally, the growth of real incomes will play an important role in determining how rapidly the quality of services is raised.

All these uncertainties make it not only difficult but also of limited value to prognosticate about the *actual* level of state and local government activity at some future date. But predictions can be made about the future cost and burden of providing the *existing* combination of services under a reasonable set of assumptions concerning the course of the nation's economy. The meaning of the projections of state and local budgets can best be viewed in terms of the three factors cited earlier to explain the historical growth of state and local expenditures—increased work loads and prices and improvements in the scope and quality of services. The impact of price and work-load changes on state and local expenditures is projected but it

* This section draws heavily on unpublished work done at Brookings by Robert D. Reischauer.

Table 9-10. Expenditures of State and Local Governments, by Function, in Fiscal Year 1973 and Estimated Cost of Providing Same Services in Fiscal Years 1981 and 1986

Billions of dollars

Function[a]	Actual, 1973	1973 services with price and work-load adjustments only	
		1981	1986
General expenditures	181.2	346.3	463.0
Local schools	48.8	81.1	108.2
Higher and other education	20.9	42.2	50.1
Public welfare	23.6	40.8	55.5
Highways and parking	18.8	42.9	54.7
Health and hospitals	13.8	27.4	38.8
Police and fire protection, and correction	11.9	23.8	34.0
Interest on general debt	6.8	14.7	18.9
Financial administration and general control	6.7	13.2	18.8
Sewerage and other sanitation	5.3	10.8	15.3
Other and unallocable	24.6	49.4	68.7
Subsidies to public utilities	2.6	3.8	5.2
Contributions to retirement systems[b]	4.8	8.8	11.8
Total	**188.6**	**358.9**	**480.1**

Sources: Actual, *Governmental Finances in 1973–74*, table 3, and *Governmental Finances in 1972–73*, table 13; projections, prepared by Robert D. Reischauer. Figures are rounded.

a. The components of total expenditures differ from the standard Census Bureau classification in that (1) public utility revenue is netted against public utility expenditure to derive "subsidies to public utilities"; (2) liquor store and trust fund expenditures are omitted; and (3) contributions to retirement systems are considered an expenditure.

b. Includes only government contributions to self-administered retirement systems; contributions to other retirement systems are included in general expenditures.

is assumed that the scope and quality of services remain unchanged. Revenues are projected on the assumption of no changes in current tax rates. Such a set of estimates provides some understanding of the pressures that will be exerted on state and local governments.[46] Projections for expenditures and revenues for 1981 and 1986 are given in tables 9-10 and 9-11.

If the scope and quality of public services are maintained at their

46. For some recent examples of analysis using a similar approach, see Schultze and others, *Setting National Priorities: The 1972 Budget,* pp. 140–43; Tax Foundation, *The Financial Outlook for State and Local Government to 1980,* Research Publication (n.s.) 28 (Tax Foundation, 1973); and Richard Pollock, "Long Run Fiscal Balance of the Hawaii State Government" (University of Hawaii, Economic Research Center, 1974; processed). For a recent example of an attempt to simulate what state and local spending in 1980 actually will be, see Ott and others, *State-Local Finances in the Last Half of the 1970s.*

Table 9-11. Sources of Revenue of State and Local Governments in Fiscal Year 1973 and Estimated Yield of This Revenue System in Fiscal Years 1981 and 1986
Billions of dollars

Revenue source[a]	1973	1981	1986
Federal grants-in-aid	39.3	74.4	101.2
Taxes	121.5	259.3	387.5
Property	45.3	86.6	117.9
General sales and gross receipts	23.0	45.0	61.9
Selective sales	19.5	34.3	48.9
Individual income	18.0	62.9	115.5
Corporate income	5.4	11.6	16.7
Other	10.4	18.9	26.6
Charges and miscellaneous general revenue	29.9	60.5	79.4
Total	**190.7**	**394.2**	**568.1**

Sources: Actual, *Governmental Finances in 1973–74*, table 3; projections, prepared by Robert D. Reischauer. Figures are rounded.

a. The sources of revenue differ from the standard Census Bureau classification in (1) the omission of insurance trust revenue; (2) the netting of liquor store expenditure against liquor store revenue and including this net amount in selective sales taxes; and (3) the omission of utility revenue.

1973 levels, state and local spending will have to increase by 8.4 percent a year between 1973 and 1981 and by 6.0 percent a year between 1981 and 1986. The "built-in" rate of growth falls in the later period because the rate of inflation is assumed to slow down.

Although the expenditure growth needed to maintain 1973 service levels in the 1980s is far higher than in the previous decade, it should not be concluded that the fiscal outlook for the state and local government sector is bleak. As the summary data in table 9-12 show, the growth of state and local expenditures needed to keep up with rising work loads and prices should be less than the growth in GNP over the next decade. Without increasing their tax burden, therefore, state and local governments will be able to provide a significant improvement in the quality of the services they provide. A qualitative improvement of about 1.25 percent a year could take place between 1973 and 1986 without adding to the revenue burden imposed by state and local governments in 1973. In contrast, given the price increases and work-load changes during 1962–72, state and local government expenditures as a percentage of GNP would have had to rise merely to provide the 1962 level of services in 1972, leaving no room for scope and quality improvements unless taxes had been increased. The future is expected to be different from the past mainly because work-load increases are likely to moderate. The growth in

Table 9-12. Summary of Revenue and Expenditures of State and Local Governments, Actual for Fiscal Year 1973 and Projected for Fiscal Years 1981 and 1986

Description	Billions of dollars			As percent of GNP		
	1973	1981	1986	1973	1981	1986
Revenue under existing tax rates	191	394	568	15.4	14.2	14.2
From own sources	152	320	467	12.3	11.5	11.6
Federal grants-in-aid	39	74	101	3.1	2.7	2.6
Expenditures (no change in scope and quality of services)	189	359	480	15.3	12.9	12.0
Revenue less expenditures	2	35	88	0.2	1.3	2.2

Sources: Tables 9-10 and 9-11.

enrollments both in local schools and in colleges and universities should be considerably less than in 1962–72. The growth in the number of welfare beneficiaries should also decline.

Thus in 1986 the 1973 revenue system will produce 18.3 percent more than is required to maintain 1973 service levels. While the calculated receipts are based on some rather rough estimates of the elasticity of taxes, fees, and charges with respect to the growth of GNP, they do suggest that without changing effective rates the scope and quality of government services could be substantially improved between 1973 and 1986. Alternatively, taxes and charges could be cut by 14.9 percent over the period and service levels maintained.

These conclusions, of course, are no more reliable than the assumptions on which they are based. One critical assumption, which deserves some explanation, is that public sector wages will grow at the same rate as those in the private sector (that is, they will keep pace with private compensation per man-hour). This is predicated on the belief that the catch-up period for public employees has largely run its course. The impact of unionization is also likely to weaken now that unions have spread to many major cities and states and now that these governments have gained some experience in collective bargaining procedures. As public employees' incomes begin to exceed those of the average taxpayer, politicians' backs are likely to stiffen when faced with demands for large wage hikes. And the Bureau of Labor Statistics has predicted a period of a relative surplus of educated manpower, which is likely to undercut wage pressure, especially in areas such as education and social services where a glut of workers clearly exists. Finally, it is assumed that state and local governments will not increase their contributions to pension plans to reduce the under-funding of pension promises.

Cyclical turns in the economy undoubtedly will mean that from an aggregate standpoint not all future years will be easy ones. Good years may tempt state and local governments to bite off more than they can chew, forcing some periodic retrenchments. This is clearly what occurred from 1972 to 1975. Faced with large surpluses, rapidly expanding tax receipts, and the new funds under federal revenue sharing, many jurisdictions raised spending and cut taxes more than was warranted in view of the cyclical nature of the economy. When the recession-inflation of 1974–75 hit they were forced into painful expenditure cutbacks and tax increases that would have been unnecessary had they responded less rapidly to the good fortune of 1972 and 1973. Furthermore, as is sometimes the case, political promises may outrun the ability of governments to deliver, thus creating the impression of unsatisfied demands and failing services. But overall, the next ten years should not be years of fiscal crisis for the state and local sector as a whole.

CHAPTER TEN

Energy and the Environment

MARC J. ROBERTS *and* RICHARD B. STEWART

AFTER A DECADE during which expenditures for environmental protection enjoyed great popularity, Americans now seem to be increasingly unsure of how to strike the right balance between environmental quality objectives and other social goals. The significant rise in oil prices brought about by the concerted actions of the oil-exporting nations, coupled with a period of near-record inflation and unemployment, has led to a general reexamination of priorities. How much can the United States afford to pay for environmental protection? To what extent do environmental and energy goals conflict? Is the world really running out of resources, and if so should America develop or conserve its own energy supplies? In this chapter we shall examine some of the critical policy problems and options posed by these questions and raise several more general points about the nature of the choices now confronting the nation.

We can view the economy as producing three kinds of outputs: energy, environmental quality, and all other goods and services. In the absence of improvements in efficiency, the more we want of any one of these the less we can have of the others. For example, given the current high price of world oil, we can have more energy at lower fuel costs by switching to coal-burning power plants. But we will pay for that either by increased air pollution or by reducing the production of other goods and services and devoting those resources instead to the production of "scrubbers" to clean power plant smokestack emissions. If, on the other hand, we can find ways to increase the efficiency with

411

which the nation produces energy and environmental quality, we can achieve to some extent all our goals simultaneously. A basic conclusion of this chapter is that there are a number of ways to improve current public policies in both the environmental and energy areas so that we can more nearly reach our goals for both with less adverse impact on other aspects of our living standards than would be possible under current policies.

But if we are to achieve such gains the United States must make more carefully considered choices both of standards and goals for domestic energy production and environmental quality and of the policy instruments used to reach those goals. And while we will argue here for the importance of proceeding in ways that minimize costs, in making these basic choices considerations other than economic efficiency must also be taken into account. In particular, energy and environmental policies can have important effects on the distribution of income. Higher energy prices, for example, would conserve energy and reduce air pollution but have a particularly acute impact on the living standards of the poor and near poor. Deregulation of the currently controlled price of natural gas would increase supplies of a particularly clean source of energy but sharply raise costs for those homeowners who years ago chose to buy a gas-heated home. There is also a question of the distribution of income among generations. Some environmental decisions are virtually irreversible, so their potential costs to future generations, whose stewards we are, must be of concern.

National security and foreign policy objectives are another consideration. Too often uneconomic policies that favor special producer interests are adopted in the name of national security. It is nevertheless a legitimate concern that we not become too dependent on unreliable overseas sources for our energy supplies. It may therefore be necessary to take some steps in the energy area that might not be warranted on economic efficiency grounds alone.

Finally, some of the decisions we make about energy and the environment have long-run effects on the nature of technological progress and even on our basic goals and preferences. It is probably true that the more experience people have with a clean environment or an unspoiled wilderness, the more highly they come to value them. And unless the economic system provides substantial rewards for cleaning up pollution, we will not channel inventiveness and scientific effort into finding better ways of doing so.

This examination of the interaction between energy and environmental problems is divided into two sections. In the first we consider the criteria that should influence policy decisions—economic efficiency, income distribution, personal preferences, technology, and national security—and then discuss the problem of setting national goals and standards and the alternative kinds of policy instruments available to achieve those goals. In the second section we treat specific suggestions for improving current energy and environmental policies in three major areas: more effective and less costly energy conversion techniques; more cost-effective ways of meeting environmental goals; and means of reducing the environmental costs of domestic energy production.

PART I. POLICYMAKING

Criteria for Making Policy Choices

Criteria for choosing social policy in the energy-environment field, or anywhere else, ultimately rest on views about the nature of the good life and the good society that cannot be proven by scientific or economic arguments. But a discussion of some of the relevant and often conflicting considerations in making decisions can serve to highlight the difficult choices we confront. In this section five such criteria are considered: short-run economic efficiency; income distribution; the impact of government programs on people's preferences and the associated problem of irreversible decisions; the implications of policies for technology and institutions; and national security and foreign policy considerations.

Economic Efficiency

The policy goal most often urged and perhaps most often ignored is economic efficiency. Yet the case for vigorous pursuit of economic efficiency in the energy-environment area is a strong one. Economic efficiency consists of maximizing the goods, services, and other amenities that can be obtained with a limited stock of resources.[1] Alterna-

1. Economic efficiency does not necessarily mean striving to maximize the gross national product. All sophisticated students of the subject agree that the GNP is simply one statistical index, which very imperfectly measures the amount of human welfare generated by the economy. In particular, it tends to ignore both residual flows and land-use implications exactly because such effects often do not pass through the market, and the GNP is a measure of market activity. See William Nordhaus

tively, economic efficiency is promoted by meeting given objectives at the lowest possible cost. Surely, if we wish both to secure a high level of environmental quality and to meet our energy needs, but have only limited resources to devote to these objectives, efficiency must be a major concern.

Economic efficiency requires first of all that the prices charged for commodities or amenities reflect all the costs incurred in producing them, including the costs of any environmental damage associated with their production. When the price of any good is set below the true cost of production, its consumption will be excessively encouraged and its production discouraged.[2] Thus, by holding domestic oil and gas prices below the world market price, as is now the case, national energy policy explicitly encourages excessive consumption of these fuels while simultaneously discouraging the new domestic production that would be forthcoming at costs above the present control price but below world market prices. Similarly, an important cause of the nation's pollution problem is that producers have no incentive to adopt production techniques that reduce pollution damages since they are not charged for those damages. Further, since goods that heavily pollute the environment are underpriced, they are consumed in excessive amounts.

Economic efficiency also requires cost-effective measures to improve environmental quality—for example, by cleaning up first at those sites where cleanup can be achieved at the lowest cost. Yet many of our environmental programs are not structured to ensure cost effectiveness. Air pollutants such as carbon monoxide, hydrocarbons, and nitrogen oxides are emitted by many sources of differ-

and James Tobin, "Is Growth Obsolete?" in *Economic Growth*, Fiftieth Anniversary Colloquium V (Columbia University Press for the National Bureau of Economic Research, 1972), pp. 1–80.

2. This statement ignores the complexities introduced by the so-called second best argument, which establishes that when some prices in an economy are distorted, it may be preferable to introduce compensating distortions in the prices of other closely related products. However, such considerations are less compelling when applied to the price level for a whole group of commodities, as in the use of energy. See R. G. Lipsey and Kelvin Lancaster, "The General Theory of Second Best," *Review of Economic Studies*, vol. 24 (1956), pp. 11–32; E. J. Mishan, "Second Thoughts on Second Best," *Oxford Economic Papers*, n.s. vol. 14 (October 1962), pp. 205–17; R. Rees, "Second-Best Rules for Public Enterprise Pricing," *Economica*, n.s. vol. 35 (August 1968), pp. 260–73; William J. Baumol and David F. Bradford, "Optimal Departures from Marginal Cost Pricing," *American Economic Review*, vol. 60 (June 1970), pp. 265–83.

ing ages and types: old and new factories, automobiles, power plants, and so forth; yet existing regulatory programs deal with the various sources of the same pollutant in a largely uncoordinated fashion. They do not guarantee, for example, that nitrogen oxides are controlled so as to allocate the cleanup burden to various sources in a cost-minimizing manner; in fact, they hinder any such effect. Yet if the regulatory program were redesigned to do just that, air quality objectives could be achieved more cheaply.

In response, supporters of current policies argue that policies aimed at efficiency would be excessively complicated and difficult to administer. It is also often argued that our comparatively crude environmental regulatory policies, while inefficient in the short run, will be best over the long run because they will promote rapid technological developments. These are both important claims and are discussed below in connection with specific options and problems.

The superiority of current arrangements is also urged by some on the grounds that an efficient distribution of cleanup burdens may well be unfair. For example, efficiency-enhancing higher energy prices may unduly burden the poor. Similarly, placing a larger obligation for cleanup on those who can do it most cheaply may seem inequitable. These arguments connect with a second policy criterion, equity.

Equity

Some economists have argued that equity and distributional considerations should not be a factor in decisions affecting the allocation of resources, and that any undesirable equity and distributional effects of such decisions should be offset by changes in taxes and transfer payments. In our view, however, it cannot be assumed that the political process will automatically correct all adverse impacts that energy and environmental policy might have on income distribution; hence, possible adverse effects must be taken into account when choosing among policy alternatives.

In some cases, by choosing appropriate policy instruments equity concerns can be met without sacrificing efficiency. For example, regulations aimed at achieving pollution control at the least cost would require those who can clean up more cheaply to do more, which some people would consider unfair. A uniform emission fee on pollutions emissions, on the other hand, would tend to produce a proportionately greater measure of control from those who could reduce pollution more cheaply, but those who controlled less would have to pay correspondingly more in the way of fees. Thus, uniform fees would lead to efficient outcomes while also being perceived as fair.

In other cases the tension between distribution and efficiency is both more serious and more difficult to resolve. In our society lower-income people tend to spend a higher proportion of their incomes on energy and energy-intensive products than do upper-income individuals.[3] As a result, a rise in energy prices has an impact that is not dissimilar to a rise in the price of bread. It is like a regressive tax, which takes a higher proportion of the income of poor people than of rich people. The effects on the poor of a sharp rise in the price of energy may be compelling enough to prompt a change in the tax structure designed to offset these effects. But the more gradual and subtle distributional impact on costs and prices resulting from measures to improve environmental quality may be harder to recognize and more difficult to offset by appropriate tax and transfer payments. Even if the costs of a program are regressively distributed, it would still be obviously socially valuable if the benefits were such that everyone gained on balance. However, many environmental protection efforts seem to be relatively more valuable to upper-income than lower-income people;[4] in that sense they are luxury goods.

Not all environmental policies benefit only the rich, of course. Improving urban air pollution, for instance, may be especially valuable to lower-income people who live in urban areas.[5] And certain kinds of recreation opportunities would be especially appreciated by lower-income urban dwellers who have limited alternatives. But many of the environmental issues surrounding the energy system involve the preservation of currently pristine and inaccessible ecosystems, such as the Colorado River or the Alaskan north slope. The benefits from such preservation, which often stem not from visiting the site but from the satisfaction of knowing it will be preserved, again seem to be especially valuable to upper-income people.

3. M. J. Roberts, "The Economic Consequences of Energy Costs," Discussion Paper 278 (Harvard Institute of Economic Research, March 1973; processed).

4. That is, willingness to pay for environmental protection seems to be a higher percentage of income among those who already have the necessities of life. This means that lower-income people may not perceive environmental protection measures to be as beneficial to them as other social and economic measures might be.

5. A. Myrick Freeman III, "Distribution of Environmental Quality," in Allen V. Kneese and Blair T. Bower, eds., *Environmental Quality Analysis: Theory and Method in the Social Sciences* (Johns Hopkins Press for Resources for the Future, 1972).

In short, programs that seek to satisfy dollar-weighted preferences for environmental quality in cost-effective and efficient terms may benefit the rich far more than the poor, while also distributing the costs of achieving environmental quality in a regressive fashion.

The Impact of Policy on Preferences

The relative value placed on environmental protection by various income groups reflects more than just differences in income; there also seem to be personal differences in tastes and preferences, perhaps in part the result of past experience and opportunities.[6] While economic analysis usually assumes that these preferences of individuals are fixed and will not be influenced by the course of public policy, surely the great public debate on environmental questions has influenced how many individuals value environmental conditions. Similarly, unless people get some chance to experience clean air and clean water, will they fully appreciate what public policy provides or fails to provide?

The effect of policy on attitudes becomes especially important in land-use decisions that are more or less irreversible.[7] It is, as a practical matter, impossible to restore a large open pit mine to its original state. Likewise, once a nuclear power plant has been built on a previously unspoiled oceanfront site, it is very unlikely that over a period of hundreds of years that site will be restored to its pristine condition.

There is every reason to expect that natural and unspoiled areas will become increasingly rare and valuable. With continued economic growth, the demand for ecological purity, and associated recreation opportunities, is likely to expand substantially, even with a constant population. The increasing crowding of our national parks suggests that society is already pushing against such limits. And technology is of very little help in expanding supply. We can find or make substi-

6. As John C. Harsanyi has pointed out in a provocative article, "Welfare Economics of Variable Tastes," *Review of Economic Studies*, vol. 21 (1953–54), pp. 204–13, if individuals in some sense shape their own preferences, the poor would be ill-advised to cultivate a taste for luxuries that would only serve to make them unhappy. In addition, lower-income urban residents are unlikely ever to have had the income and leisure to experience and come to value remote and unspoiled areas. Thus, income affects consumption in two ways: in the short run by expanding opportunities, and in the long run by altering preferences. When economists talk of "the income elasticity of demand," they are generally referring only to the short-run phenomenon.

7. In contrast to issues involving natural biochemical processes, where many kinds of residuals will gradually dissipate even after they are added to the air or the water. See, for example, Gordon M. Fair and others, *Water and Wastewater Engineering*, vol. 2 (Wiley, 1966).

tutes for coal; it is harder to find or make substitutes for the Yosemite Valley. Thus, a major consideration in decision making should be the weight given to the interests of future generations and their opportunities to experience exceptional unspoiled environments.

Energy and environmental policies also have a symbolic aspect. Society's treatment of its own resources and environment helps define the values of that society; man's relationship to nature implicitly shapes his relationship to his fellows. These considerations are difficult to quantify or, indeed, even articulate, but they have a legitimate place in the process of public policy formulation.

Technological and Institutional Issues

We have a strong long-run interest in developing and using energy technologies that will reduce the volume of wastes per unit of production and shift the mix of such residuals to substances that are less harmful to the environment. Otherwise, as the economy grows, the amount of residual flows will increase, or the costs of maintaining a constant level of environmental quality will increase substantially. The current efficiency of energy and environmental policies may be less important, therefore, than whether, in the long run, they stimulate or hinder the development of new and lower-cost technologies for reducing pollution and using energy more efficiently.

Institutional adaptation may be quite as important as technological adaptation. Government regulatory programs and practices have often persisted long after becoming outmoded because the organizations and constituencies they had created successfully preserved them. Unfortunately, there is already evidence of excessive rigidity in current environmental programs. For example, federal grants for constructing municipal waste treatment plants have benefited the construction industry and other special interests while bringing about overinvestment in operation of such facilities and their inefficient use.[8] Alternative approaches—such as using waste water to recharge underground aquifers, which could prove environmentally and economically superior in many cases but require less investment than

8. Because municipalities receive federal subsidies for construction outlays but not for operation and maintenance expenses, they tend to overinvest in construction and spend too little for skilled operation and proper maintenance. See *Examination into the Effectiveness of the Construction Grant Program for Abating, Controlling, and Preventing Water Pollution,* U.S. Comptroller General's Report to the Congress (U.S. General Accounting Office, 1969), pp. 13–20, 38–40.

current methods—have not been actively pursued. Politically en-
trenched interests that benefit from current programs have aggressively opposed any major departures.

Foreign Policy and National Security

The international aspects of the energy problem raise a variety of
additional considerations, some of them economic. The cost of producing oil in the Middle East and delivering it to the United States
is only a fraction of the present world price—perhaps $2 versus $13.
As a consequence, foreign oil-producing countries have the potential
of undercutting new domestic energy supplies (for example, coal
gasification or shale liquefaction) that could be developed at costs
approaching today's world market price. This potential threat and its
attendant risks of loss to commercial ventures may inhibit private,
large-scale investments in alternative energy sources in the United
States and demand a larger governmental role in investment decisions
than would otherwise be the case. On the other hand, for the government to bear some of the risks of private ventures is a course easily
subject to abuse and can lead to grossly inefficient investments. The
special nature of the world oil market, however, with prices so far
above costs, poses a dilemma in which conflicting considerations have
to be balanced against each other.

It also may be true that the ability of foreign oil producers to
raise or even maintain the real price of oil depends significantly on the
rate of growth of oil consumption by the importing countries. Given
the large production capacity and divergent interests of members of
the Organization of Petroleum Exporting Countries, a slow worldwide growth of oil consumption in the next five years would require
difficult decisions on the part of OPEC about who would bear the
burden of holding down oil production. It may therefore be in the
joint interests of the United States and other major consumers to take
actions on energy conservation beyond those which would make
economic sense in a world without international oil cartels.

Other issues involve national security. While the United States—
unlike Japan and Western Europe—itself still produces a major part
of its energy requirements (only 15 percent of energy consumption
now comes from oil imports), a continuation of today's low price
policy for domestic energy is likely to lead to a steady decline in the
domestic fraction and a corresponding rise in the imported fraction.

In turn, a growing proportion of imports would have to come from potentially unreliable sources in the Middle East. Since the current price of oil imports is already high, it makes no sense to try to correct this situation by underwriting the development of even higher-cost domestic sources. The existence of such high-cost supplies could not be creditably used as a bargaining device, and such projects are likely to leave the United States in the paradoxical position of preferring even higher world energy prices to protect its investment in very high-cost options. At the same time, however, both economic efficiency and national security considerations strongly argue against a policy of indefinitely holding the price of domestic energy well below world market levels. In addition, national security objectives also point in the direction of acquiring a sizable stockpile of oil to help reduce the disruptions that a sharp reduction in imports would entail.

In summary, we must realize that none of the diverse objectives for energy and environmental policy can be fully satisfied. Some trade-offs are necessary among them, even if there is no simple way to prescribe how much of one goal we should be willing to give up in order to improve our performance in other respects. Nonetheless, as a society we will have to impose some priorities and institute some policies.

Setting Standards

The first step in setting energy and environmental policy is to decide on the levels of environmental quality and the quantity and kinds of energy desired. In the case of energy, most, though not all, of these decisions can be left to the marketplace. Government has three major roles. It must ensure that the prices of various energy products fully incorporate the environmental costs associated with energy production and use; only in this way will decisions made in the market by individual consumers and business firms take into account the interactions between energy and the environment. Government may also have to strengthen the incentives for efficient energy use, where market incentives are weak—for example, by mandatory information disclosure on the energy consumption of various appliances. Finally, and ironically, it must review and correct many of its own current energy policies that distort energy prices and encourage inefficient use. Once these kinds of actions are taken, energy is a commodity whose output and allocation can be left mainly to market decisions.

Setting the appropriate standards for environmental quality is another matter. There is no way that the millions of citizens who are affected by environmental degradation can individually "buy" the level of environmental quality they want. Only collectively, through government, can consumers of environmental quality decide what they want and what they are willing to pay for it. Economists and others have sometimes spoken as if such decisions could be made through an objective process in which technical experts would calculate and balance the benefits and costs of various levels of cleanup. But in practice, the diffuse and complex nature of these costs and benefits, the necessity for subjective valuation, and the problems of distributional equity and long-run impacts on preferences and technology preclude any such purely objective process.

Today, environmental quality standards are mainly set through a complicated interactive process involving legislatures, which establish the basic structure of standards and the criteria for arriving at them; administrative agencies, which define and implement the precise standards to be achieved; and the courts, which review administrative implementation at the behest of opponents to it. One may dispute the relative role these various actors play and criticize the particular solutions that emerge; but we can offer no basic alternatives to this rather untidy approach to standard setting.

There is, however, continuing and lively controversy over the comparative roles of the state and federal governments. Environmental legislation over the past fifteen years has tended to centralize the determination of environmental quality goals and implementation strategies in the hands of the federal government. This trend developed in response to the historically inadequate efforts of state governments to deal effectively with environmental problems. In part the states lacked the trained manpower and resources to do the job; and many states were reluctant to take the initiative in cleaning up for fear industry would gravitate to areas with laxer standards.

While there is a clear national interest in ensuring a healthy environment, in preserving areas of exceptional environmental quality, and in dealing with interstate pollution, we believe that the trend toward centralized setting of standards may in some instances have gone too far. For political and administrative reasons, federal policies often exhibit uniformities and rigidities that are economically inefficient and environmentally counterproductive. For example, the uniform emission limitations mandated in the Federal Water Pollution Control Act have led to a misallocation of scarce cleanup resources and an emphasis on uniform cleanup technologies that are positively harmful to the environment in some areas.[9] In addition, such an approach runs counter to any general democratic presumption in favor of decentralized decisionmaking. It has also given the federal bureaucracy responsibility for a myriad of essentially local decisions that it is ill equipped to handle. How the centralization versus decentralization issue might be handled in the case of the nondegradation debate about air quality standards and nuclear power plant regulations is discussed below. The issue is also touched upon in the subsequent proposal for public river basin authorities for managing water quality.

The debate over the division between state and federal authority has been less sharp in the energy area, focusing mainly on nuclear safety regulation and power plant siting. However, the growing demand to tap fuel mineral resources on a massive scale in the western United States and on the Outer Continental Shelf has provoked reaction in many western and coastal states, which are threatening to impose controls to block or restrict such development. Given legitimate concerns and interests at both the local and national level, accommodating the interests of all parties within the federal system will be a major task.

Alternative Policy Tools

Once a target level of energy use or environmental protection is chosen, a strategy for achieving the goal must be found. At least six different kinds of strategies are identifiable.

—*Laissez-faire:* relying on private markets to achieve the objectives.

—*Regulation:* adopting laws and regulations that tell people what

9. For example the Environmental Protection Agency is funding a waste treatment system in eastern Long Island that consists of a massive sewer collection and treatment system that will discharge treated wastes to the ocean. Such a system will gradually lower the lake of fresh ground water on which the area relies for its water supply, cause salt water intrusion, and threaten the shellfishing industry. Superior, more sophisticated approaches such as recycling are being largely ignored.

they may and may not do with regard to their use of inputs or the production and disposal of their outputs.

—*Public enterprises:* turning over either primary production or the job of cleanup directly to the public sector, as is now the case with water-borne wastes (through sewer systems) and urban garbage collection.

—*Effluent or emission fees:* using fiscal incentives to alter the inputs and outputs of energy users and waste sources. For predictable political reasons the use of fiscal incentives has typically involved the provision of subsidies (such as tax incentives) rather than the imposition of penalties on outputs.

—*Marketable permits:* creating transferable rights granting the holder the right to emit waste into the ecosystem up to a certain amount.

—*Legal action:* as either an alternative or a supplement to other measures, private utilization of the legal system to correct misallocations could be encouraged by changing legal rules to increase the incentives of those injured by environmental degradation to sue those who injured them.[10]

Since energy and environmental problems arise for a wide variety of reasons and occur in very different economic and social contexts, no one strategy will be ideal for all purposes. To match the right problem with the right strategy or mix of strategies requires looking at the characteristics and desirability of these alternative mechanisms in various situations

The Environment

In the environmental area the issues are, by and large, quite complex, as is suggested by an examination of the difference between effluent charges and the regulatory controls that are now the most common approach.

EFFLUENT AND EMISSION FEES. When properly used, effluent or emission charges will help secure economically efficient pollution cleanup. For example, a uniform fee—say 10 cents for each pound of sulfur emitted into the air by a firm—would lead firms to

10. Indeed, for completness, there is a seventh policy device that bears mention—appeals to good citizenship and moral suasion. Examples are antilittering campaigns, appeals for water or electricity conservation in times of short supply, appeals to people to drive less during the energy crisis, and so on.

reduce sulfur emissions just to the point where the costs of removing an additional pound of sulfur equals 10 cents. The costs of eliminating an additional pound of sulfur from emissions normally rise as the percentage of sulfur removed is increased. Up to a certain point, therefore, the costs of removing sulfur from any given source are less than the charge, and it is cheaper for the firm to remove the sulfur than to pay the fee; beyond that point, it is cheaper to pay the fee than to remove the sulfur. The costs of removal for each firm, compared to the size of the fee, will therefore determine the percentage of sulfur which that firm will find it profitable to remove. Firms that can control sulfur relatively cheaply will clean up more and pay less in the way of fees, while firms with higher control costs will clean up less and pay more in the way of fees. This approach secures a given level of cleanup with the minimum commitment of resources for control, exactly because the costs of additional cleanup for all sources (the marginal cost) is equalized. Effluent fees accordingly appear to offer the advantage of decentralizing cleanup decisions (which reduces government's administrative costs and controls) in a way that guarantees that the costs to society of cleanup are minimized.

FEES VERSUS REGULATION. In contrast, the regulatory approach at first glance seems much less attractive. It requires that rules be promulgated to govern the behavior of all waste sources, thus centralizing the burden of decisionmaking. Furthermore, desires for administrative simplicity and equality of treatment tend to produce inefficient regulations that require all polluters to reduce their emissions by the same extent, regardless of whether a firm's abatement costs are high or low. The resulting inefficiency can substantially increase the cost of achieving a given level of pollution control—by billions of dollars on a nationwide basis.

Why then have most environmental programs resorted to the regulatory approach? One reason is that fees entail some uncertainty about the level of cleanup that will be achieved unless (as is unlikely) polluters' reactions to a fee schedule can be exactly predicted in advance. Proponents of fees argue that this uncertainty can be dealt with by subsequently adjusting the initial fee upwards or downwards, as appropriate. But if polluters know that the initial fee may be in force for only a short time, their immediate response will not be representative of their long-term behavior. Furthermore, if polluters make significant capital investments (or other basic changes not easily reversed) in response to an initial fee, their responses to later changes in the fee schedule will be distorted in possibly wasteful ways. Thus, in order to be confident of inducing the desired level of cleanup, the fee-setting authority will have to know in some detail the cleanup costs of the relevant polluters; this necessity undercuts some of the claimed advantages of fees in decentralizing decisionmaking.[11]

Regulation, in contrast, appears to promise greater certainty in the level of quality achieved, at the price of higher costs due to its inefficiency. Moreover, in the heyday of environmental enthusiasm between 1968 and 1972, considerations of costs were apparently less persuasive than getting the job done. And no doubt the legal background of most legislators and the political gains to be had from cracking down on polluters contributed to the almost universal choice in Congress of the regulatory approach. Moreover, the appeal of fee schemes depends on the assumption that polluters will act to minimize their economic costs, an assumption that may be at odds with reality in many instances. For example, the managers of municipal waste treatment plants may not respond to economic incentives; and large firms with some market power may prefer merely to pay the fee, rather than reduce pollution.

On the other hand, fee schemes can make administration and enforcement more effective and less costly. Fee schemes provide a continuing incentive to control emissions, while typical regulatory sanctions encourage the polluter to delay and interpose legal challenges in order to postpone as long as possible the day on which he must choose between compliance and suffering a sanction. In addition, accurate self-reporting of emissions may be encouraged by substituting fee systems for regulatory controls, whose severe and discontinuous sanctions provide a greater incentive for manipulation of emissions data.[12]

MARKETABLE PERMITS. To the extent that policymakers are unhappy about losing control over output levels as a result of employing fee schemes, an alternative (never tried in practice) that promises

11. See Bruce A. Ackerman and others, *The Uncertain Search for Environmental Quality* (Free Press, 1974), pp. 262–69.
12. See Marc J. Roberts, "Environmental Protection: The Complexities of Real Policy Choice," in Irving K. Fox and Neil A. Swainson, eds., *Water Quality Management: The Designs of Institutions* (University of British Columbia Press, 1973).

the best of both fee and regulatory approaches is potentially available: a pollution control agency directly determines how much pollution it will allow to occur by issuing a specified volume of pollution rights and creating a market for their transfer so that potential polluters must bid against one another for the right to pollute.[13] This system confronts each firm with a situation identical to the one it faces with an effluent fee. Thus, marketable permits have the same tendency as a fee system to accomplish cleanup at least cost.[14] Moreover, a marketable rights approach would in principle be superior to fee or regulatory devices in dealing with economic growth and the consequent tendency toward increased pollution. With economic growth, regulatory and fee schemes will tend to lead to a gradual deterioration in environmental quality. Unless positive action is taken to tighten regulations or increase fees, the amount of residual material per unit of production will tend to remain constant as the amount of production increases, creating increased residual flows and reducing ambient environmental quality. In contrast, under a marketable pollution rights scheme, the total quantity of pollution emissions is itself fixed. New sources can enter the system only if they buy disposal rights from existing polluters. The allocation of the burden of increasing control, in the face of increased growth, is accomplished through market mechanisms rather than by potentially arbitrary bureaucratic determinations. The price of the dumping rights will rise as economic activity grows and those who find cleanup least expensive will clean up first.

But a marketable effluent rights scheme would not be appropriate in all situations. It could only be used where there is an appropriate number of pollution sources in any given ecosystem—neither too few nor too many; lakes and rivers with a few sources, or air basins with a few major industrial sources, are examples. Finally, a marketable

13. This scheme was first proposed by John Dales, *Pollution, Property and Prices: An Essay in Policy-Making and Economics* (University of Toronto Press, 1968). See also W. David Montgomery, "Markets in Licenses and Efficient Pollution Control Programs," *Journal of Economic Theory,* vol. 5 (December 1972), pp. 395–418.

14. Indeed, it is possible to combine a marketable pollution rights scheme with various supplemental fee and bonus programs to allow, in effect, a safety value if the pollution agency guesses wrong about the costs of pollution control. See M. J. Roberts and M. Spence, "Effluent Fees and Marketable Licenses for Pollution Control," *Journal of Public Economics* (in press).

rights system requires the same kind of intensive monitoring of emissions and enforcement as the fee or regulatory approaches.

Another difficulty is that an effluent environmental control program should respond to variations in ecological conditions (such as seasonal variations in river flows) since the harm done by any given level of emissions may depend on those conditions. It would be difficult to build such variability into a rights scheme, and supplementary regulations or fees for special conditions may be necessary.

LAND-USE PROBLEMS. The application of either fee or rights schemes, or of mixed systems that combine such schemes with regulatory features,[15] is limited to situations in which there are clearly definable sources of environmental damage that can be quantified and either taxed or precisely limited. This characteristic makes them applicable to residuals but not to the wide variety of land-use problems to which the energy system also gives rise—for example, whether or not to locate an oil refinery in a particular coastal region or where to route a high voltage transmission line. In such land-use contexts, direct governmental controls of the regulatory type seem unavoidable. Regulation may also be desirable because such decisions typically have important and often irreversible long-term effects that call for a careful case-by-case examination. The possibility and likelihood of conducting such assessments would seem to be enhanced when the government takes direct responsibility for outcomes.[16]

However, the mere fact of direct government responsibility for particular land-use and other environmental decisions does not assure that such decisions will be made wisely or well. Government bureaucracies are typically plagued by tunnel vision and tend to favor certain special interests, tendencies that may often lead to disregard of important factors. Thus, the Federal Highway Administration may overstress good engineering practices and cost minimization at the

15. For example, minimal levels of cleanup could be achieved by a regulatory mechanism. But having guaranteed a minimal level, it might be desirable to provide incentives through a fee scheme for polluters to control their wastes beyond the minimal level (especially where they can do so at relatively low expense) and to develop environmentally superior technology. A mixed system may serve such varying objectives better than either a pure regulatory or a pure fee system.

16. Though the proper roles of federal, state, and local governments are not easy to determine. In part it depends on the nature of the potential environmental damage, such as spoiling the beauty of a particular local neighborhood versus destroying a national wilderness area.

expense of environmental concerns; while the Environmental Protection Agency may, as its decision to take the lead out of gasoline perhaps suggests, pursue high-visibility policies that may not give adequate consideration to economic and energy costs.

ROLE OF THE COURTS. There are two basic ways in which the courts could play a role in the environmental area. The first, and most ambitious, would be the application of traditional liability rules of nuisance against polluters, whereby the courts themselves become, in effect, regulatory agencies. But because the comparatively strict rules of proof employed in such cases make it difficult to establish a causal link between a plaintiff's injury and multiple pollutant sources, victims of environmental degradation only infrequently bring court litigation directly against private firms to recover damages or an injunction. In addition, there are difficulties aggregating what are often the individually small claims of a large number of affected parties within the context of traditional court litigation. But there is a second role that the courts have increasingly come to assume: reviewing the actions of the various administrative agencies that implement environmental policy.

The right to obtain judicial review has been extended by courts not only to regulated firms but also to environmental groups and other beneficiaries of regulatory schemes who claim that the agency has not gone far enough in protecting their interests. The courts have also given environmental and other public interest groups expanded rights to participate in agency decisionmaking processes.[17] This expansion of participation rights and judicial review has, to a degree, improved the quality of agency decisionmaking and the agencies' consideration of all relevant interests. At the same time, it has given environmental and public interest groups the ability to delay government programs or projects and thus to enjoy an enhanced measure of bargaining power with the agency—a clear example of the substantive impact of procedural arrangements.

Energy

The same tools for implementing policy are available for use in dealing with energy problems, and their strengths or weaknesses often parallel their value in the environmental context. For example,

17. See Richard B. Stewart, "The Reformation of American Administrative Law," *Harvard Law Review,* vol. 88 (June 1975), pp. 1669–1813.

if the government chooses to try to improve the energy efficiency of new cars, it could do so by regulatory devices, such as mandating a given level of fuel economy for new automobiles, or through pricing mechanisms, such as taxing new cars with low gas mileage or increasing the gasoline tax. Most of the same arguments for and against the use of regulation and fees in the environmental context are applicable here as well.

However, the nature of energy issues suggests that two policy tools, laissez-faire and public provision, are likely to have an especially significant role. First, government regulation has in important cases artificially depressed the price of energy, producing excessive consumption, unnecessary environmental degradation, and serious resource misallocation. The appropriate remedy in such cases is not more regulation. Not only economic efficiency, but also (in most instances) national security would be better served by higher energy prices that reflected all of the economic and environmental costs involved in the production of energy.

Direct public decisions about production, which occur frequently in the case of dealing with water pollution and solid waste disposal,[18] play an even larger role in the energy area for two basic reasons. First, a large percentage of fuel minerals are located on public lands in the western United States and the Outer Continental Shelf; thus there is no way for the government to avoid a major and direct resource management task in the years ahead. Second, the massive scale of new energy technologies, such as coal gasification or liquefaction, may require a significant government role in providing capital for research and development and demonstration projects (or even various kinds of guarantees for the construction of commercial facilities). The appropriate balance between public and private capital and the proper strategy to be pursued in the development of new technologies are also questions of great moment in which the government as a direct provider of both funds and research efforts will be inextricably involved.

18. Public provision of environmental cleanup is especially attractive when there are important economies of scale or important economies in serving a whole area. This may well be the case in river basin water quality management or regional solid waste collection. See Marc J. Roberts, "River Basin Authorities: A National Solution to Water Pollution," *Harvard Law Review*, vol. 83 (May 1970), pp. 1527–56. There is also necessarily a large role for the public provision of environmental amenities, such as parks, wilderness areas, and the like, because no entrepreneur is going to be able to capture through prices all the gains to society from providing such amenities.

PART II. POLICY IN ACTION

The preceding discussion, dealing with the criteria for choice, the establishment of goals and standards, and the evaluation of alternative policy techniques, has necessarily been general in character. To use the general principles set forth in order to select a set of policy techniques in a specific situation requires knowledge about the problem to which the techniques are to be applied. Environmental and energy problems vary substantially in the number of firms involved, the kinds of technology available, the likely behavior pattern of those firms, the demand structure for energy and for related environmental amenities, the relation between increased emissions and the damages they cause, the nature of the ecosystems in which those emissions occur, regional patterns of land use, and so on. To what extent is reliance on private markets feasible? Are there many or few polluters? Are they such a number that would facilitate the use of market solutions? How difficult or easy is inspection in any given context? How do the risks of inefficiency balance against the risks of failing to achieve our environmental quality objectives in any particular case? How serious are the distributional issues in a given case? These are the kinds of questions which must be answered before a particular policy and the strategies for its implementation can be chosen. It is to a discussion of a number of such particular situations that we now turn.

Conserving Energy

Our previous analysis suggests that, given sound pricing policies, there are no grounds for alarm about the world's long-run supply of energy resources, the ascendancy of energy conservation as a political issue demands that the question be examined. Current energy prices, despite their recent rise, are in fact too low from the viewpoint of energy efficiency. This is partly because utility prices typically reflect only the average costs of supplying customers. Hence, when additional output is increasingly costly (as it is today), consumers pay something much below the actual cost of new supplies.[19]

19. For example, while some gas companies import liquefied natural gas at very high prices of over $2 per thousand cubic feet, consumers pay only for the average

In addition, under most utilities' rate structures, added purchases cost successively less; this can lead to large customers paying less than the marginal costs of providing service to them. Most important, utility prices typically do not vary with the time of day, even though the system becomes fully utilized only during peak periods. Since it is the expansion of peak demand that causes a need for new generating capacity, peak power is almost certainly underpriced.

Furthermore, energy prices still do not reflect the full environmental damages caused by energy production and consumption, despite the recent price increases due to the increased costs of environmental protection efforts. There are often health and environmental costs even when ambient environmental standards are being met,[20] costs that current energy prices do not reflect. Because of the political unpopularity of higher energy prices, such prices may inevitably remain somewhat too low, thus encouraging consumers to continue to overuse energy unless other conservation measures are instituted.

Alternatively, even if energy prices were correct, the decisions made by consumers might be so imperfect that conservation policies could be justified as perfecting otherwise flawed market choices. In fact, both of these arguments seem at least partly applicable to the United States in recent years. With energy prices both low and declining, consumers and business managers have not worried much about energy conservation. Nor is it obvious that such inattention was mistaken: it could well have taken more resources to make better decisions about energy consumption than would have been gained from those better decisions.[21] As energy becomes increasingly ex-

---

cost of all supplies—less than half that figure. Hence, consumers will use the more expensive resource even when it is not worth that much to them because they pay so little for it. See Thomas R. Stauffer, "Liquefied and Synthetic Natural Gas: Regulation Chooses the Expensive Solutions," in Richard E. Caves and Marc J. Roberts, eds., *Regulating the Product: Quality and Variety* (Ballinger, 1975), pp. 171–98.

20. For example, the emissions of a large fossil fuel power plant that complied with the new source performance standards could still adversely affect visibility, even where secondary air quality standards are not being violated. Energy Resources, Inc., "A Conceptual Framework for Analyzing Alternative Nondegradation Proposals," submitted to U.S. Environmental Protection Agency (Cambridge, Mass.: Nov. 3, 1975; processed), pp. 8–6 to 8–11.

21. In Herbert Simon's terms, the "globally rational" decision is an imperfect one. A decisionmaker, with scarce time, seeks for "satisfactory" not "optimal" solutions. See his "A Behavioral Model of Rational Choice," *Quarterly Journal of Economics*, vol. 64 (February 1955), pp. 99–118.

pensive, the interests of businesses and households will tend to change, and careful decisions about energy use will become more appropriate. However, it takes time for old habits to die out. More important, it is often difficult for energy users to acquire and evaluate relevant information, as studies of the unrealized potential for energy conservation indicate.

The most obvious conservation measures are those aimed at diffusing information to enable consumers to understand and follow their own self-interest. For example, the relative energy efficiencies of various air conditioners might be publicized, information about appropriate office lighting standards disseminated, or homeowners informed about the fuel savings from insulation and storm windows. On the other hand, it may often be too expensive to diffuse information and have consumers effectively utilize it; if so, regulatory programs such as performance standards for appliance energy efficiency may be called for. These and other measures aimed at directly limiting energy use (such as automobile mileage requirements) will be necessary if, for political reasons, prices remain too low.

Conserving Electricity

Given its rapid rate of growth, at least until very recently, electricity must be a target for any serious conservation program.[22] Rather than discuss in detail product-oriented conservation programs (such as a fee or regulatory scheme aimed at improving the energy efficiency of appliances), we focus here on two less well known policies that could be undertaken by the utilities themselves to lower both total energy use and the need for new generating capacity: lowering the generation reliability of the system and other various forms of load management.

RELIABILITY. The reliability of an electric system is a function of how often its customers must do without power. Because equipment breaks down unpredictably, no utility system can ever provide perfect reliability, so a decision must be made on how much reliability

22. While overall energy use has increased at a rate of 3½ percent in recent years, until the last two years national electricity use has been growing at closer to 7 percent, reflecting the steady conversion from other sources to energy provided in the form of electricity. In the last two years, however, total electric output has grown very little, given the combined impact of higher prices and poor economic conditions. See U.S. Federal Power Commission, News Release 22392, June 1, 1976, p. 4, and FPC, *Electric Power Statistics, December 1974* (Government Printing Office, 1975), table 14, p. 14.

to provide. How should the increased probability of customer inconvenience be weighed against the economic and land-use costs of building added reserve generating capacity to take over when other equipment fails?

There are at least three reasons for suspecting that U.S. utilities have tended to overinvest in generating plants and hence in reliability. First, under public utility regulation (which allows a given rate of return on assets) utility management must increase the rate base in order to increase total profits. Providing higher reliability by constructing more plants tends to accomplish just that. Second, utility managers have every personal reason to value reliability since system failures can result in personal pressure from the press and within their own organizations. Third, the generation planning in most electric utilities is done by professional engineers whose training emphasizes the importance of technical performance and system reliability.

Until very recently electric utilities made decisions about reliability levels on the basis of very simple targets and rules of thumb.[23] In recent years formal mathematical methods (such as "loss of load probability") have been developed for estimating how often electric utility systems with different generating resources and demand patterns will not have enough capacity. These methods, while still imperfect, represent a major improvement and generally suggest the need for lower reserve requirements than did the old rules. Reserve requirements have diminished as systems have grown in size and in the number of their generating facilities and as reduced costs for transmission have made interconnection of systems over wide areas economically advantageous. However, the reliability of American utilities is still too high.[24] We believe that better planning processes,

23. For example, some companies planned on having some specific percentage of peak load demand available as a reserve, or insisted on having reserves equal to the one or two largest "risks" in the system (a risk is either a generating unit or a transmission line which could fail as a discrete unit). See, for example, Western Systems Coordinating Council, "Reply to Federal Power Commission Docket R-362—Reliability and Adequacy of Electric Service" (Montrose, Colorado: The Council, April 1, 1976; processed), pp. 3–32 to 3–35.

24. American utilities today typically plan enough plants so that only on one day in every ten years will generating capacity be insufficient—a quite conservative planning target in view of the much lower reliability levels achieved by the transmission and distribution system. Michael L. Telson, "The Economics of Alternative Levels of Reliability for Electric Power Generation Systems," *Bell Journal of Economics,* vol. 6 (Autumn 1975), pp. 679–94. Furthermore, planning is often based on very conservative assumptions about whether or not power will be available from neighboring companies, which in practice it often is.

coupled with sophisticated analysis of the social costs and benefits of various reliability levels, could significantly lower the number of new generating plants and yield substantial economic and land-use savings. The need for additional capacity could also be reduced by strengthening the interconnections among different areas of the country, so that surplus power could be more easily shifted from one area to another. Furthermore, utility systems should be encouraged to arrange for joint operation as a single system for power dispatching purposes, thus pooling capacity.[25] This can further lower the need for reserve capacity to achieve any given reliability level, thus producing additional economic savings and environmental benefits.

LOAD MANAGEMENT. The need for new generating capacity is also tied closely to increases in the peak demand on a system since additional demands at other times can be accommodated by idle generating capacity. Insofar as electric utilities can lower peak demand and spread electricity use more evenly over the day, total power requirements can be satisfied with less generating capacity, which in turn reduces environmental and economic costs.[26]

One approach to reshaping demand patterns is to vary the price of electricity by time of day and season of the year, charging more when the system is experiencing peak demands. Some such variations have been widely employed. Many utilities have summer-winter differentials, while others have offered special off-peak rates for specific uses, such as household water heating. But no U.S. utilities widely use time-of-day pricing for a whole class of customers.[27]

25. This has been done in the New England Power Exchange, but unfortunately the companies have not made corresponding curtailments in new capacity investment so the region still has one of the highest reserve margins in the country. For example, in 1975, the region had a reserve margin of 53 percent. See NEPLAN, *New England Load and Capacity Report* (Westborough, Mass.: NEPLAN, April 1975).

26. Not all utilities have the same load curves. Some have summer peaks and others winter peaks, depending on the relative role of air conditioning and heating demands. Reshaping a utility's load curve also will affect the type of generating plants built, since base load plants, designed to run all the time, are different from peaking units run for only an hour or so, and from mid-range units that have an intermediate pattern of operation. Thus, flattening the load curve could increase the need for base load capacity while lowering the need for peak capacity. See John T. Wenders, "The Misapplication of the Theory of Peak-load Pricing to the Electric Utility Industry," *Public Utilities Fortnightly,* vol. 96 (Dec. 4, 1975), pp. 22–27.

27. Unlike France, where large industrial customers have for years been charged according to a tariff that makes special assessments for daily peak load demands. Marcel Boiteux, "The 'Tarif Vert' of Electricité de France," in James R. Nelson, ed., *Marginal Cost Pricing in Practice* (Prentice-Hall, 1964), pp. 127–49. And in England and Germany, special daily off-peak rates are available to selected residential customers.

Recently, interest in such peak-load pricing—a technique long advocated by economists—has revived in the United States. Public utility commissions in several states, concerned about rising rates, have encouraged companies to undertake experiments with such rate structures. Preliminary results from one of those, the Green Mountain Power Corporation in Vermont, does suggest substantial consumer responses (although the study is open to several methodological objections). Particularly for large industrial customers, who often already have sophisticated metering systems and may have substantial capacity to readjust their electric utility use, peak-load pricing seems very much in the public interest, for both energy and environmental reasons. Other methods can also be used to try to control peak demands. For example, in Europe use has been made of "ripple control" systems, which allow a central office to turn various customers or specific devices on or off.[28]

Conserving Energy Demand in the Transportation Sector

The transportation sector of the economy accounts for approximately 25 percent of total domestic energy consumption, three-quarters of that from motor vehicles. The exclusive dependence of motor vehicles on liquid petroleum is especially significant in view of dwindling domestic supplies, increased imports, and the potential environmental consequences of offshore drilling (the source of much of the remaining U.S. reserve). Insofar as reducing oil imports is accepted as an important foreign policy goal, lowering petroleum use by motor vehicles surely becomes a central policy objective, which could have significant environmental benefits.

GASOLINE: PRICES AND TAXES. Automobile energy use depends on miles per gallon and on the total number of vehicle miles driven. Recent gasoline price increases have had a salutary effect on both. New U.S. automobile models are available with dramatically in-

28. The system works by sending low-frequency signals out over the same wires as the electricity. In Finland, for example, ripple controls are utilized to cut down on the winter electric heating peak. Calculations as to heat losses in various buildings have been made; during peak demand hours selected customers are shut off for specified periods that can be tolerated without injurious temperature declines. See Antero Johkda and Heikki Teittinen, "Effect of Offpeak Direct Electric Heating on the Fluctuation and Costs of Power Supply and Indoor Comfort," *Sahko*, vol. 44 (July–August 1971), pp. 181–88. Similar techniques could be profitably applied in the United States, again with land-use and economic gains. Another device is a special switch that disconnects all current when the subscriber uses more than a prescribed total amount. This forces customers to schedule their electricity usage more evenly, and thus limits their contribution to peak demand.

creased fuel economy, while the growth trend in automotive vehicle miles has leveled off.[29] Unfortunately, Congress has enacted price controls that keep the present price of gasoline artificially low, help discourage new exploration, and also may explain the current increase in purchases of larger new car models.

As a first step Congress should repeal the regulations on the pricing of domestic crude oil that have artificially depressed the price of gasoline. It may perhaps be possible to offset some of the adverse distributional consequences of such a move by taxing oil company profits and using the proceeds for redistributive purposes.[30] Even the additional conservation efforts that such a move would stimulate, however, would be insufficient because the price of gasoline would still not fully reflect all the social, environmental, and foreign policy costs associated with its use.

In the short run, the only feasible way to effect a substantial reduction of gasoline consumption (apart from administratively cumbersome rationing schemes) would be to increase its price sharply through an added tax, which would also decrease pollution emissions. On the other hand, such a tax would be regressive and decrease mobility, especially for lower-income groups. This would make the extension and improvement of public transportation an urgent priority. We could also compensate for some of its effects by expanded welfare programs or through a refundable tax credit equal to the amount of the tax times a weekly allowance of (for example) eight gallons of gasoline. (This measure would, however, blunt the effectiveness of the tax in reducing energy usage.)

29. The size of the long-run price elasticity of demand for gasoline, which would deter the extent of gasoline price increases required to reduce demand significantly, is disputed. See, for instance, R. G. Adams, H. Graham, and J. M. Griffin, "Demand Elasticities for Gasoline: Author Views Discussion Paper No. 279" (University of Pennsylvania, Department of Economics, 1974; processed); Federal Energy Administration, *National Petroleum Product Supply and Demand,* Technical Report 74-1 (Government Printing Office, 1974); D. N. Dewees, R. M. Hyndman, and L. Waverman, *The Demand for Gasoline in Canada 1956–72* (1974); H. S. Houthakker and P. Verleger, Jr., *A Study of the Quarterly Demand for Gasoline and Impacts of Alternative Gasoline Taxes* (Environmental Protection Agency and Council on Environmental Quality, 1973).

30. It is, however, difficult to devise a tax that would recoup windfall profits without discouraging new investment. An imperfect approximation would be to impose a lower tax on the development and production of new crude oil than the equivalent tax on old crude oil. In addition, general redistributive measures financed out of the proceeds of such a tax would not exactly match the adverse effects of higher prices because some poor people would be more seriously hurt than others.

While it has sometimes been claimed that added taxes on gasoline and other painful measures to reduce automobile use can be avoided by expanding mass transit facilities, reliance on improved public transit alone is largely ineffectual in reducing automobile usage and gasoline consumption. Instead, the carrot of public transit improvements should be combined with the stick of gasoline taxes and other measures to reduce automobile usage. The effectiveness of such measures would be enhanced by mutual reinforcement, while the adverse effects on personal mobility would be minimized.[31]

NEW AUTOMOBILE TECHNOLOGY. In the longer run, we would make substantial gains by reducing the fuel consumption of new motor vehicles. Since only about 10 percent of the car population turns over every year, it would require a number of years for such improvements to make a substantial impact. The recent rise in gasoline prices has clearly had an impact on car design as well as on driving habits. And a further increase in gasoline taxes would provide added incentives for fuel economy. But if, as is likely, it proves politically infeasible to raise the price of gasoline substantially, additional measures to improve new car fuel economy would become necessary.

In the past, modifications of new engine technology adopted in order to meet requirements in the federal Clean Air Act for reducing automotive pollutants had a substantially adverse impact on fuel economy. For example, the approximately two-thirds reduction from 1967 to 1974 in hydrocarbons and carbon monoxide emitted by new motor vehicles was achieved through modifications of the basic internal combustion engine that produced a fuel penalty of 14 percent for intermediate and standard sized cars.[32] The widespread introduction of catalytic converters in 1975 model year cars permitted a retuning of new car engines that eliminated much of this penalty (though the oxidizing catalyst does cause additional environmental problems by generating sulfur compounds whose extent and hazard are still unclear).

In the next five to ten years it should be possible to develop other

31. See Bruce F. Goeller and others, *San Diego Clean Air Project: Summary Report* (Rand Corporation, 1973); Goeller and others, *Strategy Alternatives for Oxidant Control in the Los Angeles Air Quality Control Region* (Rand Corporation, 1973).

32. Frank P. Grad and others, *The Automobile and the Regulation of Its Impact on the Environment* (University of Oklahoma Press, 1975), pp. 125, 133.

new automotive technologies that will both reduce automotive pollutants and deliver improved fuel economy.[33] However, the technical
conservatism of domestic manufacturers has thus far precluded any
major shift toward new technologies. The federal Clean Air Act
amendments of 1970, which require 90 percent reduction in automotive pollutants on a five- to six-year timetable, with a fine of
$10,000 for each car manufactured that did not achieve such reduc-
tions, has reinforced this conservatism. And by calling for immediate
reductions, such a scheme practically forced the manufacturers to
tinker with the existing internal combustion engine because there was
insufficient time to develop and tool up a new engine technology. On
the other hand, the $10,000 per car penalty lacks ultimate credibility
because applying it on a broad scale could shut down a major sector
of the U.S. economy. Hence the deadlines for achieving 90 percent
reductions have been repeatedly extended in response to plausible
claims by many manufacturers that a workable technology to meet the
deadlines was not available. The ultimate noncredibility of the
$10,000 penalty, and the fact that a firm producing a car whose emis-
sions are much lower than the uniform regulatory level receives no
advantage from superior environmental performance (and may even
be penalized if his car is more expensive as a result), mean that
domestic auto manufacturers have little incentive to invest in a four-
or five-year effort to develop and tool up an environmentally superior
technology.[34]

To encourage more technical innovation we should also seriously
consider amending the Clean Air Act to substitute a system of emission fees for pollution from new motor vehicles in place of the current rigid regulatory approach.[35] The fees calculated on the estimated
emissions from a car over its useful life could (especially if they were
fixed for a period of years) allow manufacturers greater flexibility in

33. Examples include the stratified charge engine, a three way catalyst with
sensitive carburetor feedback mechanisms, the diesel engine, and, in the longer run,
the Rankine cycle engine similar in principle to the old Stanley Steamer but with up-
to-date performance characteristics. See ibid., chap. 7.

34. Furthermore, the stringent nitrogen oxide emissions standard in the act,
whose achievement has been postponed by Congress, could, if enforced, inhibit the
use of some new and efficient technologies. Since there is evidence that this standard
is unnecessary to the achievement of acceptable levels of air quality in all but a few
cities, relaxing it may well be appropriate.

35. See, for example, Henry D. Jacoby and John Steinbruner, *Clearing the Air:
Federal Policy on Automotive Emissions Control* (Ballinger, 1973).

timing and provide sustained, credible incentives to invest in stable control technologies that would also be energy efficient.[36]

Improved fuel economy could also be achieved through encouraging the purchase of smaller cars, decreasing the weight of automobiles, making the use of radial tires standard, streamlining, and developing a continuously variable transmission. These changes together could lift the average fuel economy of automobiles from its current level of approximately 14 miles per gallon to 30 miles per gallon or more, ultimately yielding a dramatic reduction in petroleum consumption.[37] Legislation has been introduced in Congress to mandate by regulation improvements in the average fuel economy achieved by the new car fleet of each manufacturer. However, experience in controlling air pollution from new cars suggests that a regulatory approach may involve unnecessary and even counterproductive rigidities, and that it might be preferable to impose a fee on new cars that would vary inversely with the fuel economy they achieve.

While it reduces energy demand, improved fuel economy also makes driving cheaper and increases automobile use, an effect that partially offsets the energy saving of increased efficiency. Accordingly, it may be necessary to maintain a gasoline tax designed to discourage driving as part of an overall policy package for the energy-environment problems caused by automobiles.

In the longer run (say, beyond twenty-five years) it could prove necessary to provide substitutes for domestic petroleum as an energy source for motor vehicles. Some alternatives, like oil shale or coal liquefaction, while technically possible, pose formidable economic and environmental problems. A more radical approach would be

36. It has also been suggested that fees be imposed not at the time of sale but annually, and on motor vehicle owners based on the emissions characteristics of their vehicles and on the mileage driven. Such a measure would not only provide incentives to purchase low-pollution vehicles, but would encourage owners to maintain the pollution control devices on their vehicles and, in the case of older cars, to install additional control devices. However, testing machinery to measure emissions accurately is cumbersome and expensive, and most states do not have existing safety inspection systems to which such a program could easily be connected. In addition, such a fee system would be more regressive than one imposed on new cars since the poor buy relatively more used cars (although used car prices might also readjust since taxes on new vehicles will raise the demand for older ones). See, for example, Donald N. Dewees, *Economics and Public Policy: The Automobile Pollution Case* (M.I.T. Press, 1975), pp. 138–39.

37. See Sorrel Wildhorn and others, *How to Save Gasoline: Public Policy Alternatives for the Automobile* (Rand Corporation, 1974).

expanded use of battery cars, which would themselves be emission free. While such an approach would shift environmental consequences to the generating plants required to produce the electricity to run them, it may be easier to impose effective controls on a few large generating units and also preferable, from a health perspective, to be able to have the emissions occur away from population centers. Given Detroit's record in technological innovation, however, a strong federal role would be required to develop a battery car with reasonable performance and cost.

Cost Effectiveness in Meeting Environmental Standards

It is too frequently assumed that meeting energy objectives must necessarily entail a sacrifice of environmental goals. Sometimes this is true, but there is also substantial evidence that in many areas it is possible to modify programs so that existing environmental goals can be achieved more efficiently and energy objectives met without sacrifice of environmental quality.

Existing federal environmental statutes were adopted when the dominant concern was for swift and effective changes in the ominous trend of environmental degradation. The unnecessarily crude or expensive approaches that were first chosen can now be improved in a number of cost-saving ways.

Improving Air Quality

The federal Clean Air Act amendments mandate achievement of nationally uniform ambient air quality standards[38] for various pollutants within relatively tight statutory deadlines. The basic burden rests on the state governments to devise implementation plans that include emission limitations on individual existing stationary sources designed to ensure achievement of these ambient air quality standards. In addition, new stationary sources and new automobiles are subject to emission limitations set on a nationally uniform basis by

38. Ambient standards prescribe the permissible amounts of pollution in the air or water—for example, so many micrograms of sulfur dioxide per cubic meter of air—with a view to preventing adverse health or ecological effects that would result from excessive concentrations. Emission limitations (sometimes called source performance standards) limit the amount that may be discharged into the air or water from a given source of pollution. They are an indispensable first step in reducing total pollution in order to meet ambient standards.

the federal government. States are precluded from regulating emissions of new cars, but may control old-car emissions either through the retrofit of control devices or through transportation controls, such as limiting access in certain areas, preferential bus lanes, car pooling incentives, and the like. They may also require new stationary sources to install controls more effective than federal standards prescribe.

Unfortunately, the state implementation plans filed under the act do not give much attention to the goals of energy conservation or of achieving the standards at the least possible cost. In part, this is attributable to the structure of the Clean Air Act. Tight time deadlines and poor information led regulators to adopt crude rules that promised to meet objectives without much concern for costs. In addition, the statute seriously limits the efficient control of a given pollutant by subjecting different sources that emit the same pollutant to different regulatory schemes that are not coordinated to ensure cost-effective achievement of environmental goals.

Least-cost pollution abatement in a given ecosystem requires that emissions be limited more severely from those sources that can do so relatively cheaply. To those affected, such differential limits appear inequitable. Moreover, to set the appropriate limits, the regulatory agency has to know the widely differing costs of control faced by each source. Air pollution, therefore, would seem to provide an ideal arena for market incentives, rather than rule-setting, for environmental control.

In view of the lack of operational experience with fee systems, it is unlikely that Congress would simply substitute a fee approach for a regulatory approach. Since experience might help resolve some of the questions about such methods, it would be desirable to experiment with emission fees in limited parts of the country. Another approach would be to introduce fees gradually into a regulatory approach. For example, polluters could initially be required to pay a fee on emissions that did not meet applicable regulatory limitations, and then (on a phased basis) fees could be introduced on those emissions from a facility that was in compliance with regulatory requirements. Fees and regulatory limitation are not mutually incompatible control devices, and there are a number of creative possibilities for combining them to secure some of the advantages of each approach.

NONDEGRADATION. In recent months the clash between energy and environmental concerns has been particularly acute in the debate over nondegradation policies in air pollution control. In litigation brought by environmental organizations, the federal courts held that state implementation plans under the Clean Air Act amendments must ensure against "significant degradation" of existing air quality even where that air quality was superior to the nationally uniform air quality standards proclaimed under the act.[39] The courts instructed the Environmental Protection Agency to write regulations to ensure the achievement of this goal, a difficult and controversial task aggravated by the fact that the statute does not squarely address the nondegradation issue. In the meantime, Congress, under pressure from the administration, is in the process of developing more specific nondegradation legislation that largely follows the basic zoning approach finally selected by the EPA. Within certain designated critical areas ("class 1" areas, such as national parks, wildlife areas and refuges, and national monuments) only minimal degradation would be allowed; other areas would have lower designations (class 2 or class 3) and greater increases in air pollution (and hence industrial development) would be allowed.

This approach has been loudly denounced by electric power companies and other industrial interests, who claim that it would severely retard economic growth by preventing industrial development in many areas. They also object that it would introduce nationwide land-use planning in the guise of air pollution controls. Environmentalists reply that it is vital to preserve existing areas of high air quality and prevent the air quality throughout the country from being degraded to the same moderately polluted level.

The heat of debate has obscured the important fact that a nondegradation policy can be justified by two quite distinct objectives. The first is to preserve existing high levels of air quality in remote and underdeveloped scenic areas, particularly in the western United States. The second is to provide incentives to reduce the total amount of certain pollutants, such as sulfates, in the environment. We believe that there are alternatives to the present policy approach followed by the EPA and Congress that would better serve these two objectives.

The case for preserving existing high-quality environments is a

39. The Supreme Court affirmed the decision of the lower federal courts by a 4–4 vote. *Sierra Club* v. *Ruckelshaus*, 344 F. Supp. 253 (D.D.C. 1972), *aff'd per curiam*, 4 ERC 1815, *aff'd by an equally divided court*, 412 U.S. 541 (1973).

compelling one. Because environmental preferences and values are heavily shaped by experiential opportunities, it is highly desirable that governmental policies promote diversity in environmental qualities, including preservation of comparatively unsullied areas. It is appropriate that the areas of high environmental quality to be preserved be selected by the national government because such areas generate not only recreation and aesthetic benefits to those who experience them directly but also give satisfaction to those who favor preservation as a matter of ideological or moral conviction. And all of these benefits, but especially the last, accrue to citizens scattered widely across the nation. In addition, there is the interest of future generations in preserving unspoiled environments. The political process in any one state would not adequately reflect all of these interests.

However, it does not follow that there is a similar valid national interest in preserving the status quo in developed areas of the country where air pollution is not yet as high as the national air quality standards. Congress may legitimately prohibit increased pollution in Yosemite, but why should Albuquerque be prohibited from choosing more industrial development and somewhat higher levels of air pollution, so long as it stays under the national standards applicable to New York and other developed cities? The case for local diversity would be clear cut were it not for the fact that air movements transfer pollution from one region to another; this demands a concern about the total amount of pollutants emitted in the nation as a whole.[40]

The controversy focuses on the possible effects of sulfates—a term that encompasses a wide variety of airborne chemicals produced by the combination of sulfur dioxide and particulate matter. The problem is that even though these pollutants are subject to regulatory controls, emissions within legal limits can perhaps produce injurious levels of sulfates. Sulfates apparently aggravate cardiovascular diseases and produce acid rainfall that damages plants and alters atmospheric chemical processes. The available evidence suggests that,

40. Under the Clean Air Act amendments, the EPA is to promulgate primary ambient air quality standards that must be adequate to protect health with an adequate margin of safety and secondary ambient air quality standards to protect against "welfare" effects such as plant and materials damage, reduction of visibility, and aesthetic effects. The statute seems to presume that there is some point below which pollution levels are nondeleterious; but the scientific evidence is ambiguous and can be taken to indicate a continuum of effects beginning at very low levels, with no sharp breaking points.

due to the cumulative effects of discharges and the problem of long-distance transport, it may not be possible to relate closely the effects of sulfates in any one region to the discharges of sulfur dioxide in particular, and of pollutants generally, in that region. As a result, we may have to handle the problem by broadly controlling such emissions over a wide area.

Nondegradation policies do serve this general goal by prohibiting increases in pollution in numerous areas of the country, thus holding down the cumulative total. And it is obviously easier to prevent such increases from occurring in the first place than to reverse them later. But, despite these attractions, nondegradation is not the best solution to the problem of securing an overall reduction in total pollutant loadings. First, it embroils the federal government in land-use decisions that, for better or worse, are now accepted as essentially local in nature and with which the national government is ill equipped to deal. Second, a nondegradation policy does not in itself reduce total emissions, but simply prevents their increase in areas of the country that are already comparatively clean. By contrast, the health and environmental effects of sulfates are probably most severe in urbanized and polluted areas of the country, particularly the northeast, where the nondegradation policy would have less application. Third, nondegradation does not necessarily provide appropriate incentives for the development of technologies that could more cheaply reduce total pollutant loadings in areas where they are now a problem.

We suggest that a far preferable approach to the problem of total pollutant loadings would be imposition of a uniform emission fee on those pollutants, in addition to current regulatory programs. Such an approach would not only provide a broadly applicable incentive for reducing emissions but would also stimulate the development of superior control technologies. Finally, such a proposal, if limited to sources such as fossil fuel power plants whose sulfur emissions can be effectively monitored, would be relatively easily enforceable and provide a promising first step in the development of emission fee approaches.

Accordingly, we propose a two-pronged federal program to respond to the two disparate objectives underlying present nondegradation policies. First, the federal government should designate for protection existing areas of extremely high air quality. Beyond this step, the federal government should get out of the business of local land-use planning. Instead, a second basic measure to deal more feasibly and more effectively with the problem of total environmental loadings would be the imposition of a broadly based emission fee.

INTERRUPTIBLE CONTROLS FOR FOSSIL FUEL PLANTS. Another crucial issue of environmental policy concerns the methods that fossil fuel power plants must utilize to meet ambient air quality standards. Variations in meteorological conditions may require much greater reduction of emissions to achieve a given level of ambient quality when weather conditions prevent the dispersal of pollutants (for example, during inversions) than in other situations. Some polluters have argued that control methods that operate on a continuous basis (for example, through the installation of stackgas cleaners or low-sulfur fuels) should be used only to the extent necessary to meet ambient standards during favorable weather conditions. Under adverse conditions, they argue, polluters should be permitted to reduce operations temporarily or switch to cleaner but more expensive fuels to ensure a compliance with ambient standards. Such proposals for intermittent controls typically include the use of tall smokestacks to disperse pollutants and monitoring equipment and meteorological forecasts to predict adverse weather conditions that require the use of such controls.

The EPA has opposed such proposals and sought to require power plants and other large sources to install continuously operating controls sufficient to ensure that ambient standards are met under the most adverse weather conditions. Intermittent controls have been permitted only as transitional measures where continuous controls are at the moment prohibitively expensive. As a result, the EPA is seeking to force most fossil fuel power plants either to switch to low-sulfur fuel or install stackgas scrubbing systems. Such systems are relatively expensive, consume substantial amounts of energy (equal to 3 to 5 percent of the production of the plant), and have their own objectionable environmental residues (sludge). The EPA has adduced two basic justifications for its opposition to intermittent controls as a general solution.

First, it has asserted that such controls are unreliable, both because meteorological prediction is uncertain and because where there is more than one large polluter in an area, the responsibility for reducing emissions in the face of adverse weather conditions is not the sole responsibility of any one actor. These objections, in our view, are overstated. Meteorological uncertainties are also a factor in ascertaining the necessary level of continuous controls; such uncertainties are susceptible to analysis and allowances can be made for them in designing controls. And where there is more than one major polluter, the sources that wish to employ such methods could be made responsible for developing an operating system designed to fix responsibility for intermittent reductions in emissions.

The second EPA argument against the use of intermittent controls is that they do not permanently reduce the total pollution load but instead rely on dispersing it when weather conditions are favorable. This tactic would not in itself be objectionable if the dispersion reduced ambient concentrations to a level adequate to prevent any adverse effects. However, as previously discussed, emissions of sulfur dioxide and particulates that ensure compliance with present ambient air quality standards can nonetheless reduce visibility, and through the generation of sulfates, endanger human health, contribute to acid rainfall that injures plant life, and have other adverse effects. However, such effects are apparently caused by the total emission of pollutants over a wide area. Rather than insisting on rigorous controls in all regions where air quality is now somewhat better than that permitted under the national standards, we believe that the appropriate response to such concerns would be adoption of an emission fee that would provide a broadly based incentive for reduction of emissions and stimulate the development of superior low-emitting technologies.

Insistence on "scrubbers" in all areas where air quality is now better than the national ambient standards would entail substantial capital outlays, while the environmental benefits in many instances would be small, particularly when the problems of waste disposal and reduced energy efficiency associated with scrubbers are considered. It also would have the effect of committing a large portion of new industrial capacity to an inferior control technology. Over the next ten years it may be possible to devise totally new generation technologies, such as fluid bed combustion, or improved technologies in removing sulfur from fuel before it is burned.[41] These would obviate the need for the installation of scrubbers. In the interim, state implementation plans could be modified to allow sources to utilize intermittent controls or fuel with lower sulfur content on an intermit-

41. See, for example, Arthur M. Squires, "Clean Power from Coal," *Science*, vol. 169 (Aug. 28, 1970), pp. 821–28.

tent basis, subject to the pervasive incentive to reduce total discharges produced by the sort of fee system suggested above.

Water Pollution Control

Air pollution problems are the locus of the most acute interaction between energy and the environment. However, a brief review of water pollution control options poses some contrasts with air pollution problems that help to clarify some of our general points.

In the Federal Water Pollution Control Act Amendments of 1972, Congress largely repudiated the strategy of the Clean Air Act amendments, which tries to relate limitations on pollution emissions from specific sources to what is required to achieve certain ambient standards. Instead, Congress opted for imposing federally set, nationally uniform emission limitations on various categories of water pollution sources. One set of limitations ("best practicable control technology currently available") must be met by nonmunicipal sources by 1977, and a second, more stringent set of limitations ("best available technology economically achievable") must be met by 1983. The precise limitations are established by the federal Environmental Protection Agency on an industry-by-industry basis and are to be substantially uniform for all sources of a given technology, size, and age within each industry. No consideration can be given to the cost-benefit situation at any particular site.

Municipal sources of waste must achieve "secondary treatment" by 1977 and "best practicable waste treatment technology over the life of the works" by 1983. The 1983 limitations must be set with reference to a "national goal," stated in the statute, "that the discharge of pollutants into the navigable waters be eliminated by 1985."

Congress adopted this approach because it believed that the strategy of setting ambient standards first and then devising appropriate emission limitations to achieve those standards was too time consuming and offered polluters too many opportunities for obstruction and delay.[42] However, evidence is accumulating that actual implementation of the congressional program will be extremely expensive

42. Under the 1972 amendments discharges must continue to comply with ambient water quality standards established under prior law, but in most instances the technology-based federal emission limitations will be more stringent than the limitations required to meet such standards and hence will determine the required degree of pollution control.

—on the order of $600 billion to achieve "zero discharge"—and that the insistence on nationally uniform controls will in many instances result in large expenditures of resources with little or no gain in enhanced environmental quality or human use.[43]

We urge that the zero discharge goal be explicitly disavowed and that the levels of control required of sources be adjusted with a view toward ambient water quality goals and the use to be made of different waterways. The insistence on uniform emission limitations can be viewed as a form of shock treatment designed to force rapid steps to control pollution. This objective has in large measure been achieved, and the time has come to relate further control measures to environmental quality objectives. One method of accomplishing this without giving dischargers excessive scope for delay and obstruction would be to amend the statute to excuse dischargers from meeting the stringent emission limitations authorized by the current statute if they can prove that further controls are not necessary to achieve EPA-approved ambient quality standards, recognizing that where there are multiple sources, they will have to develop a joint plan to ensure that this requirement is met.[44]

In the longer run, water pollution problems represent an area in which some sort of centralized management, focused on the cost-minimizing achievement of ambient goals in a given river basin, has much to recommend it. A public basin authority, operating its own large-scale waste treatment plant or plants, would charge every polluter a fee to treat its wastes. Such an authority could also undertake measures oriented toward directly altering conditions in the river, such as programming water releases to keep up minimum flows, or adding oxygen directly to a river to support the ecological balance.[45]

Creating new institutional bases for basin management is even more important in light of several deficiencies in the way water pollution control programs have been conducted in the past. First, we have

43. See Ackerman and others, *Uncertain Search.*

44. Section 316 of the 1972 statute makes such a provision for single plants in the case of thermal pollution. Sources need not comply with uniform technology-based standards if they can demonstrate that a lesser level of control would preserve the local ecology. Of course, such a requirement can have many possible meanings in practice, depending on how it is interpreted with respect to burdens of proof, and so forth.

45. For an analysis of how this scheme might be even more effective in providing appropriate incentives than the more usual effluent fee systems, see Roberts, "River Basin Authorities."

relied very heavily on restricting pollution from clearly identifiable sources such as paper mills. Yet street dirt carried in rain-water runoffs, silt from construction sites, and nutrients from lawns and fields, may all be as important, or more important, sources of pollution in any given area. In order to develop and undertake programs designed to curtail such flows, we need an agency focused on managing the entire resource. Furthermore, our existing programs have focused very heavily on certain aspects of water pollution—such as the level of dissolved oxygen—that have been easiest for scientists and engineers to study and model but that may not be particularly important from the viewpoint of some major human uses (like swimming). One way to help redirect the focus of our efforts then, would be to expand the river basin agency proposal outlined above so that their responsibilities include not only water quality but also recreational facilities and programs designed to enhance the use of the water bodies in question. This dual responsibility might have the desirable effect of introducing considerations of human use and social valuation into the process of setting cleanup programs and priorities.[46] As Ackerman and others argued, it seems quite wasteful for society to spend significant sums of scarce money to affect the biochemical composition of an industrial river in a way that does not change its recreation value, and is a part of the river that is unappealing for recreation purposes anyway.

If, however, we are unwilling or unable to organize such new public entities, then the water pollution context would seem to be an ideal situation in which to use marketable rights schemes, at least for well-defined point source discharges. That approach would seem to be especially attractive in the case of thermal pollution. Neither technology-based standards nor state regulations allowing each facility to raise water temperatures by a fixed number of degreees (the current programs) are calculated to prevent undue temperature increases in receiving waters at the lowest control cost. What is required is a system that would effectively limit the total heat added to each stream (limits that are related to a waterway's particular eco-

---

46. Marc J. Roberts, "Organizing River Basin Authorities: Scope and Structure," Discussion Paper 174 (Harvard Institute of Economic Research, 1971; processed). Compare Ackerman and others, *Uncertain Search,* who suggest a variety of special purpose water quality agencies, each with a different mission. Of course, such an organizational amalgam does not guarantee efficacious policy where other financial and bureaucratic constraints intervene, as the limited success of the multifunctional metropolitan district commissions illustrates.

logical and hydrological circumstances), while distributing the burden of avoiding thermal discharges in a cost-efficient manner—exactly the situation that a marketable rights scheme is best equipped to handle.

Environmental Impact Statements

One of the most important policy innovations of recent years affecting both energy and the environment was the environmental impact statement process required by the National Environmental Policy Act (NEPA). These requirements have often been denounced as an unjustified obstacle to the timely development and utilization of energy resources. NEPA requires federal agencies responsible for implementing a proposed government project or licensing a proposed private project to prepare, and circulate for comment by the public and by other agencies, a detailed statement of the environmental effects of the project and of alternatives to it. Persons who believe the impact statement is inadequate can test its sufficiency by federal court litigation. NEPA has been denounced as at best useless, at worst productive of enormous delays, a weapon utilized by irresponsible opponents to block projects or exact unjustified concessions. Such criticisms were, for example, levied when the Court of Appeals for the District of Columbia Circuit enjoined an offshore oil leasing program for failure to prepare an adequate environmental impact statement,[47] and when the same court more recently enjoined the Interior Department's program for leasing coal on federal lands for failure to file an impact statement for the relevant region.[48] However, NEPA should not prove a long-term obstacle to development of energy resources. On the contrary, it should help to promote rational energy policies.

First, past delays are in part a product of the transition period, in which agencies began projects without the capacity to undertake environmental review. Yet now most federal agencies have learned to make their peace with NEPA and routinely carry out the requirements imposed by law. Unfortunately, the Interior Department, which is primarily responsible for the development of mineral re-

47. *National Resources Defense Council v. Morton*, 458 F.2d 827 (D.C. Cir. 1972).
48. *Sierra Club v. Morton*, 509 F.2d 533 (D.C. Cir. 1975), *cert. granted sub nom. Kleppe v. Sierra Club* and *American Electric Power System v. Sierra Club*, 96 Sup. Ct. 772 (1976); the Supreme Court has voted to hear the case.

sources on public lands, has thus far failed to make the necessary changes in organization and procedure to ensure regular and effective compliance with NEPA requirements. The fault lies not so much with the act, however, as with the Interior Department.

Moreover, adoption of NEPA-type procedures could significantly improve Interior's administration of its minerals policy. A recent General Accounting Office study found that the Interior Department's administration of its coal leasing program was almost totally inept.[49] There has been no overall department policy concerning the total amounts of land to be offered for lease or their location. The systematic analysis required in environmental impact statements of the justifications for the environmental consequences of agency action could, if it were undertaken by the Interior Department, significantly improve its administration of the nation's fuel mineral policies and help to ensure that leasing policies reduce adverse environmental consequences.

It is true that the quality of analysis in many impact statements is poor and their effect on agency policies uncertain, particularly where (as is often the case) they are prepared by outside consultants who are often anxious to do future work for the agency. And NEPA litigation (or the threat of it) may have been used irresponsibly on occasion by opponents of projects. But litigation is expensive; most environmental groups act responsibly in husbanding their limited resources. And while NEPA is sometimes productive of costly delay, such delay may be worth incurring in return for a procedure that focuses on the environmental pros and cons of proposed actions under circumstances that promote a broadly based and considered evaluation of the project's justifications. Since many of the decisions to which NEPA applies involve long-term commitments of resources (for example, power plants and dams), it may well be worth expending substantial resources in order to secure such consideration.

Trading Off Energy and the Environment

No matter how appropriate and cost-effective our energy and environmental programs, there will remain some conflict between the

49. Comptroller General of the United States, *Further Action Needed on Recommendations for Improving the Administration of Federal Coal-Leasing Program* (U.S. General Accounting Office, April 28, 1975).

demand for energy and environmental protection goals. Only with great caution, however, should we consider sacrificing environmental quality to expand energy supply, given the longer-run implications of such a policy. At any given point, the sacrifices in environmental quality may appear to be marginal; but their cumulative adverse effect over time could be substantial, both on the environment itself and on the values of citizens whose perception of environmental quality is influenced by the environments to which they are accustomed. Progressive environmental degradation over time runs the risk of fostering a cumulative insensitivity to such degradation that would lend a self-fulfilling quality to the prophecies of those who contend that the populace prefers a steady expansion of energy supplies at the cost of continuing erosion of environmental amenities.

Nonetheless, such considerations do not justify a flat refusal to qualify or modify present environmental standards. Our knowledge of the consequences of various forms of environmental degradation and the corresponding benefits associated with their prevention is imperfect. It is not unreasonable, therefore, to review our standards to see where they might be too high—those where, even in the longer term, the costs of meeting them at the margin are not worth the benefits we achieve. More important, a review of the deadlines that have been set for achieving environmental goals would probably reveal that substantially lower costs could be realized by the establishment of more realistic timetables, not only without sacrifice to long-run goals but, in some cases, with an increase in the likelihood of achieving them.

By the same token, in reviewing environmental standards we should be prepared to raise as well as lower them. In particular, there is a strong case for making further improvements in environmental quality and recreation opportunities in urban areas that are accessible to, and used by, lower-income residents. Such groups today often have the least access to high-quality environments, and special efforts on their behalf are needed if we believe that it is an appropriate social goal to provide some minimum level of environmental quality for all citizens.[50]

50. The notion that society should alter the distribution of a good or service to provide an acceptable minimum to all is already embodied in many areas of public policy (such as health, housing, and education). See James Tobin, "On Limiting the Domain of Inequality," *Journal of Law and Economics,* vol. 13 (October 1970), pp. 263–77.

A careful review will suggest marginal adjustments to accommodate energy concerns without undue environmental consequences rather than a wholesale revision of environmental quality standards. For example, if a stringent nitrogen oxide standard for new automobiles would lead to excessive fuel consumption, it may be possible temporarily to relax the standard and postpone scheduled achievement of current ambient standards in a few cities. Alternatively, automobiles in highly polluted areas could be required to maintain more stringent controls, while those used in less polluted areas could be allowed to have less stringent and more energy-efficient engines (instituting stricter controls on stationary sources of nitrogen oxide where appropriate).

In making these trade-off decisions, we must consider the relation between additional amounts of environmental degradation (emissions or land disruption) and the damage they cause. Such relations (called damage functions) do not all have the same shape. At some points, the impact at the margin of additional emissions or land disruption decreases as environmental damage grows because a given increment of degradation often does more harm when it occurs in a very clean ecosystem than in one that is already heavily polluted. For example, the addition of one power plant in the middle of Yosemite National Park would cause far more aesthetic injury than would such an addition in Elizabeth, New Jersey. In other situations the opposite is the case: a clean system can absorb some pollution or disruption with little damage until some threshold is reached and damages suddenly increase rapidly. For example, adding organic waste to a river can have little impact until the dissolved oxygen goes below a critical value, when some fish or other species will be wiped out. In still other cases, the incremental damages are constant (the damage function linear), and finally in some instances the system passes through successive thresholds, and marginal damages alternately rise and fall.

In deciding which standards can be relaxed, therefore, we should look for cases where degradation will cause relatively little harm (marginal damages are low and declining), provided we also consider what we gain by allowing such changes; even small losses in environmental quality are not worth allowing unless we gain significant cost saving or expansions in energy supply.

This analysis could, for example, help to resolve the question of whether energy developments (mining operations, power plants, and so forth) should be decentralized or concentrated in a few locations. If marginal damages are decreasing, there is more justification in concentrating polluting activities in already deteriorated areas. If, on the other hand, marginal damages increase due to threshold effects, then dispersing pollution in order to keep all regions below the threshold might be more advisable. In the case of western coal development or the location of nuclear power plants, for example, concentration would seem likely to prove less harmful than diffusion, since much of the social and environmental damage is caused by the initial development.

Of course, analyzing the problem in this way assumes there is some relatively easily observed and agreed upon measure of damage, which is often not the case once we move beyond physical indexes to the question of how people value various physical changes. And regardless of the shape of the damage functions, the political process may react far more strongly to concentration than to diffusion, even if the aggregate effect of the latter is larger. Among other things, concentrated havens tend to provoke groups to become politically active to prevent the project from going forward. Thus the political problems of working out apparently fair and acceptable compromises may preclude what would otherwise be an attractive location policy.

Trade-off decisions should also be influenced by whether or not the contemplated effects are irreversible. For example, if superior cleanup technology is likely to be available soon, we should be more willing to postpone investing in control devices, and to tolerate pollution emissions in the interim, so long as the harm that is caused is not permanent. Since heating a river by thermal pollution causes changes that will often reverse themselves when the pollution is ended, allowing such pollution is likely to be less objectionable than allowing the release of nutrients into a lake that will accelerate the unalterable process of eutrophication. Similarly, our willingness to allow strip-mining in various locations should depend on the extent to which the effects of such mines can be reversed by later reclamation. And when contemplating irreversible changes, we should pay special attention to preserving those areas that have special aesthetic and ecological excellence—recognizing that every area is unique in some respects and that this consideration is not a precisely definable constraint on development choices.

Another specific area in which we believe that these principles clearly imply some reconsideration of current practices is nuclear power. For various reasons, the Nuclear Regulatory Commission has imposed nationally uniform standards both with regard to radio-active discharges from atomic power plants and accident protection, and its prescription of more stringent state regulation has been sustained by the courts.[51] But would a detailed analysis show that such uniformity is really cost effective? We believe that some variations in routine radioactive release levels and plant safety could be allowed.[52] This makes good sense from an incentive perspective because the lower costs of less stringent controls will give utilities some reason to locate nuclear plants in more remote areas. Given both the prospect of growing energy demands—even if a conservation program is undertaken—and the health hazards of fossil fueled plants, we believe that the continual growth of nuclear power generation is unavoidable. But this can also be done in a way that is acceptable from a health and environmental perspective, provided that plant location and design and waste handling and storage procedures reflect the substantial hazards involved and make allowance for the inevitable imperfections of those who will operate all these systems.

There are other elements of current standards that seem excessively rigid and should be modified. A nondegradation policy that freezes existing air quality in all areas where it exceeds the federal ambient air quality standards is unwarranted; a flat ban on interruptible controls is similarly unjustified. Likewise, we should turn from the wasteful and inflexible technology based on the emission limitations of the Federal Water Pollution Control Act Amendments to controls designed to achieve realistic, cost-justified levels of water quality. In all these cases, less strict rules promise substantial economic and energy savings at very small environmental costs.

We are tolerably optimistic that it is possible to develop and implement policies that will satisfactorily reconcile and advance both our environmental and our energy objectives. But doing so will re-

51. *Northern States Power Co.* v. *Minnesota*, 447 F.2d 1143 (8th Cir. 1971), *aff'd mem.* 405 U.S. 1035.
52. Such variations probably imply more stringent rules for nuclear safety than currently exist in built-up areas and more relaxed rules in rural areas (though fears of accidents might prevent locating plants too near urban areas).

quire a level of political leadership and a degree of policy sophistication that has not been much in evidence in America in recent years.

Bureaucrats and legislators must avoid the temptation to make quick political capital by hunting for scapegoats on which to blame current problems. In that sense there are few if any culprits in the current situation, and our officials must be candid with citizens about the difficult nature of the choices involved and the necessity for higher energy costs. Only in this way will increased understanding of the interdependence of energy and environmental choices foster greater responsibility in public debate and political choice.

CHAPTER ELEVEN

Safety Regulation

NINA W. CORNELL, ROGER G. NOLL, *and*
BARRY WEINGAST

SINCE THE LATE 1960s Congress has enacted a number of laws
that expand federal intervention in private market decisions on matters relating to the safety of raw materials, processes, products, and
places of work. This legislation has increased the number of policy
instruments available to the government for dealing with safety issues
and has created several new government agencies with responsibility
for safety regulation. So dramatic has been the appearance, if not the
reality, of increased government control over product and worker
safety that these activities, along with environmental controls, are
called the "new regulation."

As used here, the term "safety regulation" refers to policies that
seek to prevent parties to private market transactions from taking
certain risks that they would otherwise assume. The distinction between safety regulation and environmental regulation is that the latter
involves limits on the risks that parties to transactions can impose on
others. In practice, the line between safety and environmental regulations is fuzzy since both attack many of the same problems. Radiation inside a nuclear power plant is a safety issue because it is hazardous to employees at the plant, while radiation outside the plant but
emanating from it is an environmental problem because it affects
everyone in the area, regardless of their employment or consumption
of electricity. Or a manufacturing process that involves the use of a

Part of the cost of preparing this manuscript was covered by a grant from the
National Science Foundation program for Research Applied to National Needs.

457

dangerous chemical may threaten workers if the chemical is released into the plant, consumers of the product if they are exposed to an unsafe amount of it, and people in general if the waste products of the manufacturing process are released into the atmosphere or waterways. Consequently, environmental, occupational, and consumer safety regulatory activities are not always clearly distinguishable.

The Scope of Federal Safety Regulation

Despite the recent burst of regulatory legislation, there is nothing new about government regulation of safety. The Food and Drug Administration is one of the oldest federal regulatory agencies; its genesis (under a different name) was 1906. Control of radiation hazards at nuclear power plants is as old as the technology, dating from the early 1950s.

The flurry of activity in creating new agencies and passing new laws has led to a dramatic change in the scope and emphasis of federal safety regulation but only an incremental increase in the number of items and activities covered by regulation. In most cases, federal concern predated the new regulatory law or the creation of a new agency. Some of the new agencies devote much of their effort to enforcing laws that were transferred to them from another agency. For example, the Consumer Product Safety Commission (CPSC), established in 1972, was assigned responsibility for the Federal Hazardous Substances Act and the Poison Prevention Packaging Act of 1970, formerly the domain of the FDA, and the Flammable Fabrics Act, previously administered by the Federal Trade Commission. In the CPSC's first two years, twenty-six of the thirty-one petitions that were granted by the agency dealt with inherited acts.[1] In some instances, new agencies were formed by pulling together offices from a variety of departments in the executive branch, as in the creation of the Environmental Protection Agency. Finally, several of the major statutes of this period are acts that amend older legislation dealing with the same class of problems. Obvious examples are the 1970 air and 1972 water pollution control acts and the Federal Environmental Pesticide Control Act of 1972, which are merely the latest in a fairly long stream of attempts to cope with these problems.[2]

1. Tabulated from data supplied by the CPSC.
2. For more detail on the history of air and water pollution control efforts, see Allen V. Kneese and Charles L. Schultze, *Pollution, Prices, and Public Policy* (Brookings Institution, 1975).

Although the proliferation of laws and agencies may not have much increased the number of regulated items and activities, it has certainly led to overlapping jurisdictions. For example, both the Consumer Product Safety Commission and the Environmental Protection Agency have jurisdiction over hazardous household chemicals, the former because of its administration of the Poison Prevention Packaging Act and the Federal Hazardous Substances Act, and the latter because of its concern with the disposal of hazardous materials. When the EPA forced farmers to stop using DDT and related compounds because of their environmental hazards and use organophosphates instead, rules were established to protect farm workers from the new pesticides, which are highly toxic. Both the EPA and the Occupational Safety and Health Administration had the authority to set the rules; they were finally set by the EPA because the OSHA's formulation was challenged in court.

Another consequence of recent safety legislation has been to shift regulatory responsibilities from the states to the federal government. The Occupational Safety and Health Act of 1970 converted what had been almost exclusively a state function into a federal one.[3] The legislation recognized the historic responsibility of the states by permitting them to submit plans to the OSHA for running their own occupational safety and health programs. The OSHA must approve state plans if they are at least as stringent as the federal program. Money has been available to the states for these activities on a fifty-fifty cost sharing basis. Because the states receive only 50 percent federal financing if they run their own programs but 100 percent if they "let OSHA do it," they have been reducing their policing of on-the-job safety and health. Of fifty-six jurisdictions entitled to submit plans to the OSHA and receive federal money, only twenty-two now have approved plans and the number is declining. North Dakota, Montana, New Jersey, New York, Illinois, and Wisconsin have removed themselves from occupational safety regulation despite having approved plans.[4]

A review of the OSHA budgets reveals that Congress indeed intended to make occupational safety predominantly a federal activity. Table 11-1 shows the budget submissions to Congress by the OSHA

3. One exception was the Longshoremen's and Harbor Workers' Compensation Act of 1927 as amended, which established federal job safety regulation for longshoremen (33 USC 941) by the Department of Labor's Bureau of Labor Standards. These responsibilities were eventually absorbed by the OSHA.

4. *New York Times,* September 21, 1975.

Table 11-1. Allocation of Enforcement Budget of the Occupational Safety and Health Administration, Fiscal Years 1973–76

Thousands of dollars

Level of government	1973		1974		1975		1976	
	OSHA request	Congressional appropriation	OSHA request	Congressional appropriation	OSHA request	Congressional appropriation[a]	OSHA request	Congressional appropriation (estimated)
Federal	23,285	26,241	24,939	29,891	37,171	41,040	48,050	52,653
State	29,975	25,000	30,080	23,000	46,000	30,371	48,500	35,600
Total	53,260	51,241	55,019	52,891	83,171	71,411	96,550	88,253

Sources: 1973 OSHA request, *Departments of Labor and Health, Education, and Welfare Appropriations for 1973*, Hearings before the Subcommittee on Departments of Labor and Health, Education, and Welfare Appropriations of the House Committee on Appropriations (hereafter Hearings), 92:2 (GPO, 1972), pt. 6, p. 454. 1973 congressional appropriation, *Departments of Labor and Health, Education, and Welfare Appropriations for 1975*, Hearings, 93:2 (1974), pt. 1, p. 438. 1974 OSHA request, *Departments of Labor and Health, Education, and Welfare Appropriations for 1974*, Hearings, 93:1 (1973), pt. 6, p. 894. 1974 congressional appropriation and 1975 OSHA request, *Departments of Labor and Health, Education, and Welfare Appropriations for 1975*, Hearings, 93:2 (1974), pt. 1, p 507. 1976 OSHA request, *Departments of Labor and Health, Education, and Welfare Appropriations for 1976*, Hearings, 94:1 (1975), pt. 5, p. 653. 1975 congressional appropriation and 1976 congressional appropriation, *The Budget of the United States Government, Fiscal Year 1977—Appendix*, p. 523.

a. These figures represent a categorization slightly different from the others and hence are not strictly comparable. The new scheme includes training expenditures for state enforcement officers as part of a category not covered here, whereas the old scheme included these as part of state enforcement activities.

for enforcement activities and the actual appropriations, broken down between federal and state activities. While the administration consistently requested more appropriations for state enforcement activities (where the federal money would be matched by an equal amount of state money), Congress consistently cut the amount slated for the states and increased the amount requested for the OSHA's own inspection staff. The final outcome of the federal appropriations process has been not only to shift responsibility from the states to the federal government, but also to cut the total amount spent on enforcement because the shift to federal enforcement reduced state matching expenditures. At the same time, federalization of safety regulation has reduced compliance costs of firms by eliminating the problem of trying to satisfy conflicting standards.

A similar shift in responsibility from the states to the federal government took place with the passage of the Safe Drinking Water Act of 1974. Until the passage of this act, the safety of drinking water supplies was a federal concern only when the water crossed state boundaries. The Safe Drinking Water Act made the safety of all drinking water supplies a federal responsibility. It requires that standards of purity be established by the federal government and that all public drinking water systems conform to the standards within a year of their adoption. Primary enforcement responsibility can be given to the states provided they establish procedures at least as stringent as those of the federal government.[5] Although the Safe Drinking Water Act provides 75 percent federal financing for approved state plans rather than the 50 percent provided for occupational safety and health regulation, the possibility of full federal preemption that has led states to abandon their own job safety programs could also lead to decisions by states to let the federal government assume total responsibility for determining safe levels of chemicals and bacteria in drinking water and for setting and enforcing standards.

Another effect of the new safety legislation has been to increase the number of regulatory rules and procedures that a specific plant or firm may face. Each law established different procedures that the responsible agency may or must use. For instance, both the OSHA and the FDA consider the presence of rats in a food processing plant an unacceptable hazard, the former because of danger to employees and the latter because of danger to consumers. If an inspector from

5. *Safe Drinking Water Act,* enacted December 16, 1974 (Public Law 93-523).

the Food and Drug Administration finds rats on the premises, the processor can be fined only if the inspector can convince the local U.S. attorney to prosecute and the case is won.[6] If an OSHA inspector finds the plant is not complying with OSHA regulations on vermin control, the manufacturer can be cited and fined virtually on the spot. Because of the overlapping regulations of the FDA and the OSHA, the same violation can lead to very different outcomes depending on which agency smells the rat.

The proliferation of regulatory tools is exemplified by the various actions that could have been taken against Life Science Products Company, the manufacturer of Kepone. Discharges of Kepone by Life Science into the public sewage system of Hopewell, Virginia, led to contamination of the James River estuary, causing large losses to the fish and shellfish industries based there. Unsafe production practices within the plant led to severe illness and disability for many of the plant's workers. Massive discharges of Kepone from the factory into the air worried those who breathed it because of its highly toxic character. Test animals have developed cancer on exposure to Kepone.[7]

At least four different federal regulatory laws are applicable in this case: the Clean Air Amendments of 1970, the Federal Water Pollution Control Act Amendments of 1972, the Federal Environmental Pesticide Control Act of 1972, and the Occupational Safety and Health Act of 1970. Only the last two laws could have brought federal inspectors directly into the plant in connection with the production of Kepone; the first two depend on there being discharge limits on Kepone or its components.

Although the Kepone plant was eventually closed by Virginia public health officials, three other authorities could also have acted. The EPA could have forced the company to register its output as a pesticide under the 1972 Federal Environmental Pesticide Control Act, which would have required the company to submit test data to the EPA on Kepone and its environmental effects. This would have given the EPA the right to inspect the plant to ensure compliance with the various provisions of the pesticide act. The OSHA could have

6. For an examination of FDA procedures and their consequences, see Melvin J. Hinich and Richard Staelin, "A Process Model of Food Regulation" (Virginia Polytechnic Institute, 1976; processed).

7. For more detail on the Kepone contamination from the Life Science plant, see the *Washington Post,* January 1, 2, 3, 4, 1976.

inspected the plant without advance warning and could have closed it under the "imminent danger" clause of the Occupational Safety and Health Act.[8] In addition, the city could have closed the factory by denying it connection to the sewer system. Before the discharges went into the James River, they passed through the Hopewell sewage treatment plant, killed the bacteria that digested the sewage, and thereby disabled the city's treatment facilities.

The federal government is obviously devoting much more attention to the problems of product and worker safety than it has in the past. This is evident not only from the number and extent of new laws that have been passed but from federal budgetary outlays to finance these regulatory activities as well. For example, the Occupational Safety and Health Administration, created in 1971, now spends over $100 million annually on federal regulatory activities that are for the most part new. Another strong signal that the impact of safety regulation has grown is that the new agencies and policies are extremely controversial. The business community, in particular, sees the new safety regulatory fervor as a source of major unnecessary increases in the costs of doing business and has said so repeatedly in congressional hearings and court appeals to regulatory decisions.

Attention to safety measures basically stems from two objectives. One is to ensure that preventive measures are taken whenever prevention is less expensive than the damages that would occur without it. A second has to do with equity: losses resulting from hazards do not fall evenly on the population, and it may be considered appropriate to forfeit some efficiency to prevent sudden drastic losses that fall on relatively few people.

Several approaches can be taken to achieve these objectives. In principle, at least, the government could choose not to intervene. The market, dominated by a principle of buyer (and worker) beware, would then determine the extent to which preventive measures should be taken. A purely market approach assigns responsibility for damages to consumers and workers, who then change their economic behavior, causing prices and wages to reflect the associated risks.

Several types of intervention can be imposed upon the caveat emptor market system. One is to establish a body of tort principles (liability laws) and to permit those damaged to sue for compensation on a case-by-case basis. A second is to establish a no-fault liability and

8. Public Law 91-596 (1970), sec. 6(c)(1) (84 Stat. 1596).

compensation system that would eliminate the need to prove responsibility on a case-by-case basis. This could be done either through some form of mandatory insurance or through a tax on injuries. Still a third option is intervention to increase the information available to those who enter the market, whether strictly caveat emptor or modified by the existence of some form of liability and compensation system. Finally, the government can set safety standards.

The Rationale for Government Intervention

The obvious and stated purpose of safety regulation is to reduce the incidence of death, illness, and injury resulting from unsafe products and work places. Presumably the decision to achieve these goals by safety regulation rests on two judgments: that in the absence of government intervention, products and work places will not be "safe enough," and that the most effective form of intervention is standard-setting regulation.

The first judgment requires an assessment of the likely performance of the purely private market system, even though, practically speaking, such a system has never existed. Common law has long held that one party to an economic transaction is accountable (liable) for some types of avoidable, damaging consequences of the transaction that are initially borne by the other party. Nevertheless, assessing the likely performance of a caveat emptor economy is instructive. If a pure market system produces less safety than consumers and workers are willing to pay for (in either higher prices or lower wages), there is a rationale for government intervention of some kind. Examination of the sources of this failure provides a set of performance criteria with which to assess the various ways the government might intervene.

The Pure Market System

Under a caveat emptor market system, any costs of accidents arising from products or employment would be borne by consumers and workers. If it were possible, at little cost, to obtain complete information about hazards, individual economic decisions would force prices of hazardous products to be lower, and wages for hazardous employment to be higher, than those for safer alternatives. The lower prices and higher wages would exactly cover the cost to consumers and workers of assuming the risks. If the cost to producers of preventing a hazard were less than they lost—in lower prices and higher wages —they could increase their profits by taking preventive measures. Thus, with complete and free information, a caveat emptor market would minimize the total cost of prevention plus compensation for hazards.[9] But since information is seldom free and is often incomplete, this happy result will not generally obtain.

INFORMATION COSTS. Information about risks is acquired in two ways: experience and study. The desirability of learning by experience depends on the nature of the decision and the extent of the risk. It is not very costly in the case of inexpensive, frequently purchased products whose potential safety hazards are minor. But experience is a costly teacher when it comes to expensive, infrequently purchased products that potentially can do serious harm.

Learning through study is an alternative to accepting the unknown risks of learning through experience. To learn this way, one must be able to acquire and understand information from secondary sources about the hazards associated with a decision.

Some kinds of safety-related information are relatively easy to obtain, for instance, from the publication of product testing results by consumer groups or from pertinent information on product packages. But a private market economy provides too little information about hazards. A firm has no incentive to advertise the potential dangers of its own products, especially when its competitors do not. Private testing organizations sell information about products to consumers,[10] but this is probably less extensive than is economically warranted. The costs of comparative testing do not depend on the number of people to whom test results will be disseminated. To avoid financial loss, independent testing organizations have to charge a price that will cover their fixed testing costs. The costs of publishing and disseminating the information to each additional person are

9. See Walter Y. Oi, "The Economics of Product Safety," *Bell Journal of Economics and Management Science*, vol. 4 (Spring 1973), pp. 3–28.

An additional problem of the unfettered market, not examined here, is that geographical immobility may prevent an effective response to unsafe working conditions. This is part of the rationale for safety regulation of coal mines.

10. To our knowledge, no private firms sell information to employees about hazards of work places. There is no way they could get full information anyway, without "planting" experts posing as employees in every firm.

thus smaller than the minimum price that must be charged if the testing organization is to stay in business. Hence, from the standpoint
of society at large, the dissemination of product safety information is
extremely restricted (usually to middle and upper income consumers)
since its price exceeds the cost of allowing one more person access to
it.

Because the private market supplies too little safety information,
a useful role for government would be to provide that information.
It could cover the overhead costs through taxes and charge only for
the costs of publication and dissemination. Alternatively, it could require that producers keep workers and consumers fully informed
about the hazards of work places and products as a necessary condition for doing buisness. The government would then assume an enforcement responsibility, checking to see that information was being
adequately communicated and spot-checking its quality by performing its own tests.

Unfortunately, making information about hazards available at a
price covering only the cost of communicating it will not necessarily
make products and work places sufficiently safe. More is involved
than simply acquiring a relevant publication or reading a more in-
formative description of a product. Once information is acquired, it
must be studied, and if it is complicated or technically sophisticated
the costs associated with understanding it can be high. If everyone
had the same tastes, income, and circumstances, a person who had
studied the information could pass on his or her findings to a large
number of neighbors and friends. An economy in learning about
hazards would result from this "delegation." And of course exactly
this occurs when a potential buyer of a car or a major appliance consults friends or relatives before making a purchase. Nevertheless
people do not all have the same preferences, are not all in the same
circumstances, and are not all equally capable of translating information, especially when of necessity it is highly technical, into practical
conclusions.

The formation of a regulatory agency is the ultimate form of delegation. One thing to be considered in assessing the desirability of a
regulatory institution is whether the costs it saves on information
generation and interpretation offset the costs it imposes because its
standards are not consonant with the differing tastes and perceptions
of risk of those it is trying to protect. Obviously, an agency need not
—and probably cannot—perfectly reflect all perceptions of risk and

tastes for safety. In some cases standards do not simply mean providing safer products at a somewhat higher cost because of the safety features, but involve banning products altogether. The benefits and costs to people of safety regulation will vary according to their attitude toward risk. The more divergent their tastes for safety, the less likely it is that the agency's standards will benefit most of them.[11]

The informational requirements for making a rational decision are more stringent than the preceding discussion suggests. Since many economic actions represent a choice among alternatives, an optimal response to risks demands that information be available for all the alternatives. For a consumer to evaluate the quality, price, and potential hazards of one product, the characteristics of other products must also be known. For this reason, requiring some producers but not others to provide information about the hazards of their products can actually be counterproductive. Without other information, a consumer might reasonably assume that an unlabeled product was of average hazardousness, or even less hazardous than average, on the grounds that the government had not chosen to make its producers advertise the risks associated with it. In this situation, the consumer might choose to buy unlabeled products and actually increase exposure to hazards. For example, requiring publication of information about potential radiation hazards of microwave ovens, but not about the chances of explosions in gas ovens, might lead to worse rather than better consumer decisions.

For the same reason, safety standards for some products but not for others will, if not related to the extent of the hazard, unjustifiably lead consumers to buy products to which no standards apply by raising the price of the products that must be made more expensively to satisfy the regulatory rules. Safety standards for automobiles, for instance, may raise prices enough so that more people will ride motorcycles; this in turn may lead to an increase in serious injuries since greater risks are associated with motorcycles than with even unregulated automobiles. Consequently, the order in which standards are promulgated or information requirements are imposed, as reflected in the priorities of the regulatory agency, should be based on the indirect effects of each standard on exposures to other hazards, as well as on the hazard the standard is designed to reduce.

11. For a more thorough treatment of this approach to understanding safety regulations, see Melvin J. Hinich, "A Rationalization for Consumer Support for Food Safety Regulation" (Virginia Polytechnic Institute, 1975; processed).

UNCERTAINTY. Complete information about the hazards of all products and occupations cannot be made available. If the nature of a hazard is uncertain, the very concept of a rational decision is not well defined.

In dealing with health and safety hazards the distinction between *risk* and *uncertainty* becomes important. Risk refers to a situation in which sufficient statistical evidence exists to allow a prediction of the probability that a particular event will occur. Life insurance companies, for example, can closely estimate the number of a given age group likely to die within a year. Uncertainty, on the other hand, refers to situations in which there is insufficient evidence to permit an estimate of probabilities, as in the case of the connection between exposure to some chemicals in the environment and the incidence of cancer in human beings.

Uncertainty covers several different circumstances. The least uncertainty occurs when a person thinks he knows how a system behaves, but has some doubts that the knowledge is precisely right. For example, even if extensive and reliable statistical tests show that the probability of a blowout for a particular brand of steel-belted tires is half as great as that of a blowout for a tire without steel belts, one cannot know exactly the advantage of steel belts for a particular set of driving conditions that was not included in the test.

Two other types of uncertainty are important in safety issues. One occurs when a person knows there is a causal link between a hazard and a damage but is unable to quantify it. Giving mice a massive exposure to a chemical and observing that in a short period of time the mice develop cancer establishes that a substance is carcinogenic. It does not establish the extent to which the carcinogenic effect depends on the dosage, the type of tissue exposed, the method of exposure, and the other features of the environment in which the dosage was administered. One may conclude that the experimental results make it more likely that the same substance in dosages comparable to human exposure levels causes human cancer, but the extent to which the likelihood has been increased is not even roughly quantifiable.

The greatest degree of uncertainty arises from the realization that not all possible causal relations have been recognized. As scientific knowledge grows, so too does the number of perceived relations between the environment and the health of human beings.

The history of the use of Freon and other fluorocarbons illustrates the progression of knowledge through the various degrees or types of uncertainty. Twenty years ago, the possibility that fluorocarbons, when released into the air, might destroy the protective layer of ozone in the earth's outer atmosphere was not suspected. The uncertainty was of the last type. As scientific knowledge increased, the possibility of a causal connection grew because laboratory experiments had shown that ozone depletion was possible. Today scientists are certain that fluorocarbons erode the ozone layer, but they are not certain of the extent of ozone depletion that can be expected or of the effect of the increased exposure to ultraviolet rays.

The literature on decisionmaking principles under conditions of uncertainty stresses the desirability of gathering more information that will reduce the amount of uncertainty and prevent catastrophic mistakes. Since the extent of uncertainty about a particular hazard, such as fluorocarbons, is likely to decline, postponing decisions, or at least avoiding decisions that are irreversible (such as consuming a known carcinogen) or extremely costly to change, increases the probability that future decisions will be more rational. And as uncertainty diminishes, past policy decisions will seem less appropriate. Consequently, flexible decisionmaking procedures, overseen by institutions capable of recognizing and responding expeditiously to past mistakes, and investment in research designed to reduce uncertainty will lead to better decisions.

These ideas add up to a plea for caution in dealing with unknown hazards. Instead of basing decisions on estimates of the expected consequences of alternative outcomes—an impossible task when probabilistic information is lacking—a more conservative course of action should be pursued. One commonly used behavioral rule of this type is "minimax regret"—that is, to adopt strategies that avoid the worst logically possible outcomes, thereby minimizing the maximum possible loss, no matter what the likelihood that the maximum loss will actually occur. The rationality of minimax regret is highly controversial, especially among economists; however, political scientists have produced convincing evidence that this decision rule is often consistent with observed political behavior.[12] If this behavior carried over into decisions about safety, it would engender a political demand

12. John A. Ferejohn and Morris P. Fiorina, "The Paradox of Not Voting: A Decision Theoretic Analysis," *American Political Science Review*, vol. 68 (June 1974), pp. 525–36, and Ferejohn and Fiorina, "Closeness Counts Only in Horseshoes and Dancing," *American Political Science Review*, vol. 69 (September 1975), pp. 920–25.

for controls on product safety more stringent than could be justified after the fact, when additional information would permit a conventional analysis of expected benefits and costs.

In sum, for several reasons people may be dissatisfied with the extent to which the private market system alone would prevent and compensate for damages from hazards. If these are the reasons for the demand for government intervention, citizens are unlikely to be persuaded of the folly of government intervention by ex post benefit-cost analyses showing that a safety policy generated more costs than benefits, since such analyses assume away the problems that led to the demand. This is not to say that safety regulation is always worthwhile; such a judgment depends on the absolute and relative effectiveness and costs of regulatory versus other forms of intervention.

The Liability System

Safety regulation focuses on preventing damages. A central policy issue is whether the problems that regulations are designed to prevent could be better handled by compensation after the damages occur, namely, by a system of legal liability.

The purpose of a liability system is not simply compensation for past damages. The possibility of having to pay for damages leads firms to invest in preventing accidents. Businesses can estimate the amount of damages they might have to pay under different operating conditions, compare these with the costs of different levels of prevention, and then choose the combination of prevention and compensation that minimizes their costs. If a businessman's selection of such a combination is to be the socially desirable one, the expected liability of the firm must equal the total expected damage arising from the firm's economic activities. Unfortunately, the liability system fails to accomplish this. One cause is damage costs that are not covered. Another is uncertainty about the extent of liability or damage.

LIMITS ON LIABILITY. The existing liability system limits compensation in several ways.

First, the maximum liability is the net worth of the defendant corporations or individuals. If a court awards compensation in excess of the net worth of the defendants, the normal consequence is a bankruptcy proceeding in which the plaintiff in the damage case eventually receives some fraction of the compensation awarded.

Second, common law sets additional limits on the liability arising from a particular action. For example, certain kinds of costs related to a hazard may not be recoverable. One cannot receive compensation for the time one spends in court litigating a civil suit, nor does one receive interest payments to compensate for the delay between the time an accident occurs and the time the liability judgment is rendered. Nor are the legal costs of initiating action covered. The liability system is very expensive to operate, especially when a case must be litigated. Court costs and legal representation for both sides can swallow up more than half the amount of damages, and it can be years before the case even comes to trial.[13]

Third, the total liability associated with a particular hazard may be limited legislatively. The Price-Anderson Act, for example, limits the liability of power companies for the damages incurred in an accident at a nuclear power plant. As with other factors that lead to undercompensation, liability limits blunt the incentive for preventive action by reducing the amount of compensation that might be avoided by prevention.

THE EFFECTS OF UNCERTAINTY AND RISK. Another failure of the existing liability system to provide appropriate incentives for prevention occurs when the costs and causes of damages are not known with certainty. For example, certain chemicals are known to be carcinogenic when inhaled, but not all people who are exposed to them develop cancer and not all lung cancer is caused by inhalation of any particular compound. Consequently, although it has been established that a worker who is exposed to carcinogenic chemicals has a higher probability of developing lung cancer than a worker who is not, to prove a causal link between the work environment and the state of a particular employee's health is very difficult.

The assessment of liability, damages, and compensation depends on both the burden and the standard of proof. The burden of proof in liability cases is upon the person claiming damage; the standard of proof is that a preponderance of evidence substantiate the claim that the damage was the direct result of a hazard that the defendant could reasonably have prevented. The standard of proof in liability law is less rigorous than that in criminal law—the standard of no

13. Department of Health, Education, and Welfare, *Medical Malpractice*, Report of the Secretary's Commission on Medical Malpractice, Publication 73-88 (GPO, 1973), and *Health Insurance for the Unemployed and Related Legislation*, Hearings before the Subcommittee on Health of the House Committee on Ways and Means, 94:1 (GPO, 1975).

reasonable doubt—but it is more stringent than the standard applied in the judicial review of decisions by regulatory authorities. In administrative processes, it is only required that substantial evidence support the decision of the administrator—that is, that a rational person could hold the same opinion as the administrator, based on the evidence at hand, even if the opinion were shaky.[14]

The liability system, by assigning the burden of proof to the person claiming injury and by establishing a standard of proof that tolerates some, though only a little, risk or uncertainty, leaves some damages uncompensated while it overcompensates others. To illustrate, suppose evidence indicates that the chances are one in ten that a particular hazard affected health. To give the firm appropriate incentives for preventive action, it should be liable for 10 percent of the damages attributable to the hazard. Of course, it is not within the realm of civil liability law to find defendants 10 percent liable; either they are liable or they are not, and when the probability is this small, they normally are not found liable.

Similarly, in some circumstances the system overcompensates for damages. The standard of proof that is applied leaves room for some probability that the cause of the damage was not the hazard at issue in the case. Suppose a particular hazard is 90 percent likely to have caused a particular damage and that this is sufficient to satisfy the standard of proof. Instead of awarding compensation for 90 percent of the damage (which provides the optimal incentive for taking preventive action), the legal system will award compensation for all of it. This is a likely eventuality in certain kinds of medical malpractice suits. One element of proof of medical malpractice is whether the doctor or hospital followed standard medical practice in treating a patient. While standard medical practice may be more likely to cure a patient than quackery, cure is not certain—especially in cases of critical injury or serious illness. Failure to adjust compensation for the risks inherent in standard medical practice leads to overcompensation. It also leads to disproportionate attention on actions to prevent malpractice claims, such as excessive testing of patients and undue timidity in using promising but nonstandard methods of treatment.[15]

14. Kenneth Culp Davis, *Administrative Law Treatise* (West, 1958), especially vol. 4, sec. 29.02.

15. See *Medical Malpractice*, Report of the Secretary's Commission, and *Health Insurance for the Unemployed*, Hearings.

Just as overcompensation for damages promotes too much attention to prevention, undercompensation leads to too little prevention. A rational business firm will invest in preventive measures so long as it expects the investment to reduce compensation payments by more than the cost of prevention. At some point, further damage-avoiding investments would begin to cost more than they were worth in reduced compensation. If the liability system awards compensation in amounts less than damages, some prevention measures, which could have reduced damages by more than the cost of prevention, will not be undertaken. Furthermore, the degree to which the liability system fails to provide appropriate incentives for prevention depends on a complicated interaction between the nature of the hazard and the legal requirements for proving damages. If the damaged party has the burden of proof, damages will probably not be assessed when the connection between the hazard and the damage, even though positive, is highly uncertain—the link between exposure to certain chemicals and cancer is a case in point. The more stringent the standard of proof, the less likely is a liability system to provide proper incentives to deal with hazards involving uncertainty.

An alternative assignment of the burden of proof would require the employer to show that the worker was not damaged by the working environment. Depending on how rigorous the standard of proof was, damages could then be awarded to workers whenever there appeared to be a connection, no matter how uncertain, between the damage and the working environment. But the amount of compensation, equal to full damages, would then be too high, since individual awards would not be discounted for uncertainty.

The workmen's compensation system offers an example of the effects both of changing the burden of proof and of limiting total liability. Workmen's compensation laws were designed to alter the liability system as it applied to accidents on the job. (It does not always cover impairment of health caused by long-term exposure to certain working conditions.) Basically, workmen's compensation laws reduce the standard of proof by eliminating the requirement that an employee show that an accident was "caused" by a failure on the part of the employer to take reasonable steps to remove hazards from the work place. Furthermore, the laws require that employers carry insurance to pay off claims that may arise under the program. Both of these changes in the liability system work to increase the amount of compensation paid and the amount of prevention that employers voluntarily choose, but their effect is lessened by the fixed upper limits set by workmen's compensation on the amount paid per claimant. Limiting the amount a worker can claim means there is less reliance on prevention than there would have been without the limits.

The existing workmen's compensation system is bound to lead to serious inefficiencies. The compensation that would give producers proper incentives for prevention is the expected value of damages, whereas the process by which damages are actually compensated is primarily a mechanism for protecting workers against loss of income resulting from accidents. The former principle requires that compensation be systematically related to the probability that the hazard caused the damage and that a particular damage actually occurred, whereas the latter principle requires that the focus be the magnitude of the loss of the damaged party.

To illustrate, suppose a work place contains two hazards to its employees: a chemical present in the plant that can reliably be predicted to increase by 2 percent the probability that a worker will die of cancer, and a particular machine that is known occasionally to inflict a minor cut on the arm of a careful operator. If a worker dies of cancer, it is quite unlikely that the work place caused it, but if the worker is cut by the machine it is certain that the injury is work related. Under the existing system, the first case would almost surely lead to no liability judgment against the employer, and the second would almost surely be covered by workmen's compensation. A substantially lower standard of proof than the present one would lead to compensation for both workers. Yet from the perspective of economic efficiency, both systems would provide a proper incentive for preventing cuts, but neither system would provide the proper incentive for preventing cancer—the former too little and the latter too much. The compensation system that achieved the proper incentive would award the heirs of every worker who was a cancer victim 2 percent of the costs associated with the worker's death and every worker full compensation for cut arms. Of course, compensation for each cut arm would be much smaller since the damages associated with premature death are normally regarded as being infinitely more serious than those arising from a minor cut.

The problem of adequate compensation versus appropriate incentives is made much more difficult if there are no reliable estimates of the probable connections between hazard and damage. Then a system of compensation that provides proper economic incentives cannot be devised. One must instead rely on appeals to principles of equity and on the likelihood that the compensation rules can be changed in response to new information. One criterion would be to assign liability to whoever is most likely to make the most efficient choice between prevention and compensation.[16] If a firm is likely to have more knowledge about the safety of its working conditions and products than employees and customers do, assigning liability to the firm will lead to lower information costs and a better choice between prevention and compensation than if workers and consumers were liable. Workmen's compensation, by lowering compensation limits, avoids the relatively high costs of operating the civil liability system, and by lowering the standards of proof, protects more people against capricious loss of income.

Although the liability system appears to be fraught with inefficiency, it is effective in some important circumstances. It does relatively well in dealing with events that have certain causes and that inflict damages that do not push against institutionalized limits to compensation. Its effectiveness is lessened by the costs of civil litigation, which makes it less efficient the lower the probable damage, and by its inability to deal with uncertainty. In general, it is more likely to deal efficiently with specific accidents than with subtle long-term health hazards.

Insurance

Another mechanism for dealing with damage costs resulting from accidents is insurance. The expected loss to each person from a hazard can be calculated by multiplying the probability of the event times the damage it causes. If each person faces a particular hazard, if the likelihood that one person will be damaged is unrelated to the likelihood that another will be similarly damaged, and if during a given period each person pays the expected loss into a common fund, in the long run the fund will have sufficient resources to pay all damages. This is the basic notion behind insurance. An insurance fund allows a large group of people to convert an occasional, large financial loss into a regular, certain, small cost—the insurance premiums. Insurance companies are profitable because people are, in general, willing

---

16. Guido Calabresi, *The Costs of Accidents: A Legal and Economic Analysis* (Yale University Press, 1970). See also Peter A. Diamond and James A. Mirrlees, "On the Assignment of Liability: The Uniform Case," *Bell Journal of Economics,* vol. 6 (Autumn 1975), pp. 487–516.

to pay slightly more than their expected loss so that they will be protected against an infrequent major setback.

If the probabilities of damage associated with various hazards are known, it will pay whoever is liable for the damages to buy insurance. Both liability and collision insurance for automobile accidents are examples. If employees could not collect compensation for work accidents from employers, insurance companies would probably be selling workmen's compensation to unions and other employee groups. Since employers are liable, they buy insurance. A better accident record can reduce an empoyer's premium, establishing incentives for undertaking accident prevention measures.

The extent to which the insurance system can go in promoting efficient accident prevention is nevertheless limited. If the probabilities cannot be estimated, there is no way to assess premiums of the appropriate size. If full damages are paid for accidents, those to whom the damages are paid—especially when serious injury is not at issue—have no economic incentive to take normal precautions against accidents. Employees may become careless; warehouse owners may not remove fire hazards. The possibility of such reactions to insurance, called "moral hazard," leads insurance companies to devote considerable effort to setting safety standards for places of employment that purchase workmen's compensation insurance. But individual and group medical insurance companies cannot—practically—monitor the behavior of each insured person to make certain that proper safeguards against illness and accident are being taken.

The Role of Regulation

The foregoing discussion leads to the conclusion that the market system plus insurance and liability laws are unlikely to generate sufficient incentives for providing economically warranted protection against hazards in at least two cases. One is when the risks of a hazard are either known or knowable but the costs of acquiring or understanding information about it are high. The other is when either the full nature of the hazard or the chance of its occurring are uncertain.

In both situations more information about health and safety hazards is likely to be especially valuable. Since the private sector normally has insufficient incentive to produce safety information, a central role of regulators is to increase the amount of information available by undertaking research, supporting the research of others, and imposing informational requirements on industry.

Once enough information is acquired, the agency has several options. The simplest is merely to disseminate the data and let people behave in ways consistent with their own tastes and attitudes toward risk. This will improve matters only if the information produced is relevant and can be obtained and understood so easily that people will use it. An agency could function as a clearinghouse for relevant product and process information: publicizing hazards as they become known, requiring that firms provide workers or consumers with information about the hazards associated with their activities, and maintaining communication with industrial trade associations that establish voluntary standards and practices. This will probably work best for products that are bought fairly frequently and for hazards that have a fairly high risk, for then people will have more incentive to use the information to their advantage.

If increasing information does not lead to economically warranted prevention, the difficulty may lie in the system of liability, compensation, and insurance. If so, altering this system may be more efficient in reducing exposure to hazards than standard-setting. One way of adding to incentives for making products and work places safer would be to increase the liability of firms, for instance, by lowering standards of proof, raising compensation limits under workmen's compensation, or imposing taxes on product- and work-related accidents.[17] Unfortunately, safety regulators are not empowered to take these actions, so they place excessive reliance on standards.

Standards can be efficient in two instances. First, when decisions are numerous and information complex, the savings in centralized information processing may be offset by the loss in efficiency that results if prevention is not based on informed, individual market decisions. Second, if the nature of a hazard is uncertain, insurance and the liability system can fail so badly that standards—if kept up to date—may be desirable.

Safety Regulation in Practice

The behavior of two major new safety regulatory agencies, the Consumer Product Safety Commission and the Occupational Safety and Health Administration, illustrates how safety regulation works in

17. For a closer examination of an injury tax, see Robert S. Smith, "The Feasibility of an 'Injury Tax' Approach to Occupational Safety," *Law and Contemporary Problems,* vol. 38 (Summer–Autumn 1974), pp. 730–44.

Table 11-2. **Budget of the Consumer Product Safety Commission, Fiscal Years 1974–76**
Thousands of dollars

Program	1974 congressional appropriation	1975			1976	
		CPSC request	Congressional appropriation	Presidential recommendation	CPSC request	Congressional appropriation (estimated)
Administration	4,350	5,410	8,406	7,635	10,103	9,738
Hazard identification	4,468	5,923	5,155	4,935	5,703	6,068
Hazard analysis and remedy	7,560	11,488	7,937	7,212	13,931	9,173
Information and education	3,410	5,054	3,685	4,736	5,922	4,459
Compliance and enforcement	9,224	14,944	11,436	12,077	14,727	12,382
Total	29,012a	42,819	36,619a	36,595	50,386	41,820

Sources: 1974 congressional appropriation, *The Budget of the United States Government, Fiscal Year 1976—Appendix*, p. 866. 1975 CPSC request, *Agriculture-Environmental and Consumer Protection Appropriations for 1975*, Hearings before the Subcommittee on Agriculture-Environmental and Consumer Protection of the House Committee on Appropriations, 93:2 (GPO, 1974), pt. 6, p. 1431. 1976 presidential (Office of Management and Budget) recommendation and 1976 CPSC request, *Department of Housing and Urban Development—Independent Agencies Appropriations for 1976*, Hearings before the Subcommittee on HUD—Independent Agencies of the House Committee on Appropriations, 94:1 (GPO, 1975), pt. 4, p. 408. 1975 and 1976 congressional appropriations, *The Budget of the United States Government, Fiscal Year 1977—Appendix*, p. 715.

a. Total appropriation also includes lapsing unobligated balances of $5,672,000 for 1974 and $335,000 for 1975

practice. The experience of these two agencies offers some basis for evaluating regulatory intervention as an alternative to the imperfect world of liability law and insurance. How safety regulation actually works can be seen in part by examining how the budgets of the agencies are allocated among various functions, how priorities are set, when and how standards are prepared, and how they are enforced. The central aim should be to give regulators the incentives and the resources to attack effectively the hazards to safety over which they have the greatest influence. This has not been achieved in the past, largely because Congress has an inappropriate concept of the problem of product and occupational safety.

Budget Allocations

Because the rationale for safety regulation rests in part on the failure of the market to provide sufficient information, the budgets of safety regulatory bodies might be expected to include substantial expenditures for producing and disseminating information, particularly in the earlier years of regulation. Examination of the budgets for the CPSC and the OSHA reveals that this is not so. Table 11-2 gives the CPSC budgets broken down by activity, and table 11-3 the OSHA budgets.

Ascertaining the preferences of an agency from the allocation of its resources is unusually difficult because the Office of Management and Budget, not the agency, submits a budget request to Congress. Only if the true preferences of the agency are revealed during its oversight hearings can the nature of the OMB revisions be at least qualitatively inferred. Fortunately for purposes of analysis, the CPSC, unlike other regulatory agencies, submits its budget requests directly to Congress, and the OMB submits a competing budget based on administration policies.

Congress and the OMB make two types of cuts in agency budget requests.[18] The first is program cuts affecting the level of activity (across-the-board cuts); the second, object or categorical cuts (removing certain tools available to the agency or changing the appropriations for specific parts of the program). The first type of cuts are related to fiscal responsibilities; the second to oversight of specific policies.

18. Richard F. Fenno, *The Power of the Purse* (Little, Brown, 1966). Fenno analyzes budgeting in Congress, but it is applicable to the OMB.

Table 11-3. Budget of the Occupational Safety and Health Administration, Fiscal Years 1972–76
Thousands of dollars

Function	1972 congressional appropriation	1973		1974		1975		1976	
		OSHA request	Congressional appropriation	OSHA request	Congressional appropriation	OSHA request	Congressional appropriation	OSHA request	Congressional appropriation (estimated)
Administration	4,024	3,546	3,719	3,530	3,530	3,967	4,265	3,877	3,973
Safety and health hazard identification, analysis, and remedy	2,220	2,800	2,983	2,955	4,355	4,939	5,640	5,153	6,747
Training, education, and information	2,294	3,294	6,517	3,491	4,491	4,892	8,911[a]	4,838	12,635[a]
Safety and health statistics	3,345	4,600	4,814	4,841	5,141	5,531	5,581	5,607	5,977
Compliance and enforcement									
Federal	16,793	23,285	26,241	24,939	29,891	37,171	41,040	48,050	52,653
State	7,781	29,975	25,000	30,080	23,000	46,000	30,371[a]	48,500	35,600[a]
Unobligated funds	...	...	99	...	...	...	6,198	...	...
Total	36,457	67,500	69,373	69,836	70,408	102,500	102,006	116,025	117,585

Sources: Same as table 11-1 (the 1972 congressional appropriation is from the first source cited in table 11-1).
a. These figures represent a categorization slightly different from the others and hence are not strictly comparable. The new scheme includes training expenditures for state enforcement officers under "compliance and enforcement," whereas the old scheme included these as part of state programs under "training, education, and information."

Table 11-2 shows the budgetary history of the CPSC during the first three full years of its operations. It began life on May 14, 1973, less than two months before fiscal 1974 began. Consequently, it had little influence on its first budget, which was put together earlier in the year from information provided by the FDA's product safety unit and thus did not reflect the perceptions of the CPSC on how the commission should be financed.

In both fiscal 1975 and 1976, CPSC Chairman Richard O. Simpson asked for an increase of more than one-third in his budget, arguing that the first budget could not be considered a "base." Congress did not see things this way. Senator William Proxmire, reviewing the CPSC budget request for 1976 in light of the 1975 appropriation of $36.95 million and an OMB 1976 recommendation of $36.59 million, commented:

The commission has the authority to submit a budget request directly to the Congress. That request is for $50,386,000, an increase of $13,432,000, or more than one-third over the fiscal 1975 budget. We certainly want to receive detailed justification for a budget increase of that magnitude.[19]

In general, the largest single budgetary item is "compliance and enforcement," which represents over one-third of the budget. This primarily finances the activities performed under acts inherited by the CPSC from other agencies. The second largest item is "hazard analysis and remedy," which refers to the resources allocated to the development of standards.

The appropriations figures show that analytical capacity does not fare well in the budget process. For fiscal 1975 the CPSC asked for a $13.8 million increase, a disproportionately large share of which was to go for standards analysis and compliance and enforcement. The final appropriations gave the agency an increase of $7.6 million, which was fairly evenly distributed. For fiscal 1976 the CPSC again asked for the largest increase for hazard analysis, the President's budget recommended a decrease of 10 percent, and the estimated appropriation provides an increase of about 16 percent. For enforcement in 1976, the CPSC asked for a 29 percent increase, the President's budget recommended a 6 percent increase, and the estimated appropriation gives an 8 percent increase.

19. *Department of Housing and Urban Development, and Certain Independent Agencies Appropriations for Fiscal Year 1976,* Hearings before a subcommittee of the Senate Committee on Appropriations, 94:1 (GPO, 1975), pt. 2, p. 817.

As Chairman Simpson put it:

Such a reduction [in analytical capability] will especially impact upon the ability of the Commission to address the development of mandatory product safety standards and will limit the overall evaluation of the offeror concept as embodied in the Consumer Product Safety Act. . . . Such a large, absolute reduction in funding, along with continued constraints on staffing, will have a devastating impact on this Commission. . . . Further, if such funding restrictions are maintained in the long term, the Commission has no choice but to consider substantial structural changes and adjustments to provide the adoption of a purely reactive approach to product safety rather than the planned and systematic standards development approach now envisioned.[20]

The OSHA's budgetary history is similar to that of the CPSC. The largest element of the OSHA budget covers compliance (table 11-3). Congress, in acting on the OSHA budget requests, has regularly added to the amounts requested for the OSHA's enforcement activities and decreased the amounts requested for supporting state enforcement activities. Standard-setting by the OSHA receives a very small portion of the budget: OSHA budget submissions by the OMB have requested between 4 and 5 percent of its budget for this purpose, and Congress has allocated between 4 and 6 percent. Information-gathering activities have not fared much better: from 1972 to 1974 appropriations ranged from 6 to 9 percent of the total budget of the OSHA.[21]

Since 1972 the OSHA process for setting standards has been all but stymied by inadequate appropriations. One major basis for OSHA standards is research by the National Institute for Occupational Safety and Health (NIOSH), which is responsible for gathering data on job-related hazards and performing scientific analyses of particular situations and substances that constitute hazards to workers, and then summarizing its findings in "criteria documents." As a result, the OSHA's ability to set standards is limited by the resources available to the NIOSH to investigate hazards. These resources have not been exactly generous.

In the health field alone, the NIOSH estimates that at least 42,000 chemicals used in industry may be hazardous to workers' health. Of

20. Ibid., pp. 821–22.
21. Because of a change in aggregation methods, the 1975 and 1976 numbers cannot be reconstructed from available publications so as to make them comparable with past years.

these, it has selected 400 as needing particular attention.[22] Its staff and research resources are not large enough to make much headway against these hazards. In fiscal 1972 and 1973, the NIOSH section responsible for preparing criteria documents had a total of thirty-one positions, including clerical and secretarial personnel, and managed to turn out thirteen documents.[23]

It seems clear that Congress places less emphasis on information gathering and evaluation capacity than safety regulatory agencies do. This suggests that Congress does not fully recognize the informational problems associated with effective safety regulation and that budgetary policies may be deflecting regulators from focusing on the very types of hazards that it makes the most sense to regulate.

Establishing Priorities

Before a regulatory agency can begin to regulate exposure to hazards, it must identify the hazards that are worth regulating. This means that procedures must be established for assessing the relative importance of hazards.

In ordering priorities, the CPSC relies heavily on a hazard index that is derived from a ranking of the severity of injuries and accident data from the National Electronic Injury Surveillance System (NEISS).[24] The NEISS provides aggregate data on the frequency and severity of accident cases from a sample of hospital emergency rooms. Each month the total number of accidents associated with each product class is reported. For each product, the number of accidents causing a particular type of injury is multiplied by an index of the "mean severity" of that injury. These calculations are summed to produce a "score" for each product.[25] The scores are used by the CPSC in deciding which products to regulate.

As calculated, the hazard index is unbelievably arbitrary. The

22. Linda E. Demkovich, "Labor Report/OSHA Launches Dual Effort to Reduce Job Health Hazards," *National Journal Reports,* vol. 6 (December 7, 1974), p. 1831.

23. *Occupational Safety and Health Act Review, 1974,* Hearings before the Subcommittee on Labor of the Senate Committee on Labor and Public Welfare, 93:2 (GPO, 1974), p. 1072.

24. A close examination of the NEISS and some of its failings can be found in Steven Kelman, "Regulation by the Numbers—A Report on the Consumer Product Safety Commission," *Public Interest,* no. 36 (Summer 1974), pp. 82–102.

25. See "Mean Severity," in Consumer Product Safety Commission, *NEISS News,* vol. 4 (July 1975).

numerical weights assigned to injuries of different severity are without any rational foundation. Thus a death is scored as 2,516 points[26] against a product, whereas a sprained ankle scores 10 points. To note that most people would gladly trade one death for 252 sprained ankles misses the main point of this fanciful scale. While considerable attention was devoted to constructing a qualitative ranking of the severity of various kinds of injuries, no effort was made to establish some foundation for aggregating injuries or even for testing the sensitivity of the hazard index to different aggregation schemes.

Another important shortcoming of the hazard index is that it takes no account of the age or frequency of use of the product. Since voluntary safety standards are changed every few years, the age of a product is important in determining whether still more stringent standards are necessary. Data on the frequency of exposure would enable the CPSC to distinguish between products that have a low accident rate per exposure but a high overall rate because they are so widely used, and products that are less frequently used but, when used, especially hazardous. This distinction is significant since it would give the CPSC some idea of how much it could influence the safety of the product. The failure of the CPSC to take account of exposure rates has led it to undertake the setting of standards for several high-ranking sources of accidents over which it is likely to have little if any control. For example, the CPSC is hard at work investigating the possibility of safety standards for matches, kitchen knives, and staircases. While many people suffer burns, cut themselves, and fall down stairs, one wonders exactly how effective the commission can be in significantly reducing the incidence of any of these accidents short of specifying that match flames be cold, knives blunt, and stairways horizontal.

Because the hazard index fails to make adjustments for age and exposure, it is unable to separate two quite distinct sources of a decline in accident rates associated with a product. Promulgation of a safety standard may cause accident rates to fall because it actually does make the product safer. But accidents may fall off because an ineffective safety standard forces up the price of the product enough to cause a major reduction in its use. Even if the purpose of the agency were narrowly defined to be the elimination of the most important sources of accidents, the latter effect could be achieved far

26. As Kelman points out ("Regulation by the Numbers," pp. 93–94), 2,516 is marked down from 34,721, which was abandoned because the agency decided it made the index too dependent on deaths.

more efficiently by simply imposing a tax or complete, unadjudicatable liability on the product, rather than by requiring that scarce resources be used to manufacture an ineffective safety device that reduces accidents only because it makes the product expensive.

The CPSC adopted the hazard index even though it was fully aware of most of the problems associated with it. While all the reasons for this decision are not known, two are clear. First, the agency was under considerable pressure from Congress to begin regulating and was afraid that if it failed to act with dispatch Congress might legislate its priorities. Second, the agency, reflecting in part the attitude of Congress, specifically rejected the use of economic analysis in setting priorities. The Bureau of Economic Analysis of the Department of Commerce has no part in setting priorities at the agency; instead it provides the CPSC with estimates of the economic impact of proposed standards. The rejection of economic analysis has effectively prevented the agency from developing a method of setting priorities that includes consideration of concepts such as the potential influence of the agency on the safety of a product or the economic benefits it might provide through regulation. Although it was correct in concluding that, because of inadequacies in the available information, economic analysis could not provide a definitive judgment on whether a product ought to be regulated, the CPSC threw out the baby with the bath by going to the extreme of regarding economic information as irrelevant.

In addition to the hazard index, the CPSC also takes action on the basis of individual case information. The Consumer Product Safety Act established a complaint process by which citizens and groups can request that the agency investigate the safety of a particular product or brand of products. Follow-up interviews from NEISS cases also suggest further action. Finally, the CPSC has field offices spread across the country that furnish information through both their contact with the public and their enforcement activities.

The flaw in these methods of generating information—and the rationale for a more systematic process such as NEISS—is that they are somewhat haphazard and may give biased signals about which products actually constitute consumer hazards. The problem is magnified if the clients of the regulatory agency are diffuse, disorganized, and perhaps unaware of its data collection processes and if the agency has a relatively small field office system, as does the CPSC.

Like the CPSC, which inherited the NEISS from the Department of Health, Education, and Welfare, the OSHA uses information systems developed by the Department of Labor on the incidence of on-the-job accidents. It too relies on complaints filed directly by workers and labor unions. It has an exceptionally large field inspection staff compared to that of the CPSC. Finally, it has developed a process for identifying target industries and target health hazards.

The OSHA's compliance activities are governed by the following set of priorities established in 1973:[27]

Priority	Category
First	Investigation of evidence of imminent danger
Second	Investigation of catastrophes and/or fatalities
Third	Investigation of complaints
Fourth	Special programs including target industry and target health hazard inspections
Fifth	General inspections and related activities

The first and third categories are not very different. Both are triggered by complaints from employees or union representatives. The fourth category, relating to "target industry" and "target health hazard," represents the OSHA's attempt to concentrate its resources on work places with the worst records. This set of priorities responds to the wishes of Congress as revealed by the legislative history of the Occupational Safety and Health Act.[28] The target industries and health hazards were identified in the following way:

On the basis of their relatively high injury rates, OSHA selected five target industries for the fourth priority category: longshoring; lumber and wood products; roofing and sheet metal; meat and meat products; and manufacturing of mobile homes and other transportation equipment.

OSHA also selected five health hazards as special targets for inspection coverage in the fourth priority category. These were asbestos, cotton dust, silica dust, lead, and carbon monoxide. According to OSHA, the selection of the health hazards was based on (1) extent and severity of employee exposure, (2) existence of standards, and (3) ability to adequately measure exposure levels.[29]

Judged by the statistics on the results of the OSHA's inspections, the agency could not have picked the worst industries and hazards as targets. From July 1973 through May 1974, it made 8,642 inspec-

27. *Occupational Safety and Health Act Review, 1974,* Hearings, p. 973.
28. Ibid.
29. Ibid., p. 974.

tions in target industries, 2,251 in industries that might have target health hazards, and 60,957 in general industries. The percentage of initial inspections (as opposed to follow-up inspections or reinspections) that resulted in citations was 60 for the target industries, 76 for those suspected of having target health hazards, and 79 for the general category industries.[30]

As with the CPSC, the OSHA method of establishing priorities, while superficially systematic and rational, is not based on a solid concept of when safety regulation may be worthwhile. It stands to reason that the most commonly known hazardous occupations and substances are probably best understood by workers and consumers, and that more effort is already being made in these cases to develop safety precautions. The most complex long-term problems are the ones least likely to be dealt with adequately. By overlooking the rationale for safety regulation, the safety regulatory authority has ignored the issue of how much improvement in safety it can bring about through regulatory intervention.

The OSHA data-gathering process suffers from other problems as well. Before it was established, job-related accident statistics were collected by the Bureau of Labor Statistics and the National Safety Council. Because new definitions and procedures for collecting data were developed when the OSHA was created, recent statistics are not comparable with the old. Thus it is impossible to tell what effect the OSHA has actually had on accident and illness rates in the aggregate or what the effect of specific OSHA standards has been.

Finally, the OSHA, like the CPSC, does not rank its priorities or evaluate its standards on the basis of economic analysis. In fact, the legislation dealing with the standard-setting process specifically rejects the weighing of costs and benefits as a criterion for judging the desirability of standards, instead specifying prevention as the only objective of the agency. As a result, both agencies throw away valuable information.

The Development of Standards

At the heart of safety regulatory policy as practiced by existing agencies is the setting of minimum standards of protection from hazards. Legislation and case law have established procedural and

30. Ibid., p. 976.

488 Nina W. Cornell, Roger G. Noll, and Barry Weingast

substantive boundaries for standard-setting activities. The effects of these rules on the standards that eventually are promulgated are sometimes quite subtle and, perhaps, even unintentional.

All regulatory agencies could adopt informational strategies rather than set standards, but in practice they rely almost exclusively on standards. For example, the Consumer Product Safety Act gives equal billing to both strategies:

A consumer product safety standard shall consist of one or more of any of the following types of requirements: (1) Requirements as to performance, composition, contents, design, construction, finish, or packaging of a consumer product. (2) Requirements that a consumer product be marked with or accompanied by clear and adequate warnings and instructions, or requirements respecting the form of warnings or instructions.[31]

The major elements of the CPSC's informational strategy have been the consumer "hot line"—a way of giving information over the telephone to consumers who call with questions—and short analyses and tips to consumers through press releases. The CPSC has not seriously considered mandatory labeling as a substitute for standards. For example, instead of regulating the design of power mowers, the CPSC could require manufacturers to label each model according to its safety devices, the kind of accidents the safety devices prevent, and the probability of serious injury, based on data from the NEISS.

One impediment to adopting this kind of informational strategy is that the members of congressional oversight committees are not enthusiastic about it. Congress has been very critical of even the current minimal reliance on information strategies. References to the hot line in the various appropriations hearings for 1975 and 1976 were all negative. For example, Congressman Bob Traxler commented: "This costs about $115,000 and on the surface it would appear to be a good idea. However, we understand that over 98 percent of the [55,000] calls received [so far] during this fiscal year represent requests for information, pamphlets, brochures, and so forth."[32] This statement reflects a House Appropriations Committee investigatory report that labeled these calls as "of an innocuous information nature," and stated that "consequently the need for this expenditure seems ques-

---

31. 86 Stat. 1212-13.
32. *Department of Housing and Urban Development—Independent Agencies Appropriations for 1976*, Hearings before the Subcommittee on HUD—Independent Agencies of the House Committee on Appropriations, 94:1 (GPO, 1975), pt. 4, p. 764.

tionable."[33] With these signals from Congress, agencies cannot be expected to place much reliance on informational strategies.

Some standards are set in response to petitions from interested parties. Surprisingly enough, industry has been quite active in petitioning for regulation of its own products. At the CPSC during its first two years, industries filed over 70 percent of the petitions received by the agency (table 11-4) and two-thirds of the petitions that were granted. Since many of these petitions requested specific exemptions from and relaxations of existing standards, the gross figures overstate the importance of business participation. Nevertheless, business petitions were the single most important source of agency actions to begin developing standards.

Table 11-5 breaks down the petitions filed under the Consumer Product Safety Act during the same two years by source and action requested. More than 40 percent of the requests to regulate a product under this act came from the industry producing the product. Among the standard-setting proceedings initiated by industry are dockets dealing with swimming pool slides, extension cords, architectural glass, glass bottles, power mowers, aluminum wiring, and fire extinguishers. Nonindustry sources are responsible for several proceedings, notably those dealing with aerosol sprays, space heaters, playground equipment, paint guns, and stepladders.

The Consumer Product Safety Act sets out detailed procedures that govern the development of standards by the CPSC. The act severely constrains the ability of the CPSC to develop its own standards by requiring that it seek out others—"offerors"—to develop safety standards that deal with the problems it has identified.[34] It may scrutinize these proposals (subject to its own resource limitations) and may contribute to an offeror's costs:

If an offer is accepted under this subsection, the Commission may agree to contribute to the offeror's cost in developing a proposed consumer product safety standard, in any case in which the Commission determines

33. Surveys and Investigations Staff, House Committee on Appropriations, "A General Review of the Operation of the Consumer Product Safety Commission" (March 1975; processed), printed in *Department of Housing and Urban Development—Independent Agencies Appropriations for 1976,* Hearings (quotations from p. 652).

34. Public Law 92-573, secs. 7(b)(4) and 7(d)(1) (86 Stat. 1213). The CPSC can develop standards if no suitable offeror outside the regulated industry can be found or if an offeror fails to develop a satisfactory standard.

Table 11-4. Petitions to the Consumer Product Safety Commission, by Source and Act, May 1973–May 1975

| | Act under which petition was filed | | | | | |
Source of petition	Consumer Product Safety Act	Flammable Fabrics Act	Federal Hazardous Substances Act	Poison Prevention Packaging Act	Administrative Procedure Act	Total
Firms and industries	22	36	23	68	0	149
Consumer groups	10	3	11	0	1	25
Individuals[a]	13	0	6	1	0	20
Government	4	2	2	0	0	8
Labor organizations	1	0	0	0	0	1
Total	50	41	42	69	1	203

Source: Tabulated from data supplied by the CPSC.
a. Affiliation, if any, not identified.

Table 11-5. Petitions Filed under the Consumer Product Safety Act, by Source and Action Requested, May 1973–May 1975

	Action requested				
Source of petition	Issue regulation	Reassign product to different law	Ban or recall product	Other	Total
Firms and industries	17	3	0	2	22
Consumer groups	5	1	3	1	10
Individuals[a]	8	0	2	3	13
Government	3	0	1	0	4
Labor organizations	1	0	0	0	1
Total	34	4	6	6	50

Source: Same as table 11-4.
a. Affiliation, if any, not identified.

that such contribution is likely to result in a more satisfactory standard than would be developed without such contribution.[35]

The commission has interpreted the intent of this passage as establishing a policy of only partial reimbursement. Without full cost reimbursement, groups other than those connected with the industry are not likely to find it worthwhile to become offerors. Peter Schuck, director of the Washington office of Consumers Union, which undertook to be offeror on the issue of power mower safety, raised this exact point with the oversight committee:

[The commission] has indicated that all other things being equal, it will look favorably upon consumer candidates to be offerors.

But therein lies the problem. All other things are not equal. In particular—and here the degree of my understatement cannot be overstated—consumer organizations are not equal to industry groups in terms of the financial resources necessary to develop a technically complicated safety standard as offeror. Indeed, I can say without fear of contradiction that so long as the funding for the offeror program remains at its present level, no consumer organization, with the possible exception of Consumers Union, can afford to be an offeror. . . . I daresay . . . Consumers Union will have to think long and hard before it makes this sort of expenditure again.[36]

The CPSC's reimbursement policy all but prevents the commission from developing the various consumer groups as a clientele and as a

35. Ibid., sec. 7(d)(2).
36. Consumer Product Safety Commission Oversight, Hearings before the Subcommittee for Consumers of the Senate Committee on Commerce, 94:1 (GPO, 1975), p. 23.

source of major input to the standards development process. It also means the industry will be writing its own standards.

The very first standards case at the CPSC made the impact of the offeror reimbursement policy abundantly clear. An industry trade association successfully petitioned the CPSC to write safety standards for architectural glass, and then submitted a proposal that it be selected as an offeror. A consumer organization—the National Consumers League—also proposed that it be an offeror in conjunction with the American Society for Testing and Materials. The CPSC, upon reviewing these and two other proposals, unanimously agreed that the NCL/ASTM proposal ranked first and that of the trade association ranked second. The NCL/ASTM insisted on full reimbursement of the costs of developing the standards, including salary for consumer representatives participating in the process. Eventually the CPSC broke off negotiations with the NCL/ASTM, expressing the belief that adequate consumer representation could be obtained free. Subsequently, the trade association won the offeror contract, settling for reimbursement of only $14,175 to pay travel and per diem expenses for the consumer representatives it intended to consult. The trade association absorbed the remaining costs, which were considerable judging from its initial reimbursement request for $451,500.[37]

Letting industry write its own standards is not necessarily fatal to the development of reasonable regulatory actions. If the commission knew what the standard ought to be, it could effectively ensure it as an outcome. The Consumer Product Safety Act requires the CPSC to develop regulations governing acceptance of offerors' proposals. These regulations include ample justification for rejecting any proposal not meeting CPSC expectations. If the commission has strong beliefs about the best way to solve a safety problem, it can invoke the act either to move the offeror closer to its own ideas or to reject the proposal as not representing satisfactory progress so that it can find another offeror or begin its own development of a standard.[38] If the commission had sufficient analytical capabilities the standards developed by the offerors might be much the same as those the commission would develop on its own.

37. "Opinion of Commissioner Barbara H. Franklin on the Selection of an Offeror to Develop a Safety Standard for Architectural Glass" (CPSC, October 8, 1974; processed).
38. P.L. 92-573, sec. 7(e)(2).

If financial and personnel resources are not abundant, the commission must limit its scrutiny of this process and hence its influence on the form, scope, and quality of the standards. Its budget shows that the resources of the CPSC are severely limited. The scarcity of analytical resources, coupled with the offeror provisions of the act, effectively relegate the commission to a judicial position. It can assess proposals on the basis of whether they address the problem the commission has cited, but it lacks the analytical resources to determine whether the standards actually solve the problem. An added difficulty is the time limit imposed by the act, which requires that the standards proposed by an offeror be adopted within thirty days.[39] If it fails to act in this time, a new regulatory proceeding, including the search for another offeror, must be opened if the product is to be regulated.[40]

Industry has several reasons for wanting a standard-setting procedure that is under its influence. First, if industry controls the standards, the economic uncertainties associated with safety regulation are reduced: industry is unlikely to impose a standard so stringent that it effectively puts itself out of business. Second, because safety standards often cannot be distinguished from design standards, the regulatory process offers the possibility of creating an enforceable cartel to reduce competition, something a voluntary trade association's standards could not do as easily because they cannot be enforced.[41]

One egregious example of the latter has already occurred at the CPSC. The offeror for developing safety standards for bicycles was the trade association for American bicycle manufacturers. The set of standards it proposed included complicated design standards that would have effectively excluded foreign-made bicycles from the U.S. market.[42] The CPSC, unaware of this feature of the proposed standards, adopted them; however, in response to heated outcries

39. An offeror must be chosen 30 days after a notice to set a standard is published. The offeror has 150 days to report a standard after being selected. Since the entire process is limited to 210 days, this leaves 30 days for evaluating an offeror's proposal. See ibid., sec. 7.

40. The agency can extend a proceeding, but to do so it must show cause, which in turn can be challenged in court and, in any event, leads inevitably to congressional criticism at the next budget hearing.

41. See Michael S. Hunt, "Trade Associations and Self-Regulation: Major Home Appliances," in Richard E. Caves and Marc J. Roberts, eds., *Regulating the Product: Quality and Variety* (Ballinger, 1975), pp. 39–55.

42. John Forester, "Toy Bike Syndrome," *Bike World*, vol. 2 (October 1973), pp. 24–27.

Table 11-6. Comparison of Occupational (OSHA) and General Population (EPA) Environmental Health Standards, 1975

	Ambient atmospheric standards	
Pollutant	OSHA (threshold level value)	Environmental Protection Agency
Sulfur dioxide, SO_2 (parts per million)	5	0.03 (annual mean)
		0.14 (maximum of 24 hrs., once per year)
		0.50 (maximum of 3 hrs., once per year)
Carbon monoxide, CO (ppm)	50	9.00 (maximum of 8 hrs., once per year)
		35.00 (maximum of 1 hr., once per year)
Nitrogen dioxide, NO_2 (ppm)	5	0.50 (annual mean)
Particulates (milligrams per cubic meter)	5[a]	0.075 (annual mean)
	55[b]	0.66 (maximum of 24 hrs., once per year)
Lead (micrograms per cubic meter)	550	1.50 (30-day mean[c])

Source: "Testimony of Samuel S. Epstein, M.D., Case Western Reserve University Medical School," in *Occupational Safety and Health Act of 1970 (Oversight and Proposed Amendments)*, Hearings before the Select Subcommittee on Labor of the House Committee on Education and Labor, 93:2 (GPO, 1975), p. 162.
a. The value for the portion of the pollutant responsible for the harmful effects.
b. The value for the total dust.
c. Standard for California.

from cyclists, it recalled the standards and started the standard development process over again. Only because the product in question had a dedicated, organized, well-informed group of consumers did an anticompetitive standard fail.

The OSHA, perhaps because labor unions are better organized than consumers, is not set up to be quite so reliant on industry for developing standards. For two years after it was established, the OSHA was permitted to adopt as its own standards that had been set either by government agencies or by certain kinds of consensus organizations. (Since 1972 the standard-setting procedure has been based on NIOSH "criteria documents.") In these two years, the OSHA adopted numerous consensus standards.

One feature of the standards the OSHA borrowed from others is that they are not as rigorous as the standards adopted by other federal regulatory agencies that regulate exposure of other groups of people to the same hazards. Table 11-6 compares OSHA standards and the standards set by the EPA for exposure to the same chemicals. In each instance the EPA standard is much more stringent.

A second feature of the borrowed standards is that they have evolved much more slowly than industry standards in response to new information. One businessman from Texas wrote to his congressman that he was caught in a bind by this kind of inflexibility:

One specific point is in regards to the pressure vessels which we manufacture in our plant for the oil and gas industry and refineries. In order to retain our certification to build pressure vessels in accordance with ASME Boiler & Pressure Vessel Code, we must construct them in accordance with the latest edition of the Code. However, the OSHA Regulations still refer to previous editions of the Code. Therefore, we could get caught in the middle in providing equipment for our customers.[43]

Now that the OSHA must rely on the NIOSH in developing standards, the process has become more cumbersome, in part because the NIOSH has produced so few criteria documents and in part because the standard-setting process is slower when the analysis is done externally. The NIOSH produced six criteria documents in 1972; by July 1, 1974, only one had resulted in a standard. (One other standard was the result of a "letter of recommendation," the procedure used when a standard is essential before all the data are collected.)

The charge of slow proceedings has also been leveled at the CPSC. Despite the statutory limit of 210 days for developing standards, the CPSC has usually taken far longer. Commenting on this performance, a report of the House Appropriations Committee in 1975 said: "The Consumer Product Safety Commission . . . has been in existence approaching 2 years and its record of achievement to date is lacking in every area of its responsibilities."[44] Senator Gale McGee, chairman of the Senate subcommittee that oversees CPSC appropriations, was also critical about the "lack of an initiative on the part of the Commission for setting new standards under the act. The charge is made that you inherited several standards from older legislative acts that were transferred to you, but you have not come up with any new ones."[45]

43. *Occupational Safety and Health Act of 1970 (Oversight and Proposed Amendments)*, Hearings before the Select Subcommittee on Labor of the House Committee on Education and Labor, 93:2 (GPO, 1975), p. 4.
44. *Department of Housing and Urban Development—Independent Agencies Appropriations for 1976*, Hearings, pt. 4, p. 629.
45. *Agriculture-Environmental and Consumer Protection Appropriations for Fiscal Year 1975*, Hearings before the Senate Committee on Appropriations, 93:2 (GPO, 1974), pt. 2, p. 1640.

One source of Congress's chagrin is the performance on the petitions reported in table 11-5. The CPSC revealed in its 1975 appropriations hearings that it had received forty-two petitions under the Consumer Product Safety Act. Four that were resolved had taken an average of 265 days, and ten more had at that time taken an average of 326 days and were still pending.[46] Of course, Congress did not look to its own budgeting decisions to explain this lack of progress, or even consider whether rapid action is a desirable characteristic of sensible safety regulation.

Compliance and Enforcement

The compliance activities of safety regulatory agencies fall into two categories. First, agencies attempt to enforce the product, process, and exposure standards that they have set by inspecting facilities and products. The standards provide a concrete set of criteria for determining whether the inspected firm is in compliance. Second, safety regulatory law contains provisions that allow agencies to take action in the absence of a standard if the hazard is determined to be sufficiently serious. Both types of activities not only weed out bad actors, but also increase the incentives of firms to reduce hazards.

As an example of the range of permissible enforcement activities, the Consumer Product Safety Act permits the CPSC to take certain remedial actions if it finds a particular product a "substantial product hazard," either because it does not meet a standard or because it possesses a "defect which . . . creates a substantial risk of injury to the public."[47] The remedial actions available include requiring the manufacturer, distributor, or retailer to take any combination of the following actions: (1) to give notice of the existence of the defect to the public, to other businesses manufacturing, distributing, or retailing the product, or to known consumers of the product; (2) to repair or replace the product; (3) to refund the purchase price of the product (less a "reasonable allowance for use").[48] The term "defect" in this section of the law has been interpreted to mean any characteristic of the product that is hazardous. It is not just applied to an atypical mistake—as it might be by the FDA on discovering botulism in a few cans of soup—but to entire product lines that are discovered to

46. *Department of Housing and Urban Development, and Certain Independent Agencies Appropriations for Fiscal Year 1976,* Hearings, pt. 2, p. 885.
47. P.L. 92-573, sec. 15(a).
48. Ibid., sec. 15(c) and (d).

be hazardous in design. To enforce this part of the law requires on-the-spot development of a performance standard for an aspect of a product that has not previously been regulated. Even though agency actions are subject to judicial review, the scope of possible procedures available to the agency, combined with the relatively low standards of proof the judiciary normally applies to administrative decisions, makes this an especially powerful tool.

One of the by-products of effective use of recall, repair, and refund requirements is the impact they can have on small businesses and on competition. The first three "substantial product hazard" cases dealt with by the CPSC demonstrate how roughly equivalent treatment of big and small firms is far more devastating to the latter than to the former.

Two of the cases dealt with products manufactured by corporations of moderate size: a proceeding on the Mini-Mac chain saw, manufactured by McCulloch Corporation, and a proceeding on Presto electric fry pans, manufactured by National Presto Industries. The third dealt with the Wel-Dex electric arc welder, produced by a small Texas firm, Relco, Incorporated.

In all three instances the commission sought essentially the same action: a notification to distributors and customers that the product constituted a hazard, and an agreement to repair, replace, or refund, in compliance with the provisions of the act. The first two cases were terminated within a few months without necessitating a formal opinion and order by the commission, as both companies agreed to undertake corrective measures acceptable to the commission.[49]

Relco, alleging that the commission had no authority to enforce the statute on products manufactured before the effective date of the act, could not agree to these corrective measures, stating that the financial stakes were too high. It would have been impractical to repair the defects cited by the commission, and replacement or refund was financially impossible. The company estimated that, of the 200,000 units it was asked to recall, if as many as 10,000 were actually returned the company would be bankrupted.[50] Nevertheless, the

49. In the Matter of McCulloch Corporation: Order Terminating the Proceeding Regarding Certain Mini-Mac Chain Saws, CPSC Docket 74-1 (May 6, 1974); and In the Matter of National Presto Industries, Inc.: Order Terminating the Proceeding, CPSC Docket 74-2 (May 9, 1974).

50. In the Matter of Relco, Inc. . . . and Wel-Dex Welder Manufacturing Company: Interim Initial Decision and Order, CPSC Docket 74-4 (April 29, 1975).

CPSC persisted in demanding the remedy it desired, rejecting proposals by Relco to limit the number of models to be recalled. In the latest order on the case, the CPSC has ordered Relco to refund the full price of all intact arc welders returned to the company and 50 percent of the price of welders either that have exhausted welding rods or that, the owners attest, were disposed of because of their evident safety hazard.[51]

A small firm, producing only a few models in its product line, is more vulnerable than a large one to any kind of action against it by either regulatory intervention or civil liability suit, for the penalties or damage awards are more likely to exceed its net worth. But regulation can be more devastating because of the lower standards of proof. In the Wel-Dex case, at the time the CPSC decided to take the product off the market, the company could not have been found liable for anything, for none of the 200,000 welders that it had sold were known to have caused a single injury. The CPSC decision was based not on any actual accidents, but on an engineering study that pointed out several design features of the device that could cause injury. Subsequently, a serious accident leading to "several days of hospitalization" was reported by the father of the victim as having occurred in September 1975. The CPSC regarded the case as significant confirmation of its earlier decision to take the product off the market, but the treatment of the incident by the CPSC clearly illustrates the differences in standards of proof between judicial and regulatory proceedings.[52] The extent of the injury and its cause were somewhat in doubt since the CPSC did not obtain direct information about the incident from either the injured party, who reportedly had moved to Saudi Arabia, or the physicians attending him at the hospital after the accident. Had the incident led to a liability claim, surely the injured party, not his father, would have been required to file the complaint, and the testimony of attending physicians would almost certainly have been sought by either the plaintiff or the defendant.

In principle, numerous enforcement actions like that against Relco would reduce competition by winnowing out small firms. In practice, agencies have not imposed a large enough number of bankrupting

51. In the Matter of Relco, Inc. . . . and Wel-Dex Welder Manufacturing Company: Amended Initial Decision and Order on Reopened Proceeding, CPSC Docket 74-4 (April 5, 1976).
52. Ibid.

penalties to make their actions constitute more than very infrequent, if random and arbitrary, events.

Although compliance activities can be the result of citizen complaints, the primary method of enforcing safety standards is through on-site inspections of randomly selected business establishments. All safety regulatory agencies suffer to varying degrees from two difficulties in undertaking enforcement activities: the problem of identifying sites to inspect and the paucity of inspectors.

Business firms do not have to report to the relevant safety regulatory agencies that they intend to enter a business that might be of interest to the regulators. Consequently, one of the main tasks of enforcement officers is to identify firms in the industries that are subject to standards. This can present major problems if, as is the case with food regulation by the FDA, the number of plants is large and unstable.

Despite relatively large budgets for enforcement in the safety regulatory agencies, field enforcement staffs are still small. The OSHA, for example, has the largest enforcement budget of all safety regulatory agencies but has fewer inspectors than some of the insurance companies that sell workmen's compensation insurance, even though it is interested in a broader range of occupational safety problems than are covered by workmen's compensation and has a bigger enforcement problem than insurers do.

A central problem for regulators is how to allocate enforcement personnel. One element of the problem has to do with the distribution of inspections by size of firm. The OSHA has attempted to spread its resources over both small and large establishments. Its field operations manual sets out the procedure for choosing industries to inspect: first to select target counties within the region, and then to inspect at least one small and one large establishment from each two-digit standard industrial classification code group in the general industry categories. Based on the history of inspection to date, a large plant is likely to be visited by an OSHA inspector about once every ten years, small plants even less often.

The infrequency of inspections blunts the effectiveness of enforcement as an incentive to comply. Equally important are the minimal consequences of being found guilty of noncompliance. From July 1972 through March 1974, OSHA cited 364,955 safety violations. Table 11-7 shows the distribution of violations by severity and the

Table 11-7. OSHA Citations, July 1972–March 1974

Severity of violation	Number of citations	Average fine (dollars)
Not serious	360,102	16
Serious	4,330	648
Willful, repeated, or imminent danger[a]	523	1,104
Total citations or average fine	364,955	25

Source: *Occupational Safety and Health Act Review, 1974*, Hearings, p. 967.
a. Willful and repeated violations can be either serious or not serious.

Table 11-8. Estimated Cost of Compliance with OSHA Standards, by Size of Firm

Number of employees in firm	Cost of compliance (dollars)
1–100	35,000
101–500	73,500
501–1,000	350,000

Source: Robert Stewart Smith, *The Occupational Safety and Health Act: Its Goals and Its Achievements* (American Enterprise Institute for Public Policy Research, 1976), p. 62.

remarkably small penalties that have been imposed. The National Association of Manufacturers has developed some crude estimates of the costs of complying with OSHA standards, which are shown in table 11-8. The small fines, the infrequent inspections, and the fairly steep compliance costs make compliance worthwhile only if an employer expects to be cited for several hundred willful, repeated, or imminent danger violations when the inspector finally arrives.[53] Anything less and it is cheaper to avoid compliance and pay the fines when one is caught. Since the total number of citations in this category during the first twenty-one months of the OSHA's inspection program was only 523, it is safe to conclude that the OSHA does not provide much incentive to improve occupational safety. Of course, the ineffectiveness of the agency's enforcement system in encouraging compliance is not particularly important if, as argued above, the standards are not rigorous enough to have much effect on job-related accidents and illnesses or are developed primarily in areas where standard-setting has the lowest payoff.

53. If a large plant is inspected once every ten years, the annualized expected cost of a willful violation is $110.40. If the complying safety equipment costs $350,000, the equipment lasts twenty years, and the firm can borrow funds for purchasing the equipment at 9 percent interest, the annualized cost of compliance is about $49,000. A firm must expect more than 400 citations when the inspector finally arrives to make the compliance actions worth taking.

Conclusions

The preceding analysis leads to both positive and negative conclusions about the present system of safety regulation. On the positive side, it is clear that there are indeed occasions when efficient governmental intervention in the form of standard-setting regulation is called for. On the negative side, the existing safety regulatory agencies, to the extent that they follow the patterns of the CPSC and the OSHA, are not designed to deal effectively with the very types of cases in which standards are most appropriate.

When targets are well chosen, safety regulatory agencies can be effective. The development of mandatory standards for baby cribs illustrates safety regulation at its best.[54]

In 1968 a presidential commission discovered that the spacing between the slats of baby cribs was so wide that, under certain conditions, the entire body of a baby could slip between the slats until stopped by its skull. The baby would then strangle as it hung outside the crib.

The crib problem had two features. First, no one was collecting data that would make the government or the industry aware of the problem, and accidents were too infrequent for the press and consumers to have become alerted to it. Second, once the problem was recognized, no one knew what kind of safety standard would deal with it effectively.

The problem was next addressed by the trade association of crib manufacturers. Without benefit of any systematic analysis, the manufacturers voluntarily adopted a standard of 3.25 inches between slats, just a little less than the former 3.5 inches. Next, the Bureau of Product Safety of the Food and Drug Administration—a precursor of the CPSC—commissioned a research project to measure the size of babies' buttocks as part of a larger project on various aspects of infant anthropometry. The study estimated that the buttocks of 5 percent of infants could be compressed by the pressure of their own weight to a diameter of 2.375 inches or less, nearly an inch smaller than the industry standard. In April 1973 a mandatory spacing standard of 2.375 inches was adopted.

54. Much of the following analysis is from Kelman, "Regulation by the Numbers," pp. 84–86.

The key to the successful conclusion of the crib slat case was the role the FDA played in generating the information and analysis that made a rational design standard possible. The essence of the crib problem was the lack of understanding of the nature of the hazard by participants on both sides of the market. Once the FDA undertook to analyze the problem, the actual promulgation of mandatory standards was anticlimactic. Since the standards imposed essentially no costs on anyone and since the industry had already established procedures for voluntary adoption of crib slat spacing standards, making the federal standard mandatory was probably unnecessary once the basis for a rational standard had been established.

One major problem with the existing agencies is that the legislation establishing them and the budget appropriation process they undergo annually are based on an implicit model of setting standards at variance with the one that accounts for the success of the crib slat case. The assumptions underlying the legislation are (1) that the essence of the safety problem is the presence of well-defined, clearcut hazards to consumers and workers that can be avoided in a rather straightforward fashion; (2) that a reasonably effective way of preventing them can be identified by a brief, cursory investigation; and (3) that the principal cause of inadequate product and occupational safety is "bad acts" by unethical businessmen. In keeping with these assumptions, agencies are pushed to develop a large number of standards, with underlying justifications that meet the loose standards of proof required in administrative procedures, in a relatively short time.

The provision in the Occupational Safety and Health Act enabling the OSHA, during its first two years, to adopt as mandatory standards the exposure limits recommended by national consensus organizations illustrates the congressional desire for speed. When formulated, these standards were not meant to be made mandatory nor were they designed to be universally applicable nor were they expected to be permanent. The result of this approach to safety regulation is that the agencies have all too often set standards for what seem to be frivolous hazards. It is no accident that some of the earliest OSHA standards were on the type and location of toilets, for example, and that the CPSC is busy regulating matches.

The main fallacy in the current approach is that the market and the liability system are far more likely to deal reasonably well with easily identifiable and easily avoidable hazards than with more complex hazards that are only partly understood. Trade associations, lacking due process procedural requirements, are likely to act more flexibly, more quickly, and more expertly than regulatory agencies in dealing with the first class of problems. Thus safety regulatory agencies have been designed to focus on issues to which they have the least to contribute.

Regulators have several different types of tasks. They are asked to be objective analysts in identifying the nature of a safety problem and its possible remedies. They are asked to be conduits of political values in deciding whether prevention of a hazard is worthwhile. And they are asked to be a police force in finding bad actors who produce products that do not meet safety standards.

All this would be difficult enough, but Congress has designed the agencies so that they cannot carry out any of these activities effectively. Regulation makes the most sense in uncertain areas the private market cannot handle. Yet the agencies have insufficient resources to do research, and in any event are made dependent on industry for information and development of standards. The agencies are ordered to ignore economic analysis in setting priorities and standards, which prevents them from developing a decisionmaking process that would lead them to attack the problems they have the best chance of solving. Finally, in enforcement activities, the agencies are hamstrung by the procedural lethargy of regulatory processes and case law in penalizing violators.

If Congress is serious about safety regulation, it should focus regulatory activities on problems the market is least able to solve. One step would be to deemphasize regulation on mundane matters. For example, the OSHA could be relieved of the responsibility of trying to prevent industrial accidents and left free to concentrate on the more complex problems of health hazards. Instead of setting standards as a means of reducing industrial accidents, either an injury tax or a strengthening of workmen's compensation would be at least as effective and probably cheaper. Even if Congress were not to entirely remove the S from OSHA, it could allocate most of the resources of the agency to health questions, saving safety efforts for exceptional circumstances.

The agencies should be given substantially larger research budgets. Research capacity should be in the agency, not separated as the

NIOSH is from the OSHA, so that its activities can reflect the priorities of the regulatory authority.The research skills should include economic analysts as well as technicians, and both should be used to aid the regulators in setting priorities as well as developing standards. One criterion for opening a proceeding should be the influence the agency is likely to have on the problem, which implies that an agency should be able to do considerable research on a hazard before formally opening a standard-setting proceeding. Hand in hand with a research strategy must come a relaxation of the time constraint on the development of standards.

Agencies should be encouraged to place greater reliance on informational strategies, especially the promotion of more effective voluntary standards by industry. This would avoid the expense of cumbersome administrative procedures and take advantage of the greater flexibility of industry in changing standards, which will be of value if growing knowledge rapidly makes each succeeding standard obsolete. Of course, because of the danger that industry might capture the coercive power of government, industry standards make sense only if they are voluntary and only if the agency has sufficient analytical capability to evaluate them.

Congress should also play a more active part in decisions on the manner and extent of enforcement of a standard. One approach would be congressional legislation of fines, or ranges of fines, for various degrees of noncompliance with a standard once it was promulgated. This would enable Congress to make a judgment about how rigorously a standard should be pursued. Fines could be raised from time to time to encourage the adoption of preventive measures. Alternatively, citizens could be offered bounties for identifying firms that were not in compliance. In general, too little use has been made of incentives for increasing safety.

Whether these actions would make regulation of product and worker safety effective is problematical. These recommendations assume, for example, that agencies can attract and retain skilled analysts in significant numbers, and that patterns of increasing lethargy and industry orientation that have become familiar in other regulatory agencies will not prevail in safety regulation as well. But carrying out these recommendations is necessary, if not sufficient, for effective safety regulation.

CHAPTER TWELVE

Income Security Policy

JOHN L. PALMER *and* JOSEPH J. MINARIK

THE OVERALL PERFORMANCE of the economy, for which the federal government has assumed greatly increased responsibility over the past forty or so years, has been discussed in chapter 7. It is this performance that determines the size of the economic pie—the total amount of national product and income that is available at any time to be allocated among various uses. This chapter focuses upon the related area of income security policy, which deals with the distribution of that income among individuals and households. The role of the federal government has increased dramatically in this area also. The primary objectives of income security policy are: (1) preventing precipitous losses in economic well-being because of largely involuntary disruptions in earnings; (2) facilitating financial access to goods or services like health care that society agrees are indispensable; (3) alleviating poverty; and (4) narrowing income differentials. These four objectives are distinct but highly interrelated; policies designed to further one are very likely to promote others. For example, we would expect the subsidization of health care expenditures

Henry J. Aaron, Michael C. Barth, Robinson G. Hollister, Joseph A. Pechman, Charles L. Schultze, and Emil M. Sunley, Jr., read drafts of this chapter and made helpful comments; numerous other colleagues provided useful comments on particular sections They should not be implicated in any statements of opinion or held responsible for any remaining errors. John O'Hare provided valuable research assistance and Robin Mary Donaldson ably performed the computer programming tasks. Support for the research on the tax system was provided by the RANN Program of the National Science Foundation.

505

to narrow effective income differentials. Similarly, programs that replace part or all of the earnings lost by a family through the unemployment, disability, retirement, or death of a breadwinner also prevent many people from falling into poverty.

It is oversimplified but still roughly accurate to say that the first three objectives are concerned principally with raising the incomes of those at the lower end of the income scale, while the fourth objective deals with the disparity of incomes across the whole scale. Further, the first three objectives are largely accepted as goals of federal policy, while income redistribution per se has not generally been a primary or explicit motivation of federal policy, though the distributional impact of various policies has often been taken into account. No doubt many advocates of the other three objectives hoped and expected that they would result in substantial income equalization; the fact that this has not occurred is probably a major factor in the recent interest in income redistribution as an explicit federal goal.

The four income security objectives may conflict with other values and goals of our economy or society. All of them involve a reshuffling of the market-determined distribution of command over goods and services, necessarily abridging individual freedom and causing some people to be treated differently from others. Sometimes they run counter to the view deeply ingrained in post-Reformation Western societies that monetary rewards ought to be tied to productive activities. Also, the growth of the economy may be slowed by the disincentive effects of certain tax or transfer policies. Such concerns contribute to our reluctance as a society to adopt a more aggressive stance toward income inequality, and they also affect our willingness and ability to pursue the other three goals.

The federal government, in its pursuit of these four objectives, can alter the distribution of income both directly and indirectly. The indirect methods are numerous and varied. Overall management of the economy and the regulation of certain types of economic activity, discussed in chapters 7, 10, and 11, have substantial distributional, as well as efficiency, consequences; for example, a sustained high level of aggregate demand has proved to be an effective means of reducing poverty. Also important are those indirect policies focused on increasing the earnings capacity of low-income workers or potential workers. These can operate on the demand side of the labor market, as in minimum wage or antidiscrimination activities, or on the supply side, as in education and training opportunities.

Effective as some of these indirect methods can be in furthering income security goals, they are not within the scope of this chapter. Here we are concerned only with the direct programmatic methods: tax collection; transfers, either of cash or by the financing or provision of certain goods and services intended primarily for current consumption; and, to a lesser extent, subsidized employment in the public sector. Even this narrower focus encompasses a broader range of activities than is usually understood by the term income security policy, which conventionally refers only to transfer programs. It is important, however, to consider certain aspects of tax and employment policies in conjunction with transfer programs, since all three have considerable independent and interactive effects on income security objectives.[1]

The tax system's potential to affect income security objectives has grown with the size of the public sector: with annual federal tax revenues of nearly $400 billion and state and local revenues $150 billion, it is now enormous.[2] The tax system affects income distribution in two interrelated ways. First, the rates, structure, and other provisions of the tax code directly affect the amount and distribution of after-tax income available to individuals and families. Second, the specific provisions of the tax law create various incentives that, in turn, affect the level, composition, and distribution of various sources of income. The effects of the latter are, of course, far more difficult to identify than the former.

The subsidization of earnings and employment has been undertaken only sparingly by the federal government since the Depression. Recently, however, greater use has been made of tax credits, both for employers (for hiring welfare recipients under the work incentive program) and for workers (the earned income tax credit in the Tax Reduction Act of 1975), as well as of public service employment. Further, proposals for greatly expanding some or all of these programs and implementing other approaches to employment and earn-

1. For a discussion of the problems arising out of the interdependencies among these once more distinct areas of public policy in several Western countries as well as the United States, see Hugh Heclo, "Frontiers of Social Policy in Europe and America," *Policy Sciences*, vol. 6 (December 1975), pp. 403–21.

2. Compare the $150 billion total involved in income security transfer programs, as defined below.

**Table 12-1. Federal Expenditures for Income Security Transfer Programs,
Fiscal Years 1960 and 1977**
Billions of dollars

Program	1960	1977
Cash programs	**22.0**	**140.9**
Means-tested	2.1	12.3
Aid to families with dependent children[a]	0.7	6.3
Supplemental security income[b]	1.4	6.0
Nonmeans-tested	19.9	128.6
Old age, survivors, and disability		
insurance[b,c]	12.9	87.2
Federal civil service retirement[b]	0.9	10.1
Veterans compensation pensions[b,d]	3.4	8.4
Unemployment compensation[a]	2.7	18.4
Coal miners' "black lung" benefits[b]	...	1.2
Public service employment[e]	...	3.3
In-kind programs	**0.6**	**42.1**
Means-tested	0.6	21.6
Food stamps[e]	0.1[f]	6.0
Medicaid[a]	0.2[g]	9.4
Child nutrition[e]	0.2[h]	3.1
Housing assistance[e]	0.1	3.1
Nonmeans-tested	...	20.5
Medicare	...	20.5
Total	**22.6**	**183.0**

Source: Derived from table 8-7 in this volume.

a. State and local administration and cost sharing. The federal financial share in Medicaid and AFDC is about 55 percent of the total.

b. Full federal financing and administration, though several states supplement the federal SSI benefits with their own funds.

c. Includes railroad retirement.

d. Includes veterans insurance programs. A small portion of this is means-tested.

e. State and local administration, full federal financing.

f. Represents the removal of surplus commodities, the precursor of the food stamp program.

g. Medical vendor payments.

h. Includes both the special milk program and the school lunch program.

ings subsidization, particularly for the low-income population, are generating more interest.

The major transfer programs financed with federal funds and serving income security purposes are shown in table 12-1. The cash programs are of two types: means-tested programs designed to put a floor under the income of recipients, thus alleviating or eliminating their income poverty; and nonmeans-tested ones that generally have eligibility criteria related to employment history and current status and are intended to replace some of a disrupted flow of earnings for people at all income levels. The noncash, or in-kind, programs support three types of consumption—food, housing, and health care—and are predominately means-tested.[3] Many of these transfer programs are administered at the state or local level; most of these have partial state and local financing.

These income security transfer programs have constituted the fastest growing share of the federal budget over the past seventeen years, rising from 24 percent in 1960 to an estimated 42 percent in 1977.[4] However, barring major changes in current policies, their share of the federal budget is expected to remain roughly constant over the next decade. While the means-tested programs have grown faster than the others (from 3 percent to 7 percent of the baseline budget), they still account for a much smaller share of the budget than the non-means-tested programs (whose share grew from 21 percent to 35 percent over the same time period). Similarly, in-kind expenditures have grown considerably faster than cash expenditures (from less than 1 percent to 10 percent of the baseline budget), but still constitute less than one-quarter of total income security expenditures.

The first part of this chapter outlines the progress that has been made in the past several decades toward the four income security objectives listed above and attempts to determine the influence of the federal government's income security programs on that progress. The second part of the chapter then analyzes some of the major issues that must be confronted in three areas of income security policy: social security, reform of the transfer system for the low-income population, and the federal tax structure.

PART I. RECENT PROGRESS: THE RECORD AND ITS IMPLICATIONS

Substantial progress has been made during the past two decades toward three out of the four income security objectives: earnings replacement, access to necessary goods, and the reduction of poverty. On the other hand, the distribution of income, after becoming substantially more even between 1929 and 1949, has remained remark-

3. Means-tested programs are often referred to as welfare programs (though this term is often applied only to the cash programs) and most of the nonmeans-tested ones as social insurance programs.

4. Calculated on the basis of the baseline budget developed by Charles Schultze in chapter 8 in order to eliminate the temporary effects of the current recession. Thus, they are not in precise agreement with the figures in table 12-1. See chapter 8 for a discussion of the sources of growth of most of these programs and the reasons why they are expected to level off as a percentage of the federal budget.

ably constant since then. Underneath this constancy, however, are a number of diverse trends within the totals. Moreover, throughout the past several decades, the budget dollars devoted to federal income security programs have grown much faster than national income.

What are we to make of this? Did income security programs have no effect on income distribution? Did they forestall a more uneven distribution? Or do our measures of distribution fail to capture the effects of the programs? In an attempt to answer these questions, and as background for our later analysis of policy issues, we turn to an examination of the past record—how have federal income security programs worked and how have they, together with other economic and social developments, affected the major objectives of income security policy?

Earnings Replacement

A number of major events can reduce the earnings or earnings capacity of families or individuals, chiefly retirement, long-term disability, unemployment, and death. Beginning in the Great Depression, the federal government has developed income security programs to moderate the effects of these events on the incomes of individuals (or, in case of death, their survivors). These programs are not means-tested: entitlement to benefits depends principally on employment history;[5] thus, people at all income levels are eligible for them.

Old age, survivors, and disability insurance (OASDI) and unemployment insurance (UI) are by far the largest public earnings replacement programs; but they are only part of a large matrix of both private and public sources of income support, as shown in table 12-2. The federal role in this area is most complex because it involves not only the specific structure of federal programs but also the appropriate mix of public and private means and the appropriate regulation of both state programs (such as workmen's compensation) and private activities (such as private pension plans).

Because of this complex of activities there is no simple way to measure progress toward fuller earnings replacement; however, the

5. If families or individuals have no earnings sources or suffer a disruption in earnings that lowers total income below some prescribed minimum, they may be eligible for initial or higher benefits from a means-tested program. In this sense the latter perform a residual earnings replacement function by placing a floor under income in general or the consumption of particular goods or services.

Table 12-2. Major Provisions for Earnings Replacement in the United States, 1976

Reason for earnings loss	Earnings replacement source[a]	Jurisdiction
Temporary unemployment	Unemployment insurance	State, federal
	Public service employment	State, federal
Disability		
Resulting from work only, total and partial	Workmen's compensation	State
	Veterans compensation	Federal
	Black lung program	Federal
Other	Sick leave	Public and private employees
Short-term	Temporary disability insurance	State, private
Long-term, total	Social security (disability insurance)	Federal
	Long-term disability insurance	Private
	Early retirement pensions	Most public and private pensions
Retirement and death		
Low-to-middle income classes	Social security (old age and survivors insurance)	Federal
Middle-to-upper income classes	Social security (old age and survivors insurance)	Federal
	Pensions	Most employers
	Annuities, life insurance, and other savings	Private

Source: Based on relevant public laws and literature.

a. In addition there are many favored tax treatments such as sick pay and pension contributions that support the earnings replacement function.

increase in expenditures in this area over the past twenty-five years is indicative of rapidly expanding protection for workers and their families. For example, expenditures under the public programs shown in table 12-2 have grown from $6.9 billion in 1950 to $31.0 billion in 1965 and to $111.7 billion in 1975 (representing an increase in percentage of the gross national product from 2.6 percent in 1950 to 7.8 percent in 1975). For the corresponding years, private employee benefits grew from $1.0 billion to $6.0 billion to $20.7 billion (from 0.4 percent of GNP in 1950 to 1.5 percent in 1975).[6] Interestingly,

6. Alfred M. Skolnik and Sophie R. Dales, "Social Welfare Expenditures, 1950–75," *Social Security Bulletin,* vol. 39 (January 1976), table 9, p. 19; and *Economic Report of the President, January 1976,* p. 171. Public service employment expendi-

payments under the public programs grew more slowly than private payments over this period, indicating a growing role in earnings replacement for the private sector. This trend is likely to continue: the social insurance programs, whose coverage is now so broad, are unlikely to continue their recent rate of growth while payments under private pension programs are expected to rise rapidly over the next two decades.

The degree of protection against lost earnings provided by UI and OASDI can be measured more precisely. Over the past thirty years OASDI has increased its coverage of the private labor force from 65 percent to near saturation, at 97 percent.[7] Table 12-3 shows the amount of earnings replacement OASDI currently provides for various types of workers and their families. The replacement rate is the ratio of the initial year's benefits to the worker's wage in the year just prior to eligibility. It provides a useful measure of the extent to which OASDI benefits alone will permit a family to maintain the standard of living achieved just prior to eligibility. It has been estimated that a replacement rate of 60–65 percent is necessary for full maintenance.[8]

Table 12-3 attests to the general high level of earnings replacement that has been achieved through social security for fully covered workers and their families. In addition to the broad extension of coverage since the early 1950s, the replacement rate for the average fully covered worker has been increased by over 30 percent. Although replacement rates fall short of 65 percent as workers' wage histories exceed the median, the presumption is that most of these families are not totally dependent upon OASDI, but have private sources avail-

---

tures are not reflected in the public program totals. Private employee benefits include payments under pensions, group life, accidental death and dismemberment, and disability insurance; paid sick leave; and supplemental unemployment benefit plans.

7. Federal, state, and local government employees are generally not required to participate, although most state and local employees have elected coverage.

8. James Schulz and others, *Providing Adequate Retirement Income* (University Press of New England for Brandeis University Press, 1974), p. 41. The figure is arrived at by adjusting the baseline rate of 100 percent for the reduced income tax burden of the elderly (OASDI benefits are nontaxable), the discontinuation of the need to save for retirement, and the lower relative expenditure needs of the elderly in order to maintain an equivalent standard of living. Similar calculations made by the Office of the Assistant Secretary for Planning and Evaluation of HEW indicate that, while 60–65 percent is appropriate for high-wage workers, the equivalent figures for median- and low-wage earners may be nearer to 70 percent and 80 percent, respectively.

Table 12-3. Benefits and Replacement Rates under Old Age and Survivors Insurance, by Age of Retirement, Second Half of 1976

| Retirement age and spouse's age | Monthly benefits for worker with median earnings | | Replacement rate[a] for worker with | | |
	Amount (dollars)	As percent of PIA[b]	Low earnings[c]	Median earnings[a]	Maximum earnings[e]
Worker retiring at					
Age 65	320.00	100.0	0.563	0.433	0.312
Age 62	252.30	80.0	0.450	0.341	0.244
Worker retiring at age 65 with spouse					
Aged 65	480.00	150.0	0.845	0.650	0.468
Aged 62	440.00	137.5	0.744	0.595	0.429
Worker retiring at age 62 with spouse					
Aged 65	410.00	130.0	0.731	0.554	0.397
Aged 62	370.60	117.5	0.661	0.501	0.358
Surviving spouse aged 65 with deceased spouse retiring in 1976 at					
Age 65	320.00	100.0	0.563	0.433	0.312
Age 62	260.20	82.5	0.464	0.352	0.252
Surviving spouse aged 62 with deceased spouse retiring in 1976 at					
Age 65	265.30	82.9	0.467	0.359	0.259
Age 62	260.20	82.5	0.464	0.352	0.252
Surviving spouse aged 60 with deceased spouse retiring in 1976 at					
Age 65	228.80	71.5	0.403	0.310	0.223

Source: Tabulation provided by the U.S. Department of Health, Education, and Welfare, Office of the Assistant Secretary for Planning and Evaluation.

a. The replacement rate is the constant dollar value of the 1976 benefit divided by the constant dollar value of the 1975 wage.

b. Primary insurance amount. The entitlement of a single worker retiring at age 65 is equal to his PIA. All other benefits are calculated as percentages of the PIA.

c. Half of the median wage for males over a continuous work history.

d. Median for all male wage and salary workers with earnings subject to the social security tax over a continuous work history.

e. Worker earning at or above the maximum wage subject to the old age, survivors, and disability insurance payroll tax over a continuous work history.

able.[9] Future targets for replacement rates in social security and the relationship of social security to private savings provisions are discussed in the second part of this chapter.

Coverage of the UI system, while not yet as full as OASDI, has expanded considerably over recent decades. In 1950, 59 percent of all wage and salary earners were covered by the permanent federal unemployment compensation system, compared to 85 percent now.[10] Legislation pending in Congress will extend coverage to nearly all members of currently uncovered groups except the self-employed.

Though replacement rates for actual UI recipients cannot be precisely calculated, it is clear that they have risen considerably in the past two decades. One recent estimate of the replacement rates for various family types in each state yielded mean values that ranged from 46 to 78 percent.[11] Although rates are considerably lower in some states than in others, these mean values are indicative of the considerable protection from short-term, involuntary unemployment now offered the vast majority of workers (and their families).[12] Among the current issues under discussion are federal minimum standards for replacement rates and what the duration of benefit payments for the longer-term unemployed should be.

Promoting Financial Access to Goods and Services

The federal government has long promoted access to certain widely valued goods and services, but only in the past ten years has this policy been explicitly articulated and vigorously pursued. In fact,

9. For example, Peter Henle, "Recent Trends in Retirement Benefits Related to Earnings," *Monthly Labor Review*, vol. 95 (June 1972), p. 19, reports that in 1972 mature private pension plans yielded a replacement rate of 15 to 20 percent to a worker with twenty years of service.

10. The primary categories of workers uncovered are state and local government employees, the self-employed, and agricultural and domestic workers. However, half of the states have extended UI benefits to some portion of state employees and a few cover the other types of workers as well.

11. Martin Feldstein, "Unemployment Compensation: Adverse Incentives and Distributional Anomalies," *National Tax Journal*, vol. 27 (June 1974), p. 236. These represent the ratio of UI benefits to a worker's previous after-tax pay and do not take into account the loss of fringe benefits with unemployment.

12. In times of high national unemployment individuals can receive UI benefits for fairly long time periods. The normal maximum duration is twenty-six weeks, but an additional thirteen weeks can be triggered by high unemployment rates. In addition, as a result of the recent recession Congress temporarily added twenty-six more

direct in-kind programs for food, low-income housing, and medical care did not exist before the beginning of the war on poverty in 1964; and they have been the fastest growing component of federal expenditures for social purposes since then.

The mainstay of federal food consumption policy is the food stamp program. Since 1974 all households in the United States have been eligible for food stamps under nationally uniform criteria if their income and assets fall below prescribed levels. The benefits vary with household size and are determined by what the Department of Agriculture considers sufficient to purchase a minimally adequate diet (currently about $2,000 a year for a family of four); they are adjusted semiannually for changes in food prices. All households, except for the very poorest, have to pay between 20 and 30 percent of their monthly income (after a considerable number of exclusions are allowed for such things as work-related expenses) in order to purchase their food stamp allotment. This insures that the transfer value of the food stamps decreases as household income increases.

Only about 50 percent of those eligible to receive food stamps actually participate in the program. Most of those who do not probably feel that participation is not worthwhile either because of the inconveniences of applying or because they consider it degrading to be on welfare. Some, however, are precluded from participation because of their inability to muster the cash to meet the purchase requirement.

Until 1968, housing assistance to the lower-income population was meager, but from 1968 to 1973 it expanded rapidly. In 1968 two new programs were enacted: home ownership assistance (section 235 of the National Housing Act) and rental assistance (section 236). These programs, as well as those already existing, have two common characteristics: the subsidies apply largely to newly constructed units and they are designed to limit the housing costs of eligible families to 20 to 25 percent of income. In general, eligibility extends to all families whose income is at or below 80 percent of the area median, though unrelated individuals in a household must be elderly or handicapped. By 1973 annual subsidized housing starts were triple or quadruple that of the pre-1968 level. The vast majority of this

---

weeks of eligibility (for a total of sixty-five) and provided the basic thirty-nine weeks of coverage to workers not eligible for regular benefits because they had worked in uncovered occupations.

assistance was going to poor and near-poor families. But because of the limited appropriations only 10 to 15 percent of those eligible for such assistance under the law actually received it.[13]

Early in 1973 the administration froze all new commitments under the major low-income housing assistance programs, citing two primary reasons: the inequities engendered by the facts that only a small percentage of the eligible population was receiving assistance and the assistance was tied to particular housing units, and the high cost of subsidies that are tied exclusively to new housing. Two approaches to a replacement for these programs are being taken. First, major experimentation is under way with a housing allowance concept. This approach is similar to the one embodied in the food stamp program: the subsidy is provided directly to the consumer and is based on family income and the cost of minimally adequate housing. Housing allowances can be used for new or existing housing as long as the housing meets certain standards. If a major housing allowance program were ever adopted it presumably would have an open-ended appropriation (as do the food stamp, Medicaid, and cash welfare programs) in order to insure that all who were eligible and wished to participate could do so. The potential annual costs of such a comprehensive housing allowance program that made up the difference between 25 percent of a family's income and the local cost of minimally adequate housing for the family (as reflected in current Department of Housing and Urban Development standards) could easily run to $15 billion.

The other approach, provided for in an amendment to the National Housing Act of 1974 (section 8), authorizes HUD to pay to the owner of eligible housing an amount equal to the difference between 15 to 25 percen of an eligible family's income and a fair market rent for the unit.[14] Since the units do not have to be new, this program is similar in effect to the housing allowance. Neither is limited by the existing stock of public housing or the speed with which new housing can be built. Both have the potential to grow, as did the food stamp

13. In dollar terms a far more important federal role in housing involves the tax subsidies to homeowners in the form of the deduction of mortgage interest payments and real estate taxes in personal income taxes and the absence of a tax on the net rental value of home ownership. These benefits are worth over $13 billion annually and are highly concentrated among middle- and upper-income families.

14. Eligibility criteria for section 8 are similar to those of the already existing low-income housing programs.

program, if money is appropriated to cover more than a fraction of those potentially eligible.

The criteria of minimal adequacy that are embodied in both food and low-income housing assistance programs are analogous. They are based on a notion of meeting certain minimum standards that are viewed as necessary for people to function in routine daily activities without obvious physical or mental distress. In each case there is a qualitative dimension (the nutritional value of the diet or the physical condition of the housing) and a quantitative dimension (the minimum cost of the necessary quantity) specified that is generally within the financial means of households with incomes above one-half the national median. Thus, these standards of adequacy would not eliminate the extensive discrepancies in the amount of the necessities of life that different households could afford to consume.

In the case of food, the quantitative dimension of the objective has been largely met as a result of the rapid expansion of the food stamp program over the past few years. Little additional effort would be required to close most of the remaining gap.[15] The universal availability and level of benefits in the program ensures financial access for all but a small minority to a diet that will meet minimum standards of nutrition.[16] In this sense federal food consumption policy has made major advances in the past decade.[17]

In contrast, progress toward the housing objective has been much more limited, as evidenced by the 90 or so percent of households eligible for low-income assistance that do not receive it. Simply increasing coverage in the existing programs (or by means of housing allowances), as was done with the food stamp program, would definitely speed progress toward the objective; but how effective this would be is unclear since the stock of low-income housing that meets the minimum standards is relatively fixed, both in quantity and in geographic location, in the short run.[18] Experience with both the newly expanded

15. The necessary steps are a more vigorous out-reach program, elimination of the purchase requirement, and, possibly, modest increases in the benefit levels for some types of households.

16. Though the extent to which food stamp users, or for that matter, nonusers, actually consume a diet that provides this level of nutrition is another issue; a more aggressive consumer education program is needed here.

17. The problems of the food stamp program are still very much in the news, however, and at this writing several reform bills were before Congress.

18. For further discussion of this problem as well as more general information on housing allowances and rent supplements, see Edward R. Fried and others,

section 8 program as well as the housing allowance experiments soon
should provide some useful guidance on these issues.

There are numerous federal programs for financing or providing
medical services, but Medicare and Medicaid are by far the most
important. The Medicare program now provides basic hospital insurance for all people who are disabled or over sixty-five and covered
by social security, and pays half the cost of a supplementary medical
insurance plan covering physicians' services and certain other benefits. Under the Medicaid program, the states and the federal government share the costs of providing basic medical care to welfare
recipients and, in many states, to the medically indigent (those categorically eligible for cash welfare but with incomes too high to
receive payments).

A large majority of the population not covered by these two programs has private health insurance, generally provided through employers. The federal government subsidizes the purchase of private
health insurance and the payment of medical expenditures through
two types of tax provisions: the income tax deduction of one-half of
health insurance premiums up to $150 plus all health expenditures
in excess of 3 percent of adjusted gross income, and the tax exemption of employers' contributions to employee insurance plans. For
fiscal 1977 the value of these tax subsidies is estimated by the Congressional Budget Office to be $6.3 billion. In contrast to the Medi-
care and Medicaid programs, the bulk of these subsidies do not go to
low-income people.

Despite the rapid expansion of health insurance over the past
decade, the combined coverage of Medicare, Medicaid, and private
insurance is still generally considered far from adequate. The most
glaring problems are these: many families are not covered by any
plan, most notably those whose head is unemployed and the poor not
on welfare in states without a program for the medically indigent;
there is a general lack of protection from catastrophic illnesses; and
out-of-pocket costs for even basic expenses required under Medicare
can be financially burdensome for some.

Unlike society's attitudes to the provision of housing or food, most
people seem to expect the federal government to promote financial

---

Setting National Priorities: The 1974 Budget (Brookings Institution, 1973), pp. 129–
45. It is interesting that housing allowance proposals generally restrict assistance to
those residing in housing that meets minimum standards, whereas the food stamp
program has no requirements for the diets of recipients.

access for all to a level of health care that is extremely high relative to any norm.[19] The history of Medicare and Medicaid and the likelihood of at least universal catastrophic coverage under some form of national health insurance in the near future testify to this. In fact, the notion that there ought to be total equality of access to medical care has considerable currency. It is frequently argued that the right to life, or at least to an equal probability of avoiding death or disability, requires equal access to medical care, and that this is a right, along with voting and justice under the law, that should be distributed equally.[20]

Clearly, considerable progress has been made in the last decade in access to health care. However, it is equally evident that we still have far to go to meet society's objective, even if it is defined well short of ensuring equal access for all. There are severe problems on the supply side of the health care market that inhibit further progress. The current debate on national health insurance is focusing on these as well as on a more precise articulation of the degree of equality of access to medical care that should be promoted by federal policy.[21]

One major issue in the federal government's role in promoting financial access is common to all three areas. Why do it through specific subsidies? Why not simply produce an income distribution through tax and transfer policies that will insure the desired degree of financial access and let people buy what they want? These questions are taken up in the second part of this chapter where the overall design of the income transfer system is discussed.

Reducing Poverty

The United States set forth the elimination of poverty as a goal in the mid-1960s in the belief that a nation capable of achieving unprecedented affluence should as a matter of duty abolish extreme

19. Federal student grant and loan programs for higher education could also be analyzed in the same terms as housing, food, and medical financing programs. The new basic opportunity grants program is means-tested and designed to promote financial access to a minimum standard amount of higher education. The equality-of-access concept it appears to embody is closer to that for medical care than for food or housing.

20. At least, as James Tobin argues, until the total amount of medical resources available is such that were they spread equally among the population only trivial needs would be unmet. See "On Limiting the Domain of Inequality," *Journal of Law and Economics*, vol. 13 (April 1970), pp. 263–77.

21. See Karen Davis, *National Health Insurance: Benefits, Costs, and Consequences* (Brookings Institution, 1975).

need. Poverty was defined in terms of a basic subsistence level of real income that varied according to the size and composition of families.[22] Since that time, estimates of the number of persons in poverty have been published annually and are considered important indicators of our economic and social progress.

A later variant of this subsistence income concept of poverty ("absolute" poverty) has been a measure of the number of persons in relative poverty.[23] Unlike the absolute poverty level, which remains fixed in real terms, the relative poverty line rises when average real incomes increase. Relative poverty is closely related to the long-standing concept of the size distribution of income. If the overall distribution of income remains constant, absolute poverty will eventually be abolished by real income growth, while the degree of relative poverty will remain unchanged.

Major reductions in the size of the poverty population and changes in its demographic composition have occurred in the last seventeen years. The former have been caused primarily by the strong economic growth of the sixties and the increased antipoverty effectiveness of public transfers in the past decade, and the latter by the differential effect of these forces on demographic subgroups of the poor and the changing demographic composition of the overall population.

Consider first the aggregate picture. Figure 12-1 shows the change in the size of the poor population from 1959 to 1975, measured as the percentage of all persons living in poverty, by the absolute definition and by one possible relative definition.[24] The absolute estimate shows a general downward trend, but with significant cyclical variation. The share of the population living in poverty fell continuously

22. Mollie Orshansky, "Counting the Poor: Another Look at the Poverty Profile," *Social Security Bulletin*, vol. 28 (January 1965), pp. 3–29. The poverty line was set as the price of a specific "market basket" of goods. It is adjusted annually only for inflation and therefore does not increase with real incomes in periods of growth (or fall in periods of recession). The market basket chosen is only an estimate of family needs and is not immune to criticism. The 1975 poverty threshold for a family of one female adult and one child was $3,660; for a husband-and-wife family of four, $5,457; and for a husband-and-wife family of seven, $8,886 (authors' estimates).

23. The relative poverty line is most commonly defined as some fraction of median income, but other definitions have been suggested. Both relative and absolute poverty can be measured as the fraction of either persons or households in poverty.

24. The concept commonly used in determining poverty status, census or family income, includes all cash receipts from employment, self-employment, interest, dividends, rent, government transfers, and regular gifts or support from friends or relatives. It does not include capital gains, the value of government in-kind transfers, or windfall gifts.

Figure 12-1. Absolute and Relative Poverty Rates, 1959–74[a]

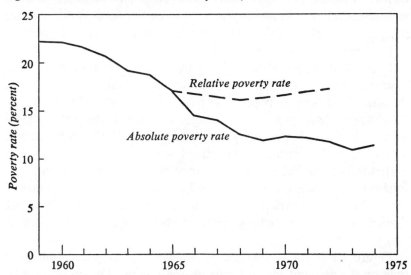

Sources: Absolute poverty, U.S. Bureau of the Census, *Current Population Reports,* series P-60, no. 102, "Characteristics of the Population below the Poverty Level, 1974" (Government Printing Office, 1976), table 1; and *Economic Report of the President, January 1976,* table B-21. Relative poverty, based on Robert D. Plotnick and Felicity Skidmore, *Progress against Poverty: A Review of the 1964–1974 Decade* (Academic Press, 1975), table 4.1 (modified and extrapolated by the present authors). Since the base year of the Plotnick-Skidmore measure was 1965, the figure should not be interpreted as implying congruence of the two measures before 1965.
a. Persons living in poverty as a percentage of total population.

from 1959 until 1969, which was a period of almost continuous economic growth. The 1970 recession brought an increase in the poverty rate, but renewed growth reinstated the downward trend until 1973. The current recession has brought a marked increase in 1974, and another for 1975 (probably to about the 1968 level) is a near certainty, though data are not yet available. This picture confirms that progress in fighting poverty is highly dependent upon the state of the economy.

The relative poverty measure used in figure 12-1 defines as poor any household whose ratio of income to its official poverty income threshold is less than 44 percent of the median of that ratio for all households that year.[25] By this measure relative poverty has changed hardly at all over the years for which adequate data are available. This lack of movement indicates that at least the lower tail of the

25. See Robert D. Plotnick and Felicity Skidmore, *Progress against Poverty: A Review of the 1964–1974 Decade* (Academic Press, 1975), chap. 2. A husband-and-wife family with two children (1965 poverty threshold, $3,223) with an income of $3,868 would have a ratio of income to their poverty threshold ("income/needs ratio") of 1.20, while a similar family with an income of $2,578 would have an in-

measured distribution of income has been relatively stable, so that as income relative to needs has grown for the general population, the same proportion of the population has remained below 44 percent of the median ratio.

In addition to general economic growth, the growth of government cash transfers also has been an important determinant of changes in the size of the poverty population over time. In 1965, 33 percent of households whose pretransfer incomes were below the poverty level were moved out of poverty by such transfers; by 1972 this figure was 44 percent.[26] This increased effectiveness of government transfers is particularly remarkable since the proportion of poor households before transfers increased between 1967 and 1973, primarily because of the increasing proportion of female-headed households, which do not share in general economic growth nearly as much as male-headed households.[27]

Figure 12-2 shows the changes in the poverty population over time by the age and sex of heads of households. The proportion of the poor who are nonaged and living in households headed by females has almost doubled since 1959, from 20.5 to 40.8 percent. Two developments account for this. First, between 1959 and 1972 the proportion of households headed by females rose sharply, from 12.0 to 16.3 percent.[28] Second, the proportion of all persons in female-headed families who were poor (the "incidence" of poverty)

---

come/needs ratio of 0.80. The cutoff at 44 percent of the median ratio was chosen because in 1965, the base year for the Plotnick-Skidmore study, 44 percent of the median/needs ratio was precisely 1.0 so that the relative and absolute poverty populations were congruent.

26. Though the effectiveness of transfers against relative poverty did not increase over this period (ibid., table 6.4). It should be noted, however, that in 1971, 20 percent of the poor received no cash transfers at all. Michael C. Barth and others, *Toward an Effective Income Support System: Problems, Prospects, and Choices* (University of Wisconsin, Madison, Institute for Research on Poverty, 1974), table 4.

27. This also appears to be a result of a general decline in the participation of the poor in economic growth over this period, even adjusting for changes in the age-sex composition of heads of households. Peter Gottschalk, "Earnings, Transfers and Poverty Reduction" (Mount Holyoke College, 1976; manuscript in preparation).

28. Most of the increase in the number of female-headed families has occurred through separation and divorce, as opposed to widowhood (which has held relatively constant) and illegitimacy (which has increased slightly from a small base). Recent research suggests that divorces and separations are more likely when a husband experiences frequent unemployment and when a wife has earned income of her own; also, the expected duration of the female headship of young divorcees is only about five or six years. Heather L. Ross and Isabel V. Sawhill, *Time of Transition: The Growth of Families Headed by Women* (Washington, D.C.: Urban Institute, 1975), chaps. 2, 7, and app. 1.

Figure 12-2. Number of Aged Poor Persons and Nonaged Poor Persons in Male-Headed and Female-Headed Households,ᵃ Selected Years, 1959–74

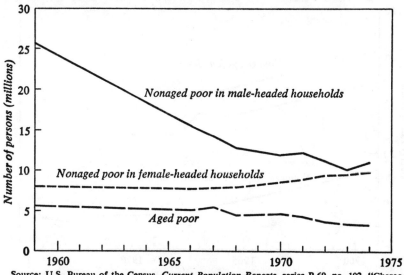

Source: U.S. Bureau of the Census, *Current Population Reports,* series P-60, no. 102, "Characteristics of the Population below the Poverty Level, 1974" (GPO, 1976), table 1.

a. "Male-headed" and "female-headed" are used according to the conventional definitions (that is, all husband-and-wife families are designated male-headed) because the data for this period do not allow a more evenhanded definition. For 1960–65 and 1969 data were not available and are extrapolated from preceding years.

decreased much less than it did for the population as a whole: for female-headed families poverty incidence declined hardly at all, whereas for male-headed families it was more than halved (from 16.9 to 6.3 percent). By 1974 a female-headed family was four times as likely to be poor as a male-headed family. Public transfer payments lifted only 23 percent of pretransfer poor female-headed households out of poverty in 1974, far below the 63 percent of the aged who were removed from poverty in 1972 by transfer payments. Moreover, the effectiveness of transfer payments in removing female-headed families from poverty has not increased since 1959, in contrast to their increasing effectiveness for other demographic groups.

A second prominent category of the poor is the aged. Figure 12-2 shows that the number of the poor who are aged has remained fairly constant, rising slightly in the mid-1960s and then falling through 1974. This constancy hardly reflects a lack of progress, however. Figure 12-3 shows that the incidence of poverty among the aged has fallen dramatically, from about 1 in 2.9 in 1959 to 1 in 6.6 in 1974. Much of this progress is due to government transfers: in 1965, 51 percent of the aged pretransfer poor were lifted out of poverty by

Figure 12-3. Poverty Rates[a] of Aged Persons and of Nonaged Persons in Male-Headed and Female-Headed Households,[b] Selected Years, 1959–74

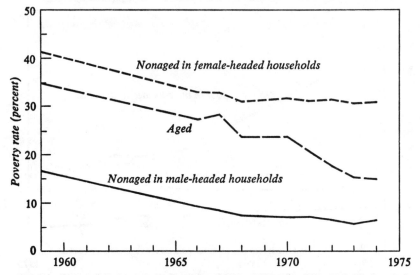

Sources: *Economic Report of the President, January 1976,* table B-21; U.S. Bureau of the Census, *Current Population Reports,* series P-20, "Household and Family Characteristics" (GPO, various years); Bureau of the Census, "Characteristics of the Population below the Poverty Level, 1974," table 1.
a. Rates for the nonaged are shown as a percentage of all persons in male- and female-headed households because of the limitations of the available data and thus are slightly understated.
b. See n. *a,* figure 12-2.

transfers, while in 1972 the figure was 63 percent. The cash transfer system is far more effective in lifting the aged out of poverty than the nonaged, and this effectiveness has increased over the past ten years.

The nonaged poor living in male-headed households constitute a declining share of all the poor, but they still account for almost half of all persons in poverty—45.6 percent in 1974. This may come as a surprise to those whose image of the poor is the broken family on welfare; but in fact the head of a family working forty hours a week for fifty-two weeks at the minimum wage of $2.20 per hour would earn $4,576, which in 1975 was almost $900 short of the poverty line for a family of four. For such a family work alone would not serve as a ticket out of poverty. In fact, even in the recession year of 1974 more than half of the male heads of poor families worked at full-time jobs, and over half of those worked for the full year.[29]

29. U.S. Bureau of the Census, *Current Population Reports,* Series P-60, no. 102, "Characteristics of the Population below the Poverty Level, 1974" (Government Printing Office, 1976), table 27, p. 93.

This employment pattern in male-headed low-income families makes it clear that it was the sustained economic growth of the sixties that was largely responsible for the reduced poverty rate in this population (before the current recession), though part of the reduction can be attributed to government transfers. In 1965, 11 percent of all poor male-headed families with children were lifted out of poverty by transfers; in 1972, 23 percent were lifted out by transfers. Thus, cash transfers were far less effective in helping the poor in male-headed families than they were for the aged, but the rate of increase in that effectiveness was quite high.

The poverty rates shown in figure 12-1 and the estimate of the antipoverty effectiveness of public transfers must be qualified in two important respects. First, the surveys on which these estimates are based are subject to significant underreporting of income by the respondents, and particularly of public transfers.[30] Second, the income measure by which poverty status is determined does not include the value of government in-kind transfers.

The in-kind programs now provide sufficient benefits to the poor that they unquestionably have a sizable positive impact on their well-being.[31] In 1974, federal food, housing, and medical in-kind transfers amounted to $22.9 billion, or 161 percent of the cash income poverty gap (the aggregate amount by which the cash incomes of the poor falls short of their poverty income threshold) in that year. In 1972, 85 percent of total food stamp bonuses, 74 percent of public housing benefits, and 75 percent of Medicaid expenditures were received by those whose pretransfer incomes were below the poverty level.[32]

30. In 1972, for example, the Current Population Survey obtained reporting of 87.0 percent of all wage and salary income, 81.7 percent of all social security benefits, and 65.5 percent of all public assistance benefits. U.S. Bureau of the Census, *Current Population Reports*, Series P-60, no. 90, "Money Income in 1972 of Families and Persons in the United States" (GPO, 1973), table K.

31. It is clear that the in-kind programs add to the real income of recipients, but one would generally expect the amount to be considerably less than the actual cost to the government, since the recipients' use of the transfer is more constrained than if it were in cash. For example, a family receiving $50 in food stamps might, if it were given $50 in cash, choose to spend $25 on food and $25 on clothing; in that case the last $25 worth of stamps would not be "worth" as much to the family as $25 in cash. The real value of the in-kind grant to the family is the amount of cash that would make it feel equally well off, and determining that value is both conceptually and empirically difficult. Nevertheless, some valiant attempts have been made, and their results are utilized below to show the impact on poverty of the inclusion of a cash equivalent value (to the recipient) of in-kind benefits.

32. *Special Analyses, The Budget of the United States Government, Fiscal Year*

One way of evaluating the impact of in-kind transfers on the poor is to determine what the effect on the poverty count would be if in-kind benefits were included in income. The available data indicate that counting in-kind subsidies, appropriately adjusted downward for their lower cash value to recipients, would reduce the poverty rate by at least 25 percent in 1971–72.[33] Since that time, in-kind transfers have more than doubled, in part because of broadened coverage among the poor. It would not be unreasonable to expect that the impact of these programs on the poor could now be nearly double that of 1971–72, indicating even greater antipoverty effectiveness of the transfer system than our earlier data. In fact, a definition of household income that both includes the recipients' cash valuation of in-kind benefits and adjusts for underreporting of cash income would probably reflect a current poverty rate close to 5 percent rather than the official level of 12 percent.

An extremely important addition to our previous knowledge about the poverty population has recently become available. Ever since poverty became a common concern, most Americans have believed that the poverty population is composed of more or less the same people year after year. The census surveys that collect poverty data report on families for only one year and so cannot confirm or contradict this conception. But one survey followed a large sample of families from 1967 through 1972 and found that a large proportion of the poor in any one year are not poor in other years.[34]

Using the census money income definition of poverty, only 20 to 30 percent of those who were poor in any one of the six years were poor in every year. On the other hand, over 50 million people, nearly a quarter of the population, were poor in at least one of the six years.

1976, table L-1, p. 198; Plotnick and Skidmore, *Progress against Poverty*, table 3.4, p. 56; Bureau of the Census, *Current Population Reports*, series P-60, no. 102, tables 40–41, pp. 121–22.

33. Timothy Smeeding, "The Economic Well-Being of Low Income Households: Implications for Income Inequality and Poverty," in Marilyn Moon and Eugene Smolensky, eds., *Augmenting Measures of Economic Welfare* (Academic Press, forthcoming), found that about 38 percent of the poor would be considered nonpoor if the cash equivalent value of in-kind transfers were included in income for 1972. A similar estimate by the present authors for 1971 yields a 27 percent reduction in measured poverty.

34. U.S. Department of Health, Education, and Welfare, Office of the Assistant Secretary for Planning and Evaluation, "The Changing Economic Status of 5000 American Families: Highlights from the Panel Study of Income Dynamics" (HEW, 1974; processed). The study was conducted under the supervision of James N. Morgan by the Survey Research Center of the University of Michigan.

Thus, the total number of people living in poverty during the six years was at least twice the number who were poor in any single year, and about seven times the number who were poor for all six years. Much of this considerable movement into and out of poverty can be explained by changes of family composition; arrival or departure of children and marriage and divorce were significant factors in major changes in household income relative to need. Changes in labor force status of family members, such as initial entry, retirement, or disability, also played an important role. Thus, for the large majority of the poor in any one year, poverty is a temporary situation.[35] The yearly "snapshot" data on poverty presented up to now in fact represent the net effect of large flows of people both out of and into poverty every year.

Narrowing Income Differentials

The distribution of annual household income in the United States is highly uneven, and, as the constancy of relative poverty suggests, there has been no general reduction in the degree of income inequality in recent decades despite major reductions in absolute poverty. Although there are controversies over the accuracy of the basic data and the different ways of measuring the distribution, there can be little doubt that the pattern of cash income receipts within the household sector has remained relatively constant since World War II.[36] Using the simplest measure of income distribution—the share of annual income received by portions of the population ranked by family income—the lowest 20 percent of the population has never varied far from a 5 percent share of total income, while the highest 20 percent has always received about 40 percent (see table 12-4). This is the net effect of the independent and interactive effects of the transfer system and the distribution of household private income.

It would be roughly accurate to describe the past two decades as a period in which a number of demographic and social changes occurred that tended to shift the distribution of private income toward more inequality, but during which the disequalizing influences were

35. Many of the more than two-thirds of the poor in any one year who did not remain continuously in poverty still had quite low average incomes over the period; the others moved into the mainstream of economic status.

36. Many of the disputes over the accuracy of available data echo those mentioned in connection with poverty, most notably the underreporting of income.

Table 12-4. Distribution of Family Income, by Quintiles and the Highest 5 Percent
of All Families, 1947–74

Percent

Year	Income rankings					
	Lowest fifth	Second fifth	Middle fifth	Fourth fifth	Highest fifth	Highest 5 percent
1947	5.1	11.8	16.7	23.2	43.3	17.5
1948	5.0	12.1	17.2	23.2	42.5	17.1
1949	4.5	11.9	17.3	23.5	42.8	16.9
1950	4.5	11.9	17.4	23.6	42.7	17.3
1951	4.9	12.5	17.6	23.3	41.8	16.9
1952	4.9	12.2	17.1	23.5	42.2	17.7
1953	4.7	12.4	17.8	24.0	41.0	15.8
1954	4.5	12.0	17.6	24.0	41.9	16.4
1955	4.8	12.2	17.7	23.4	41.8	16.8
1956	4.9	12.4	17.9	23.6	41.1	16.4
1957	5.0	12.6	18.1	23.7	40.5	15.8
1958	5.0	12.5	18.0	23.9	40.6	15.4
1959	4.9	12.3	17.9	23.8	41.1	15.9
1960	4.8	12.2	17.8	24.0	41.3	15.9
1961	4.7	11.9	17.5	23.8	42.2	16.6
1962	5.0	12.1	17.6	24.0	41.3	15.7
1963	5.0	12.1	17.7	24.0	41.2	15.8
1964	5.1	12.0	17.7	24.0	41.2	15.9
1965	5.2	12.2	17.8	23.9	40.9	15.5
1966	5.6	12.4	17.8	23.8	40.5	15.6
1967	5.5	12.4	17.9	23.9	40.4	15.2
1968	5.6	12.4	17.7	23.7	40.5	15.6
1969	5.6	12.4	17.7	23.7	40.6	15.6
1970	5.4	12.2	17.6	23.8	40.9	15.6
1971	5.5	12.0	17.6	23.8	41.1	15.7
1972	5.4	11.9	17.5	23.9	41.4	15.9
1973	5.5	11.9	17.5	24.0	41.1	15.5
1974	5.4	12.0	17.6	24.1	41.0	15.3

Source: U.S. Bureau of the Census, *Current Population Reports*, series P-60, no. 101, "Money Income in 1974 of Families and Persons in the United States" (GPO, 1976), table 22, p. 37.

approximately offset by the equalizing effect of rising government transfer payments. The distribution of household private income has become somewhat more uneven over the past two decades, largely because of growing inequality in household earnings, which constitute about 80 percent of the total. This trend, in turn, is the net result of a multitude of influences that are difficult to isolate. Of lesser importance are those that are demographic in nature; others appear to reflect changes in the underlying distributive arrangements in the labor market. Among the latter, which are causing an increased dispersion in annual earnings among prime-age labor force participants,[37] are: increased inequality in hourly wages due to the changing occupational structure of the economy and greater relative wage increases over time for the higher-wage occupations; and increased variation in the amount of time worked.[38]

There are many ways in which changes in the demographic composition of households can lead to shifts in the distribution of household income. For example, it is likely that an increase in the number of heads of household with generally lower earnings—the young, aged, and females—will increase the inequality of income. One study that attempted to isolate the effect of changes in the age, race, sex, and education of the population from 1960 to 1970 found that on balance they promoted family income inequality.[39] Another effect, resulting from some of these demographic shifts as well as changes in labor force participation rates—most notably the large decline among the aged and increase among females[40]—is the increasingly greater number of multiearner and no-earner families, as opposed to those with one earner. The impact of this influence has been to redistribute income from both the top and bottom of the household distribution of income to the middle.[41]

37. Focusing on this group allows us to sidestep the effects of the demographic changes discussed below.

38. The former two are suggested by Peter Henle, "Exploring the Distribution of Earned Income," *Monthly Labor Review*, vol. 95 (December 1972), pp. 16–27; and the latter by T. Paul Schultz, "Long Term Change in Personal Income Distribution: Theoretical Approaches, Evidence and Explanations" (Rand Corporation, 1972; processed).

39. Joseph J. Minarik, Jr., "A Microanalysis of the Size Distribution of Income" (Ph.D. dissertation, Yale University, 1974). The increase in proportion of heads of families who were young, aged, female, or black had a disequalizing effect; the increase in those with greater schooling was equalizing. The net effect was to redistribute one-half of one percent of total income from the bottom decile of households ranked by income to the top decile.

40. Labor force participation among men sixty-five and over has declined from 45.8 percent in 1950 to 22.4 percent in 1974; for married women of all ages with husband present it increased from 23.8 percent in 1950 to 43.0 percent in 1974. U.S. Bureau of Labor Statistics, *Handbook of Labor Statistics, 1975: Reference Edition* (GPO, 1975), pp. 29, 57.

41. Minarik, "Microanalysis." This occurred because no-earner households generally have low incomes, whereas multiearner families tend to concentrate in middle-income levels. There is a possibility that continued increase in the labor force participation of wives might become a disequalizing factor since they are likely to be concentrated in families where the husbands' earnings are above the median. The employment rate of such women is now lower than the average.

Given the relatively constant income distribution and the decline in the receipt of earnings in its lower tail, transfer payments can be thought of as "filling in" for the missing earnings. Recent data confirm that this is the case. Even over the short time span of 1967 to 1972, the share of government cash transfers in the total income of the lowest 20 percent of households increased from 55.5 to 60.0 percent.[42] It is clear that lower-income households are becoming more dependent on transfer income and that families without earnings are largely responsible for this trend.

There is reason to believe that simply the availability of government transfers may have caused greater reliance on them as an income source, and in some cases even contributed to greater measured income inequality. Higher social security and supplemental security income (SSI) benefits, for example, can enable the elderly to maintain their own households instead of living with their children. This turns one household into two, each with lower incomes than the initial one. Inasmuch as the number of subfamilies found by the 1970 census was significantly lower than that for 1960, it is clear that some of this breakup has occurred.[43] Similarly, more generous benefits for families headed by females make it more possible for them to live apart from relatives, and also make independence more attractive than living with a husband, if his earnings are low, since eligibility for the aid to families with dependent children program (AFDC) would be jeopardized. Finally, transfer benefits might cause some recipients to reduce their work effort, thus resulting in at least a partial substitution of transfers for earnings. There is some evidence that AFDC has a relatively weak work disincentive effect, that unemployment compensation has a moderate one, and social security a strong one.[44] It is unlikely, however, that these effects cause an ap-

42. Independent tabulations of the authors, using Bureau of the Census, Current Population Survey, 1970: Public Use Sample, tape on file in the Brookings data bank.

43. Minarik, "Microanalysis," chap. 6. The number of subfamilies decreased by 11 percent between the two years, while the total number of nuclear families increased by 12 percent.

44. For evidence on AFDC, see Irwin Garfinkel, "Income Transfer Programs and Work Effort: A Review," in *Studies in Public Welfare,* Paper 13: *How Income Supplements Can Affect Work Behavior,* Prepared for the Subcommittee on Fiscal Policy of the Joint Economic Committee, 93:2 (GPO, 1974); for unemployment compensation, see Stephen T. Marston, "The Impact of Unemployment Insurance on Job Search," *Brookings Papers on Economic Activity,* 1:1975, pp. 13–48; and for social security, see Michael J. Boskin, "Social Security and Retirement Decisions," Working Paper 107 (National Bureau of Economic Research, 1975; processed).

preciable change in the distribution of income since they are largely compensated for by transfers.

The obvious question is how the income distribution is altered if the whole range of noncash government expenditures is taken into account. This is an area in which both the conceptual and methodological problems are severe. The evidence to date is very tentative and inconsistent. Our reading of it suggests that the inclusion of all noncash expenditures in the definition of income would probably result in a modest reduction in inequality within any given year (for example, the lowest 20 percent of all families and persons probably would have 6½ to 7 rather than 5 to 5½ percent of the income) and only slightly less inequality over the time in the pretax distribution of income.[45]

This look at income distribution has focused so far on pretax income. The other important factor is the distribution of tax liabilities and its change over time. A recent study concluded that in 1966 the burden of the tax system of the United States was approximately proportional over the broad middle range of incomes, with taxes for very low and very high income households somewhat higher than the average as a proportion of their income.[46] The higher burdens on very large incomes were due largely to the progressivity of the federal income tax. Those on low incomes were due partially to the presence in those income groups of households with sizable and offsetting positive and negative incomes (due to business income and capital losses), who pay taxes higher than other households with equivalent net incomes. Beyond that fact, however, low-income households pay higher rates of taxes because of the regressivity of payroll, sales, and excise taxes.

---

45. Eugene Smolensky and others, in a series of discussion papers prepared for the Institute for Research on Poverty (Madison, Wisconsin) over the past two years, have reported minor changes in the distribution of income in both dimensions as a result of considering all public expenditures. Edgar Browning, in "How Much More Equality Can We Afford?" *The Public Interest*, no. 43 (Spring 1976), pp. 90–110, reports much greater effects in both dimensions. Both studies have their flaws, however, and we place less reliance on Browning's results because he has a less inclusive measure of public expenditures, includes an inappropriate measure of the imputed value of leisure in his income definition, considers only families and not unrelated individuals, and does not account for the changing distributional impact of public expenditures over time.

46. Joseph A. Pechman and Benjamin A. Okner, *Who Bears the Tax Burden?* (Brookings Institution, 1974), chap. 1. Most households were found to pay approximately 25 percent of their income in taxes; this result is not altered by any of a wide range of tax incidence assumptions tested in the study. The federal tax system was found to be slightly progressive.

Households with low incomes tend to consume comparatively large fractions of their income, sometimes over 100 percent when incomes are temporarily reduced. For such households sales and excise taxes can be a considerable burden. If a sales tax is universal (that is, payable on all goods) it can have the same effect as a flat-rate income tax with no exemptions or deductions for low-income households. Payroll taxes also bear heavily on those with low incomes. Again, while the payroll tax rate on employees is fairly low, the burden on the poor can be great because the first dollars of earnings are taxed with no exemptions or deductions. For the 80 percent of households not at either extreme of the income distribution, these regressive taxes were neutralized on balance by mildly progressive income taxes in 1966. However, for the past three decades the overall tax system has been moving in a regressive direction since payroll and sales taxes have been growing sharply as a share of government revenues.[47]

The net effect of government taxes and expenditures (the "fisc") on the overall distribution of income is difficult to determine because the distribution before taxes and expenditures is affected by the incentives implicit in the tax and transfer system. For this reason one cannot simply assume that the configuration of prefisc income is the one that would exist in the absence of a public sector. All that can be said with certainty is that over the past two decades the distribution of income, including transfers but before taxes, has exhibited a slight trend toward equality; and that the combined federal, state, and local tax system, which is nearly proportional and thus has little effect on the distribution, has been exhibiting a regressive trend. The distribution of income after taxes and expenditures has been very nearly constant.

Poverty and Income Distribution: A Summary

As a result of both economic growth and large increases in public transfers, considerable progress has been made against poverty over the last seventeen years, though there have been recent reverses due

47. In 1970, 18.0 percent of all government receipts were raised by payroll taxes, compared to 9.9 percent in 1950. Further increases have taken place since 1970, largely due to social security. For state and local sales taxes, the ratios are 9.6 percent and 6.7 percent for 1970 and 1950, respectively. *Survey of Current Business,* vol. 56 (January 1976), tables 3.2, 3.4.

to the recession. Poverty as conventionally measured has been reduced by about a half (from 22 percent to 12 percent of the population), and further reductions should occur as the economy recovers from the current recession. But this measure of poverty overestimates unmet needs. On the basis of an income definition that includes some valuation of in-kind transfers and makes additional allowances for income underreporting, the poverty count for 1971–72 might be reduced by as much as a third more. Considering the rapid growth of in-kind transfers in the last three years, it is quite likely that the overall incidence of poverty in the population, using such a broad income measure, will drop to below 5 percent as recovery from the recession proceeds.

Within the poverty population, the share of persons living in households headed by nonaged males has decreased (though it is still almost half), while that of persons in female-headed households has risen rapidly and that of the aged remained roughly constant. Because of the overall reduction in poverty incidence, these shares are consistent with a constant incidence of poverty among female-headed families, a sizable reduction among male-headed families, and a very large reduction among the aged. A continued high rate of divorce and separation, coupled with sustained economic growth, would maintain this trend for the near future. The transfer system has increased its effectiveness in moving aged and male-headed families out of poverty, but not female-headed families; however, a substantial proportion of the poor, particularly in male-headed families, still receive very little or no assistance. Although these year-to-year changes in the overall size of the poverty population are relatively modest, there are very large annual flows of people in and out of poverty largely because of changes in family composition and entry into or exit from the labor force due to normal life-cycle events.

The distribution of income has remained highly uneven and fairly constant over the past twenty-five years, although there have been some significant changes in the various determinants. The distribution of earnings among full-time labor force participants appears to be growing more uneven. The demographic characteristics of the population have shifted in ways unfavorable to equality primarily by increasing the share of households headed by females and the aged. An increasing number of families without earnings populates the lower tail of the distribution. Further, government transfers probably have encouraged greater formation of independent households by persons and families who have low pretransfer incomes. This process increases the number of low-income households and, thereby, the measured inequality. Government cash transfers, however, have increased sufficiently in magnitude over the past ten years to more than offset those trends, so that on balance the distribution of household money income has become very slightly more even.

Taxes and in-kind benefits are not taken into account in the above measure. Inclusion of in-kind benefits in the income measure probably would have only a minor equalizing effect on the distribution of income. Excluding taxes had little effect in 1966, but their recent trend has been in a disequalizing direction due to the growing share of government revenues raised by sales and payroll taxes. It is not possible to measure the actual redistributive effect of the fisc in any given year because the distribution of prefisc income would be different in its absence, but all evidence indicates that the distribution of income after taxes and transfers has been very nearly constant in the last twenty-five years. There are no indications that the prefisc distribution is likely to become anything but more uneven in the near future, and only a major change in tax policy is likely to make the fisc more equalizing.

Implications of the Record

This brief review has shown that, with the exception of reductions in income inequality, considerable progress has been made in the past two decades toward our national income security objectives. Protection from precipitous losses in welfare due to disruptions in the earnings of regularly employed workers has greatly expanded; the financial access of the lower-income population to certain valued goods and services has been substantially improved; and major reductions in income poverty have occurred. Expansion of the transfer system has been integral to all of this progress, yet there seems to be a prevailing negative judgment about the overall efficacy of social programs. To some extent this attitude probably stems from the belief that spending for social programs is out of control,[48] as well as a general focus on goals rather than achievements. There are, however, more specific sources.

48. See chapter 8.

First, there is probably widespread public ignorance of the facts, particularly concerning the contribution of the major means-tested noncash programs (especially food stamps and Medicaid) to the alleviation of poverty. This is not surprising, since it often takes time for perceptions to catch up to reality, especially when the reality is changing fast and requires sophisticated analysis to comprehend it. The history of these in-kind programs is recent enough that it is only now that data permit an assessment of their distributional impact, as well as that of the imputation of underreported cash income.

Next, some would argue that a successful battle against poverty requires increases in earnings and other sources of private income, not just greater reliance on income support benefits. First, it is undoubtedly true that millions of people have permanently escaped poverty as a result of increased private income, but this route out of poverty does appear (at least in the short run) to be far more influenced by general economic conditions and normal events in the life cycles of individuals and families than by expenditures on various manpower and social services.[49] Second, the reduction in poverty incidence among the aged is due to increased social security benefit levels and coverage, which do depend on earnings history. Perhaps most disquieting is that, primarily because of social trends affecting people at all income levels, there has been a marked increased reliance on public income support of female-headed families. Although this has become a phenomenon of great magnitude, it must be remembered that most female-headed welfare families remain neither female-headed nor on AFDC for many years.

A third factor in negative assessments about social programs has to do with the income security programs that primarily serve the poor. There is concern about such issues as work and family stability disincentives, gaps and overlaps in coverage, and unwarranted complexity and administrative inefficiency. These problems have become more acute as the programs have grown in number, coverage, and benefit levels. It is also true that general success of the programs in

49. In retrospect, our expectations about the effect of these services on earnings potentials appear unrealistically high, though they were never very large, either in absolute terms or as a percentage of total social expenditures; Plotnick and Skidmore, *Progress against Poverty*, p. 58, indicate that welfare and Office of Economic Opportunity (OEO) services and other employment and manpower expenditures constituted only 2.8 percent of the $74.5 billion public sector social program budget in 1965, and 5.0 percent of $184.9 billion in 1972.

eliminating poverty has focused attention on their remaining inadequacies. Unfortunately, the goal of eliminating poverty in America often seems lost in the debate over welfare reform. Some of these issues and alternative policy measures to address them are discussed in the second part of this chapter.

A fourth element in public criticism of social programs is increased dissatisfaction with social security, traditionally the one income security program that has been largely above reproach. As discussed below, social security may indeed require some major changes over the next decade; but the need for change arises not from any lack of effectiveness in the system but from some technical flaws in the current law and from the need to adapt the system to rapidly altering economic and social circumstances.

The final source of discontent (though one undoubtedly not as widespread) lies in the fact that the combined effect of social programs and the tax system has not led to a reduction in overall income inequality after taxes and transfers, or even of relative poverty. In this view, it is not that these programs are necessarily doing anything wrong, it is that not enough is being done. These critics feel that more policies should be directed explicitly at the goal of narrowing overall income differentials.

The issue of whether or not the federal government should engage in broad vertical income redistribution (and, if so, how much) has long been a subject of debate.[50] Opponents of income redistribution generally rest their case on one of two broad and interrelated arguments.[51] The first stresses that the degree of inequality now existing is necessary to provide incentives for hard work, risk taking, and accumulation—in short, all those characteristics that are essential to the promotion of economic efficiency and the continued strong growth of the economy, which are believed to benefit all in the long

50. This debate has enjoyed a strong revival in recent years. Some of the more prominent scholarly works on this subject are: John Rawls, *A Theory of Justice* (Harvard University Press, 1971); *Income Inequality*, a collection of essays by various authors in *Annals of the American Academy of Political and Social Science*, vol. 409 (September 1973), pp. 1–173; Arthur M. Okun, *Equality and Efficiency: The Big Tradeoff* (Brookings Institution, 1975); Alice M. Rivlin, "Income Distribution: Can Economists Help?" *American Economic Review*, vol. 65 (May 1975, *Papers and Proceedings, 1974*), pp. 1–15; and Irving Kristol, "Taxes, Poverty, and Equality," *Public Interest*, no. 37 (Fall 1974), pp. 3–28.

51. These arguments are advanced by Harry G. Johnson in "Some Micro-Economic Reflections on Income and Wealth Inequalities," *Annals of the American Academy of Political and Social Science*, vol. 409 (September 1973), pp. 53–60.

run. The only exception to this defense of the status quo is made for the deserving poor, those who through no fault of character or behavior find themselves unable to provide even a minimal standard of life for themselves and their families. The second argument stresses that life-cycle phenomena and the exercise of choice among alternatives provided to citizens necessarily give rise to observed inequalities of income as conventionally measured because of differences in personal characteristics and preferences. To quote Johnson: "Efforts to prevent this outcome, or to cancel it out by post facto income redistribution, run the serious risk of depriving the citizen of the benefits of freedom of choice and self-fulfillment and of eventually requiring a reversion to a more authoritative, or totalitarian, structure of society and the state. . . . The conclusion to be drawn from [these views] is that ethically-motivated social concern about inequality should properly focus on inequalities of opportunities and the knowledge and resources required to exploit them properly."[52]

Advocates of a more aggressive federal role in income redistribution through tax and transfer policies argue as follows. The existing degree of income inequality is only partially a reflection of the age distribution of the population and of differences in taste. It is in large part a result of the highly uneven distribution of earnings; as Okun has put it, "the labor market is not, in fact, a cafeteria line, and what people get on their trays bears only a slight relationship to their preferences."[53] Inequality of opportunity certainly ought to be redressed where it can be clearly identified and is amenable to acceptable social intervention. Most such efforts should promote economic efficiency as well as reduced income inequality.

Unfortunately the concept of equality of opportunity is an elusive one; it is impossible to define it with any operational precision. Okun likens it to the notion of a fair race where people are even at the starting line. The problem is to find the appropriate starting line. "The inheritance of natural abilities is on one side of the line of unequal opportunity, and the advantages of family position are clearly on the other. But much of the territory is unsettled. What aspects of the proverbial silver spoon should be regarded as creating inequality of opportunity? Does the line begin at differences in prenatal influences? Or at the benefits of better childhood health care, achieve-

52. Ibid., pp. 56, 58.
53. Okun, *Equality and Efficiency*, p. 73.

ment-oriented training, educational attainment, family assistance in job placement, inheritance of physical property?"[54] Recent evidence indicates that this unsettled territory of socioeconomic background may have a much greater effect on economic outcomes for both men and women than previous research with less appropriate data has shown.[55] Unless we as a society are willing to do away with the institution of family childrearing it will be difficult to neutralize this effect in any substantial way. This suggests that some lessening of income differentials after taxes and transfers is essential to increasing equality of opportunity and could lead to a lesser degree of pre–tax-and-transfer income inequality in the future.

Furthermore, there is no evidence that modest use of properly designed tax and transfer policies to reduce income differentials has serious effects on economic efficiency through such things as reduced savings and investment and work effort.[56] And, to the extent that there is a trade-off, we must keep in mind that both greater equality and greater efficiency are of value. Within reasonable limits, we should be willing to give up a little of the latter to get a lot of the former.

PART II. SOME MAJOR ISSUES IN INCOME SECURITY POLICY

The three areas examined here—social security, welfare reform, and the federal tax structure—do not exhaust the list of programs affecting income security objectives. In particular, the whole range of "human investment" programs and policies, which attempt to improve the earning power of low-income groups through compensatory education and skill training, is omitted. Nor do we deal with the important subject of policies designed to eliminate race and sex discrimination. This selectivity implies no judgment about the relative

54. Ibid., p. 76.
55. John A. Brittain, *The Inheritance of Economic Status* (Brookings Institution, forthcoming). This study is based on an analysis of the inequality of economic status among brothers relative to that among all men in a particular sample. Inequality among brothers was found to be much less. For different measures of economic status (residence quality, occupation, and income), as well as for composite measures, family background influences shared by the brothers accounted for one-third to two-thirds of the inequality of economic outcomes.
56. The reforms of the tax and transfer system discussed later in this chapter are advanced with these concerns in mind.

merits of direct tax and transfer policies versus the latter approaches, but only reflects the constraints of space and time available.

Social Security

A number of developments have resulted in a growing debate over reforms of the social security system, among them: the recession and the resulting financial deficits of the system; anticipated major shifts in the age distribution of the population; the automatic adjustments to the benefit formula that now result in an overadjustment to inflation for current workers and an otherwise irrational future benefit structure; the increased labor force participation of women; the advent of the supplemental security income program; and the growing coverage of private pensions. The implications for social security of many of these developments have been recognized and analyzed for some years; others have gained attention only recently.

Financing

The social security system is financed on a pay-as-you-go basis. OASDI benefits are paid out of trust funds that are replenished by the payroll taxes of currently employed workers, assessed at 9.9 percent of all covered wages up to the maximum taxable individual earnings base.[57] To insure that payments to current beneficiaries keep pace with inflation, and in an attempt to prevent the need for continued ad hoc adjustments in the revenue structure, Congress approved a set of automatic adjustments that, starting in 1974, has increased the maximum earnings base annually at the rate of the prior year's increase in covered wages. The expectation was that under normal economic conditions this would maintain a revenue flow in close approximation to the benefit expenditure requirements on a year-to-year basis. However, largely because of the recession, OASDI is currently running annual deficits.[58] Also, projections under current

57. This base is $15,300 for 1976 and is expected to rise to $16,500 for 1977. Both figures represent about 85 percent of the total wages of those covered by social security. An additional 1.8 percent is levied on the same wage base to finance Medicare. Half of the payroll taxes are paid by the employer and half by the employee (the self-employed paying about 70 percent of this total). There is general agreement among economists that most, if not all, of the employer's share of the tax is passed on to the employee in the form of lower wages. See John A. Brittain, *The Payroll Tax for Social Security* (Brookings Institution, 1972), chap. 3.

58. Annual deficits can be absorbed for a time by drawing on reserves in the trust funds that were instituted to meet just such a contingency, and this is now happening.

law indicate long-run revenue shortfalls that will increase in severity after the turn of the century. It is useful to subdivide these deficits into short-term (the next ten years) and long-term (the sixty-five years beyond that) ones, because their basic causes and magnitudes differ over these time periods, as do the type and urgency of any policy actions that might be taken to deal with them.

In 1976 OASDI expenditures will exceed revenues by $4.4 billion, which represents nearly 0.6 percent of earnings subject to the social security tax. The shortfalls will probably equal about 0.9 percent of payroll taxes in 1981, and could go as high 1.5 percent by 1985. Reserves in the combined OASDI trust funds have not yet been depleted by the current shortfalls, but they are expected to be within six years.[59] Deficits of this magnitude were not foreseen when, at the end of 1973, Congress last adjusted the OASDI tax schedule. This short-run deficit is due primarily to the recent increase in unemployment and fall in real wages, both of which have reduced payroll tax receipts considerably below what was projected and also have induced a larger number of people to retire. In addition, the incidence of disability among insured workers has, contrary to earlier predictions, been rising at a rapid rate, also contributing to the deficit.

The continuation of this short-term deficit can be predicted with a fairly high degree of certainty. (Even if the economy experiences a rapid and sustained recovery, real wage rates will be well below the 1980 level that was originally projected in 1973.) It is not particularly sensitive to either the inflation overadjustment or probable demographic changes. Furthermore, it is unlikely that a reduction in future benefit commitments would be acceptable as a method of dealing with it. For these reasons we assume that an increase in revenues to finance social security on the order of 1.3 percent of covered wages, or 13 percent annually over what current law provides, will be necessary during the next ten years, with at least half of it needed within the next five years.[60]

59. These projected deficits are much larger than those in the President's fiscal 1977 budget and the Congressional Budget Office's reports, but they are consistent with the more recent social security trustees report in which the preferred economic projections show the DI and OASI trust funds balances falling below zero in 1979 and 1982, respectively. *1976 Annual Report of the Board of Trustees of the Federal Old-Age and Survivors Insurance and Disability Insurance Trust Funds* (GPO, 1976).

60. The increase is needed not only to compensate for the continuing deficit, but also to build up again the reserves in the trust funds so that any subsequent

There are three alternative sources for the additional required revenues: increases in the payroll tax rate, increases in the maximum taxable earnings base (above the level called for by the automatic adjustment), or the use of general revenues.[61] Although until recently there has not been much resistance to either tax rate or wage base increases, arguments against them are now gaining force because of the effects of their current high levels. Concern about the payroll tax rate centers on its overall regressive impact on income distribution, and particularly the sizable burden it represents for low-income workers and their families. Any increase in the tax rate would further exacerbate this burden.[62]

Increasing the wage base in order to finance the deficit would have two important effects. First, because only a small percentage of total earnings are above the covered maximum, the base would have to be raised considerably to yield the required revenues.[63] This places the entire burden on those with earnings above the current maximum and, consequently, imposes a large increase in their yearly payroll taxes. Second, these greater contributions for high-wage workers would cause them to receive higher future benefits, thus exacerbating the long-term deficit problem in the process of dealing with the short-term one.

The third alternative of utilizing some general revenue financing for social security has long been advocated by those concerned with the distributional impact of the current tax and opposed by those concerned about deterioration of the "earned right" concept, which it is feared could lead to either less political support or a means test for the system. These fears appear to be largely ungrounded, at least

---

cyclical downturns will not immediately deplete them. If one were to adopt the view that temporary injections of general revenues rather than payroll taxes should be used to finance deficits caused by cyclical fluctuations in the economy, then a permanent payroll tax increase on the order of 8 percent (0.8 percent of covered payrolls), along with a general revenue transfer in the tens of billions, might be sufficient.

61. In his 1977 budget President Ford requested an 0.6 percent increase in the payroll tax rate, effective January 1977, which has since been rejected by Congress.

62. Methods of relieving low-income earners from the burden of existing payroll taxes are discussed on pp. 576–77 below.

63. For example, if the 0.6 percent payroll increase requested by the President were to be financed this way, the wage base would have to move to approximately $22,000 in 1977. And if the entire 1.3 percent of payroll increase were to be accomplished this way in 1977, the maximum would have to go to over $40,000. Of course, the higher the wage base moves the fewer the number of workers from which to draw additional revenues.

with respect to modest injections of general revenue financing. One approach to this was recommended by the last Advisory Council on Social Security, a public nonpartisan body appointed under statute by the President. It suggested providing general revenue financing for Medicare and gradually shifting the Medicare tax and trust funds into OASDI. This would represent no erosion of the earned right concept because, except for the establishment of eligibility, Medicare benefits are unrelated to earnings histories.

While the short-term deficit described above can be predicted with considerable certainty, the nature of the long-term deficit depends critically on the way in which the inflation overadjustment is eliminated (as well as on a number of other somewhat speculative long-run economic and demographic projections). In order to understand the issues involved, it is useful to focus first upon the behavior of replacement rates over time.

Future Behavior of Wage Replacement Rates

OASDI benefits are based on a worker's covered wage history. The first step in the computation involves determining the average monthly wage (AMW) on which payroll taxes have been paid.[64] The primary insurance amount (PIA) is then derived from the AMW by applying a benefit conversion formula that in 1976 provides for 129.5 percent of the first $110 of AMW, 47.1 percent of the next $290, and so on down to 20 percent of AMW above $1,000. Actual monthly benefits are a fixed percentage of a worker's PIA, with the amount depending on the characteristics of the beneficiary unit (as shown in table 12-3 above). This conversion formula yields a progressive replacement wage schedule since a worker's PIA rises less than proportionately with earnings. This progressive formula was instituted on the rationale, borne out by empirical evidence, that the lower the average wage of the primary earner of a family, the more dependent the family is likely to be on his or her social security benefits.

Under current law the future pattern of replacement rates for successive cohorts of retirees[65] can easily be very erratic since the rates

64. In the retirement (OA) program, for persons reaching age 62 in 1976 this is based upon the highest twenty of the past twenty-five years of earnings and is scheduled to increase to the highest thirty-five of forty by 1991. The survivors' and disability benefits have a slightly different formula for the AMW calculation but are otherwise determined similarly to OA benefits.

65. A cohort consists of all those retirees who enter benefit status in the same year.

are influenced by three independent factors. First, there is an automatic inflation adjustment, which, unfortunately, was written into the 1973 law in a way that causes an overcompensation for inflation for current workers.[66] Under this provision inflation drives up replacement rates, and the greater the inflation the faster future replacement rates will rise. Concomitantly, two forces are operating to depress replacement rates over time. The most important one stems from the combination of the constant dollar bracket widths and the progressivity of the PIA conversion formula. The growth of money wages concentrates more and more of the typical worker's AMW in lower PIA conversion rate brackets. This lowers the average conversion rate and, thus, replacement rates over time.[67]

The net effect on replacement rates of these three forces depends upon what assumptions are made about future rates of inflation and growth of wages. Cases 1–3 in table 12-5 illustrate the effects of several different assumptions on benefits for median wage earners, as well as the future revenue requirements for each. Two important conclusions can be drawn. First, various combinations of rates of wage and price increases can lead to extremely different behavior of replacement rates over time (even if they yield the same rate of growth of real wages, as in cases 1 and 2). It would be unsound policy to permit the vagaries of the economy to have such an arbitrary and unpredictable effect on the replacement rates of future retirees.

Second, the consequences for both future benefit levels and revenue requirements of the most probable future behavior of wages and

66. The adjustment operates by uniformly increasing all the conversion rates in the PIA formula by the previous year's cost-of-living increase. Thus, if inflation in 1976 is 10 percent, the conversion rate for the first bracket in 1977 will become 142.45 percent (129.5 plus 12.95), and so on, with the final 20 percent bracket becoming 22 percent. (A new 20 percent bracket is added annually at the time the maximum wage base is automatically increased.) For current beneficiaries, whose AMW is fixed, this produces the desired 10 percent higher PIA and monthly benefit. Current workers are overcompensated, however, because not only do they benefit from the higher conversion rates they will face at retirement, but their AMWs will also be higher because inflation pushes up their money wages over time. They get, in effect, a double inflation adjustment—their benefits are calculated at an increased percentage of increased wages.

67. The other depressing factor is a temporary one: the lengthening of the averaging period for the AMW calculation, which requires the inclusion of an additional and, typically, lower-than-average year's earnings in the AMWs of each successive cohort of retirees. See Lawrence Thompson, "An Analysis of the Factors Currently Determining Benefit Level Adjustments in the Social Security Retirement Program," Technical Analysis Paper 1 (U.S. Department of Health, Education, and Welfare, Office of Income Security Policy, 1974; processed).

Table 12-5. **Old Age and Survivors Insurance Replacement Rates, Tax Rate Required, and Benefit Levels for Single Median Wage Earners without Dependents, under Various Economic Assumptions, Selected Years, 1980–2055**[a]

	Current law						Altered law[b]					
	Case 1		Case 2		Case 3		Case 4[c]			Case 5[d]		
	Real wage growth 2 percent, inflation 4 percent		Real wage growth 2 percent, inflation 6 percent		Real wage growth 1.5 percent, inflation 4 percent		Real wage growth 2 percent, constant replacement rate			Real wage growth 2 percent, declining replacement rate		
Year	Replacement rate	Tax rate	Replacement rate	Tax rate	Replacement rate	Tax rate	Replacement rate	Benefit level (1976 dollars)	Tax rate	Replacement rate	Benefit level (1976 dollars)	Tax rate
1980	0.446	...	0.446	...	0.446	...	0.446	374.25	...	0.446	374.25	...
1985	0.472	10.9	0.469	10.9	0.481	11.5	0.446	413.21	10.9	0.425	397.64	11.0
1990	0.471	11.1	0.476	11.1	0.489	11.8	0.446	456.22	11.1	0.403	416.50	10.2
1995	0.474	11.5	0.492	11.7	0.501	12.5	0.446	503.69	11.4	0.383	436.36	9.8
2005	0.509	12.5	0.561	13.4	0.558	14.1	0.446	614.00	11.9	0.345	479.96	9.2
2015	0.537	15.7	0.624	17.8	0.605	18.2	0.446	748.46	13.8	0.315	533.10	9.8
2025	0.558	19.9	0.677	23.8	0.643	23.7	0.446	912.37	16.6	0.290	597.88	10.9
2035	0.575	21.6	0.721	26.7	0.676	26.3	0.446	1,112.17	17.2	0.269	676.84	10.5
2045	0.589	21.5	0.756	27.4	0.705	26.7	0.446	1,355.72	16.4	0.252	773.10	9.5
2055	0.594	22.2	0.772	28.7	0.718	27.8	0.446	1,496.84	16.3	0.245	828.86	9.4

Source: Tabulation provided by U.S. Department of Health, Education, and Welfare, Office of the Assistant Secretary for Planning and Evaluation. These estimates may not conform precisely to comparable ones produced by the Social Security Administration, but the long-run patterns of all the variables are quite similar. The assumptions concerning labor force participation and other demographics are consistent with those of the preferred alternative in the *1975 Annual Report of the Board of Trustees of the Federal Old-Age and Survivors Insurance and Disability Insurance Trust Funds*, H. Doc. 94-135, 94:1 (GPO, 1975). The preferred set of assumptions in the 1976 report yields considerably higher long-run revenue requirements, principally because of a long-term real wage growth of 1.75 percent a year and a lower birth rate. In our view these assumptions are no more justified than those used here.

a. Tax rate is the percent of payroll required to cover the current year's benefit outlays on a current cost financing basis. All replacement rates are the primary insurance amount measured against the last year's wage in constant dollars. The PIA is for a single man retiring at the age of sixty-five who earned the median wage and was covered for all years. Replacement rates would be 50 percent higher if an aged spouse were included.

b. Assumed to go into effect in 1980, with average monthly wage computed over constant period of twenty years and wage-indexed.

c. Brackets in the formula for the primary insurance amount are indexed by wage increase

d. Brackets in the PIA formula are indexed by the price index.

prices (something approximating case 1) are undesirable. As was noted earlier, replacement rates of about 65 percent are probably adequate for a median wage earner to provide for the maintenance of the standard of living achieved just prior to retirement. Under case 1 assumptions, social security replacement rates for the median wage earner will be at 50 percent and 75 percent, respectively, for individuals and couples by the turn of the century. A majority of such workers also will be receiving private pension benefits at replacement rates of about 20 percent or will have other opportunities to accumulate private savings.[68] The total level of projected adequacy is thus likely to exceed what society would consider desirable, especially in view of the increasingly higher rate of payroll taxation that would be required.[69]

For both these reasons there is a growing consensus among analysts and policymakers knowledgeable about social security that steps should be taken as soon as possible to eliminate the inflation overadjustment and otherwise reduce the uncertainty and potential instability in the future behavior of replacement rates. This requires an explicit policy decision about the desired future pattern that should be made soon, since today's benefit formula determines future financing costs. If we wait too long to act, achieving reasonable replacement rates will require cutbacks in benefit levels.

Two alternatives to deal with this problem have gained the most attention. The first would hold the average replacement rates constant at, say, 1980 levels.[70] This does not imply that the real benefit levels of each successive cohort of retirees remain constant; in fact they would increase at the rate of growth of real wage levels.[71] The future benefit levels that this would yield for median wage earners re-

68. The changing role of social security in light of growing private savings provision is discussed below.

69. Another factor is that the replacement rates for low-wage workers will be about 50 percent higher than for median workers. OASDI benefit levels that approach or exceed 100 percent and, thus, provide for a substantially higher standard of living after retirement than just prior to it seem to make little sense.

70. Average replacement rates can be held constant by fixing the averaging period for the AMW, indexing the bracket widths in the PIA conversion formula by the growth rate of covered money wages, and applying a wage or price index to workers' past earnings in order to put all years' wages on a comparable basis when calculating AMWs. Such an approach was recommended by the last Social Security Advisory Council.

71. Historically, average annual money wage increases have exceeded inflation by about 2 percent. That is why this rate was chosen for the assumption in cases 4 and 5 of table 12-5.

tiring in various future years and the consequent revenue requirements (which, as a percent of covered wages, are independent of the
rate of real wage growth) are shown in case 4 of table 12-5. Note
that even if such a measure were adopted, current projections show
long-term revenue requirements considerably higher than those
necessary to cover the short-term deficit. The annual amount is relatively small for the remainder of this century, but rises rapidly beyond then. This projected need is created primarily by the dramatic
shift in the age distribution of the population now taking place,
which will begin to have a major impact on social security financing
as the post–World War II baby-boom generation hits retirement
age.[72] Concomitant with this increased requirement for supporting
the aged, of course, would be a reduced requirement for supporting
children.

The second alternative would remove the inflation overadjustment
in such a way that average replacement rates would decline over
time with the growth of real wage levels. The future pattern of replacement rates and benefit levels for median wage earners under this
alternative are shown in case 5 of table 12-5.[73] Even in this instance,
with average replacement rates declining fairly rapidly over time,
benefit levels still increase in constant dollar terms. Revenue requirements vary from year to year, but the percentage of payroll required
is considerably less than under a regime of constant replacement
rates and even somewhat below current levels for most years. Patterns
of replacement rate behavior between this and constant ones could
be structured in line with whatever rate of increase in benefit levels
relative to real wage growth (and accompanying revenue requirements) is desired.

72. Unless birth rates increase well above zero population growth levels in the
next decade, there will be only two workers for every aged person by 2020, whereas
now there are approximately three. Thus, a much larger percentage of current wages
will have to be devoted to support any given level of benefits. Other specific assumptions concerning labor force participation rates and disability incidence underlie these projections; but because of the large number of variables that could
shift over time, projections beyond the turn of the century have a high degree of
uncertainty.

73. This alternative has been advanced by the Consultant Panel on Social Security to the Congressional Research Service. It can be accomplished by taking the
same steps described above, note 70, except indexing the bracket widths in the PIA
formula by the rate of increase of prices rather than money wages. Then, over
time, real wage growth will result in more of the typical worker's AMW being concentrated in lower PIA conversion brackets.

Individual Equity[74]

When social security was set up in 1935, the relationship of an individual's benefits to payroll taxes paid was structured to more nearly resemble a private insurance plan than does the present system. The goal of individual equity—that each worker should receive benefits reflecting a fair rate of return on his contributions—was stressed and felt to be crucial to the public acceptance of a compulsory program. Starting with the 1939 amendments, however, greater emphasis was put on the goal of social adequacy, as reflected in the minimum and dependent's benefits, the high degree of overall progressivity in the PIA computational formula, and a contributions base short of lifetime earnings for determining the AMW.[75] This emphasis on social adequacy has been an essential element in social security's ability to offer a high degree of income protection relative to need, and has constituted a major source of its popularity. But, as a result of both the expanded coverage and higher benefit levels of social security and other changes taking place in society, the goal of social adequacy is more and more coming into conflict with that of individual equity, with increasingly controversial consequences.

The pursuit of social adequacy implies that some workers are going to receive more in benefits relative to the taxes they pay than others. The progressive benefit formula ensures that this will be the case for low-wage earners vis-à-vis high-wage earners. And the fact that individual earnings provide the basis for taxation while benefits are tailored to family circumstances ensures this for single workers and two-worker families vis-à-vis single-worker families. For example, a husband and wife who have both worked enough to be eligible for the maximum social security coverage will receive only one-third more benefits than a couple in which the man is eligible for the maximum but the wife has no covered earnings; yet the former will have paid twice as much in taxes.

74. The remainder of this section on social security has benefited from drafts of a work in progress on the future of social security by Alicia H. Munnell.

75. See Joseph A. Pechman, Henry J. Aaron, and Michael K. Taussig, *Social Security: Perspectives for Reform* (Brookings Institution, 1968), pp. 33–34. Emphasizing social adequacy means insuring that benefits meet some socially determined level of adequacy even though the individual equity criterion would call for less. The difference between these two is often referred to as the welfare component of social security.

How inequitable this social adequacy emphasis is considered to be depends largely on the extent to which it produces large numbers of workers in the system who do not realize a fair return on their contributions. This is clearly not a problem for either current or immediate future beneficiaries. Calculations indicate that, even for a single worker at the maximum covered earnings (the worker who fares worst under the system) who is now at mid-career, the ratio of expected benefits to contributions, with a 2 percent real rate of return assumed on the latter, is above 1.2. This ratio ranges above 4.0 for low-wage workers with a dependent. Thus, the social adequacy goal has been pursued to date without having to compromise individual equity at all.[76]

These favorable relationships between expected benefits and contributions have been made possible by a continuing rate of growth in numbers of covered workers that has far exceeded that of covered retirees, in conjunction with the pay-as-you-go nature of social security financing. This will no longer be the case in the future, however, because of the current broad coverage of the labor force and the shifting age distribution of the population. Under the present method of financing, social security can retain its social adequacy or welfare component only at a considerable expense in individual equity.[77] If social security is to continue to be generally perceived as fair and

76. A 2 percent real rate of return would be considered fair by most; this is somewhat higher than savings accounts yielded on average over the past sixty years. These calculations are reported in U.S. Social Security Administration, "Ratios of Benefits to Contributions for Selected Retirement Cases" (SSA, 1974; processed). The method by which the short-term deficit is financed and the inflation overadjustment eliminated could lower these ratios, but is unlikely fundamentally to change the conclusion.

77. This can be illustrated in the following way. Consider a situation in which both replacement rates and the ratio of covered workers to retirees are constant over time and payroll taxes are set at the level necessary to finance the benefits on a pay-as-you-go basis. The expected rate of return in the aggregate for each successive cohort of retirees would be equal to the average annual rate of growth of real wages over their earnings history, which we can reasonably assume to be 2 percent. Thus, each cohort as a whole will receive a fair return on its contributions, having an average benefit-to-contributions ratio, as calculated above, of 1.0. However, to the extent that any retirees in a given cohort realize a ratio greater than 1.0, others must be getting less than this 2 percent real rate of return. The only way for everyone to realize a fair return is if replacement rates were the same across all wage histories and beneficiary unit types.

In fact, the prospects for today's young workers are far worse than this example indicates because the ratio of covered workers to retirees will be moving in an adverse direction for them so that future cohorts as a whole will receive substantially less than a fair rate of return.

to well serve those it covers, it is going to have to embody a judicious balancing of these two conflicting objectives. This suggests that a move toward more emphasis on individual equity may be required.[78] This can be pursued in either of two ways: on the revenue side, by the use of general revenue financing to underwrite some or all of the social adequacy component of social security (and allowing reduced taxation of those with otherwise inequitable rates of return); or on the benefit side, by moving toward a more proportional replacement rate profile within a given age cohort for workers with different earnings histories and different family situations.

The Changing Role of Social Security

A forceful argument against moving toward a more proportional benefit formula is that it would result in a reduced adequacy of social security benefits for those who could least afford it—the low-wage workers and retirees with dependents. There are, however, major changes occurring in the total income support picture for the aged and disabled that suggest that social security's future role could be more limited than its present one without sacrificing the overall adequacy of income support for the aged. In concert with other modifications to social security, these would allow for a gradual shift to a more proportional benefit formula.

The first change is the advent of the supplemental security income program (SSI), the new federal guaranteed income program for the aged and disabled. This program's target population considerably overlaps that of social security (approximately 50 percent of SSI recipients also receive OASDI), and it is often advocated as a more appropriate vehicle than OASDI for meeting social adequacy goals for the low-income aged and disabled. This view represents SSI as a more efficient use of public funds because its income conditioning ensures that benefits go only to those with a demonstrable need and its coverage of the aged and disabled poor is comprehensive. The extremely high degree of progressivity at the lower end of the OASDI benefit formula helps many of the same poor, but it does not reach

78. Recently sizable numbers of state and local public employees (whose participation in social security is optional) have either withdrawn or begun to consider withdrawing from the program, partly because they can realize a higher rate of return in private or other public programs. This may well be a harbinger of decreasing support of social security by the higher-income, more steadily employed groups, who can collectively do better in alternative plans.

others at all. Social security also augments the income of many elderly persons (for instance, retired federal civil servants) who are relatively well off because of property income or a second pension. At a minimum this argues that, if society wishes efficiently to allocate additional resources to the aged and disabled population, higher priority ought to be placed on increasing SSI rather than OASDI benefits. Even more, it provides a rationale for reducing the degree of progressivity at the bottom end of the OASDI benefit formula in favor of higher SSI benefits.[79]

The second major change is the increased eligibility of women for OASDI and other pensions in their own right. This is a direct result of the dramatically rising labor force participation rates of women, still on the increase, since World War II. Married couples in which both husband and wife work now constitute a majority of families. By 1970, 68 percent of women aged forty-five to forty-nine were insured for their own social security benefits, and conservative estimates indicate that shortly after the turn of the century 70 percent of all wives of retired beneficiaries will be entitled to benefits on the basis of their own earnings record.[80] The implication is that the secondary spouse's benefit is rapidly becoming less necessary in order to insure adequate wage replacement for husband and wife families. Proposals to reduce or eliminate it over time should be given serious consideration.[81] If this were done, however, it would be necessary to provide for coverage of the minority of wives who will not have sufficient independent earnings to qualify for social security because their work is primarily in the home. One possible way of doing this would be to credit half of the sum of a husband and wife's earnings to each.

79. If this approach were pursued, some structural changes should be made in SSI to make it more substitutable for OASDI among the low-income aged and disabled. Most important would be to lower the eligibility age to sixty-two and to provide higher benefits for recipients with dependents not eligible for SSI in their own right.

Many people would object to the expansion of a program that is means-tested at the expense of one that is not. Ultimately, it may be desirable to substitute the use of demogrants or refundable tax credits for much of the federal SSI program. This, however, must await tax reform that broadens the tax base so that only the low-income aged and disabled would be net recipients of such an approach to basic income support.

80. *Reports of the Quadrennial Advisory Council on Social Security,* H. Doc. 94-75, 94:1 (Government Printing Office, 1975), p. 76.

81. Independent of the implications of increased labor force participation of women, a reduction of the secondary spouse's benefit is advocated by many on the grounds that a 30 percent income differential (rather than the present 50 percent) is all that is required to permit two to maintain the same standard of living as one.

The final major change in the broader environment of income support for the aged is the growing ability of high-wage workers to save for retirement. Private pension coverage has been growing rapidly. Between 1950 and 1970, coverage more than doubled under employer-financed plans, rising from 22.5 percent of the private labor force to 48 percent, and the rate of asset accumulation increased about sevenfold.[82] In addition, under the recently enacted Employee Retirement Income Security Act of 1974, standards were set up to promote greater security of private pension rights, the tax treatment of self-employed accounts was liberalized, and a new tax deduction was provided for workers without coverage from employers.

Although this trend of rapidly expanding private pension coverage appears to be subsiding, the experience of the recent past and the continued growth of real wage levels indicate that middle- as well as high-wage workers will be increasingly able to supplement their social security benefits through private savings. This should eventually place an upper limit on the level of compulsory public protection through OASDI. For this reason (in addition to the equity argument advanced above) it may be desirable to reduce somewhat the degree of progressivity in the middle range of the benefit formula as real income growth occurs, as well as to slow down the rate of growth of the maximum covered earnings base. Public benefits for middle- and high-income workers as large (in real terms) as would be generated by the current automatic adjustments to the wage base and constant wage replacement rates over time may not be necessary. Furthermore they would be likely to interfere with private savings.

Private Savings, Capital Formation, and Intergenerational Equity

Recently, some economists have expressed concern that social security is causing a major reduction in private savings and, consequently, having a detrimental effect on the rate of capital formation and the long-term growth rate potential of the economy. Many proponents of this view advocate major payroll tax increases to reduce current consumption, build up large surpluses in the OASDI trust funds, and, thereby, increase the pool of savings.[83] These arguments require careful evaluation since they imply a major alteration in the present arrangements for financing social security.

82. U.S. Bureau of Labor Statistics, *Handbook of Labor Statistics, 1974* (Government Printing Office, 1974), p. 298.
83. Martin Feldstein, "Toward Reform of Social Security," *Public Interest,* no. 40 (Summer 1975), pp. 75–95.

To the extent that the anticipation of receiving social security benefits causes workers to save less toward retirement than they otherwise would, social security does lead to an overall reduction in savings.[84] The evidence is inconclusive on the extent to which this has happened in the past;[85] however, even if it has been of minor consequence, it may be of greater magnitude in the future because of the recent growth in social security benefit levels.

If social security actually does reduce savings by an appreciable amount, should surpluses be built up in the trust funds to offset this effect?[86] For this to be a wise policy, two conditions would have to be met: (1) given the projections of the effect of OASDI on personal savings, the overall future level of savings in the economy is going to be inadequate to meet desired capital formation needs; and (2) given a need for additional savings, the OASDI trust funds are the best place to accumulate it. Neither of these appear in fact to be the case. On the one hand, the more reliable studies of the capital formation issue indicate that future private savings are unlikely to fall far short of our needs, and that we can meet our future capital needs with only minor adjustments in fiscal and monetary policy.[87] And, on the other hand, even if considerable additional savings were required, increased payroll taxes are an undesirable vehicle for accomplishing this. Large increases in payroll taxes on current workers would increase the forced savings of millions of families whose current consumption needs are high relative to their income and who would not choose to increase their savings even at relatively high

84. This is because the revenues raised through the payroll tax do not represent savings: they do not accumulate in a trust fund but are paid out to beneficiaries who use most of their social security payments for current consumption.

85. Alicia H. Munnell, "The Future of Social Security" (manuscript in preparation), points out that, while using essentially the same data, different estimating techniques have yielded widely different estimates of this effect. According to Munnell, Feldstein concluded that in the absence of social security, "1969 personal savings would have been more than double the actual saving figure of $38.2 billion" (p. 171) while her own calculations for the same year found the reduction to be only $3.7 billion (p. 172). See Martin Feldstein, "Social Security, Induced Retirement, and Aggregate Capital Accumulation," *Journal of Political Economy*, vol. 82 (September–October 1974), pp. 905–26; and Alicia H. Munnell, *The Effect of Social Security on Personal Saving* (Ballinger, 1974), table 4-7, p. 68.

86. For such a step not to be counterproductive the total budget surplus (that is, federal funds plus trust funds) must increase pari passu with the OASDI trust fund surplus, and steps must be taken to maintain full employment, presumably via more expansionary monetary policy, since fiscal policy would be constrained.

87. See, for example, Barry Bosworth, James S. Duesenberry, and Andrew S. Carron, *Capital Needs in the Seventies* (Brookings Institution, 1975); and *Achieving Price Stability through Economic Growth*, Report of the Joint Economic Committee, H. Rept. 93-1653, 93:2 (Government Printing Office, 1974), pp. 93–99.

rates of return. There are other ways to increase the future savings rate that would not have such undesirable distributional consequences.

There is, however, another argument for building up surpluses in the OASDI trust funds that is based on the notion of equity across different generations of workers. If the inflation overadjustment is eliminated in such a manner as to stabilize wage replacement rates over time (see case 4, table 12-5) and if the generation of workers now entering the labor market does not save more, financing their future OASDI benefits may require sharply increased taxes for the working generations of 2015 and beyond. For this reason, it may be desirable to raise slightly social security taxes for the upcoming generation of workers (with a forgiveness for low-wage workers, paid for by general revenues) and build up budget surpluses. The resulting increment in national savings, if accompanied by appropriate monetary policy, could be translated into a higher level of national investment, and therefore a faster rate of growth in productivity and real wages. The higher real wage growth, in turn, would provide the wherewithal to moderate the tax impact on the later working generation when the upcoming one retires.[88]

Conclusions

There are two major issues in the social security system that require immediate attention. First, considerable additional funding must be provided to compensate for the short-term OASDI deficits, although this can be postponed for a few more years. One of the options—raising the wage base—has consequences that are often not fully appreciated. It raises future social security benefits for a population that otherwise would save voluntarily to supplement their benefits. Because it produces higher benefits, raising the wage base has less of a long-run impact on the deficit than it does in the short run, thus necessitating larger future tax increases than other alternatives. And, finally, it further deemphasizes the goal of individual equity by increasing future payroll taxes relative to future benefits for the part of the population that already realizes the lowest rate of return on its contributions. For these reasons, and because of the distributional

88. As noted above, allowing replacement rates to decline is an alternative to higher future revenue requirements. If the burden is going to be borne by the age cohort that causes the bulge in the distribution—either through higher taxes to build up budget surpluses or through lower retirement benefits—then the choice depends primarily on the preferred time pattern of consumption of that generation.

impact of the payroll tax, the best means of dealing with the short-term deficit may be to shift Medicare gradually to general revenue financing and the present Medicare payroll tax receipts into the OASDI trust funds.

Second, the overadjustment for inflation should be eliminated. Although it has little effect on the short-term deficit, it adds billions of dollars every year to the annual amount of the expected long-term deficit and increases the arbitrary and irrational nature of the future benefit structure. Whether the elimination of this inflation overadjusment causes future average benefit levels to rise as fast as or more slowly than real wage growth depends on how adequate future benefits will seem in light of increased potential for voluntary savings and the willingness of upcoming generations to tax themselves. Owing to the uncertainty of both the future coverage of private pension plans and the exact magnitude of the long-term deficit, it is probably best to provide for stable average replacement rates now, with the possibility of allowing them to decline at some future date.[89]

The future role and structure of social security will also be affected by major socioeconomic changes now occurring. For instance, the SSI program offers the opportunity to channel federal expenditures more effectively to the aged and disabled poor than does OASDI. At the same time, middle- and high-wage earners are increasingly gaining access to private provision for retirement and disability. These two developments imply that social security could play a more limited role in a broader system of income support for the aged and disabled that continues to provide greater income security protection. Large demographic shifts are also occurring (especially the rising ratio of beneficiaries to covered workers and the increasing participation of women in the labor force) that are contributing to inequities within OASDI. All these changes suggest that consideration should be given to moving gradually toward a somewhat more uniform wage replacement rate schedule[90] among different types of beneficiary units

89. Another possibility would be to set the automatic adjustments so as to reduce replacement rates as real wages grow and to rely on Congress to make ad hoc upward adjustments in the replacement rates if it seems indicated.

90. That is, the profile of replacement rates within a given cohort of beneficiaries, rather than the rates for representative workers of successive cohorts. One way of accomplishing this would be to engineer different rates of change over time in the replacement rates at differing points in the profile.

and workers at different wage levels and to limiting the growth of social security benefits for high-wage workers.

Current concern about our future capital formation needs does not appear to warrant, though some advocate it, raising payroll taxes and building surpluses in the trust funds beyond those necessary to provide for a cushion against temporary shortfalls. It may be desirable, however, if birth rates do not increase substantially, to build up some surpluses in the trust funds in order to distribute more equitably the added financial burden of social security benefits for the post–World War II baby boom generation.

Income Transfer Policy and the Lower-Income Population

Though substantial progress has been made over the past decade, through both economic growth and major expansions of the income transfer system, poverty has yet to be eliminated. In addition, a set of new problems has been created and some old ones exacerbated in the process. These problems stem from the interaction of the different means-tested programs and their interrelationships with other social welfare programs and tax policies that affect the lower-income population.[91] Although some people believe these problems are a small price to pay for the major advances against poverty made by the transfer system, they do require attention. They are at the heart of what many people believe to be "the welfare mess," and further alleviation of poverty will surely have to come through structural improvements in the welfare system as much as from expansion of income transfer expenditures.

Problems with Welfare

The problems of the welfare system have been debated for years and led to the introduction of the family assistance plan (FAP) by President Richard M. Nixon in 1969. However, since the sixties and even the early seventies, when debate focused primarily on the AFDC

91. In addition to the provisions of the personal income tax that exempt some initial amount of income from taxation (the low-income allowance plus personal exemptions), the other major federal tax provision affecting the lower-income population is the payroll tax. In addition, the Tax Reduction Act of 1975 provided for a temporary earned tax credit that pays a benefit of 10 percent of earnings of families with children up to a maximum benefit of $400. The maximum is reduced 10 cents for each $1 of family income above $4,000, so that there is no benefit at $8,000 or above.

program and its shortcomings, the context has changed substantially, largely because of the expansion of transfer programs and advances in our understanding of the relevant issues. Only recently has a full appreciation of the impact of the total complex of programs and policies of income security for the lower-income population been possible.[92] For example, the universal availability of food stamps and the general coverage of other transfer programs means not only that the entire low-income population is now eligible for income support, but also that we have in effect an income guarantee that is very substantial for some. The issue is no longer so much whether income support should be provided to certain groups, but rather what should the exact form and amounts be? Should the working poor population receive less assistance than AFDC families at equivalent levels of need? Is cash preferable to food stamps? Before considering some of these issues and alternatives in welfare reform, we first examine some of the most salient problems created by the present complex of programs.

HORIZONTAL INEQUITIES AND TARGET INEFFICIENCIES. People with similar needs receive very different levels of assistance, depending on such factors as their particular family structure, where they live, and how good they are at dealing with the bureaucracies that administer the programs. Except for the food stamp program— the only universal means-tested program—all the others are designed to serve specific, and often overlapping, categories within the low-income population. In addition, states vary widely in the amount of their AFDC benefit levels,[93] and in whether or not unemployed fathers are eligible for the program. Also, low-income housing pro-

92. See especially Barth and others, *Toward an Effective Income Support System; Studies in Public Welfare*, Papers 13–20, Prepared for the Subcommittee on Fiscal Policy of the Joint Economic Committee, 93:2 (Government Printing Office, 1974); and Henry J. Aaron, "Why Is Welfare So Hard to Reform?" (Brookings Institution, 1973). See also an excellent review article drawing on the above studies, Laurence E. Lynn, Jr., "A Decade of Policy Developments in the Income Maintenance System" (1975, processed), to appear in Robert H. Haveman, ed., *A Decade of Federal Anti-Poverty Policy: Achievements, Failures and Lessons* (Academic Press, forthcoming). The discussion in this section draws on the final draft of the latter paper and also has benefited from a preliminary draft of Robert Haveman's introduction to the volume.

93. For the continental United States, these range from a low of $60 a month in Mississippi to a high of $419 a month in Wisconsin for a family of four (largest amount paid). U.S. Department of Health, Education, and Welfare, National Center for Social Statistics, "Aid to Families with Dependent Children: Standards for Basic Needs, State Maximums and Other Methods of Limiting Money Payments," HEW Report D-2 (forthcoming, 1976).

grams reach only a fraction of the eligible population. This wide variation in available benefits is not only highly inequitable, it also dilutes the antipoverty effectiveness of federal welfare expenditures. Some very poor people are receiving little assistance, while others above the poverty level are receiving more. Assistance to those below the poverty level should clearly be a higher priority for the federal government.

In general it is the two-parent families, nonaged or disabled individuals, and childless couples that fare the worst, although in some states with low AFDC benefits families are well below the poverty level even when in-kind benefits are considered. In many states, even if the father is involuntarily unemployed, his family may be eligible only for food stamps and a small amount of general assistance. In the more generous states a two-parent family of four whose head is working full time could be earning $4,500 a year and be eligible only for $900 in food stamps subsidy,[94] whereas an AFDC family of the same size could have a small amount of earnings and receive benefits in cash, food stamps, Medicaid, and housing assistance worth as much as $8,000.

UNWARRANTED COMPLEXITY AND ADMINISTRATIVE INEFFICIENCY. Each program has its own independent and complex set of eligibility criteria and income definitions. In some cases the criteria are administered in an arbitrary fashion and depend on family attributes that are subject to frequent changes. Although the same families may be receiving benefits from several programs, the delivery systems are either totally separate or only partially integrated. Administrative and financial responsibilities are spread among the federal, state, and local governments with little rhyme or reason. Some programs are fully federally financed and administered with an option for state supplementation (SSI), some fully federally financed but state and locally administered (food stamps and housing programs), and some jointly financed by the federal, state, and local governments and administered at the state and local levels (AFDC and Medicaid). The results of all this fragmentation are high overhead costs, unnecessary frustrations for administrators and recipients, and large error rates in the system.

94. Under the current temporary tax provisions the family could be eligible for a $350 earned income tax credit payment. On the other hand, it also would be paying approximately $350 in payroll taxes.

WORK DISINCENTIVES. In order to deliver benefits to those with low incomes, means-tested programs scale them to family income. One consequence of this is that an increase in a family's earnings causes a reduction of its benefit. Thus, an additional dollar of earnings is actually worth less to recipients because it is accompanied by the loss of benefits worth some fraction of a dollar. If a family is receiving benefits from a number of such means-tested programs simultaneously, as is frequently the case, the value of an additional dollar's earnings can be quite low. For example, one study found that AFDC families, on the average, could expect a net gain of only 20 to 36 cents from each additional dollar's earnings if they were also receiving food stamps, and even less than this if, in addition, they were living in public housing.[95] In some cases the benefits from additional earnings may even be highly negative since eligibility for Medicaid and AFDC-UP (unemployed fathers) can cease abruptly when earnings reach a certain level, even though substantial benefits were being received at earnings just below that level.[96]

INCONSISTENCIES WITH THE TAX SYSTEM. While the federal government is providing income support to most lower-income people with one hand, it is removing support from many with the other hand. Virtually all workers, no matter how poor, must bear the burden of payroll taxes. And, although those below the official poverty thresholds do not have to pay income taxes,[97] near-poor families whose resources are sufficiently inadequate that they are eligible for income assistance do incur an income tax liability since income eligibility for means-tested programs often extends up to 150 percent of a family's poverty threshold.

These and other such difficulties with the income security policies designed to assist the lower-income population are really manifestations of a broader problem. Because of the multiplicity of highly complex programs, with overlapping target populations and a plethora of executive and legislative actors at various levels of government, the overall effects are at best difficult to understand and, in

95. *Income Security for Americans: Recommendations of the Public Welfare Study*, Report of the Subcommittee on Fiscal Policy of the Joint Economic Committee, 93:2 (Government Printing Office, 1974), p. 77.

96. The institution of a poverty line cutoff in the food stamp program, which has been proposed by the administration, would also have this effect.

97. Assuming that Congress and the President agree on permanent tax provisions that maintain the level of exempt income above family poverty thresholds.

many cases, are not those intended by the programs' designers.[98] This makes it next to impossible to implement a coherent strategy for the whole system reflecting a conscious compromise among conflicting objectives.

Furthermore, the complexity and fragmentation is placing an increasing burden on congressional committees and staff and executive officials. On the one hand, too many important details of program design and policy are left for lower-level staff experts or program administrators to work out, are dealt with in regulations, or decided without an appreciation of their consequences. Frequently these "details" determine, for example, who will receive benefits—surely a policy matter for elected officials or their appointees to decide. On the other hand, both the executive branch and Congress are constantly tinkering with the programs, often in response to dissatisfaction with the results of the above processes. In addition, the constant flow of regulations from the federal level (of which there are literally hundreds for each of these programs) has made the job of the state and local government officials and administrators a nightmare. The cumulative effects of this process are harmful to public understanding and confidence in the programs as well as to the overall design of the system.

Whither Welfare Reform?

What is to be done about all this? There is general agreement that some major actions must be taken, but, as the past seven years have shown, the disagreements over what constitutes desirable reforms are both broad and deep. Most of the debate today centers around whether to make incremental changes in the programs as they are now constituted or to undertake major structural reform. Incrementalism means different things to different people; it is a label often affixed both to approaches to reform that would sharply curtail the expenditures and numbers of recipients in present programs and to ones which would sharply expand them. In general, those who believe we are already spending too much on these programs favor streamlining and rationalizing the present set of programs in order

98. Though many problems in individual programs that are exacerbated by interactive effects are there, at least implicitly, by design. While there is general agreement on goals for the system, these goals are, by their very nature, somewhat inconsistent. Thus, what is now viewed as a flaw may be the inevitable result of an undesirable but necessary trade-off.

to reduce complexity, error, administrative overlap, and other inefficiencies and to target benefits more on the lowest-income recipients. Those who are more concerned with the inadequacies and inequities of present programs may also support such measures but, more importantly, advocate some combination of the following steps:

—The elimination of the purchase requirement for food stamps and, perhaps, eventually replacing them with their cash equivalent.

—The establishment of a federal minimum payment for AFDC with uniform criteria for eligibility and benefit determination and a requirement that all states adopt the AFDC-UP option.

—The expansion of low-income housing programs not tied to newly constructed housing to much larger segments of the low-income population.

—The permanent enactment of a work bonus or earnings supplement program similar to the earned income tax credit to help the working poor.

—The expansion of federally subsidized public service jobs targeted on the lower-income population.

—The expansion of the unemployment insurance system to meet the minimum needs of new entrants and reentrants to the labor market and of those who have exhausted their benefits.

Proposals for major structural change, on the other hand, typically involve eliminating several of the present means-tested programs in favor of a federally administered, nationally uniform, cash assistance program suitably integrated with the federal income tax system. States could supplement the federal benefits to any or all categories of people at their own expense.[99] Such a program would be similar to many existing means-tested programs in that it provides a schedule

99. A program with this structure is often labeled a negative income tax. A detailed proposal for such a program, which would replace much of the present welfare system, was developed recently within HEW and the Treasury Department. (*See National Journal Reports,* vol. 6 (Nov. 23, 1974), p. 1772.) Refundable tax credits offer an alternative structure to an NIT for providing comprehensive cash assistance. The report of the public welfare study details a proposal which would combine a small comprehensive cash assistance program with a refundable tax credit (which would substitute for personal tax exemptions) in order to achieve benefit levels that would allow for partial replacement of the present welfare system (*Income Security for Americans,* pp. 155–56). A similar refundable tax credit is also discussed in the next section of this chapter. Benjamin A. Okner, in "The Role of Demogrants as an Income Maintenance Alternative," in Irene Lurie, ed., *Integrating Income Maintenance Programs* (Academic Press, 1975), describes a large-scale credit income tax proposal which would substitute for most of the present welfare programs. Such an approach requires massive tax as well as welfare program reform.

of basic benefits to recipients who have no other income that reduces benefits as income increases. (The same schedule of basic benefits and benefit reduction rates could apply to all recipients, or there could be some differentiation.) It differs from other programs, however, in that eligibility depends primarily on income and family size and not on a myriad of other criteria. And except for medical care, benefits are solely in cash, phased down gradually as earnings increase in order to preserve work incentives, and are tied to the tax system so that they phase out entirely at the level of earnings where a positive tax liability begins. Internal Revenue Service administration is sometimes proposed.

Though a complete assessment of any incremental or major reform proposal requires analysis of its specifics, judgments about the strengths and weaknesses of these two broad approaches can be made on the basis of their general distinguishing characteristics. But, before doing so, it is necessary to discuss the merits of retention or expansion of current in-kind programs as opposed to the use of unrestricted cash assistance, since this is a central issue in the debate over incremental change versus major structural reform.

CASH VERSUS IN-KIND BENEFITS. There are substantial costs associated with providing in-kind benefits rather than an equal amount of government expenditures in cash. The administrative costs of food stamps, for instance, are higher because there are so many links in the chain. Stamps must be printed, transported, dispersed, redeemed, recovered, and destroyed, in the process involving printers, case-workers, recipients, grocers, banks, post offices, and private vendors. Such a complicated process also increases the likelihood of fraud and error. The recipients bear costs in the time and transportation necessary to obtain the stamps and the unavoidable social visibility of participation in the program. Also, they are unlikely to value the stamps as highly as cash since the latter would give them more flexibility in purchasing out of a limited income those items they believe most essential to their welfare. Sometimes this even engenders black marketeering in order to convert the stamps to cash. Finally, the purchase requirement (which is essential to the requirement that the specified percentage of income is indeed spent on food) precludes many eligible persons from participating.

All these costs are those peculiar to the individual program. In-kind benefits also contribute centrally to the problems of a multi-program system discussed above. Greater utilization of cash assistance would thus greatly facilitate a more coherent and comprehensive program structure.

For in-kind transfers to be superior to equivalent cash transfers, three conditions must be met: (1) the objective must be to increase the consumption of the particular good or service, not general income augmentation; (2) recipients either will not or cannot purchase the amount of good or service out of an income augmented by a cash equivalent; and (3) the value to society of the extra consumption (if any) of the good or service produced by the in-kind transfer above that which would be produced by a cash equivalent transfer must more than compensate for the higher costs enumerated above.

It seems clear that health care meets these criteria. The degree of equality of financial access to care and amount of consumption that society considers desirable is high. Very few low-income families would spend more than a small fraction of the cash equivalent of their Medicaid or Medicare insurance coverage on health care,[100] and many of those that did might be prone to purchase health care only as needed, ignoring both preventative measures and insurance. Publicly financed health insurance for (at least) the lower-income and aged population should be continued, but it ought to be more comprehensive and sensibly integrated with the rest of the transfer system. The latter would be far easier to accomplish with major structural reforms of the welfare system.

The case for food stamps and low-income housing programs, as opposed to unrestricted cash assistance, is much less persuasive. The expenditures needed to maintain minimum standards of food or housing consumption, as reflected in current law, are generally regular, predictable, and constitute only about a third of incomes at the poverty level. For most recipients, food stamps, in fact, are little different in their effect than a cash payment since they increase expenditures for food by at most 15 to 20 cents per dollar of benefits compared to the payment of the cash equivalent.[101] Furthermore,

100. This is even more true of higher education, since it is not an insurable item; low-income families that do desire large amounts of it would have to make outlays that would be prohibitively high relative to their annual incomes.

101. On average, about half of food stamp benefits goes toward additional food expenditures; the other half simply frees up cash income that would otherwise have been spent on food. About one-third of an equivalent cash transfer would be spent on additional food consumption.

there is no evidence that nutrition is improved as a result of this increased expenditure. In light of this and the costs of providing these benefits in stamp rather than cash form, the food stamp program appears to be little more than an inefficient general income supplementation scheme that ought to be eliminated in favor of direct cash transfers. Because of its universal coverage, cashing out the food stamp program implies instituting a comprehensive cash assistance program. Such a step neither should nor probably would be taken except in conjunction with total reform of the welfare system.

Although there is no evidence comparable to that for food stamps to indicate that the consumption of housing increases more with rent subsidies or housing allowances than with equivalent cash transfers, neither is there any reason to expect markedly different results than in the case of food stamps. Thus the superiority of in-kind benefits for housing to unrestricted cash assistance is also highly questionable.[102] As a practical matter, substituting cash for housing subsidies is a less straightforward proposition than in the case of food stamps. Housing programs serve only a small proportion of the eligible population, many of whom have incomes well in excess of their poverty thresholds, and there is considerable geographic variation in the costs of equivalent low-income housing. The issue is most appropriately framed as whether society is better served by increased cash assistance to the poor or by increased expenditures on low-income housing assistance programs. If the former takes the form of a comprehensive cash assistance program, replacing the present welfare programs, consideration should be given to providing differential cash benefit levels that depend on the local cost of meeting standards of minimal housing adequacy.

INCREMENTALISM VERSUS MAJOR STRUCTURAL REFORM. The primary advantage of incrementalism is its political feasibility. Continual marginal improvements in existing means-tested income security programs, with perhaps an occasional major change or addition of a new program, is consistent with the pattern of the past. An incremental approach avoids the politically troublesome compromises among conflicting objectives that must be explicitly made during more comprehensive change. And, since the marginal cost of

102. Of course the supply situation is different in housing than in food. Under any approach to subsidization of housing costs, the government may have to engage in some regulation and stimulation of low-income housing production.

each reform can be kept small and is decided on separately, there is no need to face up to the overall budgetary consequences of continual incrementalism. Finally, the nature of the political process is such that it is generally easier to legislate smaller new programs and modify old ones than it is to abolish the old and institute larger new ones embodying new principles.

On the other hand, the case for major structural reform, despite the severe political obstacles, seems to us to be more compelling on its merits. The existing set of means-tested programs does not reflect a consistent view of the appropriate roles of each level of government in income security policy. The variety of federal, state, and local administrative, legislative, and financial responsibilities embodied in the present system is a source of many of its difficulties. Other problems are inherent in the very nature of the individual programs—such as categorical eligibility requirements, discretionary eligibility determinations, and the in-kind form of benefits—or are the consequence of multiple programs that serve overlapping target populations. While it is possible in theory to arrive by an incremental approach at the same point a comprehensive reform would reach, in practice it seems unlikely.[103] As one author has put it: "incremental changes are likely to leave largely unsolved or even make worse the

103. An illustration of some of the kinds of problems that arise from an incremental approach is provided by the earned income tax credit. Making this a permanent program is highly touted because it targets cash assistance on the working poor in a manner that appears to promote work incentives. (And if this were the only way to provide cash assistance to the working poor it would undoubtedly be preferable to nothing.) Consider, however, the following. Because of its categorical nature it compensates only families with children for their payroll tax payments; equally needy childless couples and unrelated individuals who also pay payroll taxes are not assisted. Below $4,000 of earnings, benefits increase with earnings, so over this income range the level of assistance is inversely related to need. The phasing out of the benefit from the $4,000 to $8,000 income level imposes an implicit 10 percent tax rate on earnings, which is in addition to the nearly 50 percent tax rate already faced by many of these families. (Virtually all families in this income range are paying 6 percent in payroll taxes, the majority are eligible for the food stamp program, with its nearly 30 percent implicit tax rate, and most families with earnings above $5,500 face 14 percent or higher marginal personal income tax rates.) The earned income tax credit requires another administrative unit and delivery system to be brought into play to distribute a relatively trivial amount of benefits to a population already largely eligible for other welfare programs. And, finally, a complex set of problems arises involving how to treat the earned income tax credit payment in determining benefits for other welfare programs in which several million recipients are also participating. (Under current regulations, each of the other means-tested programs would provide for a different treatment, and in some cases this could result in temporary loss of welfare benefits worth far more than the credit.)

problems created by the existing income maintenance system; perverse incentives, horizontal inequity, inefficiency, program administration that is high in cost and low in quality, unaccountability, and stigmatization of those forced to deal with the system as it is. No one really wants such a system. Sooner or later, the cumulative effects of these problems will demand solution; the reemergence of 'the welfare mess' as a national issue is inevitable."[104] In this view an essential feature of major structural reform is that it provides a means by which the very processes of public policy decision-making and implementation are restructured. It embodies the belief that only a reshaping of the federal role,[105] the elimination of the fragmentation of policy responsibility within Congress and the executive branch, and replacing the present system with a simpler and objectively based program structure will allow substantial progress to be made toward a system of income support that adequately addresses the problems outlined earlier. Only this sort of change will produce the kind of policy control that is desirable, and both recipients and taxpayers will be better served.

As an alternative to either incrementalism or a comprehensive cash assistance program, it is sometimes proposed that the low-income population should be divided into two groups, those living in households headed by an employable adult and those not. The latter would be covered by a cash transfer program, while employable heads of households would be given manpower training and job placement assistance as needed to find a regular job, or be offered public service employment as a last resort. There are several difficulties with this approach. First, major administrative and conceptual problems would arise in making such a division of the population: any definition of employability will be inherently arbitrary and complex to administer.[106] Second, under any definition of employability that the

104. Lynn, "Decade of Policy Developments," p. 82.
105. The issue of the appropriate division of responsibility between the federal, state, and local governments in income transfer programs is treated here only as a by-product of the problems with the current system. See chapter 8 for a discussion of other important policy rationales for greater federal responsibility in the provision of income assistance.
106. That is, a person's employability depends not only on his or her personal characteristics (like health) and family circumstances (like age of children, for a single household head) in ways that cannot be entirely objectively determined, but also on the demand for labor in the local labor market. In addition, both these personal and market characteristics can shift frequently, especially for low-income people.

political process is likely to yield, a majority of employable low-income adults will be working more or less full time in normal economic circumstances. They will not require manpower assistance or jobs[107] so much as modest cash income supplementation that is related to their needs, as measured by family size as well as income. Third, unless we are prepared to make the federal government an employer of last resort for even the temporarily unemployed, a general cash assistance program with benefits related to income and family size will be necessary even in the best of economic times to provide a back-stop for families with employable heads.[108] Finally, millions of people will not fit neatly into one of the three implicit categories—living in a family whose head is nonemployable, is employed, or is not employed but employable—for long periods of time but will shift back and forth among them, in many instances several times a year.

If a comprehensive approach to welfare reform is to be taken, the most sensible approach would seem to be to provide universal coverage through an income-related cash assistance program and, in addition (rather than as a substitution), to provide as much manpower services, public service employment, and other employment assistance to the low-income population as is needed within budgetary and macroeconomic policy constraints. Clearly this must involve much more aggressive policies in these areas than those now being pursued.

New Perspectives

The most serious obstacles to basic structural reform in the past have involved the interrelated issues of costs and the anticipated work disincentive effect of the broadening of the eligibility base for cash assistance. A number of recent developments have cast new light on these issues, however, and suggest that much of the conventional wisdom about them should be reassessed.

First, the costs of expanding the system on an incremental basis have proven to be high; and although the rate of growth of expenditures is expected to level off, there is no reason to expect that in the future an incremental approach will be any less expensive than a

107. Some may argue that more higher-paying jobs are the answer, but current income inadequacies and structural problems in the welfare system should not have to await this long-term solution.
108. And, again, unless public service jobs were to pay far more than the minimum wage, additional income supplementation, depending on family size, will be necessary for some.

comprehensive one. For example, the combination of a permanent earned income tax credit covering all workers, a national minimum AFDC benefit of $3,000 annually for a family of four, a requirement that all states offer an AFDC–unemployed fathers program, and eliminating the food stamp purchase requirement would add over $5 billion annually to income transfer program expenditures if implemented now. In addition, if rent supplement or housing allowance programs actually reached the entire population now eligible for low-income housing assistance, the additional expenditures could run as high as $15 billion a year. Finally, there will periodically be multi-billion dollar tax cuts for lower- and middle-income taxpayers that are not coordinated with income transfer programs.

Might it not be preferable to use some fraction of these potential increases in income support expenditures to purchase the advantages of a more comprehensive reform of the transfer system that is integrated with the tax system? It is arguable that such a course could in the long run produce superior results at less cost than under any incremental appoach. For example, a cash assistance program, fully financed and administered by the federal government, which would preserve work incentives, replace the present federal role in the supplemental security income, AFDC, and food stamp programs, and have a benefit structure that would provide $4,000 to a family of four with no other income, could cost as little as $4 billion more in transfers and $2 billion in additional tax relief to lower- and middle-income taxpayers.[109]

Furthermore, it now appears that the issue of work disincentives for the working poor is not as critical as has been believed. First, the evidence of the New Jersey negative income tax experiment and other

109. This example does not represent our recommendation of the optimum level or structure of benefits in a reformed system. (For example, a higher basic benefit level and benefit reduction rate might be applied to those not expected to work.) It is probably the lowest level that could be considered as a replacement for present programs. The estimate is based on various plans drawn up by HEW over the past two years. The assumed tax rate on earned income is 50 percent and the year of implementation is 1979, with the costs and benefit structure specified in 1976 dollars. It also assumes an annual accounting period, a comprehensive filing unit definition, a 75 percent offset for all other types of income, and an assets test. The 100 percent federal financing would make it possible for all but a few states to supplement benefits, without additional expenditures, in order to maintain the level of benefits to which most AFDC and SSI recipients are now entitled. The tax relief is caused by an increase in the thresholds of tax-exempt income to the transfer break-even levels, by utilizing a set of standard deductions, according to family size, which are phased down at a 50 percent rate at higher levels of income.

labor supply studies does not support the contention that benefit levels as high as the poverty line and modest marginal tax rates will cause large-scale work reduction among male family heads.[110] Second, the low-income working population already faces substantial marginal tax rates through payroll taxes, food stamp eligibility, and, for many, income taxes. An appropriately structured comprehensive reform could represent a modest improvement in work incentives for those now receiving benefits and would be far superior to the addition of a new program (such as a housing allowance) to the present complex.

Finally, the fear that comprehensive welfare reform would make millions of people primarily and permanently dependent on the federal government for their means of subsistence is clearly unfounded. The vast majority of those who would become newly eligible for cash assistance are now eligible for food stamps. Furthermore, they would have substantial earnings and receive only a modest income supplement. And, as noted earlier, for the majority of those who experience poverty over a period of several years, having such a low income is a temporary phenomenon. For most recipients a reformed income transfer system would provide a cushion against short-term adversity, not a permanent source of income.

Income Distribution Policy

The issues in basic income support policy involving coverage, costs, and marginal tax rates take on a somewhat different aspect if, instead of being viewed narrowly from the perspective of welfare reform, they are considered as part of the broader question of income distribution policy. There is a tendency to lament the fact that the preservation of work incentives in an income-tested program necessitates greater costs and broader coverage at a given benefit level to families with no other income. If work incentives are ignored, a comprehensive cash assistance program that pays $4,000 to such a family of four could apply a 100 percent benefit reduction rate and, thus, provide no assistance to any family with income in excess of $4,000; whereas, with a 50 percent benefit reduction rate, assistance would be received by families with up to $8,000 of income. The latter

110. See Irwin Garfinkel and Stanley H. Masters, *Labor Supply and Income Maintenance Programs* (Academic Press, forthcoming).

alternative, however, may be desirable for considerations of vertical equity that are totally unrelated to work incentives.[111]

Viewed in this light, a tax-and-transfer system that yields a net benefit to a family with $8,000 of earned income does not have the unfortunate side-effect of alleviating poverty without destroying work incentives, but rather has a desirable effect of a policy that seeks to reduce, without drastically compressing, income differentials.[112] Transfers should be regarded as negative taxes; so a proposal that would benefit the $8,000 a year family should be viewed just as dispassionately as a proposal to decrease its tax liability through an increase in the standard deduction. From the income distribution perspective, it may be considered desirable and equitable to use tax and transfer policies to increase marginally the purchasing power of an $8,000 family while increasing it greatly for a poor family.

There is one final argument to be considered in favor of a more explicit income distribution policy and the administrative mechanism to implement it. Increasingly, the federal government is assuming responsibility for resource allocations because the private market outcomes are perceived as less than socially desirable by the general public. Energy, air pollution, and health delivery systems are but three of many new areas of government activity that have been added to more traditional ones such as transportation and water resources. Typically, the techniques employed to effect resource allocation are highly centralized bureaucratic or regulatory ones, rather than more market-oriented strategies of altering the incentive structure through fees and subsidies. But these approaches are ill suited to achieve results that often depend on the decisions and actions of many individuals. They are taken partly because they come naturally to legislators and partly because of the fear that a market-oriented approach to resource allocation will have undesirable equity conse-

111. The argument advanced here is more fully developed in Michael C. Barth, Larry L. Orr, and John L. Palmer, "Policy Implications: A Positive View," in Joseph A. Pechman and P. Michael Timpane, eds., *Work Incentives and Income Guarantees: The New Jersey Negative Income Tax Experiment* (Brookings Institution, 1975).

112. We have opted for a tax system that mildly compresses (in theory, at least) rather than totally eliminates income differentials at the upper end of the income distribution. Clearly, concerns about equity as well as the incentive effects of such taxation prevent us from raising the necessary federal revenues by taxing all income above whatever level necessary at 100 percent, with no taxation of incomes below that level. (This would be analagous to 100 percent benefit reduction rates or poverty level cutoffs in transfer programs.)

quences.[113] Unfortunately, once the bureaucratic-regulatory approach is adopted, equity concerns and general struggle over income distribution issues result in the adoption of highly inefficient policies.[114]

The preferable approach would be to use market or market-like analogues somewhat more freely in resource allocation decisions and to employ tax and transfer policies to offset or correct unwanted income distribution effects. A major obstacle to this, however, is the lack of an appropriately structured tax and transfer system that would permit comprehensive and systematic adjustments in the overall distribution of income. Thus, when Congress wished to distribute the benefits of the Tax Reduction Act of 1975 in a way that provided some compensation for the higher energy prices paid by consumers, there was no way to reach systematically the lower-income population. The result was a hodgepodge of personal income tax cuts for all taxpayers, the earned income tax credit for some low-income families, and a $50 benefit for all OASDI and SSI recipients; and much of the lower-income population ended up by receiving no benefit at all.

Tax Reform

Government could play its most significant role in influencing the distribution of income through the tax system; at present, however, government policy seems aimless. The entire tax system at all levels of government places a roughly proportional burden across the vast majority of the population. Indeed, the low-income population bears a burden that is, if anything, heavier than for most of the rest of the population, and the distributional impact of the tax system over the past two decades has shifted somewhat toward regressivity. If even a mildly progressive tax system that does not burden the poor is a desirable goal, reforms are necessary.

The primary culprit in the tax system is not a weak corporate income tax or the rate structure in the federal personal income tax but (1) state and local sales and excise taxes; (2) the narrowness of

113. These general points are made and illustrated by example in Robert H. Haveman, "Efficiency and Equity in Natural Resource and Environmental Policy," *American Journal of Agricultural Economics*, vol. 55 (December 1973), pp. 868–78. Perhaps the most striking recent example of concern over equity providing an obstacle to efficient policies is the congressional debate over energy policy.

114. Or, in many cases, the protection of the status quo for producers in highly inefficient industries.

the federal personal income tax base; and (3) federal payroll taxes. Some possible improvements in these areas are discussed below. The greatest scope for reform lies in the second area. Broadening the federal personal income tax base could increase the effective progressivity of the tax, introduce greater horizontal equity, permit rate reductions, and provide revenues to finance other reforms to reduce the tax burdens of lower- and middle-income taxpayers.

The federal personal income tax could also assume more directly some of the present functions of the income support system, to the benefit of both. While past policies have been formulated under the assumption that income taxes could at best be reduced to zero for low-income households, newer approaches use negative taxes or refundable credits to provide benefits to those with low incomes. The earned income tax credit of the Tax Reduction Act of 1975 does this on a small scale and is still in effect. We have already discussed a full-scale negative income tax as a replacement for the federal role in the present welfare system. This would provide for the more comprehensive and integrated tax and transfer system that is desirable for many reasons. An alternative to this approach, which would not fully replace the current federal role in the welfare system but would take an important step in that direction, is the use of refundable tax credits in lieu of personal exemptions in the federal income tax system; this is the final topic of this section.

State and Local Taxes

The combined incidence of state and local taxes is generally believed to be regressive,[115] and recent research indicates that the state and local tax burden has grown relative to gross national product.[116] While the major focus of this chapter is on federal policy, some discussion of the regressive aspects of state and local taxation is essential in view of the growing importance of this part of the tax system.

Almost all the states levy sales taxes, and some localities impose their own sales taxes in addition to those of the states. Sales taxes are generally assumed to be fully shifted to consumers. Because low-income households often consume most or all of their income, they

115. Pechman and Okner, *Who Bears The Tax Burden?* p. 65. Note that under certain incidence assumptions, state and local taxes are progressive at the top of the income scale, but they are invariably regressive at the bottom (ibid., table 4-10, p. 62).

116. Between 1955 and 1974 the state and local tax take as a share of GNP increased by 50 percent. See chapter 9 in this volume for a detailed analysis.

tend to pay relatively high proportions of their income in sales taxes. A remedy for this situation is to substitute other taxes, such as progressive state income taxes, and many states have done this.[117] It is important that the income tax substituted for the sales tax have a comprehensive base, to prevent the introduction of horizontal inequities. Many of the state income taxes are based on the federal income tax, whose base is now considerably narrowed; how the base could be broadened is discussed below.

The local property tax has long been considered regressive and burdensome for those with low incomes, but recent research indicates that this may be a misconception. Conventional measures of the incidence of the tax have been biased toward regressivity by measuring income over a single year rather than a longer time period; further, the tax may be borne primarily by owners of capital—corporate, partnership, and individual businesses—who tend to have high incomes.[118] The property tax is probably less regressive than many of its alternatives. Further, in the absence of federal income tax reform involving taxation of imputed net rent of homeowners, the property tax is the only tax linked to the value of the use of a home to its owner. The reduction or elimination of the tax would increase incentives for consumer investment in housing, which many economists believe is already excessively subsidized by government tax policy. The property tax is difficult to administer, however, and subject to arbitrariness because it depends on valuations of individual properties. On balance, it appears that the property tax is more progressive than was earlier thought, but still subject to problems of administration and horizontal equity.

Many states have attempted to remedy the presumed regressive effects of the property tax by adopting "circuit breaker" laws. These provisions refund some portion of property taxes to homeowners or renters[119] if the taxes exceed some fraction of income. Circuit breakers have the unfortunate effects of benefiting those with greater

117. As of 1976, forty states and the District of Columbia have their own income taxes.

118. Henry J. Aaron, *Who Pays the Property Tax?* (Brookings Institution, 1975), chap. 3. The length of the measurement period is crucial because households with incomes below their usual level often pay property taxes that are quite large relative to current income; those with permanently low incomes generally do not pay much in property taxes.

119. Not all circuit breakers cover renters; those which do count some fraction of rent as payment of the property tax.

wealth more than those with lesser wealth; benefiting those who choose to spend more money on housing more than those who choose to spend less; and benefiting those with temporarily low incomes more than those with permanently low incomes.[120] A carefully designed system of housing allowances or property tax deferral would be far superior to the circuit breaker in providing property tax relief where it is needed.

Broadening the Federal Personal Income Tax Base

Economists have observed for many years that the multiplicity of special provisions, exemptions, and deductions in the federal tax code have reduced potential revenue and thus increased the rates needed for the income tax to raise a given amount of revenue.[121] This erosion of the tax base has several undesirable effects on the economy as a whole. First, is inequitable: it benefits certain persons on an unsystematic and unintended basis. Second, it is inefficient: it encourages unproductive tax avoidance behavior and the transfer of investment to less socially productive activities. Third, it reduces output: it discourages work effort through excessively high marginal tax rates on those who do not successfully avoid taxes. And fourth, it is divisive: it alienates some groups because of the special favors extended to others, and it confuses and demoralizes all taxpayers with its complexity. A comprehensive reform of the income tax to broaden its base and lower its rates would make the tax more equitable and efficient and facilitate the raising of additional revenue to finance new programs and replace less equitable taxes.

Following are some reforms that would broaden the tax base in a manner designed to increase equity and progressivity.[122] Several tax relief and rebate schemes for distributing the additional revenues will then be explored. Illustrative revenue estimates are made at 1976 income levels.

120. Aaron, *Who Pays the Property Tax?* pp. 72–79.
121. Joseph A. Pechman, "Erosion of the Individual Income Tax," *National Tax Journal,* vol. 10 (March 1957), pp. 1–25; Joseph A. Pechman and Benjamin A. Okner, "Individual Income Tax Erosion by Income Classes," in *The Economics of Federal Subsidy Programs,* a Compendium of Papers Submitted to the Joint Economic Committee, 92:2 (Government Printing Office, 1972), pp. 13–40.
122. Most of these suggestions are from George F. Break and Joseph A. Pechman, *Federal Tax Reform: The Impossible Dream?* (Brookings Institution, 1975), chap. 6, option B. That volume is also an excellent source for information on the individual reform items.

CAPITAL GAINS. Present law provides that only half of long-term capital gains be included in adjusted gross income, that the first $50,000 of long-term gains may be taxed at an alternative rate of 25 percent, and that no tax be levied on accrued capital gains when assets change hands at death or by gift. Given reduced tax rates and a somewhat liberalized averaging procedure,[123] capital gains could be taxed as ordinary income upon realization or when assets are transferred at death or by gift. Such a reform could increase revenues by an estimated $11.3 billion.

HOMEOWNER PREFERENCES. Homeowners can now deduct both mortgage interest and property taxes from taxable income, although they are not required to include the rental value of their homes in taxable income (unlike holders of other assets, such as stocks and bonds, who must include the dividends and interest from their assets). While these deductions would be justified if the rental value of homes were included in income, the present situation bestows a double blessing on homeowners. The inclusion of imputed rent would be a very difficult process (much like the assessment of home values for the property tax), but the removal of the deductions would not.

The issue of homeowner preferences is extremely sensitive from a political standpoint, however. A total elimination of such deductions would both reduce property values and increase the out-of-pocket costs of homeowners who would have no opportunity to adjust their family budgets because of long-term mortgage contracts. These preferences could be partially removed, however. First, the deduction for the property tax could be eliminated on the grounds that it is a benefit tax—directly related to services received—and that its deduction is unjustified when the rental value of owned homes is not included in income.[124] Second, the interest deduction could be limited to the amount of business and investment income plus $2,000, which would mean that interest paid as a cost of earning money income (which is taxable) would be deductible, but only a limited amount of interest paid to obtain housing services (which are not taxable) would be deductible. Such reforms would increase revenues by $5.3 billion. If the impact of these reforms were judged too great

123. Income averaging is necessary in the taxation of capital gains to prevent inequities arising from the taxation in one year of income accumulated as a capital gain over many years. Under a progressive tax, a gain taxed fully in one year would tend to be subject to higher rates than if it were taxed as it accrued.

124. This could encourage states and localities to substitute other taxes for property taxes to maintain deductibility for their residents.

to be absorbed by the economy and by homeowners at one time, the adjustment could be eased by making the reforms apply only to new mortgages (written after a certain date) or by phasing in the reforms over a period of years.

TREATMENT OF MARRIED COUPLES AND SINGLE PEOPLE. The tax code currently produces some anomalous results in tax liabilities of married and single taxpayers. Married couples receive an "income splitting" benefit that is intended to compensate them for their family responsibilities, but in fact the benefits of income splitting do not depend on the actual responsibilities of the couple. Further, some single persons have family responsibilities to people outside of their homes, but except in certain circumstances they do not benefit from income splitting. Married couples where both husband and wife work are taxed as heavily as couples with the same income but only one earner, while the two-earner couple puts forth greater labor effort and does not have the benefit of home-produced services by one of the couple. Finally, some married couples where both husband and wife work—those with roughly equal individual incomes, especially if the incomes are relatively high and they do not itemize deductions —pay higher taxes than they would if they were single. These problems defy a total solution, but a more equitable situation than that at present could be achieved by using one rate schedule rather than the present four and by making the distinction of family responsibility on the basis of exemptions and deductions. A 10 percent tax credit for the earnings of second earners in families, with a ceiling of $1,000, could replace the present child care deduction. A tax rate schedule that steered a middle course between the present married and single schedules, together with the tax credit for the second earners, would leave revenues approximately unchanged.

PERSONAL DEDUCTIONS. Several of the current personal deductions are in need of reform. The deduction for state and local gasoline taxes is clearly uncalled for in view of the energy shortage; it is also totally unverifiable and thus a tax on honesty. The present deduction of one-half of medical insurance premiums without reference to the total amount of medical expenses could be removed. Furthermore, the present deduction floor of 3 percent of adjusted gross income, designed to screen out normal medical expenses from deductibility, is too low and allows even families with less than average expenses to receive a deduction; a 5 percent floor would be preferable. The percentage standard deduction—16 percent of income with a minimum and a maximum—could be repealed and replaced by a fixed $3,000 standard deduction. The total revenue raised by these changes would be $4.0 billion.

BUSINESS AND INVESTMENT INCOME. All percentage depletion provisions in the tax code could be eliminated. This simplification, together with the taxation of capital gains at ordinary rates, would permit the abolition of the minimum tax on preference income. The additional revenue raised on personal tax returns would be $0.8 billion. A further reform in this area, which would raise little revenue but would strengthen the integrity of the income tax, is a limit on "expense account living" through excessive deductions for unjustifiable business expenses.

ACROSS-THE-BOARD TAX RATE REDUCTIONS. If the reforms listed above were enacted, it would be possible to lower income tax rates and still maintain federal revenues at or above their present level. Some reduction would be necessary before long-term capital gains could be taxed at ordinary income rates; a 70 percent top bracket rate would be too high for taxing gains accrued over a long period, even with averaging procedures available. The ultimate choice of a precise rate structure would of course depend on the revenue productivity of reforms undertaken and the current fiscal policy situation. Under our suggested reforms, tax rates could be reduced from the present scale of 14 to 70 percent to a lower 12 to 53 percent and still increase revenues;[125] total revenues would be $142.1 billion, compared to current revenues of $128.5 billion. The distribution of the tax burden would be significantly shifted from low- to high-income households; married couples, homeowners, and recipients of property income would tend to be the most affected. These additional revenues could be returned to the taxpayers through several methods detailed below.

Payroll Tax Relief

OASDHI payroll taxes place a sizable burden on low-income taxpayers because, unlike federal personal income taxes, they apply to the first dollar of wage and salary earnings without any exemptions or deductions. Although a typical family of four at its poverty threshold, with total income in earnings of $5,500 in 1975, had no

125. This reduction of tax rates would permit the elimination of the maximum tax on earned income.

federal personal income tax liability, it paid $643.50 in payroll taxes. In fact this family's payroll tax liability exceeded its income tax liability until it earned about $15,965.[126]

The present temporary earned income tax credit was instituted to compensate certain low-income workers for these payroll taxes, but it is neither comprehensive in its coverage nor related to family size. For these reasons a preferable alternative might involve a household deduction and personal exemptions for payroll taxes similar to those in the personal income tax system, with the revenue loss to the trust funds to be made up by general revenues.[127] In order to concentrate the payroll tax relief on lower-income earners and hold down the payroll tax revenue loss, these exemptions and deductions could be phased out by, say, $1 for every $2 of earnings above the total exempt level of income.

If a household deduction of $1,700 and personal exemptions of $750 were chosen, this would totally exempt most of the poor from payroll tax liabilities. The phase-out would gradually reduce the tax relief until those at approximately twice their poverty threshold incomes would be receiving no benefit from the provision. Such a scheme would result in a revenue loss of $6.3 billion if it were put into effect for 1976; this is $5.0 billion more than would be lost by the continuation of the earned income tax credit.

Tax Credits in Lieu of Personal Exemptions

Another possible means of tax relief would be the use of personal tax credits in place of exemptions. The most common argument for the use of credits is that, unlike exemptions, they provide the same amount of tax reduction for all taxpayers, regardless of income.[128] Therefore tax credits are seen as contributing to a more progressive tax structure. The use of a $30 per capita credit in the Tax Reduction Act of 1975 suggests that there is congressional interest in the credit

126. Counting both the employer's and employee's share of the payroll tax; as noted earlier, most economists believe that both are borne by the worker in the long run.

127. This is the formulation suggested by Benjamin A. Okner in "The Social Security Payroll Tax: Some Alternatives for Reform," *Journal of Finance,* vol. 30 (May 1975), pp. 567–78.

128. A $750 exemption reduces taxes by $525 for a taxpayer in the 70 percent bracket, but by $105 for a taxpayer in the 14 percent bracket. The equal value of credits does not hold where a taxpayer is made nontaxable by a credit, as will be discussed later.

approach, and this provision remains in the 1976 tax law with some modification.[129]

In practice, there are drawbacks to the use of credits. Credits provide greater differentials between tax liabilities of families of different sizes at lower incomes, and smaller differentials at higher incomes, than do exemptions that cost the same amount of total revenue. If a $250 per capita credit were substituted for the $750 exemption in the 1976 tax law, a single individual could earn 123 percent ($3,782) of his poverty threshold and pay no income tax, but a family of six could earn 152 percent ($11,600) of its threshold and not be taxable, compared to 93 percent and 106 percent under present law.[130] At higher incomes, substituting the credit for the exemption would have the opposite effect and narrow the difference between taxes of individuals and six-member families in the 50 percent bracket from the present $1,875 to $1,250. Those who disapprove of this suggest that a personal credit be allowed as an alternative to the deduction rather than as a substitute, with the taxpayer choosing whichever would minimize his tax.

Under the tax reform package suggested above, substituting a $250 credit for the $750 exemption reduces tax liabilities by $5.4 billion; offering the credit as an alternative reduces liabilities by $8.1 billion, or $2.7 billion more. The substitution raises taxes for high-income and lowers them for low-income taxpayers, while the optional credit leaves tax liabilities unchanged at high incomes and reduces them at low incomes. In view of the fact that virtually the same result as a tax credit scheme could be achieved through the alteration of current exemptions and the tax rate schedule, the use of credits has little to recommend it unless the rate changes are politically less feasible (as some would argue). However, it is possible to use the credits in an income redistribution scheme that would not be possible otherwise, and that method is described below.

Refundable Tax Credits

While it is often said that a credit is of equal value to all taxpayers regardless of income level, in fact only those taxpayers who

129. The credit is now the greater of (1) $35 per capita or (2) 2 percent of taxable income up to a maximum of $180.

130. The calculations use the authors' estimates of 1976 poverty lines. Exemptions have in the past been set along with the standard deduction to make as many of the poor as possible nontaxable, usually accomplishing this for families but failing for individuals. Under the 1976 tax reductions, very little additional reduction would be needed to make all the poor nontaxable.

have a tax liability (before the credit is applied) at least as great as the credit realize its full worth, and those with no liability receive no assistance from it at all.[131] Thus, while a credit is responsive to differing abilities to pay above the income levels where tax liabilities are in excess of the credit, it is not responsive to the need for income supplementation below those levels. A way to render it so is to make it refundable, much like the current earned income tax credit. This would mean that a family would receive the balance of any excess of their credits over their tax liability, thus insuring that the credit is worth its full amount to persons at all income levels and yielding a more desirable distributional effect. It could also be viewed as a means of offsetting the burden of other taxes, such as state and local sales and excise taxes, on the poor.

In addition, the impact of such a refundable tax credit (RTC) on current welfare programs could be substantial and desirable. Welfare recipients would have little or no tax liability to offset against an RTC and, therefore, would receive sizable cash refunds; these refunds could be partially or fully offset by a reduction in welfare benefits.[132] This would partially "buy out" the present welfare system, reduce its costs and caseloads, and provide cash assistance to those categorically ineligible for current means-tested programs (in a way that would not subject them to higher marginal tax rates on earnings), thus reducing the inequities of the present treatment of the working poor.

As an example of how such a program would work, a $250 credit was substituted for the $750 exemption in the tax reform package with payroll tax relief but without the earned income credit or the present per capita credit. Table 12-6 shows that revenues under this package would be about $2.4 billion greater than under present law; coupled with the payroll tax relief discussed earlier, the total liability reduction would be only about $3.9 billion. Table 12-7 shows that the redistribution of income with the credits would be substantial in comparison to the 1976 law. The income and payroll tax burden on

131. For example, substitution of a $250 credit for the personal exemption would eliminate the total income tax liability (under present law) of $310 for a family of four with $8,100 of income, but would be of no help to the same family at $6,100 of income, which is already nontaxable. Between these two levels, the greater the family income, the greater the benefit derived from the credit because it results in cancellation of the total income tax liability.

132. In order to effect offsets, RTC payments could be disbursed on a quarterly basis to those without substantially offsetting liabilities and pro rated on a monthly basis for purposes of income accounting in welfare programs.

Table 12-6. Federal Individual Income Tax Liabilities under Present Law and under a Reformed Law, by Adjusted Gross Income Class, 1976

Adjusted gross income class (dollars)	Liabilities (billions of dollars)		Change in liabilities (percent)
	Present law	Reformed law	
0–2,500	−0.1	−4.2	...
2,500–5,000	0.2	−3.3	...
5,000–7,500	2.8	0.1	−94.7
7,500–10,000	6.0	3.3	−43.9
10,000–12,500	7.8	5.9	−24.0
12,500–15,000	11.1	10.0	−10.4
15,000–20,000	23.0	23.6	2.7
20,000–25,000	18.3	20.9	14.5
25,000–50,000	30.5	39.1	28.2
50,000–100,000	15.5	18.9	21.7
100,000 and over	13.4	16.5	22.5
All classes	128.4	130.8	1.8

Source: Calculated from Brookings 1972 Tax File projected to 1976. Figures are rounded.

Table 12-7. Federal Rates of Individual Income and Payroll Taxes under Present Law and under Reformed Law, by Comprehensive Income Class, 1976

Comprehensive income class (dollars)	Tax rate (percent)		Change in effective rates (percentage points)
	Present law	Reformed law	
0–2,500	10.0	−20.0	−30.0
2,500–5,000	9.9	−1.7	−11.6
5,000–7,500	14.2	7.8	−6.4
7,500–10,000	17.8	13.6	−4.2
10,000–12,500	18.9	16.3	−2.6
12,500–15,000	21.0	19.3	−1.7
15,000–20,000	21.7	21.8	0.1
20,000–25,000	22.5	24.2	1.6
25,000–50,000	23.5	27.9	4.4
50,000–100,000	28.9	34.6	5.8
100,000 and over	33.5	44.1	10.6
All classes	21.2	20.8	−0.4

Source: Same as table 12-6. Figures are rounded.
a. Includes adjusted gross income, excess of percentage depletion over cost depletion, interest on state and local government bonds, and one-half of the total estimated capital gains transferred by gift or death.

the lowest income bracket would be reduced by 30 percent and that for the highest bracket increased by 11 percent, with a smooth progression between these two extremes along the income scale. The taxes of those least able to pay would be reduced, and the benefit would accrue to all low-income taxpayers regardless of their status in existing programs.

The net costs of the package would be considerably less than the decrease in tax liabilities. Welfare costs could be significantly reduced, depending on how the tax credits were treated in the categorical programs. If welfare and food stamp benefits were reduced dollar for dollar for the refundable credits, program costs would be reduced by approximately $5 billion, with roughly one-third of this reduction accruing to state and local governments and the balance to the federal government. Accompanying the dollar savings would be a reduction in welfare caseloads of as much as 15 percent.[133] Total benefits to welfare recipients could be increased at the cost of smaller program savings.

Conclusion

It is possible to approach the subject of tax reform from a perspective totally divorced from income security considerations, and to design a simplified tax system that would be more equitable to taxpayers with similar incomes (by reducing tax preferences that favor some persons over others) but would leave the effective progressivity of the tax unchanged. Such an approach would have many benefits, including greater efficiency for the economy as a whole and increased popular confidence in the tax system.

Here we have chosen to go beyond this approach, and to modify even the reformed income tax so as to use it as an income support instrument. The income tax could be used to provide cash payments to all those with low incomes, regardless of their eligibility for present categorical programs; and the effective progressivity of the tax could be increased to raise revenues for these cash payments. Such an approach has benefits and costs. The benefits would be reduced welfare caseloads and reduced tax burdens for those with low and moderate incomes, in addition to the benefits of a simplified tax system. The costs are the inefficiencies and burdens of increased taxes for upper-income households, offset to some extent by lower marginal tax rates. We feel that the benefits of this redistributive approach outweigh its costs.

The burden of taxes on low-income households is substantial, and one of the best ways to benefit such households would be to restructure the tax system so as to reduce the burden. We have suggested several steps in that direction. The two most regressive taxes are state and local sales taxes and the federal payroll tax. Sales taxes are paid

133. Authors' estimates.

by rich and poor alike, and for the poor, who consume most of their income, this burden can be excessive. Most of the states have income taxes and could shift much or all of the sales tax burden to the more progressive income tax. Because the federal payroll tax bears on the first dollars of the income of the poor, it is especially burdensome to them. An exemption and deduction scheme is suggested here to eliminate the payroll tax liabilities of most of the poor while losing only a modest amount of revenue.

The federal income tax is the logical source of additional revenue to finance the payroll tax relief, but tax rates are too high to be raised further. The level of the rates is dictated by the narrowness of the tax base; broadening the base would reduce the inequities of the many special preferences and permit rate reductions while raising more revenues. Sufficient revenue could be forthcoming to finance the payroll tax relief described earlier.

While the various reforms suggested here were illustrated as a package, they need not be viewed as an indivisible unit. If modest tax cuts were called for by fiscal policy considerations, it would be reasonable to provide them through payroll tax relief and substitute general revenues for the shortfall. Income tax reform could proceed using any or all of the individual suggestions here, or a comprehensive reform package could be phased in gradually to cushion its effects on the economy. Finally, the additional tax revenues provided by economic growth (which raises revenues by greater amounts than income because of the progressive tax structure) could be earmarked for an income support scheme (such as the refundable credits suggested here) and phased in over time.

The revenue estimates presented here, however, do indicate that a meaningful program of income support is feasible even now. In exchange for a modest increase in effective tax rates at the top of the income scale we could provide significant tax relief for those with low and moderate incomes, simplify the tax system, and take a step in the right direction toward welfare reform.

With a broadened tax base, future growth in income tax liabilities could be returned to the taxpayers through rate reductions that would compensate the few whose taxes were increased by the reform, and through increased income support that would further shrink the welfare caseloads. We find this prospect an attractive alternative to the current tax and transfer system.

CHAPTER THIRTEEN

Congress and the President: Enemies or Partners?

JAMES L. SUNDQUIST

A BOOK that talks of what government should do must ask once more, at the close, about the capacity of government to get things done. For every public opinion poll nowadays attests to an appalling loss of confidence by the people in their governmental institutions, particularly those of the federal government in Washington.

Appalling, but hardly surprising. One need not dwell on the events that led to this unfortunate state. They are known well enough—Vietnam, a Great Society that overpromised and underdelivered, intolerable rates of inflation and of unemployment at the same time, the CIA, Spiro Agnew, Watergate, and finally the Republic's first presidential resignation.

By now, the legacy of deep distrust from these events has eroded the confidence of government in itself. The emerging political heroes appear to be those who deride the efficacy of the very administrative apparatus over which they preside or hope to preside. More than ever, candidates run against the bureaucracy, and members of Congress run against the institution in which they serve. More is heard about what the government cannot do than about what it can. Officials and candidates alike shy from risky policy departures; better to retrench, withdraw, play safe, than to attempt to use the tools of government for lofty purposes.

The author acknowledges the assistance of several persons who, in addition to the editors, offered criticism and suggestions after reading an early draft: Louis Fisher, Walter J. Oleszek, Judith H. Parris, and Jerrold E. Schneider.

Yet the needs remain. Long-standing and festering domestic problems, like poverty and urban decay, will not be solved by market forces or the states or local communities alone. And even if there were none of these, there would still be crises, foreign and domestic. The capacity of government to act decisively and effectively when it has to may be the overriding problem of the time, one that adds a new dimension to every other problem. The perplexity of what to do through public action is compounded by the conundrum of how to get it done.

Capacity in government depends, in the United States as elsewhere, on leadership. But even the ablest leaders—and the haphazard nomination and election processes of a democracy do not assure selection of the ablest—cannot transcend the limits of the institutional structures in which they labor. In the United States, that has a special meaning. The institutional structure bequeathed to twentieth century America by the eighteenth century is more complex than that of any other democratic country in the world. The United States stands alone in the degree to which governmental powers are shared among competing institutions—nation and states, Congress and the President, Senate and House of Representatives, all checked in turn by an independent Supreme Court.

The problem of governing, since the beginning, has been to assemble those dispersed powers in a working combination sufficiently harmonious to permit decisions to be made. Some of the divisions of power have been bridged in the course of past crises. A civil war and the ordeal of a great depression buried the doctrine of states' rights and established national supremacy in matters on which the nation elects to act. And with the depression and the New Deal revolution, the Supreme Court ceased trying to conform both the President and Congress to—as Mr. Justice Holmes put it—Mr. Herbert Spencer's *Social Statics*. But one great division of power remains unabridged. That is the division of national governmental authority between the President, the Senate, and the House—three competing institutions that have the power to checkmate one another on most matters if they choose to press their authority to its limits.

That division has, if anything, become more crucial because of a phenomenon peculiar to the past two decades. Since 1954 the electorate has been doing most of the time what before that date it did only on rare occasions—sending to Washington a president of one party and a Congress dominated by the other. For fourteen of the past twenty-two years, the executive and the legislature have confronted one another across not only an institutional but also a partisan political gulf, each branch compelled by the dynamics of party competition not to cooperate with the other but rather to attempt to use its power in such a way as to discredit the other. On any major issue, if a Republican president sends a bill to a Democratic Congress, the Democrats must find reason to belittle and reject it—or else they are publicly pronouncing their political adversary to be a wise and able leader and his party's policy to be the right one. Conversely, if Congress initiates a bill, or a modification of the President's bill, he is under the same compulsion to find reason to denounce and veto it.

True, both the President and Congress are able to rise above "politics" on occasion: the Marshall Plan was the joint product of President Truman and the Republican Eightieth Congress. But that was a time of crisis. And there was no such collaboration on domestic matters; Truman ran for reelection—successfully—against the domestic record of that same Eightieth Congress. In another period of divided government, from 1955 through 1960, the Democratic congressional leadership collaborated with President Eisenhower on foreign policy and on some domestic matters, including tax policy. But Congress rejected most of the President's domestic legislative program, and he vetoed what it proposed. In the end, as in 1948, the President was crusading against the record of Congress, and John F. Kennedy devoted much of his 1960 campaign oratory to decrying Eisenhower vetoes. In the past eight years, relations between the branches have fluctuated mostly between bad and worse. They collaborated on a few new departures—revenue sharing, President Nixon's "new economics of 1971," some consolidation of federal grants-in-aid, rescue of the northeastern railroads—but Congress blocked President Nixon's major reorganization plan, his welfare reform proposal, and many of his measures to dismantle the Great Society. It thwarted both him and President Ford in foreign policy as well—Southeast Asia, trade negotiations with the Soviet Union, Cyprus, Angola. Meanwhile presidential disdain for congressional initiative has been expressed in the longest list of vetoes of significant bills in the country's history.

The public tends to dismiss the denunciation and counterdenunciation that flow from divided government as so much "playing politics," and much of it is. Often, after both sides have made their statements for the media, compromises are worked out. Nevertheless, President Ford's nearly half a hundred vetoes, so far, reflect the different conceptions the two major parties have of the national interest. That, of course, is the reason for the party system, and something would indeed be lost if the parties failed to disagree or compromised too soon. To give the electoral processes vitality the parties must find ways not to conceal their fundamental differences in outlook and approach but to sharpen them as they apply them to concrete legislative issues. That this results so often in immobilization of the policymaking process is the consequence of the party system's operation within a structure of checks and balances.

If the public is really tired of political gamesmanship between the President and Congress and weary of governmental stalemate, the first step toward a solution is readily at hand. The voters can go back to doing what they used to do—elect a Congress to support whatever president they choose. Bestow some of the old power on the presidential coattails. But the results of recent elections suggest that the voters are motivated to go positively in the other direction—at least when they are choosing Republican presidents. Ticket splitting for millions of voters seems to be little short of compulsive.

"For government to function," wrote V. O. Key, Jr., "the obstructions of the constitutional mechanism must be overcome, and it is the party that casts a web, at times weak, at times strong, over the dispersed organs of government and gives them a semblance of unity."[1] With the President of one party and the majorities in Congress of the other, there can of course be no web at all. And not even the semblance of unity.

The Cult of the Strong Presidency

For the first two-thirds of this century, then, those who pondered the problem of how to unite the fragmented powers of government came to widespread agreement on what seemed a clear and feasible solution—the strong presidency. If the party is the web that unites the executive and legislative branches—when it controls them both—the leader of the party is the President. He carries the party's mandate in the presidential campaign. His program becomes the party's pro-

1. *Politics, Parties, and Pressure Groups,* 5th ed. (Crowell, 1964), p. 656.

gram, his appointees the party's spokesmen, his record the party's record. Members of Congress accept his leadership; senior members refer to past presidents they have served *"under,"* not "with." If the government is unified, it is through presidential energy, presidential skill, presidential force.

A succession of strong leaders—Theodore Roosevelt, Woodrow Wilson, Franklin Roosevelt—had dramatized the great potential of the presidential office.

The creaky machinery of the American government could be made to work after all, it seemed clear, if the President were strong enough. So half a century of agitation and effort went into building up his office. The President, a man, became the presidency, an institution. The Executive Office of the President was formed, made up of staff assistants who would extend the President's reach and his authority. In a whole series of legislative acts, he was assigned specific responsibilities of leadership. The Budget and Accounting Act of 1921 required him to devise annually a comprehensive program for the whole of the government, embodying a fiscal policy—which, before that time, a president did not have to do and usually did not. With the consent of Congress, he became the single spokesman on legislative policy for the whole of the executive branch; no agency could speak to Congress without his clearance. By the Employment Act of 1946, he was compelled to have an economic policy for maximum employment, production, and purchasing power. Before that date a president did not have to take responsibility for maintaining prosperity and economic growth, and before Franklin Roosevelt most did not. And of course he was still expected to fulfill his traditional roles of chief diplomat, chief global strategist, and—since World War II—Leader of the Free World.

Here was the answer. If parliamentary countries had a cabinet in which the powers of government were united, the United States had a presidency that served a comparable purpose. The President became the acknowledged leader of the legislative branch, as well as director and general manager of the executive. Congress waited for the State of the Union Message, the Budget Message, and the Economic Report of the President to set the agenda for its session. Then it waited for the administration bills. Presidents transmitted them with an increasing flow of special messages. It was on the administration program that media attention focused. An enterprising journal, *Congressional*

Quarterly, devised an index to measure individual congressmen by the degree to which they supported the presidential program.

Political science textbooks written during the New Deal or in its afterglow made of the strong presidency an article of faith. Thomas E. Cronin, under the title "The Cult of the Presidency," has excerpted some of the textbook language: the presidency is "the great engine of democracy," "the American people's one authentic trumpet," "the central instrument of democracy," "the chief formulator of public policy" and "chief architect of . . . foreign policy." "Presidential government is a superb planning institution." "He symbolizes the people." "He is . . . a kind of magnificent lion who can roam widely and do great deeds." "Few nations have solved so simply and yet grandly the problem of finding and maintaining an office or state that embodies their majesty and reflects their character."[2]

And what of the danger that a president might roam widely but do bad deeds? Well, wrote Louis Brownlow, the Franklin Roosevelt adviser who was one of the architects of the aggrandized presidency: "During the whole history of the thirty-two Presidents, not one has been recreant to his high trust."[3] Paul Appleby, the philosopher of *Big Democracy,* saw no danger in the presidency: "through Congress, and through elections, it is a power popularly controlled."[4] And Richard E. Neustadt, whose *Presidential Power* was at least for a time the bible of the "cult of the presidency," had no worries. A president seeking to "maximize his power" energizes the government, he wrote. What is good for the President, he concluded, is therefore good for the country.[5]

But suddenly, in the last decade, things went sour.

—and Disillusionment

After Vietnam and Watergate, it is hardly necessary to dwell upon the dangers of the strong presidency that half a century of aggrandizement has produced. Those episodes tell us that a president could, after all, be recreant. Decisions could be made by the President alone, or by him in consultation with a small group of his own selection,

2. *The State of the Presidency* (Little, Brown, 1975), pp. 25–29.
3. *The President and the Presidency* (Chicago: Public Administration Service, 1949), p. 51.
4. *Big Democracy* (Knopf, 1945), p. 124.
5. *Presidential Power* (Wiley, 1960), pp. 181–85.

confined if he chose to subordinates whom he could dominate. The President, in other words, could withdraw into a tight little circle from which critical or independent spirits could be excluded. He could defy popular and congressional opinion, if he chose. He did not even have to tell anyone what he was doing.

Most presidents don't act that way, of course. Lyndon Johnson and especially Richard Nixon are now seen as aberrations. Gerald Ford is the norm—open, outgoing, responsive. So people have stopped worrying. After all, Johnson was forced to retire and Nixon to resign, which proves, we are accustomed to saying and hearing, that the American system *did* work. Yet the experience of ten years of headstrong and unsuccessful presidential leadership compels an earnest reexamination of the faith that the strong presidency is a safe and reliable solution to our constitutional dilemmas.

In any institution, if power reposes in a single person, what happens when that person turns out to be rash or impulsive or erratic or touched with megalomania or bent on corrupting the purposes of the institution to serve his own? These traits may be uncommon, but they are hardly unknown. Hence most human institutions hedge the personal power of any individual executive by making him or her responsible to a plural body—a board of directors, a governing council, a board of trustees, or something comparable. In a parliamentary government, that plural body is the legislature itself, which selects and removes the chief executive. Among American governments, plural bodies are commonly in charge at the local level, where city councils and school boards select, control, and dismiss managers and superintendents.

The problem with the presidency, in essence, is how to pluralize the exercise of its power, and the one effective way to do that is to bring the presidency into a collaborative relationship with the leaders of Congress—one that will compel the restraint of consultation but stop short of creating a situation of perpetual deadlock. This is probably impossible to achieve with certainty under the American constitutional system, but I will return to the question later.

The Founding Fathers, no strangers to royal tyranny, considered several alternatives to the independent, one-man presidency. One possibility was a three-man executive, which was rejected on a divided vote. Another was to vest in the legislature the power to select the President, a scheme that was not laid aside until the final days of the convention. When the delegates approved the plan embodied in the Constitution, they were not unduly worried because it seemed full of safeguards. In the first place, the President would be carefully chosen by a small group of elders called the electoral college, who would be able to scour the country for a chief magistrate of proven ability, level head, and judicious mien. If they did not agree, the choice would be made by the House of Representatives. The legislative power, including the power of the purse, would be in Congress. While the executive power would be in the President, he would be hemmed in. Actual administrative authority would be in the department heads, whom the President would no doubt assemble as a cabinet for collective policy consideration. The Senate, conceived as a kind of privy council, would advise and consent on appointments and treaties.

How things have changed in the bicentennium since then! The President is selected not by a small group of electors who can carefully screen the available talent but by the people themselves, who respond initially to fleeting impressions gained in frenzied primary campaigns. There is reason to believe that in the arduous and interminable selection process the candidate of sober judgment, restrained opinion, and judicious temper, free of any trace of megalomania, is screened out, not in. Once elected, any president who may be inclined toward excess (to repeat, the aberrant president, not the norm) finds that in the use of executive power the constitutional restraints need no longer bind. The administrative authority that once reposed, by tradition as well as law, in the members of the cabinet can be drawn into the White House to virtually whatever degree the President desires. He does not have to use his cabinet as a policy council, or even assemble it for that purpose; few modern presidents—Eisenhower was the exception—have done so. The Senate does not advise on treaties, but only consents, and treaties in any case have been superseded to a large degree by executive agreements or informal executive confrontations, demarches, and détentes. In the daily clashes and crises of a shrunken, interdependent world, what counts is the actions of the President as chief strategist, chief diplomat, and commander-in-chief, and in those capacities, as long as he does not commit military forces in actual hostilities, he is under no constitutional compulsion even to consult the Senate. On appointments also, the Senate does not advise as a body and rarely withholds consent; the President's chief advisers and assistants are either exempt from confirmation or routinely approved, usually, on the reasonable premise that the President's heavy responsibilities entitle him to choose his own circle of close associates. So if a president is determined to maximize his authority for the short run—during an election campaign, say, or for the duration of a foreign crisis—he can ignore the supposedly countervailing institution at the other end of Pennsylvania Avenue.

His short-run domination may be at the expense of longer-run authority, of course, for Congress is not without means of retribution. But retribution is quite different from restraint. It operates only after the fact, after the damage has been done. The legislature has no enforceable constitutional right to intervene *during* the fact. It has no right to participate in the decisionmaking process, no right to be consulted. Presidents have even denied its right to be informed and have succeeded in defying its demand for information. True, the processes of congressional oversight can always be strengthened. The tradition by which White House advisers refuse to testify before congressional committees can be changed, by law if necessary—assuming a veto can be overridden. But even if Congress learns what is going on, it may be too late, and in any case it has no power to countermand any action of the President in his capacity as chief executive.

The effective restraining force, if there is to be one, must therefore come from within the executive branch itself. Yet here a determined president can usually take command. He can dismiss or reassign officers in the departments and executive agencies who oppose him; the Supreme Court has affirmed that power. Richard Nixon found a way to rid himself of Archibald Cox, though he lost an attorney general and a deputy attorney general in the process. It may take a little time, but the White House can always learn who in the bureaucracy is loyal and organize around the others, and it can fill key positions in the departments with its own henchmen. If necessary, it can take foreign policy out of the State Department, or any other policy out of any other department, and place it directly in the White House, and it can organize its own task forces—"plumbers," perhaps—to do jobs it prefers not to entrust to the permanent civil service.

Even the powers of Congress to take corrective action *after* the fact have their limits, for they often cannot be used directly to alter the behavior that may be deemed offensive. Congress may pass a new law, if the existing law is in fact unclear—provided each house can muster two-thirds of its members to override a veto. The War Powers

Resolution, enacted over a veto, is an example of such a clarifying law. Yet if the existing law is satisfactory but simply maladministered, changing it is obviously no recourse. If Congress, for example, feels that a president has used political criteria in adjusting milk prices, it can do nothing through the legislative route except either abandon the dairy program altogether, which it does not want to do, or attempt to set prices itself, which it cannot do with the necessary flexibility. Congress may cut appropriations for an agency it feels has abused its power, and this can work in instances where the abuse arises from an excess of governmental activity. The legislators could have dealt with Vietnam that way at any time with a simple clause in an appropriations bill—again assuming it could override a veto or outmaneuver the President in a legislative deadlock. But if the problem is the misuse of funds that Congress wants to see spent, but properly, cutting the budget only injures the program. In case of an outright violation of the law, its members can sometimes go to court, like any other citizen, and obtain an order to the President or a subordinate. Finally, there is the ultimate remedy of impeachment and removal of the chief executive. But in practice that depends on catching him in a clearly illegal act and, even then, is a process so extreme and divisive as to be beyond consideration in any but the most extraordinary circumstances.

So the corrective action often has to take an indirect form. Congress has to hold as a hostage things the President is asking for—laws, appropriations, confirmations—and use them for purposes of bargaining. At the height of Congress's feud with President Nixon, Representative William Moorhead, veteran Pennsylvania Democrat, put it bluntly: "We know there are programs coming up that he wants, and wants badly. And the only way that we will get back the programs [we want] is to hold [his programs] ransom for the programs we need."[6] Senator James Abourezk, freshman Democrat from South Dakota, was even more specific: "If the President persists in . . . defying the will of Congress . . . then this body should impound money for the White House staff, impound money for high executive branch officials, and refuse to approve any Presidential appointees."[7]

But far easier to threaten than to carry out. Bargaining—or blackmail—on a broad scale is almost insuperably difficult to organize in a Congress of dispersed power, and it often cannot be carried out

6. *Congressional Record,* vol. 119 (February 21, 1973), p. 5003.
7. Ibid. (January 16, 1973), p. 1136.

without damage to agencies and programs that have public and congressional support. To hold up all the President's appointments would mean judicial vacancies unfilled, cabinet posts empty, major agencies without direction. Also, the programs the President wants are usually programs that large segments of the public want. It would be easy for the President and his party to drum up public sentiment against Congress for impairing the normal and useful functioning of government and injuring innocent third parties in its vendetta against the chief executive. Within Congress, the committee or the house aggrieved by a presidential act may have to depend for retribution upon another committee or the other house, whose reaction may be, "Don't ask us to carry your fight against the President; we sympathize with you, but we're not going to let our program be your hostage."

Moreover, a branch made up of 535 equals has a hard time bargaining with a branch whose authority is concentrated in one executive. No one can commit Congress. No one can even speak for it. The elected leadership cannot be sure of its support. And the President can use his own bargaining devices to divide and conquer the diffused and plural legislature.

These are the dilemmas that have faced Congress since it set out a few years ago, with much public support, to bring to bay what it had finally concluded was an overgrown, overbearing, overweening presidency.

The Resurgence of Congress

Even before the full scope of the Watergate scandal had been uncovered, Congress had been aroused to an extraordinary mood of determination and resolution: the balance between the executive and legislative branches had to be restored. The turning point came at the opening of the Ninety-third Congress in January 1973, as the result of a whole series of conflicts with President Nixon that had reached a climax in the preceding autumn.

The most important of these was a conflict over spending, in which the Republican president defeated and humiliated the Democratic Congress. In the middle of the 1972 election campaign and just before Congress was scheduled to adjourn, the President challenged it with a demand that expenditures in that fiscal year be cut from the $256 billion already authorized by the lawmakers to $250 billion in order to stem inflation. If Congress could not make the cuts, he demanded that it give him a blanket authority to do so. The House of Representatives listened to pleas from its leaders that to give the President that kind of power would be to, in the words of Speaker Carl Albert, "knowingly and willingly abdicate not only our powers—but our responsibilities."[8] But then it acquiesced to the President's request. The Senate, however, heeded the pleas of its Democratic leaders and refused to go along. It agreed with the President's request but proposed a formula for making the $6 billion cut that restricted the President's discretion. That alternative the House members of a House-Senate conference committee rejected as unworkable, and Congress adjourned in deadlock.

The Senate had succeeded in preserving the prerogatives of Congress, but only at the cost of publicly demonstrating the impotence of the whole legislative branch. Here were both houses agreeing that the President was right, that aggregate spending authorizations of Congress did add up to unsound policy. But having acknowledged its cumulative mistakes, Congress then proved incapable of pulling itself together to rectify them. Accepting the President's leadership, it could not even organize itself to follow. The President won a public relations victory to exploit in the campaign, Congress suffered another loss in public esteem, and the country presumably suffered more inflation.

Confident that public opinion was behind him, the President then proceeded to rub another congressional sore by impounding still more money that Congress had appropriated. In January the administration reported that a total of $8.7 billion was being held in reserve.[9] And he was defying the Congress in other ways as well. Without consulting Congress, which by then was dominated by peace sentiment, he had stepped up the Vietnam War by renewing the bombing of North Vietnam and blockading Haiphong harbor. He was claiming for his administration an unlimited right to withhold from Congress any information on any subject, solely at his own discretion, under the doctrine of executive privilege. And he was proceeding to put into effect indirectly a reorganization of the executive branch that Con-

8. *Congressional Record*, vol. 118 (October 10, 1972), p. 34612.
9. Louis Fisher observes that this figure rested on a narrow definition of impoundment that excluded another $9 billion in impounded funds. *Presidential Spending Power* (Princeton University Press, 1975), p. 172.

gress had rejected; when they refused to consolidate seven domestic departments into four, he appointed four supra-cabinet officers in the White House to exercise, insofar as possible, the powers the four new department heads would have held.

Congress convened in January 1973 in a fighting mood. Nixon, wrote one reporter, had aroused "a snoozing Congress and made it mad."[10] "The accelerating usurpation of power by the Executive branch," said Speaker Albert, must be checked, and reversed. "The time has come for the Congress to call a halt to these wholesale executive invasions of legislative powers and responsibilities."[11] Senate Majority Leader Mike Mansfield called for "a reinforcement of the Constitution's [system of] checks and balances." Pointing out that the Democratic Senate majority had actually been increased by two while Nixon was being reelected by a landslide, Mansfield declared that "the people have not chosen to be governed by one branch of government alone."[12] But mingled with the assertive and determined words were expressions of deep anxiety. The "decline of Congress" was seen as a long-term trend, beginning at least as early as the New Deal, that had only reached its culmination with the extraordinary aggressiveness of Nixon. Editors and columnists expressed doubt that Congress could effectively assert itself against the President, or even that it genuinely wanted to, and these doubts were shared by many members. "The fault lies not in the Executive Branch but in ourselves," said Mansfield, referring to Congress's failure in the spending dispute.[13] "The Congress must regain the will to govern," said Barbara Jordan, the new congresswoman from Texas.[14]

In the ensuing months, Congress did muster a rare unity of purpose and firmness of will in its confrontation with the President, and it was aided immeasurably by the collapse of the Nixon presidency as Watergate unraveled—an unraveling to which the congressional investigative power had made its own important contribution. A president in a desperate struggle just to retain his office—and a losing struggle, as it turned out—is in no position to ward off the demands of a

10. Arlen J. Large, *Wall Street Journal*, April 13, 1973.
11. Speech of January 31, 1973, inserted in *Congressional Record*, vol. 119 (February 5, 1973), pp. 3239–40.
12. Address to the Senate Democratic conference, January 4, 1973, reprinted in *Congressional Record*, vol. 119 (January 4, 1973), p. 324.
13. Ibid.
14. *Congressional Record*, vol. 119 (April 18, 1973), p. 13170.

resurgent Congress, and so the legislative branch did succeed in reviving those of its lost powers that had been most at issue. The President voluntarily canceled the supra-cabinet appointments that had offended Congress (and had outraged the subordinated departments as well). Over the President's veto, Congress enacted the War Powers Resolution, which requires the President to report to Congress within forty-eight hours any commitment of American military forces and obtain the legislature's approval within sixty days. It passed the Congressional Budget and Impoundment Control Act to restore congressional authority over fiscal policy and spending decisions. It extended the confirmation power to the top officials of the Office of Management and Budget. It experimented with various "legislative veto" devices to give it a chance to review certain types of executive actions before they were taken. Meanwhile, in the case of the Nixon tapes, the Supreme Court had overruled unanimously the President's claim of unlimited executive privilege, although it did not define exactly what the limits are.

By the time the Ninety-third Congress adjourned at the end of 1974, then, each of the specific causes of the anger and unrest that had marked its opening had been removed. The Nixonian aggressions against the legislature had been repulsed, the offending President himself had been actually driven from office, and Congress had set up barriers through legislation that would prevent new "usurpations." Not only had the pre-Nixon status quo been restored, but also the pre-Johnson and in some respects even the pre-Franklin Roosevelt and pre-Theodore Roosevelt relations between the branches. In fact, in some matters Congress was on firmer ground than any it had ever occupied before. Yet a caveat has to be entered: if a determined President chooses to interpret even the new laws in his own way, Congress is essentially back where it started. A president can still carry the nation into hostilities, without genuine consultation with Congress but in such a way that the legislative branch can do no other than support him. And an anti-impoundment act without a loophole is probably beyond the art of draftsmanship. While the intent and spirit of these laws is clear, so have been earlier laws and the Constitution itself, and all are encompassed equally within the general limitations, discussed above, on what Congress can do whenever it feels the President has overstepped his powers.

The most significant of the new reforms is the budget legislation that forces Congress, for the first time, to assert an explicit fiscal policy. That policy may not be controlling because the President can still wield his veto power over the spending and revenue measures that embody it, but Congress is at least in a position of parity in the fiscal bargaining. No president can veto everything, and without an unlimited power of impoundment the executive has no automatic means of forcing his will upon Congress. It is significant that in the first test of nerve between the President and Congress in a fiscal policy deadlock after passage of the budget act, it was the President who flinched. President Ford demanded in the late months of 1975 that Congress in extending the tax cut also enact a tight statutory spending ceiling for fiscal year 1977. When Congress held to its position that the 1977 spending limit should be set later, in accordance with the schedule established in the new congressional budget law, the President had to yield.

Viewed in the perspective of history, the changes in the executive-legislative power balance wrought by a single Congress—the Ninety-third—are truly momentous. Ever since the era of congressional government at the close of the Civil War (when Congress succeeded in writing reconstruction policy in defiance of President Andrew Johnson), the flow of power had been all one way, in the direction of the President. In just two years, the trend of a hundred years was dramatically reversed. An extraordinary abuse of presidential power triggered a counteraction equally extraordinary, and the ponderous processes of institutional change were expedited. Congress, by now, seems satisfied. The *Congressional Record* of the Ninety-fourth Congress has contained, so far, hardly an echo of the earlier outcry against presidential "usurpations" and "invasions" and the weakness of Congress to combat them. Indeed, probably more concern is being expressed now—outside Congress, at least—about invasions in the opposite direction: it is Congress that has succeeded in thwarting the President and his secretary of state on a whole series of foreign policy issues—Vietnam, Cyprus, Angola, and trade relations with the Soviet Union.

This leads to a critical question about the flow of power back to Congress. If the legislative branch has succeeded in restoring its "constitutional prerogatives," how well is it equipped to exercise them? Constitutional law is one thing, the realities of day-to-day administration quite another. Will a greater degree of congressional participation in the daily decisions of government actually produce a superior governmental product? Two generations of political scientists before Vietnam and Watergate had taught, for the most part, that the answer to that question was no. That conclusion had not been reached casually, without a basis in the American governmental experience. The seemingly inherent weaknesses of the legislative branch as policymaker had been a major force in driving scholars and observers—and the public at large—to the strong-presidency solution. Just as that has had to be reexamined, so now the present resurgence of Congress compels a fresh look at what have been seen over the years as its endemic weaknesses, and an examination of whether those weaknesses, if they in fact exist, have been or even can be corrected.

The Endemic Weaknesses of Congress

The weaknesses that the critics of Congress have attributed to that institution can be summarized under four somewhat overlapping headings. It has been charged with parochialism in its outlook, irresponsibility in its conduct, sluggishness in its processes, and amateurism in its approach to questions. So handicapped, the analysis went, Congress can best leave the decisions of government to the executive under broad delegations, subject to continuous close oversight and residual control.

All of the attributed weaknesses, insofar as they can be shown to exist, arise at least in part from the very nature of the legislature as a plural body whose members are elected from vastly different constituencies. Hence, the shortcomings of Congress can be said to have been deliberately designed into it by the men of 1787 who created it. And the designers were not simply wrong, either. Plural legislative bodies have come into being in every democratic country for a reason—as guarantors of majority rule, safeguards against despotism. These are a democracy's supreme values, and so the defenders of the legislature can turn most of its alleged weaknesses into strengths: parochialism and amateurishness become representation of diversity and of the plain people of the land; sluggishness becomes orderliness and deliberation; the refusal to delegate discretion to administrators becomes the rule of law. If the place of Congress in the institutional scheme is lessened, the surety of its strengths is lost as its weaknesses are being circumvented.

Nevertheless, during all this century, until the divide was crossed in 1973, the consensus in the United States was that the weaknesses of Congress outweighed its strengths, and so the strong presidency of the twentieth century was born and grew, with the acquiescence, if not always the express support, of Congress itself. And corresponding decisions were being made in other countries; legislatures have declined in favor of strong executives all across the democratic world. Indeed, the decline has been steeper in other countries; the American Congress, despite the rise of the presidency, was even before its current resurgence by far the most active legislative body in the world.

Parochialism

Individual senators and representatives depend for survival not on pleasing the nation as a whole but on satisfying the limited constituencies from which they are elected. So being national-minded can be a positive hazard to a legislative career. The politically safe course for almost any newcomer to Congress is to attend assiduously to his or her duties as a delegate—interceding with the executive branch on cases involving constituents, promoting local projects, speaking and acting for the particular interests of the state or district—while leaving the statesmanship to others. Even if the member later assumes responsibility for leadership on broader questions, he had better never forget who sent him to Washington and who keeps him there.

This has its merits, up to a point. The parochialism of Congress ensures that local and narrow interests can get a hearing, that they are not ridden over arbitrarily, which is not necessarily the case in the executive branch. Yet whatever the merits of the local or regional claim, it must be pressed. Representatives of Texas must see the national interest in terms of oil, those of South Dakota in terms of cattle, and those of Detroit in terms of automobiles, while New York City representatives must look at every policy from the standpoint of the consumer. Foreign policy seen through the eyes of a constituency may predispose a representative toward the Greek, the Israeli, or the Irish view of particular problems. The budget appears as a "pork barrel" to be distributed among districts as well as a fiscal program for the country. What weapons the military forces should get are liable to be judged by what factories are located in a state or district. And so it goes across the whole range of policy. Political incentives propel the member—especially the House member who represents more specialized constituencies—from the broad to the narrow perspective. To avoid invidious reference to the living, one may reach into history for a case and come back with, perhaps, the story told by Henry Stimson about the chairman of the House Naval Affairs Committee of sixty years or so ago. Asked one day whether it was true that the navy yard in his district was too small to accommodate the latest battleships, the chairman replied, "That is true, and that is the reason I have always been in favor of small ships."[15]

Defenders of Congress argue that the national interest is, in the last analysis, the sum of the local interests. This argument, however, rests on a mythical conception of how a legislature with the work load of the American Congress operates. Decisions—except for the greatest ones—cannot really be made by the collectivity of both houses. Issues have to be parceled out instead for piecemeal action by committees and subcommittees, and these are unlikely to be fully representative. Committee assignments are determined by what the members want to do. Farm state members want to deal with agriculture while city people do not, so the agriculture committees are rural and proagriculture in their composition. The military affairs committees are dominated by partisans of the military, urban affairs committees by members from the cities, interior committees by proreclamation westerners, and so on. By custom, the judiciary committees are made up exclusively of lawyers. Within each committee, there is further specialization of subcommittees and of individual members. The decisions of the specialists have to be accepted by their colleagues most of the time without more than a cursory examination; a fresh and exhaustive review of every question by every member is obviously impossible. And through logrolling, the advocates of various local interests form coalitions of mutual support.

Specialization is properly advanced as one of the strengths of the houses of Congress, and they could not function without it. Yet if specialization is to prevail, then by definition the effective power of decision is delegated mainly to individuals and small groups who reflect the views of relatively narrow geographic segments of the population; if the sum of those views turns out in some cases to be the equivalent of the national interest, that has to be coincidental.

The presidency, in contrast, has a nationwide and governmentwide

15. Stimson testimony in *National Budget System*, Hearings before the House Select Committee on the Budget, 66:1 (GPO, 1919), p. 641.

perspective. Individual presidents have local and regional origins, it is true, but the conversion of a John Kennedy or a Lyndon Johnson to new views when he leaves the Senate for the White House testifies to the broader presidential outlook. Responsible only to the largest of constituencies, the President can, if need be, sacrifice a local interest to the general welfare. This does not mean he always does; presidents want approbation from all the local constituencies too. But he can. He can act to close outmoded military bases or agricultural research stations, for instance, and more than offset his local political losses with the credit earned from the larger public. Moreover, the hierarchical structure of the executive branch facilitates the weighing and balancing of local and narrow interests. If separate departments speak for the cities and the countryside, for the producer and the consumer, for employers and for labor, the White House and the Executive Office of the President command a broad view of the entire government and can discern from the clash of separate interests, in a judicious and deliberate fashion, where the national interest—defined by some "greatest good of the greatest number" concept—lies. The President's budget has been an important instrument of discipline, forcing the balancing of all claims within a limit set by fiscal policy. Until now, legislators faced no corresponding discipline; whether and to what degree the new requirement for a single integrated congressional budget will inspire a broader viewpoint within Congress has yet to be determined.

Irresponsibility

How does the electorate exercise control over a plural body chosen from half a thousand separate constituencies? It is not even possible, sometimes, to fix responsibility within Congress for what that body does or does not do. If a popular measure dies in committee, who killed it? Republicans may blame Democrats and Democrats Republicans, members may blame the chairman and the chairman the members, liberals and conservatives may blame the others' tactics, and so on. The individual member tells his constituents, "I did the best I could; it was the fault of all those other fellows." And from all indications, this tactic works. Even as opinion polls show public confidence in Congress as a whole to be extraordinarily low—13 percent gave it a favorable rating in one recent test—the voters tend to approve their own representatives and return them to office. And anyway, if a voter is unhappy with Congress and seeks to alter it, he can cast his ballot against, at most, only 2 of 535 members in any one election.

The members of Congress can hide not only behind one another but behind the President as well. If they intervene in a casual or piecemeal way in economic matters or in the complex world of U.S.-Soviet or U.S.-European relations, it is still the President who must bear most often the electoral responsibility for the consequences of their acts. The continuing management of the economy and of diplomacy are the President's responsibility. He is the one held accountable by the electorate for results, and normally a plea that Congress interfered is not an acceptable excuse. After all, the President was sent to Washington to lead and manage Congress too. So if the public, or any substantial segment of it, is aroused by events in Cyprus, say, or inside the Soviet Union or anywhere else, and a majority in Congress feels a surge of emotion to strike a blow, it can usually be done with relative impunity. The members reap the political reward and go on to the next item on their agenda while the administration is left to pick up the pieces of its wrecked policy and reorder its relations around the globe.

When a President exercises power, on the other hand, responsibility is clear. Further, he must take personal responsibility for the way the whole executive branch exercises its discretion. He cannot escape by putting the blame on his colleagues, as can a congressman; the plaque on Harry Truman's desk announced, "The buck stops here." And popular control—eventually, at the end of the President's term—is real: everybody can vote for president. If not for or against the incumbent, at least for or against the candidate of the incumbent party, whom the President will be supporting.

To all these criticisms of Congress as irresponsible, another has of late received fresh emphasis—its tendency to "leak." The very opening of its processes to clearer public view and the democratic extension of participation, both intrinsically desirable reforms, have made it more difficult for Congress to protect the secrecy of information. If it is conceded that a government must do some things in secret, a case can be made that Congress either must be excluded altogether from the decision process or must delegate authority to a very few to act on its behalf—an alternative that may defeat the purposes of legislative participation.

Sluggishness

It takes time for a legislature to blend and reconcile disparate views. But it takes more time in the American Congress than in other national legislative bodies because of certain peculiarities of Congress —its division into two houses that must concur on all legislative matters, the further fragmentation of power within each house among numerous committees and subcommittees, the Senate rule requiring an extraordinary majority for the closure of the debate, and the virtual absence of party discipline. In each of these respects, the United States Congress occupies a position among national parliaments that is either unique or extreme.

The result is that any piece of legislation must surmount an obstacle course of unparalleled difficulty. At each point along that course, the action may be delayed, if not killed—in the House, by the subcommittee, the full committee, the Rules Committee (or even by the chairman of one of these, through the device of not scheduling it for action), or on the floor; in the Senate by the subcommittee, the committee (or, again, by a chairman), or on the floor by a majority or by a minority large enough to forestall cloture of debate (forty-one members, or as many fewer as there are absentees at the time of the vote); or in a House-Senate conference committee. As a result, few things happen quickly. Policies eventually adopted are often approved too late; a fiscal policy designed to counter one economic trend may not win approval until that trend has disappeared and the opposite trend has set in, at which time it may be exactly the wrong policy. And in the process of overcoming the countless legislative hurdles, policies may be compromised to the point of ineffectiveness.

The assurance of ample deliberation is a virtue—but, again, only up to a point. Deliberation is not an end in itself; the end is action. After an appropriate time, the majority must have the capacity to act, or government is impotent. What is "appropriate" is always debatable, but there can be little doubt that policymaking in Congress has been delayed at times beyond the limits of reasonable deliberation to the point of outright paralysis, with consequences that can only be termed disastrous. The majority of Americans, by every measure, were ready to end discrimination against blacks in most of its manifestations by the time President Truman sent his program to Congress in 1948. Yet congressional procedures permitted the southern minority to block the major legislative remedies for a decade and a half, until the blacks took to the streets in massive protest. Can anyone measure how much unnecessary poison was injected into race relations in this country by that long delay that was broken only by extralegal action?

The inherent slowness of Congress gives the President infinite advantages as policy leader. Only the President, indeed, can be trusted with power where quickness of decision and action is imperative. This has been recognized not only in time of war but also to a degree in peacetime when the government must be able to respond quickly to events beyond its control. In foreign relations, therefore, the President has often been granted broad latitude to commit the nation, and the War Powers Resolution appears to acknowledge a continuing if limited authority even for the use of military force. The President has been granted discretionary powers in such domestic matters as prices and wage control. There is strong reason to make his economic powers permanent in a manner corresponding to his war powers—covering rates of taxation and expenditure as well as direct controls—on the ground that only the President can act quickly enough to counter sudden inflationary or recessionary trends in the economy. Presidents can procrastinate too, but unlike Congress they are not compelled to by any institutional structure. When their minds are made up, they can act within the limits of their statutory power.

Amateurism

An executive branch decision is presumably derived from expert judgments. The President is himself an amateur, and so may his cabinet members be, but they have in their employ experts on every subject of accepted governmental concern—often the leading experts in the country. From their accumulated experience in the administration of government programs, these experts can advise on the workability of proposed new policies. They can assess the side effects and predict the consequences. They may be overridden by the politically responsible amateurs for whom they work, but at any rate their judgment is normally sought and considered sympathetically.

When Congress elects to compete with the President in policy initiation, quite the opposite may be the case. Members of Congress do not have equal access to the executive branch expertise, and they may not trust it, especially when the two branches are under differing partisan control. Moreover, in those circumstances, as suggested earlier, they are under some compulsion to reject in whole or in part the executive branch's leadership. So they need experts of their own. This can be salutary. The executive branch has no monopoly on either wisdom or data, and it is good for experts in the bureaucracy to be checked and challenged by experts on the outside.

However, the solid expertise Congress needs for overruling the executive branch and substituting its own judgment is not easily or reliably assembled. The legislative branch does contain research and information-gathering organizations that match their executive branch competitors in quality of staff—the General Accounting Office, the Congressional Research Service of the Library of Congress, the new Office of Technology Assessment, and the even newer Congressional Budget Office. But the older of these organizations, at least, have not been intimate participants when the members of Congress were actually making legislative policy. They have been a step removed from the policy process, as nonpartisans in a climate of partisanship and as bodies independent of the legislative committees and subcommittees and their individual members; the heads of the General Accounting Office and the Library of Congress are presidential appointees. How the expertise of these agencies is used depends heavily on the circle of staff advisers who are at the core of the policy-making process. These are the committee and subcommittee staffs and the personal staffs of senators and representatives, who are chosen and appointed by the members of Congress themselves and who reflect the partisan orientation, and are sensitized to the political needs, of their sponsors.

Again, there are committee and subcommittee staffs that compare well with executive branch agencies in specialized knowledge and general competence. Yet even when the backup resources of the GAO, the CRS, the OTA, and the CBO are taken into account, they can rarely match their rivals in depth, despite enormous expansion in recent years. The range of responsibility of each committee is too broad, and the attention given most subjects too intermittent, to permit the engagement of specialists on each. Hence committee and even subcommittee staffs have tended to be composed of generalists, often knowledgeable about many things but usually truly expert only in legislative manipulation and in knowing where in the executive branch to turn for reliable data and the best advice. When in a period of intense and partisan interbranch competition executive branch sources dry up for them, the shortage of qualified specialists on Capitol Hill becomes more glaring and acute.

As Congress has tried during the Nixon-Ford years to remedy its shortages, the weaknesses of its personnel system have been exposed. Neither house has a merit system or central facilities for recruitment or a tenured career service. The fragmentation of the hiring process ensures that at best the structure of staff assistance will be spotty. Since each chairman has the responsibility for assembling his own staff, the competence of the staff available to cope with a given legislative issue depends on the chairman's conception of how much genuine expertise he needs. Sometimes he may not see the need for any at all; he may be content to rely for information and argument on the interest groups supporting his position—always a dubious source. Or a chairman may feel a need for expert assistance but have no acquaintance with the universe of talent in that particular area and no ready means of tapping it, in which case he falls back on amateurs. Moreover, the need is apt to develop quickly, and established experts are difficult to obtain on short notice for jobs that offer no security of tenure. So the recruitment field may be limited to persons not yet established in careers; in other words, the young and inexperienced. All this goes double for members who may try to make policy in opposition to the committee or subcommittee; they have to rely wholly on their personal staffs, who are usually even younger, even less experienced, and more transient than the committee employees.

So the men and women at the center of the advisory process are disproportionately represented by young lawyers taking a temporary fling in the glamour of Capitol Hill before settling down to practice, fledgling academicians gaining some practical experience before joining a faculty somewhere, political operatives between campaigns, students taking a year or two off before finishing their education, and even college interns enjoying a Washington semester—all overnight "experts" with responsibility for passing judgment on the advice of the genuine experts from the bureaucracy.

Finally, an element of expertise almost invariably lacking on Capitol Hill, even in experienced and permanent staff, is the comprehension of administrative necessities that can only come from responsibility for program operation. Even when the congressional majority and the President are political allies, the separation of administrative from legislative responsibility reduces the degree of attention given in the legislative process to questions of administrative feasibility—an aspect both of the administrative amateurism of Congress and of its lack of responsibility and accountability for administrative results.

Congressional Reform and Its Limits

As Congress in 1973 surveyed its loss of standing vis-à-vis the President, it was not unaware of its endemic weaknesses. "The fault lies . . . in ourselves," Mike Mansfield had said. So even as Congress looked outward and resolved to do battle with the President, it looked inward to its own organization and procedures. Since then, in internal reform as in relations with the executive, it has made more dramatic progress than at any time in more than half a century.

The new reforms—particularly the new budget process, a dramatic modification of the seniority system, and an assertion of greater power by the House majority caucus—may well prove lasting. But the reform impulse has now run up against a stubborn fact of congressional life, which has dampened the urge for further change. For the typical member of Congress, reform inevitably means a sacrifice of individual freedom and individual power. Each of the weaknesses enumerated above—parochialism, irresponsibility, sluggishness, and amateurism—results from, or is accentuated by, decentralization of power within the institution. It is the individual decisionmaker who is parochial and amateur; it is the multiplicity of veto points that makes for delay and indecision; it is the scattering of authority that hides its exercise and permits each member to escape a clear responsibility. To remedy these defects would require the individual decisionmakers in the committees and subcommittees to be effectively subordinated to some form of central authority in each House—an authority that could make timely decisions on behalf of the membership, from a national viewpoint, with expert assistance, and with clear responsibility. Congress, in other words, would have to become something of a hierarchy, like the executive branch, with a power of decision somewhere. Yet individual members cherish their independence and their shares of dispersed power. Beyond that, it is obviously impossible to go far in centralizing power in Congress without changing the fundamental character of that institution and losing the very real values that come from its pluralism and diversity.

The dilemma becomes clearer when one attempts to design the

specific nature of the centralizing mechanisms that might be employed. Powers that might be recovered from the committees, subcommittees, and individual members could be centered in the leadership of the majority party, in an authoritative central policy committee, in the majority party caucus, or in some combination of these. The alternatives are more than theoretical; each has at one time or another been tried, and a review of these experiments is revealing.

The apogee of leadership power came during a period of about twenty years with its midpoint at the beginning of this century. That was a time of tightly organized and well-disciplined party "machines" at state and local levels, held together by patronage, and the politicians who made their way to Congress were accustomed to follow leaders—or obey bosses, as the progressive enemies of machine politics preferred to phrase it. In the Senate, the majority leadership was collective, an oligarchy of like-thinking Republican stalwarts whose leading figure was Nelson Aldrich of Rhode Island. But in the House, the power of the Speaker was all but absolute. That was the time of the fabled Republican "czars" of the House—Speaker Thomas B. Reed of Maine and, after him, Joseph G. Cannon of Illinois. The Speaker held sway by virtue of his power to control all committee assignments; his chairmanship of the House Rules Committee, which cleared all measures for floor debate; and his right of recognition, which controlled access to the floor.

During the reigns of Czars Reed and Cannon, Congress was unquestionably powerful. President Theodore Roosevelt's legislative program was at the mercy of Speaker Cannon and Senator Aldrich and his fellow oligarchs. They told him what their houses would or would not accept, and they spoke with authority; they could deliver or withhold majorities. No problem of sluggishness here, but the other weaknesses remained and by the concentration of authority were even magnified. In the House in particular, Uncle Joe Cannon became parochialism and irresponsibility writ large. As the nation grew and urbanized and Cannon failed to grow and broaden with it, Cannonism became a national issue. But Cannon's power over the majority of the controlling party in the House sustained him in the office, and only his Illinois constituents could defeat him at the polls. So progressives had to aim their attack at the institution of the speakership, and in 1910, a coalition of Democrats and progressive Republicans seized the opportunity to strip that office of its most important powers. The Speaker's control of committee assignments was wrested from him, and as a safeguard against a return of Cannonism, both parties guaranteed their committee members continuous tenure, with rank determined automatically by seniority. In the Senate, too, seniority came to be the protector of individual rights.

Since that period, the antiboss, antimachine ethic of the progressive movement that toppled Cannon has become even more deeply ingrained in the American politician and in the electorate, and any return to czarism in either house has been unthinkable. Even the strongest leaders of our own era—the two Texans of the Eisenhower period, Senate Majority Leader Lyndon Johnson and Speaker Sam Rayburn—therefore fell far short of being bosses in the old sense. They could not direct the committees; quite the contrary, on every issue they were at the mercy of the committees and their chairmen in whom the power of decision actually resided. Neither Johnson nor Rayburn had at his command any sanctions to compel the making of the decisions they desired, or even to get decisions made at all. They could not depose or penalize recalcitrant committee chairmen or reconstitute committee membership. They had no significant rewards to offer beyond the original assignment to committees, and they lacked full control even over that. All they could do, really, was to use their personal prestige, extraordinarily high in Rayburn's case, and their ability to wheedle, cajole, and persuade, which was legendary in Johnson's. Rayburn through the expenditure of accumulated goodwill and Johnson through sheer animal energy could negotiate compromises and dispose a few swing votes in favor of them, but this brokerage took place only *after* the committees had acted. If a conservative Democratic committee chairman such as Wilbur Mills or Howard Smith or James Eastland or Harry Byrd chose to kill a bill in committee, there was little either of the elected leaders could do about it. Johnson freely admitted his limitations.[16] And Rayburn acknowledged as much when he personally led the fight in 1961 to reduce the power of Howard Smith, the Rules Committee chairman who had thwarted the Speaker and the party's liberal legislative proposals throughout the Eisenhower period.

16. See, for instance, the letter from Senator Patrick V. McNamara, Michigan Democrat, to Lyndon Johnson on the latter's handling of unemployment compensation legislation in 1959, quoted in James L. Sundquist, *Politics and Policy: The Eisenhower, Kennedy, and Johnson Years* (Brookings Institution, 1968), pp. 78–79.

The use of an authoritative policy committee as a central repository of power had its heyday too, even earlier than the Cannon-Aldrich period. If there was a time that can be called the golden age of congressional supremacy—when the legislature laid down the policies that governed the nation, in defiance of the President if necessary—it was during the Reconstruction Era. The instrumentality was the Joint Committee of Fifteen on Reconstruction, which came closer than any other group in the history of Congress to performing the legislative functions of a British cabinet. (President Andrew Johnson compared it, instead, to the Directory of the French Revolution.) It rejected the Lincoln-Johnson program of reconstruction and wrote its own Radical Republican alternative, which was enacted over a series of Johnson vetoes. And to put the program into effect against executive resistance the radical-dominated Congress went so far as to take from the President the power to remove cabinet officers—a type of derogation that in a later case the Supreme Court held unconstitutional—and in the end impeached him.

But the circumstances of the time were exceptional. Rarely has Congress been so ideologically cohesive, so dominated by a single faction of a single party. The two-thirds majorities necessary to override presidential vetoes could be mustered almost automatically. But that could happen only in a Congress whose natural minority had disappeared from its halls, when the Confederate states seceded. Once those states were readmitted, Congress lost its homogeneity, and its partisan majorities were no longer large enough to crush a president.

The use of the majority party caucus as the centralizing instrument had an even briefer, though distinguished, life, amounting to a single Congress, that of 1913–15. The central measures of Woodrow Wilson's New Freedom, notably tariff reform and creation of the Federal Reserve System, were enacted through the caucus mechanism. Democratic members of the regular Senate and House committees having jurisdiction over those subjects developed the bills with the leadership or collaboration of the Wilson administration—and the exclusion of Republican participants. The measures were then submitted for approval to a "binding" Democratic caucus, one that pledged the members (unless they were formally excused for any of several specific reasons) to vote for the bills on the floor. After the caucus votes the standing bipartisan committees went through the motions of considering the bills but the results were ordained. Majority party unity had been attained, a clear party policy had been adopted, and the minority was easily overridden.

There is no reason that a legislative body cannot elect to rely for policy development on the majority caucus and its subgroups rather than on standing bipartisan committees. Parliamentary democracies routinely proceed that way. But any restoration of the 1913–15 procedure would depart violently from tradition in this country. The exclusion of the minority from genuine participation in the legislative process, which raised cries of "disfranchisement" and "tyranny" and "King Caucus" in Wilson's day, would provoke louder outbursts now. The binding of individual members to follow party policy would offend the antimachine values that are the legacy of the progressive era. "I call the shots as I see them," "I wear no man's collar," "I stand on my own two feet"—these are the slogans a congressman likes to utter and a constituency likes to hear. "Rubber stamp legislature" is an effective epithet.

The use of the Democratic caucus as a regular mechanism for making policy ceased after only a brief experiment in a single Congress, despite the success of that trial. It might have survived the opposition attacks on King Caucus if the party had retained its unity on basic policy. But it did not. It fell apart on issues of preparedness; the House majority leader was among those who split with President Wilson, and from that point on the use of the caucus to establish binding policy was out of the question. The institution has never been revived. House Democrats have made no attempt for four decades to bind a caucus, and the present House majority leadership has explicitly forsworn any such possibility. As for congressional Republicans, after their vociferous attacks on the Democratic practices of the Wilson period, they abandoned even the word "caucus," preferring to call their meetings "conferences."

In its post-1972 reform mood, the House of Representatives and to a minor degree the Senate have moved gingerly in the direction of all three centralizing models. The House Democratic majority has been holding caucuses more frequently than at any time in recent decades. And while the caucus has not attempted to bind individual members concerning their votes on the floor, it has taken some other revolutionary steps. For one thing it has brought an end to the rigid seniority system that had prevailed for sixty years. Last year, it finally exercised on three occasions its option to depose committee chairmen who were out of step with the party rank and file or too old to be effective, or both. It has also undertaken in several instances to instruct committee Democrats to report bills to the floor, and so far no committee has defied it. The committees and their chairmen are now under effective control of the party caucus; their heretofore sacrosanct right to bottle up bills desired by the majority party membership as a whole has been taken from them. These changes may not appear startling or drastic, yet they add up to the first significant recentralization of the power that was dispersed to the committees in 1914–15 when King Caucus was dethroned. Following the example of the House, the Senate Democratic caucus has taken the first step toward reasserting a corresponding control over its committee chairmen; henceforth at the opening of each Congress they will be confirmed in their jobs individually by secret ballot.

The House majority caucus also transferred the task of filling the party's vacancies on standing committees from the Democratic members of the Ways and Means Committee, where it had resided since the overthrow of Cannon, to the caucus's own steering and policy committee. This is a body at once more representative and more directly subject to caucus and leadership control. The Speaker is its chairman and appoints nine of its twenty-four members, but Speaker Carl Albert—never a seeker after personal power in the Reed-Cannon or even the Rayburn tradition—has tried to develop the committee as a collective leadership structure. At the beginning of 1975, the committee attempted to act as a policy coordinator in the field of energy, where jurisdiction was divided among several standing committees—but without conspicuous success. A corresponding special committee of Senate Democrats on energy likewise had little impact. Both efforts were abandoned, and the experiment was not extended to other areas.

In one crucial field of overlapping jurisdictions, however—that of budget and fiscal policy—Congress in 1974 established a permanent coordinating mechanism. It created in each house a new bipartisan standing committee on the budget, with the Congressional Budget Office as an analytical resource to serve both. These committees have begun presenting annually to Congress a comprehensive fiscal plan governing revenues, expenditures, and deficit or surplus, which upon adoption sets limits on all subsequent fiscal actions. To the surprise of many, who predicted that the combined power of the old standing committees would be concentrated on scuttling their new rival, the system survived its trial year of 1975 and, as of this writing, the first stages of the 1976 cycle. Congress can now claim to have brought under orderly policy control the piecemeal appropriations process that so embarrassed it in its 1972 feud with Richard Nixon. The House Budget Committee recommendations of 1975 were approved, however, by only the narrowest of margins, and it is too early to say with assurance that the two houses will in the long run submit to restraint upon their freedom to appropriate as and when they please. Liberals, in particular, have expressed fear that in the long run the new process will enforce tighter budget policies than Congress has adhered to in the past and domestic social programs will bear the brunt. Advocates of a strong defense posture worry also about the budget limitations that may be imposed on them. Which is another way of saying that, in the past, liberal social programs and generous (or adequate, depending on the point of view) military spending may have cosurvived only because the appropriations process on Capitol Hill lacked discipline. If the choice turns out to be guns-plus-butter versus an orderly fiscal process, not every member of Congress will be willing to exalt the process—even with the control of inflation it implies—over the policy objective.

Except in this one field of fiscal policy, there remains no regular institutional structure in either house to deal effectively with matters that cut across the jurisdictions of two or more committees. With its power dispersed, Congress remains organized to deal with narrow problems but not with broad ones. Its structure still impels it to think parochially. It can skirmish for limited objectives but it cannot think strategically. It can, for instance, devise policies affecting energy but not a *national energy policy*. It can enact measures affecting the nation's growth but not a *national growth policy*—even though in 1970 it committed itself by statute to do so. It cannot have a comprehensive economic policy (apart from fiscal policy) or a policy on intergovernmental relations. It has no machinery for the coordination of foreign policy with military policy. The breadth of each of these policy areas, like the budget area, calls for a body of some kind with jurisdiction cutting across those of existing committees. The leadership in neither house has shown a disposition to improvise with temporary special committees for coordination purposes, and it is clear that a multiplicity of permanent committees dealing with broad, cross-cutting policy questions would create a jungle of conflicting jurisdictions that could only make the present situation worse.

Aware that Congress flounders as the nation's policymaker, many of its members have tended to blame a lack of information and analytical capacity. The last few years have seen a rapid growth of congressional staff, and the research and analysis agencies serving the legislators have been enlarged. But analysis is not decision. In the case of broad questions that cut across committee jurisdictions, institutions that use data to formulate comprehensive policy do not exist —except for budget and fiscal policy. Otherwise, despite the recent reforms, responsibility for decision remains unfixed. Congress still has no way of setting an agenda, or priorities, for its own activities, no way of assuring consistency and completeness in its consideration of the country's problems. For the good and largely inescapable reasons set out above, it does not appear likely that a much greater degree of centralization of responsibility for these purposes can be attained —in the leadership, in new committees, or in the caucuses.

In short, if presidential government has its perils, a pendulum swing to some ideal of congressional government is not the safeguard. That goal is unattainable within the American constitutional framework and tradition.

The Prospects for Collaboration

So the President and Congress are compelled to live together in a marriage arranged by matchmakers of a long-gone era, a marriage that, however loveless, is without the possibility of divorce. How can the partners live together in a reasonable degree of harmony, attaining enough unity of purpose to make the government functional?

The indispensable requisite for fruitful collaboration is that the President and the congressional majority be of the same party. When the two branches are in the hands of partisan adversaries, the President will not consult freely and share with congressional leaders his crucial decisions, which is essential to preventing the abuse of power. Nor, in those circumstances, will Congress accept the presidential leadership that is needed to compensate for the diffusion of its own internal structure. But if partisan consistency is the first requirement for interbranch collaboration, it has not always proved to be enough. Presidents and Congresses of the same party have quarreled bitterly and often. In the administrations of Theodore Roosevelt, Taft, Coolidge, Franklin Roosevelt, Truman, and Johnson, relations sooner or later degenerated into tension and hostility. Indeed, if one searches this century for periods when presidential-congressional dealings were marked by mutual respect, friendly interchange, and productive collaboration, one comes up with shockingly few years. On the Democratic side, they are limited to three periods totaling barely a decade —the first two years of Woodrow Wilson, the first four years of Franklin Roosevelt, the three Kennedy years (although this is debatable, for the Democratic conservatives were able to block much of the Kennedy program in his first two years), and less than two years of Lyndon Johnson. It was during these brief periods that most of the truly innovative, progressive legislation of this century was enacted; the slate of accumulated program ideas was swept clean on these occasions, and afterward the government could return to its normal state of deadlock and inaction. On the Republican side, only Eisenhower of the postwar presidents had a Congress of his own party, and his lasted but two years, during which time it gave him as much opposition as support. In the 1920s the Republican presidents got along reasonably well with their congressional majorities, but probably only because neither the President nor Congress had much of a program or asked much of the other. When congressional progressives did manage to enact innovative legislation, it was met with vetoes, as in the case of the farm bills killed by President Coolidge.

A development of great significance, however, suggests that, if the voters now choose to put their trust in a president and congressional majority of the same party, the chances of a durable peace between the branches will be better than at any time in this century. That development is the realignment of the parties in Congress, which reflects the changes that have been taking place in the country—the final working out, that is, of the realignment of the 1930s, when the issues of the Great Depression and the New Deal gave the United States its present party system. Since then, as new generations of voters have come along, those who were not committed by inheritance found themselves attracted to the Democratic party if they were liberals in the New Deal sense and drawn to the Republican party if they were conservatives. In this process, both parties have become more homogeneous. By now, all the northern states have realigned generally on the national pattern. So have the metropolitan areas of the South, and the realignment is progressing in the rural areas.[17]

With some time lag, these changes have affected the party composition of the Senate and the House. On the Republican side, the once deeply divided party has coalesced into a far more homogeneous group. Its western insurgent wing that was once so powerful as a dissenting force—including such great names at La Follette, Norris, Borah, Brookhart, Hiram Johnson—has vanished, its tradition absorbed within the Democratic party. A small body of northeastern urban liberals remains, but it has been dwindling too. The House "Wednesday" group of liberal-to-moderate Republicans has only thirty-three members, at least nine of whom are retiring this year— some from frustration. Already, when a Republican president is chosen, his party in Congress is able to work with him as a cohesive and like-minded body. If a Republican is inaugurated in 1977 and if that party also is given a congressional majority, executive-legislative harmony should be easily and automatically attained.

On the Democratic side, the old anti-New Deal "bourbon" wing that thwarted and frustrated Democratic presidents from Franklin Roosevelt to John Kennedy has all but disappeared in the North, melded into the Republican party. It remains in the South as a body of unreconciled dissenters from the national Democratic program, but its ranks are dwindling rapidly. As seats held by conservative southern Democrats become vacant, they fall one by one either to the resurgent Republicans of the South or to Democrats whose views are essentially those of the national party. The conservative stalwarts who once made up one-third to almost half of the Democratic strength in both houses, and by virtue of seniority held an even larger proportion of actual power, are now reduced to not much more than half a dozen in the Senate and thirty to forty in the House. And many of these are old. Moreover, since the Democratic caucus no longer is

17. This realignment process is described in James L. Sundquist, *Dynamics of the Party System: Alignment and Realignment of Political Parties in the United States* (Brookings Institution, 1973), especially chaps. 11 and 12.

forced by the seniority system to bestow automatic chairmanships upon them, a Democratic president and his congressional leaders would be able to ignore or override them.

The country has become so accustomed to seeing the President and the Congress at each other's throats that this seems almost a permanent and normal condition of American government. Some may even think it beneficial because it suggests that any future Watergates will be exposed more quickly and surely. Installing a hostile Congress just to watch the President seems hardly a necessary safeguard; a Democratic Congress was rather rough on Harry Truman. And a Congress with a majority of the President's party might actually be more effective in preventing malfeasance, as distinct from punishing it, because its leaders would be closer to the President. The isolation of the President and his immediate associates that gave the Nixon-Watergate era its distinctive character would be reduced.

The more important consideration in forming a government, in any case, is to make possible affirmative, positive action. So the quiet revolution going on within the party system, which provides a new basis for presidential-congressional collaboration, is one of hope and promise. The prospects for interbranch cooperation when the President and the congressional majority are of the same party are brighter than at any time in the memory of anyone now living, and they will become even brighter in the future as party realignment completes its course. Responsible party government under the President as party leader will be possible—not just in times of extraordinary majorities like those that produced the New Deal and the Great Society but on a continuing basis. One has to go back to the nineteenth century for a time when that could be said about either party.

There are still things that can keep this promise from being realized, of course, even if the President and the congressional majorities are of the same party. Much depends on the skill of the individual who happens to be President; many in the past have failed as party leaders. The central mechanisms for developing solidarity and capacity to act within the congressional majority still must be attended to. And it remains to be seen whether the vastly expanded congressional facilities for policy analysis, such as the new congressional budget machinery, will be a bridge between the branches, facilitating collaboration, or a barrier. Set up by a congressional majority bent upon equipping itself for confrontation with a president of the other party, will these mechanisms display an institutional bias toward confrontation even when the White House falls into friendly hands?

These are not minor considerations. But there is at least solid reason to believe that the prospect for an effective, lasting partnership between the President and Congress has never been better than it is right now—assuming, to repeat, that the voters do not choose four more years of hostility and stalemate by sending to Washington a president and a Congress of opposing political faiths.

The electorate, as always, holds the key.